The ONE YEAR® DEVOTIONS for people of *purpose*

CHARLES COLSON

WITH ANNE MORSE

TYNDALE HOUSE PUBLISHERS, INC.
CAROL STREAM, ILLINOIS

Visit Tyndale's exciting Web site at www.tyndale.com

TYNDALE and Tyndale's quill logo are registered trademarks of Tyndale House Publishers, Inc.

One Year is a registered trademark of Tyndale House Publishers, Inc.

The One Year Devotions for People of Purpose

The devotions in this book are adapted from commentaries produced by BreakPoint, a program of the Wilberforce Forum, a division of Prison Fellowship Ministries.

Designed by Luke Daab

Edited by Susan Taylor

Previously published in 2004 as *How Now Shall We Live? Devotional* by Tyndale House Publishers, Inc. under ISBN-10: 0-8423-5409-3, ISBN-13: 978-0-8423-5409-7.

The One Year Devotions for People of Purpose first published in 2006.

ISBN-13: 978-1-4143-1298-9
ISBN-10: 1-4143-1298-9

Printed in the United States of America

10 09 08 07 06
5   4   3   2   1

CONTENTS

MAY

FOREWORD

Two years ago, the Wilberforce Forum launched an intensive, one-year worldview training program for one hundred serious Christians we named "the Centurions." Our goal was to teach community leaders from coast to coast to understand, articulate, and live out a biblical worldview and then to teach it to others.

As we worked together, one thing we discovered was the importance of a daily devotional. Theologian and Wilberforce Fellow T. M. Moore writes an online devotional guide exclusively for the Centurions that offers a bracing dose of worldview thinking at least once a day. Almost to a person, the Centurions rank it among the most formative influences in their study.

This daily dose of worldview thinking is desperately needed. The biggest single challenge in the church today is helping the faithful understand that the Christian life is about far more than simply attending church on Sundays. And as shocking as this may sound, it's also about far more than fulfilling the great commission.

Christians are indeed agents of God's saving grace—instruments for bringing others to Christ. We are also agents of his common grace: He calls us to sustain and renew his creation and defend the created institutions of family and society.

The book of Genesis lays the foundation for this cultural commission. For five days, God created the heavens and the earth. On the sixth day, he created human beings—and ordered them to pick up where he left off. They were to reflect his image and have dominion, but from then on, the development of the creation would be primarily social and cultural. It would be the work that humans performed as they obeyed God's command to fill and subdue the earth.

The same commands bind Christians today. Though sin introduced a destructive power into God's created order, it did not obliterate that order. When we are redeemed, we are both freed from sin and restored to do what God designed us to do: create culture.

But we cannot fulfill this commission if we do not take religious doctrines seriously, if we "emphasize the upbeat and the encouraging and play down the business of God's wrath" (in the words of *New York Times* columnist David Brookes)—in other words, if we practice religion that is easygoing and experiential rather than rigorous and intellectual. Sociologist Alan Wolfe put it bluntly when he said that Christians have become "part of the mainstream culture, not dissenters from it."

Wolfe is right. The church *has* been mainstreamed (and the culture largely lost) because we have forgotten that God commanded us to love him with all our *minds*. We have lost the concept of worldview.

How do we get it back? Working with the Centurions has made me realize that the only way to get people thinking differently is to make a huge paradigm shift. We can do this only through regular practice. We cannot simply say one day, "I am going to start thinking differently." We have to discipline ourselves to think about cultural matters from God's perspective every single day.

That is the purpose of this book. In all my writings, I've been sensitive to and placed considerable emphasis on the fact that people are desperately hungry to discover the meaning and purpose of life. Rick Warren has attested to this in his book *The Purpose-Driven Life*, and I have found the same response to my own writings. This devotional is intended as a daily reminder that Christians must be people of purpose, acting as salt and light in the surrounding culture, making an impact for God's Kingdom. It offers a disciplined approach to helping you change how you think about art and literature, television and films, politics and bioethics, terrorism and truth. It is designed to help you learn to think *Christianly* every day of the year, to apply worldview thinking to the moral dilemmas and difficulties of your own life.

Only when large numbers of Christians begin to think this way—

and act accordingly—will the faithful stop floating lazily along in the mainstream and have the courage to leap into the cold, countercultural rapids. If enough of us take the plunge, the force of the current will inevitably reshape the surrounding culture.

Are you up to the challenge? Then grab your life jacket and turn the page. That first, bracing splash awaits you.

Charles W. Colson
July 2006

STORMING PAGAN STRONGHOLDS

TO READ: ACTS 17:16-33

He is not far from each one of us. "For in him we live and move and have our being." As some of your own poets have said, "We are his offspring." Acts 17:27-28

In a culture as hostile to Christianity as ours has become, the church's impulse may be to circle the wagons and keep strictly to our own kind.

But is this the right response? Should Christians retreat into a new isolationism? Or should we go on the offensive, infiltrating increasingly hostile territory?

In the book of Acts we find Paul as he stands on Mars Hill, disputing with the philosophers of Athens. Acts 17 says that Paul was accosted by Stoics and Epicureans. The Stoics taught that virtue lies in an act of sheer will, not unlike the teaching of modern existentialists.

The Epicureans endorsed a philosophy of eat, drink, and be merry, not unlike today's consumption-driven pleasure seekers, whose motto is, "Whoever dies with the most toys wins."

Yet Paul was willing to mingle with these pagans and unbelievers—and to use their own literature in speaking to them. In describing God as the architect of the universe, he echoed a reference to the philosopher Plato. The line "In him we live and move and have our being" was a direct quotation from a Greek poet.

Yet Paul never compromised his message. The climax of his speech was a bold proclamation of the empty tomb—unarguable evidence for Christ's resurrection.

Some mocked him, Acts tells us, but a few believed. Paul had made a dent in a pagan culture.

Each one of us has our own opportunities to mingle with nonbelievers and engage their hearts and minds. For you, it might be a neighborhood association, a PTA, or a workstation.

What matters is not where we speak but what we say.

This is no time to circle the wagons, no time to be faint of heart. It is time to storm the strongholds of pagan America.

Father, I ask for the courage to befriend those around me who may be hostile to Christianity. Help me to find ways to recast the eternal message of salvation in language they will understand.

JANUARY 2

CONFRONTING
OUR FRIENDS

TO READ: 1 SAMUEL 20:1-17

*Jonathan had David reaffirm his oath out of love for him,
because he loved him as he loved himself.* 1 Samuel 20:17

One of the best ways we can teach our kids about the value of friendship is by dusting off the best works of children's literature, like Kenneth Grahame's classic, *The Wind in the Willows*. It tells a charming story about a mole who leaves his underground home in the English countryside and makes friends with a water rat. Through his new friendship, Mole discovers a fascinating new world, populated by Badger and Otter and Toad and a host of other colorful animal characters.

The Wind in the Willows was one of C. S. Lewis's favorite children's books—and it's safe to say he knew something about the subject. Vigen Guroian, author of *Tending the Heart of Virtue*, says the story shows "how friendships can form us into stronger and more integrated persons. . . . Mole is called out of his womb-like home to become a friend to others," and his character develops precisely though learning to be a loyal and giving friend. To quote Guroian again, "Modern psychology confirms that common stock of human wisdom which says that children ought to have friends, and not just any friends, but [ones] with real virtues that in combination contribute to the moral growth of all the friends."

And when children go astray, it is often their friends who call them to accountability. In *The Wind in the Willows*, Toad suffers from uncontrollable appetites that threaten his own destruction. He is lucky to have friends who love him enough to act severely with his weaknesses.

Led by the tough-minded but loving Badger, they confront Toad about his excesses and fight off the vicious stoats (ermines) and weasels who have taken advantage of him. What else are friends for?

The view of friendship that Kenneth Grahame expresses in story form comes from ancient times. It was the Greek philosopher Aristotle who wrote that friendship "helps the young to keep from error; . . . [and] those in the prime of life it stimulates to noble actions . . . for with friends men are more able to think and to act." Even more important, friendship reminds us that in Christ, God himself has called us his friends. As Guroian writes, "Friendships sound the call to a higher and transcendent communion with God."

Why not introduce the children in your life to a hero who is not afraid to be a friend—one like Badger, who helps his friend Toad conquer the demons within. And we ourselves must remember that we have an obligation to our own friends to call them to accountability when we see them falling into sin—and to be open to the loving rebukes of friends who are concerned about our moral character.

Lord, help me not to fall into friendships that degrade my moral growth. Give me the wisdom to choose friends whose characters inspire me to follow you more closely—friends who love me enough to risk my wrath to offer necessary rebukes.

ARE ANIMALS "PERSONS"?

TO READ: GENESIS 1:24-26

*God said, "Let us make man in our image . . .
and let them rule over . . . all the creatures."* Genesis 1:26

Not long ago the California Milk Advisory Board ran what became known as the "happy cows" television ad. It featured singing, wise-cracking dairy cows contentedly munching grass in bucolic bliss. Viewers loved them, but the People for the Ethical Treatment of Animals (PETA) sued, claiming that the ads violated consumer protection laws. How? According to PETA, the ads deceive consumers about the way cows actually live. (Note to PETA: Cows don't really sing, either.)

PETA also got upset over the "Chicken Challenge" at an Illinois casino, where customers were invited to play tic-tac-toe against chickens. PETA said the game "disrespected chickens."

We laugh at stories like these, but the influence of animal-rights advocates has been growing, and their agenda is dangerous. Americans and Europeans alike are passing laws that do more than just protect animals. In Germany, for example, a law was passed declaring that animals have the same rights as humans.

Some changes in how animals are treated on farms and in labs may be needed. But the modern animal-rights movement is driven by more than just humane concerns; activists have a serious agenda—one that challenges Christianity's most fundamental doctrines.

Animal-rights activists believe there is no fundamental difference between animals and humans. The idea that humans are special in any way is called *speciesism*, defined as a prejudice akin to racism and sexism. PETA's Ingrid Newkirk even compares eating meat to the

Nazi Holocaust and says that the animal rights movement is "at great odds" with Christian teachings.

Ominously, some animal-rights activists carry their logic to extremes. If it's "murder" to kill chickens, they believe, then it's morally acceptable to stop the "murderer." In *National Review Online,* Wesley Smith writes about terrorists who employ "death threats, fire bombings, and violent assaults against those they accuse of abusing animals."

These people are dangerous in more ways than one. Charles Oliver of *Reason* magazine explains: "By placing chickens and Jews on the same ethical plane, animal rights activists may inadvertently make it easier for a future Hitler to herd millions of humans into gas chambers."

Oliver is right. The philosophy behind the animal-rights agenda is an assault on human dignity. Christians have a moral duty to respect the animal world as God's handiwork. This means finding out how animals are treated in research labs and on factory farms and helping shape laws that determine their treatment. We must make sure we and others treat animals "with the mercy of our Maker," as Christian writer Matthew Scully writes in his book *Dominion: The Power of Man, the Suffering of Animals, and the Call to Mercy.*

But *mercy* for animals is completely different from *rights* for animals—and we should never confuse the two.

Lord, teach me to be concerned enough about animal suffering to ensure that I am not contributing to it. Grant me a heart that beats with the mercy that the Creator has for his creatures.

MIRACULOUS EVIDENCE

TO READ: MARK 8:22-26

When he had spit on the [blind] man's eyes and put his hands on him,
Jesus asked, "Do you see anything?" Mark 8:23

In *An Anthropologist on Mars,* Oliver Sacks describes the case of a man named Virgil, who had been blind since childhood. At the age of fifty, Virgil underwent surgery to restore his sight.

What he experienced afterward inadvertently confirmed the Bible's account of one of Jesus' miracles.

Following the surgery, Virgil suffered from what is called "post-blind syndrome"—the inability to make sense of the panorama of colors and shapes that crowd our field of vision. As Sacks writes, Virgil would "pick up details . . . an angle, an edge, a color, a movement—but he would not be able to synthesize them, to form a complex perception at a glance." For example, when looking at a cat, Virgil "would see a paw, the nose, the tail, an ear, but he couldn't . . . see the cat as a whole."

It took time and practice, but Virgil finally adjusted to being sighted. As his wife put it, "Virgil finally put a tree together—he now knows that the trunk and leaves go together to form a complete unit."

These words ought to ring a bell for Christians. In the Gospel of Mark, we read that Jesus led a blind man "outside the village. When he had spit on the man's eyes and put his hands on him, Jesus asked, 'Do you see anything?'" The blind man replied, "I see people; they look like trees walking around" (Mark 8:23-24).

As Keith Mano writes in *National Review,* this phrase "is a clinical description. Like Virgil, the Bethsaida man can now see, but he cannot yet make sense of what he is seeing. Tree and man run together, as did trunk and tree-top for Virgil."

In short, "this is irrefutable evidence that a miracle did occur at Bethsaida. . . . No [charlatan] in the crowd could have faked it all by pretending to be blind because only someone recently given his sight" would see people who, according to Mark, "look like trees walking around." Mano concludes, "A faker, not knowing about post-blind syndrome, would have reported that Jesus had given him perfect vision."

Instead, the Gospel reports that Jesus cured the man twice: once of blindness and then of post-blind syndrome.

The story of the blind man's miraculous healing could not be understood until our own day, when modern medicine has revealed the true nature of blindness.

Do you have trouble believing in the miracles of Christ? Do your friends? If so, read the fascinating story of the two men who were healed of their blindness—both of whom saw people who "look like trees walking around."

Lord, thank you for modern medicine that offers testimony to ancient miracles.

TEACHING CIVILITY

TO READ: LUKE 6:27-36

Do to others as you would have them do to you. Luke 6:31

There's a modern-day "punishment room" that many lawbreakers fear and hate—and some would say violates laws forbidding cruel and unusual punishment.

But the judge who sends people to this ersatz torture chamber says he's only making the punishment fit the crime.

Municipal Court Judge Paul Sacco of Fort Lupton, Colorado, got tired of complaints from senior citizens about teenagers driving through their neighborhoods with boom boxes blasting loudly enough to wake the dead. So the judge came up with an original—and appropriate—penalty. Kids who violate the noise ordinance are locked in a room at the courthouse and are forced to listen to the worst music imaginable—at least to the ears of rap-loving teenagers.

One recent batch of scofflaws was shut up with the sound of Roy Rogers and Dale Evans warbling "Happy Trails to You." They suffered through Disney tunes, bagpipe music, and songs by Wayne Newton and Barry Manilow. But the teens were nearly driven mad hearing Tony Orlando and Dawn sing "Tie a Yellow Ribbon Round the Old Oak Tree" and Dean Martin crooning "The Middle of the Night Is My Cryin' Time."

The treatment is unorthodox—but extremely effective. Seventeen-year-old David Mascarenas says he's already taken his stereo out of his car. And not one survivor of this punishing ordeal has ever reappeared before Judge Sacco.

This judge may be onto a good thing. It's clear that for these kids the more informal channels of teaching civility—the home, the school, and the church—have failed. When that happens, the heavy hand of the law must take over. But instead of taking a punishing approach, Judge Sacco has opted for a teaching approach. He's helping these kids understand why laws of civility and courtesy exist in the first place.

The result is that they're learning firsthand the most universal moral code: Do unto others what you would have others do unto you.

This is a lesson in civility we all ought to take note of at a time when we Americans are encouraged to think too much of our own rights and not enough about the rights of our neighbors.

It's a lesson that dozens of Colorado kids won't soon forget—kids who still shudder at the memory of the day they were forced to listen to Roger Whitaker and Dean Martin.

As one teenager put it, "If I ever get caught again, I'd rather pay the sixty-five dollars." But I'm sure he—and his neighbors—benefited much more from a musical lesson in courtesy.

Lord, as I go into the world today, illuminate ways in which I routinely put my own "rights" ahead of courtesy, compassion, and consideration for others. Help me daily to conquer every selfish impulse as I interact with people in my office, on the road, in my neighborhood, and in my home.

JANUARY 6

TURNING HUMAN LIFE INTO A COMMODITY

TO READ: GENESIS 1:26-31

God created man in his own image . . . male and female
he created them. Genesis 1:27

A graduate student at New York University's film school, Carrie Specht, was borrowing money daily just to buy food. But rather than take another low-paying job, Carrie signed on with an infertility clinic to sell her eggs to an infertile couple.

It's the latest trend among college coeds—a trend that could change the very definition of what it means to be human.

Carrie had held a series of low-paying jobs, such as dog walking, before spotting an ad in the *Village Voice*. A clinic called Advanced Fertility Services invited "healthy, caring women" to assist infertile couples, and it offered two thousand dollars to cover "time and inconvenience."

It turned out the clinic was looking for women willing to let doctors harvest their eggs and sell them to infertile couples.

Carrie had her eggs harvested four times. They were fertilized and implanted in the wombs of anonymous recipients. Carrie has used the money—some eight thousand dollars—to pay tuition and finance film projects.

Dr. Mark Sauer, director of an assisted-reproduction program, says the average donor is a college student who is "clearly doing this because of the financial gain." But what are the ethical issues involved in the sale of human eggs?

For example, in some states there is no limit to how many times a woman may donate eggs. But what happens if two people spawned

11

from the same donor should meet and marry? It could be a genetic disaster if they had children.

Perhaps worst of all is what egg harvesting teaches women about their own worth. In an article in *Jane* magazine called "Chicks Selling Their Eggs," a young woman named Martha said, "It occurred to me that they were going to pay me money for something I wasn't ever going to use."

What we're seeing here is the triumph of a completely mechanistic view of human life. The human body is regarded not as a gift from God but as a purely physical object to be taken apart, sold, and used—just like any other physical object. Human eggs are regarded merely as a commodity.

In *Without Moral Limits* Debra Evans writes, "Women are not machines of reproduction, but are each unique, individual persons in body, mind and spirit." She's right. Genesis says we are made in the image of God—that we find our ultimate identity and worth in reflecting our Creator.

You may never be asked to sell off part of your own body—but you are almost certainly hearing arguments demanding that you accept a redefinition of what it means to be human, whether the subject is abortion, cloning, or selling human eggs. Are you prepared to make the biblical case against the commodification of human life?

Lord, open my eyes to cultural changes that defy your teachings. Give me opportunities to share these teachings with those who are being dangerously misled into believing that your gift of life is something to be sold to the highest bidder.

JANUARY 7

ARE WE ABOLISHING MARRIAGE?

TO READ: GENESIS 2:18-25

For this reason a man will leave his father and mother and be united to his wife, and they will become one flesh. Genesis 2:24

The moment Michelle Meako became engaged, she told her intended, "I want a big wedding." The couple wrote their own vows, picked out a cake, and planned a Canadian honeymoon. The couple omitted only one detail: a marriage license. They couldn't get one because Michelle and her "spouse" are both women.

Is it unjust for a government to refuse to authorize same-sex "marriages"?

In *The Clash of Orthodoxies,* Princeton philosopher Robert George writes that the matrimonial law reflects a moral judgment: that marriage is inherently heterosexual, monogamous, and permanent—a union of one man and one woman. This judgment is based on both the biblical and natural law understandings that marriage is a two-in-one-flesh communion of persons. This communion is consummated and actualized sexually—that is, by acts that are reproductive, whether or not they result in children. They unite the spouses as a single procreative unit—an organic unity achieved even by infertile couples. Only a mated pair can be a complete organism capable of human procreation.

By contrast, homosexual acts have no relationship to procreation and can't unite persons organically. As a result, these acts can't be marital—which means relationships integrated around them can't be marriages. Same-sex partners are physically incapable of marriage. It takes a man and a woman to become "one flesh."

"Okay," our secular neighbors may say, "that's your definition of marriage. But why should you be allowed to impose your views on everyone else?"

That's why we have to be ready with additional, nonreligious arguments for traditional marriage. For instance, if we expand the meaning of marriage to include same-sex unions, on what grounds could we legitimately oppose marriages of three or more people, or weddings between siblings?

Another argument, made by Bill Bennett, is the impact it would have on the shaping of human sexuality, especially among the young. "Societal indifference," he writes, "about heterosexuality and homosexuality would cause a lot of [sexual] confusion."

Since the beginning of recorded history, virtually every society and every major religion has revered and protected traditional marriage. It's the institution that nurtures, protects, and civilizes children. Marriage forms the framework of society's most basic institution: the family.

If supporters of same-sex marriage succeed, marriage will be reduced to nothing more than a legal contract between any two people based solely on feelings. True marriage would be abolished, and the damage to our society would be irreparable.

We Christians are often made to feel "intolerant" for not going along on issues like same-sex "marriage." When others try to intimidate us into silence through the "bigot" label, we need to speak out— to explain why same-sex "marriage" is impossible and how attempts to impose it will harm us all.

Lord, give me the courage to be salt and light in the world and to speak up for your truth, regardless of the consequences.

WHY MEN WON'T COMMIT

TO READ: RUTH 2:8-14

My daughter, listen to me. Don't go and glean in another field and don't go away from here. Stay here with my servant girls. . . . I have told the men not to touch you. Ruth 2:8-9

Tina wants to get married, but her boyfriend, Ted, just wants to move in. Ted is an exceptionally honest young man, so here is what he says: "Tina, I'm fond of you, and I want to live with you for the following reasons. First, it will make it easier for me to enjoy regular sex. Second, I want to protect my assets—assets I'd have to share with you if we got a divorce. Third, you already have kids, and I don't want to support them. Fourth, I'm waiting for my perfect soul mate to come along. Until I meet her, I'd like to live with you."

Ted's arguments are incredibly insulting. And yet, according to a new study, these are exactly the reasons men want to live with women—reasons that not only insult women, but also make them big losers on the domestic front.

Researchers with the National Marriage Project at Rutgers University have published a report called *Why Men Won't Commit: Exploring Young Men's Attitudes about Sex, Dating, and Marriage.* It offers the top ten reasons men are reluctant to say, "I do." Among them: They can get all the sex they want without marriage. They want to avoid the financial pitfalls of divorce. And they're afraid marriage will demand too many changes and compromises. Apparently, their live-in girlfriends can get used to their bad habits or leave.

Most galling of all is men's admission that they're waiting for their "true love" to come along. Then they'll tie the knot, buy a home, and father kids. Meanwhile, their live-ins can pick up their socks and provide sex on demand.

Grandma was right. Men won't buy the cow if they can get the milk free. Grandma was echoing the wisdom of the biblical writers. Read the Old Testament, and you'll get a picture of how carefully the ancient Israelites protected unmarried women: They knew how predatory, how utterly selfish, men can be. Taking on the responsibilities of a wife and children involved hard work that would last a lifetime. And men were motivated to shoulder those responsibilities only because their culture demanded it.

Modern women have far more freedom of movement than their sisters in the ancient world did. But human nature is still fallen. This means that men are as predatory as ever—and women today are paying the price for it in a culture that doesn't demand marriage.

The sad truth is that nearly everyone suffers from an inclination to be selfish. We need to become fully aware of relationships in which we ourselves are tempted to put our own desires above the good of others simply because we know we can "get away with it."

O God, teach me to put generosity ahead of getting my own way, remembering that Jesus was tempted by Satan to put him first—but chose instead to sacrifice himself for the sake of all mankind.

SHOULD WE BE "IN ON THE KILL"?

TO READ: PHILIPPIANS 4:4-9

Whatever is true, whatever is noble, whatever is right, whatever is pure, whatever is lovely . . . think about such things. Philippians 4:8

Americans have a fascination with television programs featuring animals chewing up and swallowing chunks of other animals—often while the animal being eaten is still alive. One cultural observer warns that this fascination borders on depravity.

Alan Jacobs is a professor of English at Wheaton College and the author of *A Visit to Vanity Fair: Moral Essays on the Present Age*. In an essay titled "In on the Kill," Jacobs describes the growing popularity of graphic shows that feature lions chewing up zebras, or tigers tearing into antelope. Some people shrug and say, "Well, that's just the way things are." Nonsense, Jacobs counters. A lioness will spend a dozen hours sleeping for every hour she spends hunting, yet how often do these programs feature sleeping cats? Far from giving us "an unedited version of The Way Things Are," Jacobs writes, "filmmakers give us pictures of predation because they, and we, are interested in predation. We would rather see a praying mantis eat the head of her mate . . . than watch a caterpillar eat a leaf."

These programs, Jacobs writes, are the modern equivalent of bearbaiting or cockfighting. A fascination with killing is deeply unhealthy and can lead to our own degradation. When we watch these kinds of programs, we render ourselves less humane by destroying the respectful kindness—the *humanitas*—that is a characteristic of the virtuous person.

Says Jacobs, "Those who can look without flinching upon animals having the flesh of their bellies eaten while they are still alive are morally numb; those who seek out such scenes for their viewing enjoyment are depraved."

When it comes to acts of cruelty, sometimes the only proper response is to avert our eyes. That's why we should resist the temptation to watch "documentaries" that revel in the cruelty of the animal world and should keep the children in our lives from becoming addicted to them.

Programs like these attack our *humanitas*—our respectful kindness—and lead not only to our own degradation but also to that of our culture.

Lord, help me to resist the temptation to view anything in films, on television—or in real life—that threatens to erode my compassion for your creation.

JANUARY 10

THE LANGUAGE OF
THE COSMOS

TO READ: GENESIS 1:1-10

In the beginning God created the heavens and the earth. Genesis 1:1

In the film *Contact,* an astronomer picks up radio signals being transmitted from outer space. The signals are mathematical formulas because, as the astronomer points out, mathematics is the only
universal language.

And the reason it is universal is that it describes the most fundamental order of the cosmos.

At least, that's what science has always taught. But today, some
mathematicians are claiming that mathematics is not necessarily
true at all—that it's merely a convention, a set of rules, like the rules
that govern baseball.

In his book *What Is Mathematics, Really?* Reuben Hersh claims that
math does not correspond to any transcendent reality; instead, he
says, it's just a human creation, much like a novel, a symphony, or a
painting.

Similarly, in *The Limits of Mathematics,* Gregory Chaitin says the traditional idea is that mathematicians have some kind of direct pipeline to God's thoughts, to absolute truth. Chaitin urges his
colleagues to abandon this way of thinking, viewing math as just another messy empirical science.

This is a stunning change. Up until one hundred years ago, no one
thought to challenge the truth of mathematics. Most of the early scientists were Christians, who said that a rational God created the universe with a rational order—a mathematical order.

As mathematician Morris Kline says, for Galileo, Copernicus, and Newton, "The search for mathematical laws of nature was an act of devotion which would reveal the glory and grandeur of [God's] handiwork."

But the new view says there is no God and that mathematics is merely something the human mind has invented. In other words, we made up rules about how to combine numbers just as we made up the rules of baseball.

But if math is simply a human creation, how do we account for its uncanny success in describing the fundamental laws of the universe? For instance, if you add five marbles to seven marbles and come up with an answer of eleven, you don't decide the mathematics was wrong; you assume you made a mistake. We all function as though mathematics is a necessary truth about reality, but without God, there's no way to explain why.

Hersh calls this dilemma a major "embarrassment."

Embarrassments like this are why Christians should never feel intimidated by secular scientists who try to make us feel ignorant for worshipping an unseen God and believing that he created the universe and all it contains. We should also teach our neighbors and our kids that Christianity is a comprehensive worldview that gives an answer for everything. It underlies the truth of mathematics—and therefore the truth of all modern science.

The "universal language" of the cosmos is the word God himself spoke in creation.

Father, thank you for the evidence of mathematical order—evidence that points to you as the author of the universe and reveals the glory and grandeur of your handiwork.

THE BEAUTY OF CHARACTER

TO READ: 1 PETER 3:3-6; PROVERBS 31:30-31

Your beauty should not come from outward adornment. . . .
Instead, it should be that of your inner self. 1 Peter 3:3-4

The women are wandering about the living room, chatting, sipping drinks, and nibbling on nachos. One by one, they disappear into another room, where a doctor injects them with a syringe full of diluted botulinum toxin type A, better known as Botox. The drug temporarily paralyzes the muscles that cause wrinkles. Within days, a wrinkled forehead becomes as smooth as a young girl's—at least for a few months. Injections must be repeated.

Millions of people ask for Botox each year, in addition to the millions who will undergo costly surgery simply to make themselves look better.

Why are we willing to spend so much for results that are so temporary? In *When No One Sees: The Importance of Character in an Age of Image,* philosopher Os Guinness says it has to do with "the modern world's obsession with physical appearance."

This obsession began, Guinness writes, when Americans started moving from the country to cities, "from small, stable, face-to-face relationships to fast, superficial, largely anonymous acquaintances." The result, he says, was "an accompanying shift from an emphasis on internal character to one's external appearance. Thus the traditional ideal of 'the strong character' has given way to 'the striking personality' and 'the successful image.'"

The dramatic increase in cosmetic procedures "is the mirror image of the decline of character," Guinness argues. Plastic surgery was once confined to those with disfiguring war injuries. Having it for purely aesthetic reasons was considered a mark of vanity, "because perfectibility was understood to lie within the spiritual, not the physical realm."

But today, even teenagers are beating on the doors of plastic surgeons, anxious to remove that small bump on the nose or to enlarge their breasts.

The danger of valuing image over character becomes clear in the political arena, where good-looking candidates are considered more electable than less attractive ones.

The same is true in other areas of life. How much wisdom and how many friendships do we miss out on because we look no further than someone's plain face or gray hair?

We need to beware of the modern tendency to admire image and personality over character and conviction. One way to do this is to make an effort to get to know our neighbors in a deeper way—one that helps us look beyond physical appearance to inward character.

To paraphrase Proverbs 31:30, true beauty proceeds from the heart—not from a syringe of Botox.

Father, help me to worry less about my looks and more about my character. Teach me to value others, not for the beauty of their faces, but for the nobility of their hearts.

SCIENTIFIC EVIDENCE
FOR BIBLICAL TRUTH

TO READ: 1 SAMUEL 17:45-51

*Reaching into his bag and taking out a stone, [David] slung it and
struck the Philistine on the forehead. 1 Samuel 17:49*

Most of us think of Goliath, the Philistine giant slain by David, as a
huge, fierce-looking man. According to a new theory, we can add one
more detail to our mental picture: glasses. Well, not glasses perhaps,
but certainly the need for an eye doctor.

Vladimir Berginer, a professor of neurology at Ben Gurion University of the Negev, in Israel, says Goliath may have suffered from a condition known as acromegaly, a disease that affects the pituitary gland.

With this condition, a benign tumor would cause the pituitary
gland to release too much growth hormone, causing the gigantism
described in the Bible. In addition, people suffering from acromegaly
often suffer from tunnel vision, which restricts their field of vision to
a narrow area directly in front of them.

According to Berginer, this condition not only explains Goliath's
great height, it also explains why David was able to defeat him so easily: Goliath never saw him coming.

Whether or not Berginer's theory holds water, it's worth noting that
scientists are increasingly using such biblical texts in their research.

This is an about-face from the way academics regarded the Bible just
a few years ago. In *Is the Bible True? How Modern Debates and Discoveries
Affirm the Essence of the Scriptures,* Jeffery Sheler points out that for more
than a century, fields such as archaeology and biblical scholarship were
dominated by "minimalists," people who believed that the Bible contains little or no history. When they applied scientific methods to the

Bible, it was usually in an attempt to disprove the truth of biblical narratives.

But the past few decades have seen what Sheler calls "refreshing winds of change" blowing across the biblical landscape. Sheler says "biblical archeology . . . [has] produced breathtaking discoveries that . . . [shed light] on the historicity of the Scriptures."

These discoveries have corroborated biblical narratives that earlier scholars had written off as myth. Not so long ago, no scholar would have dreamed of submitting a paper on Goliath to a scientific journal—not when his peers believed that Goliath was a fictional character. But the growing body of scientific evidence now means that hypotheses like Berginer's are beginning to be taken seriously.

We need to learn about and share evidence like this when we converse with friends who view the Scriptures with skepticism. Archaeological and medical evidence that support biblical truth may provoke a "holy curiosity" among our unsaved friends—one that ultimately leads to belief in God himself.

Lord, give me the courage and the words to describe scientific findings with friends who resist biblical truth—people who may one day find you through a curious mind seeking answers to scientific questions.

ERECTING BARRIERS
TO SIN

TO READ: ROMANS 7:15-25

What I want to do I do not do, but what I hate I do. Romans 7:15

Safeway offers savings on everything from steak to dog food. All you have to do is present your "Club Card" at the checkout line.

Of course, in exchange for the savings, Safeway learns every detail of your shopping habits—a loss of privacy that's increasingly characteristic of the information age.

We Americans voluntarily give up enormous amounts of information about ourselves—our names, social security numbers, and birth dates—to complete strangers. Every time we use a credit card or write a check, we leave behind clues about who we are: our likes, dislikes— even our weakness for Mrs. Fields Cookies.

That information goes into enormous databases, where people will pay handsomely for a peek at every detour your life takes.

Most of these people just want to sell you something, and they use the information for marketing surveys. But there's a darker side to information age technology. Bryan Pfaffenberger, author of *Protect Your Privacy on the Internet,* says that "for $5 you can get anybody's social security number, and for another $5, [you can] get all his residences for the past five years." With this information you can gain access to someone's credit card numbers. Medical records, salary, investments—all are available for a price.

Tragically, Americans have embraced information age technology without stopping to ask how it will shape the culture.

In *Technopoly: The Surrender of Culture to Technology,* Neil Postman warns that every technology brings with it an ideology—a set of beliefs, a way of doing things, a shifting of priorities. Information-age enthusiasts believe that the efficient collection and manipulation of information is the key to prosperity.

Corporations and governments now digitize as many of their records as possible—records that contain intimate details of our lives.

In this rush to digitize, few people paused to ask whether this was a good idea. Consequently, we've lost the ability to control who has access to our personal information.

Christians know that sinful human nature needs the restraint of law to prevent abuses of power. That's why we should support measures that would restrain those who can't resist using the Internet to pry into the most private aspects of our lives.

We must recognize, as well, that we are all vulnerable to sin—including sins the law may not necessarily discourage. In the absence of legal restraints, we must erect private barriers to sin—such as asking Christian friends to keep us accountable—knowing that we, like Paul, want to do what is good but have difficulty doing it.

Father, help me to be wary of technological advances that take no account of sinful human nature. Thank you for the gift of your Son, who frees me from the prison of my own evil desires.

IMPRESSING SECULAR CYNICS

TO READ: 1 JOHN 3:16-20

*Dear children, let us not love with words or tongue
but with actions and in truth.* 1 John 3:18

Regular readers of the *New York Times* could be excused for wondering if the wrong paper had been left on their doorstep. Instead of the usual hysteria about evangelical involvement in American public life, they read praise for that involvement.

The object of that praise was our impact on foreign policy. In "Following God Abroad," columnist Nicholas Kristof called evangelicals the "newest internationalists."

He cited the cover of the latest issue of Campus Crusade for Christ's magazine. Instead of a story about issues normally associated with evangelicals, the issue looked at rural poverty in Cameroon.

Kristof approvingly cited the list of international issues that Christians are involved in with their "growing clout": human rights in China and North Korea, sexual trafficking in Eastern Europe, slavery in Sudan, and the battle against AIDS in Africa.

Kristof acknowledges that he disagrees with evangelicals on many issues. But he hastens to add that the people he calls "snooty, college-educated bicoastal elitists" should "welcome this new constituency for foreign affairs."

Christian involvement in foreign policy is causing some Americans to reexamine their attitudes toward Christians in public life. As Kristof wrote, "I've lost my cynicism about evangelical groups, partly because I've seen them at work abroad."

There are two important lessons in these stories about newfound respect. The first is that of all people, Christians are most prepared for the challenges posed by the modern world. We are commanded to treat the obligations imposed by citizenship as an act of service to God.

At the same time, since we know that we are members of a church that encompasses people of every tribe, tongue, and nation, we are naturally concerned about what goes on outside the borders of our own country. The more you understand our worldview, the less surprised you should be at the thought of evangelicals as internationalists.

The other lesson is that the best way to get people to listen to our arguments is to show them the impact that Christian faith can have. As Kristof noted, when danger threatens, secular aid groups pull out, but Christian groups remain. That's the kind of witness that prompts a second look—and favorable words—even from the *New York Times*.

We don't have to go overseas to show that faith in Christ makes a difference in the way we treat the poor, the sick, and the suffering. There are plenty in our own neighborhoods who need our loving attention. Do the local secular cynics respect *us* because they see how we love our neighbors?

Father, I rejoice that your disciples are earning praise from those who do not follow you: Christians are not only aiding the abused of the world but are also witnessing to your existence. Help me to be such a witness to the cynics of my own town, loving the needy while showing the skeptics their need of you.

THE DUTY TO DISOBEY

TO READ: DANIEL 3:8-29

We want you to know, O king, that we will not serve your gods. Daniel 3:18

In the spring of 1963, Martin Luther King Jr. was arrested for leading a series of massive nonviolent protests against the segregated lunch counters and discriminatory hiring practices rampant in Birmingham, Alabama. While in jail, King received a letter from eight Alabama ministers. They agreed with King's goals but thought that he should call off the demonstrations and obey the law.

King disagreed, and his famous *Letter from Birmingham Jail* explains why. "One may well ask: How can you advocate breaking some laws and obeying others? The answer lies in the fact that there are two kinds of laws: just and unjust. . . . One has not only a legal but a moral responsibility to obey just laws. Conversely, one has a moral responsibility to disobey unjust laws." Then King quoted Augustine: "An unjust law is no law at all."

How does one determine whether a law is just or unjust? A just law, King wrote, "squares with the moral law or the law of God. An unjust law . . . is out of harmony with the moral law."

Then King quoted Thomas Aquinas: "An unjust law is a human law that is not rooted in eternal law and natural law."

King stood squarely in the middle of a long Christian tradition, and more than three decades after his death Christians are still influenced by his legacy. For example, those who engage in civil disobedience at abortion clinics believe that a law permitting the murder of unborn children is unjust—and therefore not a valid law at all. Thus we have the right—even the duty—to protest abortion.

As we celebrate King's birthday, it is well to remind ourselves of his great contributions, not just to the advancement of civil rights, but to the defense of a Christian view of the law. His writings are especially timely in an era when judges constantly exceed their authority—making the law for themselves, threatening the right of self-government, holding themselves accountable to no one. We've already witnessed judicial attempts to force Catholic Charities to cover birth control for its employees; how long before judges demand that Catholic hospitals perform abortions or insist that Protestant groups provide benefits for same-sex partners?

The story of Shadrach, Meshach, and Abednego reminds us that we must stand firm against all attempts to force us to do anything that would violate the laws of God. And we must join efforts to restrain out-of-control judges whose goal is to enforce not merely toleration of evil but everyone's participation in it.

Lord, give me the courage to resist demands—backed up by the force of law—that I collaborate in evil. Help me to remember that nothing—wealth, employment, social position, even life itself—is more important than obedience to you.

THE MOTHER-CHILD BOND

TO READ: ISAIAH 66:12-14

As a mother comforts her child, so will I comfort you. Isaiah 66:13

In 1963 Betty Friedan wrote a book about "the problem that has no name," referring to the alleged alienation and meaninglessness housewives experienced. The book was called *The Feminine Mystique* and is credited with igniting the modern feminist movement and helping to drive millions of women out of their homes and into the workplace.

A generation later, Danielle Crittenden has written a book about what she calls "The Problem," but it's precisely the opposite of the problem Friedan identified: it's the misery today's working mothers feel about leaving their children every day.

As Crittenden writes in *What Our Mothers Didn't Tell Us,* young women today are told to fit motherhood into their careers and are warned against letting motherhood "define them." But many women are surprised to discover that they like being mothers. "This is motherhood's greatest joy and darkest secret," Crittenden writes. "Suddenly, you can't stop thinking about your child."

Our policy makers usually ignore this intense mother-child bond. "In all the policy discussion of the problems faced by working mothers," Crittenden says, the fact that "we love our children more than anything else and want to be with them as much as we possibly can goes unmentioned." Instead, feminists try to convince mothers that "such feelings are imposed upon us by a sexist society." They dismiss full-time motherhood as "a servile and ultimately dangerous state for women to succumb to," Crittenden notes.

Polls consistently show that a majority of mothers say they'd prefer to stay home with their children if they could. That innate desire is backed up by Scripture, where some of the most striking images depicting God's nurturing concern for his people are those of mothering. For example, we read in Isaiah 66: "As a mother comforts her child, so will I comfort you" (v. 13). And in 1 Thessalonians 2 we read, "We were gentle among you, like a mother caring for her little children" (v. 7).

Christians ought to commit themselves to helping the mothers who must work to find ways to spend more time with their kids. And we should reassure mothers who choose to care for their own children that doing so does not put them in a "servile and dangerous state," as the feminists claim. Instead, motherhood is a sacred trust from God.

Lord, help me to find ways to support the mothers in my church and in my neighborhood—mothers who sometimes need assistance nurturing their children. Show me how to demonstrate respect and encouragement for the important role they are playing in their children's lives.

THE TRUTH ABOUT THE TRINITY

TO READ: DEUTERONOMY 6:1-4

Hear, O Israel: The Lord our God, the Lord is one. Deuteronomy 6:4

On American college campuses, students are receiving tracts claiming that Christians believe in three gods rather than one. The Muslims distributing these tracts are causing no end of confusion for students, including Christian students, who don't understand one of their core beliefs—the doctrine of the Trinity.

Christians believe that the one true God has forever known himself as the Father, the Son, and the Holy Spirit. It's foundational to our faith, and yet, says theologian Timothy George, it is perhaps the most neglected doctrine we hold, maybe because we can't understand it or explain it. And so, George says, "We tend to shove it to the side, until all of a sudden we find ourselves in a discussion with a Muslim who says to us, 'Oh, you Christians claim to believe in one God, but really you believe in three gods.'"

And that is exactly what the Koran teaches about Christians. We need to remember that Muhammad lived some two centuries after Augustine, who wrote one of the great treatises on the Trinity. He did so in the face of heretical beliefs about God that were circulating in his day. But those beliefs continued to spread, and eventually they reached Mecca, where Muhammad lived. According to these heretics, God has a wife called Mary, with whom he had intercourse, resulting in Jesus. It was this distortion that Muhammad heard and believed, and many others who call Christians tritheists think that we really do believe in three gods.

George insists that this is why a strong grasp of the doctrine of the Trinity is vitally important. It's "nothing other than the conceptual framework needed to understand the story of Jesus as the story of God."

Muhammad's mistaken teachings about the Trinity continue to influence millions of Muslims. At this time of great curiosity about religious teachings, Christians must reach out to their Muslim neighbors, learn what they believe, and learn how to lovingly correct their misconceptions about what we believe.

But we cannot do this unless we understand our own teachings—especially the doctrine of the Trinity. How well do you and your family understand it? Could you explain it to an unbeliever if you were challenged to do so? The doctrine teaches that there is only one true God—and yet within the being of God, there has eternally existed a bond of relationship, love, and intimacy: Father and Son and Holy Spirit.

Father, help me to remember that many of my neighbors believe false teachings about you. Be with me as I prepare to witness to them the truth about the Holy Trinity: that "the Lord Our God" is Father, Son, and Holy Spirit.

JANUARY 18

LOVING OUR (URBAN) NEIGHBORS

TO READ: MARK 12:28-34

Love your neighbor as yourself. Mark 12:31

What's the recipe for a prize-winning, faith-based program?

Take one ex-con. Add a neighborhood filled with gangs and gunfire. Throw in one conversion to Christ. Stir in nine hundred fatherless kids. Fold in dozens of baseballs, and bake in the sun for sixteen weeks. Yield: one hundred Little League teams filled with kids learning self-respect and community values. It's a terrific recipe—one cooked up by Chicago insurance broker Bob Muzikowski.

As a child, Muzikowski played baseball in city leagues. At Columbia University he began experimenting with drugs and abusing alcohol, habits that would worsen following graduation. In 1983 a Christian friend named B. J. Weber invited Muzikowski to attend the National Prayer Breakfast in Washington. "Sure, why not?" he responded.

Driving to Washington, Muzikowski stopped at a bar for a few drinks. When a fight erupted, Muzikowski jumped in, at one point attempting to swing from a chandelier. Police charged him with assault and destruction of property—for yanking down the chandelier. He never made it to the prayer breakfast.

Weber bailed Muzikowski out of jail—and then led him into a new life in Christ. He began attending Alcoholics Anonymous meetings, got married, and moved to Chicago.

It was on his way to work one day that Muzikowski first saw a derelict ball field full of trash. *The kids in this neighborhood could use a real Little League to play in,* he thought.

Muzikowski teamed up with a friend to create the Near North Little League. Initial practice sessions "were pretty wild," as coaches dealt with 250 boys who were long on enthusiasm and short on fundamentals. Each game began with a prayer. Cursing was strictly forbidden.

"While I had no illusions that I would change the world, I had no doubt that God wanted me to play baseball with [these] kids," Muzikowski says. "My faith had taught me that being a Christian means truly believing what Jesus said about loving my neighbor."

The next year, four hundred kids joined the league.

Reporters wonder why a wealthy white businessman lives among the poor, coaching other people's kids. Muzikowski answers, "Jesus didn't say, 'When you've paid someone to do it unto the least of these.' What he said was, 'When you have done it unto the least of these, you have done it unto me.'"

Muzikowski's life is a tremendous witness to the Lord he serves—and a reminder that God gifts all of us for one mission field or another—anything from an inner-city baseball field filled with fatherless kids to an elite college campus populated by thoroughly secular students. Do we know where God wants us to serve? Are we open to his call?

Lord, at each stage of my life, show me where my gifts can be of use to your Kingdom, and create in me a desire to use them.

JANUARY 19

IS LIFE "ALL ABOUT ME"?

TO READ: 1 CORINTHIANS 13:4-8

Love is patient, love is kind. . . . It always protects, always trusts, always hopes, always perseveres. 1 Corinthians 13:4-7

"I'm just not growing in this relationship," Kevin told his wife, Diane. After ten years of marriage and the birth of two children, he left his family. And he did it, Diane discovered, with his therapist's blessing.

If Diane had been up on the state of modern psychology, she wouldn't have been so surprised. One Christian psychologist says that the spread of what he calls the "selfist philosophy" has gravely damaged many American families.

In *Psychology as Religion: The Cult of Self-Worship,* Dr. Paul Vitz describes modern psychology's deep commitment to self-worship, or "selfism." All the major theories of motivation and personality, he says, assume that reward for the self is the only functional ethical principle.

These values are hostile to our ability to form permanent relationships or to commit to such values as duty and self-sacrifice. Instead, he says, "with monotonous regularity, the selfist literature sides with those values that encourage divorce" and the breaking of family ties.

Part of the problem is the nature of the therapeutic process. The psychotherapist is typically preoccupied with an individual patient, and he seldom challenges his version of the facts. He doesn't listen to children, parents, or the spouse who might be involved.

Worse, some therapists encourage divorce on theoretical grounds. They teach that if either spouse feels the relationship has stagnated, the marriage isn't worth saving.

Selfist ideals give some counselors a strong bias against parents. In recovery group settings, patients are under pressure to describe how badly their families treated them. Patients thus become self-pitying "victims"—with a strong sense of moral superiority.

With its emphasis on treating individuals in isolation and its hostility to social bonds, modern psychology has caused incalculable damage to our society.

Vitz invites his readers to imagine a different kind of therapy, one based on love, gratitude, respect, and forgiveness—a therapy that strengthens a patient's family instead of destroying it.

This approach follows the biblical vision of human relations. It does not give anyone an out if they think they're not growing in their relationships. Instead, 1 Corinthians tells us to love one another unconditionally, to be patient and kind and not insist on getting our own way.

The rise of selfism means that Christians need to be cautious about those from whom they seek counsel. And if you find yourself asking, "What's in it for me," stop and remember the rest of Paul's message: Love "always protects, always trusts, always hopes, always perseveres"—and above all, "Love never fails" (1 Corinthians 13:7-8).

Lord, let me not be influenced by a culture that urges me to indulge in an orgy of selfishness. In moments of temptation, frustration, or boredom, may I remember to embrace your command to love my family as you love me.

J A N U A R Y   2 0

APPRECIATING BEAUTY

TO READ: EXODUS 26:1-6

Make the tabernacle with ten curtains of finely twisted linen and blue, purple and scarlet yarn, with cherubim worked into them by a skilled craftsman. Exodus 26:1

There's a lot of junk out there being marketed to Christians. Nearly everyone agrees that much of it is cringe-inducing and only confirms people's worst stereotypes of Christians. What they do not agree on is what we should do about it. Any answer to that question must start with remembering the place that beauty and aesthetics occupy in a truly Christian worldview.

In an article titled "The Jesus Market" in the *Weekly Standard,* Stephen Bates gave readers a sense of just how much stuff is included in that category and how tasteless some of it can be. Christian merchandise, he wrote, is more than books and music. It's outerwear, underwear, food, knickknacks, and even rubber duckies that say, "Depend upon Christ the King."

The fact that so many Christians buy this kind of merchandise is an indication that there is something vital missing from their belief system: an appreciation of taste and beauty.

An appreciation of beauty is not optional for the Christian. It's as mandatory as the pursuit of truth and goodness, which is why aesthetics has historically been considered a branch of moral theology.

Augustine, Thomas Aquinas, and C. S. Lewis all wrote that beauty, like truth and goodness, has its origin in who God is, in his very nature. Aquinas said that beauty "participates in the divine brightness." Beauty gives us a glimpse of God's integrity, perfection, and majesty. Beauty points to the order and intelligence that sustains the universe. And it points to the source of that intelligence and order. Augustine and Lewis both wrote of the role their love of beauty had in their conversions. In *Confessions*, Augustine exclaimed, "O Beauty ever ancient and ever new! Too late I loved you!"

And in *Surprised by Joy*, Lewis described the "joy" and "longing" he felt as a boy when he listened to the music of Wagner. The feelings the music inspired provided evidence of the existence of something truly awe inspiring—the only thing that could fulfill his longing.

When we're tempted to make, or buy, some of the tackier Christian merchandise, we should remember God's instructions to those responsible for creating his holy Tabernacle: The Tabernacle and all its contents were to be made with great care, of the finest materials—pure gold, silver, and bronze, acacia wood, fine linens, all "skillfully worked" to a beautiful pattern. The same went for the clothing of the priests. Anything intended to honor and glorify God had to be of the highest quality.

As Christians we can and should do better than the kind of stuff that makes us all cringe. An indifference to beauty, after all, is as foreign to the Christian worldview as indifference to truth or to goodness.

Lord, create in me a desire to seek out and appreciate only goods that are of the highest quality—merchandise that reflects the beauty, truth, and goodness of the One I worship.

"IT IS WELL WITH MY SOUL"

TO READ: ROMANS 8:31-39

Neither death nor life, neither angels nor demons, . . . nor anything else in all creation, will be able to separate us from the love of God. Romans 8:38-39

Millions have found comfort in the great gospel hymn "It Is Well with My Soul." But many people don't know the tragic story behind the composition of the hymn, a story of a soul finding peace in God even in the midst of grief and loss.

In 1871, a Christian businessman named Horatio Spafford was hard hit by the great Chicago fire. Spafford had invested heavily in real estate along Lake Michigan, and the fire wiped out his holdings.

Only a short time earlier Spafford and his wife had suffered the loss of their son. However, the worst was yet to come.

Two years later Spafford decided to take his wife and four daughters to Europe on vacation. But last-minute business kept Spafford at home in Chicago. He sent his family ahead on the ocean liner SS *Ville du Havre*.

Halfway across the Atlantic, an English vessel rammed the *Ville du Havre* and cut her in two. In the chaos that followed, Mrs. Spafford watched helplessly as her four daughters were swept overboard to their deaths. Within just twelve minutes the ship had sunk.

The survivors were taken to Wales. From there Mrs. Spafford cabled the terrible news to her husband. The cable consisted of just two words: "Saved alone."

Spafford immediately set off for Wales to be with his wife. As his ship approached the mid-Atlantic, he looked out over the billowing waves that had taken the lives of his beloved daughters. Inspired by the sight, Spafford wrote the words of his now famous hymn:

When peace, like a river, attendeth my way,
When sorrows like sea billows roll;
Whatever my lot,
Thou hast taught me to say,
It is well,
It is well with my soul.

What an astounding sentiment! We can only imagine the grief he must have suffered—how he must have prayed and wept and searched for meaning in the tragedy. But in the end, he was able to affirm a deep faith that, for the believer, "it is well," even in the face of great personal suffering.

The greatest hymns are those that speak out of the warp and woof of a flawed and fallen world, that give expression to our deepest fears and hopes. Music helps us express thoughts too profound for simple prose and gives melody to the richest experiences of faith.

As the life of Horatio Spafford teaches us, music can flow from a wounded heart to soothe and bless Christians for generations to come.

Lord, teach me to appreciate music that points to you so that in times of sorrow, I will find comfort—and find you—in the music of faith.

CREATING AND KILLING

TO READ: PSALM 106:36-39

They shed innocent blood, the blood of their sons and daughters. Psalm 106:38

In a scene in *The Two Towers,* the second in J. R. R. Tolkien's Lord of the Rings trilogy, the traitor Saruman is torturing the noble wizard Gandalf. "What," the evil wizard asks Gandalf, "is the greatest power?"

"Life," Gandalf replies.

"You fool," says Saruman. "Life can be destroyed. Did I teach you nothing?"

Trying again, Gandalf says, "Creation."

"Yes," answers Saruman, "the power to create life."

This passage comes to mind today, the anniversary of the start of the modern holocaust: the Supreme Court's *Roe v. Wade* decision. Forty million babies have died as a result.

As terrible as *Roe* was, we are now facing an even worse horror. In *Roe* we took life—which was bad enough—but at least we were not pretending to be God. Now, with cloning, humans will play God, the author of life: We will create life for our own purposes.

Sadly, just as most Christians were asleep when *Roe* was decided, we are in danger of sleeping through the alarm of this latest moral catastrophe. We're not talking about taking the lives of millions of kids, as horrible as that is. We're talking about *creating* the lives of forty million kids—and *then* killing them, ostensibly for the good of humanity.

Where will all this lead us? In *The Abolition of Man,* C. S. Lewis offered a prophetic warning half a century before human cloning became a potential reality. "If any one age," he wrote, "really attains, by eugenics and scientific education, the power to make its descendents what it pleases, all men who live after are the patients of that power," slaves to the "dead hand of the great planners and conditioners."

Just as Lewis foresaw, the biotech revolution is moving like a steamroller, crushing everything—including ethical questions—in its path. The reason is that secular ethics have been drained of moral content. In the political debate, the utilitarians—those who demand the "greatest good for the greatest number"—have seized the high ground and offer dazzling promises of cures to come.

As Christians it's our duty to raise even bigger moral questions. We should answer those who justify the creating and killing of millions of humans on the grounds that it will "improve health" by pointing to people like Joni Eareckson Tada, a quadriplegic (and Christian) who knows exactly where such research will lead: to a culture in which some lives are considered not worth living—or saving.

History reminds us that the worst atrocities are performed in the name of humanitarian causes. And sacrificing one to benefit all soon makes all vulnerable.

Lord, let me not weaken before arguments that I—or loved ones who suffer from debilitating diseases—"deserve" the cures promised through the killing of others. Help me to boldly speak out for the truth that every life is precious.

THE COSMIC DRAMA

TO READ: GENESIS 1:31; 2:1-4

Thus the heavens and the earth were completed in all their vast array. Genesis 2:1

Is there life on other planets? Are extraterrestrials real or merely a fantasy?

"The universe is so large that it would be folly to say that we are the exception," says Rev. George Coyne, director of the Vatican Astronomic Observatory. His colleague, Rev. Christopher Corbally, suggests that belief in extraterrestrials would not conflict with Christian doctrine: While Christ is indeed the savior for earthlings, he is not necessarily the only savior for the whole universe.

These are interesting ideas. But even more intriguing is the fact that belief in the possibility of alien life originated more than two thousand years ago—by those eager to discredit religious belief.

In *Crisis* magazine, Benjamin Wiker, a fellow with the Discovery Institute, writes that historically, the idea of aliens arose among ancient materialist philosophers, called the Epicureans, "as part of an overall philosophical argument." According to Wiker, their theories were rooted "not in evidence but in the desire to rid the world of religion."

Epicurus and his disciple Lucretius taught that belief in gods who intervene in human affairs is the root of all evil, leading people to engage in such atrocities as child sacrifice. Their solution, Wiker says, was to eliminate religious belief by embracing a materialist view of the universe. They got rid of the need for a divine creator by asserting that everything in the universe came into being as a result of the chance jostling of brute matter—that is, atoms. "Because the number of atoms in a limitless universe is infinite," Wiker writes, "the random motion of the atoms must have produced a 'plurality of worlds.'" These worlds—like Earth—contained, as Lucretius put it, "various tribes of men and breeds of beasts."

Early Christians viewed these claims with skepticism. First, they believed that anything that lived independently of air and water had to exist in the air—and hence would, by definition, be a spirit and not some kind of embodied extraterrestrial. Second, they believed the teachings of Genesis: that God, not chance, created the universe and human beings. Most important of all, Wiker writes, early Christians believed that "the incarnation of Christ was the union of God's divinity with our humanity." Humans "were thereby placed at the center of the cosmic drama, which made no room for questions about the redemption of other intelligent beings—even angels."

Today we're witnessing a resurgence of interest in the possibility of extraterrestrials. As was the case two thousand years ago, those who reject belief in God are at the forefront of the search for "little green men."

It's a reminder that no matter how convincing the evidence seems, Christians must always be skeptical of teachings that contradict the Holy Scriptures—and must examine the true motives of those who try to alter our beliefs.

Father, forgive me for the times I have been too quick to accept ideas that minimize your Son's sacrifice. Give me discernment in sorting through cultural teachings that uphold biblical truth—and those that seek to tear it down.

HOW TO FIND HAPPINESS

TO READ: MATTHEW 6:19-22, 31-34

Seek first his kingdom and his righteousness, and all these things will be given to you as well. Matthew 6:33

Harvard psychology professor Daniel Gilbert is working on a fascinating project: He's studying happiness—scientifically.

Gilbert and his associates are doing research on what they call "affective forecasting." That is, they're trying to find out how we predict what will make us happy and whether our predictions are accurate. Their research has led them to believe that we often don't know what we want—even when we think we do.

Reporter Jon Gertner writes in the *New York Times Magazine*, "What Gilbert has found . . . is that we overestimate the intensity and the duration of our emotional reactions—our 'affect'—to future events. In other words, we might believe that a new BMW will make life perfect. But it will almost certainly be less exciting than we anticipated; nor will it excite us for as long as we predicted."

On the other hand, bad things don't always hurt us as much as we fear they will; we have a remarkable ability to adapt even to the worst circumstances. Gilbert's associate George Loewenstein told the *Times,* "In the same way that our eye adapts to different levels of illumination, we're designed to . . . go back to the happiness set point. Our brains are not trying to be happy. Our brains are trying to regulate us."

What all of this means, the researchers say, is that humans tend to make bad decisions because they're wrong about what will or will not make them happy. It's a little sobering to realize how many of our important decisions are based on wrong thinking and transitory emotions. Bad choices in all of the major areas of our lives—education, career, marriage, and more—can be traced back to mistaken beliefs about what will make us happy.

When we seek God's best instead of our own, we find a higher standard by which to make our decisions—a standard that doesn't change when our feelings do.

The truth is that spending our whole lives chasing what we want is the best way *not* to find happiness. As C. S. Lewis put it in *First and Second Things: Essays on Theology and Ethics*, "You can't get second things by putting them first; you can get second things only by putting first things first."

This study is bona fide research that validates what the Bible teaches. Science confirms that chasing our own personal desires is a dead end. Seeking the Kingdom of God first is the choice that brings true and lasting satisfaction.

Lord, when I am tempted to "buy" happiness through a bigger home, a faster car, or a different spouse, help me to remember that lasting joy can be found only in your presence and your purposes.

PROMOTING MARKETPLACE MORALITY

TO READ: LEVITICUS 19:9-13

Do not defraud your neighbor or rob him. Leviticus 19:13

What would it take to prevent another Enron scandal?

Recently, experts in business ethics gathered at Rice University to work on an answer. Rice professor Duane Windsor suggested that what's needed is "more fear of a loss of reputation."

The schools will be asking these questions for years: How could the auditors be so negligent? What new regulations are needed?

The most crucial question is one that secular observers may be unwilling to ask: Has value-free postmodernity—the fruit of modern secularism—undermined the moral foundation essential for democratic capitalism?

As theologian Michael Novak argues, western liberal democracy is like a three-legged stool. One leg is political freedom; the second, economic freedom; the third, moral responsibility. Weaken any one of those legs and the stool topples.

Enron's collapse exposes a decayed third leg—the leg of moral responsibility.

Enron's leaders were the best and the brightest, pillars of the community. Enron's chairman, Kenneth Lay, boasted that he hired only graduates of the top business schools.

Enron's collapse exposes the glaring failure of these business schools. Ethics historically rests on absolute truth, which our elite schools have systematically assaulted for four decades.

But the Enron debacle does offer a good chance for Christians to contend for the biblical worldview in the marketplace. The Scriptures endorse concepts such as private property, contract rights, and the discharge of debts—all essential to free markets. The Bible also demands justice, warning of God's judgment against oppressors who withhold wages or take advantage of the needy.

The scriptural system, in short, balances the acquisition of wealth with a demand for both justice and compassion. It requires people to subordinate self-interest to moral demands.

Through the centuries Christians have fought to bring these moral demands to bear in the marketplace. For example, in nineteenth-century England following rapid industrialization, conditions in the coal mines and factories were deplorable. The great Christian statesman Lord Shaftesbury led a crusade against these conditions, exposing what William Blake's poem *Jerusalem* called "the dark Satanic mills."

The lesson of history, which our neighbors need to understand, is that capitalism is healthy only when it is subject to moral restraints derived ultimately from religious truth.

It is these moral restraints that have been dangerously loosened, as Enron reveals. The resulting chaos can lead only to bureaucratic regulations and the loss of freedom—unless we rebuild the third leg of Michael Novak's stool.

When we read about scandals like Enron, we should also examine our own lives, asking ourselves if we are fair and generous with those who depend on us. Do we pay babysitters, gardeners, and cleaners an appropriate wage? Those of us who run businesses must make sure our employees work in decent conditions and earn a decent salary, knowing that a watching world will judge not only us but also the God we say we serve.

Lord, let me bring glory to you, not through public gifts to charity, but through private payment of all my debts.

JANUARY 26

SHOULD CHILDREN BE "THE ULTIMATE SHOPPING EXPERIENCE"?

TO READ: 1 KINGS 3:16-28

[The king said,] "Cut the living child in two and give half to one and half to the other." I Kings 3:25

Don't all parents want to give their children the best chance at success in life?

According to the *Washington Post* magazine, the answer is "not necessarily," especially if it gets in the way of what's most important to the parents.

The article tells the story of newborn Gauvin Hughes McCullough and his two mothers: Sharon Duchesneau, his birth mother, and Candace McCullough, his adoptive mother. Yes, Duchesneau and McCullough are lesbians, but that's the least remarkable part of Gauvin's story.

Duchesneau and McCullough are also deaf. From the moment they decided to have a child, they set out to maximize the chances that the child would be deaf also.

Sperm banks told them that deafness was a condition they screened out in potential donors. Disappointed, they turned to a deaf male friend. Even so, that wouldn't guarantee that Gauvin would be deaf like his "mothers." They had to wait several months after Gauvin was born for an audiologist to confirm success: the baby was deaf.

Why would parents, especially those who have experienced the challenges posed by a disability like deafness, wish this condition on their children?

Increasingly, deaf people see deafness not as a disability but as a culture. They regard treatments, such as cochlear implants that enable deaf children to hear, as a kind of cultural genocide.

This view perfectly reflects the postmodern obsession with identity politics. We belong to the "culture" we build out of our own grievance groups, defined by sexual orientation, gender, disability, etc.

Tragically, Duchesneau and McCullough are hardly alone in practicing what can only be called eugenics. Soon, thanks to advances in genetics, parents won't have to live with the uncertainty of "success" that this couple did. Not only will they be able to prevent disabilities and illnesses, they will be able to enhance physical and mental attributes and choose things like size and hair color. Children will become, as one commentator put it, the ultimate shopping experience—designer babies.

Thus we will have gone from seeing children as charges, whose well-being we are supposed to put above our own, to the means by which we achieve self-fulfillment and what we think is best for us.

Today expectant parents are confronted with technological "advances" intended to guarantee a "perfect" baby. And if the child is revealed to be "imperfect"? Parents are encouraged to abort and try again. We need to seek the treasure of God's wisdom—that we may be delivered from "the way of evil."

Lord, help me to offer your wisdom to loved ones experiencing complicated pregnancies and to employ that wisdom myself when I must make difficult decisions regarding the health of loved ones in my care.

JANUARY 27

ABUSING OUR BODIES

TO READ: 1 CORINTHIANS 6:19-20

Honor God with your body. I Corinthians 6:20

For years, Seattle ferryboats regularly transported up to 250 passengers across Puget Sound. Then ferry officials noted something odd: The seating no longer seemed to accommodate as many people as it once did. Many passengers ended up standing or sitting on the floor.

To put it politely, people just aren't fitting into the seats the way they used to. As a result, Seattle planned to spend millions of dollars to install bigger ferry seats.

Since the 1950s, public seating has followed what's called "the eighteen-inch rule": Seats measuring eighteen inches across have been considered adequate to accommodate most derrieres. But now, in an era known for Big Gulp drinks, Double Whopper burgers, and supersized fries, the eighteen-inch rule is being, shall we say, stretched.

Seattle ferry officials first tried reducing the number of passengers allowed on each ferry, but that outraged some commuters—so much so that they organized a petition denouncing what they labeled the "Butt Police." So ferry officials decided the only solution was to simply enlarge the seats—at taxpayer expense, of course.

The "reshaping" of America is causing problems everywhere. According to Michael Fumento of the American Enterprise Institute, America is the fattest nation on earth. Builders of everything from cars to sports arenas to movie theaters are having to design bigger seats to accommodate bigger—well, bigger Americans.

Of course, some people have weight problems for medical reasons, but according to the National Academy of Sciences, at least two-thirds of Americans are overweight—mostly for *non*medical reasons. And the cost of our collective weight gain goes beyond dollars. The Centers for Disease Control says that more than 300,000 of us die prematurely every year of weight-related illnesses.

These statistics are a sobering reminder that good stewardship of our bodies requires moderation and exercise and that overeating is unhealthy.

In an era of slogans such as "keep your laws off my body," Americans are making sacred the notion that what we do in private is nobody else's business and that private conduct is irrelevant to public matters.

But as Seattle's million-dollar ferry renovation reminds us, private behavior *does* have public consequences.

The next time we reach for a second helping of Ben & Jerry's Chubby Hubby ice cream, we ought to remember the lesson of those too-small ferry seats: What we do behind closed doors—or in the case of the refrigerator, before an *open* door—can have an impact on society at large.

Lord, help me to fill the emptiness inside, not with unnecessary food but with a rich relationship with you.

JANUARY 28

A BIBLICAL VISION
OF SEXUALITY

TO READ: 1 CORINTHIANS 6:13-18

Flee from sexual immorality. I Corinthians 6:18

In Africa, the scale of the AIDS epidemic boggles the mind. According to epidemiologists, fifteen thousand people, most of them in developing countries, are infected with HIV every day. It's estimated that in sub-Saharan Africa between 12 and 25 percent of the adult population are infected, with total infection rates as high as 39 percent.

In some parts of Africa, between half and three-quarters of all deaths are caused by AIDS. Sadder still, orphans of AIDS victims are three times more likely to die before the age of five—often from starvation—than non-orphans.

The impact of AIDS goes beyond personal tragedies. It can be felt in the economic and political spheres as well. AIDS has a tremendous impact on the already depressed economies of sub-Saharan Africa.

And if that weren't bad enough, Tommy Thompson, secretary of Health and Human Services, warns that communities ravaged by the disease would become fertile breeding grounds for terrorists.

Given the scope of the problem, it would certainly be wise to consider every possible approach—including the involvement of the church. The people of Uganda and other parts of East Africa learned recently how important this help can be. Trans World Radio, a Christian broadcaster, aired a radio special called "The Honey That Kills." In East Africa, "getting honey" is slang for having sex.

Instead of talking about condom use, the program told listeners about one sure way to avoid infection: biblical standards of chastity and fidelity. In addition, Trans World Radio enlisted local churches to minister to AIDS patients and spread the word about chastity. This program is part of the reason that Uganda, uniquely among African nations, has experienced what the United Nations characterizes as a major turnaround in the battle against AIDS.

It makes perfect sense. Christianity strikes the ideal balance between compassion for the victims and honesty about the epidemic.

As Eugene Rivers, a Boston pastor deeply involved in the issue, says, "Promiscuity, infidelity, [even] rape" are at the heart of the AIDS epidemic in the developing world. Therefore, a real solution to the AIDS problem must include a "biblical vision of human sexuality and behavior and responsibility." As he puts it, the AIDS pandemic cries out for a biblical answer.

At a time when it's considered impolite, or even intolerant, to cite Christian arguments in public discourse, issues like AIDS are a reminder of what not citing these arguments can cost: a chance at a real solution to the greatest health crisis of our time. Christians must boldly and unapologetically make these arguments and insist that scarce government funds go to AIDS programs that have proven their worth.

The lives of millions depend on it.

Lord, at a time when many "experts" pretend there is no link between promiscuity and disease, bless the efforts of the real authorities on human sexuality: those who honor your teachings.

LEARNING TO FEAR EVIL

TO READ: PROVERBS 1:1-7

The fear of the Lord is the beginning of knowledge,
but fools despise wisdom and discipline. Proverbs 1:7

A few years ago, on the one hundredth anniversary of Alfred Hitchcock's birth, his fans celebrated with birthday parties, film festivals, and sales of macabre memorabilia such as shower curtains from the Bates Hotel.

Why is it that Hitchcock's films continue to grip our imaginations? The answer lies in the worldview that undergirds his movies.

Hitchcock didn't consider himself an explicitly Christian filmmaker. But he once acknowledged to the great French director François Truffaut that "one's early upbringing influences a man's life and guides his instinct." Hitchcock's own Catholic education developed in him, as he put it, "a strong sense of . . . moral fear—the fear of being involved in anything evil."

This background is evident in Hitchcock's films. As Maria Kuntz writes in *Crisis* magazine, the archetypal Hitchcockian situation "involves an ordinary man or woman suddenly [thrown into] an out-of-the-ordinary situation. . . . This disruption," she writes, "is caused by some manifestation of evil: a malevolent person . . . political agents [or] a sinful past."

For example, in a film called *I Confess,* a man confesses to his priest that he has just murdered a man. Through a bizarre set of circumstances, the priest himself is accused of the crime and must make a fateful decision: Should he break his vows and turn in the killer—or be hanged for the crime himself?

In Hitchcock's films, resolution of the plot often requires the hero to overcome some shortcoming or sin. For example, in the film *North by Northwest*, Cary Grant plays an irresponsible playboy who, through a case of mistaken identity, is pulled into a Cold War plot involving the sale of state secrets. Grant is given a choice: He can back out and save his own skin or help both his government and the woman he loves—but at the risk of his own life.

These moral dilemmas are what make Hitchcock's films so popular even today. As Kuntz writes, Hitchcock's films "are not theological ruminations about the nature of evil, but a presentation of its horrific consequences."

Hitchcock's films remind us of the power of art to communicate a fundamentally Christian worldview.

This weekend, why not rent a couple of Hitchcock's earlier films and watch them with your family or some unsaved friends? Then discuss the portrayal of real good and real evil. It's a wonderful way to point people to the only solution for evil: the cross of Jesus Christ.

Lord, thank you for artistic gifts that when well-used can be a witness to the wisdom of fleeing evil. Teach me how to use the creative gifts of others to bring loved ones into your Kingdom.

HAVE WE ADAPTED
TO EVIL?

TO READ: EPHESIANS 4:17-19

Having lost all sensitivity, they have given themselves over to sensuality so as to indulge in every kind of impurity, with a continual lust for more. Ephesians 4:19

The latest fad in the world of toys is pop musician action figures. From Art Asylum comes an Eminem figure swinging a chainsaw, his face distorted with rage and malice. The next Eminem action figure will include a dead woman in a car trunk, thus memorializing the lyrics and cover of the rapper's first album.

You would expect widespread shock and outrage over this. But nobody seems to care. Commenting on Eminem's fantasies of incest, one music critic writes that Eminem is just "one of those charming rogues"—"indubitably dangerous" but "good-hearted." If these things bother you, he says, you need to "disable your prejudgment button." *Prejudgment* means judging before the facts are in, but the music critic isn't asking us to delay judgment about whether the music is evil; he more or less admits that it is. What he means is that we should delay judgment about whether or not evil can be fun.

In *What We Can't Not Know*, Jay Budziszewski says we shouldn't be surprised by any of this. Our society has been desensitized to evil. Desensitization is one of the ways that an organism adapts to its environment. If you touch the tiny creature called a hydra once, it flinches. But if you touch it fifty times, by the fiftieth touch the flinch is much less pronounced. Eventually the hydra stops flinching.

Like the hydra, we, too, have been desensitized. "Mainstream" movies outdo the ancient Roman amphitheater by showing every spurt of blood close up and ten feet tall. Video games allow players to feel that every time a victim is stabbed, shot, dismembered, or decapitated, they are doing the killing themselves. Lust and gore beyond the dreams of cruelty fall into our waiting hands.

You see what has happened. We were touched by abomination, and we flinched, but nothing seemed to happen. Then we were touched again and again, and by the five-hundredth touch, we stopped flinching. But something *has* transpired. We have become the sort of people who endure the abominable touch and cease to notice.

In a culture that celebrates violence, we need to ask ourselves if there are any ways in which we are allowing ourselves to become desensitized to evil—through the games we play, the films we watch, the books we read, or even the toys we buy.

By the grace of God, the task before us is to become *re*sensitized. Instead of "adapting" to our fallen society, we need to seek to be salt and light so that our culture might be redeemed.

Lord, help me to drive from my life anything that desensitizes me to evil—and darkens my understanding of the God of righteousness.

ARE HUMAN
REMAINS "ART"?

TO READ: PHILIPPIANS 2:5-11

[Jesus] made himself nothing, taking the very nature of a servant,
being made in human likeness. Philippians 2:7

In Germany the corpses of some two hundred people are artistically arranged at Mannheim's Museum of Technology and Labor.

The "artist" is a German doctor who has been labeled a real-life Dr. Frankenstein, and the display has stirred up an international debate about the sacredness of the human body.

One cadaver, called "The Muscleman," features a skeleton whose muscles have been cut off and hung on a hanger. A corpse called "The Runner" features muscles sliced into strips that appear to be blowing in the wind as he runs. Then there's a cadaver of a pregnant woman, her abdomen sliced open to reveal the corpse of a five-month-old fetus.

The artist, Dr. Gunther von Hagens, says all of the corpses came from volunteers who gave permission for their remains to be used this way. He preserved the cadavers using a technique he invented called plastination. Von Hagens calls the corpses "anatomical artwork" and says they're meant to help people understand the beauty and vulnerability of the human body.

German theologians are outraged, calling the exhibit immoral and voyeuristic. Even the German prime minister got in on the act, saying the exhibit is "degrading to human dignity."

The critics are right. Dr. von Hagens's grotesque work is a product of his materialist worldview. His comments suggest that he views the human body as nothing more than a complex mechanism, a complicated network of cells. So he sees nothing wrong with putting corpses on display like so many stuffed owls or racks of deer.

But the Scriptures teach us that our bodies are of much higher value. In fact, the high view of the human body came largely from the New Testament teaching of the Incarnation. In the ancient world it was considered too degrading to think a god would take on human form. The Incarnation was a radical idea—and led, in the Christian tradition, to a great respect for the human body as such.

As the influence of Christianity declines, one of the cultural effects we'll see is a lack of respect for the human body. Using human cadavers in ghoulish works of art is only one way the materialist worldview is expressed. We also see it come into play when scantily clad models are used to sell cars or when doctors kill healthy fetuses and sell them for parts.

Christians ought to stand against the materialist ethic in all of its expressions. This means everything from speaking out against merchandisers who "sell" the human body along with their products, to refusing to allow our children to wear sexually explicit clothing.

Because God took on human form, the human body is sacred—and it ought to be treated that way.

Lord, teach me to honor you by respecting the dignity of my own body and the bodies of others. May I treat them not as sources of entertainment but as sacred reminders that you took on human form yourself.

UNCONVENTIONAL (LITERARY) WEAPONS

TO READ: 2 SAMUEL 12:1-15

There were two men in a certain town, one rich and the other poor. 2 Samuel 12:1

The great nineteenth-century evangelist Charles Finney once declared, "I cannot believe that a person who has ever known the love of God can relish a secular novel."

Ironically, it was during Finney's lifetime that Christians turned a secular novel, *Uncle Tom's Cabin,* into a great weapon for Christ.

Probably no other novel has made such an impact on a nation. *Uncle Tom's Cabin* sold 300,000 copies in its first year and two million copies by the end of the decade. These are incredible figures, considering that America's population was less than a tenth of the size it is today. The book helped millions of Americans understand for the first time what a terrible thing it was to be a slave.

Today "Uncle Tom" is a derogatory term applied to blacks who treat whites with fawning subservience. But in Harriet Beecher Stowe's novel, Tom is a Christlike figure. He suffers the worst evils imaginable yet refuses to strike back.

The book seared the consciences of Stowe's readers and helped them realize that slavery was a great evil, not merely a problematic social institution.

Antislavery activists had been trying to get that message across for almost thirty years. But nothing they did had the impact of this book. In fact, most abolitionists didn't read novels. Like Charles Finney, they considered novels frivolous, if not downright immoral.

Uncle Tom's Cabin is a reminder that one of the reasons we read fiction is because it helps train the moral imagination. As the late writer and thinker Russell Kirk put it, the battle for our hearts and minds is fought in the "land of the human imagination."

Biblical figures understood the power of a good story. Remember the prophet Nathan, who confronted King David about his affair with Bathsheba? Nathan did not offer David a dry lecture on the sin of adultery. Instead, he spun a story about a rich man who took the only lamb belonging to a poor man. In order to get past David's defenses, Nathan told an allegorical story.

Harriet Beecher Stowe received much of her insight into slavery from carefully documented abolitionist accounts. She then used her creative ability to teach the message that all men and women are created in God's image and are infinitely precious to him.

Modern Christians ought to use the same strategy as we fight modern social evils such as abortion, pornography, and the breakdown of the family. We must use books, film, music, and television to shock Americans out of their complacency—and fight modern evils through the weapon of a great story.

Lord, as I participate in the fight against modern social evils, help me to choose weapons that will be most effective in winning the first important battle: the battle for the terrain of my neighbors' hearts.

FEBRUARY 2

WIRED FOR COMMUNITY

TO READ: PSALM 68:4-6

God sets the lonely in families. Psalm 68:6

U.S. News & World Report notes that Americans are getting married later in life. And in *Business Week*, reporter Michelle Conlin writes: "The U.S. Census Bureau's newest numbers show that married-couple households . . . have slipped from nearly 80 percent in the 1950s to just 50.7 percent [of the population] today. That means that the U.S.'s 86 million single adults could soon define the new majority. . . . What many once thought of as the fringe is becoming the new normal."

As a result, the way we view many things—singleness, marriage, friendships, and institutions—is changing dramatically. For instance, *U.S. News & World Report* focused on the "Tribal Culture," in which single friends form highly organized groups that serve as a kind of substitute family. At Web sites such as Friendster.com, literally thousands of people meet to form social networks.

The existence of these "tribes" tells us something about the way we're wired: Humans are social beings. We need family and community—even in a culture that prizes autonomy above all things. But *Business Week*'s reporter sees a quite different meaning in the trend she calls "the new normal." Conlin argues that benefits such as insurance and Social Security, which have always gone to married couples, should also be extended to singles, cohabiting couples, and homosexuals living together. She writes, "Just because matrimony is good for society doesn't mean that outmoded social benefits are."

There's a genuine cause for concern when people cite widespread singleness as an excuse to promote policies that denigrate traditional families. The benefits we give to two-parent families should have nothing to do with how many families there are. It's a recognition of the great importance of a stable family structure to our society, in all kinds of areas—the strength of the workforce, the emotional health of kids, and even the physical health of adults. These benefits are one way that we encourage standards that reflect the way we were designed to live—standards like lifelong faithfulness to one person, and a committed mother and father for every child. The more we ignore these standards, the weaker our culture becomes.

"The new normal" may change a lot of things, but it shouldn't change the way we look at a God-ordained, time-tested institution. Tribes may have their place in the chaos of postmodern culture, but they are no substitute for marriage and the family.

In this area, as in so many others, Christians should not be overly influenced by our post-Christian culture. While autonomy may be highly valued by others, Christians know that God put us in families for a reason. No matter what our current living arrangements are, no matter how difficult some family members may be, we must never forget our God-given need of—and obligation to—our families.

Dear heavenly Father, help me to be willing to fulfill my need for community, not just through friends and colleagues, but also through family relationships. Open my eyes to the needs of my family—and my need of them.

F E B R U A R Y   3

FADS IN FAITH

TO READ: JEREMIAH 14:11-16

*[The prophets] are prophesying to you false visions, divinations,
idolatries and the delusions of their own minds. Jeremiah 14:14*

Nerissa Rosete thought she'd found the house of her dreams in
Orange County, California, and put down a twenty-thousand-dollar
deposit. A few days later, after a consultant looked at the property,
Rosete voided the contract and forfeited half the deposit.

Why? Because the spiritual energy wasn't right. Rosete's house, you
see, had feng shui problems. Followers of feng shui—a three-thou-
sand-year-old Chinese practice—believe that decorations, furniture
arrangement, and direction of rooms can affect vital energy called
"chi." And, they're quick to add, "good chi" makes the difference between success and failure in life.

Feng shui practitioners will tell you that "the northern area of a
room governs an occupant's career, the south fame and fortune, the
east health and the west creativity and children." Likewise, couples
seeking to have a baby should place red or yellow candles in the
southwest corner of the bedroom.

Just as important is avoiding bad feng shui, and that's why Rosete forfeited ten thousand dollars rather than complete the purchase. Her feng
shui consultant saw the steeply receding backyard and warned her that
the decline would cause all the positive energy to rush out of the house.

According to the *Los Angeles Times*, an increasing number of prospective buyers hire feng shui consultants to look at homes they're
considering purchasing. Some buyers even demand certificates at-
testing to the home's worthiness. And sales contracts are sometimes
contingent on a feng shui inspection.

Sellers hire consultants to help their home have more feng shui appeal. They will do everything from redecorating to remodeling so the owners can say "Good chi here!" to prospective buyers. In addition, builders are incorporating the ideas into new homes—and not just those in Asian neighborhoods.

You don't have to be in the market to buy a new house to feel the need for chi. People who want the benefits of feng shui are redecorating and remodeling even if they don't find the results particularly comfortable.

Fads like feng shui make demands of people that would be ridiculed as absurd if we were talking about Christianity. Yet its devotees ask us to believe things that require far more credulity than biblical faith. And such beliefs have nothing to say about how we ought to live or about our eternal destiny—which makes them poor substitutes for biblical faith, in terms of both eternal salvation and creating an ordered society.

In a diverse society like ours, new and unusual beliefs confront us constantly. When we hear about ideas like the need for good chi, we need to be on our guard. Prophets of false visions, idolatries, and delusions were around three thousand years ago—and they're still around today.

Lord, help me to be a witness to your truth wherever I encounter untruth; give me the words to encourage unbelievers to substitute the Good News for good chi.

FEBRUARY 4

EUGENIC NIGHTMARES

TO READ: PSALM 139:13-18

*You created my inmost being; you knit me together
in my mother's womb. Psalm 139:13*

"It is better for all the world . . . [if] society can prevent those who are manifestly unfit from continuing their kind. . . . Three generations of imbeciles is enough."

If you think that this quote came from a Nazi document, you're wrong. It's from Oliver Wendell Holmes's 1927 majority opinion in *Buck v. Bell,* which upheld a Virginia law mandating the sterilization of the "feebleminded."

Twenty years later we had Holmes's words thrown back in our faces by Nazi defendants in the Nuremberg trials: While the Nazis' worst crimes may have ended at Auschwitz, they began in America. That's the conclusion of Edwin Black's *War against the Weak: Eugenics and America's Campaign to Create a Master Race.* Black contends that American "corporate philanthropies helped found and fund the Nazi eugenics of Hitler and Mengele."

Eugenics originally referred to the use of selective breeding to "improve" the human race. Of course, the definition of "improve" reflected the bigotry of the eugenicists. Blacks, Jews, Eastern and Southern Europeans, the mentally retarded, and even people with brown hair were targets of the "improvers."

Thus, between 1900 and the midsixties, "hundreds of thousands of Americans . . . were not permitted to continue their families by reproducing." The tools of American eugenics included forcible sterilization, commitment to mental institutions, prohibitions against marriage, and even dissolution of existing marriages. One Michigan legislator went so far as to introduce a bill calling for the electrocution of severely retarded infants.

Eventually American eugenics, with help from the Carnegie Institution, the Rockefeller Foundation, Margaret Sanger, and others, found its way to Germany. While "Nazi eugenics quickly outpaced American eugenics in both velocity and ferocity," Black writes, the connection between the two was never lost.

The Holocaust and other crimes of the Third Reich made *eugenics* a bad word, and the American connection was swept under the rug. But the attempt to play God "never really stopped."

Today it takes the form of "human genomic science and corporate globalization." Instead of racist declarations, we have biotech promises: miracle cures and ever-increasing life expectancies.

While the word *eugenics* is never used, that's what it is. We are intent on draining "imperfections" from the gene pool. Even today, children whose "deformities" are discovered in utero are rarely permitted to be born.

Christians need to pull the truth about eugenics out from under the rug and hold it up as a reminder of where playing God leads us.

We must also carefully examine our own attitudes, given that we are bombarded daily with news stories that promote the deadly view that some humans—based on such standards as size, age, race, intelligence, and state of health—are unworthy of protection.

Lord, knowing as I do that all humans "are fearfully and wonderfully made," let me never absorb the view that some of those you knit together are not worthy of the life you gave them.

SHOULD WE JUST "ACT NATURALLY"?

TO READ: GALATIANS 5:13-26

The fruit of the Spirit is love, joy, peace, patience, kindness, goodness, faithfulness, gentleness and self-control. Galatians 5:22-23

In the film *Analyze This,* a psychiatrist suggests to his patient, an angry mobster, that hitting a pillow will make him feel better. But instead of punching the pillow, the mobster pulls out a gun and shoots it. "So, do you feel better?" the psychiatrist asks.

"Yeah," the mobster says, smiling. "I do."

The scene is funny, but it perpetuates a widespread—and erroneous—notion that venting anger helps us get rid of it. Contrary to what we've all heard, psychologists are now finding that venting anger actually increases aggression.

Pop psychology has perpetuated the notion that "getting your anger out" is good for you, that it helps defuse rage. But recent studies conducted at Iowa State University and at Case Western Reserve University found that venting anger actually makes people more aggressive. As the *New York Times* reported, the studies found that human subjects who pummeled a punching bag became more aggressive than subjects who did not. As one researcher put it, "They keep trying to get this emotional release [through walloping a punching bag], but it never happens."

Instead, the opposite happens: Hitting things seems to give people "permission to relax their self-control," as the *News York Times* put it—and thus leads to escalating aggressiveness.

The theory of catharsis became popular through the psychological theories of Sigmund Freud. According to Freud, when we repress anger, pressure builds like steam in a kettle, and the best way to relieve the pressure is to release it by hitting a punching bag or smashing a piece of china.

Unfortunately, our culture has been slow to grasp the folly of this idea. In fact, "self-expression" of all kinds is usually seen as a good thing. But the most recent findings of social science support the notion of self-restraint over self-expression. They confirm the biblical insight that giving in to our impulses is a bad idea. Self-control, in fact, is part of the fruit of the Spirit, says Paul in his letter to the Galatians. And in James 1:19-20, James warns Christians of the great damage we can cause when we fail to control our tongues.

Acting out anger only makes it worse, for whatever you act out, you are practicing. And whatever you practice, you grow better at doing.

What we ought to be practicing are the biblical virtues—practicing them until they become second nature. And then, when we act naturally, what people will see in us is the fruit of the Spirit—not unrestrained rage and broken china.

Lord, when I'm tempted to act out my anger, remind me to practice peace, patience, and self-control instead.

FEBRUARY 6

PARENTS OR PRISONS?

TO READ: DEUTERONOMY 22:13-30

The girl's father will say to the elders, "I gave my daughter in marriage to this man, but he dislikes her. Now he has slandered her." Deuteronomy 22:16-17

In nearly every respect, our prisons are a cautionary tale about the dangers of weakening traditional family structures.

The link between family breakdown and crime is now indisputable. It has been estimated that between two-thirds and three-quarters of all inmates grew up in something other than an intact two-parent home. In some juvenile corrections systems, like that of Wisconsin, the number is closer to 90 percent.

Economist Jennifer Roback Morse summed up this link in *Policy Review:* "Without parents—two of them, married to each other, working together as a team—a child is more likely to end up in the criminal justice system at some point in his life." "More likely," in this case, means at least twice as likely.

The problems don't end there. As Morse puts it, "If a child finds himself in the criminal justice system . . . the prison will perform the parental function of supervising and controlling that person's behavior." This supervision is, to put it mildly, a poor substitute for the mixture of loving discipline that real parents can provide.

What's more, prisons abound with what Morse calls "family substitutes"—fellow inmates who teach young offenders how to become "better" criminals.

Every twinge of fear you feel when you go out at night is partially attributable to the effects of family breakdown. The same is true of every one of your tax dollars that goes to law enforcement and corrections instead of to other worthwhile purposes.

If the effects of family breakdown are indisputably calamitous, why are we so intent on accelerating the breakdown? Whether it's the refusal to treat two-parent families as the normal standard in textbooks or the deconstruction of marriage inherent in the campaign for same-sex "marriage," the effect is the same: The one institution that we depend on to instill "the basic self-control and reciprocity that a free society takes for granted," in Morse's words, is diminished.

That's because marriage—the decades-long commitment to labor together as a team and make the sacrifices necessary to raise good kids—is hard work. If people are taught that marriage is merely one lifestyle choice among many, they are more likely to opt for an easier way of living. Then, as Morse demonstrates, it will be a case of sowing the wind and reaping the whirlwind.

In Deuteronomy we learn how seriously God intends couples—and the culture in which they live—to take their marriage vows. This is why we must think carefully and prayerfully before we ourselves enter into marriage—or decide to break our marriage vows. If our marriages fail, we risk not only damaging our children but also driving up the crime rate.

Father, help me to remember that marriage is not so much about contentment as about commitment; not so much about satisfying my own personal desires as about satisfying my family's physical, emotional, and spiritual needs.

FEBRUARY 7

THE WOMAN ON THE BUS

TO READ: PSALM 9:1-20

The Lord is a refuge for the oppressed, a stronghold in times of trouble. Psalm 9:9

Half a century ago, Rosa Parks changed the course of American history when she refused to give up her bus seat to a white man.

Most people know the story of the seamstress who helped ignite the civil rights movement, but many people don't know that Rosa Parks is a devout Christian and that it was her faith that gave her the strength to do what she did that day in 1955.

In her book *Quiet Strength: The Faith, the Hope, and the Heart of a Woman Who Changed a Nation,* Parks says her belief in God developed early in life. "Every day before supper and before we went to services on Sundays," Parks says, "my grandmother would read the Bible to me, and my grandfather would pray. We even had devotions before going to pick cotton in the fields. Prayer and the Bible," she recalls, "became a part of my everyday thoughts and beliefs. I learned to put my trust in God and to seek Him as my strength."

Parks's husband, Raymond, had been an early activist in the fight for civil rights, and Parks joined him in his work. But she says she never planned to be arrested for breaking a racist law. On December 1, 1955, Parks was sitting on a bus in the front row of the section reserved for blacks. But when a white man got on, there were no more seats in the white section, so the bus driver told Parks to move back.

Parks was convinced that to do so would be wrong—and she refused to get up. "Since I have always been a strong believer in God," she says, "I knew that He was with me, and only He could get me through that next step."

Parks's behavior throughout her arrest was above reproach. Because of this and because of her well-known exemplary character, Alabama civil rights leaders thought Parks's arrest signaled the right time to act. They launched the famous Montgomery bus boycott, which lasted more than a year, and the rest is history.

The story of Rosa Parks is a reminder of what a central role Christian faith has played in the civil rights movement.

When you hear the familiar refrain that Christians are bigots, tell those who taunt you who were really behind the great civil rights advances of this generation: Christians. And make sure the children in your life know about the unimpeachable Source of Rosa Parks's quiet strength. Her brave, dignified example just might encourage them to seek out that same Source for themselves.

Lord, help me to remember that you are my refuge and my strength only if I turn to you in times of trouble. Help me to develop the habit of putting my trust in you during times of peace so that I will not give in to fear during times of peril.

FIGHTING IRRATIONAL FEARS

TO READ: LEVITICUS 26:14-17

You will flee even when no one is pursuing you. Leviticus 26:17

A few years ago, ABC's news magazine *20/20* broadcast a report about a link between phthalates, chemicals used to soften plastic, and the appearance of kidney tumors in mice. The report strongly suggested that children who suck on toys containing phthalates are risking their health. Americans reacted with panic. But it turned out that reports of deadly rubber duckies and Barbie dolls were greatly exaggerated.

Science writer Michael Fumento points out that while massive doses of phthalates did cause tumors in rodents, "other studies showed the chemical caused *no* harmful [effects] in guinea pigs" and monkeys or in human cells.

20/20 isn't the only news outlet to run scary stories with little basis in fact. Not long ago the UN estimated that some 110 million land mines are buried around the world. It turns out the estimate was a little bit off—by about 100 million mines.

Killer Barbies? Land mines under every step? Why do so many Americans uncritically swallow such exaggerated and alarmist reports?

One possibility is that many of us live with an inchoate sense of anxiety, even dread. We can't say why we feel this way, and we can't point to anything we've done that would merit death from land mines or chemicals, yet the sense of unease is there.

Endless gloom-and-doom reports reinforce this sense of dread. And where does it come from? Perhaps from displaced guilt. For all our noisy protestations, we know there's something wrong with how we have ordered our society. We know that if we were living as we ought, men would not abandon their families, women would not line up in front of abortion clinics, and kids would not open fire on their classmates and teachers in schoolyards.

We see the consequences of our sin and folly, but we don't admit the connection between cause and effect, at least not openly. We know we deserve God's judgment, but instead of saying so, we look for punishment in all the wrong places. Stories of killer toys and poisoned apples feed our sense of guilt and impending doom.

And we shouldn't be surprised, because this is precisely what God told us would happen. In Leviticus 26, he warns the Israelites that if they do not follow his commandments, they will live in such fear that they will flee even when no one is pursuing them. Our irrational fears are the inevitable consequence of disobeying God's law.

Do you suffer from unfounded fears? We need to examine our lives to make sure that there is no unacknowledged sin that we are holding back from God's forgiveness.

Ultimately, the only healthy fear is fear of the Lord.

Lord, I don't want to live with dread and guilt. Teach me to confess every sin to you and seek your forgiveness so that I may enjoy your perfect peace.

CREATING REAL COMMUNITIES

TO READ: HEBREWS 10:23-25

Let us not give up meeting together, as some are in the habit of doing,
but let us encourage one another. Hebrews 10:25

Writer Elisa DeCarlo was a problem drinker who participated in an on-line support group for others with drinking problems. One day DeCarlo found a shocking message from a man known to her only as "Larry." Like other members of the online support group, Larry had shared details about his life: his divorce, his custody battle over his five-year-old daughter, Amanda—and of Amanda's tragic death in a fire.

But then Larry confessed that he'd actually murdered his daughter and bragged that he got away with it by feigning "shock, surprise, and grief."

DeCarlo was horrified by what she read. But almost as horrifying were the reactions of other members of the group. Some insisted that the confession must be a guilt-induced fantasy—even though Larry denied making it up. Even worse, other members insisted on absolving Larry of any guilt. Besides, they said, it wasn't their place to judge.

In the end, DeCarlo and two others tipped off the police—to the outrage of their e-mail companions. They sent the tipsters vicious e-mails, vilifying them for breaking faith with their fellow group members.

DeCarlo denies that she broke faith. Instead, she says, she *lost* faith in the authenticity of virtual communities. She says the incident taught her that the sense of community she felt online was "for the most part, illusory."

Those who celebrate "virtual communities" created online forget that it takes more than shared interests to create a real community. It requires the kind of proximity and everyday contact that enable your neighbors' concerns to become your own. Real-life friendships require transparency and openness in our dealings with one another. Real-life friendships deter wrongdoing because it's much harder to hide our actions from real-life friends.

True community is impossible when your "neighbors" are "just words on a screen," as DeCarlo put it.

Clearly, the people in Larry Froistad Jr.'s online support group did not seem real to him. That's why—although he was careful to cover his tracks with his real-life neighbors—he apparently felt free to let his guard down with online friends. And it appears that his online buddies experienced this same loss of realism.

Froistad was arrested and convicted of murder, but his story is a reminder of why the Bible urges us not to forsake gathering together.

Do you spend as much time with real-life friends as you do with online ones? Do you meet regularly with Christian friends who hold one another accountable?

Only in close communion with one another, in which we can truly know and care for one another, can true community exist.

Lord, help me to be an encouragement and a "spur" to friends with whom I meet and pray regularly. Make me ever mindful of the dangers of trying to go it alone—or of trying to get along with only virtual friends.

THE LOST RITUALS OF COURTSHIP

TO READ: SONG OF SONGS 1:1-4

*Let him kiss me with the kisses of his mouth—for your love
is more delightful than wine.* Song of Songs 1:2

A Valentine card made in the nineteenth century—hand painted with birds and flowers and featuring tender words of love—recently sold at auction for nearly forty thousand dollars.

How the language of love has changed. Today you'll find cards reading, "Love ya, baby!" and "Be my love slave!" Others are even more charming. "What is the true nature of romance?" asks one card. The answer inside reads, "These questions are best pondered naked."

Have Americans lost the ability to engage in true romance?

It's not just the cards. Hike down to the local mall, and you'll see other symbols of modern "romance" in the windows of Victoria's Secret: a row of plastic torsos wearing garter belts, thong underwear, and push-up bras.

At the bookstore you'll find books and magazines featuring—yes, you guessed it—advice on how to have better sex. Or you and your sweetie could rent the film *Valentine,* in which a psycho butchers girls who were mean to him in high school.

How romantic.

How did Valentine's Day become little more than a holiday celebrating sex and violence? Some believe our culture's loss of courtship rituals has led directly to the loss of romance. The purpose of courtship was to gently woo and win a maiden's heart. But these days, men anticipate sex within a few days—sometimes within a few hours—of meeting a woman.

Where's the incentive to write poetry that reflects the emotional or spiritual side of romance? There is no emotional or spiritual side. How sad that on Valentine's Day young lovers think the right thing to do is to give each other not lacy hearts but racy underwear.

God's outlook on romance is so much richer. The Bible teaches that couples are to put aside their own selfish desires and focus on the interests of the loved one. Passion can reach its full potential only when it's combined with restraint—that is, within the boundaries of marriage. Song of Songs reminds us of how exciting true love can be.

Sad to say, that's not the view teenagers get when they wander into stores on Valentine's Day—because the stores equate romance with sex.

From time to time we need to examine our own attitudes toward romance, love, and sex to make sure we're not absorbing our culture's tragic teachings. In an era of "hooking up," we ought to create opportunities in our congregations and with sister churches for young people to meet and interact in a godly way.

A hundred years from now nobody will be paying forty thousand dollars for a Valentine that reads, "Be my love slave!" But those who rediscover the lost rituals of courtship will find, as Song of Songs 1:2 says, that true love is "more delightful than wine."

Lord, show me ways to share with others—young and old, saved and unsaved— the ancient language and lessons of romantic love.

REVERSAL OF FORTUNE: CHRISTIANITY VERSUS ISLAM

TO READ: PROVERBS 9:7-9

Do not rebuke a mocker or he will hate you; rebuke a wise man and he will love you. Proverbs 9:8

Among the reasons Osama bin Laden gave for his jihad against the West is "the tragedy of Andalusia."

He was referring to the reconquest of southern Spain in 1492. For nearly seven centuries Moorish Spain embodied the Islamic world's cultural superiority over Europe. While much of medieval Europe lived in squalor, Muslim Cordoba boasted street lighting, public baths, and at least seventy libraries.

Islamic greatness at the time wasn't limited to Moorish Spain. Bernard Lewis, an authority on the Islamic world, writes in *What Went Wrong?: Western Impact and Middle Eastern Response,* that a thousand years ago only China approached the achievements of Islamic civilization. Name the area—science, math, architecture—and the Islamic world ran circles around the West.

"Suddenly," Lewis tells us, "the relationship changed." For the last five hundred years, the Islamic world has lagged behind the Christian West politically, culturally, and economically, becoming "poor, weak, and ignorant" in comparison.

While the twentieth century saw advances in freedom and democracy in the West, Lewis says, the same period saw a "string of shabby dictatorships" in the Islamic world.

One of the major reasons for the reversal of fortunes, writes Lewis, is that the Muslim world, instead of turning its gaze inward, chose to blame its decline on external forces, specifically the Christian West.

But there's more to it than Islam's wrapping itself in victim status. The difference has to do with the Christian worldview's capacity for self-criticism and reform.

It's no coincidence that the period that witnessed Islam's decline and Christianity's ascent began with the Reformation. The Reformation ideal of the church's always being reformed was a bulwark against the kind of cultural stagnation that has plagued the Islamic world. And this idea of perpetual reformation wasn't limited to the Protestant world; the Catholic Church also embraced reform.

The reforming mind-set not only affected Christianity but also created the foundation for the modern world. The dynamism and freedom that characterize the West are the product of Christianity's reforming itself and moving forward culturally. As historian Samuel Huntington has noted, Western Christianity shaped the basic institutions in most of the world's truly democratic societies.

By contrast, when Muslims speak of reform, they mean moving back culturally to the legal and social arrangements of Muhammad's day.

The ascendancy of the West is the story of the difference that Christianity makes, and we Christians ought to apply its lessons to our personal lives as well. Are we open to the regular correction of our own hearts and minds? Do we let trusted friends help us identify ways in which we need to change?

Father, when I fail you, let me not be caught blaming everyone but myself. Help me in the difficult task of subjecting myself to correction from mature Christian brothers and sisters. Teach me to wisely advise those who come to me for godly criticism, helping them to move forward into dynamic obedience to Christ.

RESISTING UNJUST RULERS

TO READ: AMOS 5:21-24

Let justice roll on like a river, righteousness like a never-failing stream! Amos 5:24

What would happen if the Supreme Court declared an act of Congress unconstitutional— and the president told the Court to go jump in a lake? It actually happened once—some 150 years ago.

In 1857 the Supreme Court ruled on the case of a Missouri slave named Dred Scott. Scott's master had taken him into the free state of Illinois. Because of the Missouri Compromise and a law passed by Congress, residents in free states could demand their freedom. So Scott sued for his freedom.

Scott's owner, John Sandford, challenged the constitutionality of the Missouri Compromise, arguing that slaves were private property protected by the Constitution against deprivation without due process of law. Therefore Congress lacked the constitutional authority to ban slavery in Illinois or anywhere else.

The Supreme Court ruled in Sandford's favor. It not only sent Scott back into slavery but also claimed he had never actually been free. The Court also ruled that Congress lacked authority to forbid or abolish slavery in federal territories—meaning that the Missouri Compromise was illegal.

Abraham Lincoln believed that *Dred Scott* was an outrage, in part because it claimed authority to decide for the other branches of government once and for all what the Constitution required. In so doing, it placed the other two branches in a position of inferiority and subservience.

Once Lincoln became president, he ignored *Dred Scott*. His administration treated free blacks as citizens, issuing them passports and other legal documents. In open defiance of the ruling, he signed legislation that restricted slavery in the western territories.

Thomas Jefferson also believed that the president and Congress were in no way inferior to the Supreme Court. He told a friend the Constitution "has wisely made all the departments coequal and co-sovereign within themselves." In so doing, the founders took into account fallen human nature. Both Jefferson and Lincoln believed the courts were quite capable of violating the Constitution—and undermining constitutional government.

Today we're so accustomed to the idea that the Supreme Court has supreme authority that we're shocked at the very idea that a president or the Congress might stand up to the Court when it abuses its power.

We need to get over our shock. Never before in our history have judges been so out of control, attempting to force "gay marriage" on Americans and demanding that Catholic Charities provide contraceptives to its employees in defiance of church doctrine.

A good way to celebrate Lincoln's birthday is to remind our neighbors that nowhere in the Constitution does it say the courts have the kind of authority they claim to have. And we should vigorously support politicians who have the courage to stand up to judicial arrogance—just as Lincoln did.

Lord, give your people the wisdom and courage to stand up for your righteousness by taking on lawless leaders who disregard it.

DARWIN'S GOD

TO READ: 1 TIMOTHY 6:13-21

*Turn away from godless chatter and the opposing ideas of
what is falsely called knowledge.* 1 Timothy 6:20

Ever since the Scopes Trial we've heard about the dangers of bringing religion into the classroom. References to God are forbidden, particularly in the study of origins. Evolution—chance plus time without a Creator—is the reigning orthodoxy.

But as it turns out, evolutionary theory—beginning with Charles Darwin himself—rests not on a scientific foundation but on a theological one. And on that hangs a fascinating tale, told in depth by Cornelius Hunter in his book *Darwin's God: Evolution and the Problem of Evil.* Hunter explains how theology—that is, the study of the nature of God—plays a central role in modern evolutionary theory.

For example, in his 1980 essay "The Panda's Thumb," Harvard paleontologist Stephen Jay Gould explained his certainty about evolution by using what Hunter calls negative theology. Negative theology is a form of theological reasoning that makes claims about what God would not do. For instance, suppose we assume that God would make only perfectly designed organisms. That belief supports a positive claim about the outcome of God's creative activity: If God created them, organisms ought to be perfectly designed. The negative expression of that same belief says that God would not make imperfectly designed organisms.

With that negative theology, Gould arrives at a scientific conclusion. He writes, "Odd arrangements and funny solutions are the proof of evolution . . . paths that a sensible God would never tread but that a natural process"—namely, evolution—"follows perforce." If we see what we regard as a biological imperfection, argues Gould, we can then conclude that evolution is true because God would not have done it that way.

But wait a minute. Evolutionary biology is a science; according to Gould and others, science and theology have nothing to do with each other. When creationists or intelligent-design advocates combine them, evolutionists cry foul. So what's a theological premise doing in Gould's scientific argument?

This is where *Darwin's God* is so valuable. Hunter shows that negative theology has always been a part of evolutionary theory—nowhere more so than in Charles Darwin's own work. It's simply false that science and theology have nothing to do with each other. "A particular doctrine of God," explains Hunter, "is a prerequisite for evolution's success."

Today Darwin's followers are celebrating his birthday. We should note the occasion by pointing out that Darwin's ideas are still being hotly debated. To our children we should make an additional point: The Scriptures warn that there will always be people attempting to present their own false ideas as knowledge—in this field and in many others.

"Keep God out of the equation," the Darwinists demand. But God is already in the equation—Darwin himself put him there.

Lord, thank you for Christian thinkers willing to boldly challenge the claims of those who, for a century and a half, have used Darwinist teachings to attack you and deceive your followers. May I never be taken in by their false ideas or fear their contempt more than I value your approval.

OF MARTYRS AND
MARSHMALLOWS

TO READ: SONG OF SONGS 8:6-7

Place me like a seal over your heart, like a seal on your arm;
for love is as strong as death. Song of Songs 8:6

A California pet store once offered the perfect Valentine's Day gift for
the person who has everything: designer hermit crabs whose shells
had been hand-dipped in 24 karat gold.

Gold-plated crustaceans are indeed an offbeat gift idea. But how
many of us know that Valentine's Day began as a symbol of Christian love?

Early church records are sketchy, but it's believed that several men
named Valentine were martyred in the third century during the reign
of Roman Emperor Claudius II, a ruler known for his brutal persecution of Christians.

One of these Valentines was a priest who secretly married couples
against the wishes of Claudius, who believed that unmarried men
made better soldiers. Two other Valentines—a priest and a bishop—
were beheaded by Claudius late in the third century.

Historians are not certain which Valentine began to be celebrated,
but they know why the church chose to celebrate him on February 15.
In ancient Rome, February 15 was the eve of a pagan festival called
Lupercalia, during which the Romans worshipped a goddess of marriage, childbirth, and sexuality, and lightly struck young women with
februa, strips of goat hide, to promote fertility.

Brian Bates, a professor at the University of Sussex, writes that during Lupercalia, "young men and women drew lots for sexual partners,
in preparation for a day of sanctioned license the following day."

As Christianity spread throughout the ancient world, the church began replacing pagan festivals with holy days. In an effort to control the more lewd aspects of the Lupercalian festival, the church fathers replaced that pagan holiday with the feast of Saint Valentine in honor of one of the martyred Christians. Instead of drawing the names of sexual partners out of a box, young men were encouraged to pick the names of saints—and then spend the following year emulating the saint whose name they drew.

The focus on love lingered on but was sanctified from mere sexual license to chaste romantic love. Not surprisingly, the romantic aspect is what became popular, not the more somber love of the Christian martyr.

In the midst of our romantic celebrations, Christians ought to remember that the love between husbands and wives is meant to reflect the love between God and his church. Throughout the Scriptures the imagery of married love is perhaps the most compelling symbol of the relationship between God and his people.

So while we're buying roses, chocolates—or maybe even one of those gold-plated hermit crabs—we ought to remind ourselves and our kids about the Author of *all* love: not Hollywood or Hallmark but God himself.

Lord, thank you for love songs that teach us what love and courtship, passion and marriage are all about and lyrically point us to you, who created men and women for each other.

GUARDING GOD'S CREATION

TO READ: PSALM 50:10-12

Every animal of the forest is mine. Psalm 50:10

Jo Kwong was helping her five-year-old twins find a suitable program one Saturday morning. As she began channel surfing, Kwong recognized the characters from Ted Turner's cartoon series *Captain Planet*. So did her daughters. "I want to watch that!" one of them exclaimed. Kwong, an environmental researcher, explained that *Captain Planet* teaches things about the environment and human nature that are simply not true.

Puzzled, one of the girls asked, "You mean, the power is not with us?" She was referring to a phrase used in the cartoon. As Kwong writes in a magazine called *The Freeman*, "I realized I was experiencing one of my worst nightmares: the brainwashing of my children through environmental 'education.'"

Kwong is right to worry. There is a concerted effort today to bombard our kids with a litany of dire predictions about ozone holes, vanishing rain forests, and the extinction of endangered species.

The result, Kwong writes, is that "children are being scared into becoming environmental activists." They're being "taught that human beings are evil."

Behind this radical view of nature is the age-old worldview of pantheism: the belief that the universe in its entirety is divine. British author John Fowles claims "that all species are equal." In Fowles's words, "We think, what a miserable little worm or what a horrible flea, but you get to the point where you realize it's all one . . . what Christians call pantheism."

History itself refutes the absurd belief that fleas and worms are equal with humanity. Mankind has always stood above nature with a power that no other part of nature has.

The Bible teaches that humans are unique because we are indelibly stamped with the *Imago Dei,* the image of God. God commands us to be responsible stewards over his creation—not to plunder and needlessly destroy but to guard and protect.

Christians believe the world has value because it is God's creation. And as his creation it deserves to be treated with respect. In Psalm 50 the Lord says, "Every animal of the forest is mine," and the Old Testament warns against the mistreatment of animals.

But at the same time there is a real difference between mankind and the rest of creation, which serves as God's gracious provision for the human race. The apostle Paul tells us that God "richly provides us with everything for our enjoyment" (1 Timothy 6:17).

We need to instill in our children the biblical perspective of responsible stewardship. Only then can they resist a pantheistic ideology that denies humanity its proper place in God's creation.

Father, help me to be alert to media messages that denigrate the nature and value of those for whom your Son died. Teach me tactful ways of discussing environmental fallacies with friends who are unaware of them and of the pantheistic worldview that undergirds them.

BORN OR MADE?

TO READ: ROMANS 1:21-32

God gave them over in the sinful desires of their hearts to sexual impurity for the degrading of their bodies with one another. Romans 1:24

It has become the mantra of the gay lobby: Sexual orientation is in our genes—our biology is destiny.

According to gay activist Denny Lee, "When people understand that being gay or lesbian is an integral characteristic, they are more open-minded about equality for gay Americans."

The problem is, there's no evidence that homosexuality *is* an "integral characteristic."

Radical gays are fond of quoting studies purporting to prove that gay people are born, not made. For example, some years ago Simon LeVay of the Salk Institute announced that he had found a significant difference in the brain structure of homosexual and heterosexual men, but subsequent research by others failed to duplicate LeVay's findings.

The same goes for the research of Dean Hamer, who claimed to have found a "gay gene." Hamer, who is gay, was subsequently investigated by the Office of Research Integrity of the U.S. Department of Health and Human Services.

Then there's a 1993 study on twins and sexual orientation by Boston University psychiatrist Richard Pillard, who claimed to have found evidence that homosexuality is a family trait. But Dr. Paul Ewald, an Amherst College biologist, told the Boston University *Daily Free Press* that Pillard's research made no such genetic connection.

Dr. Ruth Hubbard of the Council for Responsible Genetics says the gay hype over genetics "is due to the fact that there is money to be made through biotechnology." And she adds, "There's no such thing as a gay gene. It is a waste of time and money" to look for one.

So why are researchers hunting for it?

If gays can prove that homosexuality is genetic, there would be, they believe, no excuse for making moral distinctions between homosexual and heterosexual behavior. But wait a minute: Suppose there was a genetic connection. Would that justify gay "marriage"? Suppose we found a gene for heterosexual behavior? Does that mean rape would be condoned? No! Nor does it mean homosexual behavior is inevitable and acceptable. We are more than the sum of our genes.

When the press trots out all the same tired claims about gay genes, Christians need to speak out, telling people about couples such as John and Anne Paulk, now on the staff of Focus on the Family. John and Anne both came out of the homosexual lifestyle, married, and raised a Christian family.

We can also tell people about the phony research about so-called gay genes—and the truth about how God heals homosexuals through groups such as Exodus, Regeneration, and Love in Action.

True hope for homosexuals lies not in a gay gene but in the gospel.

Lord, give me wisdom in telling others about the existence of biblically based treatment programs for people suffering from sexual brokenness. Bless and protect the work of these ministries, whose counselors faithfully serve you and yours in the face of tremendous hostility and hatred.

SEEKING WISDOM

TO READ: PROVERBS 8:1-11

Wisdom is more precious than rubies. Proverbs 8:11

More than 225 years ago, Paul Revere made his famous midnight ride to tell Americans that "the British are coming!" It was important, life-changing news.

How times have changed. Today, "the news" is brought to us every hour on the hour—whether something important is happening or not. And at least one historian says that all of this daily "news product" is making us dumb.

In *How the News Makes Us Dumb,* C. John Sommerville observes that people used to exchange news only when something really important happened. But what defines "breaking news" today? On the typical morning news program we may find out that the president has a new dog. We learn what the weather was like yesterday in Bucharest, or we discover what some film critic thinks of the latest flick.

In other words, most of what's called news today is really just a flood of trivia—inconsequential data that we will soon forget. Sommerville calls this the "flotsam and foam" of history. If you don't believe it, check out a newspaper from fifty years ago. How much of what you find is truly newsworthy? And how much of it influenced the course of history? Not much.

But if nothing truly important happens most of the time, why do reporters behave as though they have earth-shattering news for us every single day?

Sommerville suggests it's because news has become an industry. And, he says, "you can't have a news business unless you pretend that the news is important every day. If publishers waited for something really important to happen, they might be idle for weeks, and their capital assets would get rusty."

That's why the media spend so much time convincing us that all "news" has the same value. No longer is it focused on the occasional life-changing event. It's excitement, entertainment, and above all, constant change.

This is why Sommerville says the news is making us dumb. The very dailiness of the news causes us to lose perspective. And when every story has equal value, we lose the ability to distinguish what is truly important from what is merely sensational.

All of this makes the news industry a natural antagonist to biblical wisdom. As Sommerville puts it, "News is only aware of change, while religion tries to concentrate on the eternal."

Sommerville helps us to put the news in perspective. Do we seek biblical wisdom as often as we tune in the news? How much of what the media label news can we easily live without?

If we can break our addiction to nonstop news, we just might discover the kind of wisdom that is "more precious than rubies."

Father, in a world that constantly tries to distract me from you—and tries to replace eternal wisdom with worldly trivia—help me to remember that even the best-informed minds are foolish if they lack your wisdom.

FAITH ATTACKS

TO READ: ACTS 17:22-31

God did this so that men would seek him and perhaps reach out for him and find him, though he is not far from each one of us. Acts 17:27

At a major university, one young woman stayed after class to talk with the professor. "In today's lecture you said you're a Christian," she blurted out, almost in tears. "I've never heard any other professor say that, and every day at this university I feel as if my faith is under attack."

The professor was Jay Budziszewski of the University of Texas, whose book *How to Stay Christian in College* deals with the reality of the college experience. The university campus has changed dramatically, he writes. And Christian parents had better prepare young people to defend their faith in a hostile environment.

Take postmodernism, one of today's intellectual fads. The best way to define postmodernism is that it's a reaction against modernism, which began in the Enlightenment when many intellectuals proclaimed freedom from God and sought to find truth "by reason alone." Postmodernism represents the collapse of that hope, insisting that human reason alone is incapable of coming up with any universal truths.

In postmodernist lingo, we can have no "grand metanarrative," that is, no big story that makes sense of reality. So if a Christian talks about the biblical worldview of creation, fall, and redemption, he's likely to be shot down precisely because what he's telling is a "metanarrative" that claims to describe ultimate reality. Big stories, you see, have been ruled out of bounds.

But if there's no big story making sense of reality, then reality itself dissolves into bits and pieces. And that's exactly what postmodernists say. They think truth is in pieces because they don't believe in a coherent reality that's the same for everyone.

Postmodernists think personality is in pieces as well, because they don't believe in a self—a core identity—that's responsible for everything we do. They think life is in pieces because they don't believe it has any ultimate purpose or meaning.

How can Christian students respond to these challenges? They can begin by acknowledging a grain of truth in postmodernism. That one cannot know truth by reason alone. But the postmodernist is wrong to succumb to despair. There *is* a metanarrative that explains reality. We must make the case for it just as Paul did when he preached to the Greeks.

Christian students can be confident that biblical faith has answers to the intellectual challenges they face on campus. If they do their homework, they'll discover that God's truth has an answer for every ideology—in the classroom and in the world beyond.

The rest of us need to remember this too, because a culture that is increasingly hostile to Christian truth will challenge us to defend it. We need to prepare now for ways to defend the metanarrative of our faith.

Lord, help me to remember that the angry defenders of the "bits and pieces" approach to reality are in desperate need of your truth, meaning, purpose—and hope.

THE BRUTALITY OF DIVORCE

TO READ: MALACHI 2:13-16

"I hate divorce," says the Lord God of Israel. Malachi 2:16

The ceremony featured a bride and groom, rings and vows, candles and music. But this was no wedding. It was a divorce ceremony.

As Phil Penningroth gave his soon-to-be ex-wife a nonwedding ring, he solemnly vowed, "Barbara, I release you as my wife and will love you as my friend."

"Phil," Barbara replied, "I release you as my husband, and I will love you as my friend." As columnist and marriage expert Maggie Gallagher put it wryly, "Life is sometimes better than parody."

Gallagher recently wrote *The Case for Marriage,* a book about how destructive divorce can be. So when the Penningroths appeared on a television talk show recently, Gallagher was invited to attend too. She listened to the Penningroths talk about their attempts to reach healing and forgiveness with their unmarriage vows—but she wasn't impressed.

Gallagher later commented in the *Washington Times,* "There's something brutal at the very heart of the divorce process that Phil and Barbara . . . were trying very hard to deny with their prettied-up ritual. . . . Divorce says: 'I'm not going to take care of you, I won't be responsible for you, you aren't part of my family, I'm free to find someone better to love.'" After dumping his wife, Phil Penningroth seemed to be saying, "Make me feel better about this," Gallagher wrote.

The spurned spouse is not the only one who suffers. Children of divorce abuse more drugs, commit more crimes, and fail in school at higher rates than children whose families are intact. They're also at higher risk of poverty, child abuse, mental and physical illness, premature sexual behavior, and suicide.

No wonder God says, "I hate divorce."

As for the couples themselves, studies reveal that the stress of divorce puts both men and women at significantly higher risk for a whole host of physical illnesses—not to mention emotional problems.

"How," Gallagher asks, "can a few words mumbled over a candle . . . somehow massage away the sting of divorce?"

Studies that document this destruction put the lie to the secular teachings that claim the route to happiness is putting personal desires above everything else—including marital and family commitments. The effects of divorce, we were told, are minor and short-lived.

Many of us know people who are considering divorce. During difficult times, we may even contemplate breaking our own marriage vows. We must take seriously not only God's hatred of divorce but also the empirical evidence that backs up his desire to keep couples and families intact whenever possible. And we must lovingly share this evidence with family, friends, and colleagues who are tearing their marriages asunder.

The Case for Marriage documents that couples who stay together are happier, healthier, and financially better off. In this matter, as in so many others, biblical teachings are being proven true.

Lord, let me not be misled by cultural lies promoted by those who hate your teachings. Give me wisdom in exposing these destructive falsehoods to couples around me—husbands and wives who need to know the impact of divorce and of the help available from the One who created marriage in the first place.

FAMILIES AND MARKETS

TO READ: PROVERBS 1:8-19

*Listen, my son, to your father's instruction and
do not forsake your mother's teaching.* Proverbs 1:8

Jennifer Roback Morse, an economist and the author of *Love and Economics,* says that the family plays a unique and indispensable role in building a healthy marketplace.

This might sound obvious, but the significance of this statement is lost on most economists. To the extent that they take the family into consideration at all, they see it as a group of consumers. They think, for instance, that tax relief for families is good for the market because it gives families more money to spend on goods and services.

This may be true, but it's a very inadequate explanation. When Morse says that "the market needs the family," she means the family's role in molding character and transmitting morals and values. A culture in which the family is so weakened that it cannot effectively perform these most basic of functions will feel the consequences in the marketplace.

The most obvious example of the relationship between the family as moral tutor and the marketplace is promise keeping. As Morse puts it, "The market order needs people who will keep their promises," people who are "trustworthy and who can trust." In other words, people who have consciences.

Without conscience there's no reason to believe that the other party will honor agreements. And a marketplace where no one's word is good must depend solely on the courts to enforce contracts. That market cannot operate in an efficient manner—if it can operate at all. Without the goodwill and trust that are enforced by conscience, the energy and resources that would otherwise be devoted to entrepreneurship are spent on keeping a wary eye on the other guy.

The source of a well-formed conscience is, of course, the family. It's in the family, first and foremost, that we learn self-control and regard for others.

In the first two years of life, children are taught to pay attention to what others, particularly their mothers, think about them and their actions. Later the family builds on this lesson and provides conscience with a specific content, such as the Ten Commandments and other moral precepts. The family upholds and reinforces these standards. And in this environment, young people learn to be the kind of people that you can trust in a healthy marketplace.

Parents of young children need to remember this if they are tempted to work longer hours than are necessary outside the home. And if we hear people denigrating the worth of full-time child rearing, we should point to the research that reveals why the whole society should highly value it: It molds the morals that make for a strong and healthy economy.

Lord, help me to support and encourage mothers and fathers in my church who are putting the building of their children's characters above the building of their own careers—or of luxurious homes.

FEBRUARY 21

PRAYING FOR THE PERSECUTED

TO READ: ACTS 12:1-5

Peter was kept in prison, but the church was earnestly praying to God for him. Acts 12:5

What comes to mind when you imagine persecution today? Who are the more than 200 million Christians suffering persecution?

The face of suffering is a child's face. In Buddhist Burma, militia and insurgents using rocket-propelled grenades destroyed a Christian hospital and an orphanage. In North Korea, great-grandchildren are punished for a great-grandparent's "crime" of following Christ.

Several Muslim countries have intensified persecution since September 11, mistakenly equating Christianity with the United States. Attackers beat, burned, and sexually abused a nine-year-old Pakistani girl, saying it was "revenge for the American bombing of Iraqi children . . . because you are an infidel and Christian."

"The face of suffering is a female face," observes Marli Spieker, founder of Trans World Radio's *Women of Hope* program. In Indonesia she met a young woman who had refused to deny Christ. So a jihad member put a gun into her mouth and said, "Let's see your God help you now." Then he pulled the trigger. Miraculously, the young woman survived, but she was horribly disfigured.

It's the face of Soon Ok Lee, a Christian and former prisoner in a North Korean concentration camp. She testified before the Senate that Christians are assigned to the cast iron factory, the most dangerous place in the gulag. She saw a group of elderly Christians killed one by one, doused with molten iron because they would not deny Christ.

The suffering faces are from every race. Many leaders of China's unregistered church have been arrested, beaten, and tortured. In Vietnam, Christians are denied jobs, promotions, and medical benefits—even water from the community well. When a Vietnamese pastor was beaten to death, authorities pressured his brother to sign a confession that he had done it.

News dispatches from around the world read as follows: "Mexico: Armed Assailants Kill Evangelical Pastor." "Israel: Bible Shop Trashed." "Nigeria: Two Catholic Priests Assassinated."

In the body of Christ, when one suffers, we all suffer. And therefore, we feel it when our brothers and sisters are persecuted.

Irina Ratushinskaya, the Russian dissident and gifted poet, was in prison for seven years because of her Christian faith. She says that every day in that cold, dank gulag she felt the prayers believers around the world offered for her.

Christians living safely in the West have an urgent duty to "pray without ceasing" for brothers and sisters across the globe who are being tortured and killed for their faith.

Lord, I come before your throne today to ask you to intercede in the lives of your persecuted followers, whose names and faces are known to you. May mistreated believers around the world feel my prayers—and the prayers of all who bring their needs before you.

SERVANT LEADERSHIP

TO READ: MATTHEW 20:25-28

Whoever wants to become great among you must be your servant. Matthew 20:26

It was 1783, and the Revolutionary War had just ended. Many of the officers in the Continental Army had fought for years without pay. Rumor had it that the Continental Congress planned to disband the Army and renege on its debt to the veterans.

As weeks passed, the mood of the soldiers grew ugly. Finally, some of the officers issued an ultimatum: If they did not receive their pay, they were prepared to march on Congress and seize control of the government.

To head off the crisis, General George Washington—whose birthday is today—addressed the soldiers in a makeshift chapel in Newburgh, New York. Washington counseled patience and reminded the men that he, too, had served without pay. He urged them "not to take any measures which, viewed in the calm light of reason, will . . . sully the glory you have hitherto maintained."

The men continued to glare angrily at the general. Washington then began reading a letter from a congressman. But as he read, he stumbled over the words and finally had to stop. Washington reached into his pocket and pulled out something his men had never before seen: a pair of spectacles. He begged their indulgence saying, "Gentlemen, you must pardon me. I have grown gray in your service and now find myself going blind."

These words of humility instantly dissolved the hostile mood. The soldiers began to weep. After Washington left, they agreed to give Congress more time. Thomas Jefferson later remarked that "the moderation and virtue of a single [man] probably prevented this Revolution from being closed, as most others have been, by a subversion of that liberty it was intended to establish."

What the founders of our country understood is that *character is the first requirement of leadership*. It was Washington's character that earned the admiration and trust of the mutinous officers. His humility, coupled with a reminder of the price he himself had paid for his service, drove his men on to greater sacrifice.

That's a lesson we must relearn today, when so many of our leaders at every level are caught up in corruption. A nation whose leaders do not lead through their own example of virtue and character cannot inspire sacrifice for the common good.

Wherever God has placed us in positions of leadership, over many or over few, we must continually strive for the kind of humility Washington modeled—seeking not power and privilege but the perfection of our characters and the willingness to pay whatever price servant leadership demands—just as Washington did.

Lord, give me the wisdom not to seek leadership positions I should not have. Where you have placed me in authority, teach me to lead with a servant's heart.

IS RELIGION AN "OBSESSIONAL NEUROSIS"?

TO READ: DEUTERONOMY 6:13-19

*Do what is right and good in the Lord's sight,
so that it may go well with you.* Deuteronomy 6:18

The late Dr. David Larson was a medical researcher who liked to tell people his favorite book of the Bible was Numbers. "Like the Count on Sesame Street," he said, "I like to count." Among the things he liked to count most were health risk factors—especially the ways commitment to religious faith can help people live longer.

Psychiatry has long held that religion is harmful to people, but Dr. Larson's research provided dramatic evidence that this stereotype is off target.

He confronted that stereotype when he began his psychiatric training as a young man. In fact, one of his professors, knowing Larson viewed religion to be a potentially helpful factor in patients' lives, urged him to give up his plans of becoming a psychiatrist. "For psychiatric patients," the professor said, "religion can only be harmful."

The psychiatrist was stating the conventional wisdom handed down from Sigmund Freud, who viewed religion as "a universal obsessional neurosis."

But Larson refused to be deterred. As he continued his research, he noticed a surprising pattern: Religion was not associated with mental illness after all. In fact, the published data showed that religion actually helped protect against both mental and physical disease.

For example, studies have shown that older adults who frequently attend religious services may have healthier immune systems. Heart patients with strong religious beliefs are much more likely to survive surgery. Churchgoing folks also have lower blood pressure, even with risky behavior such as smoking factored in. Most dramatic of all, the simple act of attending church each week is linked with reducing risk of earlier death by about 25 percent.

Religious commitment also protects people from addictions and mental disorders. Consider the fact that alcohol abuse is highest among those with little or no religious commitment. Among youth, studies have found an inverse correlation between religious commitment and drug abuse. The nonreligious are also much more likely to suffer from depression and commit suicide.

The scientific data provide a wonderful tool for apologetics. Christians believe that God created humans to have communion with him and to live according to his laws. If we live contrary to God's plan, the consequences are invariably harmful. The research clearly shows that if we ignore biblical principles, we pay a steep price in terms of stress, depression, family conflict, and even physical illness.

It's empirical evidence that a biblical view of human nature does indeed conform to reality.

Lord, thank you for medical research that affirms the truth of your Word. Recall it to my mind if I ever begin to think I don't really need to go to church, socialize with other Christians—or obey all of your commands.

GENETIC WITNESS

TO READ: PSALM 145:5-12

All you have made will praise you. Psalm 145:10

Biologists have recently developed technologies that allow them to sequence, or read, large amounts of DNA. DNA carries the information to build proteins, the nano-level machines that do the work inside cells. Biologists can now "read" the entire genomes of microbes—their complete volume of DNA—and compare that information to other known genomes.

Think of this as comparing the words in a library of books. Just as we have dictionaries that contain the words in the English language, so biologists have computer databases that record the DNA sequence they've discovered. Anyone who wants to publish a newly discovered gene sequence records it in these databases.

One such database is called GenBank. If you've found a new gene, you can take that information to GenBank and look for matching sequences. Like a student who looks up unfamiliar words in the dictionary, a biologist compares newly discovered genes to those already recorded in GenBank. The comparison then tells them what their gene does. It may match the ones that make a protein for metabolism, or transport, or some other cellular job.

Many of the genes that biologists have discovered have no matches in GenBank. They are unique, and no one knows what they do. As biologists have compiled the "words" in the genetic library of microorganisms, they have found that many of these microbes belong only to the species in which they were found. These sequences have been dubbed "orphans." Russell Doolittle, of the University of California, notes that "in every genome examined so far, at least a quarter of the genes remain 'hypothetical,' in that no function can be ascribed." We don't know what these genes do in the cell.

Biologists are fairly certain that these orphan sequences truly are genes because they share the features that identify known genes. The sequences, says Doolittle, "look conventional in every way," but, he adds, "where these unique sequences are coming from and what they do remain baffling mysteries."

The main evolutionary theory for the origin of genes says that new genes arise from already existing genes. But the orphan genes don't have detectable evolutionary parents. If they did, they wouldn't be orphans.

Where did these genes come from? What do they do? No one knows.

The best way to keep evolutionary theory honest is to challenge it with the puzzles it faces. When we do so in this instance, we see the case for intelligent design—for a Creator who gave us these purposeful genes.

News like this should delight every Christian. Like the psalmist, we should rejoice at evidence that points to God's inventive power.

Lord, thank you for genetic puzzles that confound evolutionary theories and confirm Christian teachings—puzzles that hint at the "splendor of your Kingdom."

MELODY OF FAITH

TO READ: JOHN 15:9-14

Love each other as I have loved you. John 15:12

Among the nominees for the Academy Awards' 2003 Best Picture honor was *The Pianist,* which tells the true story of one man's survival during the Nazi occupation of Poland. But how much better the film would be if its makers had not omitted a key historical fact.

The Pianist is based on composer Wladyslaw Szpilman's memoir. The Jewish Szpilman avoids the fate of the rest of his family—who perished in Treblinka—through a series of improbable events: being selected to work on a construction crew and then as a clerk.

While searching for food, Szpilman is stopped by a German officer who asks him his profession. The officer then takes him to a piano, where Szpilman plays Chopin. The German hides and feeds Szpilman until the war's end.

As Michael Oren writes in *The New Republic,* the image we are given is one of a "monster transformed by music." But that image, Oren notes, is a "misrepresentation."

The German soldier in question was Wilm Hosenfeld, "an ardent Catholic who abhorred Nazism." Hosenfeld wrote in his diary that the war happened because "humanity had to be shown where its godlessness was taking it." Our "denial of God's commandments" and unwillingness to "love one another" condemned us to die "innocent and guilty alike."

This faith is why Hosenfeld "repeatedly risked his life to rescue others, Poles and Jews, from extermination." It's why survivors, including Szpilman, tried to get Hosenfeld released from a Soviet labor camp, where he died in 1952.

In the film, the only suggestion of Hosenfeld's true motivation is when he tells Szpilman: "You must survive. God wills it." But without knowing about his faith, audiences can't possibly make sense of this remark. Why must Szpilman survive? Is it because he can play Chopin flawlessly or because he is made in God's image?

In suggesting the first answer, the filmmakers are following the Romantic ideal of the artist as a visionary, prophet, and even redeemer. The irony is that no one better articulated this vision than the German composer Richard Wagner—Hitler's favorite composer.

This is not to say that Wagner or Romanticism should be blamed for the crimes of the Third Reich. But they are reminders that the kind of heroism displayed by people like Hosenfeld and other "righteous Gentiles" was more often than not a function of their faith. Risking their lives to rescue others was a matter of love for their neighbor, not a refined aesthetic concept.

We Christians need to take advantage of every opportunity to tell people why we live the way we do. For instance, if we are given credit for being especially kind or generous, we should make sure the credit goes to the One who commanded us to behave that way: Jesus Christ.

Lord, let my behavior each day be such that it excites the curiosity of those around me, creating a willingness in them to hear about the Father who commands it.

FEBRUARY 26

THE CHALLENGE
OF WILBERFORCE

TO READ: GALATIANS 6:7-10

Let us not become weary in doing good. Galatians 6:9

Roe v. Wade has been the "law of the land" for more than three decades. Is it time to give up on our battle to stop the legalized murder of unborn children?

When we get discouraged, it's time to remember the lessons of history—specifically the lessons of eighteenth-century England.

In 1787 William Wilberforce, a member of Parliament and a Christian, decided to take on one of the most entrenched moral evils of the day: the British slave trade. Wilberforce knew this would be no easy task because the British Empire depended heavily on it.

First, Wilberforce educated himself thoroughly, learning all about slavery and conditions on slave ships. Then he began working with a small but influential group of friends who were equally committed to abolition. They supervised government inquiries into the slave trade and exposed the horrors of it. Then Wilberforce and his allies began educating the public about those horrors.

In 1788 a vote restricted the number of slaves a ship could carry based on the ship's tonnage. That first victory was a small one, but it proved that the slave industry was vulnerable.

For the next nineteen years Wilberforce introduced bills that would ban the slave trade. And year after year his opponents found ways to defeat them, often by playing dirty. But after nearly two decades of hard work, it became clear that the logjam was breaking up. The public would no longer tolerate commerce in human misery.

This change in attitude, writes Kevin Belmonte, author *Hero for Humanity: A Biography of William Wilberforce,* grew directly from "the sustained campaign to convince the public of the slave trade's immorality."

Finally in 1807—twenty years after Wilberforce began his battle—the House of Commons voted by an overwhelming majority to abolish the slave trade.

What is the lesson of Wilberforce's life? Despite repeated losses, he kept working. By God's grace, his cause made incremental gains. He didn't demand all or nothing but eventually carried the day.

This is what we have to remember when we become discouraged over abortion: We're making progress. More college students now say they're pro-life than proabortion. Congress recently passed both the Born-Alive Infants Protection Act and a ban on partial-birth abortions.

Wilberforce understood that while people may ignore the truth, they still recognize it when they see it. So he looked for ways to remind people of what they already knew in their hearts. Modern Christians must do the same, fighting as intelligently and tirelessly as Wilberforce. Gradually, slowly, we're winning the hearts and minds of the next generation.

Father, when it comes to fighting modern evils, give us the determination and persistence of Wilberforce. Help us not to grow discouraged over temporary setbacks but to soldier on under your direction—until we reap the harvest of victory.

DETESTABLE ART

TO READ: EZEKIEL 7:20-22

*They were proud of their beautiful jewelry and used it to make
their detestable idols and vile images. Ezekiel 7:20*

Jose Milicua, a Spanish art historian, recently uncovered evidence of
what were called "colored cells," used during the Spanish Civil War by
anarchist forces in Barcelona. The prison cells, inspired by the work
of artists such as Wassily Kandinsky and Salvador Dali, were em-
ployed in what their designer called "psychotechnic torture" of prisoners. The cells' floors were arranged in a way that forced prisoners to
stare at the walls. The walls were curved and utilized mind-altering
geometric shapes, "color, perspective, and scale." Lighting created the
illusion that the shapes were moving. This produced feelings of confusion, depression, and distress among the prisoners.

Spain's leading newspaper, *El Pais,* insisted that the creators of
such "revolutionary and liberating [artistic] languages" as surrealism
"could never have imagined that they would be so intrinsically linked
to repression."

Maybe not—but they knew what they were doing. For surrealism
and other kinds of modern art, shocking conventional sensibilities
was an important, if not the most important, function of art. In their
conception, art is supposed to confuse, disorient, and distress. And so
what happened in the Spanish "colored cells" differed only in degree,
not in kind, from what was happening in art galleries.

What's more, the artists, like the creators of the "colored cells," saw
a connection between their creations and politics. Art can be a tool
for transforming the larger culture.

Just about the only connection they did not draw was the one between art and beauty. That connection was severed when the West turned its back on the Christian tradition. And this connection is central to the Christian understanding of art.

When we see and appreciate beautiful things, we recognize that beauty isn't accidental. We know it's a product of intelligence—the artist's—and that the artist is the product of an even greater Intelligence: the Creator of all.

This recognition is why Thomas Aquinas defined beauty as "that which, when seen, pleases," because we recognize "God's good and orderly creation" in artistic efforts.

Much of twentieth-century art is the story of a rebellion against "any hint of the sublime or beautiful rooted in creation." Is it any wonder that rejecting the tradition that taught us how to think and create—a tradition based on a Christian worldview—would produce ugliness?

Sometimes Christians attempt to separate their "spiritual lives" from their livelihoods, unwilling to let their religion "intrude" on their work—especially creative work. But the story of "psychotechnic torture" shows that when our work rebels against God's holy standards, it can cause great harm to others—and becomes detestable in God's eyes.

Father, teach me to use the gifts you have given me as a way to point people to Christ—not drive them away. Let my hands never produce anything that is detestable to you.

RESISTING EVIL

TO READ: MATTHEW 5:38-48

If someone strikes you on the right cheek, turn to him the other also. Matthew 5:39

During Black History Month, children hear a lot about Jackie Robinson, who broke baseball's color barrier in 1947. Robinson is remembered for his quiet dignity in the face of racial bigotry on the ball field. But many kids have never heard about the source of Robinson's ability to turn the other cheek: his faith in Jesus Christ.

Robinson was born in 1919 into a culture steeped in racism. And from early childhood it infuriated him. Historian Jackson Lears, writing in *The New Republic,* says Robinson had "a reputation as a mad brawler, always ready to smash in the teeth of any white man who insulted him." Later, at UCLA, he gained a reputation as a thug.

But it was also at UCLA that Robinson began to encounter the forces that would free him from some of his rage. One was a nursing student named Rachel Isum, whom he later married. The other was a black minister named Karl Downs, whose hard-hitting sermons taught Robinson that Christianity was not a synonym for racial submission.

By 1945 Robinson had developed a firm conviction that God had an important purpose for his life. That purpose became clear when Robinson was summoned to the office of Branch Rickey, general manager for the Brooklyn Dodgers. Rickey was determined to make history by putting the first black player on a major-league team. But first Rickey made certain Robinson understood what he would face: everything from racial epithets to physical assaults to hotel clerks refusing him accommodations.

Rickey challenged Robinson, telling him he was "looking for a ballplayer with guts enough not to fight back"—a phrase that has since become legendary. Rickey also handed Robinson a copy of Giovanni Papini's *Life of Christ*, and he reminded Robinson of the words of Jesus: "Do not resist an evil person. If someone strikes you on the right cheek, turn to him the other also" (Matthew 5:39).

Robinson's struggle began as soon as he walked onto the ball field wearing a Dodgers uniform. During his ten years with the Dodgers he endured racist remarks, death threats, and unfair calls by umpires. But Robinson's faith helped him keep his anger in check. Every night he got on his knees and prayed for self-control.

"Through all the frustrations," writes Lears, "his Christianity sustained him."

At times, we all face attacks and insults we consider unjust. We're tempted to strike back through words and actions. Like Jackie Robinson, we need to turn to Christ for help in keeping our anger from spilling out—and spoiling our witness.

Christians ought to spread the word about Robinson's Christianity. Americans deserve to know the full story of the hero whose faith helped him overcome racial prejudice to make baseball history.

Father, when I am tempted to use powerful fists—or a clever tongue—in response to insults, help me to remember that your Son endured far worse with forgiveness—and love.

CLASHING CREATION STORIES

TO READ: PSALM 119:89-100

You established the earth, and it endures. Psalm 119:90

It's a classic story of creation—one you may be familiar with but probably have never heard spelled out quite this way: "In the beginning was no intelligence or purpose; there were only particles and impersonal laws of physics. These two things plus chance did all the creating. Without them nothing was made that has been made. The particles combined to become complex living stuff through a process of evolution. Primitive humans, not having science to tell them what had happened, dreamed up a Creator they called God."

As Phillip Johnson writes in *The Right Questions,* this is the "creation story" of evolutionary naturalism. And once we understand that—really understand what they're saying—we will have the enforcers of Darwinism on the run.

Johnson explains that at the root of all secular learning there is "an unacknowledged creation story" that is the precise opposite of the biblical one. But don't expect to hear it told forthrightly at Harvard or Berkeley or anywhere else. To state its elements this explicitly would be to reveal that it is merely a story. "A foundational story," Johnson writes, "is much more powerful when it is pervasively assumed." If its elements are never evaluated, it appears to be an unavoidable implication of reason itself.

The secular creation story originated with Charles Darwin, whose evolutionary theories appeared to make God unnecessary as Creator. Religious belief, intellectuals assumed, would die out as soon as people became better educated.

A modern evangelist for the secular creation story is Harvard geneticist Richard Lewontin. The primary job for science educators, Lewontin maintains, is to get the public "to reject irrational and supernatural explanations of the world . . . and to accept a social and intellectual apparatus, science, as the only begetter of truth." At least he's honest about what evolutionists are up to.

"To put it simply," Johnson writes, "Christians have been losing because they have not found the best way to state the question. They do battle on ground that favors the agnostics." We must understand that the debate is not a clash between science and religion or between reason and faith. It is a clash between two religions—Christianity and naturalism—and two definitions of science—evolution and intelligent design.

For too long, Christians have allowed themselves to be intimidated by people with a string of degrees next to their names—people who sneer at biblical truth and attempt to teach our children to do the same. We owe it to our children and to ourselves to learn as much as we can about evolutionary teachings and to make sure our children know the truth: Evolutionary naturalism isn't based on science but on irrational belief.

Lord, I ask you to guard our children against those who would drive them away from you through secular fairy tales that masquerade as science.

LEADING BY EXAMPLE

TO READ: 1 CHRONICLES 11:15-19

[David asked,] "Should I drink the blood of these men who went at the risk of their lives?" 1 Chronicles 11:19

When money from oil and manufacturing poured into Malaysia, its leaders had a choice: They could use the funds to build an economy that would benefit all Malaysians, or they could use the funds to line their own pockets and the pockets of their families and friends—something called "crony capitalism." Malaysian leaders chose the second course, and their actions brought Malaysia to the brink of economic ruin.

It's a perfect illustration of the wrong way to lead.

Where can we find examples of the right way to lead? One place we find them is the Scriptures. Remember the tale of David when he was battling the Philistines? Philistine soldiers had surrounded him and trapped him in the cave of Adullam.

David was desperately thirsty, and he said, "Oh, that someone would get me a drink of water from the well near the gate of Bethlehem!"

Three of his soldiers, overhearing him, got up, broke through the Philistine lines, drew water from the well near the gate of Bethlehem, and carried it back to David.

But instead of drinking it, David dumped the water out on the ground. His men were astonished and probably outraged, but David said, "God forbid that I should do this! . . . Should I drink the blood of these men who went at the risk of their lives?"

David was saying, "Yes, I want that water badly, but I am not going to take it at the expense of the lives of my men." More than he wanted water, David wanted his men to know that he put their interests first and that only the Lord was worthy of the sacrifice they had made. And so David poured out the water before the Lord.

There is a long tradition in the military that when an officer takes his troops into the field, he makes certain, always, that his troops are fed first. That tradition follows right from the story of David. Leaders are to pour themselves out for those whom they serve. In the spiritual realm, they do so with the authority that God has given them to lead, by being utterly selfless.

We must never forget this principle of leadership, whether we're leading Third World nations, American businesses—or our own families. We must never abuse our positions of leadership in order to serve our own interests. Leadership is a holy trust to serve those who depend on us.

Father, remind me daily to be the kind of leader who reflects the approach modeled not only by David but also by your Son: one willing to subdue self-interest in the interest of loving service.

MARCH 3

GOD'S SIGNPOSTS

TO READ: PSALM 104:1-35

He wraps himself in light as with a garment;
he stretches out the heavens like a tent. Psalm 104:2

Did God create the heavens and the earth? Or is the universe nothing more than an accident that "just happened"?

In *The Question of God*, Harvard psychiatrist Armand Nicholi sets up a debate over this question between two deeply influential men: a famous psychiatrist and a famous professor of medieval literature. Their positions were unequivocal—and mutually exclusive. Today, Dr. Nicholi writes, we need to ask ourselves how much of what they believed was based on evidence and how much on emotion that caused them to distort reality?

To the question, is there a God? psychiatrist Sigmund Freud answered no. Belief in what he labeled "an idealized Superman" is "patently infantile" and "foreign to reality." Freud "strongly advised us to face the harsh reality that we are alone in the universe," Nicholi writes. "In short, Freud shouted, 'Grow up!'"

Nicholi goes on to say that Oxford don C. S. Lewis answered the question of God with a resounding yes. Lewis pointed to the fact that the universe is filled with "signposts" such as the "starry heavens above and the moral law within," "all pointing with unmistakable clarity to that Intelligence." Lewis shouted, "Wake up!"

Freud attacked the Scriptures as being "full of contradictions, revisions, and falsifications." Religion, Freud wrote, is "the universal obsessional neurosis of humanity," and the teachings of Jesus are "psychologically impossible and useless for our lives." Freud was convinced, Nicholi writes, that psychoanalysis "has shown us that a personal god is, psychologically, nothing more than an exalted father," a "projection of powerful wishes and inner needs."

Lewis offered evidence that God does exist. He wrote, "He left us conscience, the sense of right and wrong: And all through history there have been people trying . . . to obey it."

Nicholi notes also that Lewis countered Freud's wish-fulfillment argument by pointing out that the "biblical worldview involves a great deal of despair and pain and is certainly not anything one would wish for."

Neuroscientists have recently found evidence that the brain is genetically programmed for belief. This confirms what Christians have always believed about the *Imago Dei*—the image of God—being implanted in us. And it may explain why Freud was preoccupied with God to the end of his days, determined to prove he doesn't exist.

How much have you been influenced by Freud's "religious" teachings over the years, perhaps without fully realizing it?

Read *The Question of God* to learn more about how two brilliant men resolved questions of faith. Their answers will help you witness to skeptical friends—and help them determine whether belief in God is really "patently infantile" or the Way, the Truth, and the Life.

Lord, thank you for Christians who use their intellectual prowess to witness to the truth that we are not alone in the universe. Help me to exploit my own gifts to do the same, to reach the unsaved in the setting in which you have placed me.

BOGUS REPENTANCE

TO READ: ACTS 2:29-39

Repent and be baptized, every one of you, in the name of Jesus Christ for the forgiveness of your sins. Acts 2:38

Novelist F. Scott Fitzgerald once wrote that "there are no second acts in American life."

To see just how wrong he was, turn on your television. A few years ago sports broadcaster Marv Albert pled guilty to misdemeanor assault-and-battery charges stemming from sexual encounters in a Virginia hotel room. Prior to his arrest Albert was NBC's top basketball announcer. After he pled guilty, NBC fired him. Dick Ebersol, the president of NBC Sports, called Albert's dismissal "something we had to do."

Then, a couple of years later, NBC quietly rehired Albert, assigning him to less important broadcasts. Eventually NBC returned him to his old job. In the calculations of his employer, Albert's expertise and popularity with fans outweighed the disgrace of having pled guilty to assault.

Albert isn't the only one who has made a comeback in recent years. Less than a year after a scandal that made her name synonymous with a sexual act, Monica Lewinsky reemerged as a spokeswoman for Jenny Craig Weight Loss Centers. And unlike Albert, who expressed some regrets for his conduct, Lewinsky was back without having expressed the slightest remorse.

Her restoration prompted *Los Angeles Times* television writer Howard Rosenberg to call it "a shame" that Lewinsky profited "from the infamy she attained when helping put the nation through enormous agony."

Rosenberg cited Lewinsky and Albert as proof that "the U.S. is either a very forgiving or forgetful nation in which fame tends to assume a life of its own if it exists long enough."

He's right. Fame is the quality we seem to admire most, even if a person is famous for all the wrong reasons. Albert's and Lewinsky's public restoration shows how little Americans care about the need for repentance and remorse before restoration.

We no longer require people caught in scandal to prove they are truly sorry for what they did, much less pay a meaningful price. Instead, all we require is that they keep a low profile for a time before reemerging, good as new.

Theologian Dietrich Bonhoeffer called this kind of bogus restoration "cheap grace." Restoration without repentance doesn't change lives or behavior. Worse, it blinds people to the need for true repentance and amendment of life. That's a problem, because God isn't as lenient as Jenny Craig.

If our neighbors are to understand what restoration really means, we must teach them. Part of that teaching should come in the form of repenting of our own sins. When we offend others, we must humbly ask their forgiveness, thus giving witness to our willingness to put repentance before self-regard.

Our unsaved neighbors need to know that there *are* second acts with God. But the curtain rises only after we've repented.

Father, let me never cheapen your sacrifice by taking it lightly, refusing to repent of sins your Son suffered and died for.

A DANGEROUS CORRELATION

TO READ: 1 CORINTHIANS 10:14-22

The sacrifices of pagans are offered to demons, not to God,
and I do not want you to be participants with demons. 1 Corinthians 10:20

Some twenty-five years ago a Stanford astronomy professor surveyed members of the American Astronomical Society on the subject of UFOs. About thirteen hundred astronomers responded.

Although nearly all so-called UFOs can be explained by natural causes, a small percentage can't be. Hugh Ross, a Christian, an astronomer, and the author of *Lights in the Sky and Little Green Men,* says researchers call these unexplainable phenomena "residual UFOs." In the Stanford study, sixty-two astronomers, or 5 percent, said they'd seen residual UFOs. But here's the interesting part: Astronomers with just a few observation hours per year witnessed UFOs, while those logging more than a thousand hours per year saw nothing.

This reverse correlation "demonstrates that something besides observing time determines who sees" UFOs and who does not, Ross writes. The most important factor, according to Ross, appears to be the activities these astronomers pursue. Those who are deeply involved in cultic, occultic, or certain New Age pursuits often see UFOs, whereas astronomers who avoid those things do not.

Twenty years of study have led Ross to believe that the principle is universal. Whenever he says this on television or on the radio, he hears from people who claim they're the exception. But upon deeper investigation, Ross writes, it turns out the person actually is mixed up in some way with occultic or New Age activities.

According to Ross, these UFO encounters "strike witnesses with intense fear, distress, and anxiety." Others experience nightmares, visions, hallucinations, and personality changes. Significantly, Ross writes, "Many who have had close contact with a residual UFO adopt new belief systems." He points to the many UFO-related cults and religions—cults whose teachings deny the divinity of Christ and the need for a Savior.

For these reasons and many others, Ross is convinced that the so-called UFOs are actually evidence of demonic activity. He points to Scriptures that warn that demons can attack only those who through their pursuits and friendships invite them. This, of course, is exactly what the victims of UFO phenomena do.

Skeptics often claim that UFO events are simply hoaxes. Ross agrees. But humans may not be the perpetrators. The nature of these UFOs and the impact they have on people are far beyond human capability. Witnesses instead appear to be the victims "of a hoax perpetrated by superhuman authors," according to Ross.

Ross's book is a warning to strictly avoid anything related to occultic activities, no matter how "innocent" they may seem. And the next time your family watches a film about "friendly" aliens or reads about the latest UFO sighting, share Ross's conclusions with them. If Ross is right, there's nothing friendly about them.

Lord, thank you for Christian researchers whose investigations give us one more powerful witnessing tool—one that warns that we are to worship you alone.

THE MAINSTREAMING
OF PEDOPHILIA

TO READ: 1 CORINTHIANS 6:9-11

Do not be deceived: Neither the sexually immoral nor idolaters nor adulterers . . .
nor homosexual offenders . . . will inherit the kingdom of God. I Corinthians 6:9-10

How does the unthinkable become thinkable? Through slow, persistent, and quiet change.

Most Americans view pedophilia—the sexual exploitation of children—as an abomination. But gay activists are now openly advocating it, calling it "intergenerational intimacy." As Mary Eberstadt writes in the *Weekly Standard,* the "social consensus against the sexual exploitation of children . . . is apparently eroding."

The process of erosion began some twenty years ago, when academics began questioning the almost universal condemnation of pedophilia. Soon, filmmakers and advertisers joined in, giving us movies like *Lolita,* which depicts a sexual liaison between a twelve-year-old girl and a forty-year-old man. More recently, advertisers such as Calvin Klein have pushed the envelope, using childlike models in sexually explicit poses in billboards and advertising.

Most Americans didn't fully wake up to the danger until 1998. That's when the American Psychological Association published the results of a study that argued that sex between adults and children is not always harmful, and that what have been called "willing encounters" should be relabeled as "adult-child sex."

The public was outraged. But, shockingly, mainline newspapers allowed homosexual activists to use their pages to attack not the study but people like radio host Laura Schlessinger, who criticized the study.

As one example, in *National Journal,* Jonathan Rauch wrote approvingly of the study and called the Congressional vote condemning it "faintly sinister." Mainline publishers also helped lower the deviancy bar by publishing novels with sympathetic portrayals of men having sex with boys as young as seven—novels that are available at your neighborhood bookstores.

In their 1979 book *Whatever Happened to the Human Race?* C. Everett Koop and Francis Schaeffer predicted that things considered unthinkable in the seventies—things like pedophilia—would be quite thinkable in the nineties. This would happen, they wrote, because "the consensus of our society no longer rests on a Judeo-Christian base, but rather on a humanistic one." Humanists view people as products of chance, not as creations of God—which means there are no transcendent standards. Standards fluctuate depending on what is viewed as "necessary, expedient, or even fashionable."

Christians cannot ignore this issue. The next time you see an ad exploiting children, speak out. Write the advertisers, boycott their products, and inform your lawmakers.

Living as we do in a depraved culture, we should also examine our hearts to make certain we are not gradually becoming more "tolerant" on any matter God calls an abomination. God help us if we allow the barbarians in our midst to convince Americans that child molestation is just another fashionable trend of the twenty-first century.

Lord, I ask you to protect innocent children from those who would abuse them. Let me never indirectly participate in their exploitation through the products I purchase. Show me what role I should play in promoting a culture that defends childhood innocence.

ARE WE STILL "PEOPLE OF THE BOOK"?

TO READ: DEUTERONOMY 5:6-21

You shall not make for yourself an idol in the form of anything in heaven above.
Deuteronomy 5:8

When media critic Neil Postman died in 2003, the press recalled his warnings about the dangers of mass communication.

In Postman's devastating critique of television, titled *Amusing Ourselves to Death,* he declared that television turns even the most tragic news into mere entertainment delivered by "talking hairdos."

Postman's book was reviewed in all the right places—but not once did we learn where Postman got his ideas. It turns out he got them from the Bible.

Postman's thesis is that different media encourage different ways of thinking. The printed word requires sustained attention, logical analysis, and an active imagination. But television, with its fast-moving images, encourages a short attention span, disjointed thinking, and purely emotional responses.

Postman says he first discovered the connection between media and thinking in the Bible when, as a young man, he was struck by the Old Testament words "You shall not make for yourself a graven image." Postman says he realized that the idea of a universal deity cannot be expressed in images but only in words.

As he put it, "The God of the Jews was to exist in the Word and through the Word, an unprecedented conception requiring the highest order of abstract thinking." This is the God Christians worship today—a God known principally through his Word.

Many religions have a set of scriptures, of course. Yet most teach that the way to contact the divine is through mystical visions, emotional experiences, or Eastern-style meditation. Judaic Christianity insists on the primacy of language.

Christians are meant to have an ongoing conversation with God. He addresses us in the language of Scripture, and we address him through the language of prayer. This emphasis on the Word has had a deep impact on Western culture. Reading was once confined to the elite. But it was the Reformation that first aimed at universal literacy so every person could read the Bible.

Here in the West we are in danger of coming full circle: The visual media may ultimately undermine literacy. If that happens, can biblical faith still flourish?

Neil Postman's writings remind Christians of the dangers of television. We need to learn when to turn it off, lest we lose our historical reputation as the "people of the book."

Lord, help me to remember that no matter how "Christian" the programming, television is no substitute for seeking you through the holy book you gave us and for which many have died copying, translating, preserving, sharing—and reading.

THE CHURCH BEHIND BARS

TO READ: HEBREWS 13:1-3

Remember those in prison as if you were their fellow prisoners. Hebrews 13:3

Journalist Ted Conover wanted to write about America's prisons. But he didn't interview guards and inmates to get the story. He wanted the inside scoop, so he went behind bars. No, he didn't commit a crime. He went on the payroll at a maximum-security prison.

After a year as a corrections officer at Sing Sing, Conover wrote *Newjack: Guarding Sing Sing,* a book that affirms what Prison Fellowship has proclaimed for twenty-five years: Only faith can make the difference in America's darkest places.

Originally built in 1828, Sing Sing is one of America's most storied prisons. When French historian Alexis de Tocqueville visited there in 1831, he observed that "whilst society in the United States gives the example of the most extended liberty, the prisons in the same country offer the spectacle of the most complete despotism."

Unfortunately, Tocqueville's words still ring true today.

Conover discovered that not only do our prisons dehumanize offenders, they also sow seeds of inhumanity in the hearts of corrections officials as well. Despite his best efforts—and even though he knew his time there was short—Conover was deeply disturbed by the experience. He became a man his wife and children did not recognize.

What did Conover conclude about our penal system? In an interview with Diane Rehm on National Public Radio, Conover offered two observations:

First, our system is in desperate need of reform. America's growing prison population illustrates an "absurd overreliance on incarceration."

He's right, of course. Prison is a "blunt instrument" that doesn't suit all crimes and all offenders. The one-size jail cell truly does not fit all—which is why Prison Fellowship has pursued and supported efforts to find alternative sentencing options.

Second, only religion made a lasting difference in inmates' lives. Conover found that the religious prisoners were the only ones with hope.

Conover's book is a great apologetic for the Christian faith—written by a secular journalist.

We ought to treat prisoners the way the early church did—praying for them, visiting them, and demonstrating Christ's compassion.

Newjack is a reminder that if we want to put a dent in crime statistics, we need volunteers to take the gospel message to those inside prisons (and to their often needy families on the outside), unleashing faith—which will transform the world of crime one life at a time.

Father, help me to remember that many of your Son's first followers were locked behind bars. Open my mind and heart to ways I can demonstrate compassion to contemporary inmates and their families—people who deeply and desperately need it.

ARE EMBRYOS
FULLY HUMAN?

TO READ: LUKE 1:39-44

When Elizabeth heard Mary's greeting, the baby leaped in her womb. Luke 1:41

Two intellectuals—one a Christian philosopher, the other a scientist—recently debated a timely moral question: Is the human embryo a tiny human being worthy of protection, or is it just a cluster of cells we can and should use in research?

Now you might assume that the Christian argued theology and that the scientist kept to empirical facts. If so, you would be wrong.

The moral boxing match took place in the pages of the *Wall Street Journal.* In the left corner, defending embryo destruction, was David Baltimore, president of the California Institute of Technology and a Nobel Prize–winning scientist. In the right corner, defending the inherent dignity of embryos, was Robert George, distinguished moral and political philosopher.

George pointed out that embryos possess the "epigenetic primordia" for internally directed growth and maturation as distinct, self-integrating, human organisms. Each embryo is therefore already—and not merely potentially—a living member of the human species.

As George put it, "The being that is now you or me is the same being that was once an adolescent, and before that a toddler, and before that an infant, and before that a fetus, and before that an embryo. To have destroyed the being that is you or me at any of these stages would have been to destroy you or me."

Baltimore could deny none of this. Instead, he made his appeal based on subjective feeling. "To me," Baltimore said, "a tiny mass of cells that has never been in a uterus is hardly a human being."

The past warns of the danger of making personal opinion the basis for defining humanity. Sixty years ago the Nazis justified horrific medical experiments on Jews because to them, Jews were "hardly human beings." A hundred and fifty years ago, white Southerners enslaved black Africans because in their opinion, Africans were "hardly human beings."

It's worth noting that George, a Christian, confronted his opponent—a man of science—with facts of science that utterly devastated the case for killing embryonic humans. In doing so, he proved that Christians have nothing to fear from science. The Judeo-Christian worldview always conforms to reality. We should not be surprised, then, that science backs up biblical doctrine—doctrine that teaches that our humanity begins at conception.

George is right: Biologically, human embryos are fully human. Only two questions remain: (1) Will we protect them, or will we allow some humans, because of their age, size, stage of development, or condition of dependency, to be killed to benefit others? And (2) Would you be willing to accept such a benefit—if your life depended on it?

Lord, in a culture that puts a high value on science—and almost none on the authority of Scripture—teach me to turn science itself into a witnessing tool, using the secular to illuminate the sacred.

JUST WAR AND CHRISTIAN LOVE

TO READ: ROMANS 13:1-5

*If you do wrong, be afraid. . . . He is God's servant, an agent
of wrath to bring punishment on the wrongdoer.* Romans 13:4

Not every American supported retaliation against the perpetrators of
the September 11 terror attacks. Those opposing military action included pacifists who believe military action is unbiblical. Among
them was Rev. Joseph Kotva of the First Mennonite Church of Allen-
town, Pennsylvania. He told the city's newspaper, "We believe all [re-
taliation] does is escalate the violence. Someone has to have the
courage to say that [the violence] stops here."

Kotva's words illustrate the pacifist argument against the use of
force—that it is antithetical to loving your neighbor as yourself, and
that love and war are never compatible. But while we can respect the
conviction of honest pacifists, they're missing an important part of
the picture.

Wars fought to take what doesn't belong to us, to expand our borders, or for revenge are indeed unjust. But war can be fought with
good intentions.

As Darrell Cole, a professor at the College of William and Mary, argues in *First Things*, the failure to fight a just war may be a failure to
love. He writes: "We . . . fight just wars because they're acts of charity.
[Fighting just wars] . . . is something Christians ought to do out of
love for God and neighbor."

What makes a just war an act of love? It brings justice, restrains
evildoers, and promotes the peace and well-being of the community.

This has always been the understanding behind just-war theory.

Thomas Aquinas in the *Summa Theologica* puts his discussion of just war in his chapter on charity, the love of God and neighbor. Aquinas applauded those who wielded the sword in protection of the community. Aquinas wrote that "retaliation should be sought out of the love of justice."

John Calvin agreed, calling the soldier an "agent of God's love," and soldiering justly a "God-like act." Why? Because "restraining evil out of love for neighbor" is an imitation of God's restraining evil out of love for his creatures.

A world where Christians refused to fight just wars would be a world where evil would reign unchecked by justice and where the strong would be free to prey on the weak.

Christians should "restrain evil" in their private lives as well by keeping a watchful eye on our neighbors' homes, reporting white-collar crime at the office, and restraining schoolyard bullies. We should also pray daily for our soldiers, who are risking their lives to make the world community safer.

Fighting just wars when necessary takes sin seriously and provides—as strange as it may sound—a loving response.

Lord, I pray for the safety of soldiers, police officers, and others willing to sacrifice their own safety for the well-being of the community. Give me the courage to restrain evil in my own life in appropriate ways out of love for my neighbors—even if doing so commands a cost.

PREPARATIO EVANGELICA

TO READ: MATTHEW 15:10-20

Out of the heart come evil thoughts. Matthew 15:19

It's well known that J. R. R. Tolkien rejected allegorical interpretations of The Lord of the Rings—for example, the notion that the ring represented the atom bomb. But Tolkien's Christian faith was a different matter. And it's no surprise that his faith found its way into the story.

Tolkien told a friend that The Lord of the Rings is a "fundamentally religious and Catholic work; unconsciously so at first, but consciously in the revision." For instance, when Gandalf calls himself a "servant of the Secret Fire," that fire, Tolkien told a friend, is the Holy Spirit.

The good news is that when The Lord of the Rings was made into a film, the connection between Tolkien's faith and The Lord of the Rings wasn't lost on director Peter Jackson and his cowriter Philippa Boyens. They told columnist Terry Mattingly that while they didn't set out to make a religious film, they understood the role that Tolkien's beliefs played in his life and work.

And knowing what he believed, they decided to honor the things "that were important to Tolkien." Thus, they said, "some of the messages and some of the themes" in the films "are based on his beliefs." Principal among these beliefs is the Christian idea that, as Alexander Solzhenitsyn once put it, "the line between good and evil runs through every human heart," and oscillates back and forth.

The cinematic version of The Lord of the Rings is more than a story about good versus evil. It's a story, says Mattingly, that offers modern audiences "another chance to understand the timeless roots of sin." Characters wrestle with the evil within them. Even when they seek to do good, they must guard against the possibility of doing the right thing for the wrong reasons or in the wrong way.

In some ways The Lord of the Rings—both the film and the book—is what the church fathers called *preparatio evangelica,* preparation for the gospel. It's a story where the characters, while not possessing the fullness of Christian revelation, can nonetheless glimpse this truth. Understanding their world and their thoughts prepares us to understand the fullness of Christian revelation.

Why not rent the film, invite a friend to watch, and then discuss *The Two Towers* with you? We should all be prepared to take advantage of the opportunities offered by the interest in Tolkien's world, one that helps us—and our neighbors—better understand why the Word became flesh.

Lord, thank you for cultural messengers who offer signposts to the truth. Teach me how to follow up on their signposts, offering the spiritually lost not mere hints of your reality but the full message of your salvation—one that directs them to a great and joyful destination: your eternal Kingdom.

FIGHTING TEMPTATION

TO READ: 1 CORINTHIANS 10:11-13

When you are tempted, he will also provide a way out so that you can stand up under it. 1 Corinthians 10:13

When young people head off to college, they face a host of new temptations—especially sexual temptations. Students need to know how to defend themselves against the standard "lines" they will encounter.

Even more important, they need to understand that many of the most common lines express a false worldview. As Jay Budziszewski points out in *How to Stay Christian in College,* this is especially true at college because ideas are the stock and trade of higher education.

Take, for example, the argument for sexual experimentation. It says that "in order to make wise choices about sex, you have to experience it." This isn't just a "line" a guy might use with a girl; it's a false theory of knowledge. It says that personal experience is the only way to know anything and that the test of experience is how you feel.

That's a principle many people rely on when making decisions. Is abortion wrong? "Depends on how it makes you feel," they say. Is God real? "Well, try it, and see how it makes you feel."

But as a theory of knowledge, this principle is clearly inadequate. In reality, experience sometimes limits our ability to make wise choices. Consider drug addiction or suicide. We can't become addicts to find out whether it's a good idea to be addicted. And we can't commit suicide to learn more about it.

In these cases experience prevents you from being able to choose wisely. Addicts can't choose wisely because they're hooked, and suicide victims can't choose because they're dead.

Over the centuries there have been quite a number of cases like this—

experiences that make it harder to choose wisely, behavior that subtracts from wisdom rather than adding to it. That's one reason Scripture identifies some behaviors as sin and warns people not to try them.

Sex outside of marriage is one of these. The best way to understand it is to stay away from it—to avoid experience and instead to determine what's right and wrong through rational evaluation in the light of biblical revelation.

At college, temptations gain most of their strength from false ideas. God promises that he will provide a way out of every temptation, and part of that means preparing our minds to refute false ideas.

If you know Christian young people who are heading off to college, make sure they know that temptation there is not a possibility—it's an absolute certainty. We must give them the tools they need, both intellectual and spiritual, so that they can successfully fight it.

The rest of us need to sharpen those tools as well, remembering that there is no time in life when temptation does not pursue us.

Lord, teach me to choose the right weapons at every stage of life to resist the onslaught of temptation.

BE NOT AFRAID

TO READ: JOHN 14:25-31

Do not let your hearts be troubled and do not be afraid. John 14:27

On August 6, 1944, German troops occupying Poland conducted one of the most draconian security sweeps of the entire war. Nazi soldiers smashed down doors and rounded up thousands of men.

In a Warsaw apartment, a young man called out to God as he heard the troops approaching. Amazingly, the Nazis missed the door leading to his apartment, and his life was spared. That young man was Karol Wojtyla—today known as Pope John Paul II.

In *Great Souls: Six Who Changed a Century,* former *Time* magazine senior correspondent David Aikman recounts this dramatic scene, and he helps us understand why simply doing our duty can turn ordinary men into great heroes.

The Nazis occupied Wojtyla's beloved Poland until 1945, when the Soviets forced them out and took their place. At that time Wojtyla began a college course in moral theology on "the right to life." As a Christian persecuted for his faith under the two worst totalitarian regimes of the century, Wojtyla deeply believed in the inherent dignity of the human person.

In addition to his studies and parish work, Wojtyla wrote brilliant plays, poems, and essays. But most of all, Aikman says, "he prayed—constantly. Before lectures, between lectures, or after lectures—on his knees in the chapel."

When he became pope in 1978, the result of all that prayer was evident in his inaugural address. "Be not afraid!" he said. He recognized that fear is a sin because it denies the sovereignty of God. And he recognized that as a leader of the church—and unwaveringly opposed to the Communist Empire—he had to give people the courage to resist evil.

And courageous he was. When Russian tanks were poised to invade Poland, the pope announced he would go and stand with his people if the Soviets crossed the border. The Soviet tanks did not move.

John Paul II casts a heroic shadow across Eastern Europe: Along with Ronald Reagan, he was the most significant influence in bringing the Soviet Empire to its knees.

And that brings us to a great paradox of heroism: True heroes don't set out to become heroes. They simply do their duty.

Today some Christians say we should abandon politics because we're losing the culture war. If we're tempted to listen, we should remember how this pope gave people great courage to endure far worse assaults on their faith and on humanity than American Christians face. And in doing so, he changed the world.

Being a hero isn't about success or power; it's about doing our duty faithfully—and having the courage to stand against all odds.

Father, give me the courage I need each day to simply do my duty—not in the cause of becoming a hero but in the cause of serving Christ.

SYMPHONIES TO SORROW

TO READ: MALACHI 4:1-6

He will turn the hearts of the fathers to their children . . .
or else I will come and strike the land with a curse. Malachi 4:6

When rocker Aaron Lewis of the band called Staind was thirteen years old, his parents divorced. In a song called "For You," Lewis sings, "To my mother, to my father/It's your son or it's your daughter/Are my screams loud enough for you to hear me?/Should I turn it up for you?"

Chad Kroeger, singer/songwriter for the band Nickelback, describes the pain of his father's abandonment with lyrics like these: "You left without saying goodbye/Although I'm sure you tried/You call and ask from time to time/To make sure we're still alive/But you weren't there right when I'm needing you most."

Whenever he sings that song, Kroeger told the *Washington Times,* fans begin to cry and tell the rocker they've been through the same heartbreak themselves.

These musical laments are a far cry from what the so-called experts tell divorcing parents to expect. As Maggie Gallagher writes in *The Abolition of Marriage,* one of the driving ideas of the postmarital culture "is that the happiness of adults is so crucial to their success as parents that divorce will make them even better parents." The notion that "divorce is better for kids than staying in a troubled marriage is now the conventional wisdom," writes Gallagher.

But are most kids really better off when their parents divorce? Does divorce actually lead to less hostility between parents?

According to Gallagher, all too often parents fight even more after divorcing than they did while they were married. In fact, she notes, "children whose parents were divorced, separated, or remarried [are] twice as likely to need psychological help as children whose parents [stay] in marriage with minor or moderate conflicts." And that's not counting all the other problems that afflict children of divorced parents in higher numbers: teen pregnancy, criminal behavior, drug use, and poor health. Children who do worst of all, Gallagher says, are those from "high-conflict divorced families."

Of course, divorce can sometimes benefit kids, but only when there is a long-term, high level of hostility or violence—and most marriages don't fall into that category.

As the songs of modern rockers indicate, children continue to feel pain from their parents' divorce even many years later. This is one of the reasons God condemns divorce so strongly.

The poignant lyrics of Aaron Lewis, Chad Kroeger, and others are reminders that all of us need to make our families a high priority. Those who are considering marriage should look beyond the romance and consider how serious a commitment marriage should be.

Just ask the real experts on divorce: young people who have experienced their parents' marital breakdown and are now writing rock-and-roll symphonies to sorrow.

Lord, let the message behind the music of divorce reach a wide audience. Show me how I might help children in my own congregation who are suffering from the pain of family destruction.

SPERM ABUSE

TO READ: EPHESIANS 4:17-24

They are darkened in their understanding and separated from the life of God.
Ephesians 4:18

Some years ago Peter Wallis and Kellie Smith of Albuquerque met at work, started dating, and eventually moved in together.

Then Kellie told Peter she was pregnant. What happened next shows the chaos that ensues when a culture enshrines sexual autonomy.

When Wallis found out Smith was pregnant, he was furious. As he told Barbara Vobejda, a staff writer for the *Washington Post,* "I felt shocked, overwhelmed and rather betrayed."

Wallis contends that he and Smith had an understanding that their sex would be nonprocreative. He filed suit against Smith, charging her with "intentionally acquiring and misusing" his semen. He maintains that she stopped using the Pill without his knowledge or consent. For her part, Smith says that she was on the Pill but, like a small percentage of women, got pregnant nonetheless.

Incredibly, a New Mexico court agreed to hear the case.

This bizarre story marks the intersection of two cultural trends: First, in this age of sperm banks and the buying and selling of sperm, semen becomes a commodity. An owner, therefore, has the right to dispose of it as he sees fit.

Second, and even more important, Wallis's claim is the inevitable result of the disconnect between sex and procreation. The sexual revolution convinced Americans of the very un-Christian belief that sex should have no consequences beyond pleasure. We think we should be free to enjoy ourselves without encumbrances. This attitude is at the root of the pressure for abortion on demand because requiring a woman to carry a child to term is viewed as punishing her for her sexuality.

The problem is that we have tried to have it both ways. We deny the connection between sex and procreation or "cure" it with abortion when it comes to women, and yet we insist on this connection when it comes to men. Peter Wallis's absurd suit exposes this preposterous double standard.

The confusion here is, as Paul wrote in Ephesians 4, the natural consequence of rebellion against God.

Christians—especially Protestants—tend to reflect very little about the God-ordained link between sex and procreation. To a certain extent we have unthinkingly accepted the teachings of our secular culture: that sex is intended for pleasure, not necessarily procreation, and that procreation is a problem to be "fixed."

When we hear of strange suits like the one in New Mexico, let's use the occasion to help our neighbors understand how and why they come about. They're the natural consequences of abandoning our historic Christian belief—of our desire to rewrite the moral and biological laws of nature to suit ourselves. The result is chaos.

Father, let me not be deceived by the tragic teachings of a darkened culture—one that invites us to worship, not at the foot of the Cross, but at the altar of autonomy.

MARCH 16

CAMPED AT
DEATH'S DOOR

TO READ: PSALM 116:1-19

Precious in the sight of the Lord is the death of his saints. Psalm 116:15

For years *Tuesdays with Morrie* dominated the *New York Times* Best Sellers List. It records the slow death of Morrie, a professor at Brandeis University who was suffering from Lou Gehrig's disease. One of his students learned of his illness, got in touch with him, and arranged to talk with him weekly. Morrie had no religious beliefs, which made the entire chronicle of death a meaningless exercise in pain and suffering.

Many people loved the book because they found the professor a heroic and sympathetic character. Even so, the book is emblematic of existential despair.

Riding to the rescue, like the cavalry of old, came Richard John Neuhaus, a Catholic priest with an uncanny knack for speaking to the needs of modern American life.

On January 10, 1993, Neuhaus collapsed in his apartment. An undiagnosed cancerous tumor had burst, and Neuhaus found himself camped at death's door for a year.

He came within a whisker of dying, and everything that could go wrong did. But after his miraculous recovery, he wrote about his experience.

Much of *As I Lay Dying* consists of Neuhaus's fascinating philosophical ruminations about death. But in the end he comes to the realization that he really doesn't have to worry about those things. It can be interesting to speculate about whether personality or consciousness continue after death, what form we are in, or what part of us survives. But in the final analysis, Neuhaus came to realize that what matters is Jesus. "In the destiny of Christ is my destiny," he writes. "When I die, in His body, body and soul are reunited. The maggots should enjoy me while they can—they will not have the last word."

We don't just wither away through terrible dehumanizing experiences, the way Morrie did; life is not a cruel hoax but a gift from a loving and gracious God who superintends our birth, life, and death. As the psalmist says, "Precious in the sight of the Lord is the death of his saints."

Do you dread suffering and death? *Tuesdays with Morrie* helps us understand why some people want to take a pill and end it all or become advocates of assisted suicide. By contrast, *As I Lay Dying* exhilarates us because it reminds us that Christians have a great hope.

If you've read *Tuesdays with Morrie*, try reading *As I Lay Dying*. You'll see two worldviews in stark contrast—and you'll see the hope of the gospel shining brightly in the dark passage of life each of us will one day walk.

Father, when I am sick or injured and the "anguish of the grave" comes upon me, free me from the chains of fear. Comfort me with the knowledge that when your Son willingly sacrificed his life, he freed me from the "cords of death."

IRISH WITNESSES

TO READ: ACTS 18:24-28

[Apollos] was a learned man, with a thorough knowledge of the Scriptures. . . .
He vigorously refuted the Jews in public debate, proving from the Scriptures
that Jesus was the Christ. Acts 18:24, 28

In A.D. 406, the Dark Ages began with a cold snap when the Rhine River froze over, allowing barbarians to cross a bridge of ice from ancient Germany into Roman territory. When they reached Rome, the barbarians looted and burned the city, wiping out centuries of learning.

Who emerged from the rubble, rebuilding Western civilization brick by brick? The Christian church.

The dramatic story is told in a book by Thomas Cahill titled *How the Irish Saved Civilization*. As the Roman Empire was crumbling, Cahill writes, its neighbors to the north—the Irish—were hearing the gospel message from a young missionary named Patricius, whom we know today as Saint Patrick. The Irish of the fifth century were barbarians descended from the Celtic tribes that had invaded Western Europe nine hundred years earlier. The Irish were still illiterate warriors—pagans who practiced human sacrifice and slavery.

But when Saint Patrick brought the gospel to Ireland, he did much more than deliver the Irish from pagan superstition: He helped transform their entire culture. Christianity gave the Irish a love of learning.

Christianity comes to us foremost in a book—the Bible. As a result, Christianity tends to foster literacy and learning. As Cahill writes, the Irish "enshrined literacy [as their] central religious act." Irish monks considered it part of their Christian duty to copy all books in danger of being lost as the Roman Empire crumbled.

Then they staged a second Celtic invasion: Everywhere they went, they established monasteries and carried on their tradition of copying and preserving the Bible and every other book they could find.

"These scribes," Cahill says, "served as conduits through which the ... Judeo-Christian cultures were transmitted to the tribes of Europe." They "reestablished literacy and breathed new life into the exhausted literary culture of Europe."

Without them, Cahill concludes, "our own world would never have come to be."

Those Irish monks are a potent reminder of how important literacy is to our faith. We worship a God who expressed himself principally through the written Word. Of all the world's religions, Christianity alone insists on the primacy of language.

St. Patrick's Day is a good time to think of ways to continue this tradition. We can support efforts to teach the world's peoples how to read, and encourage Christians who are translating the Scriptures into every language. Finally, we can send copies of the Bible to all who need them—the Scriptures that confirm that "Jesus was the Christ."

Lord, may I never become indifferent to the need to arm myself with the glorious weapon of your Word or to seeking ways to place the gospel into the hands of those who lack it.

THE ECOLOGY OF LIBERTY

TO READ: PROVERBS 22:1-16

A generous man will himself be blessed, for he shares his food with the poor. Proverbs 22:9

It was one of the earliest—and most graphic—attempts to blame too many people for too much pollution. In Paul Ehrlich's classic book *Population Bomb,* the author described an evening he spent in Delhi, India: "The streets seemed alive with people," he writes. "People eating, people washing . . . people defecating and urinating. . . . As we moved slowly through the mob . . . the dust, noise, heat, and cooking fires gave the scene a hellish aspect." What was Ehrlich's solution? Compulsory population control.

One astute observer, theologian Michael Novak, says the problem is not too many people; it's too much poverty. And the most effective way to lift the poor out of poverty and thus cut down on pollution is by promoting capitalism, private enterprise, and freedom—what Novak calls "the ecology of liberty."

As Novak writes in *National Review,* "Where people are poor, environmental conditions tend to be abysmal. And if the twentieth century proved anything, it was that the best way to end poverty isn't red—the color of socialism—but blue, the color of liberty, personal initiative, and enterprise."

For instance, more than a billion people worldwide live without clean drinking water. This is especially true in Africa, thanks to perpetual civil wars, dishonest governments, and badly managed finances.

Although Africa faces technical challenges to clean water, there is no reason these challenges cannot be conquered there as they have been elsewhere, Novak writes. But this will happen only if other obstacles—political, cultural, and economic—are addressed through economic incentives.

For instance, Africans have become accustomed to subsidized or no-cost water. Meanwhile, those who pollute water—farmers and industries—pay no price for doing so. The result: They continue to treat water with reckless disregard.

The solution is to create incentives for conscientious use and penalties for irresponsible use of water. Those who build and maintain treatment facilities could be offered financial incentives. Polluters could be penalized.

As Novak observes, "Blue Environmentalism encourages the highest possible level of practicality and private enterprise." This is why one of the guiding principles of "Blue Environmentalism" must be liberty. We must create markets that feature a healthy dose of both positive and negative incentives that work in the interest of both people and the environment.

Many of us send money to overseas missions that feed the poor. But if we really want to lift them out of poverty and pollution, we must promote "the ecology of liberty"—and share not only our food but our technological and economic knowledge as well.

Lord, we are often encouraged to view the faraway poor as dirty, ignorant masses that are polluting "our" planet. Help me to see them as individuals made in your image, and that part of loving you with "all our minds" means devoting ourselves to figuring out ways to lift "the least of these" permanently out of poverty.

EMOTION VERSUS TRUTH

TO READ: JOHN 14:1-11

*[Jesus said,] "I am the way and the truth and the life.
No one comes to the Father except through me." John 14:6*

The weeks following the terrorist attacks on America saw a noticeable increase in church attendance. Americans who hadn't been inside a church for years suddenly felt the need to go. Millions watched televised memorial services from the National Cathedral in Washington and St. Patrick's in New York.

This turning to religious faith caught the notice of many cultural commentators. Columnist Peggy Noonan spoke for many people when she wrote, "God is back." A new survey, however, paints a somewhat different picture.

Poll results released by the Pew Forum on Religion and Public Life suggest that the post–September 11 spike in religious influence flattened out within a few months.

What's even more noteworthy is what Americans believe about the relationship between religion, morality, and truth. For instance, 60 percent of Americans believe that growing up in a religious home makes it more likely that a child will be a moral adult. Yet less than half say that a belief in God is necessary to be a moral person.

Similarly, more than three-quarters of all Americans agree with the statement "Many religions can lead to eternal life." What's even more distressing, according to Pew, is that nearly half of the "highly committed" evangelicals polled agreed with that statement.

The inevitable conclusion from these polling results is that religion in America has succumbed to what has been dubbed "Oprahfication," which takes its name from the talk-show host.

Columnist Terry Mattingly defines Oprahfication as the assumption that "all truth is based on human experiences, feelings and emotions ... as opposed to the claims of religious doctrine, transcendent faith, or cultural traditions."

Thus, the important thing about a religion is how it makes us feel, not whether it's true. In fact, questions about truth claims are considered impolite, uncivil, and even intolerant. If a particular belief makes a person happy, who are we to judge?

As Mattingly notes, this is the direction that American religion, including evangelicalism, is headed, and the numbers bear him out. It's this worldview that causes people to see all religions, even those with diametrically opposed doctrines, as equally valid.

We Christians need to help people understand that religion is not a matter of sentiment; it is a matter of truth. Insisting that the truth claims of Christianity, and of other faiths, be taken seriously isn't "intolerant." On the contrary, it accords them the respect they deserve—something our "Oprahfied" religious culture can't and won't do.

Oh, God, in a culture that rejects the very idea of truth, let me never be afraid to proclaim what I know to be gloriously, "intolerantly" true: that no one can come to you except through the sacrifice of your Son, Jesus Christ.

TWO ARE BETTER THAN ONE

TO READ: ECCLESIASTES 4:8-12; 1 THESSALONIANS 5:11

Two are better than one. . . . If one falls down, his friend can help him up.
Ecclesiastes 4:9-10

We've been hearing for years that children reared in single-parent homes are at higher risk of poverty, drug abuse, and involvement in crime. But for babies, a parent's marital status can literally make the difference between life and death.

In *The Case for Marriage,* authors Maggie Gallagher and Linda Waite examine hundreds of studies that cast light on how family formation affects children's health. Their conclusion? Divorce, they say, "appears to be literally making some children sick."

For example, one study tracked the health of children before and after their parents' separation. It found that divorce made it 50 percent more likely a child would have health problems. For babies, the risks are even greater. One study found that white babies born to unmarried mothers are 70 percent more likely to die in the first year of life; black infants born out of wedlock, Gallagher and Waite note, are 40 percent more likely to die before their first birthday.

College-educated white mothers are the demographic group whose babies have the lowest infant-mortality rate. But even among them, the authors say, "being unmarried increases the risks a baby will die by 50 percent."

When babies survive infancy, their parents' marital decisions follow them into childhood and even adulthood. A Swedish survey found that adults raised in single-parent homes were one-third more likely to die over the sixteen-year study period than were adults from intact families.

What is it about marriage that so dramatically affects children's health? Well, part of it is likely the greater income married parents enjoy, which means they can better afford private health insurance. But Gallagher and Waite also found that "the lack of emotional support from a partner may also make it harder for a single mother to manage a child's health problems effectively."

This conclusion echoes what we read in Ecclesiastes: "Two are better than one, because . . . if one falls down, his friend can help him up. But pity the man who falls and has no one to help him up!"

Many single moms do a heroic job. But clearly they have a tougher time. The empirical evidence makes it clear that in most cases, married parents—a mom and a dad—are better for kids.

Parents cannot go back in time to remake bad decisions about marriage, divorce, and childbearing. But single parents ought to be able to turn to their churches for assistance if they need it. And if we see single parents struggling to rear their children alone, we ought to offer a helping hand, remembering that we are commanded to "encourage one another, and build each other up."

Lord, I ask for your blessing and protection on the single parents I know, and on their children. Show me ways to encourage and assist them without giving offense. Give these parents patience and wisdom as they bring up children precious in your sight.

BUILDING COMMUNITIES
OF VIRTUE

TO READ: ACTS 2:42-47

*They devoted themselves to the apostles' teaching and to the fellowship,
to the breaking of bread and to prayer. Acts 2:42*

There is one country whose flag you will not see flying outside the United Nations headquarters: "Cyber Yugoslavia," population 16,573. That's because it exists only in cyberspace.

The lack of any physical contact between its "citizens" hasn't stopped "Cyber Yugoslavia" from adopting the trappings of real countries: a flag, a constitution, and even a national anthem of sorts. The plan is to petition for UN membership as soon as its "population" reaches five million.

While it may sound bizarre, the people behind this "virtual nation" are not alone in how they have forgotten the requirements for creating real communities.

"Cyber Yugoslavia" is a clever gimmick, but it is the poster state for the Internet age and for what happens when people are linked together by only their keyboards.

As Quentin Schultze writes in *Habits of the High-Tech Heart,* Americans imagine cyberspace as a "location for recreating community." We see this belief on display in the millions of Web sites that bill themselves as either a community or a part of a larger community.

The problem is that while information technology can help us communicate with others, it cannot build what Schultze calls "communities of virtue." "Virtual communities" he says, cannot build "moral lives of gratitude and responsibility."

The reason is that social networks based on shared interests, like the Internet, do not require us to think about more than ourselves. On the contrary, in cyberspace it's easy to forget that anyone else—any real people—really exists. There is no need to be neighborly, hospitable, or generous—not just because you can't be held accountable but because it is not possible. The "community" is not held together physically, and the mode of interaction precludes acts of meaningful self-denial. The practice of virtues like self-denial shapes character and builds friendships—friendships that, in turn, hold us morally accountable. That just can't happen in cyberspace.

It's actual communities that require us to think about the needs and interests of others. And it's in real communities, starting with the family, that character is formed. For all the talk about Internet diversity, only a real community—one based on shared space, not just shared interests—can teach us how to live with people who are different from us.

As Schultze reminds us, this is the biblical model for community. Is it messy? Sure. But if our goal is real virtue, then there is no avoiding real people.

Lord, help me to get over any reluctance to interact with the diverse members of your Body and not merely socialize with those with whom I have much in common. Teach me the joys of loving and being loved by members of your flock from every social and economic level: breaking bread together, teaching and being taught, meeting one another's needs—and celebrating our common citizenship in your Kingdom.

WHAT'S BEHIND HUMAN NATURE?

TO READ: COLOSSIANS 3:5-15

You have . . . put on the new self, which is being renewed in knowledge in the image of its Creator. Colossians 3:9-10

MIT professor Steven Pinker has written a book that won't make him any friends in the politically correct crowd. But Pinker, who believes in evolutionary psychology, gets the most important question wrong: the "why" behind all the "what" he is describing.

In *The Blank Slate: The Modern Denial of Human Nature,* Pinker rebuts the most widely held explanations of why people behave as they do—that is, what we call human nature.

These explanations include the "blank slate," which holds that we are almost entirely a product of our environment and are infinitely malleable. Another explanation, the "noble savage" idea, imagines primitive cultures as peaceful and naturally cooperative in contrast to the conflict and competition of civilization.

For Pinker, much of human nature is intrinsic, hardwired into us. In other words, we're the product of our genes. He asserts that people, irrespective of environment, behave similarly in similar situations.

Pinker's rejection of the blank slate is most forceful in his chapter on gender. Men and women, he says, are psychologically, not just physically, different. They have different aptitudes, they see the world differently, and they have different approaches to solving problems. These differences aren't learned; they're inherent and rooted in biology.

Thus, attempts to ignore these differences, such as trying to have both sexes equally represented in all academic fields, are doomed to failure.

Ideas about the "noble savage," says Pinker, are equally wrong-headed. Studies of primitive tribes show that deaths from warfare are between three and thirty times as high as in the civilized West. Rape and murder are also more prevalent.

Pinker's book brings to mind something evolutionist Richard Dawkins once wrote: "Biology is the study of complicated things that give the appearance of having been designed for a purpose." Pinker, too, says we should ignore what nature itself seems to be telling us.

Human nature as Pinker describes it conforms neatly to Christian ideas: We are male and female and have a capacity for both good and evil. Nevertheless, Pinker attributes human nature to evolution.

Pinker's Darwinism leaves him unable to provide a coherent explanation for things such as self-sacrifice, true altruism, or mercy. Readers are left with no basis for why we should do good and not evil and no alternative to the nihilism that Darwinism leaves in its wake.

Pinker is right: We aren't blank slates. But it isn't evolution that did the writing. It was the Author of life.

We should remember this if we are ever tempted to blame or credit anything but ourselves for the decisions we make. We were made by a purposeful God, not by mindless evolution. We sin because of the Fall; we overcome it through God's mercy.

Father, thank you for the gift of life and for the sacrifice of your Son, who brought us back into communion with you. Help me daily to set my heart on "things above" and to put to death my "earthly nature."

MARCH 23

SEEKING WISDOM

TO READ: ECCLESIASTES 1:1-18

The eye never has enough of seeing, nor the ear its fill of hearing. What has been will be again, what has been done will be done again; there is nothing new under the sun. Is there anything of which one can say, "Look! This is something new"? . . . I have seen all the things that are done under the sun; all of them are meaningless, a chasing after the wind. . . . I applied myself to the understanding of wisdom, and also of madness and folly, but I learned that this, too, is a chasing after the wind.
Ecclesiastes 1:8-10, 14, 17

In 1730 a London wag began publishing the *Grub Street Journal*. Its purpose was to expose how unreliable newspapers were by showing how rival editors printed conflicting reports of the same events. The *Journal* became extremely popular, but ironically, people kept right on reading the discredited newspapers.

As C. John Sommerville writes in *How the News Makes Us Dumb*, "Even when we catch the papers in distortion . . . we still come back to them for more. We know it is insubstantial fare, like enchanted food, but we still need that daily fix."

How right he is. Sommerville played the *Grub Street* game in his own book. Here's what he found: The *Wall Street Journal* announced one day, "Scores on College Entrance Tests Fall." On the same day, *USA Today* announced: "SAT Scores . . . Up."

On the same day that the *Washington Post* announced, "Iran Offers to Accept Iraqi Kurds," the *New York Times* announced: "Iran Is Said to Close Its Border to Iraqi Kurds."

If I were a Kurd, I'd be a little nervous about that.

As bad as these headlines are, "the news" is inaccurate in a much deeper way. Newspeople claim to give us "all the news, all the time," as CNN puts it. But this is absurd. By definition, "the news" is limited to whatever some editor decides to include in today's broadcast or newspaper.

But what about the thousands of other events that were not included? Some of those may ultimately be judged far more important than the ones that grabbed the day's headlines.

As Sommerville says, "Historians may eventually tell us that the world turned a corner at just that time. Maybe in some embassy or boardroom or laboratory or monk's cell some lever was pulled that set history on a new course."

But these historic moments will never be "news" because they went unnoticed when they actually occurred.

In *Surprised by Joy*, C. S. Lewis urges against making young people read newspapers because "nearly all that a boy reads . . . will be known before he is twenty to have been false in emphasis and interpretation, if not in fact." Moreover, "most of it will have lost all importance. Most of what he remembers he will therefore have to unlearn; and he will probably have acquired an incurable taste for vulgarity and sensationalism."

The next time you're tempted to catch your fourth "news update" of the day, admit it: You're addicted. Balance television watching by reading good books, especially well-written histories. They will help you keep perspective and balance—and you may acquire something the Bible describes as being "better than jewels": wisdom.

Father, help me to remember—each time I turn on the TV or open a newspaper—that much of what I learn there is vanity, madness, and folly. May I seek to fill my mind not with trivia but with truth.

EVIDENCE FOR THE RESURRECTION

TO READ: ACTS 2:22-47

Those who accepted his message were baptized, and about three thousand were added to their number that day. Acts 2:41

As a newspaper reporter covering the courts, Lee Strobel saw how circumstantial evidence is used to expose what really happened during a crime. So, in the midst of a spiritual quest, Strobel began to wonder: *Could circumstantial evidence verify that the resurrection of Christ really happened?*

Strobel asked philosopher J. P. Moreland: "Can you give me five pieces of solid circumstantial evidence that convince you Jesus rose from the dead?"

Certainly, Moreland responded. First, there's the evidence of former skeptics. Some of those who were most hostile to Jesus prior to his death became his most ardent supporters afterwards.

Second, the ancient Jews had a number of important religious rituals, including offering animal sacrifices, obeying the Mosaic law, and keeping the Sabbath. But within five weeks of Jesus' death, more than ten thousand Jews had suddenly altered or abandoned these rituals. Moreland asked, why would they relinquish rites that had long given them their national identity? The implication is that something enormously significant had occurred.

Third, we see the emergence of new rituals: the sacraments of Communion and baptism. The early Jews baptized in the name of the Father, the Son, and the Holy Spirit, which, Moreland said, "meant they had elevated Jesus to the full status of God."

Fourth, we see the rapid rise of a new church, beginning shortly after the death of Jesus. Within twenty years this new church had reached Caesar's palace in Rome and eventually spread throughout the Roman Empire.

Fifth, the most convincing circumstantial evidence of all is the fact that every one of Jesus' disciples was willing to suffer and die for his beliefs. All but one died a painful martyr's death. Would they have done this for a lie? Of course not. They did it because they were convinced beyond a doubt that they had seen the risen Christ.

Even if we doubted two-thousand-year-old evidence, we have all the circumstantial evidence we could possibly want right in front of us. It is, Moreland said, "the ongoing encounter with the resurrected Christ that happens all over the world, in every culture, to people from all kinds of backgrounds and personalities. They all will testify that more than any single thing in their lives, Jesus Christ has changed them."

Some of the most powerful witnesses to Christ today are persecuted believers around the world—in Sudan, North Korea, and China—believers who are willing to suffer and die rather than dishonor Christ.

What kind of testimony are you giving to the reality of the Resurrection? If you have recently come to faith in Christ, have people seen an alteration in your lifestyle?

Father, as I prepare for Easter, I pray that I would be a better witness to your Son's sacrifice, that unbelievers around me would be inspired to examine Christ's claims through the circumstantial evidence of my life.

DEMYSTIFYING MOVIE MAGIC

TO READ: EPHESIANS 5:1-14

Have nothing to do with the fruitless deeds of darkness, but rather expose them.
Ephesians 5:11

A father was watching a videotape of *The Wizard of Oz* with his six-year-old daughter, Ashley. Ashley enjoyed the film—until the Wicked Witch of the West stole Dorothy's dog, Toto. At that point Ashley burst into tears. Hours later the little girl was still worried about Toto.

Ashley's reaction is not uncommon among young children. That's why parents need to demystify the magical power of the movies.

First, parents can reduce the impact of films by demystifying the medium itself. For example, Ashley's parents could explain that underneath the costumes and makeup are ordinary people. They could tell her that right after the frightening scene was shot, the director yelled, "Cut!" Then the actresses who played Dorothy and the witch probably took off their costumes and went to have lunch together.

A second way to demystify movies is to identify the way the filmmaker manipulates the plot's *moral* perspective. Leland Ryken, a professor of English at Wheaton College, points out that our response to films can be swayed when a movie treats "immoral acts with a comic tone that prompts [us] to acquiesce." In the film *Indiana Jones and the Last Crusade*, there's a scene in which Indy and his father discover that they've been sleeping with the same woman, and the discovery is treated humorously. The underlying message is that promiscuity is no big deal.

Third, we can identify the way the *techniques* of filmmaking are intended to affect us. Music, camera angle, background scenery—all of these can help manipulate the reactions of the viewer. For example, most Americans disapprove of adultery, yet millions of moviegoers loved *The Bridges of Madison County*—a film that celebrates adultery. One poll showed that almost half the people who saw the film thought the adulterous wife should have run off with her lover. The sentimental musical score, the lovely bucolic setting, the attractive actors—all of these helped reinforce the message that the adulterous relationship was a good thing.

Film is powerful because it seems so real. This apparent reality is why movies can have such an impact on our thinking—sometimes without our realizing it.

If you enjoy taking youngsters to movies, tell them to watch for the ways the filmmaker uses things like music and camera angles to influence the audience. Then, over a pizza, compare your reactions. Did everyone discern the filmmaker's moral messages? Were they biblical or unbiblical?

Finally, no matter how realistic a film may seem, we all need to remember: It's just a movie.

Lord, let me never underestimate the power of film to influence my thinking. Help me to teach discernment to those under my influence, that they may never be morally manipulated by movie magic.

ARE "THE PEOPLE" STILL IN CHARGE?

TO READ: PSALM 58:1-5

Do you rulers indeed speak justly? Do you judge uprightly among men?
No, in your heart you devise injustice. Psalm 58:1-2

We Americans think we enjoy self-government. We have all the trappings of self-government, like elections. But in reality, we have gradually lost many of our rights to govern ourselves. We are, in a sense, a nation run by a handful of judges who often enforce not the law but their personal opinions.

Here's a case in point: Beginning in 1997, federal judges began ruling on a series of state laws enacted to outlaw partial-birth abortion. As moral philosopher Hadley Arkes writes in *Natural Rights and the Right to Choose,* these laws were written with great care, and yet abortionists went to court claiming the statutes were confusing. In crediting their claims and being willing to act on them, Arkes writes, "Judges had to be willing to break from the conventions that defined quite sharply in the past the 'ethic' of judges in a democracy."

In a democratic regime, Arkes explains, judges are supposed to confine themselves to cases in which the law is actually being enforced on particular persons. But in these cases, abortionists simply said they were confused by the statute. And if judges are "willing to pass judgment on a statute, without the occasion of a case, then the judges" cast themselves in the role of legislators: "Lacking any record of a case, they would simply" vote on their sense of whether the legislation was constitutional.

In fact, the judges "would be legislators on a more exalted plane," Arkes notes. In striking down a statute, their own votes would override those of lawmakers who, representing millions of citizens, had passed the law.

This kind of power has always been viewed as deeply problematic. In a democracy, a sense of propriety obliges judges to work under a discipline that confines the reach of their power. So long as judges use restraint, power remains in the hands of the people elected to office.

But these were the very constraints judges willingly threw off in the partial-birth abortion cases. Judges found a reason to strike down every single law without exception. And, Arkes writes, they would not even bother to justify this extraordinary unconcern for the restraints on their office.

Christians need to be concerned about all the issues judges will rule on in the next decade, and they need to insist that lawmakers confirm only judges willing to exercise judicial restraint.

In our own lives, we need to ask ourselves if we, too, sometimes abuse the authority God has given us over employees, family members, and others. Sad to say, the desire to impose our own views is common to us all, and we must ask the Giver of all authority for help in overcoming it.

Lord, teach me to recognize the times when I exploit the authority you give me. Show me where to use my gifts in fighting the battle against earthly rulers who recognize no authority beyond their own beliefs.

LOVING CORRECTION

TO READ: 1 CORINTHIANS 5:1-5

It is actually reported that there is sexual immorality among you. 1 *Corinthians* 5:1

Some people argue that it doesn't pay to exercise church discipline these days—because people outside the church get too upset.

Consider the case of Catholic Archbishop George Pell of Sydney, Australia. Pell denies Holy Communion to homosexuals who don't accept church teachings on homosexuality. A biblical approach to sexuality is "essential for human well-being [and] for the continuity of the human race," he notes.

Pell has sponsored AIDS hospices and shown compassion to those infected with this deadly disease. Nevertheless, homosexual activists are outraged over his views and loudly protested his appointment as archbishop in 2001.

Then there's Cardinal Juan Luis Cipriani of Lima, Peru. Cipriani announced that politicians who oppose church teachings on abortion would be denied communion. Who became outraged over this? Americans United for Separation of Church and State.

When the Southern Baptist Convention took steps to cut ties with churches that allow homosexuals to serve as pastors, critics couldn't wait to wrap the "narrow-minded bigot" label around them.

But aren't these churches simply upholding their standards? Churches have never portrayed themselves as democracies. The church is hierarchical and authoritarian and ultimately answerable only to God. So why should anyone join a church and then expect to be permitted to flout its authority? After all, if you fail to attend enough meetings, you can be thrown out of the Rotary Club. Yet the minute churches impose discipline on their members, they're charged with everything up to and including fascism.

Shouldn't the church have at least the same right to set its own standards as a country club? If people don't like them, they're free to leave—assuming they're members in the first place.

Whether church members like it or not, the church must discipline its members. When we fail to discipline, the church does not become more "relevant" to the watching world; it simply loses its moral authority.

Discipline should be applied not only to enforce right doctrine but also to uphold right behavior. As theologian Greg Bahnsen put it: "Discipline guards the purity of the Church, preserves the Church by removing evil, and provides severe but loving correction for one who is in danger of falling into perdition." Without effective discipline, there can be no accountability and thus, no spiritual growth.

When we hear about cases of church discipline, it ought to serve as a reminder that we are all witnesses to Christ and our behavior should always reflect that. If it does not, we must be willing to submit to church discipline ourselves when it is carried out in the manner the Scriptures prescribe.

Church discipline is a mark not of intolerance and repression but of obedience to God and loving pastoral care for Christians.

Lord, let my church have the courage to discipline members who require it. Help me to remember that such discipline is designed to bring us closer to you.

LUKEWARM COMMITMENT

TO READ: REVELATION 3:15-22

*Because you are lukewarm—neither hot nor cold—
I am about to spit you out of my mouth. Revelation 3:16*

Columnist Jonathan Rauch believes that America has made "a major civilizational advance" in recent years. Rauch, a longtime atheist, is thrilled about a phenomenon he calls "apatheism."

It's not that people don't believe in God anymore, Rauch writes in the *Atlantic Monthly*—the majority still say they believe. But statistics show that they're going to church less, and when they do go, it's more to socialize or enjoy a familiar ritual than to worship. And as Rauch observes, they're refraining from sharing their faith with their friends and neighbors.

On the whole, the people Rauch describes haven't put much thought or effort into their faith. They're looking for comfort and reassurance, not for a God who asks anything of them. Hence the rise of "apatheism," which Rauch defines as "a disinclination to care all that much about one's own religion, and an even stronger disinclination to care about other people's."

Rauch thinks this is great because he believes that "religion, as the events of September 11 and after have so brutally underscored, remains the most divisive and volatile of social forces." If you must have faith, he argues, it's better to be lukewarm about it than to be "controlled by godly passions."

There are several problems with Rauch's analysis, but the main one is that the "apatheism" he describes looks very much like selfishness. And it's selfishness, not religious faith, that is a truly disruptive force.

True faith takes us out of ourselves, leading us to serve God and other people. It's selfishness, not tolerance, that dictates that we direct our own lives and stay where we're comfortable. Selfishness makes us keep our faith strictly personal, afraid to integrate it with the rest of our lives or even talk about it for fear of being judged harshly.

In Jonathan Rauch's ideal world, without the "godly passions" he deplores, there would have been no Mother Teresa, Corrie ten Boom, or William Wilberforce able to identify evil and stand against it.

Rauch may not like the idea of a world controlled by "godly passions," but if he were to see a world controlled entirely by human passions, he might not think it was such a great civilizational advance after all.

What about you? Are you known for your "godly passions" or for a laid-back, lukewarm faith? Do you stand boldly against cultural evils, or do you sit quietly because you're concerned about what the neighbors might think?

Father, forgive me for letting the concerns of the world—and its pleasures—cool my commitment to you. From this day forth may the watching world see me "on fire" for you, burning brightly in your service and shedding light on your truth.

HOW DEVOTED DADS
POINT TO CHRIST

TO READ: EPHESIANS 6:1-9

Fathers, do not exasperate your children. Ephesians 6:4

What do Blaise Pascal, Alexis de Tocqueville, and G. K. Chesterton have in common?

All were prominent Christians. But these champions of our heavenly Father had something else in common as well: All had exceptionally close relationships with their earthly fathers.

In *Faith of the Fatherless,* psychologist Paul Vitz says he initially set out to examine the lives of prominent atheists of the last four centuries. He discovered that all had fathers who were weak, abusive, missing, or dead. Then he began to wonder whether what appears to modern eyes to be defective fathering simply reflected the social conditions of the time.

To find the answer, Vitz compared the family conditions of prominent atheists to those of prominent theists from the same period. What he found is startling: Every theist he studied had a strong and tender bond with his father or with a father substitute. And as adults, these men became known for taking on the intellectual forces of atheism.

For example, Blaise Pascal, the great French philosopher and mathematician, was homeschooled by his Catholic father. Their relationship was close and affectionate. As an adult, Vitz writes, Pascal wrote "a powerful and imaginative defense of Christianity."

John Henry Newman, a Catholic cardinal, also had a lifelong, loving relationship with his father. Vitz notes that Newman developed a "clear and critical understanding of modernism" and wrote rational responses to it.

Tocqueville, author of *Democracy in America*, loved his father deeply. He argued that religion is absolutely necessary in the public life of a nation—a view that was, Vitz writes, "really quite unusual" at a time when atheistic views of culture "were becoming standard in Europe."

William Wilberforce, Britain's great abolitionist, was also a devoted dad. When his son Samuel was away at school, Wilberforce found time to write him more than six hundred letters, in which he poured out his love. Samuel later became a bishop who was "well-known as one of the major debaters in the conflict . . . over Darwinian evolutionary theory," Vitz writes.

Christian apologist G. K. Chesterton was deeply attached to his father, who was Chesterton's constant companion when he was a child.

In light of Vitz's research, we can hardly overstate the importance of good fathering. His book helps us understand why the Scriptures command fathers to provide diligent spiritual leadership to their children—and why, in Ephesians, fathers are specifically instructed to avoid exasperating their children.

Fathers—and father figures—should ask themselves daily whether or not they are modeling the patient love of our heavenly Father. It's a question with eternal consequences.

Lord, help me not to abuse the power I have over the children in my life by provoking them to such a degree that they are tempted to reject us both.

VAN GOGH'S
STARRY WITNESS

TO READ: MATTHEW 13:1-24

*The one who received the seed that fell on good soil is the man
who hears the word and understands it.* Matthew 13:23

Most of us are familiar with at least a few of Vincent van Gogh's paintings, such as *The Starry Night* and his Sunflower series. But did you know that van Gogh's works are reflections of his deep religious faith?

This is something art historians usually overlook. In fact, historians often present van Gogh's faith as an obstacle he had to overcome so that he could grow as an artist. But art historian Kathleen Powers Erickson disputes that idea. In *At Eternity's Gate: The Spiritual Vision of Vincent Van Gogh,* drawing on the artist's own letters, Erickson argues that van Gogh's faith was at the very foundation of his artistic vision.

As a young man, van Gogh, who was born on this date in 1853, was a lay missionary to impoverished coal miners in Belgium. He read the works of evangelical preacher Charles Spurgeon and attended revival meetings.

Van Gogh's hopes for becoming a pastor were dashed when he was denied admission to seminary. Devastated, van Gogh left Christian ministry and turned to art.

Erickson writes that for a time, van Gogh abandoned the institutional church. He attempted to forge a new—but not wholly orthodox—synthesis between Christianity and the new forces of modernism.

Van Gogh struggled with mental disease, and during his stay at St. Remy's hospital he created some of his greatest art. According to

Erickson, it was here that van Gogh returned to the Christianity of his youth. He painted pictures with explicitly biblical themes, such as *The Good Samaritan* and *The Pietà*. One of his most moving paintings of this period is *The Raising of Lazarus*. The painting is in varying shades of intensely bright yellow, with a pulsating sun filling the scene with light. Lazarus has a thin red beard—just as van Gogh himself did. It's clear the painting is a self-portrait, at once a meditation on Scripture and a personal testimony to faith.

Erickson writes that van Gogh considered the sun—and sunflowers—to symbolize the light of God and his presence in the world. By the same token, his wheat fields—with their sowers and reapers—are taken directly from Christ's parables about the Kingdom of Heaven.

When art critics dismiss van Gogh's faith, they not only misinterpret his work, they also diminish the power of his paintings.

Van Gogh, who struggled with poverty and mental illness during his short life, still managed to honor and worship Christ through the artistic gifts God gave him. Are we willing to do the same with our own gifts—even under difficult circumstances?

To learn more about the faith of van Gogh, read *At Eternity's Gate*. You'll discover how the man who painted powerful and moving starry nights used his paintbrush to point art lovers toward the Son.

Lord, thank you for the gifts you have given me. Help me to use them to produce an eternal crop for your Kingdom.

COURTING A LIFE MATE

TO READ: SONG OF SONGS 7:10-13; 8:4

Do not arouse or awaken love until it so desires. Song of Songs 8:4

In *I Kissed Dating Goodbye,* Joshua Harris describes why as a teen he gave up dating: He believed that dating relationships were inherently unhealthy.

Harris, now happily married, suggests a series of steps that people can take to explore whether a friendship should lead to courtship and perhaps marriage.

When we meet someone special, he says, we should first seek a deeper friendship. Although romance may seem more exciting, "it can also foster illusion and infatuation, obscuring the true character of each person."

Instead of dropping regular routines in order to spend time together, the couple should "find activities that pull [them] both into each other's world of family, friends, work . . . and ministry."

Both parties should then consult trusted advisors about the advisability of moving beyond friendship. These mentors can ask the hard questions, such as "Are you mature enough to marry?" or "Are you attracted to his looks or to his character?"

Four "green lights" can help someone decide whether to stop the relationship or keep on going. (1) Is this person a Christian? (2) Do you have a realistic vision of what lifelong marriage is all about? (3) Does your romance meet with the approval of parents and godly friends? If *you* think you're ready for marriage but no one else does, that's a red light, and you may need to reconsider. (4) Do you have a sense of God's peace about your plans, or do you feel apprehensive?

If all the lights are green and the couple agrees to move forward, Harris writes, they enter into a time of "principled romance," the testing and heart-winning stage of courtship. They ought to look for activities that allow them to spend time together among family and friends. They may also spend some limited time alone together in appropriate settings.

After that, it's time to fish or cut bait—to get engaged or perhaps break off the relationship.

Harris's proposals may sound Victorian, but they offer a refreshing contrast to today's secular approach to dating and marriage, helping us understand why the Song of Songs warns us not to awaken love until the time is right. Love too soon may bring grief instead of the joy God intends.

Harris's book, although intended for teens, is a sobering reminder that "principled romance" is God's desire for all of us. In a culture that cares little about honorable relationships, the church must redouble its efforts to help members of all ages seek romance in appropriate ways. We must help them avoid awakening love until the right time—and prepare them for true love, which, as Solomon puts it, is "much more pleasing . . . than wine."

Lord, thank you for a modern take on an ancient teaching. May this book be a convincing witness to young people who are eager to experience romantic love. Protect the young people of my own church from destructive dating advice offered by a depraved and deceitful culture.

SHAPING OUR CULTURE

TO READ: JOHN 15:1-11

This is to my Father's glory, that you bear much fruit,
showing yourselves to be my disciples. John 15:8

In their prophetic book *Boiling Point: Monitoring Cultural Shifts in the 21st Century,* George Barna and Mark Hatch write that the changes coming in the next ten years may create a society that is radically different from the one in which we now live.

First, they say, many important changes will occur in demographics. The census bureau predicts that by the year 2010, whites will drop to 68 percent of the population and Hispanics will overtake African-Americans as the nation's largest minority group. Also, certain parts of the nation will likely become ethnic colonies. Maryland and the District of Columbia will become a center for African-Americans, while Texas, New Mexico, Arizona, and California will develop into Hispanic colonies.

We can also expect a widening gap between rich and poor, a larger percentage of the population to be senior citizens, and further diversification of the family structure—all important considerations for ministry.

Second, technological advances will fuel the most dramatic changes, the authors say. For example, nanoprobes may be developed that can be injected into our bodies to clean arteries, strengthen bone tissue, or perform diagnostic tests. And gene manipulation may allow parents to screen out defects in their children before they're born. Therapeutic cloning to replace damaged body parts may gain congressional approval as Americans embrace "quality of life" over the inherent "dignity of life."

With "smart houses," computers will control all the functions of your home. Businesses will rely more and more on the Internet, and online transactions will be the norm. Computer chips may even become so powerful that artificial intelligence will be virtually indistinguishable from human thought.

Where will Christians be in all these changes? Barna and Hatch suggest that we have two options: either to be the victims who are trampled by the inevitable march of progress or to be the innovators who help to direct and shape these coming changes. Clearly, the second option is better.

As Barna and Hatch write, "If the role of the church is to influence all dimensions of culture rather than to be shaped by the culture, then we must be alert and assertive in representing God to the best of our ability in the world."

Barna and Hatch contend that the church is the biggest wild card in predicting the future of our nation. That's because historically the church has had such enormous influence in shaping the direction of the culture.

The authors have written their book to help Christians deal with impending cultural shifts. Are we up to the task?

Father, give me wisdom in discerning cultural trends and teachings. Lead me to seek out wise sources—those that investigate and interpret social shifts according to your Word. And then, armed with the truth, may I bear fruit for your Kingdom, helping to shape my society in a way that honors you.

THE CRUCIFIXION
OF CHRIST

TO READ: JOHN 19:1-37

Then Pilate took Jesus and had him flogged. . . . Finally
Pilate handed him over to them to be crucified. John 19:1, 16

Former journalist Lee Strobel covered many trials in which a jury's decision hung on the medical evidence. Was it possible, he wondered, to examine two-thousand-year-old medical evidence and determine whether or not Jesus really died on the cross?

For an expert opinion, Strobel went to Dr. Alexander Metherell, a research scientist. Metherell is convinced there's no way anyone could have survived what the Romans put Jesus through.

First, there was the flogging. Soldiers used whips of braided leather thongs. The metal balls woven into the lash caused deep bruises that broke open during the torture. Often the victim's back was so shredded that his spine was exposed.

Those who didn't die from the flogging went into hypovolemic shock brought on by blood loss. There would be a loss of blood pressure leading to faintness and collapse. And the loss of fluids would result in tremendous thirst.

The Gospels indicate that Jesus was in shock as he carried his cross to Calvary. He collapsed on the road, and Simon of Cyrene had to carry the cross for him. Later, Jesus said, "I thirst."

Then there was the agony of the crucifixion itself. The Romans drove spikes through the wrists and feet of Jesus—spikes that traveled through the median nerves. This caused such enormous pain that a new word was invented to describe it: *excruciating*. The word literally means "out of the cross."

Metherell believes that Jesus, like other crucifixion victims, eventually died of asphyxiation. The stresses on the muscles and diaphragm put the chest in the inhaled position; in order to exhale, the victim had to push up on his feet to ease the tension in the muscles for just a moment. It would be enormously painful, and exhaustion would eventually set in.

As breathing slowed, the victim would go into respiratory acidosis, leading to an irregular heartbeat and eventual cardiac arrest. Then, in the case of Jesus, to ensure that he was dead, a Roman soldier thrust a spear into his side.

Flogging, massive blood loss, shock, crucifixion, stabbing: Could Jesus have suffered all this and survived?

Not a chance, Metherell told Strobel. Besides, Roman soldiers had good reason to make certain Jesus was dead: Had he survived, they would have been executed.

The better the science, the greater the support for what Christians have long believed by faith: that love drove Jesus to willingly endure an excruciating death so that you and I might live.

How often do you think about the sacrifice Jesus made on your behalf? Do you obey his commands?

Father, thank you for loving us so much that you offered the most precious gift you had: the life of your own Son.

APRIL 3

A SENSE OF THE DIVINE

TO READ: REVELATION 4:2-8

Holy, holy, holy is the Lord God Almighty, who was, and is, and is to come. Revelation 4:8

Imagine finding yourself walking on pink, rubbery grass, surrounded by purple mountains and tubular trees. Suddenly, a creature walks up to you. It looks like an otter, but it's the size of a polar bear. Then this odd creature begins speaking to you. The experience is bizarre, beautiful, and yet somewhat frightening.

If you've read C. S. Lewis's space trilogy, you will recognize the creature as a "hross." By introducing us to these and other fantastical creatures, Lewis takes us away from the constraints of the world we know and reveals the vastness of God in a way unlike any we have ever known.

The hero of the space trilogy, Professor Ransom, is both an everyman character and a kind of Christ figure. In the first book in the series, *Out of the Silent Planet,* Ransom is kidnapped and taken to Mars. In the second book, *Perelandra,* Ransom travels to Venus, a paradise featuring an Adam and Eve who have not yet sinned.

In the final book in the series, *That Hideous Strength,* we find the magician Merlin awakening at a critical moment to help battle the forces of evil on earth.

Through these novels, Lewis takes us to worlds of unspeakable strangeness and beauty. Because the space trilogy is science fiction, the books are written with a kind of plausibility. We know they are not true, but they almost could be. We get the feeling that the strange creatures and landscapes really could exist, if not on Mars or Venus then perhaps on another planet.

These literary adventures give us an experience of what Lewis calls the *numinous*, a sense of wonder and awe in response to the presence of something utterly beyond us. Lewis's hope is that we, like Ransom, will find in this experience a sense of the divine presence of God.

The Ransom character experiences this when he meets the beautiful yet frightening angelic beings called eldils. Although Ransom has no concern for his safety, the encounter leaves him troubled. These angels are unlike anything else he has ever known; they powerfully reflect God's majesty and holiness. They are only partially visible, but they reflect God simply by their very being. Just being in their presence recalls to Ransom's mind his own shortcomings. By giving us experiences of the numinous, Lewis does Christians a great service.

Unfortunately many churches today so stress the personal aspect of God that we've lost that sense of awe and wonder, the sense of otherness that is appropriate when speaking of the holy Ruler of the universe. "Happy clappy" songs and relentlessly upbeat sermons do little to recall to our minds our shortcomings and need of a Savior who suffered for us.

Perhaps one reason people crowd our churches for Easter services is because those services *do* focus on the majesty of a holy God "who was, and is, and is to come." How often does your church inspire awe over God's majesty the rest of the year?

Lord, may I who am unworthy worship you in a way that reflects the fact that you are worthy to receive "glory and honor and praise" forever and ever.

SHUTTING OUT STIMULATION

TO READ: COLOSSIANS 3:15-24

*Whatever you do, work at it with all your heart,
as working for the Lord. Colossians 3:23*

Why would anyone want to watch a race between a human and a giraffe or eavesdrop on a blind date between annoying strangers?

The public has a seemingly insatiable appetite for "reality TV," and as one network executive told the *New York Times,* "We've got a responsibility to satisfy that appetite."

Gloria Goodale reports in the *Christian Science Monitor* that the public constantly bombards producers with new ideas. Favorites include people falling off of buildings or out of airplanes, and street fights between homeless drunks—already an Internet favorite. The producers have said no to these and other dangerous and degrading ideas, but how long will that last among people who think they have "a responsibility to satisfy that appetite"?

The title of a new book by Richard Winter, a psychiatrist and associate professor of practical theology at Covenant Seminary, gives away his diagnosis for the sorry state of TV and why we watch it. The book is titled *Still Bored in a Culture of Entertainment.*

"When stimulation comes at us from every side," he writes, "we reach a point where we cannot respond with much depth to anything. Bombarded with so much that is exciting and demands our attention, we tend to become unable to discriminate and choose from among the many options. The result is that we shut down our attention to everything." That is, we get bored.

Overstimulated and bored, we start looking for anything that will give our jaded spirits a lift. Winter says that boredom explains the rise in extreme sports, risk taking, and sexual addiction. "The enticements to more exciting things have to get louder to catch our dulled attention," he writes. And so reality TV gets more risqué and more degrading by the day—a trend that shows no signs of abating.

Winter, who notes that boredom is part of life in a fallen world, says we must recover a sense of passion and wonder. Engaging the world rather than passively watching it can mitigate much of our boredom.

He writes, "Finding interest and joy in life involves active engagement with the world. . . . [T]he person who wants to be involved with life knows that it is necessary to move toward someone or something, to want to understand and know."

And engagement with the world, that is, wanting to understand and know, is also central to developing a Christian worldview.

Your boredom can be a wake-up call to pursue passion, wonder, and a Christian worldview—with all your heart, soul, mind, and strength.

Lord, teach me to shut out all outside stimulation so that I might go into my prayer closet, be still, and know that you are God. And then, refreshed, may I throw myself into passionate pursuit of the work you intend me to perform— joyously, as though I perform it directly for you.

INTO THE VERY PRESENCE OF GOD

TO READ: MATTHEW 26:57-68

They spit in his face and struck him with their fists. Matthew 26:67

It was early morning Iraqi time. Crouched in a modified tank, NBC News correspondent David Bloom picked up his phone and played back his messages. One was from Jim Lane, a New York financier. The two were sharing a daily, long-distance devotional time using Oswald Chambers's classic *My Utmost for His Highest*. Lane read the message for April 5, based on a passage from Matthew: "Because of what the Son of Man went through, every human being can now get through into the very presence of God."

Moments later, Bloom climbed out of the tank, took a few steps, and collapsed. Soon after, he was ushered into the presence of God.

David's death from a pulmonary embolism devastated his family, friends, colleagues, and millions of TV viewers. At age thirty-nine, David was a rising star at NBC. Viewers looked forward to watching Bloom file his reports while bouncing across the desert on his "Bloom-mobile," face streaked with dirt, hair snapping in the wind. He loved his job, and everyone knew it.

But what most viewers did not know was that David was a committed Christian. But while he had a strong understanding of the gospel growing up, it wasn't until he was in his late thirties, according to Lane, that Bloom "effectively came to a saving knowledge of Jesus and started a real faith journey."

On the day Bloom died, Lane says, "David was in a very good place, at peace with himself, his faith, and his family." That peace was reflected in the last message he would ever send to his wife, Melanie—one that reveals that in the middle of a desert battlefield, his own mortality was very much on his mind. Bloom wrote: "When the moment comes in my life when you are talking about my last day, I am determined that you and others will say, 'He was devoted to his wife and children; he was admired; he gave every ounce of his being for those whom he cared most about—not himself, but God and his family.'"

At the end of the April 5 devotional reading, Oswald Chambers writes: "The cross of Christ was . . . not only a sign that our Lord had triumphed, but that He had triumphed to save the human race." Those who knew Bloom thank God for that triumph in the short life of this ebullient, gifted man.

What about you? Will you be remembered for your devotion to Christ and your willingness to serve His cause with gusto? Do you live as though each day were your last?

Father, may I never forget the agony your Son endured for my sake—so that I might one day be ushered before your throne. I pray that my life will be a daily witness to my devotion to you and that on the day of my earthly death, those who know me will celebrate your triumph in my life.

IS ISLAM TOLERANT?

TO READ: LAMENTATIONS 3:59-63

You have seen the depth of their vengeance,
all their plots against me. Lamentations 3:60

In nearly every discussion about Islam we're told that Islam is a "tolerant" religion.

One example people often cite of Islam's tolerance is the treatment of Jews and Christians living in Islamic societies. We are told that Jews and Christians were freer to practice their faith in places like medieval Baghdad and southern Spain than Jews were in Christian Europe.

There's no denying Christians weren't as tolerant as they should have been. But according to historian Bat Ye'or, this characterization of Islam's treatment of Jews and Christians is "a radical distortion of what happened." In her book *The Decline of Eastern Christianity under Islam,* Egyptian-born Ye'or says that Islam's regard for its Christian subjects could best be described as one of contempt.

How could it be otherwise? As she reminds us, Islam's spread was the product of a "military conquest," not peaceable conversions. The degree of massacre, enslavement, and other brutality exceeded anything being done in Christian Europe.

For those Christians who survived the initial conquest, life wasn't that much better. There were pockets of relatively good treatment. But on the whole, *tolerance* is hardly the word to describe the treatment. Hundreds of thousands of Christians and Jews were traded as slaves; they were required to wear distinctive clothing; and they were denied the protection of Islamic law.

The closer we get to our time, the worse things seem to get. In 1916, 1.5 million Christian Armenians died at the hands of their Turkish

Muslim rulers. No less lethal is the treatment Sudanese Christians have received from the Islamic government since it tried to impose Islamic law on them. At least two million have died, and thousands have been sold into slavery.

If you're looking for a place where Christians are doing the same thing to Muslims, you won't find one. What accounts for the difference? Historian Richard Connerney writes that in Islam, "the themes of religion, politics, and law are inseparable." According to Connerney, conquest and jihad are woven into the fiber of the religion. Thus, belligerence toward people of other faiths and cultures is, arguably, inherent to Islam.

In contrast, although Christians have mistreated non-Christians, a fair examination of Christian history and doctrine shows this conduct is in violation of Christian beliefs, not in their furtherance.

Christians should respect and love Muslims in their midst. But we should insist on an accurate telling of the story. To do otherwise would be to fail to learn from history—including biblical history. And we know what happens to those who do that.

Lord, like the prophets of old, your people must sometimes shout the truth to those unwilling to hear it. Make me willing to boldly stand for historical truth— and lovingly witness to your truth without offense.

APRIL 7

AMERICA'S AWAKENING CONSCIENCE

TO READ: ROMANS 2:12-16

When Gentiles, who do not have the law, do by nature things required by the law,
they are a law for themselves, even though they do not have the law, since they
show that the requirements of the law are written on their hearts, their consciences
also bearing witness, and their thoughts now accusing, now even defending them.
Romans 2:14-15

The film *Life Is Beautiful* caused a great stir because it suggests that even during the Nazi Holocaust there were signs of light in the darkness.

We in America have seen a holocaust of astounding proportions perpetrated against the unborn for more than thirty years. Nevertheless, as was the case fifty years ago in Germany, there are signs of light today, a cause for hope: A recent study by the proabortion Alan Guttmacher Institute reveals that the number of doctors performing abortions and the number of women seeking abortions is declining. And the number of abortion providers and facilities is at the lowest level since 1974, the year after *Roe v. Wade*.

Nationwide the number of abortion providers dropped 14 percent between 1992 and 1996 alone. Abortion advocates complain that fewer communities want to have abortion facilities in their midst; town after town is rejecting zoning requests to open up new clinics along Main Street.

What's responsible for this dramatic change? Abortion supporters blame antiabortion violence. But this is not the reason. Despite massive publicity suggesting otherwise, aggressive acts against abortionists are actually down sharply. The real reason for the decline is that abortion is being exposed for what it is, and cultural attitudes are changing.

Medical schools are increasingly refusing even to teach the techniques of death. Only about one of every ten OB/GYN programs trains its students to perform first trimester abortions, and even fewer teach mid- and third-trimester techniques.

Anecdotal evidence is flooding in as well. One doctor went on television to speak out against partial-birth abortion, despite a warning from hospital administrators that they might revoke his privileges if he did so. The doctor spoke out anyway, and in the end, the hospital administrators were persuaded by his arguments.

What does this increasing disdain for abortion amongst women, doctors, and communities tell us? It tells us that although people's hearts have been hardened, the truth has not been forgotten. Fewer doctors are going into this abominable trade because the truth is penetrating their consciences. Remember what Paul said in Romans 2, referring to the Gentiles: The law is written on their hearts and accuses them.

We Christians must advance our arguments all the more enthusiastically. We are winning the hearts and minds of the culture. We must also pray for the hearts of our countrymen. If we do, we may see the light overcome the darkness in our land.

Lord, thank you for empirical evidence that people cannot live outside your laws without suffering the torment of an outraged conscience. Bless those who are courageously speaking out for the truth. When it comes to friends who have been involved in abortions, help me to lovingly explain why their hearts accuse them—and how they can relieve their remorse and find healing through your forgiveness.

EVIDENCE FOR
THE EXODUS

TO READ: EXODUS 1:6-14

They put slave masters over them to oppress them with forced labor. Exodus 1:11

For most of the past century, scholars regarded the story of the Exodus as a myth—a story meant to inspire awe and devotion but not grounded in history. As justification for their skepticism, scholars point to the lack of references in Egyptian chronicles of the period to either the Hebrews' sojourn in Egypt or the Exodus.

But in *Is the Bible True? How Modern Debates and Discoveries Affirm the Essence of the Scriptures,* author Jeffery Sheler points out that although there may be no specific mention of the Hebrews in ancient Egyptian records, there is much indirect and circumstantial evidence.

One surviving document refers to a people called the "apiru," who were workers in an unidentified building project. This document dates from the reign of Rameses II, the pharaoh of the Exodus. Scholars have noted the similarity between *apiru* and *Hebrew* (there is no *h* in Semitic languages). Many consider the document a reference not only to the Hebrews in Egypt but also to their forced labor.

Even those who don't go that far say that this document, along with others, attests to the presence of a large Semitic population in Egypt at the time of the Exodus.

What were they doing there? Forced labor. James Hoffmeier, a Wheaton College professor, points out that "the practice of using forced labor for building projects is only documented for the period of 1450 to 1200 B.C., the very time most biblical historians place the Israelites in Egypt."

As for the absence of references to the Exodus, Sheler points out that Egyptian chronicles were much more propaganda than history. And what ancient despot would want to memorialize an embarrassing defeat?

A writer for *Bible Review* magazine offered a humorous translation of what this chronicle of defeat would have said: "Rameses the Great ... before whom all tremble in awe ... announced that the man Moses had kicked his royal [seat] for all the world to see."

Unlike other faiths, biblical faith is rooted in history. Christians believe that God has acted in history just as he acts in our lives today in order to accomplish his purposes.

Are you embarrassed when critics mock Christians for believing in certain passages of Scripture, such as the parting of the Red Sea? You shouldn't be, simply because scholars cannot yet explain these events. If anyone should squirm, it's the secular critics who deny the accuracy of biblical accounts based on no evidence whatsoever, only to be proved wrong later.

Modern archaeology is confirming what we already know: that we can have absolute faith that God's Word—all of it—is true.

Lord, thank you for archaeological evidence that confirms the truth of the Scriptures—not for our sakes but for the sake of those who have been taught that your Word is a lie.

THE LEGACY OF
DIETRICH BONHOEFFER

TO READ: MATTHEW 16:24-27

[Jesus said,] "If anyone would come after me, he must deny himself and take up his cross and follow me." Matthew 16:24

Some sixty years ago a Lutheran pastor named Dietrich Bonhoeffer was involved in a failed plot to assassinate Adolph Hitler and was executed by the Nazis for treason.

In *The Cost of Discipleship*, Bonhoeffer paints a vivid picture of what it was like to be true to the Christian faith under a hostile regime. Under persecution, Bonhoeffer discovered that even though God's grace is freely given, it also extracts a high cost.

Costly grace led Bonhoeffer to return to Germany and suffer with his fellow Germans when he could have stayed safely in America. Costly grace led Bonhoeffer to continue preaching the Word of God even though the Nazis tried to suppress his work. Costly grace led Bonhoeffer to stand against a turncoat church that mixed Nazi doctrine with Christian truth. Along with other faithful believers Bonhoeffer signed the Barmen Declaration, which boldly declared their independence from both the state and a co-opted church.

Costly grace led Bonhoeffer to attempt to smuggle Jews out of Germany. Costly grace led the young pastor to set aside his commitment to pacifism and join in the assassination plot against Hitler—which led to his execution by the Nazis.

But even in prison Bonhoeffer's life shone with divine grace. He comforted other prisoners, who looked on him as their chaplain. He wrote many moving letters that were later collected into a volume called *Letters and Papers from Prison*.

On the morning of April 9, 1945, Bonhoeffer knelt and prayed and then followed his captors to the gallows, where he was hanged as a traitor.

British journalist Malcolm Muggeridge wrote a tribute to Bonhoeffer in *A Third Testament*. Writing about World War II, Muggeridge said: "Looking back now across the years ... what lives on is the memory of a man who died, not on behalf of freedom or democracy or a steadily rising gross national product, nor for any of the twentieth century's counterfeit hopes or desires, but on behalf of a cross on which another man died two thousand years before.

"As on that previous occasion, on Golgotha," Muggeridge adds, "so amidst the rubble and desolation of 'liberated' Europe, the only victor is the man who died, [just] as the only hope for the future lies in his triumph over death. There can never be any other victory or any other hope."

The lesson of Bonhoeffer's life and death is that God's grace is never cheap. It demands from us everything—even our lives. But in return it gives us a new life that transcends even the most oppressive political conditions.

Have you counted the cost of following Christ? Are you—like Bonhoeffer—willing to lose your life in service to him?

Thank you, Father, for the life and witness of Dietrich Bonhoeffer, who counted the cost of serving your Son and willingly paid it.

DUTCH DISASTER

TO READ: ROMANS 2:6-11

There will be trouble and distress for every human being who does evil.
Romans 2:9

As America moves closer to embracing same-sex "marriage," one can almost picture folks in the wedding industry rubbing their hands in delight. After all, if we legalize gay "marriage," we'll have more weddings than ever, right?

Wrong. We will end up having fewer marriages, not more. Just ask the citizens of Holland, where marriage is going the way of typewriters and buggy whips.

In the *Weekly Standard*, Stanley Kurtz, a research fellow at the Hoover Institution, points out that in recent decades, at a time when parental cohabitation was sweeping across northern Europe, the Dutch clung to the last, ragged remains of their religious traditions. Yes, Dutch couples cohabited, but when they had children, they usually got married.

But during the mid-1990s, the rate of out-of-wedlock births began to shoot up. By 2003, the rate of increase had nearly doubled to 31 percent of all Dutch births.

What accounts for this phenomenon? Gay "marriage." These were the years, Kurtz notes, "when the debate over the legal recognition of gay relationships came to the fore in the Netherlands." The debate came to an end when Holland legalized full same-sex "marriage" in 2000.

Kurtz says the conjunction of these two social phenomena is no coincidence. During Holland's decade-long drive to legalize same-sex "marriage," gay advocates openly scorned the idea that marriage ought to be defined by the possibility of childbearing. Love between two partners—*any* two partners—was the real basis of marriage, they said. Thus, as one gay "marriage" advocate told the Dutch parliament, "There is absolutely no reason, objectively, to distinguish between heterosexual and homosexual love." Dutch leaders bought this argument. Marriage would be reduced to—as Kurtz put it—"just one choice on a menu of relationship options." In marriage, as with cheeseburgers, you could have it your way.

Then a funny thing happened on the road to redefining marriage: Dutch people simply stopped getting married, even when they had children. This really ought to come as no surprise. After all, Kurtz writes, "Spend a decade telling people that marriage is not about parenthood, and they just might begin to believe you. Make relationship equality a rallying cry, and people might decide that all forms of relationships are equal."

What's happening in the Netherlands gives us clear evidence of what gay "marriage" does: People stop getting married, and children suffer.

Here in America we must do everything we can to strengthen marriages. We do this by making sure we honor our own marriage vows (and those of others) and by getting involved in political efforts to retain a definition of marriage that reflects the truth: Marriage can take place only between one man and one woman.

If we fail to do this, American families—already deeply damaged by divorce and illegitimacy—will be destroyed.

Father, help me to live out my marriage vows in a way that witnesses to your definition of matrimony: one man and one woman in lifelong, faithful companionship. Give me words that will clarify the issue for those who have been deceived by the rhetoric of evil: Society cannot "redefine" marriage without real and tragic consequences.

USURPING PARENTAL RIGHTS

TO READ: LUKE 17:1-4

Jesus said to his disciples: "Things that cause people to sin are bound to come, but woe to that person through whom they come. It would be better for him to be thrown into the sea with a millstone tied around his neck than for him to cause one of these little ones to sin." Luke 17:1-2

The announcement from her daughter's school got Debra Loveless's attention. The Gay, Lesbian, and Straight Education Network, or GLSEN, planned to conduct two assemblies aimed at "preventing discrimination based on sexual orientation and gender/identity expression in K-12 schools."

Loveless requested school officials at Metro High School to exempt her daughter from attending because of her religious beliefs, and they granted her request. Later, at the invitation of a school board member, Mrs. Loveless herself attempted to see what was being taught in the assemblies. But when she arrived at the school, an armed security guard ushered her back out, saying school officials wanted her to leave the school grounds.

What would Loveless have witnessed had she not been ordered to leave? A GLSEN conference held at Tufts University in March 2000 provides a picture. Workshops at the conference, attended by both teachers and teens, included "From Lesbos to Stonewall: Incorporating Sexuality into a World History Curriculum" and "Early Childhood Educators: How to Decide Whether to Come Out or Not."

The *Weekly Standard* magazine reported on a workshop titled "What They Didn't Tell You about Queer Sex and Sexuality in Health Class: A Workshop for Youth Only, Aged 14 to 21." In it, Michael Gaucher of the Massachusetts public health agency asked kids how they knew whether they had sex. One student asked whether oral sex counted. Gaucher responded, "If that's not sex, then the number of times I've had sex has dramatically decreased, from a mountain to a valley!"

Clearly, GLSEN's agenda is more than simply teaching kids to get along with one another. Considering the content of past GLSEN assemblies, Loveless was right to be concerned. And as a citizen, she also had a right to know what was going on without being ejected by an armed guard. The American Center for Law and Justice filed suit on behalf of Loveless, asking for an injunction to prevent school officials from prohibiting parents from attending school assemblies, regardless of whether their child is present or not.

Metro High School has taken its role of acting *in loco parentis* much too far—usurping the rights of parents to know what their kids are learning. As Francis Manion of the ACLJ, put it, "Parents do not abandon their rights as parents once their children go to school."

He's right. Parents should not allow secretive school officials to push them aside. After all, parents—not the schools—are ultimately responsible for their kids.

Do you know what your own children are being exposed to at school? What about at camps, at extracurricular lessons—or even in your own home? Those who want to influence our kids—for good or ill—go where children go or attempt to reach them at home through television, computers, and radios. We must be constantly vigilant against those who want to win over our kids not for Christ but for the kingdom of evil.

Lord, give me the courage to stand up to those who—pretending to have the best interests of children at heart—attempt to lead them into sin.

RUNNING FROM
OUR CONSCIENCE

TO READ: HEBREWS 9:14-28

*How much more, then, will the blood of Christ . . . cleanse our consciences from
acts that lead to death, so that we may serve the living God! Hebrews 9:14*

At a meeting of fellow abortionists, a physician and a nurse are describing a survey of the abortionist's present and former staff. The
survey reveals that no matter how much we try to block it, God's law
really is written on our hearts.

In *What We Can't Not Know,* J. Budziszewski writes that some of the
staff reported that they refused to look at the aborted fetus. Others
looked but felt "shock, dismay, amazement, disgust, fear, and sad-
ness." Two thought that abortion "must eventually damage the
physician psychologically." Others described dreams about vomit-
ing up fetuses.

Budziszewski also describes the strange appeal of RU-486, the
abortion pill. RU-486 can cause severe bleeding, cramping, and nau-
sea. The expulsion of the embryo may take several days, and the
woman may be able to recognize the remains of her child. Researchers
in clinical trials of RU-486 argued that for some women, these dreadful burdens are what make RU-486 attractive. They welcome the increased suffering because they regard it as a price they ought to pay, a
kind of atonement for having an abortion. But if abortion is just another "procedure," as abortion supporters claim, why are women trying to "atone" for their act?

You may have friends who say they don't feel guilty about their
abortions. That may be true—but conscience is not necessarily about
what people feel. Budziszewski quotes a proabortion counselor who

said to a proabortion journalist, "I am not confident even now, with abortion so widely used, that women feel it's okay to want an abortion without feeling guilty. They say, 'Am I some sort of monster that I feel all right about this?'"

That's a revealing question. Plainly, if a woman feels guilty for not having *feelings* of guilt, she must have guilty *knowledge*; she must know that what she did was wrong.

Paul says that God's law is "written on the heart." Although we can become desensitized to evil, we can't really forget that it *is* evil. We can drive our consciences underground—but we can never erase them.

How can people involved in abortion get over their guilt? The Christians in their lives must lovingly teach them that atonement is possible only through repentant faith in Christ. We need to remember that atoning gift when we ourselves sin—as every Christian does. Instead of enduring the pangs of guilt or trying to "fix" the sin ourselves, we must drop to our knees and ask God to cleanse us through the blood of Christ, which was spilled for this very purpose.

If we refuse his gift, we will pay price after painful price in a never-ending cycle—because we cannot pay the one price God demands.

Lord, help me to get beyond my anger at those who kill the innocent unborn and those who make use of their services. Let me be willing to exploit the witness of their own guilt to bring them into saving knowledge of you, the One who forgives even the most heinous sins and exchanges guilty knowledge for joyful absolution.

THE HALIFAX SCENT POLICE

TO READ: TITUS 3:1-11

Remind the people to be subject to rulers and authorities, to be obedient, to be ready to do whatever is good, to slander no one, to be peaceable and considerate.
Titus 3:1-2

When seventeen-year-old Gary Falkenham put on some Aqua Velva deodorant before school, he had no idea he would run afoul of the law. But Gary lives in Halifax, Nova Scotia, where a recent law bans cosmetic fragrances.

The case highlights the absurdity of using law to deal with matters of social conduct.

Gary's typing teacher took offense at the scent of his toiletries, and instead of asking Gary to wash the scent off, she invoked the new law and had him removed from school. At least ten more students were suspended for the same reason.

And it's not just teachers who are invoking this law. The *Boston Globe* reports that an eighty-four-year-old woman was "booted out of City Hall for wafting her customary cologne . . . and another woman was ordered off a city bus for smelling too sweet."

Perfume prudery has even caught on in the private sector: Halifax's major newspaper, the *Chronicle-Herald,* declared "strong mouthwash" off-limits for employees.

Many of us have experienced too much perfume in a closed space—and it's not pleasant. But the experience is no worse than encountering those who *fail* to use deodorant or mouthwash. By and large, people try to use a moderate amount precisely because they are concerned for their neighbors' sensibilities and sensitivities.

In this case the Canadian concern for politeness, animated by environmentalist fervor, resulted in a ban on fragrance. But as any civil libertarian can tell you, introducing law into the realm of manners and personal restraint is not always benign. The impulse to make manners the province of law doesn't just stop with Right Guard. Canadian radio also censors "Dr. Laura" Schlessinger's broadcasts—and *Focus on the Family*—when their "religiously derived views" express what censors consider "hate speech."

Yes, this happened in Canada, not the U.S. But trendy ideas are often born in more liberal cultures and quickly migrate here.

Social scientist James Q. Wilson reminds us that there are only two restraints on behavior. One is internal—the restraint of conscience. The other is external—the law, enforced by government. The heavy hand of the law steps in when internal restraints fail. The fewer inner restraints we have, the greater the force of law, so that eventually, the state can come to control personal conduct—even to the extent of regulating the use of deodorant.

We Christians should ensure that our conduct is such that it "spreads everywhere the fragrance of the knowledge of [Christ]," remembering that we are "the aroma of Christ among those who are being saved and those who are perishing" (2 Corinthians 2:14-15). We might also tell our neighbors why a healthy society requires civil citizens: It's because the death of manners can eventually lead to the birth of tyranny.

And that's a stench no perfume can disguise.

Lord, let me take the lead in modeling considerate, conscience-driven conduct, demonstrating to those around me that those who follow the law you wrote on our hearts have little need of external threats.

OVERCOMING ADDICTION

TO READ: PSALM 42:1-11

*As the deer pants for streams of water, so my soul pants for you, O God.
My soul thirsts for God, for the living God. Psalm 42:1-2*

Kevin, a deacon at his church and the father of three, was hunched over his computer late one night. He wondered how his wife and his church friends would react if they could see him now, because Kevin was searching for sex on the Internet.

Online sex is a disturbing—and growing—phenomenon that affects many Christians.

Focus on the Family conducted a survey recently to find out how widespread the problem is, and the results were shocking. It appears that one out of five adults—nearly 40 million people—may have visited a sexually oriented Web site. And of those who identify themselves as "born again" Christians, nearly 18 percent confessed to visiting such sites.

What's behind this voracious appetite for Internet sex? It's partly that the Internet acts as a pipeline for pornographers, allowing them to pump raw moral sewage directly into our homes. But the Internet would not be able to sell this product if the craving for it did not already exist. The authors of a recent book say that sexual addiction—like all addictions—represents a deep hunger for God.

In *The Sacred Romance*, Brent Curtis and John Eldredge point out that humans are designed for intimacy with God. Sometimes we allow the world to drown out God's voice. But our need for communion with him never goes away. Instead of seeking fulfillment in Christ, addicts try to fill their emptiness with other things: pornography, an affair, or a fantasy life.

As the authors put it, "We put our hope in . . . some form of immediate gratification, some taste of transcendence that will place a drop of water on our parched tongue. . . . This taste of transcendence, coming as it does from an obsession with . . . pornography . . . has the same effect on our souls as crack cocaine." The addiction "attaches itself to our desire [for God] with chains that render us captive."

That's why addiction expert Gerald May calls addiction "the most powerful psychic enemy of humanity's desire for God."

Nothing can free the captives of addiction except God—something even the secular world has begun to recognize. Joseph Califano, who served in President Carter's cabinet, once said he was stunned to discover that nearly every ex-drug addict he meets cites religion as the key to breaking his addiction.

If you or someone you know is struggling with sexual addiction, a Web site called PureIntimacy.org, run by Focus on the Family, offers help.

Those seeking insight and restoration from addiction will learn how God's power and love can free them from the chains that bind them.

Father, teach me to recognize every attempt to quench my thirst for you with something that will never truly satisfy. Remind me to rely on the strength of your Son, who understands our temptations because he was tempted and whose love can break the bonds of even the strongest addiction.

CAN WE COMMUNICATE WITH THE DEAD?

TO READ: 1 CHRONICLES 10:8-14

Saul died because he was unfaithful to the Lord . . . and even consulted a medium for guidance. 1 Chronicles 10:13

More than three thousand fans packed San Francisco's Masonic Auditorium. Many had driven for hundreds of miles to see their idol. Some waved signs reading, "We Love You John!"

Then the man they came to see strode onto the stage—one uniquely suited for our credulous age.

John Edward is America's most famous medium. Every night, more than 600,000 American households watch *Crossing Over* on the Sci-Fi channel, eager to watch Edward and his "guests"—by which he means spirits—minister to loved ones left behind.

Belief in mediums and spiritualism has grown markedly in the past decade. Half of all Americans believe that it's possible to communicate with the dead. A third claim to have done so.

This isn't the first surge of interest in mediums and spiritualism in the English-speaking world. The first few decades of the twentieth century saw a comparable enthusiasm for séances and psychics. People who wouldn't have been caught dead in a Christian church sat around tables holding hands with their eyes closed, waiting for something to happen.

That surge, like the present one, followed periods in which faith in the biblical God was declared to be untenable. Science, in the form of Darwinism or positivism (the belief in natural, empirically verifiable phenomena), promised substitutes for the old beliefs.

What happened in both instances was a rise in superstition. Then as now, occult practices and beliefs began to flourish, even among the educated. People who dismissed the Resurrection and the Virgin Birth toured the country lecturing about communicating with the dead.

Rejecting the biblical God doesn't change the fact that as humans, we are incorrigibly religious and need to believe in something. Nor does it mean that questions such as, is there life after death? cease being important. It simply means we've been cut off from the real answers to these questions. And that makes us vulnerable to superstition and irrationality.

Are you one of the thousands who tune in to watch John Edward? Are you among the millions who believe they have contacted the dead—perhaps at a séance or through a psychic channeler? If so, be warned: The Bible says these practices are extremely wicked—and extremely dangerous.

We ought to help our neighbors understand that the answers they seek cannot be found through cable television mediums; they can be found only through faith in the One who really did "cross over"—from death to life.

Father, empower me, through your Holy Spirit, to witness effectively to those who seek spiritual answers through satanic sources. Let me be a witness as well to Christian friends who believe there is no harm in "parlor games": séances, table turning, and fortune-telling. Thank you for the promise that the blood of Jesus cleanses all of our sins—if we are willing to confess them.

APRIL 16

A JEALOUS GOD

TO READ: LEVITICUS 18:21-30

Do not give any of your children to be sacrificed to Molech,
for you must not profane the name of your God. Leviticus 18:21

On March 1, 2004, the California Supreme Court ruled that Catholic Charities must include contraceptives in its prescription drug coverage, despite Catholic teaching to the contrary.

California law states that if employers offer prescription drug coverage, they must include contraceptives. The law exempts "religious employers" like churches—and Catholic Charities argued that, as an "arm" of the Catholic Church, it *was* exempt. But the court rejected this argument, saying that the law affects "a nonprofit public benefit corporation and its employees, many of whom do not belong to the Catholic Church."

Justice Janice Brown, the sole dissenter, replied that the ruling defined "religious employers" too narrowly. The ruling reflects "such a crabbed and restrictive view of religion that it would define the ministry of Jesus Christ as a secular activity," Brown contended. She called the law "an intentional, purposeful intrusion into a religious organization's expression of its religious tenets and sense of mission."

That's exactly right. As legal philosopher Robert George of Princeton notes, this ruling should be seen as part of a larger attack on the Catholic Church for "its resistance to the new liberal orthodoxy." If the church can be forced to fund contraceptives, then it will eventually be told it must pay for abortions and provide "spousal" benefits to same-sex partners. And, George reminds us, what applies to the Catholic Church will also apply to Protestants.

The ruling did more than provide a glimpse into a possible future where religious liberty will have been effectively eradicated. It also provides us with an insight into the nature and priorities of the "new liberal orthodoxy."

To put it in biblical terms, the new liberal orthodoxy is a "jealous god" that will countenance no rival truth claims. Given a choice between imposing its views on religious organizations or helping working people afford prescription drugs, it chooses ideology over people. It can be compared to Molech, the Canaanite god who demanded the sacrifice of innocents.

This is strong language, but protecting the freedom to worship our God begins with understanding how far our opponents will go in service to theirs.

Following the ruling, Catholic Charities faced a choice between two options: violate Catholic teaching, or drop prescription drug coverage.

The choice between obeying Caesar and obeying Christ is one that Christians have faced down through the centuries. Today, religious groups of every stripe must join forces to fight government's immoral decrees. But in the event we lose—if we are ordered to violate God's commands—we must respectfully decline.

Lord, as we resist attacks on your people and your doctrines, make us as wise as serpents and innocent as doves. Give us the willingness to give Caesar what belongs to him—but give us, as well, the courage to refuse Caesar's demand that we give him what belongs to you alone.

THE HILLARY AD

TO READ: ROMANS 1:28-32

*They are gossips, slanderers, God-haters, insolent, arrogant and boastful;
they invent ways of doing evil; they disobey their parents;
they are senseless, faithless, heartless, ruthless. Romans 1:29-31*

It was one of the most outrageous political ads of the season a few years ago. It opened with images of Hillary Clinton, then running for the U.S. Senate. An announcer says, "It's rumored Hillary Clinton is a lesbian. It's rumored that Hillary Clinton supports homosexual marriage. It's rumored that Hillary Clinton will leave her husband after taking office. It was rumored Bill Clinton had an affair with Monica Lewinsky. Sometimes rumors are true."

The ad finishes with the question, "Shouldn't you know the truth?"

The commercial was sponsored by a group called the Christian Action Network. Its president, Martin Mawyer, defended the ad on the grounds that certain rumors about Mrs. Clinton do exist and that she ought to be made to respond to them.

That's nonsense. Repeating wild rumors on television through tasteless ads that hint and wink is unfair. Merely repeating rumors with no evidence to back them up is not the way to get to the truth. Christians have a right to speak out about political candidates and the issues—just as every American does. But with that right goes a concomitant responsibility, and that's the need to behave responsibly.

This responsibility falls more heavily on Christians than on other citizens. First, the Bible strongly condemns gossip and warns us to avoid those who persist in spreading it. In Romans, Paul associates gossip with those who are insolent and haughty, full of envy, and haters of

God; he warns us that we should not approve of those who practice these things.

Second, we should avoid rumor-mongering because it's a terrible witness. Openly criticizing a candidate's character or views is one thing, but slinking around behind her back and repeating vicious gossip is another thing altogether.

Christians are not immune to the temptation to gossip—about our friends, about people at church—or about the private lives of politicians. We need to see gossip and malice the way God does—on a par with murder. Proverbs 19 warns us not even to associate with those who gossip.

When Christian radio and television stations are offered ads that feature vicious gossip, they ought to reject them on biblical grounds. And when Christians receive letters that spread rumors of any kind—especially from an organization that calls itself *Christian*—they ought to take a minute to mail off not a check but a letter of rebuke.

Lord, help me to guard my tongue when I am tempted to gossip about friends and neighbors, colleagues, and celebrities. When others bring "juicy" gossip and slander to my ears, help me to do what is nearly impossible without your power: change the subject.

MUSICAL DISHARMONY

TO READ: PSALM 92:1-5

It is good to praise the Lord and make music to your name. Psalm 92:1

From outside a massive church building, you'd never guess there's a crack about to split the congregation in two. The disagreement isn't over church doctrine or missions policy; it's over the style of music used for the worship service.

The congregation has always sung traditional anthems of the church from well-worn hymnals. But some members complain that the church is losing people to other congregations that offer a more contemporary style of worship—with Scripture songs, guitars, and drums.

The disagreement has erupted into a full-scale war, and similar conflicts are tearing churches apart all across the country. How can we bring peace to these war-torn churches? Is there a right and wrong kind of music for worship?

The way to forge a peace treaty is to ask some fundamental questions: What's the biblical standard for judging any kind of music? As Christians, how do we choose which music we listen to at home? Do we simply gravitate toward the music we like, or do we try to appreciate truly good quality?

Good music is a bit like good food. What we like is not necessarily what's good for us by objective standards of nutrition. If we're smart, we cultivate our tastes so that we learn to like broccoli and carrots, not just pizza and ice cream.

In the same way, the music we like is not necessarily what's good for the soul. We should cultivate our tastes so that we learn to like music that is good by objective standards of beauty—music that is truly excellent.

Perhaps you thought that taste means merely personal preference. But Christian authors J. I. Packer and Thomas Howard write in *Christianity: The True Humanism* that "taste is a facet of wisdom: It is the ability to distinguish what has value from what does not."

In music, we should be learning to distinguish what has objective value from what does not. For example, good music should fit the message, treating serious themes with a somber tone and cheerful themes with a light tone. Good music should be emotionally powerful without lapsing into sentimentality.

Churches that unite behind objective standards of beauty such as these can heal the rift that divides so many congregations. And they might discover that they've been fighting the wrong battles. By objective standards, old music may be either good or bad—and the same is true of contemporary music.

How does your congregation make decisions about what songs to sing? Are there standards in place to ensure that only the best-quality music—traditional or contemporary—is used in worship?

Christians should unite behind the goal of discerning real beauty, remembering that we worship the God of beauty.

Lord, you are "my strength and my song." Teach us to lift our voices with melodies pleasing to you—songs that reflect your glory and your beauty.

REDEEMING THE CULTURE THROUGH ART

TO READ: MATTHEW 18:23-35

The master called the servant in. "You wicked servant," he said, "I canceled all that debt of yours because you begged me to. Shouldn't you have had mercy on your fellow servant just as I had on you?" Matthew 18:32-33

Bryan Coley, artistic director of a theater company called Art Within, has an intriguing theory: He believes that the next Billy Graham will be a playwright, and he could be right. The arts and media have tremendous influence in our culture today, helping to shape the values of millions.

Imagine, Coley says, what could happen if the church launched thousands of Christians into careers in which they could shape the ideas that pour into our culture.

All too often, Christians have just one kind of response to the garbage we see in the arts and media: We criticize, ban, and boycott. By contrast, Art Within goes beyond criticism by creating plays that present a Christian worldview. They take as their motto a line by Michelangelo: "Criticize by Creating."

Take the issues of cloning and embryonic stem-cell research. Those who hope to profit from this research minimize the humanity of the embryo; they try to convince the public that the potential benefits far outweigh any human-rights concerns.

To address this debate, Art Within offered a new theatrical adaptation of *The Island of Dr. Moreau,* a classic story by H. G. Wells about an arrogant scientist whose goal is to create humanlike creatures out of animals. This leads to a race of deformed beast-people. The play is a powerful warning against pushing science beyond moral limits—of breaking through biological barricades simply because we can.

If Bryan Coley is right—that the next Billy Graham may be a play-wright—it's because people absorb moral propositions much more easily through images and the medium of storytelling than through dry theological treatises. Stories shape our thoughts, move our emotions, and enlarge our imaginations.

Think of how Jesus made use of images and stories. He could simply have said, "God forgives your sins, so forgive others." Instead, he told the parable of the unmerciful servant. Why? Because a story gets at aspects of truth that are beyond the power of didactic teaching.

Arts are an important way to understand God and his creation. In a post-Christian culture, those who blend artistic gifts with Christian faith can help lead us back to a biblical worldview. That is why the church should encourage them.

As Coley puts it, "If I do not use my talents to criticize by creating, then my son, now two years old, will live in a society where Christian ideas are a foreign language."

We all have a role to play in redeeming the culture through the arts—arts that point to the greatest Artist of all: the God who created the heavens and the earth.

Father, thank you for the artistic gifts of those throughout the centuries—including Jesus—who pointed their cultures toward you. Teach me how I might use my own artistic gifts, or those of others, to criticize my own culture—and point it toward your truth.

BABIES A LA CARTE

TO READ: PSALM 5:4-6

You are not a God who takes pleasure in evil. Psalm 5:4

A few years ago Lisa and Jack Nash of Denver, Colorado, announced that their new baby, aptly named Adam, had been conceived solely to be a donor of cells for his older sister.

The story began when the Nash's daughter, Molly, was diagnosed with Fanconi anemia, a hereditary and always fatal disease. Doctors determined that the best hope for Molly was a cell transplant from a relative whose cells matched Molly's but without anemia.

Since they had no other children, the Nashes decided to have one to save Molly. Any child conceived naturally would have been unlikely to provide Molly with the cells she needed. So by in-vitro fertilization, the Nashes produced fifteen embryos, which they sent to a genetic testing facility. Only one of the embryos had the "right" genetic material. It was implanted in Mrs. Nash, who subsequently gave birth to Adam. Adam's stem cells were taken from his umbilical cord and implanted in his sister, and Molly is now a healthy little girl.

Naturally the Nashes are pleased at the outcome. But thoughtful Christians should respond differently to what happened here.

Instead of being an end, with all the God-given dignity that implies, Adam was a means—valuable only insofar as he carried the right genetic material. If he hadn't, he would have been rejected—like the other fourteen discarded embryos. How will he feel when he's old enough to understand this?

The technology and the worldview that made Adam possible won't be limited to noble purposes like preserving life. We're fast approaching a world that will see kids' purpose as merely enhancing their parents' sense of fulfillment. Even if they aren't conceived as a source of spare parts, they will still—through genetic manipulation—be made to embody their parents' ideas of an ideal child. Parents' creating the personality of their kids fits our narcissistic culture, but it is dehumanizing in the extreme.

It turns children, as technology critic Jeremy Rifkin puts it, into "the ultimate shopping experience."

Most Christian parents would never conceive a child merely for spare parts and trash its fully human, embryonic siblings. But some of us do press our kids to look a certain way, engage in certain sports, or pursue a particular career. This is every bit as dehumanizing as designing a child before birth. It's a form of idol worship in which children are forced to worship at the altar of their parents' desires.

Lord, help me to become knowledgeable about where modern technologies are leading, and give me courage enough to stand against accusations that I'm hopelessly reactionary. And when it comes to those you have put in my care, may I never try to force their God-given gifts into a mold of my own making, compelling them to serve me instead of you.

DOES BELIEVING MAKE IT SO?

TO READ: JOHN 14:1-7

*Jesus answered, "I am the way and the truth and the life.
No one comes to the Father except through me." John 14:6*

When Julie went away to college, she witnessed to her three room-mates. She was excited when they all seemed open to the gospel. But to her surprise, they responded just as warmly when Sally said she believed in "the god within all of us" and when Amy said she believed that God is a "force"—like in *Star Wars,* and when Ruth said she was a "very spiritual" person but didn't believe in any god at all.

What baffled Julie most was when the others agreed that "we're all saying the same thing in the end."

How can Christian students like Julie make sense of the bewildering range of beliefs they encounter in this post-Christian age? In *How to Stay Christian in College,* Jay Budziszewski explains that Julie had run into the powerful myth that "truth is whatever you sincerely believe." It holds, then, that if you believe it, then it's "true for you"—and rules of logic and evidence don't apply.

The "myth of sincerity" is especially potent when it comes to life's big questions—about God and morality. Consider abortion, for example. A few years ago, abortionist James McMahon said, "I frankly think the soul or personage comes in when the fetus is accepted by the mother." In other words, unborn babies become human only when their mothers sincerely believe they're human.

Students encounter the same reasoning on college campuses. If a classmate sincerely believes her unborn child is human, friends will call the child a "baby" and congratulate her. But if she doesn't, they call it a "fetus" and encourage her to have an abortion.

This is such an obvious fallacy. Can we really make something true just by believing it? How about a concrete example: If you sincerely believe your onion rings are French fries, do they become French fries?

When it comes to concrete, familiar objects, no one falls for the sincerity myth. We all know that there's an objective reality that exists on its own, despite what we may believe about it—and no matter how sincere we are. If we accept the idea of objective truth when we are dealing with trivial questions, then logically, we have to accept it when dealing with big questions about God and morality as well.

Stories like Julie's remind us that we all need to be aware of the fuzzy thinking people engage in when it comes to religion. We need to learn how to gently cut through logical inconsistencies, and we must train the teens in our lives to recognize these fallacies when they encounter them at college.

With a little help, they can learn to cut through the fables with the sharp edge of biblical truth.

Lord, help me to arm myself with the sword of truth, that I may ably slash through spiritual lies.

MODELING MORAL ABSOLUTES

TO READ: PSALM 25:1-22

Good and upright is the Lord; therefore he instructs sinners in his ways.
He guides the humble in what is right and teaches them his way. Psalm 25:8-9

Not long ago the National Association of Scholars surveyed a random sample of graduating seniors about what they had learned in college about ethics and morals in the workplace. Their answers make it clear that we should brace for more corporate scandals in the future.

Nearly all respondents said that college had prepared them ethically for their professional lives. That sounds good until you understand what they meant by "ethically." Three quarters reported learning that "what is right and wrong depends on differences in individual values and cultural diversity."

New graduates cited "recruiting a diverse workforce in which women and minorities are advanced and promoted" as business's top ethical priority.

By contrast, "providing clear and accurate business statements to stockholders and creditors" lagged far behind. Honesty and transparency barely outpolled "minimizing environmental pollution by adopting the latest anti-pollution technology and complying with government regulations."

To be fair, "clear and accurate business statements" was the top choice for students going into business. But even among these students, nearly six in ten chose something besides honesty as their top ethical priority.

No wonder we hear about companies cooking the books. While a diverse workplace is desirable, how can anyone seriously believe that it's more important than telling shareholders the truth?

It should surprise no one that businesspeople who are taught that there are no moral absolutes will cheat and cut corners. NAS president Stephen Balch correctly points to a link between the poll results and "the ethical laxness behind the recent scandals." What is surprising is that many people, especially our educated elites, can't or won't see the connection.

That's why there is no substitute for teaching a belief in moral absolutes. Of course, this starts at home, but schools—from elementary through graduate—also have a role to play. As Balch explains, schools can confirm the values and beliefs that students bring to the campus, or they can undermine them by providing students with "sophisticated excuses for succumbing to the temptations of greed and power."

Are we taking the time to teach moral absolutes to the children and young people in our lives? Clearly we can't always rely on schools to do this. For that matter, are we ourselves modeling to our families and neighbors God's commands for how to treat those with whom we do business? Are your business decisions above reproach? Do you pay your bills on time? No Christian should ever be caught returning a product they have damaged or broken and asking for a refund.

If Christian parents, grandparents, and teachers don't do all they can to ethically train the children and young people in our lives, we should not be surprised when they grow up making excuses for their ethical laxness—laxness that will, in time, bring on the next round of corporate scandals.

Lord, you have said that no one whose hope is in you will be put to shame. Help me never to put my trust in a lesser standard than your holy one and, in doing so, discredit myself and defame the name of the God I worship.

REMEMBERING THE PERSECUTED

TO READ: 2 TIMOTHY 3:10-15

Everyone who wants to live a godly life in Christ Jesus will be persecuted.
2 Timothy 3:12

Some Chinese Christians have been "tortured to death in prison using molten metal being poured over their heads," says Nina Shea of Freedom House's Center for Religious Freedom. White House sources confirm that President Bush discussed human rights violations against Christians when Chinese President Jiang Zemin visited him.

How widespread has persecution become? Missiologist David Barrett estimates that there may have been as many Christian martyrs in the twentieth century as in all nineteen previous centuries combined.

The organization Open Doors evaluates countries by their levels of persecution. Topping their list is North Korea, where Keston Institute, a British-based human rights group, says people caught with a Bible are "detained, tortured, sent to a re-education camp, or summarily executed."

Numbers three and four on the list are Marxist countries also: Laos and Vietnam. Number two is Saudi Arabia, site of Islam's sacred cities, Mecca and Medina. Arrests, torture, and prison are common, and authorities can impose the death penalty for converting from Islam to another religion.

For several years Christians applauded a new openness in the former Soviet Union. But according to the Keston Institute, which has monitored the region for decades, things are changing. Headlines on its Web page include "Belarus: Repressive Religion Law Gets President's

Signature," "Uzbekistan: [Is] Being Protestant a Crime?" and "Russia: Escalation in Missionary Expulsions."

The Russian Federation requires religious congregations to register. The process is long and cumbersome, and bureaucrats use any pretext to refuse legitimacy. One group "was refused for not including page numbers on a document." And registration doesn't mean that much. Even after registering, the Moscow Salvation Army was disbanded by court order.

In some countries the problem may not be official persecution but populist vigilantes. Compass Direct, a Christian news service, reports a number of anti-Christian assaults in Pakistan, with radicals "targeting Christians in retaliation for President Musharraf's support for the U.S. war on terrorism." After a Karachi court released a Christian who had survived a massacre, a contingent of the police force rearrested him. One local paper reported, "The police beat up and abused his lawyers when they tried to prevent their client from being taken away."

These are great evils and grave injustices. God warns us in 2 Timothy that all who faithfully follow Christ will endure persecutions, just as Paul did. All Christians have a responsibility to pray for persecuted Christians throughout the world and, as we're able, to work for human rights.

Father, I pray for dear brothers and sisters in Christ who are suffering so terribly. I ask that you will rescue them from your enemies and give them what you gave Paul: endurance to carry on in the face of evil—persevering until you bring them safely into your heavenly Kingdom.

CREATING LASTING RELATIONSHIPS

TO READ: 1 JOHN 4:7-12, 19-21

We love because he first loved us. 1 John 4:19

After breaking up with his girlfriend, Wei-Li Tjong, a young New York attorney, set out to meet someone new. Tjong did what increasing numbers of people his age are doing: He placed an Internet personal ad. The ad included what he admits was a flattering photo at one of the many Web sites devoted to matchmaking.

Within two months Tjong went out with more than seventy women—sometimes more than one a night. By his estimate, a third of these had "gone home with him," a euphemism for having sex.

The spread of what the *New York Times* calls "hyperdating" is, according to Robert Rosenwein of Lehigh University, redefining our ideas about intimacy. Traditional dating was, in Rosenwein's words, "a very long process where you disclose things over time." Hyperdating speeds things up considerably.

Rosenwein's assessment is correct, but the ability to do instant couple matching and mating raises important questions. If the article is correct about the way technology is shaping people's expectations, then we're trading something very important for the convenience provided by technology.

For starters, notice how many of the women Tjong had sex with on their first and only date. Hyperdating may claim to be about relationships, but judging by the facts, it's largely about casual, meaningless sex. Even more troubling is how unromantic this kind of experience is. In the hyperdating world, people are commodities. It requires strategic planning, a flair for marketing, and cold calculation to stand out in the sea of personal ads.

This is dehumanizing—self as commodity—and not that different from the way we market consumer goods. It has nothing to do with building lasting relationships. And it certainly has nothing to do with intimacy. Hyperdating lacks the patience required to truly know a person. And it is a pale imitation of true romantic love, which, as C. S. Lewis writes, is a foretaste of the love of God. In *The Four Loves*, Lewis says that in romantic love, we place the other person's interest at the center of our being. We love that one special person as we love ourselves.

Doing that requires an investment of ourselves, including our time, and that leaves us vulnerable. But as Lewis put it, "The only place outside Heaven where you can be perfectly safe from all the dangers and perturbations of love is Hell"—or in this case, the hyperdating scene.

There's nothing wrong with the desire for companionship, but hyperdating robs it of intimacy—the very thing that makes companionship desirable in the first place.

Whatever our marital status, we all need to examine our relationships from time to time to make certain we are giving our friends and loved ones the time and attention they deserve. If we are single and dating, we must ask ourselves, are we obeying God's command to love those we date as he loves us—or treating them like consumer goods?

Father, you call us to love one another—without exception. Let me never be found hating brothers and sisters for whom your Son died—or treating friends of either sex more as commodities than as companions.

FENCES FOR TEARING DOWN

TO READ: NEHEMIAH 9:5-6

You made the heavens, even the highest heavens, and all their starry host, the earth and all that is on it, the seas and all that is in them. You give life to everything.
Nehemiah 9:6

Imagine waking up tomorrow morning to find that your neighbor had moved his chain-link fence all the way across your yard—and right up against your door.

"What's up with the fence?" you ask.

"Not to worry," he says. "Just ignore the fence. I'm only claiming physical reality for my domain. And since you're such a spiritual person, you don't care about that, right? You still have your personal, subjective, religious yard. Isn't that great? Now we won't come into conflict with each other! Like the poet Robert Frost said, 'Good fences make good neighbors.'"

This sort of arrangement is exactly what prominent scientists like Harvard paleontologist Stephen Jay Gould have proposed as the proper relationship between science and religion. In *The Wedge of Truth*, Christian thinker Phillip Johnson challenges scientists like Gould to admit that their fence-building proposal is a bad idea, for both religion and science. There can be a proper balance between science and religion only if there's an open, honest relationship between them.

To see why, start with the quote from Frost: "Good fences make good neighbors." We often hear this line quoted as if Frost thought it were true. But he actually used it as a shallow cliché. In his poem "Mending Wall," he wrote:

Before I built a wall I'd ask to know
What I was walling in or walling out,
And to whom I was like to give offence.

When Gould proposes to keep peace between science and religion by putting a fence between them, we need to look at where he wants to put the boundary. Phillip Johnson points out that Gould's boundary line claims the whole realm of knowledge for science, effectively "walling out" religion and putting it into a private, subjective ghetto.

Religion, claims Gould, cannot include anything about real history, including the life of Jesus, because history belongs to science. Gould calls this his "first commandment" of the relationship of science and theology. It's a view widely shared by scientists today.

Johnson exposes Gould and others for "dressing up naturalistic philosophy as if it were science." He encourages believers to take on this specious argument wherever we encounter it—in school, perhaps, or in casual conversations with our neighbors.

Too often our children are bullied into accepting philosophy as science. We need to give them—and ourselves—the tools to challenge "scientific" claims and teach them to pry the nails out of fences that shut out not only true academic debate but truth itself.

Lord, when secular scientists fence you out, help me to open a gate into their minds. If they have closed their minds to you, show me a way to engage their hearts. Teach me, in the face of their loud contempt, to quietly witness to the truth: that the heavens above, the earth below, the seas and all that is in them, were designed by a God of boundless love.

CORRODING THE CONSCIENCE

TO READ: TITUS 1:15-16

To the pure, all things are pure, but to those who are corrupted and do not believe, nothing is pure. In fact, both their minds and consciences are corrupted. Titus 1:15

It's a cartoon staple: When chipmunks Chip and Dale race up a tree, Donald Duck saws off the branch they're sitting on, but the branch doesn't fall to the ground—the tree does.

The cartoon is funny, but in real life if someone saws off the branch we're sitting on, there are dire consequences. This is just as true with the law as it is with trees.

As moral philosopher Professor Hadley Arkes notes in *Natural Rights and the Right to Choose,* many of our elites "have gradually talked themselves out of the ground of their rights, without being quite aware of it." They can "no longer offer a moral defense of those rights." In effect, "they have talked themselves out of the premises on which their own freedom rests."

This has happened, writes Arkes, because our politicians and our culture have indirectly absorbed the teachings of academics who claim that "God is dead," truth is gone, and everything is permitted.

Much of the language of our laws is rooted in layers of moral understanding and religious persuasion that many no longer recognize. And yet, Arkes says, "My colleagues . . . speak firmly of 'rights,' or of the 'injuries' done to 'persons' . . . serenely unaware that their language here is grounded in understandings that they have professed, at least, to have rejected long ago."

Both politicians and the man on the street have absorbed this moral relativism, Arkes observes: Most Americans can no longer give account of the premises of this regime in which we live and thus cannot offer a moral defense of it or the rights it was meant to secure.

This has had enormous consequences on our laws, for if there are no fixed moral truths, the law has no authority. It simply turns into a system of power without the least pretense of finding a moral justification for itself. It is precisely this approach to the law that allows judges—and the culture they influence—to question, for instance, whether the sick, the handicapped, or the unborn among us are fully human.

We must teach our fellow citizens why our laws must be based on something greater than naked power—and make certain that we ourselves, in our private lives, are not allowing our consciences to be corrupted by a moral relativism that rejects the truth and denies God.

What happens if Americans abandon the grounding of moral truth? We will, like Donald Duck, end up sawing down the very tree we sit in—the moral basis that undergirds our freedoms. And then, our freedom and our civilization will come crashing down.

Father, may I never forget that the serious consequences of ignoring your fixed laws—the corruption of both my mind and my heart and, in the end, separation from you.

WHO REALLY GETS INTO HEAVEN?

TO READ: JOHN 11:17-27

[Jesus said,] "I am the resurrection and the life. He who believes in me will live, even though he dies." John 11:25

In recent years, films like *City of Angels, What Dreams May Come, Ghost,* and *Meet Joe Black* have sought to reassure viewers that death is not something to fear by presenting a benevolent afterlife.

This may sound encouraging, but Hollywood's conception of life after death bears little resemblance to the biblical one. For starters, in movies God is conspicuous by his absence. Even when characters do invoke him, the films have nothing to say about who he might be, much less what he might require of those who seek admission to his heaven.

What's more, there is no connection between the lives characters live on earth and their state after they die. Angels simply accompany the departed to the afterlife with no explanation regarding why that person deserves either heaven or hell.

Even when some standards are present, they often seem arbitrary. The knowledge that there's life after death doesn't seem to change anyone's behavior. It certainly didn't stop many of the characters in these films from sleeping around.

This only goes to show that if we want to make sense of death and find hope, there's no substitute for Christianity.

History demonstrates this truth. Prior to Christianity, only the gods were viewed as immortal. The idea that human consciousness could even survive after death was unthinkable. But Christianity, with its teaching that in "dying, [Jesus] conquered death," changed all of that.

As Notre Dame theologian John Dunne says, it was Christianity that enabled us to understand that death, like birth, is an event to be lived through.

This teaching didn't simply make people feel better about themselves; it also helped them to love their neighbors and build civilized societies.

As sociologist Rodney Stark points out, "The Romans threw people out into the street at the first sign of disease, because they knew it was contagious and they were afraid of dying." By contrast, Stark writes, the early Christians took care of their sick because they thought, *So what if I die? I have life eternal.* This concern for their neighbors, even at the risk of their own lives, is the reason that even today so many hospitals bear Christian names. It's one more worldview witness: Only Christianity enables humans to live rationally, purposefully, and sacrificially.

We should share this message with our neighbors—both for their sakes and society's. Films that portray phony visions of God and his heaven present a perfect opportunity to open such a discussion. Unsaved friends just might remember our description of the true heaven—and the true God—when like the biblical Mary and Martha, they suffer the loss of loved ones.

Father, thank you for the gift of your Son, who gives my life meaning and motivation to live for others. If I lose my life in the process—so what? I will be with you for all eternity.

FAITH IN THE WORKPLACE

TO READ: 1 PETER 4:10-11

Each one should use whatever gift he has received to serve others, faithfully administering God's grace in its various forms. 1 Peter 4:10

When Tom Winston became a Christian, he knew he'd have to quit his job. He wasn't doing anything exactly immoral—Winston was a bus driver. But his route included gambling tours to Atlantic City, where his passengers, many of whom were poor and desperate, gambled away their money. When it came to those gambling runs, Winston said, "I decided I didn't want to use my gifts to lead people astray."

So Winston quit his job and formed his own bus company, called Universal Tours. Gambling runs are strictly off-limits. So are smoking, drinking, and swearing. But passengers *will* find some very good reading material on their seats: the Bible.

Does this "Christianized" approach to business drive customers away? Do they think Winston is trying to "impose his morality" on them? Far from it. Customers appreciate Winston's business practices—so much so that Winston now grosses half a million dollars in annual revenues. People are eager to support businesses that put principles above profits.

Winston isn't the only businessman who puts his money where his faith is. Robert Ukrop, chief operating officer for the Ukrop supermarket chain in Richmond, refuses to sell alcohol. He also closes his stores on Sunday. That's somewhat of an inconvenience for customers, of course. Yet when the *Richmond Times-Dispatch* surveyed local supermarkets, Ukrop's had 36 percent of the market. Its nearest competitor, which *does* sell alcohol and is open on Sundays, had only a 24 percent share.

Robert Trumble, a business professor at Virginia Commonwealth University, explains that "people relate to certain values and they go and buy at Ukrop's because of that." He added, "When I moved down here, there wasn't one person who didn't tell me to shop at Ukrop's."

It seems we can't open a newspaper today without reading about the latest business scandal. As a result, consumers are eager to support businesses structured along biblical moral standards—even if they're not as convenient.

God surely delights in Tom Winston, Robert Ukrop, and other businessmen and women of integrity, people who put their gifts—and their money—where their faith is. They remind us that whatever business we are in and whatever gifts we have, we must make sure we're using them not to lead people astray but to lead them closer to Christ.

Father, thank you for the gifts you have given me. Teach me to consider how my use of these gifts may be harming others. Help me to be willing to put obedience to you—and love for my neighbors—above all else.

RESTORING SHALOM

TO READ: NUMBERS 5:5-10

When a man or woman wrongs another in any way . . . he must make full restitution for his wrong. Numbers 5:6-7

A nineteen-year-old man stood nervously in a Houston courtroom, waiting to hear his sentence. He had been found guilty of stealing his grandmother's car and wrecking it.

The sentence turned out to be simple but eloquent. State District Judge Ted Poe took the keys to the young man's own car—a purple Trans Am—and handed them over to the defendant's grandmother. Until the grandmother's own car could be repaired, she would have the use of her grandson's car.

Outraged, the defendant turned to his lawyer and demanded, "Can he do that?"

Yes, Judge Poe can do that. And his sentence is a superb example of how judges can put biblical ideals of justice into action.

This is not the first example of Judge Poe's creative—you might even say poetic—justice. Once, instead of sending a wife beater to prison, he sent the man to the steps of city hall, where he was required to confess his crime and apologize to his wife—in front of TV cameras.

In another case Judge Poe ordered a shoplifter to spend seven days standing in front of a K-Mart wearing a sandwich board that read, "I stole from this store."

In a case involving a drunk driver who struck and killed two people, Judge Poe sent the offender to prison for twenty years and ordered that photos of the victims be hung in the man's cell.

Some critics have grumbled about Judge Poe's creative sentences, calling them cruel and unconstitutional. But Judge Poe says his ideas come straight from the Bible. In the book of Numbers we read that if one man wrongs another, he is to confess his sin and make full restitution.

There's also the biblical concept of restoration. As Poe puts it, "Jewish and Christian law teaches that if you do a crime, you get right with the victim."

The principles that Poe is working from come from the biblical concept of *shalom*—a term commonly translated "peace." But it means more than that: It means the existence of right relationships, harmony, and wholeness. When offenders commit crimes, they're not only breaking a law, they're also violating the shalom of the community. Restoring shalom requires confession, restitution, and reconciliation.

This concept applies to more than just criminal offenders. Christ's teachings are clear: We are all to seek right relationships with one another, be willing to confess our sins to each other and ask forgiveness—to make reconciliation with all members of the body of Christ our constant goal.

Is there someone with whom *you* need to restore shalom?

Father, how hard it is to reconcile with those we have offended and who have offended us. When I am tempted to allow relationships to remain broken, help me to remember that if Your Son could forgive those who whipped and crucified him, I have no excuse for not forgiving others.

APRIL 30

WHY ATHEISTS REJECT GOD

TO READ: PSALM 14:1-3

The fool says in his heart, "There is no God." Psalm 14:1

"Religion is nothing but a crutch." How often have we heard someone direct that sneering remark at the faithful?

The jibe reflects the teachings of Sigmund Freud—that belief in God is nothing more than wish fulfillment, the projection of a childish need for security. But as it turns out, Freud's teachings were based not on psychoanalytical evidence but on his personal hostility toward religion.

In *Faith of the Fatherless,* psychologist Paul Vitz describes Freud's theory that religious people suffer from unconscious and infantile needs. According to Vitz, Freud's "interpretation of religion is . . . unsupported by psychoanalytic theory or clinical evidence." It's "not really a part of psychoanalysis—and hence cannot claim support from psychoanalytic theory." Instead, Vitz writes, Freud's rejection of religion is "rooted in his personal predilections."

Freud himself acknowledged this, telling a friend that his views on religion "form no part of analytic theory. They are my personal views."

Nevertheless, Vitz writes, "Freud implies . . . that he is very familiar with the psychology of belief in God." In reality, "Freud had very little psychoanalytic experience with patients who believed in God or were genuinely religious."

Why was Freud so hostile toward religion? Vitz's own research provides an answer. In a study of more than a dozen of the world's most influential atheists, including Freud, Vitz found that all had defective relationships with their fathers—fathers who were weak, dead, abusive, or who abandoned their children. Clearly, one's relationship with one's father can have a tremendous impact on one's attitude toward God.

This finding is certainly true of Freud. He despised his father, a devout Jew who was a weak, passive man unable to support his family. Moreover, Freud claimed his father was a sexual pervert. According to Vitz, in Freud's mind his father's passivity and perversion were "clearly connected to Judaism and God."

No wonder Freud, in proposing the Oedipus complex, placed father hatred at the center of his psychology. Freud's story illustrates the fact that for many atheists, barriers to religious belief are not rational, based on empirical evidence. Their atheism is based on a nonrational need to reject God.

It's a rare Christian who hasn't encountered atheists who express tremendous hostility toward the God they insist doesn't exist. It would be funny were it not so tragic. If we have relatives, colleagues, or neighbors who fall into this category, we ought to pray for them and for wisdom for ourselves in witnessing to them.

When you hear those old stereotypes about religion being a "crutch" for people with "infantile" needs, be sure to set people straight: It's atheists who engage in unconscious "wish fulfillment." And that's a "crutch" that only the healing love of Christ can overcome.

Lord, help me to be sensitive to the backgrounds of those to whom I would acquaint your love. Give me the strength to respond to contempt with compassion, knowing that the goal is to win not arguments but souls.

WHY WE LIKE MYSTERIES

TO READ: EXODUS 20:1-17

You shall not murder. Exodus 20:13

W. H. Auden, a great poet and Christian convert, once jokingly said that the reading of detective stories is an addiction like tobacco or alcohol.

What is it about mysteries that appeals to so many people? After all, mystery novels follow a fairly conventional formula: Someone is murdered, a detective hunts for clues, and the killer is finally brought to justice.

The reason people love mysteries, Auden believed, is that they tap deeply into the needs of the human heart. They address our acute awareness of the difference between good and evil, guilt and innocence. Mystery novels feed our God-given desire for justice and moral closure.

Mystery novelist P. D. James, a member of the Church of England, points out that the finale of any mystery is a kind of last judgment. There's a moral rebellion expressed in the murder itself and in the confusion that occurs in its aftermath. Finally, the moral order is restored. What was done under cover of darkness is now revealed in the light. Evil is punished, and the innocent go free.

As Auden put it, mystery novels allow us to indulge in "the fantasy of being restored to the Garden of Eden, to a state of innocence."

Phrases such as *moral rebellion* and *moral order* are clues that the mystery genre presupposes a moral universe. In fact, moral absolutes are essential to the mystery genre. Take them away, and the mystery story falls apart. Why? Because if there is no such thing as real evil, there's no such thing as real guilt. There would be no point in tracking down a murderer because murder would not be wrong.

In an age that rejects absolute moral truths, the popularity of the mystery novel is a healthy sign because it points to the existence of a moral order and, hence, the truth of Christianity. Because we are made in the image of God, we inherently crave to know that moral universe. We yearn for justice and absolute good. That's why—despite the corrosive relativism of the modern age—we like books that paint a picture of a moral universe, where evil is punished and righteousness triumphs.

It's fun to escape into stories that feature a body in the library or beneath a rosebush. But they can also serve a serious purpose: training our minds and imaginations to recognize the realities of the moral universe.

If you or someone you know is addicted to whodunits, make sure you seek out the best. Look for Brother Cadfael mysteries by Ellis Peters, or try a few by Ngaio Marsh, Josephine Tey, or Dorothy Sayers. And then, as odd as it may seem to use murder mysteries as witnessing tools, help your mystery-loving friends to consider why they—like Auden—are addicted to literary murder.

Father, thank you for literature that offers clues to the moral universe you created—stories that describe our fallen nature, our craving for your justice, and our longing for the ultimate moral closure you promise. Teach me how to use these stories to witness to salvation through Christ, "the mystery that has been kept hidden for ages and generations" (Colossians 1:26).

A NATION OF VICTIMS

TO READ: ROMANS 16:1-16

Greet my dear friend Persis, another woman who has worked very hard in the Lord.
Romans 16:12

Social scientist Charles Sykes tells the story of a man who embezzled two thousand dollars and used it for gambling. When he was fired for his crime, the man began looking for someone to blame. Going to court, he successfully argued that his gambling behavior was a handicap protected under the Americans with Disabilities Act, and his employers were forced to reinstate him. It's a classic example of how deeply victim psychology has permeated our culture.

How did a country known for its rugged individualism turn into a nation of professional victims? Psychologist Paul Vitz says we can thank the rise of what he calls "selfist psychology."

In *Psychology as Religion: The Cult of Self-Worship,* Vitz argues that modern psychology has embraced narcissism and self-worship, or selfism. Selfism's fixation on personal rights has produced a citizenry who pledge allegiance not to family, church, or community but to "actualizing" themselves.

In view of the many rights Americans now presume themselves to have, Vitz writes, it's inevitable that one of them will eventually be violated. When that happens, too many of us enroll ourselves in the victim-of-the-month club.

There's no shortage of categories: We're victims of racism, sexism, looks-ism, size-ism and age-ism. We're victims of cigarette, alcohol, sex, and gambling addictions. Some people claim to be victims of compulsive gossiping, shopping, eating, and chronic-lateness syndrome.

What's happening here? Are folks being abducted by a deranged shopping cart, one that snarls, "Take me to Wal-Mart, and nobody gets hurt"? Do roving gangs of Hershey bars fling themselves into the mouths of helpless victims? As Vitz writes, "We now have so many addictions that the total accounts for well over 100 percent of the American population." It would be funny if it weren't so serious.

The obsession with individual rights reveals how deeply selfist psychology conflicts with Christian teachings. Where selfism demands rights, Christianity encourages duty. The selfist says, "What's in it for me?" The Christian wonders, "How can I serve others?" The selfist whines, "I'm a victim." The Christian acknowledges, "I'm a sinner."

One way to fight the temptation to seek our identity in a victim group is to consciously deepen our commitment to communities that selfism has done much to destroy: family, church, and neighborhood. That is what the early church did. At the end of Paul's letter to the Romans, he warmly greets the many friends and family members who worked and suffered on his behalf—and praises their hard work and commitment to one another.

It's easy to skim over these lists of friends, but Paul's words should give each of us pause. If he were writing about your congregation, would he commend your hard work—or would you be among those he criticized for creating "dissensions and obstacles"?

Father, if I catch myself venturing into the land of victimhood, remind me that I should be committed not to avoiding responsibility but to responsibly serving the One who became a sacrificial victim for us all.

CHRIST'S "FIGURATIVE FINGERPRINTS"

TO READ: PSALM 22:14-18

They have pierced my hands and my feet. . . . They divide my garments among them and cast lots for my clothing. Psalm 22:16-18

Former journalist Lee Strobel has covered more than one murder trial in which a killer was convicted because he left his fingerprints at the scene of the crime.

A few years ago Strobel was searching to see whether or not the claims of Jesus Christ would hold up under rigorous investigation. Is there, he wondered, a type of historical evidence that's analogous to fingerprints—evidence that could establish whether Jesus is, or is not, the Messiah?

For the answer, Strobel went to theologian Louis Lapides. Born in a Jewish home, Lapides grew up rejecting Jesus as the Messiah. But later he became a Christian, and during his spiritual journey he carefully examined the Old Testament prophecies about the Promised One.

What he found stunned him. For example, Isaiah 53 says, "He was despised and rejected by men, a man of sorrows, and familiar with suffering . . . he was led like a lamb to the slaughter . . . he was assigned a grave with the wicked . . . he bore the sin of many, and made intercession for the transgressors."

As Lapides told Strobel, "Here was the picture of a Messiah who would suffer and die for the sins of Israel and the world—all written more than seven hundred years before Jesus walked the earth."

Ultimately Lapides found some forty-eight major predictions. In Isaiah he read that the Messiah would be born of a virgin; Micah identified Bethlehem as his birthplace. Psalms foretold his betrayal, accusations by false witnesses, and the method of his death (in Psalm 22)—even though crucifixion wasn't invented until long after Psalm 22 was written.

The specificity was impressive. But Strobel asked Lapides: Is it possible that Jesus fulfilled these prophecies by accident?

"Not a chance," Lapides replied. "The odds are so astronomical that they rule that out." Statistical calculations by mathematician Peter Stoner confirm this: The probability of any one person's fulfilling forty-eight messianic prophecies is one chance in a trillion, trillion, trillion . . . and seven more trillions!

"The odds alone say it would be impossible for anyone to fulfill the Old Testament prophecies," Lapides declared. "Yet Jesus—and only Jesus throughout all of history—managed to do it."

Evidence like this gives backbone to our beliefs, and comfort in the face of condescending attacks on our willingness to worship an unseen God.

If an unbelieving friend says there's no solid evidence that Jesus was the Christ, tell him or her about the forty-eight Old Testament prophecies . . . and invite him or her to do the math. It's a kind of historical fingerprint—a fingerprint that identifies Jesus as the one and only Messiah.

Father, thank you for ancient evidence of your plan to save sinners through the sacrifice of your Son—the one and only Messiah. Help me to use these prophecies to witness to those who find it hard to believe in anything—or Anyone—without solid proof.

THE COURTS' ASSAULT ON OUR CHILDREN

TO READ: PSALM 82:1-8

Defend the cause of the weak and fatherless. . . . Deliver them from the hand of the wicked. Psalm 82:3-4

New Jersey Superior Court Judge Bruce Gaeta didn't see a problem with the tryst between a forty-something middle-school teacher and her thirteen-year-old student. Gaeta dismissed the relationship as a way for the boy "to satisfy his sexual needs."

At sentencing, Gaeta said, "I really don't see the harm that was done here, and certainly society doesn't need to be worried." Instead of the plea bargain of three years in prison—down from a possible twenty—the woman received only five years probation.

The resulting uproar led to a disciplinary review of the judge—and his swift reassignment. An appellate court reversed Judge Gaeta's decision, and the teacher was sent to prison after all. But while justice was eventually done, Judge Gaeta's decision reveals a real problem in our judicial system today: a lack of understanding of the threat posed by the sexualization of children.

The law is intended to protect us against real threats, whether they are corporations disclosing operating losses or adults having sex with children. But when it involves one of our nation's great idols—unfettered sexual license—this understanding of law is crumbling.

This unwillingness to recognize the threat to children led the U.S. Supreme Court to strike down provisions of the Child Pornography Prevention Act. Because no actual child is used in the production of virtual pornography—computer images created to look like children having sex—the majority could find no reason to ban it. Missing from their reasoning, however, was how images of children—real or virtual—gratify the violent lusts of pedophiles and inflame them to violate real children.

Similarly, the Court found the Child Online Protection Act unconstitutional because it called for measures deemed not the least restrictive—meaning inconvenient for adults—as a means of preventing children's access to pornographic Web sites. The justices decided that adults' right to easy access to pornography trumped society's rights to shield kids from filth.

Christians understand that shame is one of God's great roadblocks, a deterrent to people who want to destroy others or themselves. Unfortunately, many Americans have so embraced sexual sin that their consciences are unable to guide their decisions—even where children are concerned.

As Edmund Burke put it, society cannot exist without restraints on human will and appetite. But when it comes to sex and children, we seem determined to remove all restraints. We need to elect leaders who will appoint law-abiding—not law-bending—judges. And we need to get senators to confirm those judges—for the sake of our kids.

Lord, keep my conscience razor sharp. Help me to make the case to my neighbors that in a fallen world, human appetites need strong restraints. Give me the courage to resist and, when necessary, even defy judges who pervert the law, delivering innocent children into the hands of the wicked.

THE COLD, UTILITARIAN CALCULUS

TO READ: LUKE 12:6-7, 22-34

Are not five sparrows sold for two pennies? Yet not one of them is forgotten by God. . . . Don't be afraid; you are worth more than many sparrows. Luke 12:6-7

In 1995, Christopher Reeve tragically injured his spinal cord in a riding accident. The actor who once portrayed Superman is a quadriplegic, unable to eat or wash or dress by himself. He requires technology and constant supervision to stay alive.

Reeve wants to walk again. Stem cells torn from cloned embryonic humans, he believes, will heal his spine. So Christopher Reeve has become a vocal advocate of cloning and stem-cell research. He has testified before the U.S. Senate, making a thoroughly utilitarian argument in favor of cloning and embryonic stem-cell research. "Our government is supposed to serve the greatest good for the greatest number," Reeve said. This is, at best, a naive and, at worst, a dangerous argument coming from a man in a wheelchair.

Jonathan Imbody, of the Christian Medical Association, pointed this out in a letter to the *Washington Times*. "Sadly," Imbody wrote, "Mr. Reeve did not seem to grasp the grim irony that severely disabled individuals like him would hardly fare well in the utilitarian calculus of anticipated benefit for the most people. Spending limited healthcare resources on intensive and expensive therapies to benefit a few would simply never pass the test. If public policy truly were reduced to 'the greatest good for the greatest number,' racism and exploitation would flourish, eugenics would rule, and the fittest and favored would be released once and for all from the burden of 'useless eaters.'"

In utilitarianism, cold calculations determine life and death. If

America were the utilitarian society Reeve advocates, he wouldn't be here to make his arguments. He would have been taken off life support long ago, and the millions spent to sustain him would have been used to help thousands of others with a better chance of being cured. And if health spending is used to benefit the greatest number of people, medical help wouldn't go to the thousands with spinal cord injuries; it would go to the millions with cancer.

We can be thankful that we don't live in that kind of utilitarian society. We live in one that still clings—however perilously—to the dignity of life assured in the Christian worldview.

As Richard Doerflinger of the U.S. Council of Catholic Bishops puts it, "Our government is not supposed to serve the greatest good for the greatest number. Our government is supposed to protect the vulnerable *individual* from the rich and powerful who may find it expedient to forget his or her dignity."

That dignity is assigned to each of us by God himself.

Father, if I ever allow my mind to fall in step with those logical-sounding "greatest good" arguments—arguments that leave the dignity of certain persons or groups in the dust—remind me of your Son's teaching: that you put tremendous value on every human you create—sick or healthy, male or female, elderly or embryonic.

THE STORY BEHIND "AMAZING GRACE"

TO READ: ROMANS 5:6-11

We also rejoice in God through our Lord Jesus Christ, through whom we have now received reconciliation. Romans 5:11

The great revival hymn "Amazing Grace" may be the only Christian hymn to find its way into the counterculture. In 1975 Joan Baez unexpectedly sang the song in concert. Judy Collins likes to sing it. Former President Clinton had the song performed during his second inaugural ceremony.

The hymn's popularity among graying baby boomers would no doubt have surprised its composer, John Newton. Newton was a mere boy when he went to sea on his father's ship. As a young man, he reveled in a life of great debauchery. His duties included helping capture West Africans and transporting them to the West Indies to be sold. The horrors of slavery evidently did not bother Newton, for he quickly rose to become the captain of his own slave ship.

Then God's grace intervened. During a voyage in 1748, a terrible storm arose. As the fury of the waves threatened to capsize the ship, Newton searched for something to take his mind off his fear. He snatched up a copy of *The Imitation of Christ,* the classic Christian devotional by Thomas à Kempis, a fifteenth-century Dutch monk. The sea eventually grew calm, but the experience changed Newton forever. As Kenneth Osbeck writes in *101 Hymn Stories,* "The message of the book and the frightening experience at sea were used by the Holy Spirit to sow the seeds of Newton's eventual conversion."

Yet Newton continued as captain of the slave ship for several more years. He attempted to justify his way of life by improving conditions aboard ship. But eventually he realized that slavery itself is abhorrent to God.

Newton finally left the slave trade for good and became a powerful crusader against slavery. The former sea captain was ordained an Anglican minister in 1764 and over the next forty years wrote hundreds of hymns. It is believed that the melody Newton used for "Amazing Grace" is a West African chant he had heard rising up from the ship's hold on one of his voyages as a slave trader.

John Newton knew well "how sweet the sound" of God's grace is— for he was painfully aware that he "once was lost" before God found him, that he "was blind" before God made him see.

Not long before his death at the age of eighty-two, Newton exclaimed: "My memory is nearly gone, but I remember two things: that I am a great sinner and that Christ is a great Savior!"

We express Newton's joy over God's free and undeserved grace every time we sing "Amazing Grace." It's precisely our unworthiness that makes God's grace so amazing.

Father, we never know when we might be sowing the seeds of conversion. Teach me to be aware that a stray word, a simple song, or the book I put into someone's hands may become the catalyst, through your grace, for bringing that person to Christ.

SETI AND THE SEARCH FOR DESIGN

TO READ: AMOS 5:8-9

He who made the Pleiades and Orion . . . the Lord is his name. Amos 5:8

SETI (Search for Extra-Terrestrial Intelligence) is a research project that takes data from the giant Arecibo radio telescope in Puerto Rico and parcels it out in small packets to personal computers all over the world. Those computers then use their idle processing time to search for signals. Anyone with a PC can join, and millions have.

To the Christian, SETI is important for two reasons. The first reason is the basic logic underlying the research program. Imagine going out to the Mojave Desert with millions of other people. Each person is given an acre of ground to search carefully. "Look for something," you're told, "that could not have been produced by natural forces." Eventually, someone finds a bottle cap, another person finds an old tire, and so on.

These objects are special because they display the hallmarks of intelligent design. Bottle caps and tires cannot be produced by any combination of natural forces.

Exactly the same logic motivates SETI. If you set the tuner of your car radio between stations, what you hear is static—random noise lacking any pattern. But at some points on the dial, a strong, narrow-band signal occurs, carrying information.

That's what SETI is looking for—a pattern that could have been produced only by an intelligence.

But if it's possible to find intelligent design in the data gathered by radio telescopes, couldn't we also find design in biological objects? Is it possible that even bacteria display the hallmarks of intelligent cause? The logic is precisely the same. And this forces scientists to acknowledge the basic presuppositions we hold as Christians. The worldview implications are enormous.

That's the second reason SETI is significant. Anyone who has read astronomer Carl Sagan's novel *Contact*, about the discovery of extraterrestrial intelligence, knows how that story is permeated by openly religious concerns. As physicist Paul Davies notes, "Underlying the narrative is the sub-theme that the universe as a whole is a product of intelligent design, and the aliens hint at how the hallmark of this design is written into the very structure of the universe." The separation between the "scientific and religious aspects" of SETI, Davies continues, "is really only skin-deep."

SETI is important to us because the whole research program would be impossible apart from the logic of intelligent design. The fact that scientists are openly pursuing it gives us a chance to point out to our neighbors that there is a basis for intelligent design and that the only compelling source of that design is the God of the Bible.

Thank you, Lord, for the patterns that permeate the heavens and the earth—are glorious blueprints that point to you as the holy, intelligent Architect.

CHINA'S PERSECUTED CHURCH

TO READ: MATTHEW 10:27-39

Do not be afraid of those who kill the body but cannot kill the soul. Matthew 10:28

Nicholas Kristof's column in the *New York Times* opens in a remote region of China, where police are unsuccessfully interrogating a woman named Ma Yuqin. As Kristof relates, "She never broke when she was tortured with beatings and electrical shocks. Even when she was close to death, she refused to disclose the names of members of her congregation or sign a statement renouncing her Christian faith."

The physical torture almost killed her. But the mental torture was even worse. Throughout her ordeal, Ma Yuqin could hear the sounds of her son being tortured in the next room. Each could hear the screams of the other—additional incentives to betray their friends and their faith. Recalling this, Ma Yuqin began to sob. "They wanted me to hear [my son's] cries," she said. "It broke my heart."

As Kristof relates, this kind of treatment is common in China. Citizens whose only crime is worshipping God are burned by cigarettes and beaten with clubs.

These brave, faithful Christians bring home to us—their brothers and sisters who live in safety far away—the reality of persecution. It puts faces and names to those who suffer in such terrible ways and whose faith grows as a result.

Look what's happening in China as a result of their faithfulness: Tens of millions of Chinese now embrace Christ as the church spreads by the blood of the martyrs. The word *martyr* means "witness," and by their suffering, martyrs bear witness that the gospel is true. We can, and sometimes do, ignore this fact when times are good. But when our faith is threatened, when we're forced to make the choice, the truth becomes clear and powerful. It empowers the ordinary and the innocent to suffer and die with confidence.

Our faithful Chinese brothers and sisters live out the words of Jesus, who told us not to fear those who kill the body but cannot kill the soul. We should pray especially for these faithful members of Christ's body in China. Their sufferings rival those of Christians who died in Rome under Nero, in Germany under Hitler, and in Russia under Stalin.

If such persecution ever came to Western shores, would your faith be strong enough to endure to the end? Would you acknowledge Christ before men—no matter what the cost?

Why not send a note to the Chinese Embassy in Washington, D.C.? Tell China's leaders: "We know about the torture. We're outraged. We want it to stop."

As Ma Yuqin notes, China's leaders fear foreign pressure almost as much as they fear Christianity itself—a faith so powerful that people will suffer torture and death rather than betray the Lord who redeemed them.

Father, I am humbled by the witness of those who stand fast against terrible persecution. I pray you will give them the strength to endure. Comfort them through the knowledge that their brothers and sisters are daily praying for them. Let their unwavering bravery inspire me to determine how I might follow you more closely, drawing on your strength and knowing that Christ will one day present before your glorious throne all who are faithful to you.

CREATED IN GOD'S (INVENTIVE) IMAGE

TO READ: 2 CHRONICLES 2:11-17

Now let my lord send his servants the wheat and barley and the olive oil and wine he promised, and we will cut all the logs from Lebanon that you need and will float them in rafts by sea down to Joppa. You can then take them up to Jerusalem.
2 Chronicles 2:15-16

In 1968, Stanford professor Paul Ehrlich declared that "the battle to feed humanity is over." He predicted that during the 1970s, "the world will experience starvation of tragic proportion [and] . . . hundreds of millions of people will starve to death."

As it turned out, almost none of the dire predictions associated with what Ehrlich called "the population bomb" came to pass. That's because the doomsayers didn't understand what it really means to be human.

Ehrlich's was only the most dramatic expression of a worldview that saw reducing birth rates as the key not only to humanity's but to the entire planet's fate as well. In this view, people were akin to parasites. They consumed resources and gave little, if anything, back. Thus, population had to be contained both for our sakes and for the sake of the earth.

The fear was so acute that groups like Planned Parenthood recommended making abortion not only legal but compulsory.

It turns out that all we really had to fear was our irrational fear about population growth. The only deaths from starvation since *The Population Bomb* was published have been the result of war and man-made famines.

Natural resources haven't run out either. In 1980, economist Julian

Simon made a wager with Ehrlich that any five metals Ehrlich picked would be cheaper in 1990 than 1980. Simon won the bet hands down. Today, if you adjust for inflation, many natural resources, including oil, cost less than they did in 1980.

The population doom-and-gloomers were wrong about almost everything. Yet their predictions and policy recommendations shaped an entire world's attitude toward population. Their naturalism—the belief that the natural world is all there is—caused them to see man as just another animal, one that consumed food and other resources at a much higher rate than other animals.

This static understanding of man made no allowance for human ingenuity. It never stopped to consider that our God-given intelligence would enable us to find a way to feed our growing population or help us find resources where previous generations hadn't thought to look. Instead, it made us the equivalent of sheep, rabbits, and other animals. That's why they were so spectacularly wrong—and why we shouldn't listen to them now.

Any account about the nature and destiny of man must start with the biblical account of who man is. Only man, among the creatures of the earth, is created in the image of God. Any worldview that doesn't acknowledge this fact and grasp its implications will inevitably fall into error.

The problem isn't people. The problem is not appreciating the true significance of our humanity. Those of us in the West, who have the benefit of education and abundance, ought to use our own creative gifts to help our brothers and sisters in the developing world cultivate theirs.

Lord, help me to remember that all human beings—including those far away and unseen—are of great value to you. May I always view them as individuals of unique and intrinsic worth, stamped with your creative ingenuity, and deserving of my respectful and resourceful love.

A JUST WAR
JUSTLY FOUGHT

TO READ: 1 SAMUEL 18:6-7

When the men were returning home after David had killed the Philistine,
the women came out from all the towns of Israel to meet King Saul with singing
and dancing, with joyful songs and with tambourines and lutes. 1 Samuel 18:6

At the Bagram air base in Afghanistan, hundreds of American soldiers poured out of CH-47 Chinook helicopters. They had just returned from a week of heavy fighting, going after Taliban and al Qaeda diehards in mountain hideouts.

"We were hailed on, snowed on, shot at, and mortared at, but we did the right thing at the right time," one officer recalled. In the battle's aftermath, according to the *Washington Post,* the men were sunburned, exhausted, and elated.

That "right thing" was killing hundreds of enemy fighters—which leads to a question: Even when we believe a war is just, is it right for soldiers to feel "elated" about what they do? Shouldn't they be more regretful?

Not at all, responds a man who survived the front lines of World War I. In *Mere Christianity,* C. S. Lewis writes, "War is a dreadful thing, and I can respect an honest pacifist, though I think he is entirely mistaken. What I cannot understand is this sort of semipacifism . . . which gives people the idea that though you have to fight, you ought to do it with a long face as though you were ashamed of it."

"It is that feeling," Lewis notes, "that robs lots of magnificent young Christians in the Services of something they have a right to, something which is the natural accompaniment of courage—a kind of gaiety and wholeheartedness."

Lewis had no delusions about war. He had seen firsthand the arrival of mechanized warfare in which one side could slaughter huge numbers of men. Lewis lost friends in both world wars, and he himself was badly wounded.

And yet Lewis apparently never lost his belief in the nobility of a just war justly fought. But although he encouraged soldiers to take pride in fighting the forces of evil in the moral enterprise that is war, he also warned against letting this pride turn into a love of killing: "We may kill if necessary, but we must not hate and enjoy hating. We may punish if necessary, but we must not enjoy it," he warns. "Even while we kill and punish we must try to feel about the enemy as we feel about ourselves—to wish that he were not bad, to hope that he may, in this world or another, be cured: in fact, to wish his good."

This is what the Bible means by loving our enemies, he added.

Those of us at home are not exempt from practicing this difficult form of love. We should ask God's forgiveness if we ever catch ourselves experiencing ungodly hatred for our enemies—or a depraved delight in their deaths.

Lord, as we continue fighting the war on terror, I pray not only for the physical safety of my country's soldiers but also for their spiritual welfare—that they will never allow the grim joy that comes from fighting for a righteous cause to turn into a soul-destroying love of killing.

MAY 11

THE CRIME-FIGHTING CHURCH

TO READ: MATTHEW 25:37-46

Whatever you did for one of the least of these brothers of mine, you did for me.
Matthew 25:40

A few years ago, an Arizona boy called Lenny suddenly embarked on a life of crime. He broke into neighbors' homes at night, broke TVs, and smeared food on the walls.

Lenny ended up before Judge William O'Neil. It was the best thing that could have happened, to both Lenny and the community, because Judge O'Neil believes in restorative justice—a way of dealing with crime that brings healing and reconciliation.

"When I became a presiding judge," he told BreakPoint, "I said I want a fuller background study in order to rehabilitate the child. We can't prevent the crime that's already happened, but we can work to prevent future crimes."

When the probation officer dug into Lenny's background, he uncovered shocking details. Lenny's parents had been contemplating divorce. One day Lenny came home from school to find his father dead. He had shot himself in Lenny's bedroom. His blood was splattered all over the walls.

The family was too poor to paint over the bloodstains. Although the walls were washed, an ugly stain—one that haunted Lenny—remained. The result was that each night he crept into the homes of intact families and let his rage explode.

Judge O'Neil realized that this didn't excuse the crime but it did explain it. So he told Lenny that he would have to pay back his victims. Lenny mowed lawn after lawn, including those of his victims. Every two weeks, Judge O'Neil wrote Lenny an encouraging letter.

The victims were so pleased with Lenny's work that they told him they didn't need any further restitution. His grades went back up. And those letters of encouragement? Lenny used them to cover the bloodstains on his bedroom walls.

It's a wonderful story of healing and restoration. But busy judges cannot get involved with every young lawbreaker the way Judge O'Neil did. And that's where the church comes in. If judges are going to do more than simply lock kids up, they need committed volunteers—people willing to help determine the type of community service a juvenile should perform and make sure he performs it. Volunteers can also restore what Judge O'Neil calls "a cycle of normalcy" to a teenager's life by modeling appropriate ways of dealing with anger and by demonstrating what healthy marriages look like. They share family meals with kids, and they invite them to church.

If we truly want to change the culture, every church ought to teach its members how to fight crime by restoring both victim and offender.

Father, you have said that what I do for "the least of these" I do for you. Let me never forget the rest of your Word: When I neglect the hungry, the thirsty, the sick, the stranger—and children headed for prison—I am neglecting you. Help me to remember that you do not tell me to look after "the least of these" only if I have time; you told me to make them a lasting and loving priority.

WHY WE BELIEVE IN UFOS

TO READ: 1 TIMOTHY 4:1-7, 16

The Spirit clearly says that in later times some will abandon the faith and follow deceiving spirits and things taught by demons. 1 Timothy 4:1

The calls were coming thick and fast to a local news station. Callers claimed that a brilliant light had appeared in the night sky moments before. It hovered for a minute and then suddenly shot off at incredible speed.

What was it? Some callers were certain they had the answer: a UFO—an Unidentified Flying Object.

Well, maybe it was . . . for about five minutes. After that, it would probably be an *identified* flying object: a comet, perhaps, or a satellite.

In *Lights in the Sky and Little Green Men,* astronomer Hugh Ross writes that 99 percent of all UFOs are later found to have a perfectly rational explanation. But the fact that so many people think they may have seen a UFO shows how completely our age accepts the possibility that intelligent life exists elsewhere in the universe.

According to Ross, half of all Americans believe UFOs are real, not simply the product of someone's overactive imagination. One recent poll indicates that 13 percent of our neighbors believe they have actually seen a UFO. One researcher estimates that during the 1970s, around one hundred UFO sightings worldwide were reported every night.

Since the so-called flying saucer age began in 1947, the U.S. Air Force and private investigators have looked into thousands of UFO reports. They concluded that nearly all can be explained by natural or man-made causes.

For instance, people often report the planet Venus as a UFO because they don't realize how bright the planet can appear at certain times of the year. The same goes for stars close to the horizon: Atmospheric turbulence and columns of warm air cause them to twinkle rapidly in red and blue colors.

What else gets people into a UFO panic? Meteor swarms, hot ionized gas, ball lightning, reflected light, military aircraft, high altitude ice crystals—even flocks of birds, who sometimes carry phosphorescent dust on their bellies and wings.

Why do people automatically think "UFO" when they see something strange? A big part of the answer is that in recent decades we've been hit with a deluge of cultural mythmaking about alien life. Every summer, for example, Hollywood gives us another blockbuster about extraterrestrials: films such as *E.T., Signs, Contact,* and *Independence Day,* to name just a few.

Second, God designed humans to *want* to believe in something.

Many of us have casually accepted the idea that there really is something, or someone, "out there." Others have never given the matter much thought—and we should. Christians need to examine the credibility of any cultural teaching that contains a spiritual component, if only so that we can discuss it intelligently with our neighbors.

As G. K. Chesterton put it, when we reject the God of the Bible, we don't believe in nothing; we believe in everything—including Little Green Men.

Lord, you warned us that many would attempt to draw your followers away from belief in you alone. Open my eyes to any teaching, however innocuous it may first appear, that will eventually ask me to substitute a celestial lie for your holy truth.

GODLY LEADERSHIP

TO READ: DANIEL 2:19-23; 4:17; 5:17-22

He was driven away from people and given the mind of an animal; he lived with the wild donkeys . . . until he acknowledged that the Most High God is sovereign over the kingdoms of men and sets over them anyone he wishes. Daniel 5:21

If you saw the movie *Saving Private Ryan,* you witnessed a reenactment of the D-day invasion up close, in brutal detail. Imagine how General Eisenhower, in command of the invasion, must have felt as he sent those young men onto the beaches. What an awesome responsibility.

In many ways, what happened behind the scenes is as powerful a story as the battle itself, and it illustrates several biblical truths about true authority.

A man who was with Eisenhower in the days prior to the Normandy invasion paints a dramatic picture. England's General Montgomery was urging Eisenhower not to invade; other generals were advising the opposite. Eisenhower never said a word. He paced back and forth in the room while all eyes were on him. The fate of the whole war—perhaps the fate of the entire world—was in his hands.

Finally Eisenhower stopped his pacing, turned to the generals, and spoke: "All right," he said, "I have made a decision. Here is what we will do." He could not have been entirely sure that he was right, but he certainly could not convey any sense of doubt either. He gave an impressive example of a leader who exercises authority without being authoritarian.

How do we strike that balance? We are all leaders in one arena or another, whether we are CEOs of corporations or parents of small families. We all need to know the biblical principles of leadership and authority. And the key to avoiding authoritarianism is having a profound awareness that even though you lead others, God is leading you. Just as others submit to your authority, you submit to his.

Scripture teaches that all true authority comes from God. That means even secular leaders like Eisenhower, whether they realize it or not, point beyond themselves to the true Source of their authority.

Christians must do even more: We must consciously strive to get our own egos out of the way and use our positions of authority to show others that we are accountable to Someone beyond ourselves.

By our gentleness and respect we show those under our authority that we, too, are under authority. What ultimately commands respect from others is not bluster or bullying but humility and a sober sense of responsibility.

Whether you lead a prayer group or a national ministry, you should seek not power but authority, a moral authority that comes from God. And it comes as a direct consequence of putting him and others first.

Lord, I know that my authority comes from you and must reflect your holy nature. I am ashamed of my failures, and I beg you to make me fit to serve those you have entrusted to my care. Day by day, help me to slay every thoughtless, selfish, arrogant, or impatient impulse. Pierce my heart with the needs of those I seek to lead. And if I fail to follow your example of sacrificial leadership, then, for the sake of your name and your Kingdom, relieve me of command.

ARE FATHERS EXPENDABLE?

TO READ: PROVERBS 3:11-12; MATTHEW 7:9-11

The Lord disciplines those he loves, as a father the son he delights in. Proverbs 3:12

Are kids better off without their fathers?

The American Psychological Association, or APA, recently published a study suggesting that fathers and even marriage are unnecessary for healthy child development. The study removes any lingering doubts about whether the APA is really about legitimate science and scholarship.

In an article called "Deconstructing the Essential Father," Louise Silverstein and Carl Auerbach set out to rebut what they call the "neoconservative defense of fatherhood." They claim that fathers do not make a "unique and essential contribution to child development." They claim there's not a shred of evidence that "marriage enhances fathering or that marriage civilizes men and protects children." After all, the authors say, in-home dads might strain the family budget by spending money on themselves once in a while. All kids really need, they say, is some "responsible, caretaking" adult.

The authors candidly acknowledge that they hope to influence public policy "that supports the legitimacy of diverse family structures," such as gay parents, unmarried parents, and single moms. At least they're honest about their intentions—but the evidence that they're wrong is overwhelming.

That body of evidence indicates that children raised in homes without fathers are more likely to commit crimes, abuse drugs, have children out of wedlock, live in poverty, drop out of school, and commit suicide. Boys who grow up without their fathers are at least twice as likely as other boys to end up in prison. Sixty percent of rapists and 72 percent of adolescent murderers never knew or lived with their fathers. And the issue is unrelated to class, race, or sex. For instance, affluent white girls raised without a father in the home are five times more likely to become mothers while still adolescents.

Scripture, history, and tradition support the overwhelming scientific evidence. The family—led by a married mother and father—is the God-given structure for child rearing. When we substitute anything else, we run the risk of serious problems.

Of course, intact traditional families have problems too. But only someone blinded by a political agenda would not see that those families are still the best environments for children.

In a culture that encourages selfish behavior, fathers must make a special effort to obey the "fathering" commands of Scripture: provide for and discipline their children, avoid discouraging them, and teach them about their heavenly Father.

By God's grace, many godly single parents manage to overcome the challenges of solitary child rearing, and Christians must be ready to assist these families when they need help. But when we see so-called family experts making phony claims about expendable fathers, we must tell our policy makers the truth—that human fathers, just like our heavenly One, are irreplaceable.

Lord, I implore you to give me wisdom when it comes to the children in my charge. Teach me to instruct and discipline them lovingly and judiciously, not drive them to discouragement and despair. Help me to be willing to put their needs before my own and to steer them daily into a closer relationship with, and joyful obedience to, their heavenly Father.

WAGING CULTURE WARS

TO READ: 2 CORINTHIANS 6:14–7:1

Come out from them and be separate, says the Lord. 2 Corinthians 6:17

Some cultural commentators suggest that we Christians should abandon our corrupt society and find some place where we can live godly lives. But when great culture wars are raging, Christians have no business fleeing the field of battle. William Wilberforce, the great British abolitionist and member of Parliament, taught us this lesson some two hundred years ago.

When Wilberforce began what he called his "two great objects"—abolishing the slave trade and the "reformation of manners"—his circumstance could not have been more daunting. England's economy was heavily dependent on the slave trade.

The prospect of reforming manners, or "morals" as we would say today, was no less daunting. Public drunkenness and crime were rampant. The elite of Wilberforce's day, like those of our own, were contemptuous of morality. In fact, it was fashionable among the landed gentry to be loose in morals and skeptical about religion.

Yet, fifty years after Wilberforce began his twin crusades, all of this had been turned around. Slavery had been abolished in the British Empire, and piety and virtue went from being despised to being fashionable.

This remarkable turnaround would not have happened if Wilberforce had allowed the inevitable setbacks of any great struggle to cause him to quit.

In an essay on Wilberforce, theologian Os Guinness points out some principles that enabled the great leader to change the world in which he lived. First, Wilberforce's faith gave him the perspective to define his purposes not by the standards of the world but according to God's purposes. This gave Wilberforce the courage to go on even when the odds were so heavily against him.

Second, despite setbacks, Wilberforce never stopped believing in the power of ideas. He knew that while people may ignore the truth, they still recognize it when they see it. So he looked for ways to remind people of what they already knew in their hearts.

For instance, he collaborated with Josiah Wedgwood, the English potter, to create an antislavery tract in, of all things, a dinner plate. The plate had a picture of a kneeling slave in shackles with the inscription "Am I not a Man and a Brother?"

Because he loved his neighbor, Wilberforce never gave up trying to persuade people to do the right thing. His life should serve as an example for all of us. Yes, the prospect of turning around our culture may seem overwhelming. But withdrawal from the fray is inconsistent with loving our neighbor—whether that neighbor is an unborn child or the abortionist who takes his life.

We cannot choose between living godly, righteous lives or participating in the culture. For our neighbors' sakes, as well as for God's, we're called to do both.

Father, may I never be so overwhelmed by the evil of my culture that I'm tempted to flee from it altogether. Show me which of my gifts I should take into the public square and use to pursue your justice through the persuasion of my neighbors.

THE TRAUMA OF DIVORCE

TO READ: MATTHEW 19:3-9

Jesus replied, "Moses permitted you to divorce your wives because your hearts were hard. But it was not this way from the beginning." Matthew 19:8

Some years ago, in a book called *Divorce: How and When to Let Go,* the authors wrote: "Your marriage can wear out. People change their values and lifestyles. . . . Getting a divorce can be a positive . . . growth-oriented step . . . a personal triumph."

It's a measure of America's own growth that most of us now see this advice as flawed and foolish.

In *The Family You Want,* John Huffmann Jr., a pastor, writes that divorce is "one of the most painful topics one can address in contemporary America."

It was a painful topic for ancient Israel, as well. The rabbis haggled over how to interpret the teachings of Moses. Moses said a man could divorce his wife only if he found out something "indecent" about her. Some scholars interpreted this to mean adultery alone. But others taught a more liberal interpretation. As Huffmann explains, these rabbis taught that if a wife so much as spoiled a dish of food, talked to a strange man, or spoke disrespectfully of her in-laws, her husband could divorce her. The institution of marriage had become so precarious that some women hesitated to marry at all, a situation that we find today as well, even within the church.

When the Pharisees asked Jesus, "Is it lawful for a man to divorce his wife?" he acknowledged that Moses gave permission for divorce—but he also pointed out that the reason for this was the people's hardness of heart.

As Huffman points out, Jesus "seems to underscore the word

permitted." Jesus makes it clear that God hates divorce and does not intend for marriages to be torn apart. He reminds us of God's ideal for marriage: that which God has joined together, no man should separate.

The Lord's teachings on divorce were, Huffmann notes, "extremely sensitive to human pain and also very strong in the warning that he gives." Divorce was "a concession to human weakness," an acknowledgment of human sinfulness. Jesus "refuses to back away from the truth that divorce is a symptom of sin."

Even under the worst of circumstances—adultery, abuse, and abandonment—God does not command divorce. He merely permits it. And divorce is always traumatic.

In this age of no-fault divorce, Christians ought to do everything possible to protect their marriages. Many churches now offer programs not only for the newly engaged and married but also for couples who want to strengthen unions of long duration.

We ought to take advantage of them, even if our marriages seem strong. God does not want us stumbling into the gloomy realm of divorce but rather living in the light of marital love.

God, help me to shut out the cultural clamor that says divorce is pain-free and perfectly proper. Teach me ways to cherish my spouse and to nurture my marriage, knowing that in a fallen world, temptation comes, sooner or later, to nearly every union.

WINNING THE "SEX WAR"

TO READ: 1 CORINTHIANS 6:9-11, 18-20

*You are not your own; you were bought at a price. Therefore honor
God with your body.* 1 Corinthians 6:19-20

The *New York Times* recently announced it was changing the heading
"Weddings" in the Sunday Style section to "Weddings/Celebrations."
The change will allow the newspaper to put same-sex unions on the
same social footing as heterosexual marriages.

A *Times* spokesperson says the change is meant to "acknowledge
the newsworthiness" of what the paper calls "a growing and visible
trend in society"—that is, "public celebrations of commitment by gay
and lesbian couples."

To qualify for listing, the same-sex couple must either enter into a
legally recognized civil union or "celebrate their commitment in a
public ceremony."

This decision by the *Times* is an example of a larger pattern of trying
to convince people that same-sex unions are essentially interchange-
able with heterosexual marriages. According to this argument, insisting there are important differences is little more than prejudice and
bigotry.

But as Peter Kreeft, professor of philosophy at Boston College,
notes, not only are the differences real, but it is gay rights advocates
who have placed them at the heart of their identity. In *How to Win the
Culture War*, Kreeft recalls a conversation he had with a gay activist.
When Kreeft noted the biblical distinction between loving the sinner
and hating the sin, the activist rejected the idea. He said that attacking homosexuality is the same as attacking homosexuals.

Kreeft says this identification between homosexuals and their sin is almost unique. Neither cowards nor adulterers would maintain that cowardice or adultery is all there is to them. It is only in the case of homosexuality and homosexuals that making a distinction between person and activity is regarded as a rejection of who they are.

Kreeft then notes a sad irony: This bid for equality ends up diminishing homosexuals. Instead of recognizing their inherent dignity and their capacity to rise above their urges and desires, they insist on being defined by whom they sleep with—nothing more. As Kreeft observes, Christianity thinks more highly of them than they do of themselves.

We can't win the culture war, Kreeft says, unless we win the "sex war," because erroneous thinking about sex lies at the heart of culture wars. It's reflected in the battlefields of abortion, homosexuality, and family.

Winning this sex war means not only honoring God with our own sexual decisions; it means changing the way we and our neighbors *think* about sex. That requires patience and a willingness to sacrifice and do more than say no to all forms of sexual sin. We must demonstrate how God's yes to passion in its proper context is superior to the "growing and visible trend" the *Times* wrote about.

Father, thank you for creating men and women for one another. Let me not be deceived by arguments intended to make me think otherwise. I pray for your strength to resist sexual sin, and for neighbors in the grip of sexual disorders. Bring into their lives someone who will lovingly lead them to a place where they can receive help and healing through your power to break the strongest sexual chains.

RESPONDING TO THE "LAST ACCEPTABLE PREJUDICE"

TO READ: MATTHEW 5:1-16

[Jesus said,] "Blessed are you when people insult you, persecute you and falsely say all kinds of evil against you because of me." Matthew 5:11

Princeton University has a strict code of conduct that demands respect for all members of the campus community. The code is rigidly enforced—except when it comes to one group: Christians. Bigotry against Christians, and particularly Catholics, is the last acceptable prejudice.

That bigotry was recently on graphic display at Princeton's Bernstein Gallery. Hanging on the walls was a collection called "Ricanstructions" by New York artist Juan Sanchez. To call this art *offensive* would be a spectacular understatement.

One piece depicts a torn image of the Sacred Heart of Jesus. Another features naked female torsos arranged in the shape of a cross. A third links together sacred Catholic devotional items under the title "Shackles of the AIDS Virus."

Catholic and other students protested to Anne-Marie Slaughter, dean of the Wilson School. They explained why the art was so offensive and asked her to remove it. After all, the art desecrates actual sacred objects such as the cross. To their surprise, Slaughter acknowledged that she would probably not allow the school to sponsor art that desecrated, say, Muslim symbols. But instead of removing "Ricanstructions," Slaughter held a forum to let all sides—including the artist—have their say in the matter.

Princeton student Matt O'Brien responded that Catholics are not suggesting that their beliefs ought to be free from criticism; they only want Catholic symbols to enjoy the same protection from abuse that all other campus groups expect.

Slaughter's response? She was sorry the art had caused "pain" to Catholic students. Nonetheless, she said, she was committed to exhibiting art that had "educational value." "Ricanstructions" was going to stay.

The exhibit has "educational value," all right: It's teaching students that tolerance and respect are worthy goals—except when it comes to Christians.

Aspects of "Ricanstructions" represent those who hold to the Catholic faith as murderers—the ones responsible for deaths from AIDS. As Princeton professor of politics Robert George explains, "Like the ancient canard about Jews using the blood of Gentile children in the Passover meal, it is an outrageous allegation that people of the slandered faith, acting on the principles of the faith, are responsible for killing people."

George is right. If Princeton is serious about showing equal respect for all, Slaughter should explain why defaming Catholics is acceptable while an attack on anyone else is a conduct-code violation.

Jesus warned us that his followers would earn the hatred and contempt of the world, so we should not be surprised at attacks like these. While we should insist that Christians receive the same respect as others, we must also remember to do so in a way that does not tarnish the name of the One we serve.

Father, give me the courage to speak boldly against attacks on you and your teachings while never forgetting your command to love my enemies and pray for my persecutors. Remind me, in the heat of battle, that the ultimate goal is not winning skirmishes on earth—even for your sake—but securing souls for heaven.

ABORTION'S TRUE COSTS

TO READ: GENESIS 17:15-21

*[God told Abraham,] "I will bless [Sarai] and will surely give you a son by her.
I will bless her so that she will be the mother of nations; kings
of peoples will come from her." Genesis 17:16*

Many Christians are familiar with the 1977 book by the late Sheldon
Vanauken called *A Severe Mercy*. It's the story of the spiritual pilgrimage that he shared with his wife, Davy, at Oxford University. In his final book, *The Little Lost Marion and Other Mercies*, Vanauken recounted
a more private chapter of Davy's life.

During the 1930s, when Davy was just fourteen, she bore a baby
girl and placed her with adoptive parents. But Davy never stopped
loving the blue-eyed baby she'd given up. Following Davy's death in
the 1950s, Sheldon Vanauken began searching for the child Davy had
named Marion. In 1988 he finally found Marion, by now a middle-
aged woman who, Vanauken writes, resembled his beloved wife.

Meeting Davy's daughter, now married and the mother of three
children, gave Vanauken a greater insight into what he calls a "wholeness of vision" regarding abortion.

In *The Little Lost Marion*, Vanauken writes: "Had the frightened
young girl who was Davy lived in this decade instead of that remote
one, she would perhaps have confided in a school counselor, who
quite likely would have told her of the possibility of a quick and easy
abortion. . . . What frightened fourteen-year-old would not clutch at
the way out that the . . . counselor held out to her?"

But a wholeness of vision requires looking beyond the immediate
concerns of a crisis pregnancy to the full and future implications of
abortion. To achieve this, Vanauken writes, "I must see not only the

frightened fourteen-year-old Davy ... but also the warmly alive Marion and her family."

While he can feel sympathy for the frightened young girl, Vanauken says, now "I know Marion and her children, too." Had Davy undergone an abortion, Marion and her "three bright and beloved children would never have existed at all."

"I glimpse," Vanauken writes, "what [John] Donne meant in saying that any man's death diminished him. I should be diminished if half a century ago Davy had clutched at the straw of abortion. And all the folk who have touched or shall touch the lives of Marion and her children and their children-to-be would be diminished."

Today, when we are assaulted by the mind-numbing abortion statistics, we need to remind ourselves that each abortion represents the loss of an individual: a person who won't live and bring love into the lives of others. A person who, like both the biblical Isaac and the modern Davy, will bear children of their own, who will love and be loved and perhaps accomplish great things.

This is the message we need to somehow communicate to those who are considering aborting other Marions. That each abortion is a tragic loss—one that diminishes us all.

Lord, according to your Word, every child ever conceived is one that you cherish and wish to bring into your Kingdom. Teach me to never put any earthly priority—fear, family embarrassment, ambition, or the deadly idea that "certain people" should not have so many babies—above that reality. I pray that you will bring into the life of every frightened, pregnant girl someone who will offer comfort, help—and a realization of the tremendous value you place on both her and her unborn child.

MOTHERS AND CULTURAL MESSENGERS

TO READ: PROVERBS 29:15-17

The rod of correction imparts wisdom, but a child left to himself disgraces his mother. Proverbs 29:15

What is America's greatest source of strength and inspiration? According to the U.S. Congress, it's American mothers. Stay-at-home moms, Congress declared, are "doing so much for the home . . . and [for] religion," which leads to "good government and humanity."

As you may have guessed, the *present* Congress has said no such thing. But Congress *did* use these words some ninety years ago when it created Mother's Day. The words reflect the then widespread belief that full-time mothers were performing a vitally important task.

How times have changed. Within just a few decades it now appears that few mothers believe this truth anymore, which is another indication of the power of cultural messages.

In 1914, when the first Mother's Day was celebrated, virtually every cultural messenger, from women's magazines to Congress, praised mothers who devoted themselves to their children. But by the 1950s, cultural messengers had another story to tell. Instead of honoring full-time mothers, the messengers began scorning them as "parasites" who wasted their brains. For editorial writers, Mother's Day became an occasion to celebrate the mom who brought home a paycheck, not the hardworking mother at home.

The message sank in: By 1996, more than two-thirds of married mothers of young children worked outside the home at least part-time.

In *There's No Place Like Work*, Brian Robertson writes that decisions about child care and work are formed "in response to subtle and not-so-subtle messages of cultural acceptability."

If, for example, we hold up as cultural heroes young mothers who put their careers ahead of family, he says, "We should not be surprised that fewer women are devoting themselves to [their] children . . . even if such devotion is necessary."

The good news is that more and more mothers are telling cultural messengers to get lost. In 1997, the number of married mothers of young children who worked for wages declined for the first time since the 1950s. And a *USA Today* poll reveals that a solid majority of mothers working full-time would prefer to work part-time—or not at all.

Robertson speculates that these changes may represent a growing hostility by mothers to the idea that the workplace is where they ought to be seeking fulfillment.

It's not easy for mothers to ignore cultural messengers who say they're wasting their time at home. But we ought to give full-time mothers all the support they deserve. And whether we're mothers or not, we should all try to be fully cognizant of the cultural messages that may be influencing us—for good or for ill—whether we realize it or not.

Maybe Congress should pass a new Mother's Day resolution, like the one they passed in 1914, to honor moms who willingly sacrifice a career for the sake of their kids.

Feminist leaders would be outraged—but millions of mothers would be eternally grateful.

Lord, remind me, in a culture that offers instant and changing "wisdom" in the news media, to seek out wisdom's one true source: your Word.

THE WAR OF THE WORLDVIEWS

TO READ: PSALM 111:1-10

The fear of the Lord is the beginning of wisdom. Psalm 111:10

A few years ago government researchers in Finland announced that a woman's risk of dying within one year after an abortion was four times higher than the risk of dying following childbirth or miscarriage.

The study flies in the face of claims made by abortion advocates, who insist that abortion is much safer than childbirth. But unless you subscribe to a pro-life newspaper or scan conservative Web sites, you probably did not even hear about this study—or heard only stinging condemnations of it.

The same thing happened when the late Mother Teresa spoke at the 1994 National Prayer Breakfast. She gave an impassioned defense of the sanctity of human life. The crowd interrupted several times with prolonged applause while then President and Mrs. Clinton sat in embarrassed silence. But most Americans never heard about that, because the press spiked it.

Why does this happen? In the *Washington Post,* the late Michael Kelly explained: "Most journalists learn to see the world through a set of standard templates into which they plug each day's events." In other words, adds John Leo of *U.S. News & World Report,* "There is a conventional story line in the newsroom culture that provides a backbone and a ready-made narrative structure for otherwise confusing news." There's a "disconnect between journalists and their readers," which explains why the "'standard templates' of the newsroom seem alien to many readers."

"Alien" is an appropriate word. Peter Brown, an editor at the *Orlando Sentinel*, conducted a poll comparing the views of journalists with average Americans. The poll revealed that journalists are less likely to attend church and perform volunteer work and are far more likely than other Americans to approve of abortion.

These differences are crucial because journalistic values "determine which stories are selected and omitted, which facts will be highlighted, and how important the stories will feel to readers," Leo says.

We have to be aware of these journalistic templates as we consume the news each day. The fact that they exist is one reason Christian- and conservative-run media are so important. And it's why we ought to encourage young believers to consider pursuing careers in journalism.

The "template" that Christian journalists use is a worldview that respects truth and recognizes that the fear of God really is the beginning of wisdom.

God, give me wisdom when hearing—and evaluating—what the world calls news. Help me to remember that what is important in your eyes—accounts of persecuted believers or stories that, if made public, would point the world toward your existence and your loving concern for us—don't fit into the "narrative structure" of those who determine what is "newsworthy." Remind me that when I encounter news stories whose claims conflict with your Word—such as articles contending that abortion does not harm women physically or psychologically—they are probably not true.

EMOTION VERSUS BELIEF

TO READ: JOHN 9:35-41

Then the man said, "Lord, I believe," and he worshiped him. John 9:38

Neuroscientist Andrew Newberg once conducted an unusual experiment: He took brain scans of Tibetan Buddhists while they meditated. After they reached their deepest stage of meditation, he injected them with a radioactive dye and observed the changes to their brain. Newberg found decreased activity in the parietal lobe during deep meditation. The parietal lobe regulates our sense of self as apart from the rest of the world.

This led Newberg to speculate that this decreased activity accounts for the sensations and feelings people associate with religious experience. As he writes in *Why God Won't Go Away,* "The brain is set up in such a way as to have spiritual experiences and religious experiences." This, he concludes, "is why so many people believe in God."

Neuroscientists believe that changes in the frontal lobe account for "divine feelings of love and compassion"; in other words, that your belief that God has changed your life is a product of your temporal lobe, which "weights experiences with personal significance."

Research like this is flawed in its understanding of what religious belief is about because it reduces all religions to a series of emotional experiences. This reductionism ignores the very important differences between religions.

Being a Christian isn't about an experience or an emotion. It's about affirming or confessing certain things to be true about what God has done in Jesus Christ and in history. Almost uniquely among the world's religions, Christianity uses creeds and confessions drawn from Scripture to define who is inside and outside of the fold. There is nothing subjective about Christianity's great statements of faith such as the Apostles' and Nicene Creeds. Nor is there anything warm and fuzzy about the Westminster and Augsburg Confessions.

This is the point that is missing in all the talk about brain functions. Researchers may or may not be right about the activity of the brain in "religious experience." But it tells us nothing more about the causes of the experience or, in the case of Christians, the basis of faith, which is not an emotion but a historical fact.

We Christians have to set the record straight—starting with ourselves. Many studies show that Christians increasingly think of faith only as an emotional experience, just as the researchers do. We gravitate toward churches that stress the emotional over the intellectual and to congregations that prefer throbbing music and emotional preaching to solid teaching and sturdy doctrines.

Before we can tell our neighbors what faith really is, we need to make sure we ourselves avoid the error the neuroscientists committed: forgetting that it is the words *I believe,* not *I feel,* that are the true mark of the Christian.

Lord, many try so hard to discredit you, especially in the world of science. Keep us from being deceived by researchers determined to "find" natural explanations for the supernatural work of the Savior. Help me to remember that faith has nothing to do with "divine feelings" and everything to do with belief in God the Father, God the Son, and God the Holy Spirit.

SURPRISE CONVERTS

TO READ: JOHN 3:16-21

God so loved the world that he gave his one and only Son, that whoever believes in him shall not perish but have eternal life. John 3:16

The women gather at the Old Country Buffet in a Boston shopping mall. They laugh and chat as they dig into roast beef and ice-cream sundaes. They could be any group of young moms and college students enjoying a night out. But they're not. These women are recent converts to Islam who are celebrating the end of Ramadan and a month of fasting.

They symbolize a curious new phenomenon in the wake of September 11: a surge of Islamic conversions.

"I said the testimony, and poof, I was a Muslim," says Tiffany Motschenbacher, a University of Massachusetts theater major. She adds, "I used to feel something was wrong with me because I couldn't grasp the concept of God. Now I finally had peace of heart."

When it comes to Islamic conversions, you can't help but count the ironies: Throughout history, Islam has spread through violent conquest. Today—after Islamic radicals killed thousands of our neighbors—Americans are voluntarily converting.

Another irony: Around the country, some so-called seeker-friendly churches try to attract people through pop music and sanctuaries that resemble shopping malls. Meanwhile, Islam—which on September 11 suffered a huge public-relations debacle—attracts converts through rigid rules of conduct, dress, and life.

Islam is now the fastest-growing religion in the United States. More than 30 percent of mosque attendees are converts. What is going on?

First, the 9/11 attacks sparked an interest in learning more about

285

Islam, a religion that appears exotic to Western eyes. Second, during times of crisis, religions with clear definitions of right and wrong look increasingly attractive. Karen Courtenay, one of the new converts who gathered at the Old Country Buffet, told *National Post* that many converts are attracted to "Islam's rich mysticism and clear theology and rules," its family values, sense of community, and moral certainty.

It's clear that Christians must educate themselves so we can explain the difference between Islam and Christianity. New converts to Islam often display a faulty understanding of both faiths. For example, Lisa, one of the diners at the Old Country Buffet, said, "I liked the fact that to become a Muslim, you don't have to disrespect Jesus. He is still a prophet, just not the Son of God." She doesn't seem to realize that placing Muhammad above Christ is the ultimate disrespect.

We also ought to rethink our seeker-friendly approach and make sure we boldly teach our doctrines—what C. S. Lewis called "mere Christianity."

We can offer our searching neighbors the simple, magnificent truth to which no Muslim may lay claim: "God so loved the world he gave his one and only Son" so that we might live.

Father, help me to faithfully teach and live out the doctrines of Christianity, especially to the children in my life. When it comes to Muslim neighbors, colleagues, and family members, help me to find ways to graciously witness to the truth: that you are the only true God and that salvation is found only through your Son, Jesus Christ.

LIFE LESSONS FROM *PEOPLE* MAGAZINE

TO READ: JOB 28:27-28

*He looked at wisdom and appraised it. . . . "The fear of the Lord—
that is wisdom, and to shun evil is understanding." Job 28:27-28*

Imagine going through one of life's most painful experiences, such as divorce. You need perspective and, if possible, a little encouragement. Do you consult your pastor? a trained professional? How about your favorite movie star? Don't laugh. In today's celebrity-obsessed culture, that's not so far-fetched.

A recent *People* magazine cover story titled "Friends Despite the Split" tells us that those old-fashioned, nasty Hollywood divorces are now passé. Instead, "a new celeb smart set" has discovered the benefits of civility, even in the wake of broken vows.

Some of this civility may come from concern for a couple's children. But other factors include "an aversion to outrageous attorneys' fees," and of course, "concern [for] their own image."

As evidence of the "smart set's" new savvy attitude, *People* recites the experiences of several celebrities who have already made the transition from spouses to "good friends."

Celebrities who have publicly humiliated and betrayed their former spouses are held up as examples of how to handle divorce. And readers are assured that "lousy husbands" can make "great friends."

One might sensibly ask: Given the short duration of most Hollywood marriages, why would anyone care about how the "celeb smart set" copes with divorce?

In *Life: The Movie,* social-critic Neal Gabler shows how America's obsession with celebrities' lives transcends mere entertainment. Their stories have become "something very close to social myth."

In other words, the stories we read in celebrity magazines eventually become less about the celebrities themselves and more a model of some aspect of our own lives. The result is that along with their entertainment, people "receive instruction on how to deal with adversity." When stars fail, the author says, their failures become lessons in real life for the rest of us.

Thus, a woman struggling with loneliness takes comfort from an actress's "struggle to find love." A man struggling to recover from a bruising divorce may look at how his favorite celebrity coped with his own broken marriage.

This kind of celebrity worship is, Gabler observes, merely a substitute religion—serving some of the same purposes that traditional faith once served.

Christians need to see celebrity culture for what it is and make sure we don't slide into celebrity worship ourselves. And we must help our neighbors see the false worldview it represents. When it comes to solving our problems, we won't find the help we need in the pages of *People* magazine or in the mouths of secular celebrities but in the pages of God's Word.

Father, I'm thankful for the fact that I need only turn to you, your Word, and your faithful followers for the wisdom I need. May I constantly impress your insights on my heart and share them with neighbors who are desperately seeking wisdom, not through fear of you but through a fascination with the foolish.

THE SIREN CALL
OF MAMMON

TO READ: 1 TIMOTHY 6:6-12

People who want to get rich fall into temptation and a trap and into many foolish and harmful desires. 1 Timothy 6:9

Someone once asked John D. Rockefeller Sr., one of the richest men in history, how much money it takes to make a man happy. Rockefeller's famous reply was, "Just a little bit more."

In *The Call*, theologian Os Guinness cites this exchange to illustrate the difficulty of resisting the siren call of money.

Throughout history, Guinness writes, people have always understood that the pursuit of money is insatiable: "As we seek money and possessions, the pursuit grows into a never-satisfied desire that fuels avarice—defined in Scripture as a vain 'chasing after wind.'" In fact, the Hebrew word for money, *kesef*, comes from a verb meaning "to desire" or "languish after something."

Jesus personified money by calling it *mammon*, the Aramaic word for wealth. His point, Guinness writes, is that money "is a power in the sense that it is an active agent with decisive spiritual power." It can be "a genuine rival to God." Money itself is not evil, of course; it can be used for great good. It is the *worship* of money that becomes sinful and destructive.

Individuals and societies that devote themselves to money are soon devoured by it, Guinness warns. This leads to commodification—the process by which money "assumes such a dominant place in a society that everything (and everyone) is seen and treated as a commodity to be bought and sold."

Buying, selling, and marketing are legitimate in their place,

Guinness writes, but "not everything can or should be given a market value. The sign of a good society is the level and number of things acknowledged to be beyond market values—and thus appreciated for their own sake," not merely for financial rewards.

The early Puritans understood that a proper sense of calling could protect them from the insatiable desire to accumulate wealth. Guinness defines calling as "the truth that God calls us to himself so decisively that everything we are, everything we do, and everything we have is invested with a special devotion . . . lived out in response to his summons and service."

Do you have a sense of God's calling? Do you hesitate to respond to God's call because you can make far more money doing something else?

We must constantly remind ourselves of God's calling on our lives and be aware of the power "mammon" can have over us. According to Os Guinness, a proper view of calling means "that for followers of Christ, there is a decisive, immediate, and moment-by-moment authority above money and the market. The choice between Masters has been made."

Lord, the next time I think I must have something—a new car, new clothes, new furnishings for my home—remind me that the only thing I really need is you. Help me to be faithful to your call on my life—willing to worship and serve not mammon but the God who richly blesses those who follow him.

WHO'S IN CHARGE?

TO READ: ISAIAH 41:1-4

Who has done this and carried it through, calling forth the generations from the beginning? I, the Lord—with the first of them and with the last—I am he. Isaiah 41:4

The problem with many recent films and television shows isn't just what's there—violence and nudity—but also what is *not* there: namely, the notion that someone is in charge of the universe.

Christians call this idea Providence. John Calvin defined Providence as a "governing activity" rooted in the idea that God is the "Creator and Preserver [of the universe] . . . [and] that he sustains, nourishes, and cares for everything he has made."

Historically, belief in Providence went beyond matters of religion. Belief in a governing activity enabled the various plot strands in drama and comedy to come together in a satisfying ending, an ending that left the audience thinking that the world had order and wasn't spinning out of control.

As Thomas Hibbs of Boston College points out, we see Providence at work in the movies of Frank Capra, for example. Whether or not the movies had a religious reference, as with *Mr. Smith Goes to Washington,* the message was the same: Some force is at work rewarding good and punishing evil.

But as Hibbs chronicles in *Shows about Nothing,* since the early 1970s, much of what we watch is characterized by what Hibbs calls a "demonic anti-providence." We see this in films like *The Silence of the Lambs* and *Hannibal.* You can find something similar in TV shows like *Seinfeld,* which advertises itself as a show about nothing.

The world we see on-screen is often one where "ultimate justice is elusive" and "where we are tempted to see the underlying force as malevolent and punitive." As a result, says Hibbs, this worldview sees "violence and ineradicable guilt as the underlying truth about the human condition." In place of the hero, we have what Hibbs calls the "demonic anti-hero," who is bound by no moral code and, in fact, invites the audience to celebrate his liberation from morality.

The demonic anti-hero and the worldview that produced him are products of cultural attitudes toward belief in God. Although most Americans profess to believe in God, this deity is a far cry from the God of Scripture. More than a century of naturalism has eroded our belief that God is providential; that is, that he is in charge of all events, rewards good, and punishes evil. What we see on-screen not only reflects these beliefs, it also reinforces them.

This is why whenever we turn on the TV or take in a film, we must remind ourselves that the concoctor of every plotline holds a certain view of the world and wants to share it, often in manipulative ways.

Understanding the impact of media starts with asking whether, according to the drama, anyone is really in charge.

Father, teach me to be aware of cultural couriers bringing dark and deceitful messages: that you are not there or that you have abandoned us. Thank you for the evidence offered through the cosmos and through your Christ that you created the heavens and the earth—and will never forsake us.

WHEN CHRISTIANS SHOULD DISOBEY

TO READ: ACTS 5:17-33

Peter and the other apostles replied: "We must obey God rather than men!"
Acts 5:29

A few years ago, *First Things* ran an article with a startling title: "When the Court Should Not Be Obeyed." The author, Russell Hittinger, argued that the Supreme Court, by its rulings on abortion, has raised questions about its own legitimacy. Remember, the first responsibility of government is to protect the lives of innocent people. Yet when it comes to abortion, the government supports wielding lethal force against the innocent for private purposes.

So, Hittinger argues, our government has abrogated its first responsibility—and thereby given up its claim to our obedience.

Is this truly a time when the Court should not be obeyed?

The abortion issue brings into sharp focus the issue of civil disobedience. In biblical teaching, God has ordained certain authority structures—the family, the church, and the state—and we are commanded to honor and obey them. But none of these structures has ultimate authority over our lives. Only God does.

That means that if any earthly power oversteps its proper jurisdiction, Christians have not only the right but also the duty to peacefully resist.

We should never take lightly the duty to disobey. Christians are justified in disobeying the civil law only when it contravenes a higher law. Civil disobedience should stem only from submission to God, never from defiance of government.

The classic New Testament example is the situation in which Peter and John were ordered to stop preaching about Jesus. Their response was, essentially, "Punish us if you must, but we will never stop preaching the gospel."

How does this teaching apply to American Christians in the face of courts that are perverting laws, making them contrary to the laws of God, and aggressively interfering with the people's right to self-government?

If courts continue to do this, we could encounter cases where unjust laws are imposed on us. At the moment, democratic processes are still available to change the law, particularly with respect to abortion. And so long as this is true, we must work within the constitutional process.

But if at some point the courts were to close the doors altogether, then the church might have to make a deliberate decision to separate itself from government.

This is what happened in Nazi Germany. In 1934, the confessing church signed the Barmen Declaration, which rejected Hitler's moral authority to rule. It was a courageous act, and many Christians went to prison for it.

Hittinger has raised one of the most difficult questions Christians will ever have to face. In the final analysis, Christians must remember that our ultimate allegiance is to the One who rules over all temporal kingdoms of this world.

Lord, give me the discernment to know if and when I should disobey my government. If earthly leaders demand that I defy my heavenly Father, give me the courage to refuse.

FROM PRISON TO PRAISE

TO READ: MARK 14:22-26

[Jesus said,] "This is my blood of the covenant, which is poured out for many."
Mark 14:24

Fifteen years ago, Jonathan Aitken was a rising member of Parliament, one of its most influential young conservatives. He had wealth, position, charisma, and enormous gifts as a writer and a businessman. Many speculated that he would one day become prime minister.

But Aitken's charmed life began to unravel when he brought a libel suit against a newspaper. On the witness stand, Aitken was caught telling a lie. The trial was dismissed, and he stood accused of perjury.

It was his downfall, however, that brought about his salvation. Aitken, up to this time a churchgoing Anglican, now began searching for deeper spiritual reality. A London prayer group began ministering to him. In his cell on the day of his indictment, Aitken meditated on the Gospel of Mark.

"This should have been a time of deep despair, the worst day of my life," Aitken later wrote. But "not so. For I had such an overwhelming sense of God's presence in the cell with me that I was at peace."

We see the same pattern so often when people are behind bars: At the nadir of their lives, they reach out to God in earnest. The loss and disgrace drive them to their knees. As Aitken discovered, "There are times when such suffering has to be part of the repentance."

When the judge pronounced sentence—nine months in prison—Aitken blew his family a kiss and was "taken down," a phrase the British use for walking down a flight of stairs to the cells below the courtroom.

To those who reckon without God, this may sound like the end of the story. But it was really just the beginning. After being released from prison, Aitken began working for his doctorate in ministry, planning to enter full-time Christian service. Because of his very public fall and redemption, the former cabinet minister may well become one of the most powerful Christian witnesses in England.

Stories like these remind us that throughout history, God has often used prisons to prepare people for his service—people like St. Paul, whose letters from prison later became part of the New Testament, and like John Bunyan, who wrote *The Pilgrim's Progress*.

These dramatic stories remind us that God continues to work his will in the most unlikely ways, raising up people from the crucible of prison to be his leaders.

Aitken's story is a reminder of what can happen when we are at our lowest point—when we have failed miserably, shamed our families, and ruined our lives: We cry out to God and he wraps his arms around us. He invites us to let him turn our greatest tragedy into his glorious triumph. In doing so, he confounds human wisdom, converting earthly defeats into heavenly victories.

Father, it grieves me to recognize that every day I fail you in some way. Let me never forget that your Son's blood, poured out for me, means there is no sin, no failure, that you will not forgive if I confess it and repent.

DECAY, WORLD-WEARINESS —AND CHRIST

TO READ: JOHN 6:35-59

Jesus declared, "I am the bread of life. He who comes to me will never go hungry, and he who believes in me will never be thirsty." John 6:35

Today marks the birthday of G. K. Chesterton, a larger-than-life apologist for the Christian faith and a literary phenomenon who wrote books and essays on every topic imaginable. But it was in his masterpiece *The Everlasting Man* that Chesterton took on the mantle of prophet.

The most striking chapter for today's readers is "The End of the World," in which Chesterton describes the Roman Empire just before Christianity emerged. With magnificent roads, aqueducts, and architecture stretching from the Middle East to England, the Roman Empire was certainly mankind's crowning achievement. But as Chesterton observes, "a dreadful secret seemed to be written ... across those mighty works of marble and stone, those colossal amphitheaters and aqueducts: Man could do no more."

Rome's accomplishments represented the limit of what man was capable of two thousand years ago. Romans sensed this, and beginning to look for "stimulants to their jaded senses," they turned to violent entertainments and orgies. Of course, those diversions didn't satisfy them either. Their philosophers and wise men seemed to have run out of anything wise to say, becoming mere sophists and clever rhetoricians. Irony and cynicism set in. The great empire began to crumble from within.

Then, into this decay came a band of people talking about the death and resurrection of the Messiah, sent by the Creator of the universe. This outrageous and utterly original message was like a splash of cold water in the face of a world-weary populace. Christianity presented a basis for true hope and a clear alternative to the decadence surrounding them.

The situation in America today is remarkably similar. There is deep dissatisfaction among people, a sense that our prosperity somehow isn't enough. The hope and optimism of a few decades ago have given way to a kind of cynicism. Nihilistic philosophies such as deconstructionism deny the existence of objective truth or wisdom, and a self-referential cleverness seems to be the pose de jour.

The Good News that Christians believe today is the same that the Roman Christians had two millennia ago. If our world has bumped up against the limits of its achievements and is still dissatisfied and hungry, perhaps people will be willing to see that the answer they are looking for has to come from beyond this world. We need to understand why people feel so dissatisfied and empty—and teach them how to fill themselves with living water.

Prosperity alone cannot satisfy. We need something transcendent, something that comes from beyond our human horizons. His name is Jesus, the King of kings, who rose from the dead.

Father, as I make my way through a culture festering into decay and decadence, filled with prosperous yet discontented people, let my life be a witness to the vital life-giving qualities of the body and blood of Christ, which slake my thirst for the transcendent and satisfy my hunger for eternal significance.

HONORING OUR SOLDIERS

TO READ: 1 SAMUEL 30:1-20

David fought them from dusk until the evening of the next day. . . .
David recovered everything the Amalekites had taken. 1 Samuel 30:17-18

America's colleges and universities insist on "diversity." But *diversity* is almost always a code word for ideological conformity, including conformity in professions.

This becomes glaringly obvious in the blacklisting of ROTC programs on many campuses. Even where those programs are permitted, ROTC students are often treated with disdain. It's a matter that deserves our attention—not only because of what we owe soldiers of the past but also because of what we owe soldiers of the present: soldiers who recently left the neatly manicured lawns of their schools for the gritty battlefields of Iraq.

One of them is Lt. Dustin Ferrell, whose story is told by William McGurn in the *Wall Street Journal*. Dustin joined the ROTC at the University of Notre Dame. As he told McGurn, ROTC helped him prepare for "a calling," that is, leading Marines. "And that's exactly what he was doing in southern Iraq in the early days of the war when his Humvee crashed," McGurn writes. Badly wounded, Dustin needed a battlefield tracheotomy to save his life. His jaw was shattered, and most of his teeth were knocked out. His driver was killed.

All of this means Dustin knows a good deal more about the reality of war than campus critics who can't stand the sight of a uniform on the quadrangle. As Dustin told McGurn, "It always troubled me that the critics [of ROTC] would go on and on about how they despised war—as though we don't despise war." And he adds: "I don't have a problem with people who choose pacifism. But we're idealists, too.

And the officers I know believe that in choosing to serve we're living up to our ideals, not putting them aside."

Dustin is right. The Scriptures teach that God ordained government to promote good and restrain evil. It's his instrument for maintaining order in the world, whether it be through kings, judges—or soldiers. In fact, the military—because of the sacrifice soldiers make for others—may be the highest of callings.

Father Theodore Hesburgh, president emeritus of Dustin's alma mater, put it this way: "As long as we live in a world stained by original sin, nations will need armies. And as long as we need armies, it should be part of any school's mission to ensure that their ranks are filled with the likes of Lt. Dustin Ferrell."

That's an important lesson for Memorial Day. We need to help our neighbors understand why a broken world needs armies and navies—and why we should demand that our universities create an honored place for them: a place that recognizes the "special grace" of their profession.

Father, I ask your blessing on all those who risk their lives in our military services. I pray that you will protect those who are willing to lay down their lives to protect their neighbors. Comfort those who have lost loved ones in war, and guide our leaders as they make crucial decisions about how to restrain evil and promote good.

THE SIN OF HUBRIS

TO READ: OBADIAH 1:1-4

The pride of your heart has deceived you. Obadiah 1:3

Have you heard the story about the sailor who leads his crew on a sea voyage, only to end up in disaster? Sounds like the film *The Perfect Storm*. But an even better version of this story is thousands of years older: *The Oresteia* by the Greek playwright Aeschylus. Both *The Oresteia* and *The Perfect Storm* teach poignant lessons about the dangers of pride. Both stories describe men of astounding determination.

In *The Oresteia*, King Agamemnon leads a confederation of Greeks on a voyage to besiege Troy and recover his brother's wife, Helen. But the gods raise a massive storm that threatens to end the war before it begins. Agamemnon refuses to be stopped. And rather than risk his fragile coalition, he makes the fateful decision to sacrifice his daughter to appease the gods.

The Greeks cross the Aegean Sea and ultimately defeat the Trojans. But their success is mixed—particularly for Agamemnon, who returns home only to be murdered by his vengeful wife.

It may seem difficult to relate to this classic figure, but the Greeks surely recognized the king's tension between his family and his job. How many of us today face the same dilemma?

It's easier, perhaps, to relate to the fishermen of *The Perfect Storm*: They need money. A run of bad luck prompts the captain to make one last trip for the season. He finds little success, and the fishermen plead with him to turn back. Yet he presses on, far out to sea. They fill the hold of the *Andrea Gail* with fish only to find their path home blocked by a storm of incredible power. Waiting out the storm's fury would cost them their catch, so they sail on—into disaster.

We can't help but be sympathetic. Relating to such a fateful choice is, of course, the point of tragedy. But tragedy also helps us recognize error and how to avoid it.

Agamemnon's refusal to take no for an answer led to his tragic fate: his daughter's death and his own. Similarly, the *Andrea Gail*'s captain wouldn't listen to reason; it cost him his own life and those of his crew.

We often hear words like *gumption* or *chutzpah* used to describe this kind of thinking. But the Greeks called it by a better word—*hubris*—which means excessive pride, an unwillingness to admit limitations.

Is there any area of your life in which you have difficulty taking no for an answer? Do those close to you think this is a good thing, or do they express concern?

In the Christian view, pride is a deadly sin, for it is often self-destructive. We may be created in God's image, but we are *not* "the measure of all things."

Lord, I pray that the sin of pride will never make me blind and deaf to your loving leadership. If I am tempted to reject any view but my own, I pray you will remind me how deceptive—and destructive—excessive pride can be, and how much you hate it.

RADICAL OBEDIENCE

TO READ: LUKE 4:16-19

He has sent me to proclaim freedom for the prisoners and recovery of sight for the blind, to release the oppressed. Luke 4:18

The letter was addressed to the Texas Board of Pardons and Paroles, and its contents left the board flabbergasted. The inmate was asking permission to turn down his parole—and stay in prison. The story behind that letter is a remarkable tale of one man's radical obedience to Christ.

James Peterson, convicted of embezzlement, knew he needed to turn his life around, so he signed up for a Prison Fellowship program called the InnerChange Freedom Initiative. It's a program at the Jester II Prison in Sugar Land, Texas, and its goal is nothing less than the transformation of inmates' hearts.

Some eighty volunteer inmates—thieves, murderers, and drug dealers—get up at 5:30 A.M. each day for devotions. They spend the day working and attending classes to develop their life skills and spiritual maturity.

Later in the program, inmates must perform community service, and they're encouraged to make restitution to their victims. Each inmate is matched with a church volunteer who mentors him during his remaining time in prison and during the final stage of the program—his first six months after release.

James was faithfully working through the in-prison portion of InnerChange. But then the parole board recommended that he be allowed to leave prison ten months early. James desperately wanted to go home, but he knew that if he left before completing the InnerChange program, he would likely fall right back into the patterns of behavior that had led to his incarceration.

He spent weeks praying about the matter. InnerChange had been featured on ABC, CBS, and in the *New York Times*. James knew that the whole world was watching—and that the program's testimony and reputation hung in the balance.

James finally made his decision: To spend an additional ten months in prison to finish the work that God had begun in him. As James put it, "There is nothing I want more than to be back in the outside world with my daughter Lucy." But, he said, "I realized that this was an opportunity to . . . become a living [witness] to Jesus Christ for my brothers and to the [watching] world. Every day . . . that I wake up here at Jester II, inside the razor-wire fences, I will be crucifying my selfish wants and desires.

"I consider it an honor," James wrote, "to stay here with [my brothers] until I complete [my] commitment."

What a tremendous act of obedience.

James Peterson gives us a glorious witness to the power of the risen Christ, who sets the captives free—even behind bars.

Father, Jesus warns us that faithfully following you means putting you before everything else: family, freedom—even life itself. Help me to be willing to ask myself daily what you demand of me and to be willing, as James Peterson is, to crucify my own wants and desires in order to follow your commands.

JUNE 2

WHY WE SUFFER

TO READ: EPHESIANS 6:10-18

Our struggle is not against flesh and blood, but against . . . the powers of this dark world and against the spiritual forces of evil in the heavenly realms. Ephesians 6:12

In the Washington, D.C., suburbs, a pair of snipers strikes at random, killing one stranger after another and throwing their families into the grip of sudden, agonizing grief.

Suffering is a part of every life. When it strikes, people often question the reality of God—his nature, his power, his very existence. Why does a good God allow this?

The problem of human suffering fascinated two of the last century's most influential thinkers: Sigmund Freud and C. S. Lewis. But as Harvard psychiatrist Armand Nicholi notes in *The Question of God,* these two men drew very different conclusions about God from their own encounters with pain.

Both Lewis and Freud experienced profound suffering. Lewis lost his mother when he was a child, endured the horrors of World War I, and watched his beloved wife, Joy, suffer an excruciating death from cancer.

Freud lost a daughter and a grandson and suffered from a painful cancer.

Human suffering led Freud to conclude that God does not exist— that no loving God would permit people to endure such pain if he had the power to prevent it. He believed that men's fates were determined by "obscure, unfeeling, and unloving powers."

Lewis concluded otherwise—but not without a struggle. After his wife's death, Lewis wrote that the danger was not ceasing to believe in God but "of coming to believe such dreadful things about Him." Like

Freud, he wondered how a loving God could allow him to suffer so terribly—and why evildoers appear to go unpunished.

As Nicholi notes, "Freud argued that the notion that good is rewarded and evil punished by 'the government of the universe' just does not square with reality."

By contrast, Lewis pointed to biblical teachings about a "Dark Power" abroad in the universe, "a mighty evil spirit . . . the power behind death and disease and sin." We are, Lewis concludes, living in "enemy occupied territory."

Lewis also reminds us of the relationship between evil and free will. The human tendency to abuse free will—to rebel against God and to violate the moral law—is what leads to human suffering.

No life is free from pain—including yours. How you respond to it "determines how it influences the quality of" your life, Nicholi concludes. "If we believe, like Lewis, that a Supreme Being loves us and ultimately controls our destiny, we may endure with patience and hope. But if we hold to the materialist worldview, we are left with Freud's [despairing] exhortation to [simply] submit to the harsh realities which confront us."

Dear Father, I know that in a fallen world, no one is exempt from pain. When times of sorrow come, help me to remember not only the origin of all evil but also the Source of all solace. Give me the strength to faithfully endure, and may I not forget for a moment that, in the end, you will destroy all evil and wipe away every tear.

JUNE 3

SPEAKING THE TRUTH

TO READ: JOHN 8:42-59

"I tell you the truth," Jesus answered, "before Abraham was born, I am!"
At this, they picked up stones to stone him. John 8:58-59

It was 1966, and then little-known Russian writer Alexander Solzhenitsyn had been invited to do a public reading at the Soviet Union's Lazarev Institute. But that night, instead of simply reading from his novels, Solzhenitsyn launched into a vicious extemporaneous attack on the KGB and the entire censorship apparatus in his country.

Former *Time* magazine senior correspondent David Aikman describes the scene in *Great Souls: Six Who Changed a Century.* Solzhenitsyn is celebrated for his willingness to speak the truth.

Recalling that extraordinary night, Solzhenitsyn recalls: "Almost every [sentence] scorched the air like gunpowder! How those people must have yearned for truth!"

Aikman says that evening marked the beginning of something. Solzhenitsyn, he writes, "seemed to be responding to a new sense of calling, not simply to write the truth in defiance of the authorities, but to stand up in public against the authorities themselves."

Solzhenitsyn's stature as a truth-telling prophet is unparalleled in the twentieth century. In the midseventies, when Solzhenitsyn won the Nobel Peace Prize, Malcolm Muggeridge called him "the greatest man now alive in the world."

Born in 1918, Solzehnitsyn grew up under the Leninist regime. Although he was raised a sincere Orthodox Christian, it wasn't long before Solzhenitsyn espoused the Marxist views of the Soviet government.

But in 1945, in a letter to a friend, he made the mistake of criticizing Stalin. Solzhenitsyn was promptly sentenced to eight years in Soviet labor camps, where he met several Christians. These friends helped him to see the "ultimate folly" of Marxist thinking. And then one night he was marvelously converted to Christ. Soon after, God miraculously healed him from cancer—and Solzhenitsyn knew God had a purpose for his life.

He continued to speak the truth about God, about the camps, and about the Soviet regime, indifferent to the danger such talk posed to him.

His brave writings culminated in *The Gulag Archipelago,* which diplomat George Kennan hailed as the "greatest and most powerful single indictment of a political regime in modern times." It brought Solzhenitsyn to the West's attention, focused on the horrors of Communism, and played a key role in the unraveling of the Soviet Union itself.

Solzhenitsyn's willingness to speak the truth shook an entire evil empire, one built upon lies—especially the lie that there is no God.

Our children need to learn about genuine heroes whose words and deeds have changed the world forever—because these people were willing to speak the truth, no matter the cost.

Are you?

Lord, how fearful I am sometimes of telling the truth—even when the cost is nothing. Give me the courage to follow the truth—even when the cost is everything.

JUNE 4

MEN AND POSTABORTION SYNDROME

TO READ: PSALM 103:13-18

As a father has compassion on his children, so the Lord has compassion on those who fear him. Psalm 103:13

For Brian Taylor, Father's Day is a reminder of something he deeply regrets: In 1994, he pressured his then-girlfriend, Tara, to have an abortion.

At the time it seemed like the right thing to do. Taylor was starting medical school, and fatherhood did not fit into his plans. But almost immediately after the abortion, Taylor began to suffer from what one psychotherapist calls a "politically incorrect trauma"—postabortion syndrome.

Taylor's distress began during his first medical school class, which happened to be on embryo development. He learned that the unborn baby's heart begins pumping blood just twenty-one days after conception, that the brain begins to function at forty days, and that the baby begins to suck his thumb as early as eight weeks.

That fall, Taylor recalls, "I barely slept four hours a night. I lost weight." One day, as he watched a father walking down a street with his young son, Taylor began to cry. Shortly afterward, Brian and Tara were married and became Christians. They began attending a Bible study in Virginia especially for couples who have had abortions. Slowly, they began to recover.

Today, Brian is among a growing number of men who are speaking out about the pain and grief fathers experience when their children are lost through abortion.

Psychotherapist Anne Speckard, who specializes in postabortion syndrome treatment, says, "Men naturally have a protective paternal response," which is why they're traumatized when their child is killed. Men who suffer from postabortion syndrome experience rage, grief, sexual dysfunction, and feelings of powerlessness.

The fact that men suffer when their unborn children are killed should come as no surprise to Christians. The Scriptures make it clear God intends fathers to protect, provide for, and sacrifice for their children. When they do the opposite, they suffer physical and emotional consequences.

The church ought to take an active role in helping men who have lost unborn children. If you have participated in the abortion of your own child and now regret it, you should know that healing is available through Christ. Pro-life organizations like Care Net and Fathers and Brothers offer materials and training for postabortive-men's Bible studies.

These groups help men understand what society calls "politically incorrect" grief over their children's deaths—and then experience the forgiveness that only God can provide.

Heavenly Father, I know that for the unmarried, news of an unexpected pregnancy often brings great fear—fear that can overwhelm the protective feelings men have for their children. I ask you to lift up the voices of men who are telling the truth about the trauma that comes from failing to protect their babies from the violence of abortion. I pray that you will bring their message to young men who need to hear it—so that paternal pity conquers their panic while heavenly peace calms their souls.

IDEOLOGY AND WORLDVIEW

TO READ: GALATIANS 2:15-21

If righteousness could be gained through the law, Christ died for nothing!
Galatians 2:21

Many Americans are confused about how Islam—a religion that we've been told stands for peace and morality—can spawn the vicious murder of innocents in the name of God. The key to understanding those who commit atrocities and those who support them has to do with the Islamic worldview.

For most Muslims in America, Islam is simply a religion. Muslims believe in the six articles of Islam and practice the required "Acts of Worship," which include prayer five times a day, fasting through the month of Ramadan, and if possible, a pilgrimage to Mecca, where Muhammad founded the religion in A.D. 622.

There is, however, another aspect of Islam that many seem reluctant to acknowledge. Islam is also an ideology with a clear sociopolitical agenda.

As Dr. Samuel Schlorff, an expert on Islam with Arab World Ministries puts it, "The truth is that there is another side to Islam, a side that embraces violence 'in the way of Allah.' . . . It holds that all men are created to live in submission to Allah, as prescribed by Islamic law. Muslims believe that Islam's destiny is to extend its control until the whole [world] is subject to Islamic law in an Islamic state, and this includes the use of force."

Islam, we're often told, is related to the Arabic word meaning "peace." A better translation is "surrender" or "submission"—the kind of peace that occurs when a vanquished soldier lays down his arms in submission. And so the very name *Islam* has militaristic connotations—and in this lies the root of radical Islam. That root then grows in the soil of the Islamic worldview.

Christians believe in the doctrine of original sin, but Muslims believe in the inherent goodness of people. Christians understand that we are incapable of following God's law and are thus in need of salvation. Muslims believe that we don't need salvation—that all people need is guidance through the Islamic law, an all-encompassing system that controls every aspect of everyday life.

As Schlorff puts it, "The model requires a Muslim government to provide the legal and social framework necessary to facilitate submission to the law. There is no separation between the sacred and the secular, between church and state." All people are called to submit; those who refuse are living subhuman lives and are impeding Islam's utopian vision for the world.

Christians should respect law-abiding Muslims in America. But we should never forget that the differences between their beliefs and ours are vast.

Father, let me be willing to speak the truth about you, no matter how "intolerant" others claim the truth to be. When it comes to my Muslim neighbors, may I be caring enough to offer myself in friendship, and gentle enough that they will one day be willing to listen to my witness: that they will never experience real peace until they surrender to your truth, your love, and your salvation through Christ alone.

A SUMMONS TO GRATITUDE

TO READ: HEBREWS 12:1-7, 28-29; 13:1

Let us fix our eyes on Jesus . . . who for the joy set before him endured the cross. Therefore . . . let us be thankful. Hebrews 12:2, 28

The film *Saving Private Ryan* opens with a harrowingly realistic reenactment of the D-day invasion of Normandy. We see the action through the eyes of Captain John Miller, played by Tom Hanks. Following D-day, Hanks learns that he is to lead a search party to find a certain Private Ryan, whose three brothers have just been killed in action. The last living son is to be sent home to his grieving mother.

No sooner do Miller and his party begin their search for Ryan behind German lines than we see a Pandora's box of moral questions opened: Why are all these men risking their lives to save one man? Don't they have mothers, too? Are they just pawns in some cynical public-relations maneuver by the Pentagon?

As first one and then another of the soldiers in the rescue party are killed, the questioning intensifies. After all, just how much is one man's life worth?

The answer comes in a stunning scene at the end of the film. It's now fifty years later, and Private Ryan is visiting Captain Miller's grave. "I lived my life the best I could," he says to Miller's gravestone. "I hope in your eyes I've earned what you've done for me."

But we can see that he has gnawing doubts. Clearly distraught, Ryan turns to his wife: "Tell me I've led a good life," he implores. "Tell me I'm a good man."

"You are," she answers him.

But the answer is not convincing. How could it be? Behind Ryan's question is the inescapable reality that however good we are and however much we have accomplished, we can never repay such a debt. How could we? We have to admit with humility that we cannot: We can only express our gratitude. In fact, columnist George Will has called the film "a summons to gratitude" for the generation that died so we might live.

The parallel to the gospel is powerful: God himself gave his Son's life that we might live.

Are you grateful for the price Christ paid for you? How do you express that gratitude?

If you happen to watch *Saving Private Ryan* with friends today, on the anniversary of the D-day invasion, bring that final scene to their attention. Ask them that question: "Just how much is one man's life worth?" Then offer the answer: "It's worth the Son of God, sacrificed on the cross for us."

Father, I thank you for the overwhelming gift of your Son and for the price he was willing to pay for me on the cross. Give me the wisdom and the willingness to express my gratitude daily, running with perseverance the race you have set for me.

FADS AND FASHIONS
IN BELIEF

TO READ: ACTS 8:26-39

*Philip began with that very passage of Scripture and told him
the good news about Jesus. Acts 8:35*

A walk down the aisle of a grocery store, especially the upscale kind, will tell you that candles aren't about soft lighting anymore. They're about achieving tranquility and a sense of well-being. They come in scents such as balsam, lavender, sandalwood, and jasmine, to name but a few. Practitioners of aromatherapy maintain that each of these scents can produce a distinct emotional state.

Aromatherapy has its roots in New Age practices. Enthusiasts call it a "complementary medicine" and tout it as a treatment for everything from impotence, insomnia, and heart disease to cancer.

To put it mildly, scientists are skeptical of these claims. Researchers have concluded that any benefits from the scents are a matter of wishful thinking.

What keeps fads like this going is the increasing willingness of many to believe almost anything, especially if it promises some of the benefits traditionally associated with religion. If it promises inner peace or a way to make sense of the world, it will attract followers.

The word that describes these fad-based faiths is "credulity," which means a tendency to give unreflective credence to claims that are dubious if not ridiculous. Those who believe in things such as aromatherapy are unconcerned with the reasonableness of their health claim because they're not really concerned about truth; they're intrigued by the promised benefits. If one promise turns out to be empty, they simply move on to the next one.

By contrast, biblical faith begins with the question "Is this true?" Christians aren't out simply to satisfy our desires. Instead, we examine claims to see if they conform to reality—whether they accurately describe us and the context in which we live our lives.

Stated another way, faith doesn't believe for belief's sake. It believes because it knows that some things are true.

This belief in truth is why Christianity is an oasis of reason in a desert of credulity and superstition. Like the Ethiopian eunuch, we must actively seek out the truth and, once we find it, lose no time in joyfully acting on it. This duty applies not only to our faith in Christ but also to every detail of his teachings—from how we should treat our families to how we should view our possessions to how we should conduct our sex lives.

The distinction between true faith and "belief in anything" is something we must also make clear to our neighbors. We should gently disabuse them of the idea that believing in scents or stars—or crystals or UFOs—is in any way comparable to faith in Christ.

They need to know that true faith is the difference between wishful thinking and the real thing.

Lord, may I never slide into the habit of embracing fads and fashions in belief without first holding them up to the strong light of truth. No matter how large or small the truth claim, give me a determination to discover whether or not it conforms to reality—and to firmly reject it if it does not.

CAN WE CREATE A "PEACEABLE KINGDOM"?

TO READ: ISAIAH 11:6-9

The wolf will live with the lamb, the leopard will lie down with the goat. Isaiah 11:6

In January 2004, the body of a cyclist was found in a California state park.

For the citizens of Boulder, Colorado, the news brought back frightening memories. Thirteen years earlier a mountain lion had killed a teenage jogger. The story of that attack is the subject of *The Beast in the Garden,* by David Baron—a story that reveals how faulty worldviews can literally kill you.

Baron writes that for five years prior to the fatal lion attack, wildlife experts had warned Boulder-area residents that an assault was likely. They proposed a series of modest measures, such as a study of the mountain lion population, to lessen the likelihood of an attack. But their warnings and proposals were ignored or discounted.

Why? Because of worldviews that many residents embraced. Boulder is known for its liberalism, especially in environmental matters. These views led Boulder-area residents to believe that they could create a sort of paradise where people and wildlife could exist in harmony. They ignored warnings that the area's out-of-control deer population was an invitation to mountain lions. No one would agree to a controlled hunt of deer.

Mountain lions were eventually spotted in the area, but the residents continued to ignore the danger. Even after a lion had eaten several neighborhood dogs, most Boulder residents were more concerned about the lion's well-being than about their own safety. At a meeting, one resident, who mentioned her affinity for "Lakota spirituality," told game officials that everything—rocks, dirt, lions, and humans—is "connected."

Even after the Boulder teenager was killed, the anticipated anti-lion backlash never materialized. In fact, one of the teenager's teachers complained that rather than collect the teen's body for burial, authorities should have left it behind so the lion could finish eating it!

The Romanticist worldview embraced by Boulder residents led them to think they could create a peaceable kingdom where the poodle could lie down with the lion. That same worldview caused them to see man, and the civilization he creates, as the serpent in the garden.

A more realistic understanding of the relationship between man and nature seeks a way to protect both people and lions. Baron uses the idea of "conservation," derived from the biblical ideal of stewardship, as a model for managing this relationship.

Of course, doing this would challenge liberals' cherished assumptions. They won't do it because they would rather stay "connected" to the beast—the one that views them as dinner.

We need to listen closely for the inevitable (and wrongheaded) spiritual element when people argue that humans and animals can all live together peacefully—even when evidence proves them fatally wrong. It's one more area in which we may have absorbed the culture's unbiblical teachings without realizing it—and the consequences can be deadly.

The lion won't lie down with the lamb—or the poodle—until the second coming of Christ.

Lord, teach me to examine every cultural teaching against the wisdom of your Word, lest I risk not only the security of my soul but also the safety of my skin.

IS NATURE ALL THERE IS?

TO READ: ISAIAH 44:12-20

They know nothing, they understand nothing; . . . their minds [are] closed so they cannot understand. Isaiah 44:18

Shortly before Carl Sagan's death, the astronomer worried about what he saw as an epidemic of irrationality infecting the world. In particular, Sagan was disturbed because so many people still believe in God—even though he'd told them billions and billions of times that nature is all there is.

Sagan recommended what he called a "baloney detector kit"—an imaginary device that would help people see through false claims and faulty logic. But as Phillip Johnson points out in *Defeating Darwinism,* Sagan was highly selective when it came to his targets. If we really want to get our money's worth, Johnson says, we need to aim our baloney detectors at a few targets Sagan missed.

For example, let's look at some of the false claims and faulty logic used to support evolutionary theory. Science textbooks and museum exhibits are prone to a very selective use of evidence. According to Johnson, they often highlight fossils that can be interpreted as possible transitional forms between reptiles and birds or between fish and amphibians. What they *don't* tell you is that transitional fossils are actually quite few in number—and even those few are hotly contested.

On the other hand, textbooks often *ignore* the huge amount of evidence that contradicts evolutionary theory. A prime example is the near silence about the Cambrian explosion, where the basic animal groups all appear suddenly in the fossil record, without any evidence of evolutionary ancestors.

We can also use our baloney detectors to distinguish between genuine scientific theories that invite testing by observation and experiment—and ideas that cannot be shown to be either true or false. Ideas that are not testable are philosophy, not science, Johnson points out—even when they come from eminent scientists.

Sagan was right about one thing: We *do* need baloney detectors. But we don't need to beam them on Christian beliefs, as Sagan urged. Instead, let's use them to get an honest take on the fossil record and to separate science from philosophy. We should also encourage robust debate between creationists and evolutionists. Such debate keeps both sides from ignoring evidence that does not appear to fit their theories.

Sagan's arguments are an example of how aggressively those who reject God will attempt to get others to do likewise. *Defeating Darwinism* was written especially for youth. Why not give a copy to a teen you know to read over summer vacation? It will help kids recognize when evolutionists are trying to give them a snow job.

And that's no baloney.

Lord, help me to remember that those who argue hardest against you are in the greatest need of you. I pray that you will guard the minds of youth who are exposed to false teachings—teachings designed to close their minds to the heavenly Creator and open them instead to worship of the god of naturalism.

RESISTING THE FASCINATION OF EVIL

TO READ: JAMES 1:13-15

Each one is tempted when, by his own evil desire, he is dragged away and enticed. Then, after desire has conceived, it gives birth to sin. James 1:14-15

The scene opens with a sleek, black car being ferried on a barge across a roiling, underground river. It's clearly a depiction of the River Styx from Greek mythology, where souls were ferried across to Hades, the realm of the dead. Then we hear the Shakespearean tagline: "Something wicked this way comes."

It's a commercial for Lexus cars, and you couldn't ask for a better illustration of an advertiser's attempt to sell products by appealing to our fascination with supernatural evil. All of the Lexus ads in the series contain macabre themes, and each ends with the words "Something wicked this way comes." As columnist Bob Garfield puts it, the ads suggest that the car "has a touch of evil."

That "touch of evil" is not there by accident. Ad makers are paid to hook people at the deepest level—and that means our spiritual nature. They are deeply attuned to our spiritual hunger, and they've become adept at exploiting it. The need for salvation is imprinted on the human soul. But if we reject God, we will have to feed our spiritual hunger some other way.

That's why some people are so fascinated with the evil side of the supernatural—and that fascination is what advertisers are tapping into when they create eerie ads that hint at dark, satanic themes.

It's not just advertisers either. Over the past twenty years, we've witnessed the rise of pop music that contains occult and satanic imagery. There's also the huge growth in supernatural fiction and games.

Are all of these just harmless thrills? No. Music and ads hinting that wickedness is fun are deliberately appealing to the darker passions of human nature. They can arouse in us the desire for wicked things—and that in turn can lead to wicked acts. As the Scriptures put it, "After desire has conceived, it gives birth to sin."

The Lexus ad series is a reminder that no part of culture is religiously neutral, no part free from the need for an informed Christian critique.

Are you fascinated with evil? Do you indulge this fascination—or do you flee it?

We ought to call companies to account when they use dark, supernatural themes to sell their products. And when these ads appear on TV, we need to teach the kids in our lives to analyze what ad makers are doing. They must learn to see through the message of ads that exploit our spiritual hunger—and suggest we satisfy it in the realm of evil.

Father, may I never be deceived by the attempts of advertisers, filmmakers, and musicians to entice me into the world of evil. Help me to resist their appeal by filling my mind and heart with your abundant goodness.

WHO ARE THE REAL HEROES?

TO READ: 2 SAMUEL 10:6-14

Let us fight bravely for our people and the cities of our God.
The Lord will do what is good in his sight. 2 Samuel 10:12

A few years ago Deb and Collin Stolpe were driving to a new home in a small bus. It was cold outside, so the couple allowed their baby potbellied pig, Snort, to sleep in the bus with them. During the night, Snort awakened the couple with loud squeals and oinks. They instantly realized that something was wrong: Deb's vision was blurred, and Collin went into convulsions.

They called an ambulance, and later doctors diagnosed near-fatal carbon monoxide poisoning.

When the story became public, newspapers hailed Snort as a hero.

It's a heartwarming story, but should we really apply the word *hero* to a pig?

That's a good question. What is a real hero?

As Dick Keyes explains in *True Heroism in a World of Celebrity Counterfeits,* our culture has stretched the meaning of the word *hero* to include all kinds of people.

Sometimes we call people heroes because, like violinist Isaac Stern, they have great talents. But great talent doesn't necessarily make a great person. As G. K. Chesterton notes, "If a man were to shoot his grandmother at a range of 500 yards I should call him a good shot, but not necessarily a good man."

Many people look up to celebrities as heroes. But as Keyes explains, you can be both talented and a celebrity and still be a public menace.

For example, Pete Rose was a talented baseball player—but he also deserved to go to prison.

Then again, some people are attracted to power and charisma. How else can we explain why millions followed evil leaders such as Hitler, Lenin, and Mao Tse-tung? However, most of us realize that evil people cannot be heroes.

Who is a real hero? It is someone we are drawn to for his or her high moral character: someone who personifies moral ideals that we respect, admire, and want to emulate. As Keyes points out, those who are almost universally accepted as heroic are those who are known not for their abilities or renown but for their moral qualities developed over a lifetime—people such as Mother Teresa, Winston Churchill, and Corrie ten Boom. They are people like the biblical Joab, who risked his life to serve God.

It's important to understand what genuine heroism is about because our heroes become a concrete personification of our own ideals. When large numbers of people hold up the wrong people as heroes—Adolf Hitler, for example—entire civilizations can become corrupted. Before we lift up somebody as a hero, we need to take moral stock of that person's life.

Who are your own heroes? your children's heroes? Are they moral champions—or just champions?

We make a mockery of real heroes when we use the term lightly—when we lump together people such as Mother Teresa ... with potbellied pigs.

Father, help me to remember and to teach my children that, for good or ill, we become like those whom we celebrate.

MAINSTREAMING EVIL

TO READ: 2 PETER 2:1-16

With eyes full of adultery, they never stop sinning; they seduce the unstable.
2 Peter 2:14

He was an eighteenth-century French aristocrat so utterly evil that his name spawned the adjective *sadistic:* the Marquis de Sade, whose vivid writings associated sexual gratification with torture and cruelty.

Astoundingly, Sade's reputation is currently being rehabilitated. In trendy academic circles, it has become chic to cast the Marquis de Sade as a herald of liberation.

Sade was an egocentric pervert who spent much of his life in prison for corrupting young girls, brutalizing prostitutes, and committing other acts too revolting to describe. His books feature graphic accounts of sexual perversion, exploitation, rape, and torture. Small wonder that his books circulated only underground.

But in the early twentieth century, literary critics began to revive Sade's works. In 1909 one writer called him "the freest spirit that has ever lived." And in the 1960s, a torrent of essays appeared, transforming Sade from a moral monster into a master of French literature. In recent years, two flattering biographies and an Oscar-nominated film were aimed at general audiences.

The appeal of Sade is not merely that his books are pornographic. As literary critic Roger Shattuck explains, Sade had a philosophical goal: namely, to "systematically invert every human virtue—above all, Christian virtue." In Sade's books, virtue is punished while vice is rewarded because, as Sade argued, nature itself has no morality—and since humans are merely part of nature, morality is nothing more than a social construction. To be true to our real selves, we ought to shrug off the shackles of conventional morality and be like the beasts—governed solely by instinct, by sex, and by cruelty. Thus Sade defended crime and violence as a necessary part of nature.

This is nothing less than an inverted form of salvation—liberation through cruelty and sexual excess.

The world is full of offers of false salvation, all speaking to a deep-rooted sense that something is wrong with the human condition, all offering some way to restore human nature to its wholeness. Sade was nothing less than an "evangelist," Shattuck says, for a worldview that defines human beings as merely part of nature and defines salvation as a return to nature: an amoral sphere red in tooth and claw. Sade's vision of cruelty and depravity was the logical consequence of the philosophy of naturalism—that nature is all that exists.

Francis Schaeffer urged Christians to practice pre-evangelism by pressing people to the logical consequences of their own beliefs. Many today accept some form of naturalism, and we need to press them to see the consequences of that belief—that humans are brutes and thus, brutality is only natural.

Lord, help me to remember that false prophets are a plague of every generation. Teach me to discern and acknowledge my own evil desires—and to recognize for what they are: the tempting teachings of evangelists for evil—those who would "liberate" me through a surrender to sin.

BUILDING UP THE BODY

TO READ: EPHESIANS 4:10-16

It was he who gave some to be . . . pastors and teachers, to prepare God's people for works of service, so that the body of Christ may be built up. Ephesians 4:11-12

Cracks were forming in the marriage of a young woman we'll call Susan. But she didn't feel comfortable discussing her troubles with her minister.

Fortunately Susan had an alternative. Her church had just begun a mentoring ministry in which mature married couples counseled engaged couples and newlyweds. Susan and her husband patched up their marriage, with wisdom and help from a couple whose own marriage had weathered thirty years of marital storms.

In *Marriage Savers,* Michael McManus explains how couples with solid, seasoned marriages provide a great resource for strengthening other marriages and preventing divorce.

Mentoring programs have proven their worth: Couples who go through mentor-assisted programs greatly increase their chances of staying married. That's because these programs involve much more than taking compatibility tests. They entail frank discussion with older couples who have what McManus considers the equivalent of a Ph.D. in matrimony. These folks can draw on years of experience to teach younger couples how to resolve conflicts, improve communication, and cherish one another.

But how many churches think of calling in older, married couples to mentor the engaged or newly married? Hardly any. And that's partly because most pastors view premarital and marriage counseling as their own preserve. It's also because even the happiest couples tend to focus on their imperfections instead of their strengths and so feel unqualified to advise others.

But, McManus argues, young couples can more easily identify with a married couple than they can with their minister. And lay mentors often find it easier to be vulnerable than a minister might be—freer to disclose their own sins and reveal how they've struggled with and solved their own marital problems.

Mentoring is a role the early church specifically delegated to mature laypeople. In Ephesians, Paul tells pastors and teachers to "prepare God's people"—that's the laypeople—"for works of service."

In Titus 2:4, Paul is even more specific. He says older women are to "train the younger women to love their husbands and children." The older generation was expected to mentor the younger one.

Churches ought to tap into that huge, unused reservoir of counseling resources—ordinary, happily married couples.

Why not encourage your pastor to read *Marriage Savers* and begin a mentoring program at your church? And if you have been happily married for a long time, why not consider becoming mentors yourselves?

You can help heal the cracks in foundering Christian marriages—and turn your church into a real marriage saver.

Lord, help me to be willing to exploit the wisdom gained through decades of married life and love. At a time when so many marriages tragically break down, show me how to build up the body of Christ by strengthening the attachment between husbands and wives who follow you.

JUNE 14

OUR CHRIST-HAUNTED CULTURE

TO READ: JOHN 4:1-30

Whoever drinks the water I give him will never thirst. John 4:14

Leslie Bohem, who wrote the miniseries *Taken* for the Sci-Fi Channel, says that stories about aliens and abductions go back a long way. He told the *Observer* that these stories go "back thousands of years to the stories of the incubus and succubus"—ancient demons. Bohem said that he doesn't want to "step on any religious toes," but he sees echoes of these stories in, of all things, the biblical story of the Virgin Birth.

He's right about this extraordinary connection. Stories about aliens are, indeed, indebted to the Christian story. In many cases, these stories simply recast biblical narratives.

For instance, in the first hour of Bohem's story *Taken*, a lonely woman finds an injured stranger—an alien in human form. Out of kindness, she takes care of him.

The stranger, who calls himself John, tells the woman things about herself and her life—things that she's never shared with anyone. These insights into people's souls lead her to suspect the truth about John.

Eventually, John goes home, but not before leaving her with child—a very special child named Jacob. The biblical allusions go beyond the child's name. This one story contains allusions to the story of Elisha and the Shunammite woman (2 Kings 4) and the story of Jesus and the Samaritan woman at the well. As well, the existence of alien visitors becomes an explanation for evil and suffering. Abductees' misfortune is the fault of powerful beings who have, for their own unknowable purposes, interfered in the lives of ordinary people. This plot element mimics the story of Job.

The fact that these allusions are very likely unintentional testifies to the way that the biblical narratives have shaped our thinking and our society. The biblical stories are woven into the warp and woof of Western culture. Even when we don't acknowledge them, they shape how we think and feel.

That's why, when our post-Christian culture tries to create alternative narratives to make sense of our lives and the world around us, they almost always end up sounding like biblical ones.

Stories about alien visitors resonate with us because they allude to the biblical stories that are—even if not directly—at least indirectly in our consciousness.

And that's what you would expect in our "Christ-haunted culture," to paraphrase Flannery O'Connor. Christ and his story are still the measure of what we regard as true.

If you have unsaved friends who enjoy science fiction, share books or films that echo the biblical narrative. And then, share and discuss this mystical phenomenon with those people.

It just might get them to musing not only about why our culture is "Christ haunted" but also about the "who" of Christ himself.

Father, open my eyes to evidence of how those who do not know you nevertheless thirst for you, and help me to use it to point the way to the One who offers "a spring of water welling up to eternal life."

BUILDING A FIRM FOUNDATION

TO READ: MATTHEW 7:24-29

Everyone who hears these words of mine and puts them into practice is like a wise man who built his house on the rock. Matthew 7:24

A syllabus for a course at the University of Maine contains the following warning: "Any language that may be deemed sexist, racist or homophobic, or may be found offensive by any minority group, is prohibited. Use of such language can result in immediate failure of that paper and possible future action."

Ironically, the course in question isn't called "Contemporary Feminism" or "Queer Theory 101." It's a class called Speech Communication.

Harvey Silverglate is the coauthor of *The Shadow University,* a book about restrictions on the liberties of college students. Silverglate says 90 percent of the nation's colleges have adopted speech codes. Ostensibly, the aim of these codes is to preserve the peace. But Silverglate notes that they are really little more than attempts at mind control, designed to preserve a secular orthodoxy on campus.

He cites the example of a religion professor who quoted biblical passages that describe the role of women and the sinfulness of homosexuality. He was brought up on charges of hostility to women and gays.

The ability to punish politically incorrect speech might seem like a victory for secular liberalism. But as philosopher Russell Hittinger points out, these codes are actually an admission of weakness. He explains: "Once upon a time people really did believe that the modern ["isms"] would provide an order of truth to replace the older worldview of [Christianity]." In other words, it was the belief that "isms" such as Marxism and Darwinism were true that made them so powerful.

But today this faith in secular ideologies is in tatters. It's difficult to find anyone who will argue that any secular ideology describes reality and provides a sure foundation for organizing our lives.

What happened? In a word, postmodernism—the belief that there are no universal truths or norms. As Hittinger points out, secular liberalism not only does not make claims about absolutes; it denies, as an article of faith, that absolutes exist—even liberal absolutes. In an ironic twist, liberalism, which tried to reduce religion to a private matter, has itself been reduced to a private matter.

This leaves liberals ill-equipped to engage Christians in debates about the fitness of their belief system. Does that mean they're willing to concede the argument to Christians? Not at all. As Hittinger put it, "My fellow faculty is scared down to their socks of Christianity."

Knowing that they can't beat the Judeo-Christian tradition in a fair fight, they seek to suppress it instead through speech codes.

Christians should be concerned about the imposition of this kind of censorship. But we should also take comfort in knowing that we alone have our spiritual home built on a firm foundation. All others will be overthrown.

Christians should make it clear that we welcome the very debate our opponents fear—and we should prepare well for them. We know that it's not *our* belief system but *theirs* that has been tried and found wanting.

To those who find that assertion offensive, we ought to graciously ask, "What are you afraid of?"

Lord, may I be robust in opposing official attempts to stifle your truth, and gentle in witnessing to those who, as they watch their own spiritual homes collapse, desperately need to hear of the firm foundation found in you.

THE CHRISTIAN METANARRATIVE

TO READ: 1 CORINTHIANS 15:42-57

It is written: "The first man Adam became a living being"; the last Adam, a life-giving spirit. I Corinthians 15:45

If the average person were asked to name the top religion stories of the past year, chances are he'd remember a scandal involving priests or maybe a campus kerfuffle between Christian and non-Christian students.

In *How the News Makes Us Dumb,* John Sommerville says there's a good reason why religious controversies get publicity while the good works of the church are ignored. It's because religion and the news are polar opposites in their approach to life. "Religion celebrates what we believe to be settled and even eternal," Sommerville says. But the news is about change and excitement. So reporters yawn when Christians go to church or volunteer at soup kitchens.

Before news became an industry, Sommerville writes, society was held together not by news but by its cultures. People shared "fairly settled assumptions about what was reasonable, natural, expected or good." Scholars call this a culture's metanarrative—a narrative that "binds our thinking."

In Western culture, the Bible provided this metanarrative. Even nonbelievers were familiar with its stories and ways of structuring moral and social reality.

But the daily news industry changed all that. Those in the news business tend to be far less religious than most Americans, and they're distrustful of a culture built on the Judeo-Christian narrative. These elites think it's their job to make us aware of the cultural restraints on our thinking, Sommerville says. That's why they sponsor "a continuous referendum on our cultural inheritance."

The result is that many people accept the idea that we should be constantly reevaluating what we believe and understand about the world—including our religious beliefs.

It's proper for news outlets to raise questions about dominant ideas—to reform or reshape traditional culture. But news stories cannot replace a culture's metanarrative, because, by its very nature, the news gives priority to the shocking and the new. It is a cycle of endless deconstruction.

The good news is that Americans are recognizing that the "news" is becoming little more than vulgar entertainment, largely irrelevant to our lives.

In the end, Sommerville says, we must use news for the limited purposes for which it is suited—and realize our need for the more settled culture the news constantly questions. We should balance our bloated appetite for news with a cultural diet rich in books, reflection, and discussion. And we should put the news through a mental metanarrative grid—asking ourselves if the "news" being offered up reinforces our cultural story—and our view of Christianity—or tears it apart.

The news may make us dumb—but reading and discussing great books, especially the Bible, leads to the kind of wisdom that brings real understanding.

Lord, let my mind not be distorted by what the world calls "news," often written and delivered by those who would destroy the grand Christian narrative.

JUNE 17

CALLING EVIL BY ITS NAME

TO READ: GENESIS 3:1-24

Have you eaten from the tree that I commanded you not to eat from? Genesis 3:11

A few years ago America witnessed the dying spasm of sixties' utopianism as visions of peace and love degenerated into mayhem and violence. By the end of Woodstock 1999, teenagers faced off against the police, looting, destroying property, and setting fires.

In a microcosm, Woodstock illustrates the complete failure of utopian visions of society—and their tendency to devolve into chaos and violence.

Utopianism is one of the most pervasive myths of our age. It lies at the heart of the great "isms" of the twentieth century, from National Socialism to Marxism. Utopianism denies the biblical doctrine of sin by defining the human dilemma not as moral rebellion against God but as ignorance, poverty, or oppression. The answer, then, is simply better education, income redistribution, or political reform.

The promise is that if we reform unjust social structures, natural human goodness will flourish.

But how realistic is this utopian vision? To be blunt, the entire twentieth century is a record of its failures. Everywhere utopian schemes have been tried—from Nazi Germany to the Soviet Union to Cambodia—they have produced tyranny and famine, secret police, and labor camps. Why? Because utopianism rests on the denial of a central Christian truth: the Fall. Christianity teaches that God created the world good and that one of the good things he created was free will. But the first humans exercised their free will to reject God's commands, which brought sin and evil into the world, resulting in suffering and death.

Modern thinkers often criticize the doctrine of sin as pessimistic and negative. But ironically, this doctrine is precisely what undergirds liberty. America's founders instituted a balance of power among three branches of government precisely on the grounds that—due to the tendency to sin—power should not be concentrated in any one person or group. They built structures designed to limit the effects of the Fall while maximizing liberty.

By contrast, utopians deny the reality of evil and thus build no safeguards against sin—which gives free rein to evil and tyranny.

Ever since the vaunted "idealism" of the sixties, utopian ideas have moved into the mainstream: into education theory, psychology, government policy, and even the general culture, with the result that no one is responsible and everyone is a victim.

Nowhere does the clash of worldviews have greater social impact than in the denial of sin and the consequent loss of moral responsibility. Christians must learn to detect false ideas and to show why they are wrong. If we fail to recognize prevailing worldviews, we ourselves will be sucked into false thinking unawares—and lose our distinctive message.

And that would be disastrous, both for ourselves and for our country.

Father, open my eyes to all attempts to airbrush the Fall out of history, human behavior, and human societies. Help me to identify utopian ideas that I may have unconsciously accepted and replace them with a fuller understanding of the reality of human sin—and of the only true "utopia" available: your holy Kingdom.

JUNE 18

CRIME AND NEIGHBORHOOD COHESION

TO READ: PHILIPPIANS 2:1-7

Each of you should look not only to your own interests,
but also to the interests of others. Philippians 2:4

Roberto Rivera, who grew up in a racially mixed, big-city neighborhood, remembers one of his old neighbors, a woman named Mrs. Greene. She was one of those people who minded everybody else's business. All the neighborhood kids hated her. But Rivera now acknowledges, "It was Mrs. Greene, more than any other factor, that kept my neighborhood safe."

Researchers from elite universities are now confirming Rivera's belief: It's the Mrs. Greenes of this world who keep crime at bay.

Mrs. Greene had three children of her own, but she considered everyone else's kids her business too. "If she saw you doing something stupid or dangerous, she wouldn't hesitate to call you on it," Rivera recalls. "Even worse, you could count on her telling your parents."

As a child, Rivera found Mrs. Greene annoying. But her presence also made him feel perfectly safe, despite the fact that he lived in an inner-city neighborhood. Why? Because he knew Mrs. Greene wouldn't let neighborhood problems get out of hand.

Apparently a lot of other Mrs. Greenes have the same effect. Researchers from Harvard and the University of Chicago recently conducted the largest study ever undertaken of the causes of crime and delinquency and published their conclusions in *Science* magazine.

They studied 343 Chicago neighborhoods of tremendous racial, ethnic, social, and economic diversity.

The researchers found that some of the poorest black neighborhoods also had very low crime rates. This meant that—notwithstanding conventional wisdom—both race and poverty could be eliminated as causes of crime.

The researchers concluded that by far the largest predictor of the violent crime rate was what they called "collective efficacy"—shorthand for a sense of trust, common values, and cohesion in neighborhoods. The more cohesion, the less crime.

Robert Sampson, formerly a professor of sociology at the University of Chicago and coauthor of the study, emphasized that cohesion is the product of "a shared vision, if you will, a fusion of a shared willingness of residents to intervene." In other words, crime is most effectively combated by people like Mrs. Greene—adults who intervene when they see kids cutting classes, spray-painting graffiti, or loitering on street corners.

Preventing crime requires two things: a moral vision of what is required to maintain neighborhood peace, and the willingness to work at it.

What are you doing to help keep *your* neighborhood safe? Do local children know they can rely on you for help?

If we're going to make our streets safe, then like Mrs. Greene, we must all become our brothers' keepers.

Father, no matter where I live, help me to be willing to get to know my neighbors, for if I don't know them, I will fear them, and if I fear them, I cannot love them.

JUNE 19

CRIME AND PUNISHMENT

TO READ: GENESIS 4:1-16

The Lord said [to Cain], "What have you done? Listen! Your brother's blood cries out to me from the ground." Genesis 4:10

In Lowell, Massachusetts, a woman pushed her grocery cart into the store's express line—with one more item than she was supposed to have. It was enough to infuriate the woman in line behind her.

The two customers had words. Out in the parking lot, they had a few more. And then, customer number two—who has a long criminal record—lost it. She grabbed customer number one by the hair and beat her senseless.

A radio talk-show host referred to the incident as "Express Line Rage." Some callers actually applauded the attacker. Of course, none of us appreciates it when shoppers abuse express lines. But that's no excuse for beating people up.

Incredibly, some people want us to believe that those who lose their tempers are not obnoxious or criminal—they're just sick. For instance, a few years ago a psychologist told Congress that road rage is a "certifiable mental illness"—one from which more than half of all Americans suffer. And not long ago, *Monitor on Psychology* ran an article about "counterproductive workplace behavior"—otherwise known as "desk rage." If you've ever pounded on your keyboard and shouted four-letter words, the men in the white coats may come looking for you.

But what happens when we redefine all unacceptable behavior as mental illness?

C. S. Lewis anticipated this shift in the modern view of crime and punishment in an essay called "The Humanitarian Theory of

339

Punishment." Traditionally, Lewis wrote, punishment is understood as a matter of balancing the scales of justice. But the "humanitarian theory of punishment" jettisons that standard.

Denying that punishment is an objective matter of justice, this theory removes criminal activity from the realm of morality and applies a therapeutic response. But as Lewis explains, punishment without a sense of objective morality ultimately sows the seeds of Orwellian tyranny: "If crime and disease are to be regarded as the same thing," he says, "it follows that any state of mind which our masters choose to call 'disease' can be treated as a crime; and compulsorily cured."

Lewis's warning has become horrifyingly real in North Korea, where Christian believers are considered mentally ill; the government attempts to torture them into "sanity."

That's why we Christians must help our neighbors understand the dangers of redefining every crime—all sin—as a mental disorder. And we need to guard against the temptation to do this ourselves when we "lose it," remembering how God punished Cain when he exploded in rage.

When one person beats up another for sneaking an extra bag of Doritos into the express line, we ought to call the attack by its proper name: not a mental illness to be treated but a crime to be punished.

Lord God, your Word says that when sin crouches at my door, I must master my desires, not allow them to master me. Help me to master my own particular demons, and if I fail, help me to recognize my sins with remorse, not recast them as mental maladies.

WITNESSING TO
THE TRUTH

TO READ: JOHN 8:31-37

You will know the truth, and the truth will set you free. John 8:32

In the 1942 tearjerker film *Now, Voyager,* suave actor Paul Henreid says to Bette Davis: "Shall we just have a cigarette on it?" As the two gaze into one another's eyes, Henreid puts two cigarettes into his mouth, lights them, and hands one to Davis.

It was the ultimate in sophisticated romance.

Flash forward fifty-seven years. In the hit comedy *My Best Friend's Wedding,* Julia Roberts sits on the floor outside a hotel room, smoking an illicit cigarette. Her friend yanks open the door and snatches the cigarette. "I want you to quit this [stuff] before it kills you," he snarls.

It's the ultimate in social condemnation.

What happened between 1942 and 1997 to generate such a change? The answer shines a spotlight on how we may one day win the abortion debate.

As Frederica Mathewes-Green writes in *Building a Culture of Life: 30 Years after Roe v. Wade,* our grandparents embraced values that we now recognize as damaging, like smoking and heavy drinking. Those attitudes, says Mathewes-Green, were celebrated in films in much the same way promiscuity is today. For instance, in the Thin Man films, the heavy drinking of both Myrna Loy and William Powell was treated as comic relief. Anyone who objected to this view was dismissed as a moralizing busybody.

But something happened on the way from the Bijou to the multiplex. Americans began losing friends to lung cancer and emphysema.

Drunk drivers killed thousands of people. As a result, cigarettes are no longer considered glamorous. Excessive drinking is no longer considered funny. And for the most part, Hollywood has stopped suggesting that they are.

It's important to understand, Mathewes-Green points out, that it wasn't all those warning labels on cigarette packages that got people to quit smoking. And it wasn't temperance unions that convinced people to stop getting drunk. It was social pressure and truth itself.

That's where the abortion debate comes in. Modern films portray sexual romps as great fun. Those who object are dismissed as moralizing busybodies. But just as media messages about drinking and smoking gradually changed, we will one day see changes in how Hollywood portrays sexuality, predicts Mathewes-Green. This will happen as more and more people are harmed by promiscuous behavior, watch friends die of AIDS, and see sisters damaged by "safe, legal abortions."

The day will surely come when abortion won't be portrayed as a noble decision by brave women who are harassed by religious crazies. Eventually, the truth will come out—and we'll even see it on the silver screen.

We need to be aware of moral messages in films—messages that may be as small as a cigarette in the hand of a glamorous star. And we must make certain that we ourselves do not make any kind of sin look attractive to others. We will ultimately regret it—and so will those who take our ungodly "advice."

Lord, protect me from cultural influences that suggest that disregarding your laws carries no consequences. Help me to be a witness to your truth, letting unsaved friends—especially those with whom I watch movies—understand not only the tragedy of sin but also the Way we can break free of it.

CAESAR AND CHRIST

TO READ: LUKE 20:19-26

Give to Caesar what is Caesar's, and to God what is God's. Luke 20:25

Puritans and Quakers left England to escape laws that insisted they believe and worship the way the state demanded. In North America they were free to worship as they wished. We've defended that right over the years as a precious American birthright.

But the sad truth is that it's a liberty denied to much of the world.

In 1998, Congress passed the International Religious Freedom Act, which established the U.S. Commission on International Religious Freedom. The commission's mission is to expose religious liberty violations around the world and then recommend action.

Every May the commission reports to the president on countries that stifle religious freedom and suggests specific foreign policy changes. While the president doesn't have to follow the recommendations, he is nonetheless bound by law to take action against nations that won't grant their people religious freedom.

Since much of the religious persecution in the world is directed against Christians, the commission's report is a powerful tool for protecting the lives of thousands of believers. Governments that deny religious freedom fall into two broad categories. Both violate the principle Jesus gave to us: "Give to Caesar what is Caesar's and to God what is God's."

In the first category are nations that believe Caesar is God—that is, that the state is supreme over all and deserves loyalty. This includes China and Russia, but the worst offender is North Korea. Life for Christians there is brutal because they will not worship the state.

In the second category are governments that believe that God is Caesar—that is, that the government is God's representative on earth. Countries like Sudan, Iran, and Saudi Arabia see their primary purpose as enforcing religious law.

The commission's work is vitally important. Americans care deeply about religious liberty, and people around the world need to hear our voices being raised. But—and this may not surprise you—the media typically ignore the commission's report. Where are all the so-called defenders of the First Amendment and human rights?

When the secular press suppresses stories of persecution, we need to make it our business to find out about it through Christian Web sites and magazines—and find ways to help those who are suffering for their faith. As Christians, our citizenship goes beyond our national borders. The Scriptures tell us that we are to remember the brethren who are being mistreated as if we are suffering with them. Therefore, we are all part of the persecuted church—brothers and sisters to those who are oppressed because of their faith in Christ.

Lord, show me how I can use my freedom to help your imprisoned followers around the world. Guide me into actions—sending food, calling ambassadors, writing letters, creating a Web site, organizing my church—that will honor your command to care for all members of the body of Christ.

THE GIFT OF MUSIC

TO READ: JOB 35:9-11

No one says, "Where is God my Maker, who gives songs in the night . . . ?"
Job 35:10

When George went shopping for CDs, he was greeted at the store by a life-sized cutout of a beautiful young singer wearing a tight-fitting, low-cut dress. The size and placement of the cutout made it hard for George not to look at it. Since he knew that the singer was all of sixteen, George left without buying anything.

Sadly, this kind of marketing is all too common in the pop music field—but George was not shopping for popular music. He was in the *classical* section of the record store.

Instead of baring their souls for the sake of music, classical artists have taken to baring their skin for the sake of sales. Plunging necklines and even partial nudity have become common on classical CD covers.

Patrick Kavanaugh, the artistic director of the MasterWorks Festival, wonders "why so many brilliant classical musicians have stooped to disrobing in order to sell Bach partitas." Case in point: violinist Lara St. John. The cover of her 1996 recording, *Bach: Works for Solo Violin,* featured St. John naked, with only "her strategically placed violin to cover her."

While the cover created a ruckus, the CD sold "phenomenally well for a classical recording" and set a precedent that other record companies were prepared to follow.

This "sex sells" approach diminishes and demeans the music. As John Kasica of the St. Louis Symphony told Kavanaugh, this approach "draws all your attention to the performers rather than to the music." It takes "away from the depth of the music itself" and turns artistry into, at best, a secondary concern.

This type of marketing diminishes the music in another way, as well. Violinist Lisa-Beth Lambert, of the Philadelphia Orchestra, says that selling a "spiritually uplifting product" through such "degrading means" is "incongruent."

She's right. Names like Bach, Beethoven, and Mozart are rightly regarded as synonymous with "genius." Their output represents highwater marks of Western civilization.

What Lambert calls the music's "spiritual uplift" is a function of how, in the creation of great art, man reflects his own creation in the image of God.

Great music provides us with a glimpse of transcendence. As the writer of Job notes, music is a gift from God. This is why the Bach violin works that St. John plays were signed with the letters *SDG—soli Deo gloria*—by their composer. It was a recognition that his music was a creative gift of the God who "gives songs in the night."

Christians should be outraged by vulgar musical marketing, not only because it's another example of our culture's obsession with sex, but also because it illustrates our culture's inability to recognize what's worthwhile, trading the exhilaration of great music for the titillation of plunging necklines.

Lord, help me to care enough about my culture to reject any product that turns your gift of sexuality into a crass marketing tool. Lead me to examine my life and my purchases to determine whether I am recognizing and supporting what is good and godly—or what is cheap and tawdry.

THE CHRISTIANITY
OF WESTERN ART

TO READ: 1 KINGS 7:13-24, 45

Huram was highly skilled and experienced in all kinds of bronze work. | Kings 7:14

Not long ago one of the hottest tickets in New York was for an exhibit of 118 drawings by Leonardo da Vinci, whom the *New York Times* calls "the Great Oz of European art."

The exhibit, according to the *Times,* offered "an organic picture of the history of one man's polymathic life." The term *polymathic* refers to da Vinci's wide range of interests: anatomy, geometry, mapmaking, architecture, and science.

All of these were on display in the paintings. But there was another equally important subject on display, one whose significance seemed to elude critics and commentators: da Vinci's Christianity. Many of the drawings have Christian themes and imagery. One drawing is of St. Peter. Another is titled *Adoration of the Magi.* Several drawings depict the Madonna and Child.

Da Vinci's personal life remains a mystery. But that has not stopped people from speculating on everything from his sexual orientation to the impact of his being left-handed. Yet, there was almost nothing in the exhibit on what role, if any, da Vinci's religion may have played in his artistic vision.

This omission is far from unusual. Christianity's role in the development of Western art is rarely, if ever, mentioned by art elites. This is especially maddening since, as Bryan Appleyard of the London *Times* has written, "Western art was Christian, is Christian, and, for the foreseeable future, can only be Christian." The messages and images contained within the Gospels, he writes, "determined the way we think [and] the way we create."

Neil McGregor, director of Britain's National Gallery, agrees. "All Western art flows from Christianity.... It is the fundamental element of Western culture."

This relationship is most obvious in works with explicitly Christian themes. Yet even here, critics rarely make the connection.

This reluctance to acknowledge the Christian content of Western art is not new. For most of the past century, art critics, who were secular in orientation, "[re-wrote] art history as the development of pictorial method," what Appleyard calls the "heresy of formalism."

This heresy is still with us. The result is that Christianity's cultural contributions are ignored, even air-brushed out of history.

Christians ought to learn about these contributions and help others appreciate them—contributions that helped make Western society great. We ought to point out the great trouble God went to in order to ensure that his temple reflected his glory—using the best craftsmen and artists available, and directing that the best materials—gold and silver, cedar and olive wood—be used.

And we ought, as well, to actively support modern artists who work to glorify God by directing art lovers to the heavenly Artist, from whom spring their gifts.

Father, show me how I might support Christian artists struggling to learn their craft. Teach me to appreciate works of art created by painters, sculptors, and stained-glass makers who wish to worship you through the work of their hands.

JUNE 24

THE MYTH OF MORAL NEUTRALITY

TO READ: 1 TIMOTHY 6:3-5

If anyone teaches false doctrines . . . he is conceited and understands nothing.
1 Timothy 6:3-4

Relativists believe they've discovered the ultimate weapon against the sense of right and wrong: the accusation of "intolerance."

If you think public officials should tell the truth, you're "intolerant and judgmental." If you say man cannot live without God, you're "intolerant and arrogant." If you believe that marriage means one man and one woman, you are "intolerant and prejudiced."

Like a powerful acid, the accusation of intolerance eats away at traditional morality. It seems that in today's culture the only way to be tolerant is to be morally "neutral"—to avoid moral judgments altogether and let everything slide.

University of Texas Professor Jay Budziszewski sets forth the ultimate defense against the relativist's ultimate weapon: the power of logic. Those who shout "intolerance" are abusing the word in three ways, he says—and all three are logical fallacies.

The first of these, what Budziszewski calls the "Let-it-Be" Fallacy, is that tolerance just means tolerating: the more you tolerate, the more tolerant you are. But logically that can't be true; if it were, you would have to tolerate even intolerance.

According to the "Skeptical" Fallacy, having convictions about right and wrong is intolerant, so the more you doubt, the more tolerant you are. But that can't be true either, because if it were, it would be wrong to hold the conviction that tolerance is good.

According to the "Apologetic" Fallacy, speaking out about your convictions is the most intolerant you can be, so the more timid you are, the more tolerant you are. But this mistake is silly too, because if it were true, you would be too timid to speak out even about the importance of being tolerant.

Clearly, the relativist's idea of "moral neutrality" contradicts itself at every point. So why do we constantly hear the accusation of intolerance?

The accusation is applied selectively as a way to demoralize Christians and other defenders of traditional morality. Accusers, too, make judgments about right and wrong; it's just that their moral judgments are the only ones they want people to be able to make. They judge that public officials don't have to be honest, that people can live without God, and that the definition of marriage isn't limited to a relationship between a man and a woman.

We need to know that it isn't intolerant to make moral judgments, because we have to make judgments just to know what to tolerate.

We need to pray for wisdom and courage when we are attacked by those whose true goal is not tolerance but the shutting down of any talk of the biblical truth they hate.

True tolerance is not a total lack of judgment. It's knowing what should be tolerated—and refusing to tolerate what we shouldn't.

Lord, when I encounter those who hate your truth, remind me that the real enemies are "spiritual hosts of wickedness," not humans whose depraved minds have been "robbed of the truth." Give me, I pray, the courage to publicly counter their claims and the willingness to privately share both your truth and your love.

PREACHING "SERMONS IN STONE"

TO READ: 1 CHRONICLES 22:1-5

David said, "My son Solomon is young and inexperienced, and the house to be built for the Lord should be of great magnificence and fame and splendor in the sight of all the nations." I Chronicles 22:5

In the spring of 2003, officials announced the winner of the competition to design a replacement for the World Trade Center and the accompanying memorial. At the heart of architect Daniel Libeskind's plans is a 1,776-foot spire, one of several glass towers surrounding an excavated pit that serves as a memorial to those who died in the attacks.

In addition, there are two ground-level parks. One is positioned in such a way that every September 11 a wedge of light falls on it "from the time that the first plane hit the Trade Center's north tower until the time that tower fell."

The *Post* praised the way the plans balance "the competing claims of past, present, and future." Other critics went beyond the aesthetics.

As the *Times* put it, some critics see in the "vast emptiness of the pit" a confirmation of the "1960's counterculture thesis that only by personal experience can one ever really know the world." Others call the design "anti-authoritarian" and a "[rejection] of dogma."

This is worldview language. Yet few of us pay much attention to the buildings in which we live, work, or even worship. That is unfortunate, because architecture is more than a matter of concrete and steel; it also embodies ideals and values.

The clearest examples of this are the great medieval cathedrals. As one architect writes, "The cathedral was literally an image of heaven."

Its proportions and its geometric ratios were "imitations of the ultimate harmony that the blessed will enjoy in the world to come."

A counter-example is modernist glass-and-steel boxes like the old World Trade Center that took the saying "form follows function" to an inhumane degree. This reflects a worldview that was the product of Enlightenment rationalism. Buildings were "machines" in which to live and work and were stripped of any human or spiritual aspect.

Unfortunately, even church buildings fell into this modernist trap. They became like school auditoriums or gymnasiums. "Form follows function" meant emphasizing acoustics and rapid egress over theology and aesthetics—a thoroughly utilitarian worldview.

Many churches would argue that they can't afford anything else. But the medieval idea of "sermons in stone" was not limited to cathedrals. Even the smaller parish churches, many of which are still standing, testified to the builders' beliefs.

Will ours? When we build new sanctuaries, do we insist that their designs honor and reflect the Architect of the Universe—the God who created a world of quite unnecessary beauty?

If we don't, our architectural horrors may ultimately affect our faith. As Winston Churchill once said, "We define our buildings, and our buildings define us."

Exactly so.

Lord, may I not be blind to the splendor of your creation, nor of the need to glorify your grandeur in creations of my own. Help me to remember that architectural ugliness dishonors both you and the creative gifts you give us—and that the form our church buildings should follow is not unsightly utilitarian function but fervent appreciation for the God of beauty.

SURRENDERING TO SACRIFICE

TO READ: JOHN 15:1-14

Greater love has no one than this, that he lay down his life for his friends. John 15:13

In an Army recruiting ad, a young soldier is running alone across the desert. He says, "Even though there are 1,045,690 soldiers just like me, I am my own force. . . . And I'll be the first to tell you, the might of the U.S. Army doesn't lie in numbers. It lies in me. I am an Army of one."

The type of radical individualism promoted in this ad undermines two essential military principles: a unit's cohesion and its willingness to follow strong leaders into combat. So why did the army suddenly decide to promote this vision of the self-centered soldier?

Since 1995 the army has fallen short of its recruiting goals three times and barely met them three others. Army officials recognized that the situation demanded a change in the way the army communicates with young people.

Linda Wolf, head of the agency that created the campaign, explains that the ad is aimed at young adults "who don't like being told what to do. They really want to be in control. They really want to make the decisions themselves. And the whole idea of 'an Army of One' does just that."

Unfortunately, the change of direction this ad illustrates also reveals the army's embrace of an aspect of today's dominant secular worldview, which exalts radical, personal autonomy as the ultimate goal of life. By embracing the same kinds of self-gratifying, narcissistic appeals as popular culture, the army is promoting military service as an expression of personal freedom.

In marked contrast, the Marine Corps still promotes what retired General Charles Krulak calls "the qualities America holds dear: honor, courage, commitment." In the late nineties, in the midst of great recruiting shortages, then-Commandant Krulak actually raised recruiting standards and toughened physical-training requirements. He refused to integrate men's and women's training programs or barracks. And in spite of—or perhaps because of—this tough approach, the Marine Corps achieved all its recruiting goals.

General Krulak said it best: The Marines "recognize what Generation X and Generation Next want and haven't been getting. They want standards. Instead of softening up, we tightened up," he said.

Krulak is right. Marine recruiters recognized our need to be part of something bigger than ourselves. This is true for civilians, as well. We all need to be aware of cultural messages that urge us to embrace radical autonomy and an attitude of self-centeredness. We must instead be willing to live and work cooperatively and, at times, sacrificially with others—family and colleagues, church and community—or for fellow soldiers in battle. How else can we obey Christ's command to love one another?

When it comes to soldiers in foxholes or civilians in office parks, arrogance and ego do not hold us together. Rather, we need to embrace a commitment to one another and a regard for the common good.

Father, help me to resist the temptation to be a spiritual lone wolf. Teach me to embrace not self-centeredness but self-sacrifice, and surrender not to personal sovereignty but to the service of others.

THE GOD WHO
INVENTED TIME

TO READ: GENESIS 12:1-9

The Lord had said to Abram, "Leave your country, your people and your father's household and go to the land I will show you." Genesis 12:1

Imagine a world where the calendar marks months but not years. There could be seasons, but no sense of past, present, or future—just an endless succession of days.

That's exactly what the world was like until God spoke to Abraham, a Sumerian living four thousand years ago in what is now Iraq. In *The Gifts of the Jews: How a Tribe of Desert Nomads Changed the Way Everyone Thinks and Feels*, historian Thomas Cahill writes that when God called Abraham out of Sumeria, he also called the whole world into time and history.

According to Cahill, many things we take for granted—our concept of time, progress, history, and even our notion of what it means to be human—we owe to the Jews and to the God of the Bible.

Before Abraham the world had no concept of history as we think of it. Everything was just part of the great circle of the seasons, never changing or progressing. The idea of progress from past to future did not exist.

Cahill writes that "thumbnail sketches of each [king's] reign are arranged . . . without the least regard for what may in fact have occurred in Sumerian history." Some kings were said to have ruled for hundreds of years—others for thousands!

When Moses wrote Genesis, it was the first time anyone had written a history that included a true sense of time and accurate dates. The Old Testament writings represent the first attempt to get facts, genealogies, and chronologies right—in short, history as we know it today.

Similarly, the story of Abraham's journey, being called from Sumeria to the Promised Land, represented a pronounced break with the familiar, cyclical mindset. Abraham was called by God to leave his home and go to a strange place. God told him that he would raise from Abraham's seed a great nation. Cahill says the concept of a distant, unseen future and a personal or national destiny was unheard of prior to this time.

For Christians, the idea of history and time is especially important. God's promises to Abraham articulate our great hope in the anticipation of "the fullness of time."

Cahill doesn't believe the Bible to be the Word of God. But the central tenet of his work is right on track. Much of what we take for granted today actually began when the God of the Bible spoke to a wandering Jew named Abraham.

Thank you, Father, for the witness of secular historians whose work reinforces the truth offered through your Word.

DEFECTIVE DATING ATTITUDES

TO READ: 1 THESSALONIANS 4:1-8

It is God's will that you should be sanctified: that you should avoid sexual immorality. I Thessalonians 4:3

Eric and Jenny were Christian kids who started out going to the movies together or playing a round of putt-putt golf. But the longer they dated, the more intimate they became until, finally, they began sleeping together.

After they broke up, the pain lasted for years.

Their story is told in a book by Joshua Harris called *I Kissed Dating Goodbye.* "Eric and Jenny probably had good intentions," Harris writes. "But they founded their relationship on our culture's defective attitudes and patterns for romance." These attitudes lead to what Joshua calls "The Seven Habits of Highly Defective Dating."

First, he says, dating leads to intimacy but not necessarily to commitment. When something happens to break the couple up—such as one member departing for college—the other partner may be devastated. "Dating encourages intimacy for the sake of intimacy—two people getting close . . . without any real intention of making a long-term commitment," Harris says.

Second, dating tends to skip the "friendship" stage of a relationship. Dating tends "to move a guy and a girl beyond friendship and towards romance too quickly."

Third, dating teens often mistake physical passion for love. Passion can distort one's perspective and lead to unwise choices.

Fourth, dating isolates couples from other relationships. Young

357

couples think nothing of sacrificing other friendships, family time, and church activities.

Fifth, dating distracts teens from their main responsibility: to prepare for the future. Maintaining a relationship takes a lot of time and energy—time that is often stolen from developing gifts, going on summer mission trips, or preparing for college.

Sixth, dating can cause discontent with God's gift of singleness. Singleness is a season of our lives in which we have tremendous opportunities for growth, learning, and service. But if we spend all that time dating one person after another, we miss its blessings.

Seventh, dating creates an artificial environment for evaluating someone's character. As James Dobson puts it, dating is designed to *hide* our flaws, not expose them. That's why young people ought to get to know each other "in the real-life settings of family and friends," says Harris.

Harris might well be on to something. If you are dating, Harris's advice is worth serious consideration. If you're a youth leader, read Harris's book, and ask the teens in your church to do something unthinkable: to take a different view of dating. Encourage kids to go out in groups, to focus on bearing one another's burdens and lifting up one another in prayer.

This way, they'll avoid the pitfalls of early dating and prepare themselves for the greatest romantic adventure of all—a happy and lasting marriage.

Lord, I pray that you will give me a passion for purity in all my relationships. Help me to recognize and avoid all situations that lead to sexual temptation. Teach me to be willing to put the good of others ahead of my own desires, living up to the holy standards to which you call us.

JUNE 29

UPHOLDING "EMPHATIC NOTIONS" OF RIGHT AND WRONG

TO READ: ROMANS 3:20-26

Through the law we become conscious of sin. Romans 3:20

In Georgia a controversy raged over whether the Augusta National Golf Club should be forced to accept women members; editorials denounced the club's insistence on the right of free association.

In Colorado the wife of a shop owner handed a brochure to an employee describing religious programs that help homosexuals leave the gay lifestyle. For this expression of her religious beliefs, the woman was forced, under local gay-rights laws, to undergo "counseling."

It seems that when it comes to sexual privacy, no one is allowed to pass judgment on others. It's a different story when it comes to other kinds of privacy rights—like the right of freedom of association or religious expression.

Moral philosopher Hadley Arkes says this state of affairs came about through the loss of understanding of natural law and thus, of natural rights.

In *Natural Rights and the Right to Choose,* Arkes notes that natural rights are the rights that are the same in all places and at all times. America's founders referred to natural rights as "self-evident truths." They knew that laws that ignored natural rights were unjust.

Today, secular scholars are hostile toward any notion of moral truths that are binding on all people. Instead, they suggest that we have nothing more than opinions about right and wrong. Humans have no fixed nature, they claim, and thus settled rights cannot arise from that nature.

The founders argued that the purpose of government is to secure the rights we already possess by nature and that God has given to us. Today, writes Arkes, secular scholars insist that we would be better off if politicians abandoned "fables about our natures, and such emphatic notions of right and wrong."

But if the Constitution really is based on truth, then we can't somehow "advance" beyond it. Attempts to do so will inevitably lead to tyranny. For instance, in 1973, the Supreme Court discovered a Constitutional "right to privacy." This "right" has enabled judges to overturn laws in the name of a whole new array of rights—including the right to partial-birth abortion.

But without a transcendent standard, there is no consistency. Private corporations and clubs are attacked for daring to define their own character. But in the name of an alleged right to sexual privacy, the law is used as a sledgehammer to punish people who criticize the sexual behavior of others.

Christians must understand how the denial of the logic of natural rights threatens not only our rights to free speech and religious practice but the right to life itself.

We must ask ourselves, as well, if we are ever tempted to ignore God's law when we disagree with it—as many judges do—or worse, privately exchange God's commands for our own.

Lord, open my eyes to the arguments of many—including some who write or interpret our laws—that have already begun to lead us down the path to tyranny. Put in my heart a love of your laws and a fervent willingness to obey every one of them.

THE GOSPEL ACCORDING TO TOLKIEN

TO READ: 2 CORINTHIANS 12:5-10

My grace is sufficient for you, for my power is made perfect in weakness.
2 Corinthians 12:9

The worldwide popularity of the Lord of the Rings films reminds us of the captivating power of a well-told story. The response to this particular story is especially encouraging and reveals that even in a world steeped in moral relativism, people still hunger for tales of the absolutes: the triumph of good over evil.

Some people view Tolkien's tale of wizards, hobbits, and elves as escapism for those fleeing reality. But in *The Gospel according to Tolkien,* Ralph Wood argues that The Lord of the Rings actually helps us to "escape into reality."

Wood points out that, far from being a shiny, happy escape fantasy, The Lord of the Rings deals effectively and movingly with subjects such as death, war, tyranny, temptation, hopelessness, and the sinfulness of human nature. "Far from encouraging us to turn away from such evils," Wood notes, Tolkien "forces us to confront them. Rather than grinding our faces in these horrors, however, it suggests a cure for the ills of our age."

That's because Tolkien's work, though not explicitly Christian, is grounded in his Christian understanding of the world. While The Lord of the Rings depicts evil as horrifyingly real, it also shows the power and strength of goodness. The heroic actions of small, ordinary creatures against a huge, overwhelming threat echo the biblical themes of God's strength being made perfect in weakness and the last becoming first. As Tolkien wrote elsewhere, a crucial theme in his work is "the ennoblement [or sanctification] of the humble." At the same time, as characters struggle against their own personal temptations, they show the weakness and fallibility of the human heart and our need for guidance and grace.

C. S. Lewis wrote of The Lord of the Rings, "As we read we find ourselves sharing [the characters'] burden; when we have finished, we return to our own life not relaxed but fortified." Lewis and Tolkien knew, and Ralph Wood reminds us in his book, Christians ought to encourage a certain kind of escapism; that is, the escape from a narrow, earthbound view of our own circumstances. This form of escapism helps us to look at the bigger picture and understand the eternal moral truths governing our lives.

Tolkien's books and, now, the films, are giving people a whole new perspective on reality—a perspective that prepares them for a better understanding of the God who is ultimate reality.

Why not invite a skeptical friend to watch one or all of the three The Lord of the Rings films with you? Discuss with the issues afterward over coffee. And later, when you're alone, spend some time musing over your own "thorns in the flesh," as Paul described them, and how, through dependence on Christ, they can be used for God's glory.

Lord, let me see my weaknesses not as sources of frustration but as opportunities to throw myself wholeheartedly on your strength. Teach me to find ways of escaping the limitations of my earthbound perspective in order to more fully comprehend eternal realities.

SIN AND REDEMPTION IN SCIENCE FICTION

TO READ: REVELATION 19:17-21

The beast was captured, and with him the false prophet who had performed the miraculous signs on his behalf. Revelation 19:20

If you want to get depressed in a hurry, watch science-fiction films.

Think of *Blade Runner,* the definitive science-fiction film of our time. It portrays Los Angeles as a decayed ruin populated by swarms of wretches who speak an unintelligible street dialect. Announcements urge people to flee the wreckage of civilization by settling on other planets.

In theological terms the vision of the world one often gets from sci-fi films such as this is of one devastated by human sin but without any hope of redemption: It's existential despair.

We see this same grim vision of the future in *The Matrix* and the Terminator films, where human folly and hubris have destroyed civilization and led to mankind's enslavement and possible extinction. Other science-fiction/fantasy films, such as *The Crow* and *Strange Days,* depict a world where chaos, not order, is the rule. Human civilization is an out-of-control dystopia, with zombielike people escaping into drugs and virtual-reality games.

On the surface the worldview of many sci-fi films resembles a Christian one. The characters' predicament isn't purely the product of some malevolent force. Instead, it's the tragic consequence of willful human action: in effect, a punishment for sins.

But the similarity is only superficial. As Thomas Hibbs of Boston College writes, this is nihilism, not Christianity. While the films see "violence and ineradicable guilt as the underlying truth about the human condition," they're missing a belief in Providence: the idea that there is a God who "sustains, nourishes, and cares for everything He has made."

This lack makes sense when you recall how naturalism—the belief that nature is all there is—permeates science fiction. Without God, redemption is not an option.

Instead of heroes acting on Providence's behalf, we are left with protagonists who are scarcely more sympathetic than the films' bad guys or who are like the cop in *Blade Runner*, described as a "one-man slaughterhouse."

What's more, in these films the forces of evil and darkness are almost never defeated decisively. Part of this, of course, is deliberate to allow for sequels. But it's also because in a world without Providence, evil can never be decisively defeated.

Given the popularity of science fiction, it's important to understand the worldviews at work in these films and to help our kids contrast them with Christian doctrines of sin and redemption. If we do, they and we will realize that our future isn't nearly as depressing as it might seem when we go to the movies.

Lord, I pray that I will not be overly influenced by the dark portrayals of the future I see on film—or in the news and in books. If I find myself growing depressed over depictions of impending horrors, remind me to return to your words of hope: that you will one day destroy all evil and lead the faithful into a joyful eternity.

JULY 2

DEVELOPING A PASSION
FOR PURITY

TO READ: PSALM 119:1-16

How can a young man keep his way pure? By living according to your word.
Psalm 119:9

How many people think it's their job to guard other people's purity? Joshua Harris, the author of *I Kissed Dating Goodbye,* thinks it's everyone's job.

Most Christians claim they desire purity in their relationships, but, Harris asks, "do we live the kind of lives that foster this purity?"

Many teens think they're pure enough if they refrain from going "all the way." But that's not good enough, says Harris. True purity is not some point on a sexual scale. It's "a direction, a persistent, determined pursuit of righteousness."

We cannot simultaneously explore the boundaries of purity—getting as close to the sexual edge as possible—and also pursue righteousness. That's why Harris advises teens against "dating": They struggle against their desire to be physically intimate. The longer they date, the stronger the desire becomes.

If we really want purity, he says, we have to change both our attitudes and our lifestyles. The secular world says it's okay to fool around, to "try out" people emotionally and sexually. But God says to guard the sacredness of sexual intimacy between husband and wife—and that means before marriage as well as after.

You may be thinking, *One little kiss can't possibly do any harm.* But look at it this way: Harris writes that God designed sex "to end in full consummation. . . . Physical interaction encourages us to start something we're not supposed to finish. It awakens desires we're not allowed to consummate, turning on passions we have to turn off."

And that's why, he says, "I avoid one-on-one dating. . . . It encourages physical intimacy and places me in an isolated setting with a girl."

"Can't I handle it?" Harris asks. "Yeah, maybe I could . . . but that's not the point. I won't stick around to see how much temptation I can take."

Harris urges teens to adopt a lifestyle that promotes purity instead of threatening it. Young men "need to stop acting like 'hunters' trying to catch girls and begin seeing [themselves] as warriors standing guard over them," he says. And young women must not, by actions, words, or choice of clothing, deliberately stir up lusts in their brothers in Christ.

I Kissed Dating Goodbye offers insights into a Christian view of sex and dating. Those who read it—young men and women alike—will increase their chances of "keeping their way pure" while they are single and also increase the odds of finding happiness in marriage.

Father, give me the desire to pursue your righteousness more than members of the opposite sex. Help me to desire to be not merely "pure enough" but someone who passionately seeks purity with all my heart.

JULY 3

LITERARY STEPS
TOWARD GOD

TO READ: LUKE 15:11-32

This brother of yours was dead and is alive again; he was lost and is found.
Luke 15:32

In the mid-1990s in Iran, Professor Azar Nafisi committed an act of subversion against the oppressive Islamic regime: She started a reading group.

As Nafisi recounts in *Reading* Lolita *in Tehran,* after being driven out of the university where she had taught literature for many years, she began to teach female students in her home. For two years the women met weekly to read and discuss "forbidden" Western classics such as *The Great Gatsby, Pride and Prejudice,* and the novels of Henry James and Vladimir Nabokov.

Nafisi writes, "The novels were an escape from reality in the sense that we could marvel at their beauty and perfection, and leave aside our stories about the deans and the university and the morality squads in the streets. . . . Curiously, the novels we escaped into led us finally to question and prod our own realities, about which we felt so helplessly speechless."

These books brought the real world to them and helped them gain insight and perspective. In particular, reading taught these women the virtue of empathy. If the chief sin of their oppressors was to judge people unfairly, Nafisi argues, the study of literature was a safeguard against falling into the same trap. As she told her university class, "A good novel is one that shows the complexity of individuals. . . . Empathy lies at the heart of *Gatsby,* like so many other great novels—the biggest sin is to be blind to others' problems and pains. Not seeing them means denying their existence."

Nafisi's compelling story illustrates one of the reasons we need art and literature in our lives. C. S. Lewis made much the same point in his essay "Christianity and Culture." Lewis wrote that culture may teach us truths about the world that point us toward the God of all truth. "Culture," he wrote, "is a storehouse of the best (sub-Christian) values." While these values cannot by themselves save anyone, Lewis noted, they *can* help us reach a greater understanding of what salvation is, why we need it, and how to find it. Many stories from the Bible—such as the Parable of the Lost Son—serve the same purpose: They point to our need to repent.

The arts can never be a substitute for faith, but they can guide us more deeply into faith.

If you have friends who are resistant to the gospel, be subversive: Give them a great novel. Even better, start a book club and invite your unsaved friends to join. Books can reach people whom a conventional presentation of the gospel may never reach—including members of a secret reading group in Tehran.

Father, I marvel at the tenacity of the human spirit—of the desire, even under desperate circumstances, to seek the truth about reality. Give me, I pray, the imagination to reach out to my own neighbors for you through art, music, or literature that creatively points to the God of all truth.

JULY 4

CHRISTIAN PATRIOTISM

TO READ: PSALM 122:1-9

Pray for the peace of Jerusalem: "May those who love you be secure." Psalm 122:6

Every Fourth of July, Coney Island hosts a hot dog–eating contest. Contestants gather from around the country to prove that they can stuff themselves with more hot dogs in twelve minutes than anyone else.

It seems that downing hot dogs and lemonade is the quintessential American way of expressing patriotism on the Fourth of July: Family picnics and fireworks celebrate the founding of our country.

Augustine would tell you that is exactly the right way to express patriotism. No, he didn't write about the finer points of American hot-dog eating; he said the best way to develop patriotism is by loving your own family.

Christians are commanded to love the whole world. But that's utterly impractical. No finite human being could possibly love every other person in the world. So God has placed us in concrete relationships where we can learn to love. As Augustine puts it, it's as though God had cast lots and assigned each one of us to a particular family, a particular church, and a particular country.

We cannot love the whole world, but we can love the particular people in the relationships where God has placed us—moving outward from family to church, community, and nation, in an ever widening circle.

That's how Christian patriotism is built.

It's easy to love people in the abstract. It's much harder to love the real flesh-and-blood people we interact with in our families, churches, and communities.

C. S. Lewis explained that we are constantly tempted to love only what is lovable—to love our wives only when they're kind and beautiful, to love our husbands only when they're successful, to love our children only when they're pleasant. But that's not the way God loves. God loves us even when we're unlovable—just because he has chosen us to be his people—and he commands us to do the same.

We're to love our families even when they're unlovable—just because they're ours. We're to love the church—just because we belong to one another as the family of God. And we're to love our country— not because it's the best and most democratic country in the world (which it may not be at times) but because it's the place God has put us. That's tough love of country: being utterly honest about our nation's flaws and shortcomings, and yet still continuing to love it. We must pray for the peace and security of our country, just as David did for Jerusalem.

When we gather together with our families and relatives on the Fourth of July and renew our bonds of love with them, we should remember that we are practicing, at its most basic level, true patriotism.

Lord, let me not long to be a member of another family, another church, or another land. Teach me to love the members of my own family, my own church, and my own country, remembering that you placed me among them for a reason.

JULY 5

LEARNING GRATITUDE

TO READ: MARK 6:34-44

Taking the five loaves and the two fish and looking up to heaven, he gave thanks.
Mark 6:41

Have you ever thought about what life was like for your great-grand-parents? If you have, you would probably agree with Gregg Easterbrook, of the Brookings Institution, that our ancestors would consider the world we live in today to be a kind of utopia.

Yet all of the progress we enjoy hasn't made Americans any happier. In fact, the opposite is true—it has made us more unhappy.

In *The Progress Paradox: How Life Gets Better While People Feel Worse,* Easterbrook says the average Westerner lives better than 99.4 percent of all the human beings who have ever lived. Life expectancy has nearly doubled in the past century and continues to increase. Real per capita income has doubled since 1960.

In the period following World War II, the average new American home was eleven hundred square feet; today it's twenty-three hundred. For most of our history the average home had one room for every two people; today there are two rooms for every one person.

By any measure of affluence—health care, leisure, technology—the average American enjoys a quality of life beyond anyone's wildest dreams even a few decades ago. But the percentage of Americans who characterize themselves as "happy" hasn't changed since the 1950s, and the percentage of those describing themselves as "very happy" is down and continues to decline.

The percentage of Americans and Europeans who suffer a bout of depression has climbed to 25 percent and shows no signs of abating.

An estimated 7 percent of all Americans suffer at least one incidence of major, debilitating depression a year.

For some people, depression is the product of genetic and other biological factors. But for many others, being depressed in the midst of unprecedented prosperity can be traced to spiritual, cultural, and moral factors. For the former, medical treatment is indicated. For the latter, what's needed is a change in worldview.

A good place to start is with a sense of gratitude. As Easterbrook notes, the Roman orator Cicero called gratitude not only the "greatest of virtues, but the parent of all others." Similarly, the philosopher Immanuel Kant called ingratitude the "essence of vileness."

How often do you think about—and thank God for—the manner in which you live? Many of us thank him for simple meals, as Jesus did. But do you also thank him for being able to live a lifestyle that would be, to someone of Jesus' day, one of spectacular abundance?

Knowing that we are better off than nearly every other human who has ever lived should inspire daily prayers of thanksgiving. And it should prompt us to generosity rather than to a desire for more.

Lord, I live in a culture that tells me I never have enough. Help me to remember how little I actually need and how much I have to be grateful for. Give me a spirit of generosity for those around the world who lack even the life-sustaining basics: bread and water and a roof over their heads.

MODERN PAGANISM

TO READ: LEVITICUS 20:1-5

Any Israelite . . . who gives any of his children to Molech must be put to death.
Leviticus 20:2

When you hear the word *pagan,* what springs to mind? Do you think of ancient tree worshippers dancing by moonlight?

An authority on the subject says that notion is out of date. These days, says Dr. Robert George of Princeton University, the term *pagan* ought to conjure up images of affluent, well-educated Americans—including many who go to church.

Paganism, George says, is not confined to the past, with primitive peoples offering sacrifices to the sun or praying to golden calves. Instead, the temptation to worship false gods is "a permanent threat" and "a constant temptation."

The essence of paganism is idolatry—the worship of false gods in place of the one true God. But the sad fact is that many modern Christians fall into pagan practices and don't even know it, and some attend churches that actually promote it.

How do you know if you're among them? There's a foolproof test, George says: "False gods demand the blood of innocents. Where the innocent and just are slain . . . the god being worshipped is not the God of Israel." When Christians of the past burned heretics, persecuted Jews, and enslaved Africans, they were serving not the biblical God but false gods.

The false gods of modern pagans are even more bloodthirsty. "Today," George says, "the unborn, the partially born, and the handicapped newly-born are . . . sacrificed to the false gods of choice, autonomy, and liberation. They're sacrificed on stainless steel altars, by priests robed in surgical whites." And advocates of assisted suicide and euthanasia are often their fellow believers.

By contrast, George notes, faithful Christians and observant Jews worship the Lord of life—the God who "endows every human being—however humble, however poor, however afflicted—with a sublime dignity." It is for this reason "that the life of every innocent person is . . . equally inviolable under the moral law."

Modern pagans—including most secularized Christians and Jews—wrap their pagan ideology in a cloak of virtue. They speak of compassion even as they rationalize their "choice" to kill the innocent. In reality, they're worshipping not the God of compassion but false gods of depravity and death.

The sobering question we must ask ourselves is, *What God do we really worship: the biblical God and all he requires or a pagan god who demands the blood of innocents?*

It is a fact of history that every civilization that has sacrificed children to the gods has been destroyed. The God of the Bible has brought judgment on even the most powerful empires.

Today's false gods masquerade under the names of "choice" and "compromise." But as Professor George notes, "A pagan culture is . . . a culture of death."

Father, may I never slide into pagan beliefs and practices unawares. Teach me to see through sophisticated rhetoric that calls evil good—and demands the blood of innocents at the altar of autonomy.

IN SICKNESS AND
IN HEALTH

TO READ: 1 CORINTHIANS 7:10-16

To the married I give this command (not I, but the Lord): A wife must not separate from her husband. . . . And a husband must not divorce his wife. 1 Corinthians 7:10-11

Forty years ago a study called the Hammond Report analyzed the smoking habits of half a million people. It concluded that smoking is dangerous to one's health. That warning ended up on every pack of cigarettes sold. Ten years later a researcher took another look at the Hammond Report and found something that had been overlooked—something just as hazardous as a pack-a-day cigarette habit: divorce.

As Linda Waite and Maggie Gallagher write in *The Case for Marriage*, an enterprising surgeon general might wish to slap divorce decrees with a warning label that reads, "Not being married can be hazardous to your health." Research is proving that those who get—and stay—married can count on much better health than those who don't.

How much better? Waite and Gallagher found that divorced, single, and widowed people are "far more likely to die from all causes," including heart disease, stroke, car accidents, murder, and suicide. As for cancer, being married dramatically increases the odds of survival. "Even sick people who marry live longer than their counterparts who don't," they write.

This happens in part because when people get married, they typically adopt a healthier lifestyle. Men especially give up what Waite and Gallagher call "stupid bachelor tricks." They give up drinking and driving, fighting at bars, and abusing drugs, they say. Wives not only discourage such behavior, they also improve their husband's health by cooking healthful meals, encouraging regular sleep, and scheduling doctor appointments for them.

Nagging, of course, can be irritating, but it works an important benefit in marriage. Husbands can improve their wives' lives, for example, by encouraging them to give up smoking and to get regular exercise. The emotional support a spouse can supply means that spouses recover more quickly when illness strikes, and this emotional support boosts the immune system. Recent divorce, on the other hand, is known to lower immune functioning.

Even monogamous marital sex can help couples ward off illness. These health benefits come about because marriage seems "to provide individuals with a sense of meaning in their lives," according to Waite and Gallagher. A wife feels licensed to nag in a way that a girlfriend doesn't, precisely because both husband and wife know their lives are intertwined.

Once again, scientific evidence is backing up biblical truth. This is wisdom we ought to share with our friends, especially those who are thinking of cohabitation or divorce. They need to know that anything other than faithful, loving marriage can be bad for their health.

If you are ever tempted to contemplate divorce, this evidence is a sobering reminder of one reason God commands us not to abandon our spouses or cheat on them. It can literally kill us.

Lord, thank you for the gift of marriage. Help me to cherish this sacred gift—appreciating, loving, and nurturing the spouse you gave me until death—not divorce—parts us.

JULY 8

PATCHING UP
BROKEN LIVES

TO READ: JAMES 2:12-26

What good is it, my brothers, if a man claims to have faith but has no deeds?
James 2:14

Jerry Bush grew up in one of the toughest housing projects in Washington, D.C. By age seventeen Jerry was pushing drugs, and it wasn't long before he was serving time.

Jerry was the kind of young man for whom the prison gate usually becomes a revolving door. But thanks to a faith-based program, Jerry ended up outside the prison gates—permanently.

Soon after his release from prison, Jerry was sitting in his front yard when a stranger approached. It was Curtis Watkins of the East Capitol Center for Change. "Would you like to turn your life around?" he asked.

Watkins invited Jerry to visit the center and see about getting a job. Although skeptical, Jerry showed up a few days later. Almost before he knew it, Jerry found himself promising to abstain from drugs and violence and to perform community service in exchange for a job.

A year later Jerry was studying to become an electrician and coaching a neighborhood football league. As he told *Insight* magazine, "These same kids used to see me doing bad stuff. Now they listen to me."

People like Jerry Bush and Curtis Watkins, who run urban ministries, are the real experts on the problems that plague the inner city—and on how to patch up broken lives.

As Joe Loconte writes in *God, Government, and the Good Samaritan,* "The problems of urban America are ravaging minority populations. Out-of-wedlock births, incarceration rates, illiteracy, unemployment—

all disproportionately affect Blacks and Hispanics. But policymakers have largely turned a blind eye . . . to the best place for help in turning things around: the Church."

Many who lead minority churches agree. A study of twelve hundred congregations revealed that nearly two-thirds of pastors from black churches were thinking of applying for government funds for social-service projects.

These numbers should surprise no one. Surveys indicate that "African-Americans are among the most religious and socially conservative groups in America," Loconte writes. "Many have built extensive social-service ministries saturated in religious instruction."

Changing people from the inside out isn't easy. Bob Woodson, founder of the National Center for Neighborhood Enterprises, says that changing people like Jerry requires "people who are in their lives twenty-four hours a day, seven days a week." It requires a willingness to make judgment calls about behavior and lifestyle choices—and to address what Woodson calls the true causes of youth violence: moral, spiritual, and social emptiness.

Christians ought to promote faith-based efforts because the real answer to our cities' needs lies in ministries that restore urban neighborhoods by reshaping human souls. And we ought to be able to give firsthand testimony to their efficacy—because we are involved in them ourselves. We cannot claim to care for the poor around us and then do nothing to meet their many needs.

Lord, no matter how busy my life is, your Word insists that I make time to help the poor. Make me willing to help them cheerfully, not just with money but also with my time, my talents—and my love.

THE LOSS OF MODESTY

TO READ: PROVERBS 11:12-23

Like a gold ring in a pig's snout is a beautiful woman who shows no discretion.
Proverbs 11:22

The *Chronicle of Higher Education* reports that "a small but growing number of women" are writing "sex-related opinion" columns in college newspapers. The subjects include health-related matters, as well as discussions of the pitfalls in relationships between men and women on college campuses.

But as the *Chronicle* notes, what draws attention to these columns isn't the "soft cuddly" pieces. No, what attracts attention are the sexually explicit ones.

One of these columns is published in the *Daily Kansan,* and as one Kansas University official put it, the paper's sex columnist, Meghan Bainum, "has no shame."

Bainum's discussion of specific sexual practices, and even personal mutilation, goes beyond frankness all the way to exhibitionism. It's easy to see why some high school principals asked the university not to send their schools the newspaper on the days that Bainum's column appears.

But Bainum is a shrinking violet compared to her counterpart at Yale, Natalie Krinsky. Some of Krinsky's material is so explicit that it borders on pornographic in its detail.

Our culture's disregard for modesty helps us understand the emergence of columns such as these. When the Kansas official talks about having no shame, he is describing a cultural attitude, not just an individual one.

In *The Repeal of Reticence,* art critic Rochelle Gurstein writes about the demise of what she calls "reticence." *Reticence,* which comes from the Latin word that means "to keep silent," is the belief that there are some areas of life that should remain private and not be subject to public inspection.

This belief governed Western culture for millennia. Then, what Gurstein calls the "party of exposure" labeled modesty, discretion, and similar behavior as the stuff of prudery and elitism. Modesty and reticence came to be regarded as something to be overcome.

The result is our "anything goes" public square, in which everything is grist for the entertainment mill. Shows like *The Osbournes* and other so-called "reality television" programs would be impossible without the triumph of exposure over reticence and modesty.

Of course, our culture has paid a price. In Gurstein's words, if something is not "mean, ugly, or indecent" in our public sphere, then it must be "inane or vacuous."

If anyone accuses you of being "too modest" or "a prude," instead of being embarrassed, you ought to be proud. It is not easy to maintain modesty in a culture that celebrates exposure. Discretion in clothing, language, and behavior is not something we ought to "get over."

When it comes to sexually explicit advice columns, we Christians need to help our neighbors understand why those columns are wrong: It's not only that their graphic nature is offensive to us but also because we know that the subject matter deserves better than co-eds talking dirty.

Lord, help me to appreciate what true modesty is in your eyes. I ask your wisdom when it comes to deciding what clothing I should wear, what behavior I should engage in, and what subjects are fitting and appropriate when I converse with others. May I value not merely the outward appearance of modesty but also purity of heart.

DO CHRISTIANS "DESERVE" PERSECUTION?

TO READ: HEBREWS 11:32-40

They were stoned; they were sawed in two; they were put to death by the sword.
Hebrews 11:37

In June 2002, Martin Burnham, an American missionary, died in a battle between his Islamic kidnappers and Filipino troops sent to rescue him. Burnham's death made him the newest member of what the *Te Deum,* an ancient hymn, calls "the white-robed army of the martyrs"—an army that, according to a recent estimate, is a staggering seventy million strong.

What's even more staggering is that according to the same estimate, 45 million, or two-thirds, of all Christian martyrs died in the twentieth century. These estimates are contained in a book titled *The New Persecuted: Inquiries into Anti-Christian Intolerance in the New Century of Martyrs,* written by Italian journalist Antonio Socci.

Socci estimates that an average of 160,000 Christians have been killed every year since 1990 in places such as Algeria, Nigeria, Sudan, and Pakistan. The "global persecution of Christianity is still in progress but in most cases is ignored by the mass media and Christians in the West," Socci asserts.

Socci's book has many critics up in arms. For writing about persecution and identifying Islamic extremism as the "main danger" to Christians worldwide, Socci has been accused of promoting anti-Islamic prejudice. Others question Socci's figures, saying that many of those he has called martyrs died in "conflicts that had little to do with religion."

Even if Socci were off by two-thirds, that still leaves fifteen million martyrs this past century, more than enough to warrant the label "persecution." How many Christians have to die before the world takes notice?

Others argue that by portraying the twentieth century as a century of massacres, Socci diminishes the significance of the Holocaust. But as Ted Olsen of *Christianity Today* notes, talking about the millions of Christians killed for their faith doesn't diminish the evil of the Holocaust any more than noting "the millions who died during Stalin's purges."

What's really bothering many of Socci's critics is the idea of Christians as victims instead of victimizers. Like commentator Tommaso Debenedetti, they see the book as part of a "right wing plot" to "deflect accusations of intolerance" away from Christians.

According to some critics, even if Christians *are* being persecuted, we had it coming. That's why Olsen is right when he asks, "How long until people start arguing that the murder of millions of Christians worldwide isn't that big a deal because of the Crusades and Inquisitions?"

For the sake of our suffering brothers and sisters, we must arouse public opinion and the power of civilized governments against all Christian persecution: the kind that prompts the killing and the kind that prompts the willingness to turn a blind eye.

Lord, the example of your first followers reminds us that those who love you have always paid a terrible and glorious price. Comfort those who have lost loved ones to persecution. Show me specific ways that I might boldly proclaim the truth about persecution despite accusations of prejudice. Thank you for the thrilling witness of those willing to die rather than betray you, and for the eternal reward you prepare for your "white-robed army."

WHY CHILDREN NEED "AUTHORITATIVE COMMUNITIES"

TO READ: DEUTERONOMY 4:1-15

Watch yourselves closely so that you do not forget the things your eyes have seen or let them slip from your heart as long as you live. Teach them to your children and to their children after them. Deuteronomy 4:9

A few years ago, James Davison Hunter wrote in *The Death of Character* that people act morally because they have learned to subordinate their own opinions and desires to the requirements of their religious communities.

The social implications of Hunter's work were clear: Weaken the "authoritative communities" that produce character, and it's harder to produce the kind of people necessary to sustain a self-governing society.

Other experts agree. One study shows that we not only *need* "authoritative communities"; we are also made to be a part of them.

The study is titled *Hardwired to Connect: The New Scientific Case for Authoritative Communities*. Jointly produced by Dartmouth Medical School, the YMCA, and the Institute for American Values, the study examines scientific data in search of an answer to the question, why, in a period of unprecedented affluence, do "large numbers of American children suffer from emotional and behavioral problems"?

The answer is that "children are hardwired for enduring connections to others and for moral and spiritual meaning." And they're not experiencing these connections because the groups and communities that best provide this "connectedness" are under stress.

The use of the word *hardwired* refers to the increasing evidence that the "mechanisms by which we become and stay attached to others" have a biological basis.

Of course, *what* our children are connected to is as important as being connected itself. The study emphasizes the role of "authoritative communities" in providing our children with "moral and spiritual meaning."

These communities—like the family and the church—are characterized by their transmission of a "shared understanding of what it means to be a good person," the establishment of "clear boundaries and limits," "teaching love of neighbor," and the encouragement of "spiritual and religious development."

Clearly, undermining "authoritative communities" like the church and the family is bad for everyone. That is why Christians must fight cultural innovations that threaten to further weaken the family. We must do what it takes to keep our own families intact and try to keep extended family in our children's lives. We should also make sure our churches are the kinds of "authoritative communities" described by the study. Do we expect members to subordinate their opinions and desires to God's "decrees and laws," as Deuteronomy puts it? Or do we, in a desire to be "seeker friendly," avoid seeming "dogmatic" at all costs? Do we undermine the health of the church community by constant church hopping?

As the study makes clear, we're not doing our kids—or "seekers"—any favors by adopting an easy approach. Instead, we should model the kind of community that promotes the well-being of both our children and our society.

Lord, help me to be willing to put a healthy connection to my communities—family, church, and neighborhood—ahead of a desire for independence and having my own way.

AVOIDING
"DECEIVING SPIRITS"

TO READ: 1 TIMOTHY 4:1-7, 16

The Spirit clearly says that in later times some will abandon the faith and follow deceiving spirits and things taught by demons. 1 Timothy 4:1

Every year more than a million people report seeing UFOs. Are these people crackpots and attention seekers? Or is there something real behind their claims?

Hugh Ross, a Christian physicist and astronomer, has studied UFO phenomena for years and has concluded that some "UFOs" are real—and dangerous.

In *Lights in the Sky and Little Green Men,* Ross says that after exposing all the frauds and natural causes, researchers "agree that there must be something real at the bottom of some UFO reports."

First, there is physical evidence. In the vicinity of reported UFOs, researchers have found deep soil compressions—including crushed rock—and altered soil and rock chemistry. Pilots encountering UFOs report disruptions in radar, radio, and compass operations. People who say they have witnessed UFOs experience temporary blindness, burns, and internal bleeding.

And yet, Ross writes, UFOs must be nonphysical because they disobey the laws of physics. For instance, they may be detected by radar without being seen, or they are seen but not detected by radar. They make impossibly sharp turns and sudden stops, disappear and reappear.

Then there's the fact that ten times as many UFO sightings occur at 3:00 A.M. than at either 6:00 A.M. or 8:00 P.M. They appear in remote areas far more often than in densely populated ones.

If some UFOs are real, as Ross believes, who or what is behind them?

According to Ross's intriguing theory, "only one kind of being favors the dead of night and lonely roads. Only one is real but nonphysical, animate, powerful, deceptive," and "bent on wreaking psychological and physical harm." It seems apparent, says Ross, that the activities we attribute to UFOs must, in reality "be associated with the activities of demons."

Other researchers—including secular scholars—have come to similar conclusions. They attribute UFO phenomena to demons or to an equivalent cause—for example, malevolent beings from another dimension. Physicist Jacques Vallee concludes: "The UFO phenomenon represents evidence for other dimensions that simply cannot be understood apart from their psychic and symbolic reality. What we see here is not an alien invasion," Vallee writes. "It is a spiritual system that acts on humans and uses humans."

Astronomer and agnostic J. Allen Hynek says that UFOs cause physical effects "in the same way that a poltergeist can produce very real physical effects."

Whether or not demons are behind some UFO sightings, Ross's research is a sobering reminder that a fearful battle for our allegiance is being waged in the spirit world. Scripture warns that "deceiving spirits" will attempt to mislead the faithful and that—in some cases—they will succeed. We must be constantly on guard against these attempts and rely on the power of Christ to protect us.

Father, there is much we do not understand about the spirit world. When it comes to phenomena humans cannot explain—activities attributed to "poltergeists," "UFOs," or other supernatural beings—I pray that you will open my eyes to— and restrain unhealthy curiosity about—all things "taught by demons."

BREAKING THE BONDAGE OF PORNOGRAPHY

TO READ: MATTHEW 5:27-29

Anyone who looks at a woman lustfully has already committed adultery with her in his heart. Matthew 5:28

"Ted" was well respected in his community and in his profession. But one day Ted discovered the Internet—and Internet pornography.

Within six months, porn was controlling Ted's life. As he puts it, his mind had "become a garbage can."

What makes this story noteworthy is that Ted is also an evangelical Christian. And the sad truth is that growing numbers of Christian men share his problem.

Cultural and technological factors have taken pornography from the margins of society to the mainstream—including, tragically, the church. A recent survey conducted by the National Coalition for the Protection of Children and Families provides us with a clue as to how big the problem may be.

The coalition surveyed students at five Christian colleges. Sixty-eight percent—more than two-thirds—of the male students said that they had intentionally looked for pornography on the Internet. Ten percent of those surveyed admitted to frequent use of pornography, and five percent acknowledged having a problem with pornography. Like any poll, these numbers understate the incidence of actual use.

Another Christian college, Seattle Pacific University, examined all the Web sites accessed by its students during a three-week period. Officials were dismayed to learn that nearly 7 percent of all sites visited were pornographic. In response, officials installed blocking software that kept students from accessing pornography on campus computers.

Technology alone will not solve the problem because there's no blocking software for the human heart. That's why, as Steve Watters of Focus on the Family writes in the Webzine *Boundless,* Christian colleges across the country are creating "special chapels, accountability groups and innovative dorm programs."

Why are Christian men so vulnerable to Internet pornography? Barbara Steffens of the coalition points to several possible factors. There's the technology: temptation is only a few clicks away. As a result, very little stands between a man and his worst impulses.

Second, Steffens adds, few churches are prepared for the challenges posed by Internet pornography. People aren't comfortable talking at church about their struggles with sexual temptation for fear of being judged. Even if they are prepared to talk, there's often no one to hold them accountable in a meaningful way.

What is your church doing to confront this challenge? An entire generation of Christian men is at risk of experiencing the same hell that Ted did.

If this is an area of temptation for you, know that God has the power to break your bondage to pornography and to heal your heart. But you will need to seek help—as Ted eventually did. He is now helping others to understand that by the grace of God and the help of our brothers, we can empty that garbage can forever.

Lord, in a world in which pornography forces its way into our very homes, I ask you to protect me and my family from this filth. Help me to remember that your power, forgiveness, and everlasting love await all who bring their addictions to your holy throne.

CHRIST'S OFFENSIVE
TRUTH CLAIMS

TO READ: JOHN 14:5-14

*[Jesus said,] "I am the way and the truth and the life.
No one comes to the Father except through me."* John 14:6

"You Christians are so arrogant," the young man said. "You think Jesus is the only route to God. It's an insult to anyone who follows another faith." Then he fired his parting shot: "It's intolerant religious views like yours that lead to hatred and violence."

In an age that celebrates "tolerance" and "pluralism," the claim that Christ is the only way to God is considered grossly offensive. Rabbi Shmuley Boteach speaks for many when he calls Christian truth claims "spiritual racism."

In *The Case for Faith,* former journalist Lee Strobel says the exclusive truth claim of Jesus "is among the biggest obstacles to spiritual seekers today." To get to the heart of the truth claims issue, Strobel interviewed theologian Ravi Zacharias, who grew up in India among Muslims, Hindus, and Sikhs.

First, Zacharias told Strobel, we have to understand that all truth claims are, by definition, exclusive. Any time you make a truth claim, you're saying that whatever contradicts that claim is false. Many Christians don't realize that every major religion makes truth claims—just as Christianity does.

For instance, Muslims "radically claim exclusivity," Zacharias noted, "not just theologically, but also linguistically." And Buddhism was born when Buddha rejected fundamental assertions of Hinduism. As for Hindus—they're "absolutely uncompromising" on several fundamental issues, including doctrines involving karma and reincarnation.

Atheists make their own truth claim: There is no God. By definition, they're intolerant of the viewpoint of anyone who does believe in God.

The trick for Christians is to witness to the claims of Christ in a loving, inoffensive manner so that we don't turn people off. We need to be tactful of cultural sensibilities. And we also need to witness to the truth on a related matter: the accusation that Christianity's truth claims lead to violence and hatred.

When they do, the violence comes not largely from Christians but from those who resist the message of Christ and hate the messenger.

As Zacharias put it: "I know of no Christianized country where your life is in danger because you are from another faith. But today there are many countries . . . such as Pakistan, Saudi Arabia, and Iran—where to become a follower of Christ is to put your life . . . at risk." Resistance to the truth, he added, "can be so strong that it can engender violence and hate even when the person has done absolutely nothing wrong."

Nothing, that is, except to believe what Jesus claimed: "I am the way and the truth and the life. No one comes to the Father except through me."

Father, give me a patient spirit and persuasive words when ministering to the lost. If they become hostile, help me to remember that they are lost. May I never give them reason, by word or deed, to doubt the validity of the truth I long for them to believe: that the only way to you is through Christ.

CAN FAITH AND DOUBT COEXIST?

TO READ: JOSHUA 24:13-18

[Joshua said,] "If serving the Lord seems undesirable to you, then choose for yourselves this day whom you will serve." Joshua 24:15

Theologian Lynn Anderson remembers the time a brilliant novelist came to the small Canadian town where he lived as a boy. One day, as he visited with Anderson's family, the writer asked Lynn, "Do you really believe the Bible's true? babies born from virgins? dead people coming out of the cemetery?"

"Yes," Lynn answered, "That's what I believe."

The writer responded, "I'd give anything to believe that because . . . the only people who really seem to be [happy] are the people who say they believe what you believe. But I just can't believe because my head keeps getting in the way!"

It's a common argument. But as Anderson told former journalist Lee Strobel, quite often it's not that people *can't* believe in God; it's that they *won't*.

In *The Case for Faith,* Strobel asks Anderson to explain what he means. "I started thinking about what [the novelist] would lose if he followed Jesus," Anderson says. For instance, "he was part of a guild of brilliant writers who all think religion is a total crock. I really believe his professional pride and the rejection of his peers would have been too high a price for him to pay."

Unfortunately, the writer isn't alone. Anderson says he once counseled a wealthy man who slept with every woman in town yet was miserable. "You've got to help me," the man told Anderson, "but don't give me any of that God talk because I can't believe that stuff."

Anderson told the man his problem was not that he could not believe but rather that he was afraid to give up all the money—some of it made dishonestly—and all the women. The man reluctantly agreed.

"When you scratch below the surface," Anderson concludes, "there's either a will to believe or there's a will not to believe." Scripture backs up this idea. Abraham is called the "father of faith," not because he never doubted but because he never gave up on God. Joshua said, "Choose for yourselves this day whom you will serve."

"Faith, at its taproot," Anderson adds, "is a decision of the will."

Anderson is right. We all need to guard against the temptation to elevate earthly things above worship of a holy God—even briefly: things like wealth, friendship, intellect, professional advancement, and the need to not look "foolish" for believing in God.

If you have a friend who says he just can't get beyond the "intellectual objections" to faith in God, dig a little deeper. Try to find out what's really stopping him. Then, lovingly show him it's not the mind that's holding faith hostage but the heart.

And then, pray that he will have the courage to act on it.

Lord, you have promised us that nothing can separate us from your love—except our own pride and passions. Give me the courage to never be ashamed of my faith—to be willing to openly acknowledge my commitment to you no matter what the cost.

GUARDING AGAINST
PRIVATIO

TO READ: HEBREWS 3:12-14

*Encourage one another daily, as long as it is called Today,
so that none of you may be hardened by sin's deceitfulness. Hebrews 3:13*

A Los Angeles woman became alarmed when strange men began hanging around her apartment, leering at her and making suggestive comments. Finally, she discovered what they were looking for: They had been lured to her home by a series of pornographic Internet advertisements.

The awful truth was that the woman had not placed the ads. She was a victim of a twisted revenge scheme that only the Internet could make possible.

The ads purported to describe the woman's kinky sexual fantasies—and they provided her name and address. The ads were posted by a man whom the woman had met at church. She had refused to go out with him—but he wouldn't take no for an answer. He was so persistent that the woman finally asked the elders of the church to eject him from the congregation, which they did. Those Internet ads were the man's twisted form of revenge.

The man was prosecuted, but his actions were hardly unique. Christian Wolf, an attorney who specializes in Internet issues, notes that people are increasingly settling scores, real or imagined, by "spreading false or misleading information on the Internet."

Two factors virtually invite people to abuse the Internet this way: easy access and anonymity. A famous *New Yorker* cartoon tells it all. It features one dog telling another dog that on the Internet "no one knows you're a dog."

This combination of access and anonymity reduces our sense of accountability, and it can easily loosen moral and cultural restraints that normally rein in bad behavior. Just as people are more likely to be offensive while making an anonymous telephone call than when talking face-to-face, so people are more likely to make rude statements sitting alone before a computer screen.

Centuries ago, Augustine preached against the dangers of what he called *privatio*, best translated as "privacy." Augustine knew that people acting in isolation and anonymity are more likely to give in to their worst impulses. The stuff we see online today vindicates that judgment.

We all appreciate our privacy. But we must guard against *privatio*—the isolation and anonymity that breaks down normal inhibitions. We must take care to nurture those forms of social interaction that increase rather than decrease our sense of accountability to one another.

Do you get together often with other believers to share your burdens and pray with one another? Do you have someone to whom you make yourself accountable and who is accountable to you? How much time do you spend online with strangers? If they met you in real life, would you be exactly what they expected?

The Internet is convenient—and fun—but we cannot allow it to take the place of face-to-face contact. Doing things *off*-line is one of the best ways to keep all of us *in* line.

Father, help me to remember that I have a deep and daily need of flesh-and-blood brothers and sisters—and that they have need of me, lest we drift into isolation and fall into sin.

PRIVATE VIRTUE AND PUBLIC DUTY

TO READ: 2 PETER 1:3-11

Make every effort to add to your faith goodness; and to goodness, knowledge; and to knowledge, self-control. 2 Peter 1:5

We often hear that a person's private conduct is unrelated to the performance of his or her public duties. This is especially true if the private failings involve sexual misbehavior. Advocates of this point of view never tire of telling us about former presidents whose marital infidelities didn't prevent them from political greatness.

What would America's founders think of such an assertion? They would have been shocked.

In *On Two Wings,* theologian Michael Novak makes a compelling case for the biblical origins of the American experiment. As he puts it, today the manner in which the story of America's founding is told cuts off "one of the two wings by which the American eagle flies." That cut-off wing is America's "compact" with the biblical God. The founders believed that there is a God who brings down the mighty and lifts up the poor. They relied upon this belief, and this conviction is, as Novak writes, "an indispensable part of their story."

America's founders did not make distinctions between private and public conduct. Novak tells the story of a prominent Boston doctor, Benjamin Church Jr., whose fellow Bostonians were shocked when they discovered Church was selling his services to the British.

In a letter to James Warren, Samuel Adams offered an explanation that would be incomprehensible to many contemporary Americans: He linked the doctor's treason to his reputation as an adulterer.

Adams wrote, "He who is void of virtuous attachments in private life, is, or very soon will be, void of all Regard for his country. . . . There is seldom an instance of a man guilty of betraying his Country, who had not before lost the feeling of moral obligations in his private connections."

In other words, if a man won't honor private obligations, why should we believe that he will honor his public ones?

Our culture has forgotten that the American experiment is a moral exercise, not just a political one. As such, it assumes certain things to be true about human nature and, as Novak tells us, about the authority of the God of the Bible.

These beliefs run contrary to contemporary thinking. That's why the ordered liberty the founders envisioned has degenerated into a demand for personal autonomy that asks nothing of its citizens—not even virtue.

Novak reminds us that private virtue, rooted in biblical faith, is essential for the American experiment to work as the founders intended. It's vital that Christians understand this often ignored "wing" on which our way of life depends—the wing that teaches us that without virtue, there can be no greatness.

Lord, give me a passionate desire for virtuous conduct in all aspects of my life, public and private, seen and unseen. Help me to remember during times of temptation that I can never be good—never mind great—without loving and imitating your holiness.

DARWIN AND MORALITY

TO READ: ECCLESIASTES 2:1-11

I thought in my heart, "Come now, I will test you with pleasure to find out what is good." But that also proved to be meaningless. Ecclesiastes 2:1

Who was the first Darwinist? No, it's not a trick question. But a recent book tells us that it wasn't Darwin.

That book is *Moral Darwinism: How We Became Hedonists* by Benjamin Wiker. Wiker calls the Greek philosopher Epicurus, who lived in the third century before Christ, the "first Darwinist." Actually, Wiker says, it would be more accurate to say that Darwin was an Epicurean—probably the most influential one ever.

What he means is that Darwin represented the culmination of what Wiker calls "Epicurean Materialism." While Epicureanism is commonly associated with hedonism, the fact is that Epicurus "offered the first thorough-going materialist view of the universe where the mere chance interaction of brute matter swirling about created all things."

So human beings are "just one more soul-less product of evolution," and "there is ultimately no good and evil." This account of the universe was the "foundation" of Darwin's system and his materialistic explanation for the world.

Wiker writes that Epicurean materialism is "fundamentally antagonistic" to Christianity. For two thousand years these worldviews have contradicted each other with regard to God, nature, human nature, and morality.

Just as Epicurean materialism provided the foundation for Darwinism, Darwinism is the foundation for "one of the two sides in the culture war": the side "that champions sexual freedom, abortion, [and] euthanasia."

A materialistic worldview undermines the very basis for morality by denying that we are distinct from the other animals and created in the image of God. Instead, we are considered the product of chance and impersonal forces.

But if that's so, why prohibit murder? Nobody talks about "murdering" a dog or a fly. The very idea of murder assumes that there's something unique about being human.

What's true about murder goes double for human sexuality and familial relationships. If there is no God, soul, or afterlife, all that's left is hedonism. In a world that is amoral, how we should live becomes a matter of "continually balancing bodily pleasures and pains." Morality and the distinction between good and evil are purely human creations with no intrinsic authority.

We ought to be prepared to highlight for neighbors and friends the moral and cultural dead end to which materialism leads. And we should point out to the children in our lives how desperately unhappy are those who wallow—as the author of Ecclesiastes did—in hedonistic self-indulgence.

A world in which good and evil are products of the "random jostling of brute atoms" is not a place where most people want to live.

Lord, how many desperate attempts have been made to encourage evil and excuse defiance. When I am tempted to seek happiness through self-indulgence, remind me of the joy of "heavenly hedonism": the willingness to throw myself sacrificially into your holy service.

LITERARY WITNESS

TO READ: MARK 4:1-20

He taught them many things by parables. Mark 4:2

The great nineteenth-century American evangelist Charles Finney once declared, "I cannot believe that a person who has ever known the love of God can relish a secular novel." He then went on to denounce Lord Byron, Walter Scott, even Shakespeare.

Such attitudes may strike some as strange, yet historically some American evangelicals have been suspicious of secular literature. To give us the tools we need to know whether that attitude is justified, Louise Cowan and Os Guinness have written *Invitation to the Classics,* which can help Christians understand not just what classic books to read but also how they can lead us to a richer understanding of the gospel.

One wonders what Finney might have made of Fyodor Dostoyevsky, who often wove profoundly Christian themes into his otherwise "secular" novels. Interestingly, the works of both Shakespeare and Dostoyevsky led Louise Cowan back to Christian faith. Cowan had read all sorts of theological works, and even the Bible itself, but had failed to regain her faith. Then she read *Hamlet* and other Shakespearean plays and was struck by the frequent Christian themes.

Dostoyevsky's novel *The Brothers Karamazov* led Cowan to explore Christianity further. "Not until a literary work of art awakened my imaginative faculties," she writes, "could the possibility of a larger context and reason alone engage my mind. ... I had to be transformed in the way that literature transforms—by story, image, symbol—before I could see the simple truths of the Gospel."

We live in a technological society that rejects anything that we can't measure and verify. People are crying out for something more, for language that speaks to the soul.

Scenes from some of the greatest works, the grand inquisitor scene in Dostoyevsky's *The Brothers Karamazov* in particular, can etch moral truths deeply into the soul. Irina Ratushinskaya, the great Russian poet, imprisoned by the Soviets, grew up in Odessa with atheist parents who never allowed her a Bible. But she read literature—Pushkin, Dostoyevsky, Tolstoy—in which she saw the gospel and which led to her conversion.

Jesus himself, who could have used any teaching style he wanted, often chose to use stories—including the parable of the sower—to help his listeners understand spiritual concepts.

If the last time you picked up a classic was when you had to in college, why not consider becoming reacquainted with great literature? Allow its rich, evocative words to penetrate your imagination and your soul. And then you can pass on these stories as a witness to unsaved friends. They may stimulate a hunger for other good books—and in turn, whet their appetites for the Good Book.

Lord, teach me to be open to any good thing—even seemingly secular things—that could, with a little imagination, be used to lead the unsaved into your Kingdom.

ASTRONAUTS WHO FOUND GOD

TO READ: ISAIAH 42:5-9

This is what God the Lord says—he who created the heavens and stretched them out. . . . "I, the Lord, have called you in righteousness." Isaiah 42:5-6

On July 20, 1969, Neil Armstrong and Buzz Aldrin landed on the moon—the first astronauts to take that "giant leap for mankind." But before they emerged from the spaceship, Aldrin pulled out a Bible, a silver chalice, and sacramental bread and wine. On the moon, his first act was to celebrate communion.

Frank Borman was commander of the first space crew to travel beyond the Earth's orbit. Looking down on the earth from almost 250,000 miles away, Borman radioed back a message quoting Genesis 1: "In the beginning, God created the Heavens and the Earth." As he later explained, "I had an enormous feeling that there had to be a power greater than any of us—that there was a God, that there was indeed a beginning."

The late James Irwin, who walked on the moon in 1971, later became an evangelical minister. He often described the lunar mission as a revelation. In his words, "I felt the power of God as I'd never felt it before."

Charles Duke, who followed Irwin to the moon, later became active in missionary work. As he explains, "I make speeches about walking on the moon and walking with the Son."

Guy Gardner, a veteran astronaut, speaks in churches on the reality of God.

What is it about being in space that seems to spark our innate religious sense? Two centuries ago the philosopher Immanuel Kant said there are two things that "fill the mind with ever new and increasing admiration and awe: the starry heavens above me and the moral law within me." Reflection upon these things, Kant wrote, leads our minds to contemplate God himself—the moral law revealing his goodness, the heavens revealing his power.

As the psalmist put it, "The heavens declare the glory of God" (Psalm 19:1).

Clearly, space travel has provided an unexpected dividend: astronauts who powerfully encounter the God who created the heavens and the earth.

Most of us will never travel in space. Many of us live lives that seem dull and dreary in comparison with the exhilarating experiences of those who escape the bonds of the earth's orbit. If we ever begin to feel spiritually run down, perhaps we ought to go outside on a clear night and gaze at the vast array of stars. Whether we are astronauts or not, the heavens above inspire a sense of awe about God's creation—and about the Creator himself.

Lord, thank you for the faithfulness of those who have lived great adventures— and witness to the greatest adventure of all: relationship with the One who created the heavens above and stretched out the stars.

IS MORALITY AN ILLUSION?

TO READ: JEREMIAH 17:1-13

*I the Lord search the heart and examine the mind, to reward
a man according to his conduct. Jeremiah 17:10*

When C. S. Lewis wrote *That Hideous Strength* in 1946, human cloning was the stuff of science fiction. But the book was prophetic: scientists today are debating whether or not to clone humans.

Lewis's novel was prophetic in other ways as well—especially concerning the nature of morality. Scholars in a new field called evolutionary psychology are working busily to deconstruct moral behavior, exactly as Lewis anticipated. As Andrew Ferguson recently explained in the *Weekly Standard*, evolutionary psychologists see morality as "an illusion fobbed off on us by our genes." But where does this line of argument lead?

Think about the emotion of guilt. Maybe you have a habit of running red lights. Now, suppose you're getting away with it. But you have a growing sense of unease . . . guilt feelings, in other words.

Evolutionary psychology holds there's nothing real about this feeling, that there's no objective basis to guilt and that humans have such emotions only because of our evolutionary past. In other words, if it was adaptive in the past to feel bad when our ancestors behaved certain ways, then that's what natural selection favored. But environmental conditions change, and what we regard as "right" and "wrong" can shift.

Lewis saw this argument coming more than fifty years ago and put it into the mouth of Professor Frost, the most terrifying character in his novel. Frost tries to win over a protagonist by telling him to forget about fundamental human motivations like "right" and "wrong."

"Motives are not the causes of action," says Frost, "but its by-products . . . when you have obtained real objectivity, you will recognize, not some motives, but all motives as merely animal."

Guilt? Remorse? According to Professor Frost, such things don't exist. They're illusions, tricks of the mind.

By the same token, what evolutionary psychologists call "discoveries" aren't genuine knowledge; they're speculation. As Andrew Ferguson points out, much of evolutionary psychology rests on surmise and guesswork about what may be "adaptive."

In reality, our moral sense is grounded not in what we adapt to but in what is right and true. It may be adaptive to kill unwanted infants as rats do when they're overcrowded. But it's morally wrong because infants bear the image of God.

Lewis saw where God-denying science ultimately leads: to hideous and unspeakable horror. This is why Christians must learn the theories of evolutionary psychologists and how to effectively combat their arguments when they drift into the public square. In the end, they're nothing more than the latest effort to get around God's teachings.

Morality is not an illusion: The Scriptures make it clear that we are all morally aware—and that God will hold each of us responsible for disregarding morality or pretending it does not exist.

Father, may I be a fervent advocate of your truth and a witness to the horrors awaiting us—both in this life and the next—if we ignore it.

THE SANCTION OF EROS

TO READ: PROVERBS 5:1-23

May you rejoice in the wife of your youth. . . . May you ever be captivated by her love. Proverbs 5:18-19

Sheldon Vanauken, best known as the author of *A Severe Mercy,* also published a collection of essays called *Under the Mercy.* In one essay, called "The Loves," Vanauken describes how a Christian friend named John shocked him by announcing that he was leaving his wife to marry another woman. John explained his sudden change of heart by saying, "It seemed so good, so right. That's when we knew we had to get the divorces. We belonged together."

Vanauken then describes a conversation with a friend named Diana who left her husband for another man. Diana defended herself with virtually the same words: "It was just so good and right with Roger that I knew it would be wrong to go on with Paul."

As Vanauken explains, both John and Diana were "invoking a higher law: the feeling of goodness and rightness. A feeling so powerful that it swept away . . . whatever guilt they would otherwise have felt" for what they were doing to their families.

When Christians marry, they often say, "till death do us part." But what many of them unconsciously mean is, "till failing love do us part."

In reality, many people love their spouse not as a person but as someone who evokes certain feelings. Their vow was not so much to the person as to that feeling.

So when such people fall in love with someone else, they transfer that vow to the other person. And why not, says Vanauken, "if vows are nothing but feelings?"

Vanauken dubs these thrilling emotions "The Sanction of Eros."

When John and Diana spoke of the goodness of their love, they were appealing to something higher than judgment, higher even than their own desires. But as Vanauken points out, "The sacred approval they felt could not possibly have come from [God,] whose disapproval of divorce is explicit in Scripture. It is Eros, the pagan god of lovers, who confers this sanction upon the worshippers at his altar."

"The pronouncement of Eros that this love is so good and so right that all betrayals are justified is simply a lie," Vanauken writes. Tragically, few people are prepared "for the amazing sanction of Eros." Those caught in its thrall are convinced that their love is different, even sacred.

It's imperative that pastors warn engaged couples about this deadly appeal. At some point, Eros will almost certainly beckon with an exciting new love—and the feelings of rightness, even sacredness, may be overwhelming. If you have not already encountered this kind of temptation, you must prepare for it.

Couples need to know that it is only when Christ is at the heart of their marriage that they will be able to resist this ancient pagan call.

Father, in a culture that celebrates endless "romance," let me not be fooled by passionate feelings—sensations that, if not taken to the foot of the cross, may ultimately drive me away from my spouse—and out of fellowship with you.

ART'S ENDURING POWER

TO READ: PSALM 96:1-13

*Sing to the Lord a new song; . . . proclaim his salvation day after day.
Declare his glory among the nations. Psalm 96:1-3*

In recent years, thousands of Japanese have been hearing the gospel of Jesus Christ in a new way—and they're embracing it.

The evangelist responsible for leading this spiritual awakening may surprise you: He's none other than Johann Sebastian Bach.

That's right. The German composer who died 250 years ago is bringing Christianity to Japan through the beauty of his music. Now there are reports of thousands of Japanese, inspired by his cantatas, converting to Christianity. It's a testament to the power of art steeped in a biblical worldview.

Christianity has never been widely embraced by Japanese culture. When European traders and missionaries came to the island nation in the seventeenth century, they met with mixed success: Commerce thrived; the gospel languished. But Japan eagerly embraced the music of Western culture.

Shinichi Suzuki even developed a method of learning to play classical instruments that became famous worldwide. But now, through a resurgence in Bach's popularity, that music is providing a foothold for evangelism that trade and traditional approaches have never provided.

Bach's popularity is so great that the classes at the Felix Mendelssohn Academy in Bach's hometown of Leipzig, Germany, are filled with Japanese students. These students are learning about more than the music of the great composer—they are learning about the spirit that moved him to write: that is, Bach's love of God.

Writing on this resurgence of Bach's music for *Civilization,* the magazine of the Library of Congress, Uwe Siemon-Netto reports that his Japanese interpreter asked to start the day with one of Bach's cantatas. She selected one whose lyrics declare that God's name is Love. "This has taught me what these two words mean to Christians . . . and I like it very much," she said.

What began as an interest in the brilliance of the music has led to an understanding of the richness of God's grace. Masaaki Suzuki, founder of a school for Bach's music in Japan, says that "Bach is teaching us the Christian concept of hope." And Yoshikazu Tokuzen, of Japan's National Christian Council, calls Bach nothing less than "a vehicle of the Holy Spirit." And the revival his music is causing indeed confirms that.

At the end of every one of Bach's works, he inscribed the initials *SDG*—shorthand for *soli Deo gloria,* "to God alone be the glory." Little could he have imagined what purposes God would have for his work, even hundreds of years after his death.

We Christians ought to open our eyes—and ears—to the way God can use the arts to witness to his glory. If we have unsaved friends who love great music, that music may ultimately become a "vehicle of the Holy Spirit"—just as the composer may have intended.

Father, some people are reached through their minds, others through literature, and still others through great music. Help me to be willing to get to know my unsaved neighbors well enough to discover their interests—interests that may become vehicles for bringing them to Christ.

WHY ATHEISTS HATE GOD

TO READ: 1 SAMUEL 3:11-18

[Eli's] sons made themselves contemptible, and he failed to restrain them.
1 Samuel 3:13

Does belief in God come from an "infantile need for security"?

In *Faith of the Fatherless,* New York University psychology professor Paul Vitz reminds us that atheists have always argued that religious belief arises from psychological factors instead of from the nature of reality. But after he became a Christian, Vitz began to wonder if psychological factors could explain a predisposition to *rejecting* God.

Vitz studied the childhoods of more than a dozen prominent atheists. He became convinced that their rejection of God is linked directly to a defective relationship with their earthly fathers. By defective, Vitz means either that the father died or that he abandoned or abused his child.

For example, Friedrich Nietzsche, a philosopher famous for saying, "God is dead," lost his father when he was four years old. Vitz writes that Nietzsche had "a strong, intellectually macho reaction against a dead, very Christian father," whom he perceived as weak and sickly.

French existentialist Jean-Paul Sartre lost his father when he was a baby. His mother remarried when Sartre was twelve, giving him a stepfather he resented. Not long afterward, Sartre concluded, "You know what? God doesn't exist."

Joseph Stalin hated his father, who beat him unmercifully. "It is not difficult," Vitz writes, "to understand why communism, with its explicit rejection of God and all other higher authorities . . . had great appeal for [Stalin]."

Adolf Hitler also received terrible beatings from his father, who died when Hitler was fourteen. And the father of China's Mao Tse-tung was a tyrant who taught his son "his first appreciation of revolution and rebellion in his own family setting."

America's most famous atheist, Madalyn Murray O'Hair, despised her father; her son William reports that O'Hair once tried to kill the old man with a butcher knife.

After studying these "major historical rejecters" of God, Vitz concludes that "we find a weak, dead, or abusive father in every case."

Given the tremendous impact men have on their children, Christian fathers must take their responsibilities seriously. The Scriptures make it clear that God will hold poor fathers accountable—as he did Eli. Those of us who suffered under indifferent or abusive fathers must forgive them—and not allow their bad example to negatively affect our relationship with God or with other family members.

Of course, no matter what our family background is, each of us is still ultimately responsible for the decisions we make. But Vitz's research shows that when we witness to atheists, we must compassionately take into account the likelihood that they have painful memories of their fathers.

Clearly, our relationship with our earthly fathers affects—for good or ill—our relationship with our heavenly Father.

Lord, I pray that the fathers I know will treat their sons and daughters with patience, wisdom, and respect, not abusing their power or frustrating their children by demanding too much, too little, or the wrong things. I pray for your healing for those harmed by wicked, absent, or neglectful fathers and that by turning to their heavenly Father, they will find their unmet need for a devoted earthly father richly answered.

FIGHTING MORAL ILLITERACY

TO READ: PSALM 78:1-8

[The Lord] decreed statutes for Jacob and established the law in Israel, which he commanded our forefathers to teach their children. Psalm 78:5

A few years ago the Josephson Institute of Ethics released the findings of its survey, "Report Card on the Ethics of American Youth." The survey identifies what the institute calls "shocking levels of moral illiteracy" among American kids.

Ninety-two percent of kids surveyed admitted to lying to their parents; seventy-eight percent admitted lying to a teacher. Seventy percent said that they had cheated on a test, and half of them said that they had done so more than once. Twenty-five percent said that they would lie to get a job.

The *Atlanta Constitution* summarized the findings as follows: "America's next generation [believes that] it's perfectly acceptable to lie and cheat." This is true despite the fact that three quarters of all the states now mandate that students be taught about "values" like honesty, trustworthiness, and respect for others.

Why haven't these programs worked? Why are kids increasingly willing to lie and cheat? As James Davison Hunter writes in *The Death of Character,* most character education is ignorant about why people behave morally. While these programs tell students that, for instance, honesty is better than dishonesty, they don't provide a justification for these beliefs he notes.

They don't provide a justification because they can't—not legally. As Hunter points out, character is intimately linked to tradition and communities. The first provides the justification for the moral teachings, and the second reinforces those teachings.

Hunter is, of course, describing religious communities. But religion is the one issue schools can't mention. The courts have decreed that government must not only be neutral between religions—like Christianity and Judaism—but also between religion and irreligion.

What's more, this moral education emphasizes the role of the autonomous individual, operating independently of any group that might hold him accountable. This leaves appeals to personal gratification and fulfillment as the only justification for moral action—with the results the Josephson Institute documents.

Surveys like these demonstrate why Christian parents must make certain their children receive moral training at home and at church. We must be involved in our congregations deeply enough so that our children feel a sense of community with those with whom they worship, and will—during church potlucks, softball games, and weddings—desire to live up to the standards of that community.

Second, we must help our neighbors understand that helping kids become morally literate requires changing how we teach them about right and wrong. This doesn't mean turning classrooms into Sunday schools. But if we want to give our kids reasons for acting morally that actually work, we must get over our phobia about religion's role in public life.

The lives and souls of our children—and our neighbors' children—are in the balance.

Lord, help me to remember the importance of my role in my church community. May I be a model of moral literacy for the children in my life—at home, at church, and in my neighborhood—teaching and reinforcing your statutes to the next generation.

IS GLUTTONY A RIGHT?

TO READ: PROVERBS 30:7-9

Give me neither poverty nor riches, but give me only my daily bread. Proverbs 30:8

A few years ago a federal court ruled that gluttony is a protected human right: The appellate panel ruled that even if you gorge yourself up to three times your normal size, you cannot legally be deprived of a job.

The court case involved a Rhode Island woman who weighed more than three hundred pounds and had been denied employment at a school for the mentally retarded. School officials said the woman's immense size prevented her from performing all aspects of her job, such as picking up patients.

This was not a case where the woman suffered from a medical condition; she simply overate. Nevertheless, the judges ruled that she was a victim of discrimination. In other words, it is now possible to eat your way into a protected group with all the same legal rights as the blind or the deaf.

To assert those rights, there are even special organizations like the National Association to Advance Fat Acceptance. The mayor of Ithaca, New York, declared one month of the year "Size Acceptance Month." He made the announcement just before shoveling a piece of chocolate cake into his mouth at a public meeting.

Gluttony was once counted one of the Seven Deadly Sins. Now it's a civil right.

Admittedly, many of us find it difficult to practice self-control in a consumerist culture. Every time we turn on the television, we are regaled with images of people eating and drinking with exquisite

413

enjoyment. Every time we drive down the street, we're lured by golden arches and cookie franchises.

Laws are supposed to remind us what we ought to do. But the pro-gluttony ruling sanctions giving in to what we want to do—even if it's unhealthy. Folks who binge on candy and chips can now do so with the confidence that even the courts will defend their right to self-indulgence.

Christians ought to view the temptation to overeat as a challenge to build character, not fat reserves. Living in an affluent culture as we do, many of our temptations come not because we have too little but because we have so much. Unlike people in poor cultures, Americans can afford to buy all the food we want—including the high-calorie junk food that puts on the pounds.

Proverbs 30 reminds us that both poverty and riches can be a trap. Poverty may tempt us to steal, but riches tempt us to gluttony.

Philippians 3 condemns gluttony as a form of idolatry. People whose "god is their stomach" are headed for eternal destruction.

This is a message our affluent society desperately needs to hear. The last thing we need is false compassion that turns human weakness into a civil right.

Lord, I confess that I sometimes eat far more than my daily bread. Make me willing to turn over to you my desire to abuse food—a sin that endangers the health of both body and soul.

THE ORIGINS OF EVIL

TO READ: MARK 7:14-23

It is what comes out of a man that makes him "unclean." Mark 7:15

Jackson Carr, of Lewisville, Texas, was an outgoing, fun-loving first grader with a passion for Hot Wheels and riding his bike. Two thousand miles away, in Bellingham, Washington, Michael Busby, age eight, had the same kind of winning personality.

Tragically, both boys were viciously murdered in the same week. Police say that Jackson Carr's fifteen-year-old sister stabbed him in the neck while their ten-year-old brother held him down. The sister later led authorities to Jackson's muddy grave.

Michael Busby's mutilated body was found in an isolated field near his home. He had been bound with duct tape, strangled, beaten, and slashed repeatedly with a razor blade. The killer, still not satisfied with torture, finally killed Mikey with a massive injection of insulin.

Police soon arrested a sixteen-year-old neighborhood boy, who confessed, saying that Michael had been "bugging him."

Stunned, grief-stricken residents of Lewisville and Bellingham are asking themselves, *How could this happen? How could our kids commit such heinous crimes?*

When people encounter this kind of violence, they tend to look in all the wrong places for answers. One Bellingham minister, for example, accused "the system." "Isn't it clear," he asked, "that [the alleged killer] . . . wasn't receiving enough support?"

Others, believing that human nature is innately good, insist that violence is caused by some social or economic factors. The eighteenth-century French philosopher Marquis de Condorcet wrote glowingly of "the indefinite perfectibility of the human race." And Karl Marx believed man would create a perfect society once the evil capitalists were destroyed.

But crime begins—and ends—in the human heart.

Crime is a place where the secular and biblical worldviews come into sharp conflict. The biblical worldview includes original sin, the Fall, and human depravity. So when we see kids killing kids, we have to point out the gruesome truth: Sin is in all of us. Every human heart is desperately wicked. If a society fails to understand this, it simply perpetuates the horrors.

Kids killing kids is an indescribable horror, but it's not new. It's simply another consequence of human depravity. When we fail to see this, we find ourselves in an impossible situation. We keep trying to solve the world's problems looking in all the wrong places instead of looking straight into the human heart.

We need to remember this if we are ever tempted to excuse our own sins by saying that something, or someone, else is responsible for them. And we should help our neighbors understand that only a Christian worldview realistically understands human sin—and recognizes that in the gospel there is an answer: redemption through Christ.

Father, when moral horrors occur in my neighborhood, help me to be a sensitive witness to the truth: that evil arises not from poverty, environment, or government structure, but out of human hearts. Give me the wisdom to identify to the unsaved the sublime solution to human depravity: salvation through your Son.

DESIGNED FOR A PURPOSE

TO READ: MARK 9:42-50

If anyone causes one of these little ones who believe in me to sin,
it would be better for him to be thrown into the sea with a large millstone
tied around his neck. Mark 9:42

Slumber parties, holding hands, and playing with each others' hair: This is typical teenage girl behavior. While boys tend to rough-house, girls tend to be more affectionate. It has always been innocent—until now, writes *Washington Post* writer Laura Sessions Stepp. Nowadays, "sexual preference is a shifting concept" among adolescent girls, and in our sex-charged culture, affectionate behavior between girls goes well beyond child's play.

It's hard to tell whether these girls are acting on attraction or simply vying for attention. In one Washington, D.C., school, a group of girls charged boys ten dollars to watch the girls make out. "In the protean world of young female sexuality, where all forms of expression are modeled," Stepp writes, "nothing is certain."

Researchers say this malleability of female sexuality is to be expected. Lisa Diamond of the University of Utah conducted a study of women ages sixteen to twenty-three who were attracted to other women and found that over eight years, two-thirds of them changed labels "from unlabeled to bisexual, lesbian to bisexual."

This phenomenon among young women is partly about how the growing acceptance of homosexuality affects them. When the Edmund Burke School in Washington, D.C., held a "diversity day," students gathered in a circle and were asked to step into the middle if they considered themselves homosexual. Nobody moved.

Then they were asked to step forward if they thought of themselves as bisexual. Of the sixty students present, fifteen stepped forward.

But are they really bisexual, or are they merely pursuing acceptance? "Most of these girls aren't gay," said one girl. "They're just doing it because their friends are doing it."

"These girls say they don't know what they are and don't need to know," writes Stepp. "Adolescence and young adulthood is a time for exploration." That statement gets closer to the heart of the matter: They don't know, and in schools and in popular culture—think of Britney Spears kissing Madonna—they're encouraged to try it all.

Today's sexually charged culture treats the options of gay, lesbian, bisexual, and transgendered lifestyle as all equal, all accepted choices. It's a degraded view of sexuality that could tempt kids into sinful experiments.

We need to train kids as never before that God designed them in his image and has a specific design for our relationships. They shouldn't be encouraged to try out everything—only to be left, in the end, with nothing.

Father, I know that what humans intend for evil, you intend for good. Help me use unsavory secular teachings as an occasion to explain to the youngsters in my life that you created not "shifting sexuality" but males and females designed to cleave together for high and holy purposes in marriage.

THE CALL TO POWER

TO READ: JOHN 17:13-19

[Jesus said,] "They are not of the world any more than I am of the world."
John 17:14

In the first chapter of *In, But Not Of,* Hugh Hewitt writes, "Among men alive at the time I wrote this book, three had done more to shape our world than any others. . . . It is hard to imagine a more unlikely trio." One of these men spent years in a prison camp and later became a math teacher. Another one, a bishop from a working-class background, didn't get his dissertation published until he was forty years old. And the third had a film career that began promisingly but never reached stardom.

But Alexander Solzhenitsyn, Pope John Paul II, and Ronald Reagan weren't content to stay in obscure positions. Their ambition benefited not only themselves but the rest of the world as well. "Had [these men] chosen different paths—easier paths—the Soviet Union might well still be where it was," Hewitt points out.

A radio talk-show host, columnist, and law professor, Hewitt wrote his book as a practical guide for students and young adults who want to make an impact on the world for Christ. As his examples show, he thinks that one of the best ways to do this is to pursue power—in business, in the cultural arena, and especially in "the sphere of political and public affairs."

But how do we reconcile Hewitt's ideas with biblical teachings? We know that Christ called us to serve, not to be served, and we often translate that to mean that we're supposed to shun the spotlight. We fear the corruption that worldly power can bring.

Sometimes, however, power also brings great opportunities for service. For instance, Christians in public life help preserve our freedom of worship and speak up for persecuted Christians abroad. Power is never to be an end in itself, but when people accept it with humility and trust in God's guidance, they can use power legitimately as a means to an end: building God's kingdom.

Hewitt acknowledges the temptations that power brings—which means Christians in powerful positions must commit themselves to a higher level of accountability. "Plant yourself in a church," he writes, "and hedge yourself with close friends who can keep you anchored when the particular dangers of living in the world come close, but do not allow yourself the easy way out—of easy volunteer work or a life of prayer for the world but no action."

Like Moses, some Christians dislike the thought of serving in leadership positions. If we are asked to serve as leaders—in church, in our professions, or in politics—we must prayerfully consider whether this is where God wants us to serve him.

If you know a student or young professional whom God may be calling to a life of public service, you might want to give him or her a copy of Hewitt's book. That young person needs to understand how to participate *in* the world without being *of* it.

Lord, help me to remember that ambition is nothing to be ashamed of if I am committed to harnessing earthly power in service to you.

JULY 30

CRUEL AND UNUSUAL PUNISHMENT

TO READ: 1 THESSALONIANS 5:11-22

Test everything. Hold on to the good. Avoid every kind of evil. | Thessalonians 5:21-22

When Edward Bello committed his most recent crime, he expected to go to prison. Instead the judge sentenced him to nine months with no television. He said he wanted "to create a condition of silent introspection" in order to induce Bello to change his behavior.

Bello's lawyers were outraged. They appealed on the grounds that making Bello keep his seven TV sets turned off is "cruel and unusual punishment"—and thus violates the Constitution.

When our founders outlawed cruel and unusual punishment, they were thinking of things like floggings and amputations. Equating a ban on TV with torture is a sad sign that television has become far too important in our culture—important and destructive.

TV critic Michael Medved says the problem with TV isn't just the programming: The problem is the medium itself. Medved notes that families began falling apart around 1960—the time the first generation raised on TV hit adolescence. These kids grew up on the wholesome sitcoms of the 1950s. Yet by 1965 the family, by every measure, had undergone massive deterioration.

The principal cause, Medved says, "was that most . . . influential of all American institutions: television." He argues that television encourages attributes that are "deadly to the survival of marriages and families."

For example, TV encourages impatience by showing programs that solve every imaginable problem in thirty minutes. "And the whole point of commercials," Medved adds, "is to make you want things and to want them now." Both of these elements undermine the quality of endurance necessary for family life.

Television also promotes depression. The focus of TV news is relentlessly negative, Medved observes. If a father works three jobs to support his kids, it's not news. But if the same father shoots his children, we watch the gory details on dozens of stations for days.

Finally, TV leads to selfishness because it creates what Medved calls "the syndrome of entitlement," the sense that we're all entitled to "ceaseless arrays of ecstatic pleasures"—just like the characters on TV series such as *Friends* or *Sex in the City*. Programs like these teach that if some aspects of our lives—like our marriages—are not endlessly exciting, we ought to replace them.

In short, Medved concludes, television undermines those attributes most necessary for family survival: patience, sacrifice, optimism, and deferred gratification.

He's right. We ought to take a good look, not just at *what* we watch, but at *how long* we watch. Do the programs you choose make you less satisfied with the good things God has given you? Do they make you crave things you do not have? Do they make you less patient or more depressed? If so, given Paul's command to "avoid every kind of evil," perhaps it's time to "kill your TV," as one wag put it, and take your family out for a walk.

Father, help me to meet my need for relaxation not through idle amusements but through healthy activities that build up my brothers and sisters in Christ, nurture my commitment to my family, and honor you.

PUTTING AWAY CHILDISH THINGS

TO READ: 1 CORINTHIANS 13:11-13

When I became a man, I put childish ways behind me. 1 Corinthians 13:11

When J. M. Barrie wrote *Peter Pan*, the story of a boy who refused to grow up, he was writing fiction to amuse children. Barrie might be surprised to learn that today increasing numbers of young "adults" are modeling themselves after Peter Pan.

The *New York Times* chronicled the emergence of this new cultural trend. Known variously as "Peterpandemonium" or "Rejuveniles," it's characterized by "grown-ups who cultivate juvenile tastes in products and entertainment."

For instance, Target stores sell underpants depicting Scooby-Doo and SpongeBob SquarePants in adult sizes, along with "fuzzy pajamas with attached feet." American Greetings, the maker of the Strawberry Shortcake doll, runs ads saying: "Who knew you and your daughter would have the same best friend?"

A surprisingly large part of the audience for children's television shows like the Teletubbies are "young adults." And more people between the ages of eighteen and forty-nine watch the Cartoon Network than watch CNN.

To Frank Furedi, a professor of sociology at the University of Kent in England, this trend represents "the self-conscious cultivation of immaturity." For many young people, he says, there's "nothing attractive about [being an adult] anymore."

Furedi rightly criticizes the influence of the media, which equates youth with relevance, and maturity with obsolescence. The media, more than any other institution, has been shaped by the "youth culture" of the 1960s. This youth culture valued play and self-fulfillment over the everyday obligations that are the stuff of adulthood.

As a result, according to Brian Page, a professor of anthropology at the University of Miami, "play has become the primary purpose and value in many adult lives. It now borders on the sacred."

If play is life's "primary purpose and value," is it any wonder that so many young people cultivate immaturity?

It's not that play is a bad thing. Our ability to laugh and be amused is the result of our being created in the image of God. We laugh because we, unlike the rest of creation, see the relationship between different things. When we play, we sometimes experience what C. S. Lewis called "joy," the sense that something greater than ourselves calls out to us.

This kind of play requires wonder, not the refusal to grow up or to create a new never-neverland. It understands the difference between "being like a child" and being just plain childish—something Paul says we ought to get over when we grow up.

We need to evaluate our priorities now and then to make sure our values are not being warped by a culture that does not value adult behavior. If we find ourselves enjoying too many childish things, perhaps we ought to ask ourselves why.

Lord, give me the courage to face the adult world and its responsibilities as I should. Help me to remember that the joys of adulthood are deeper and richer than those of childhood and that rather than clinging to youth, I should put away childish things in favor of thinking, speaking, reasoning—and playing—as an adult.

NO HOSPITALITY

TO READ: ROMANS 12:9-13

Practice hospitality. Romans 12:13

A recent ACLU report complains that access to abortions is "increasingly jeopardized by the imposition of religious beliefs in the health care context."

This deceptive language suggests that a Catholic or Presbyterian hospital is imposing its beliefs on a pregnant woman by refusing to kill her unborn child. A "no" response is equated with "imposing." The reality is that the ACLU would impose its zeal for killing the unborn on those who disagree.

Naturally the report doesn't put it quite that way. The ACLU Web site says, "It is often . . . appropriate to accommodate an individual health professional's refusal to provide a service." That sounds good—until you read the fine print. It goes on to say, "but only if the patient is ensured safe, timely, and feasible alternative access to treatment." In other words, if the woman can't get an abortion nearby, medical personnel at a religious hospital must perform it even though it is against their deepest convictions.

While the ACLU concedes that an individual health-care professional might be excused, it concedes nothing to the institution. The report states that hospitals "operating in the public world and serving and employing a religiously diverse population . . . ought to play by public rules." To do otherwise is viewed as a violation of "reproductive rights" and a failure "to provide basic health care."

Wait a minute. Public rule number one is the First Amendment, guaranteeing the free exercise of religion. Clearly the ACLU and the abortion industry want to eviscerate the exercise of religious conviction in faith-based medical centers.

For centuries, Christians have established hospitals to heal the sick and care for the dying. They're motivated by a concern for the ill—and also by the desire to obey God. The Scriptures command, "Practice hospitality." The ministry of hospitality means gracious, tender care for friend and stranger alike.

Hospitality does not mean doing anything and everything to please a guest. If a friend comes to us and asks for a gun to kill himself, we invite him in, comfort him, and encourage him to choose life. We don't give him what he wants; we give him what he needs. In the same way, we don't kill an unborn child because the child's mother says she doesn't want to give birth to that child.

A pregnant woman and her child deserve real hospitality that affirms life and gives wise counsel. Hospitals must remain free to minister in the name of Christ. Christians ought to do what they can to keep hospitals that way—and also consider ways we can help those the ACLU cheerfully abandons in favor of abortion uber alles: mothers and their unborn children.

Father, I ask you to strengthen doctors, nurses, and hospital administrators who are facing pressure to collaborate with evil. I pray that I will not succumb to similar pressure—whether it be killing the unborn directly or supporting those who do through my taxes. Let me count as nothing the threat of job loss, financial ruin, or even prison, compared to obedience to a just and holy God.

THE MORALITY OF ANGER

TO READ: 1 SAMUEL 11:1-15

*When Saul heard their words, the Spirit of God came upon him in power,
and he burned with anger.* 1 Samuel 11:6

"We learned in our class that if you believe in peace, you can stay alive," said the eleven-year-old boy. "We learned that you should always find a peaceful way to solve your problems because you should never be violent."

Ironically, the boy lives a stone's throw from the Pentagon, where terrorists murdered more than a hundred people who were peacefully going about their business on September 11, 2001.

In *Why We Fight: Moral Clarity and the War on Terrorism,* William Bennett writes that teachers who cultivate these ideas in children's minds are seeking to "prevent another generation of young people from learning the proper uses of righteous anger."

The very idea that rage can be righteous has become a foreign concept. And Bennett wants to know why the country's elites "seem to back away from any hint of righteous anger as if it were some kind of poisonous snake. Why wasn't anger itself considered a moral response to the unprovoked attack on September 11?"

The answer, in part, is that these elites embrace an ideology, rooted in the Vietnam era, that sees America as an imperialistic power intent on imposing its will on others. Moreover, because they do not believe in the doctrine of the Fall, they see all wars as the result of misunderstandings. They believe all violence is wrong and that wars never solve anything. Instead of getting angry or waging another "imperialistic" war, we should blame ourselves: We should figure out what we did to make the terrorists so mad.

This view has so permeated our culture that many citizens hesitated to express anger over the terror attacks. But the morality of righteous wrath has been accepted throughout history as necessary for justice. "As the ancients recognized," Bennett notes, "anger is a necessary power of the soul, intimately connected with the passion for justice." The demand that we stifle our rage and negotiate with fanatics bent on wiping us out is thus immoral because it is a denial of justice.

If in our schools no "distinction is made among kinds of 'peace,'" Bennett warns, "children are deprived of the tools they require to distinguish a just from an unjust peace ([for example,] peace with honor from the peace of the grave.) They are robbed of the oldest and most necessary wisdom of the race, which is that some things are worth fighting and dying for."

In our private lives, we need to examine our own use of anger. Do we engage in righteous wrath over moral evils—or just lose our tempers over minor irritations?

We must make sure that we understand why—in the face of great evil—getting angry isn't wrong. It's the necessary prologue to justice.

Lord, how often I am tempted to shrug off staggering evils that harm others but explode over trifling annoyances that affect me personally. Show me when it is proper to "burn with anger"—and how to respond to those who inspire it.

AUGUST 3

CATERING TO CRUDENESS

TO READ: 1 THESSALONIANS 5:16-24

Test everything. Hold on to the good. Avoid every kind of evil. 1 Thessalonians 5:21-22

A few years ago a series of ads for Candie's shoes made the old ads about the Tidy Bowl man look positively genteel. One Candie's ad featured actress Jenny McCarthy wearing a pair of bright orange, high-heeled sandals that matched her T-shirt. Jenny is glancing up from her newspaper with an embarrassed smile on her face. And no wonder: The camera has caught her sitting on the toilet.

What's the point of using bathroom images to sell shoes? The answer is that manufacturers have decided one way to appeal to the lucrative youth market is with smirking, in-your-face vulgarity.

It used to be that ads for children's products had to pass muster with parents—or parents wouldn't shell out money to buy the product. But these days many youth have money of their own, so advertisers have felt free to ignore parental standards and appeal directly to the kids. Their ads began speaking the language of immaturity—exploiting the silly, the childish, even the vulgar.

It started in the 1970s with products such as the Garbage Pail Kids. Many parents were shocked and outraged. But today it's commonplace to see toys that are deliberately gory and disgusting. Manufacturers and ad makers alike know that for a certain stage of adolescence, the highest compliment a kid can give is *"Ooh, gross!"*

The Jenny-on-the-john ads are an example of how advertisers cater to kids' bad taste. But bad taste is more than merely an aesthetic issue. Deal Hudson writes in *Crisis* magazine that the problem with bad taste is not simply that "it promotes inferior art" but also that it promotes "inferior manners and morals." As Hudson warns, "Vulgar TV and banal music" can lead to "brutish manners and even violent behavior."

Because of original sin, we're all born with base tendencies. Good taste must be taught and cultivated. But some advertisers are teaching just the opposite: They're affirming *bad* taste by catering to kids' most vulgar instincts.

That's why we ought to speak out when we see ads that cater to crudeness and explain to our kids why gross is *not* cool. We ought to remind them that the apostle Paul taught us to "hold on to the good" and to "avoid every kind of evil." That goes for us as well: Advertisers don't hesitate to sell vulgarity to adults, either. We ought to train ourselves to recognize and reject it.

When we see crude ads like the ones with Jenny McCarthy sitting on the john, we need to help our kids to be intelligent, discerning consumers, willing to rebel against advertisers who would manipulate and exploit them for a few bucks and a pair of shoes.

Lord, help me to shut out of my life anything that would make my mind and heart coarse—television programs, magazines, and films that smear vulgarity across the screen and call it "art." Strengthen me so that they don't lead me away from the God of beauty and purity and leave me unfit to associate with your children.

ARE CHRISTIANS TOO CREDULOUS?

TO READ: PROVERBS 3:1-10

Trust in the Lord with all your heart. . . . Do not be wise in your own eyes.
Proverbs 3:5-7

If someone asked you what you'd call a person who believes in astrology, reincarnation, and communicating with the dead, you'd probably say "a New Ager." You might be surprised to learn that sometimes the correct answer would also be "a born-again Christian."

Many Americans are gullible when it comes to spiritual matters. If a certain belief promises to enhance our sense of well-being, to make sense of our lives, or to give us warm, fuzzy feelings, it will find adherents—no matter how bizarre or irrational the claims may be.

Astonishingly, a prominent sociologist of religion says that among the credulous are many people sitting beside you in the pews every week.

In *Spiritual Marketplace: Baby Boomers and the Remaking of American Religion,* Wade Clark Roof reports that 25 percent of born-again Christians interviewed in a recent study believe in the possibility of communicating with the dead. A third believe in reincarnation and astrology, and half say they believe in psychic powers. Just as troubling as this trend toward syncretism (mixing different beliefs or practices) is the departure from historic Christianity. Half of those Roof interviewed told him that "the various religions of the world are 'equally good and true.'" As Roof put it, what is true of Americans in general is increasingly true of those who describe themselves as born again. The problem is that "they trust their own experiences more than anything else."

This reliance on subjective experiences rather than on the

unchanging truth of the Scriptures is what leads to credulity and syncretism. Belief systems based on personal experiences alone place no priority on objective truth. Too often, instead of asking, "Is this true?" people ask, "How does it make me feel?"

It's the perfect belief system for an age that places the self at the center of the universe. Each person becomes the judge not only of what's true "for him" but also of what's right. Right and wrong, like truth, become about what we feel.

As Roof and others have noted, the past few decades have seen a shift in the way American Christians define being *born again* and *evangelical.* Such terms are no longer a matter of believing certain doctrines or teachings; rather, they're a matter of having a particular life-changing experience.

While personal transformation is an important part of being a follower of Christ, Christianity is about more than feelings or experiences. It's about affirming what the Scriptures teach about God, the person of Jesus Christ, and the origins and destiny of man. Believing means not only saying yes to what the Scriptures say is true but also saying no to whatever contradicts those teachings.

This is what our churches and our Bible study groups need to hear. Trusting their experiences has led many people to put their trust in myths. Have you? When you hear something new, do you ask, "How does it make me feel?" or "Is it true?"

Lord, help me to remember that true Christian faith involves being wise not in my own eyes but in yours and that means clinging to your great unchanging truth, not to my own changeable and gullible feelings.

CRAVING SPIRITUAL MILK

TO READ: 1 PETER 1:18–2:8

Like newborn babies, crave pure spiritual milk,
so that by it you may grow up in your salvation. 1 Peter 2:2

Wesleyan University in Connecticut, originally a Methodist college, recently became embroiled in controversy over a course titled Pornography: Writing of Prostitutes. The course requires students to create their own works of pornography.

Across the country, colleges such as Northwestern, Columbia, and New York University are also offering "porn studies."

How did undergraduates go from studying Homer to creating pornography? The answer is that sexual liberation has become nothing less than a worldview—a vision of reforming human nature and creating a new society. It's a worldview that begins with the assumption that humans are products of Darwinian evolution and concludes that we find our identity by delving into the biological, the natural, the instinctual—especially the sexual instincts. Liberating our sexuality thus becomes the high road to healing and wholeness.

For Margaret Sanger, an early champion of birth control, the drama of history consists in a struggle to free humanity from biblical morality. "Through sex," she wrote, "mankind may attain the great spiritual illumination which will transform the world, which will light up the only path to an earthly paradise."

The same quasi-religious fervor motivated Alfred Kinsey, who likewise saw history as a moral drama, with science competing against religion and superstition. He spoke as if the introduction of biblical sexual morality were the watershed of human history, a sort of "Fall" from which we must be redeemed through sexual liberation.

Another architect of the sexual revolution was Wilhelm Reich, who taught that all dysfunctions are a symptom of sexual failure—and can be cured by sexual release. A book about his philosophy is aptly titled *Salvation through Sex.*

These are the ideas that have filtered down to our colleges, which explains why they're offering courses on pornography. The goal of sexual liberation is not merely titillation or sensual gratification but a complete worldview that aims at freeing the inner self from the evils of repression and restoring its original wholeness—and then renewing all society.

Of course, these grandiose claims are completely contrary to the facts. Social science has uncovered clear evidence that sexual licentiousness is devastating to any society. The decline of sexual morality in America since the 1960s has produced an epidemic of abortion, sexually transmitted diseases, and children born into fatherless homes, with all the attendant social pathologies, such as increased drug abuse and crime.

If we want to stand against the sexualization of American culture, it's not enough to express moral outrage. We must fight the battle on the level of worldview versus worldview. We must be ready to show that true liberation is not about the gratification of our sexual instincts but the satisfaction of our deepest spiritual hunger.

Father, help me to be vigilant against those who would twist the salvation message and then offer it to me, hoping that I'll bite. May I always desire to "rid myself of all deceit" and "crave pure spiritual milk"—that is, the salvation and true satisfaction that can be found only through your Son.

REDEEMED BY ART

TO READ: 2 CORINTHIANS 5:11-21

If anyone is in Christ, he is a new creation; the old has gone, the new has come!
2 Corinthians 5:17

A man in Austria named Jack Unterweger murdered a woman in 1976 and was sentenced to life in prison. While there, he made good use of the library and began to write. In time he became a best-selling author, surprising the public with his compelling insights into the world of crime.

He portrayed himself as a victim, abandoned by his prostitute mother and raised in foster homes where he was abused. He became a media darling, and soon the public demanded his release. So after fifteen years, the prison gates were flung open, and at age forty, Jack Unterweger was a free man. When he assured the media that he would never spend another day in prison, they declared him "redeemed by art"!

Almost immediately a wave of murders of prostitutes began. As a writer with expert knowledge of the subject, Unterweger was hired by a German magazine to cover the story. A retired police officer read about the case and notified authorities that the killer was using the same methods as a man he had sent to prison years earlier—the same Jack Unterweger.

While searching the writer's apartment, police found receipts from a trip to America, and Los Angeles police had three murders that fit Unterweger's MO exactly. When the FBI got involved, profilers said all the murders were the work of one man.

Airline tickets and credit card records revealed that Unterweger had been in each location at the time of the murders. But the media refused to believe it. Unterweger was covering the case, they said. He had a right to be there. There was just one problem: The writer had arrived before the murders occurred.

The evidence became conclusive: Unterweger had killed twelve women. He was charged, tried, convicted, and sentenced to life in prison. Art had not redeemed him after all.

Indeed, art has no power to redeem. True literature and art can uplift the spirit. But over the years, many have been tricked into believing that art can also transform the heart.

Can a guilty man be redeemed? Absolutely. It happens every day—but not by art. No one will ever be redeemed by art or social engineering or charity or good works—or sitting in a church pew, for that matter. Not a murderer—not any of us.

The real answer is nowhere more clearly put than in the Scriptures, which say, "If anyone is in Christ, he is a new creation." And that's the greatest artwork of all.

Father, how foolishly and tragically gullible are those who put their trust in anything or anyone but you. Help me to bring good out of evil by using stories like this one as a witness to the power of Christ alone to redeem lives.

AUGUST 7

ABUSING OUR POWER

TO READ: JONAH 4:1-11

*Nineveh has more than a hundred and twenty thousand people who
cannot tell their right hand from their left, and many cattle as well.
Should I not be concerned about that great city? Jonah 4:11*

Most Christians are aware of the dangerous agenda of the animal
rights movement and how most militants—driven by a naturalistic
logic—place animals and humans on the same moral plane.

But Matthew Scully, author of *Dominion: The Power of Man, the Suffering of Animals, and the Call to Mercy,* thinks that many Christians tend
to dismiss the topic too quickly. Christians talk about being good
stewards, he says, but what does being a good steward actually mean?
How often do we give examples of how the duty of Christian stewardship over animals is ignored—or abused?

Scully raises a good question. Christians need to be in the vanguard
when it comes to protecting animals from abuse, because they are part
of God's creation. While animals are certainly not morally equivalent
to humans, they nonetheless have certain rights that we must recognize and respect, just as earlier generations of Christians did.

St. Francis of Assisi was famous for his passionate concern for animals. In *The Problem of Pain,* C. S. Lewis calls the suffering of animals
"appalling." "Animal pain," he wrote, is "begun by Satan's malice and
perpetrated by man's desertion of his post." William Wilberforce, the
great abolitionist, took a public stand against cruelty to animals. And
Malcolm Muggeridge asked, "How is it possible to look for God and
sing His praises while insulting and degrading His creatures?"

When it comes to animal welfare today, Christians have allowed the
secular world to set the agenda. Their faulty logic—that humans and

animals are morally equivalent—becomes clear when militants raid restaurants to "rescue" lobsters, demand that cockroaches be treated "humanely" on film sets, or compare eating meat to the Holocaust.

People like this give the animal rights movement a bad name. And it's partly our fault, because Christians have ignored the debate over animal welfare—except to criticize radical groups such as People for the Ethical Treatment of Animals (PETA).

Good stewardship means doing more than criticizing or simply feeling bad about animal abuse. When God reasons with Jonah, he makes it clear that he is concerned not only about the enormous number of humans who would die if he destroyed Nineveh but also about the huge number of cattle that would perish.

We need to get involved in shaping laws that determine animal treatment. But first we must make it our business to find out how the fish of the sea, the birds of the air, and the cattle of the earth are treated on factory farms, in research labs, and by commercial fishermen.

We have a duty to prevent the needless torment of animals—torment that, as Lewis observes, we Christians perpetrate when we desert our posts.

Father, forgive me for ignoring the suffering of the animals you created. Show me ways through which I can lessen their torment, not out of sentimental feelings or false beliefs about their equality, but because you care enough for them to command me to do it.

AUGUST 8

SOMETHING BEAUTIFUL
FOR GOD

TO READ: TITUS 1:5-9

*Since an overseer is entrusted with God's work, he must be blameless. . . .
He must be hospitable, one who loves what is good,
who is self-controlled, upright, holy and disciplined. Titus 1:7-8*

The pharmacist waited on his customers and then turned to a small woman in her thirties waiting quietly in the background. She stepped forward with a long list and a shy smile. Would the pharmacist be willing, she asked, "to do something beautiful for God?"

A few minutes later the woman walked out of the pharmacy with her arms full of donated medical supplies to care for the sick and dying. The world would later come to know that young woman, who had just begun her ministry to the poor in Calcutta, as Mother Teresa.

In *Great Souls: Six Who Changed a Century*, journalist David Aikman describes how Mother Teresa never relied on worldly power. Instead, she relied on the moral authority that came from God—authority she gained from living out the gospel as she ministered to the poor. And she was persistent.

On one occasion, the young Mother Teresa "came across a dying woman whose body . . . had been eaten by rats and ants." When the staff of a nearby hospital balked at accepting the woman, Aikman writes, "Mother Teresa simply refused to move until they changed their minds."

Mother Teresa relied on her moral authority once again in 1971 when she defied the Indian government, which was encouraging abortions for women who had been raped by Pakistani soldiers. "What you are going to help them to do is to commit murder—and

439

this will be with them for life," she told the authorities, and she herself took in scores of unwanted children.

How does one earn moral authority? By being faithful—by doing one's duty.

The great paradox of heroism is that we cannot achieve it if we set out to become heroes. Rather, as God calls us, we submerge our ambitions in obedience to him and do our duty.

We Christians must contemplate the difference between power and moral authority. Politicians can gain political power. But the minute they leave office, they lose it. If Christians are obedient to a transcendent calling, God confers authority that will only grow over time. If we are faithful to God's commands, we will, at the very least, become powerful witnesses in our own neighborhood. Or we may, as Mother Teresa did, become witnesses to the whole world.

Father, help me to remember that no matter how much I do for the poor, I will never be a worthy witness to your character if my private life is in shambles.

AUGUST 9

EXPLOITING THE GENERATION GAP

TO READ: PROVERBS 4:1-10

Listen, my sons, to a father's instruction; pay attention and gain understanding.
Proverbs 4:1

Imagine that strangers approached your twelve-year-old daughter and said they wanted to talk with her about her problems at home, at school, and with boys. You'd probably be pretty upset. After all, who has the right to give your daughter advice—especially on what's going on at home? Shouldn't she be talking to *you?*

Not according to a magazine called *CosmoGirl!* The way the editors see it, parents are preachy and out of touch with what teenage girls need to hear. And *CosmoGirl!* aims to fill that void.

CosmoGirl! is the brainchild of the Hearst publishing empire, which publishes *Cosmopolitan* magazine. *Cosmo,* of course, played a big role in launching the sexual revolution back in the sixties.

Hearst is capitalizing on a lucrative trend in magazines aimed at teens. *CosmoGirl!* is loaded with horoscopes, celebrity gossip, and articles on love and sex. In one issue a columnist told girls how to get their own way when their parents disapprove of their plans.

When *CosmoGirl!* launched in 1999, its Web site announced: "We can help you with questions about your changing body that you feel funny about asking your doctor or mom." . . . "[Are you n]ervous about the pressures that boys may be putting on you? [Are y]our parents totally stressing you out? You can look to *CosmoGirl!* for realistic advice."

The Web site boasts that the editor of *CosmoGirl!* is "someone who's young enough to understand . . . and can tell you the real deal—without being preachy like a mom." This trend to reach over parents' heads and appeal directly to kids has become pronounced over the last thirty years. Before then, parents were the recognized arbiters of what messages their kids were getting—and of what they purchased. But today companies market directly to kids without much concern about whether or not parents approve of either the messages or the products.

And what is *CosmoGirl!*'s message? That kids can't trust their parents. After all, if they trusted their parents, they probably wouldn't be buying magazines like *CosmoGirl!* So companies have a huge stake in keeping children divided from—and at odds with—their parents. It's a cynical ploy, and one that Christians must stand against.

Our best defense is to take an active interest in our children's lives. Remember, kids turn elsewhere for advice only when they don't get satisfactory answers at home. If you create a world that is loving and honest, you can neutralize the lure of magazines.

We all need close relationships with those who can give us wise advice—and they, in turn, may sometimes need wise and loving advice from *us*. When you have problems and need advice, do you turn to a magazine—or to a wise Christian friend?

When it comes to our children, we should remember that even teenagers long for an honest, open relationship with their parents. No matter what the media tell you, that's worth far more than a whole truckload of makeup tips, celebrity gossip—and unbiblical advice.

Lord, remind me, when I need a reminder, to make time to listen to my children—to seek them out even when I am busy, to listen to their heartaches, and to offer wise council that reflects your wisdom.

RITUALS AND ROMANCE

TO READ: GENESIS 29:1-14

*When Jacob saw Rachel daughter of Laban . . . he went over and rolled
the stone away from the mouth of the well and watered his uncle's sheep.
Then Jacob kissed Rachel. Genesis 29:10-11*

Courtship has changed a lot in recent years, and not for the better.
Consider a couple of recent personal ads from the *Washingtonian* magazine: One Romeo says he's looking for a "drop-dead gorgeous, sensitive, passionate" woman to share his Caribbean holiday. Another,
who describes himself as a "financially secure" executive, wants you
to call if you're a "strikingly beautiful woman" who enjoys "fast boats
and overseas travel."

It would appear that men who offer financial incentives in exchange for female companionship view romance through a crass economic lens. How on earth did this happen?

Historian Beth Bailey observes that until the start of the twentieth
century, dating as we know it did not exist. If a boy wanted to get to
know a girl, he had to wait until she invited him to her home. But between 1890 and 1925, young women began moving from farms to the
cities. Jammed together in crowded rooms, they no longer had parlors into which to invite gentlemen callers. As a result, Bailey writes,
"a 'good time' . . . became identified with public places and commercial amusements."

The move from private parlors to public dance halls, she says, "fun-
damentally altered the balance of power between men and women."
Men no longer had to wait for women to invite them to their homes.
Instead, women now waited for men to invite them on dates.

Little by little, Bailey writes, dating "moved courtship into the world of the economy. Men's money was at the center of the dating system." This led to a view of "dating as a system of exchange best understood . . . as an economic system." In a sense, the author says, a woman was "selling her company to [a man]."

The implications of this arrangement have recently become chillingly apparent. The results of a survey of boys indicated that more than half of them thought if a man spends "a lot of money" on his date, it's okay to demand that she have sex with him. Other research finds that many young women agree. How tragic.

The biblical view of courtship and marriage teaches couples to put aside their own selfish desires and focus on the interests of the loved one. But the cold, hard world of economics teaches the opposite: that we're entitled to a "return on our investment."

Today's young women might consider taking a leaf out of their great-grandmothers' etiquette books. Instead of letting a man pay for an expensive dinner, suggest options that cost little or nothing: Take in a free concert, lecture, or ball game, or attend church activities together.

As for all those rich Romeos trying to buy a woman's company through vulgar classified ads? They should remember that the economics of courtship works both ways. They may find the "drop-dead gorgeous, sensitive, passionate" woman they're looking for—only to find that she's a gold digger who takes them for everything they've got.

Lord, help me to reject the selfish values of my culture and be willing to engage in "sacrificial" romance, because that is the best training for a marriage that is both sacrificial—and romantic.

A DANGEROUS COMPROMISE

TO READ: COLOSSIANS 1:24–2:5

I tell you this so that no one may deceive you by fine-sounding arguments.
Colossians 2:4

Does calling yourself "born again" make you a Christian?

In *Spiritual Marketplace: Baby Boomers and the Remaking of American Religion,* sociologist Wade Clark Roof chronicles the shift in religious attitudes in contemporary America. Roof finds that as a result of the baby boomer "quest culture," many Americans understand religious faith as some sort of emotional personal experience, which they describe as spiritual. All sorts of strange beliefs can fit under that heading.

By describing themselves as spiritual rather than religious, these people tell us a lot. The word *religion* comes from the Latin word for "to bind." But boomer spirituality distrusts authority and dismisses the importance of belonging ("binding oneself") to a particular church or denomination.

Their emphasis on being spiritual carries with it a syncretistic approach to belief. In other words, instead of adhering to a specific set of doctrines, they feel free to pick and choose from various belief systems or to create their own tailor-made religion.

Unfortunately, syncretism has found its way into evangelical circles as well. Roof says that many people who describe themselves as "born again Christians" actually hold beliefs that are at odds with biblical Christianity. Some 25 percent of those interviewed in Roof's study believe in the possibility of communicating with the dead. A third of them believe in reincarnation and astrology, and half say they believe in psychic powers.

Moreover, half agreed with the statement "The various religions of the world are 'equally good and true.'" This prompted Roof to characterize this brand of so-called born-again Christianity as "markedly different" from earlier varieties. As columnist Terry Mattingly puts it, "Born again . . . doesn't mean what it used to mean." It also tells us that polls of born-again voters can be very misleading.

Actually, it's not that born-again Christianity has changed. It's that Roof's subjects, like many of those who claim to be born-again Christians, actually practice an entirely different faith. The situation Roof describes is analogous to the circumstances theologian J. Gresham Machen confronted in the 1920s and 1930s. Liberal theologians had introduced new doctrines and ideas into the church and had often claimed biblical warrant for those ideas. As a result, many people were confused by these teachings.

In *Christianity and Liberalism,* Machen showed that while those ideas might be attractive, they weren't Christianity. In the same way, while the mixture of Christianity and other religions may suit the spirit of our age, it simply isn't born-again Christianity.

We need to remind others and ourselves that Christianity is more than a spiritual experience. It's a worldview—a set of beliefs about the God who acted in history, beliefs revealed through Scripture and transmitted by our two-thousand-year-old heritage of Western civilization. It is these beliefs, not our "spiritual" feelings, that define what it means to be a Christian—no matter what the spirit of the age may tell us.

Lord, may I cling closely enough to you, your Word, and your followers that I am not taken in by the "fine-sounding arguments" of the modern age.

AUGUST 12

WORSHIPPING THE GOD OF TECHNOLOGY

TO READ: ISAIAH 2:12-22

In that day men will throw away to the rodents and bats their idols of silver and idols of gold, which they made to worship. Isaiah 2:20

A congregation was faced with a financial dilemma. They had just installed an expensive, high-end audio and video system for their sanctuary and were way over budget. To solve the problem, the congregation decided to lay off one of its two pastors. Technology, they were forced to conclude, was a higher priority than pastoral care.

In another church, the pastoral staff no longer makes decisions about what to preach. The authority falls instead to the technologists who run the high-tech worship services. Their ability to get images to project during the services dictates the preaching topics.

In *High-Tech Worship? Using Presentational Technologies Wisely,* Calvin College professor Quentin Schultze does not suggest that there's anything wrong with the use of worship technology, but he does urge churches to ask some pertinent questions before purchasing high-tech equipment: What is the purpose of worship? How should we worship? How will technology enhance—or detract from—our worship?

"Worship," he writes, "is a natural response of praise to God as our Creator, Redeemer, and Comforter. We worship because we recognize by grace what God has done, is doing, and has promised to continue doing. . . . God promises to carry through on His gift of salvation. Worship, therefore, is partly a memorial that enables us together to thank God for His 'covenant fidelity.' " Worship is the result of a worldview that recognizes God as the One who made us, provides for us, and gives our lives meaning and direction. Worship is not about us and our well-being but about God and his glory.

Schultze suggests we take into account our own church's worship tradition and the congregation's personality and goals. Only after doing that are we prepared to think wisely about the impact technology may have on us as we worship. Schultze recognizes that congregational singing often benefits when everyone looks up at words on a screen. But if we're not careful, he warns, worship through technology "can be reduced to engineering maximum impact on audiences. This mechanistic concept assumes that worship should be like a machine, calculated and packaged to meet spiritual and religious needs." When that happens, technology robs us of true worship.

Many Americans firmly—and wrongly—believe that technology can *improve* virtually everything. But it does *change* almost everything, for technology is not neutral. Technology changes the way we view the world. When it's used in worship, it can change the way we view God, ourselves, and our faith. Technology must always be a means, not an end.

How does your church use technology? Schultze's book is a reminder that Christians must be wise stewards of all things, including technology. We must remember that when we place anything above God—be it gold, silver, or technological nuts and bolts—we're engaging in idol worship.

Father, let me not be seduced by the promises of technological "improvements" to my church. Give wisdom to the leaders of my congregation that they would fully comprehend how every proposed purchase will affect our worship of you—the God who has been worshipped in low-tech ways for generations before us.

BIBLICAL STUMBLING BLOCKS

TO READ: DEUTERONOMY 7:1-11

*You must destroy them totally. Make no treaty with them,
and show them no mercy. Deuteronomy 7:2*

Do unbelievers ever ask you thorny questions about the nature of God? Some people, for example, wonder how God could order Israelite soldiers to slaughter the children of their enemies.

The idea that a good and loving God would do such an apparently wicked thing is a stumbling block to faith for many people. That question nagged so much at journalist Lee Strobel that he went to theologian Norman Geisler for some answers. In *The Case for Faith,* Strobel describes their conversation and what he learned.

Strobel reminded Geisler of all the times God commanded the Israelites to kill children. In Deuteronomy 7, God commanded Israel to "totally destroy" the Canaanites and six other nations. In Exodus, God ordered the execution of every firstborn Egyptian son. He also ordered Israel to destroy the Amalekites—including women and children.

Strobel asked, "Can people be expected to worship [God] if he orders innocent children to be slaughtered?"

The answer, Geisler told him, is that God's character is absolutely holy; he must punish sin and rebellion. The Bible shows that the Amalekites were utterly depraved—and their goal was to wipe out God's chosen people. So God used the Israelites as his instrument of judgment.

"But why did innocent children need to be destroyed?" Strobel asked.

First, Geisler says, "God is sovereign over all of life, and he has the right to take it if he wishes." Second, for good or ill, children throughout history have always shared the fate of their parents. Third, given the violent and depraved nature of the Amalekite culture, "there was no hope for these children."

In a sense, Geisler added, "God's action was an act of mercy," in that some Christians believe that a child who dies before the age of accountability goes to heaven. In any event, it is the prerogative of a merciful God to make that decision. Finally, the Amalekites were given plenty of time to repent, and they chose not to. God's holy nature demanded that he deal with their persistent evil.

It was much the same with the Canaanites, who practiced incest, bestiality, cultic prostitution, and child sacrifice. The Bible says their culture was so evil that it nauseated God. So he destroyed the Canaanites, but the righteous among them were spared. The point, Geisler said, is that "whoever repented, God has been willing to save."

God also destroyed the Canaanites for a reason that will resonate with modern parents: God wanted Israel, in the words of Norman Geisler, to be "relatively free from the outside corruption that could have destroyed it like a cancer."

Sometimes it isn't easy to understand and accept what God determines. But even in our confusion—or personal distress—we must be willing to trust in the rightness of God's righteous decisions.

Lord God, may I never feel ashamed when others ask me how I can worship a God whose holy nature at times demands "no mercy" on evildoers. Help me to remember that, while your actions may sometimes confound me, your holy character contains no contradictions.

AUGUST 14

WHAT MAKES
THE MATRIX POSSIBLE?

TO READ: 2 CORINTHIANS 1:3-11

He has delivered us from such a deadly peril. 2 Corinthians 1:10

Millions of Americans have watched a box-office smash called *The Matrix,* starring Keanu Reeves. Filled with thrilling special effects and martial-arts sequences, *The Matrix* has spawned two sequels.

Although the film is full of references to cyber culture and Eastern mysticism, it's a story that would be impossible without Christianity.

The Matrix tells the story of humanity enslaved by a set of machine masters. To keep people from rebelling against their captors, the machines have created an alternate reality called the Matrix that prevents people from knowing who is actually in control.

But there's a problem with the machines' otherwise flawless plan: Seers have foretold the coming of "the one" who will deliver humanity from its bondage. This sounds familiar, doesn't it?

But as it turns out, the way "the one" delivers his people isn't what we might expect. His companions speak to the deliverer in cryptic phrases: "I can only show you the door, you must walk through," or "When the time comes, you won't need to dodge the bullet." His power to deliver lies in his ability to ignore what he believes is real and, therefore, to shape reality for his own purposes.

This is straight out of Zen Buddhism, which teaches that salvation comes through our understanding that all human experience, including suffering, is illusory. In other words, slavery is unpleasant because we're attached to the illusory idea of freedom.

The problem is that if you believe that suffering is illusory or the product of our attachment to the idea of freedom, there's little incentive to deliver anyone, starting with yourself. There's no real hope for redemption. That's why the film's hero, in order to save the day, ultimately has to act in a manner much more consistent with the biblical salvation account, including sacrifice and even resurrection.

This reliance on Christian themes in film plots should not surprise viewers: It was Christianity that gave humanity the idea of a savior in the first place. Before you can believe in a savior of any kind, however, it's necessary to believe in a God who both cares about his creation and continues to work through history on behalf of his people.

This conception of God was unknown in the pagan world. Pagan gods were capricious and cruel or incapable of feeling anything.

Christianity revealed to the world a personal God who not only saw our suffering but also intervened dramatically to deliver his people—first during the Israelites' exodus from Egypt and then, decisively, through the death and resurrection of his own Son.

These events changed not only history but our stories as well. With Christ there was a basis for hope, for belief in something more than fate or the whims of the gods. Belief in the Christian God made happy endings for the human drama possible.

Lord, help me to watch films discerningly and use them as witnessing tools to those who see only a good story without realizing that sometimes they are seeing a flickering imitation of your Great Story.

AUGUST 15

FASHION'S FEROCIOUS ASSAULT

TO READ: 1 TIMOTHY 2:9-10

I also want women to dress modestly, with decency and propriety. I Timothy 2:9

What do clothing manufacturers consider appropriate attire for young girls these days?

You may not want to find out.

The chain store Hot Topic, which carries clothing for teens, offers stripper-inspired thong underwear featuring such decorations as the Cat in the Hat and the words "Pay up, sucker!" Other stores carry T-shirts announcing to the world that the little girl wearing one is a "porn star."

The marketing of sex to kids is nothing new, but these efforts are increasing, and they're aimed where many kids are most vulnerable: fashion. In the past few years GapKids has sold terry-cloth bikinis for preteens, according to the *Washington Post*. In Canada, the *Ottawa Citizen* reported that a seven-year-old girl accessed a hard-core pornography site by typing in the Internet address printed on her T-shirt.

This blatant pitch to kids underscores the problems facing parents these days.

First, marketers aim this sexual imagery directly at kids, bypassing parental authority and protection. A recent PBS *Frontline* exposed the advertising world's efforts to create and sell to a parallel culture for youth.

And why not? According to Michael Wood, vice-president of Teenage Research Unlimited, a company that studies teenage trends, girls twelve to eighteen currently spend more than thirty-seven billion

453

dollars on clothes. With money like that, it is easy to see why companies such as Playboy, that have always put the bottom line before responsibility, are willing to exploit our kids for profit.

As Helen Isaacson, president of Playboy's product marketing, told the *Wall Street Journal*, "We need to develop a buzz in the younger market and then move up."

How despicable. This debate is not simply about the appropriateness of certain clothing. Playboy is not just selling a bathing suit; it's selling a lifestyle that revolves around sex without consequences and devoid of emotion and meaning. This is grooming young girls to be the sexual objects young men want them to be and doing it under the guise of playfulness and fun.

The divorce of sexuality from the Christian ideals of fidelity, selflessness, and sacrifice has resulted in many of our culture's woes. Playboy is selling poison to our children, not fun. When children believe the messages about sexuality embodied in the logos on skimpy outfits, they are internalizing patterns of thinking and behavior that will make it difficult to build lasting relationships. They are setting themselves and others up for a lifetime of suffering.

We need to make sure the young people in our lives understand this. And we must all take care to dress fittingly for every occasion, avoiding inappropriate choices in an effort to look more youthful or to gain the attention of the opposite sex. God wants us to clothe ourselves in good deeds—not in attention-getting garb.

Father, help me to protect my children from those who would draw them into an ugly world of sexual exploitation by marketing to their need for acceptance. Give me the words to help my children understand that the God who designed their sexuality also designed the conditions under which it can be most beautifully enjoyed.

AUGUST 16

IS HOMOSEXUALITY CONTAGIOUS?

TO READ: EZEKIEL 18:19-28

The soul who sins is the one who will die. Ezekiel 18:20

A few years ago the *Atlantic Monthly* described an audacious new claim that many things once thought to be genetically based are in fact caused by germs.

There's a widespread consensus these days that ulcers, for example, are actually caused by a virus. But some biologists think there may be evidence of a viral cause for heart disease, cancer, Alzheimer's, psychiatric illnesses—even homosexuality.

Biologist Paul Ewald of Amherst College says the idea came from considering the Darwinian idea of "evolutionary fitness." If Darwin were right, then genetic traits that reduce the chances of an organism's survival or reproduction would be wiped out by natural selection.

But why have some diseases lasted so long and become so common? If natural selection were doing its job, the genes that predispose people to heart disease and cancer ought to have been weeded out long ago. No, that idea has been discredited, and the failure of the standard Darwinian paradigm is now causing biologists like Ewald to search for alternative causes to these diseases.

And yet, the germ theory seems just as preposterous as the old genetic theory. A virus for depression? for homosexuality? There's virtually no evidence for such a theory. The frequency and distribution don't even come close to fitting the pattern of an infectious disease. Only someone totally committed to scientific naturalism would even think of reducing complex moral and psychological conditions to a viral infection.

That's the real weakness of the germ theory. Biologists are facing pressure to come up with such strange theories not because of the evidence but because they are already committed lock, stock, and barrel to a form of reductionism that refuses to see human beings as anything more than part of material nature. Therefore, if genetics fails to explain something, there must be some other natural cause—say, a virus. There's simply no room in today's scientific world for the idea that human beings are more than nature—that depression or homosexuality might have a spiritual component.

We know that people may be depressed because they are lonely or feel that life has no meaning. It's time to make the case that the spiritual dimension is real—that it can even have scientifically measurable effects.

The late Dr. David Larson of the National Institute for Healthcare Research has collected several studies showing that people with strong religious commitments suffer less depression and stress and mental disorder than those without such a commitment. In one Gallup survey, they were twice as likely to describe themselves as "very happy."

The scientific explanation bandied in the *Atlantic Monthly* is just the latest fad—an attempt to explain all of our existence by natural causes. But the time has come for scientists and researchers to look beyond genes and viruses and finally admit what their own research shows: Humans are spiritual and responsible beings.

And the Scriptures warn that God will hold us accountable for our actions even if scientists do not.

Lord, how fanatically the secular world seeks answers to every human problem—answers that dismiss your existence. May I never be found blaming germs, genes, or other fashionable theories for my failures when the real cause is old-fashioned sin.

AUGUST 17

SMUGGLED THEOLOGY

TO READ: LUKE 12:22-34

Where your treasure is, there your heart will be also. Luke 12:34

There's a story about a public-school librarian who did all she could to keep Christian literature out of the library. Ironically, she went out of her way to order plenty of copies of The Chronicles of Narnia by C. S. Lewis. These children's stories are wonderful allegories of the gospel message, but the librarian did not realize that.

This story illustrates how successfully Lewis was able to, as he put it, "smuggle ... [theology] into people's minds ... without their knowing it."

Perhaps the best example of how Lewis did this is *The Lion, the Witch, and the Wardrobe.* The story features four children in wartime Britain who enter a world called Narnia through a clothes wardrobe. The children encounter talking beasts, dwarves and giants, and even talking trees and river gods. An evil White Witch holds Narnia prisoner by keeping the land in perpetual winter—until a majestic lion called Aslan offers himself as a sacrifice and thereby lifts the curse that has long held Narnia.

Like that hostile librarian, many people who love the Narnia books have no idea that Aslan is an allegorical representation of Christ.

In his essay "Sometimes Fairy Stories May Say Best What's to Be Said," published in *Of Other Worlds: Essays and Stories,* Lewis explains that he communicated the gospel message in story form because fairy tales "could steal past a certain inhibition which had paralysed much of my own religion in childhood." Why, Lewis asks, does "one find it so hard to feel as one was told one ought to feel about God or about the sufferings of Christ?" The chief reason, Lewis suggests, "was that one was told one ought to."

But, Lewis proposes, suppose one could cast biblical truths into an imaginary world. Suppose we could "strip them of their stained-glass and Sunday school associations." Could we then make them for the first time appear in real potency? Given the enormous popularity of the Narnia books, it would seem that Lewis accomplishes this goal. Children and even adults condition themselves to receive explicit truth by ingesting it implicitly.

When children come to love stories that exalt self-sacrifice, virtue, and nobility, they can't help but respond to the Great Story that proclaims those very things. We need to get these books into the hands of children—and perhaps reread them ourselves if we find our own faith becoming a bit stale.

Because the Narnia books do not evoke certain prejudices about church, readers who would never touch a Bible can hear and be touched by the truth. As E. L. Mascall put it in *Theology* magazine, in Lewis's fantasies "fiction and theology are so skillfully blended that the non-Christian will not realize that he is being instructed until it is too late."

Father, guide me in offering the right books to youngsters who come from homes hostile to you. I pray that the message of these books will be smuggled past their prejudices and will prepare their hearts for an understanding of who and what their treasure should be: the gift of your Son.

AUGUST 18

KEEPING OUR VOWS

TO READ: JEREMIAH 3:1-10

If a man divorces his wife and she leaves him and marries another man, should he return to her again? Jeremiah 3:1

The minister was outraged, and he didn't care who knew it. His question for Dr. Laura Schlessinger was this: Was he out of bounds to sue a couple he had recently married—a couple who had promised never to divorce? The pastor explained to Dr. Laura that the divorcing couple had begged him to marry them. They promised they would never part. But part they did—just eighteen months after the ceremony.

The minister asked, "Do you think taking them to court for some token amount would be a good idea? After all, they made a promise to God, to me, and to the guests at their wedding that they would stay married until death." And he added: "I provided a service on the condition that they were marrying for life. They are breaking the contract, and I want compensation for wasting so many hours on that wedding."

When Dr. Laura posed this question to her radio audience, the response was overwhelming. One woman said, "I think [everyone] who attended should be able to sue for fraud." She labeled the wedding "a deceitful attempt to extract cash and gifts from unsuspecting friends and family."

Another had an even better idea: When one marriage partner dumps the other, she said, the minister should invite all the wedding guests back and "unperform" the ceremony. The departing spouse would be forced to explain why he or she is leaving, buy presents for the guests, and pay all the expenses of the "unceremony."

These ideas may sound humorous—in a vindictive sort of way—but they do raise a serious question. Why can't people keep their marriages together?

Mike McManus, author of *Marriage Savers*, suggests that divorce is partly the fault of the church. McManus maintains that if churches really wanted to keep marriages from unraveling, they would introduce the bride and groom to programs with a proven success record. For example, for engaged couples there's a program called PREPARE. The couple fills out a questionnaire, which provides an objective snapshot of the state of their relationship. Then older married couples teach them concrete strategies for tackling weak areas. PREPARE's questionnaire can predict with 80 percent accuracy which marriages will end in divorce.

The church ought to be a force for preserving the institution God has ordained as the basis of the social order. God frequently uses the concept of divorce to symbolize the brokenness of the relationship between himself and his people, as he does in Jeremiah.

Instead of getting angry about America's tragic divorce rate and suing couples for breach of contract, we ought to do everything we can to help build unbreakable marriages.

Lord, we desecrate your church when we do so little to help the body of Christ build healthy marriages. Show me how I can work with fellow Christians to make it harder for couples to wed unless they appreciate the seriousness of breaking the marital contract—a contract they signed and sealed in your presence.

BECOMING COMMUNAL CHRISTIANS

TO READ: ACTS 4:23–5:6

Those who owned lands or houses sold them, brought the money from the sales and put it at the apostles' feet, and it was distributed to anyone as he had need.
Acts 4:34-35

For many Christians the word *church* means the buildings where Christians meet on Sunday—a place to go to satisfy our spiritual needs. This confusion limits our ability to have an impact on the culture and to spread the gospel.

Focusing on *our* needs is a manifestation of a philosophy that has gripped American life—what sociologists call "radical individualism." Two decades ago, sociologist Robert Bellah wrote *Habits of the Heart: Individualism and Commitment in American Life,* in which he stated that radical individualism was the defining reality of American life. People were so absorbed in themselves that they saw everything in terms of how it would satisfy their personal needs or desires. Bellah argued that this individualism was invading the church, even shaping our ideas about religion. As evidence, he described an interview he had with a woman named Sheila Larson. When Bellah asked her to describe her faith, Larson told him, "It's 'Sheilaism,' just my own little voice."

We so privatize our faith—which becomes little more than simply listening to "our own little voice"—that we undermine the authority of and our need for the church.

Evangelical Protestantism has been especially susceptible to this focus on self. Bellah describes it as the "near exclusive focus on the relationship between Jesus and the individual." Accepting Jesus, he says, as "one's personal Lord and Saviour [has been] almost the whole of piety." Bellah argues that this leads people to believe that if they're "alright with Jesus," they don't need the church.

But seeing Christianity as exclusively, or even primarily, a personal relationship with Jesus falls woefully short of historic Christianity. Reformers such as Luther and Calvin said that participation in the life of the church was not optional for Christians; Calvin claimed that anyone who called himself a Christian while withdrawing from the church was a "traitor."

The Reformers understood that there is a social and communal dimension to Christianity—a dimension that is not optional. This dimension includes matters of discipline and doctrine. Being part of the church means that you don't have the final say in what you should believe or how you should live.

As Bellah reminds us, these are fighting words for many Christians who have appropriated to themselves final authority in these matters. But if Christians hope to have any impact on our culture, we must begin to "recapture God's vision for His people." We must mimic the first Christians, who put themselves under the authority of church leaders—leaders who did not hesitate to discipline unfaithful members, as the story of Ananias and Sapphira reminds us.

There is no room for "Sheilaism" in the evangelical church. Christian identity is not a matter of *me*. It's a matter of *we*.

Lord, let me not fall prey to the idea that I can "go it alone" with you, abandoning your precious flock to get along as well as it can without me. Show me what role I should play in the life of my church, and make me willing to place myself under the authority of those charged with having the "final say" in what I believe and how I behave.

FIGHTING OFF THE "PLANNERS AND CONDITIONERS"

TO READ: PROVERBS 15:3-12, 26-29

The heart of the righteous weighs its answers, but the mouth of the wicked gushes evil. Proverbs 15:28

One of the fiercest ongoing battles in Congress is over stem-cell research and cloning: whether to permit them, whether to fund them, whether this type of research offers any real hope.

If our leaders are smart, they'll heed the warning of an Oxford don who saw it all more than fifty years ago. C. S. Lewis wrote prophetically, "If any one age really attains, by eugenics and scientific education, the power to make its descendents what it pleases, all men who live after are the patients of that power," slaves to the "dead hand of the great planners and conditioners."

Just as Lewis predicted, the biotech revolution is moving like a steamroller. We glibly toss about the term *bioethics,* but sadly, the "bio"—the technology—has overpowered the "ethics."

The reason is that secular ethics has been drained of moral content. The utilitarians—those who demand the greatest good for the greatest number—have seized the high ground, offering dazzling predictions of cures for deadly diseases. Unused embryos will be destroyed anyway, they say—so using them to help the desperately sick is the "pro-life" position.

This is not so. Predictions of what embryonic stem-cell research may accomplish are grossly overstated. In fact, experiments to date have led to some grotesque results. Proponents claim that only embryonic stem cells can meet their research needs, yet researchers have achieved promising results from placental and adult stem cells, the use of which presents no ethical dilemmas.

And what about those "leftover" embryos, which are "just going to be destroyed anyway"? Couples who have adopted and given birth to them ought to show off their beautiful "post-embryos," who are now healthy children.

Missing from the discussion is the fact that the scientists involved in embryonic stem-cell research are poised to make huge profits from these deadly studies. Christians must remind their neighbors that the worst atrocities are performed in the name of humanitarian causes: Sacrificing one to benefit all soon makes all vulnerable. We must, as the psalmist writes, "pursue righteousness" and have discerning answers ready to respond to those whose mouths "gush evil."

We must raise the question C. S. Lewis posed in *The Abolition of Man*: What does it really mean if we set ourselves up as the master of the future destiny of the human race? His answer is chilling: If man with his technology makes the ultimate conquest over nature, he will soon find that nature has conquered him. "If man chooses to treat himself as raw material," Lewis wrote, "raw material he will be," manipulated by dehumanized conditioners.

In our lifetimes, democracy has triumphed over tyranny. What an irony it would be if, by exchanging moral truth for the cold calculus of utilitarianism, our generation ushered in a new and even more terrifying form of tyranny.

Father, may my desire for healing therapies for myself or those I love not tempt me to sacrifice something far more valuable than a cure for "the greatest number": my humanity.

THE MILITARY VALUES GAP

TO READ: EXODUS 12:21-32; 15:3-5

At midnight the Lord struck down all the firstborn in Egypt. Exodus 12:29

A few years ago a report by the Triangle Institute for Security Studies pointed to a widening "values gap" between the U.S. military and American civilians. For instance, many more elite officers identify themselves as "conservative" and "Republican" than do their civilian counterparts. Military officers, the report says, "tend to take a negative view of civilian society, viewing it [as suffering from] a moral crisis." These officers "believe civilian society would be better off if it adopted more of the military's values and behaviors."

This values gap has already "taken a toll on the traditional principle of civilian control over the military," the study concludes.

Civilian control of the military is a defining characteristic of American life and is grounded in certain assumptions. One of them is that those in uniform respect the civilians they are taking orders from, as well as the society they are safeguarding. Without this respect, why would they defer to civilian leadership?

During the 1990s the principle of civilian control was the subject of more ongoing strain than at any time in American history, typified by open dissent between military and civilian leaders over issues such as allowing homosexuals to serve in the military. Then Secretary of Defense William Cohen initiated a campaign to "reconnect" soldiers and civilians.

The real solution is much more fundamental. We need to reconnect civilians themselves to their own moral traditions. Until recently, virtually all Americans, in and out of uniform, had high esteem for such virtues as attention to duty, honor, and sacrifice. Today, the military and the church seem to be the only institutions to still cherish these values. If there is a gap today, it's not the military that has changed but the civilian culture.

This "values gap" reveals that the culture war runs far deeper than surface political battles between religious conservatives and secular elites over issues such as abortion and cloning. The struggle goes to the heart of what kind of people we are—and to the very security of our nation.

The military has continued to preserve concepts like honor and decency and sacrifice—and the result is that they are drifting further and further away from America's mainstream. In weaker nations, this kind of values gap would result in a military coup. That's not a risk here. But we do risk a demoralized military: Soldiers will begin to wonder if it's worth risking their lives for a country that no longer appreciates them.

If your neighbors tell you that Christians are narrow-minded bigots who want to force their morality on everyone else, set them straight: Explain that we are trying to protect those values most essential to a free society—and that means keeping our military willing to fight for it.

We should remember, as well, the sobering lesson of Exodus: When the people are corrupt, no army, however strong, can protect it.

Lord, thank you for soldiers and sailors who love their country enough to be willing to die for it. Help my fellow countrymen—and me—to be worthy of such sacrifice.

BIBLICAL MIRACLES

TO READ: EXODUS 14:19-31

All that night the Lord drove the sea back with a strong east wind and turned it into dry land. Exodus 14:21

Sometimes miracles enhance our faith—but sometimes the accounts of biblical miracles can be a stumbling block to belief. The skeptic asks: What about Jonah and the whale? What about Noah and the Flood? What about the parting of the Red Sea? These stories are held up as so preposterous that no one could possibly take the Bible seriously.

But scientists who study these events say they are not as impossible as they might seem. Sometimes they are just special instances of the application of perfectly normal laws of nature.

Take the parting of the Red Sea. The Bible says God used the east wind, blowing all night, to push the waters back. It's a well-known fact that a steady wind blowing over a body of water can change the water level. So two oceanographers decided to see if the same thing could happen on the narrow sliver of the Red Sea reaching up into the Gulf of Suez. That's where many scholars believe the Israelites crossed as they were fleeing from Pharaoh's army.

Writing in the *Bulletin of the American Meteorological Society,* the scientists concluded that a moderate wind blowing constantly for about ten hours could very well have caused the sea to recede a mile or two. The water level would drop ten feet, leaving dry land for the Israelites to cross. According to one scientist, "The Gulf of Suez provides an ideal body of water for such a process because of its unique geography."

Later, an abrupt change in the wind could cause the water to return rapidly—in a sudden, devastating wave. It could easily have trapped Pharaoh's troops, just as the Bible describes. The study, of course, doesn't prove that the crossing of the Red Sea happened exactly that way. It merely shows that God could have used perfectly normal forces to perform his miraculous deliverance.

A skeptic may argue that if there's a natural explanation, it wasn't a miracle after all. But if it were only a natural event, isn't it strange that the sea parted just when Moses held out his staff—and that it fell back just when Pharaoh's soldiers were at exactly the right place in their hot pursuit?

No, God may use a natural process to accomplish his goals, but it's still a work of his hand, in his timing, and for his purposes.

Our kids can't help but see that the secular world is deeply skeptical about biblical miracles. And many adult Christians privately feel embarrassed when they are challenged about some of the more impossible-sounding miracles of the Bible—challenged by intelligent people who suggest we're fools for believing in such nonsense.

Emerging scientific evidence is giving us and our children the confidence we need to tell a cynical world, "Yes, miracles—God's miracles—really do happen."

Lord, forgive me for ever feeling ashamed of your Word. May I always remember that even without "hard" evidence, I can be confident that every Word of your holy Scriptures is true—because you say it is.

FIGHTING THE ENEMIES OF MARRIAGE

TO READ: GENESIS 19:1-11, 24-25

Then the Lord rained down burning sulfur on Sodom and Gomorrah. . . .
Thus he overthrew those cities. Genesis 19:24-25

"So what if gays and lesbians want to marry? That doesn't do anything to *your* marriage."

We hear that argument often as Americans consider legalizing same-sex "marriage." Stanley Kurtz of the Hoover Institution offers Christians the best argument for keeping marriage between one man and one woman. In the *Weekly Standard,* Kurtz asks, "Will same-sex marriage undermine the institution of marriage?" His answer: "It already has." How? By taking the gap that exists between marriage and parenthood and making it even wider.

"If marriage is only about a relationship between two people and is not intrinsically connected to parenthood," writes Kurtz, "why shouldn't same-sex couples be allowed to marry?" It follows, Kurtz adds, "that once marriage is redefined to accommodate same-sex couples, that change cannot help but lock in and reinforce the very cultural separation between marriage and parenthood that makes gay marriage conceivable to begin with."

He offers Norway, the most conservative of the Scandinavian countries, as exhibit A. Prior to 1993, when the courts imposed same-sex "marriage," Norway had a low out-of-wedlock birth rate. The traditional link between marriage and parenthood was still in place. But once same-sex "marriage" was legalized, Norway's out-of-wedlock birth rate shot up as the traditional link was broken and cohabitation became normal. Gay "marriage" wasn't the only factor, but it appears to have been the decisive one.

As it turns out, that was the plan. Kurtz cites Kari Moxnes, a Norwegian feminist and vocal enemy of marriage. She says, "Norwegian gay marriage was a sign of marriage's growing emptiness, not its strength." And according to Kurtz, Henning Bech, a gay Danish social theorist, "dismisses as an 'implausible' claim the idea that gay marriage promotes monogamy." According to Bech and Norwegian sociologist Rune Halvorsen, "The goal of the gay marriage movements in both Norway and Denmark . . . was not marriage but social approval for homosexuality." The same is true in this country.

Kurtz continues, "If, as in Norway, gay marriage were imposed here by a socially liberal cultural elite, it would likely speed us on the way toward the classic Nordic pattern of less frequent marriage, more frequent out-of-wedlock birth, and skyrocketing family dissolution."

"In effect," he concludes, "Scandinavia has run our experiment for us. The results are in." The verdict: Gay "marriage" will destroy true marriage.

This should hardly surprise us. Christians know what God says about men and women, marriage and sex. We should know by now that when we try to replace his teachings with human doctrines, an entire culture ends up paying a terrible price. That's why we must learn the prudential arguments against same-sex unions and promote them in the public square—before we all suffer the deadly consequences.

Father, I pray that you would bring help and healing to those ensnared by homosexual desires. I pray as well that you would open the eyes of my countrymen to the deceitful arguments others are offering to justify their own agendas. Help us to boldly and lovingly speak the truth about the nature of marriage—and about the tremendous need to protect it.

AUGUST 24

COUNTERFEIT CONSCIENCE

TO READ: JUDGES 21:24-25

In those days Israel had no king; everyone did as he saw fit. Judges 21:25

In 1999 the Montana Supreme Court issued a troubling ruling: It claimed that the state constitution's guarantee of privacy ensures a woman's absolute right to an abortion.

Even more disturbing was the way the court defined the word *conscience.*

The opinion involved a challenge to a 1995 Montana law prohibiting physician's assistants from performing abortions. In overturning the law, the court said that when the Montana constitution uses the term *right to privacy,* it means a right to personal autonomy—including so-called procreative autonomy. The court argued that a woman has a "moral right to decide . . . whether to continue a pregnancy."

"The fundamental right to personal and procreative autonomy and . . . to individual privacy," the court said, "prohibits government from dictating, approving, or condemning values, beliefs, and matters ultimately involving individual conscience." Using the court's absurd logic, a state could not prohibit sexual harassment or even rape. But what really stands out is the court's degraded understanding of "conscience."

This faulty understanding of conscience is illuminated by political philosopher Robert George. As George explains, modernists define the concept of conscience as little more than self will: Conscience merely "licenses behavior by establishing that one doesn't feel bad about doing it." Or, in the words of philosopher Russell Hittinger,

471

conscience is reduced to being "the writer of permission slips" for our behavior. This is what people have in mind when they say, for example, "My conscience does not tell me that abortion is wrong; therefore, abortion is not wrong for me." What they mean is, "I don't feel bad about it, so it's not wrong."

In contrast, the Christian understanding defines conscience as a monitor and guide to our behavior. As John Henry Newman wrote, "Conscience has rights because it has duties. . . . It is a stern monitor." What Newman meant is that the function of conscience is to identify what our specific duties are under the moral law. These duties include both negative prohibitions and positive requirements such as feeding the hungry, helping the poor, and visiting prisoners. These positive duties are every bit as binding as the prohibitions.

Modern culture's failure to see the connection between duty and conscience mirrors a period of time in ancient Israel. Recall the last verse of the book of Judges: "In those days Israel had no king; everyone did as he saw fit." In other words, in the absence of moral leadership and example, people lose a sense of duty and abandon themselves to their own autonomous choices. The good news is that by the same token, leadership— not a king as in Old Testament times but the leadership of godly men and women in the church—can help restore a proper definition of duty and conscience. Each of us should consider ourselves leaders in this area, letting young people see that our consciences are in good working order. They should see us actively engaged in ministry and should also see us resisting the temptation to do what is forbidden—even seemingly minor things such as speeding on the way to a church-run camp.

There's no time to lose. As the current state of abortion law amply demonstrates, a failure to understand what conscience really means can literally make the difference between life and death.

Lord, may my conscience never become so corrupted that I use it to write permission slips for sinful behavior rather than allow it to guide me into goodness. May those under my influence never see me doing what I see fit instead of following your commands.

A U G U S T   2 5

LETTING KIDS BE KIDS

TO READ: JOHN 16:16-33

You will grieve, but your grief will turn to joy. John 16:20

In Salt Lake City a first-grader began compulsively throwing away all of her dolls, even the ones she loved. Her horrified parents finally discovered why: The little girl's teacher had said the world is so crowded and miserable that the only solution is to stop having children. This sensitive child decided that the responsible thing to do was not even to pretend to raise babies.

It used to be that parents and teachers "tried to keep childhood a carefree golden age," writes Marie Winn in *Children without Childhood.* The goal was to "shelter children from life's vicissitudes" as long as possible and give them time to grow up before having to face adult problems and pressures. But the contemporary approach operates on the belief that children must be exposed early to social problems in order to survive in this complex world. School curricula and library books for children all the way down to toddlers cover the gamut of issues: AIDS, death, divorce, pollution, sexual abuse, global warming.

As Michael and Diane Medved write in *Saving Children,* "Kids arrive for kindergarten fed on Sesame Street warnings about 'uncomfortable touches' and armed with a fingerprinted 'stolen child' identification card." The message kids absorb from this is that the world is a dangerous place and they'd better know how to protect themselves. The unspoken subtext, of course, is that no one is willing or able to protect them.

The upshot is that such programs often give children an even greater sense of fear and insecurity. Instead of preparing kids to meet the problems of adulthood with some confidence, these programs burden kids with a paralyzing fear and despair. For example, studies show that school programs warning children about sexual abuse only made the children paranoid. By contrast, gentle instruction from sensitive parents about being cautious may spare children that paranoia.

The best way to prepare kids for adulthood is to give them back their childhood. Let them draw pictures, read stories, and play make-believe—confronting evil mostly in a symbolic form of dragons and trolls and wicked witches that safely disappear with the words *The End*. Years spent in positive play help build the strength of character children will need to confront the intractable problems of adulthood without collapsing into despair.

And the best antidote to despair is an abiding Christian faith, which teaches kids that no matter how dark things look, ultimately evil will suffer defeat, and good will prevail. Jesus said, "In this world you will have trouble. But take heart! I have overcome the world" (John 16:33). That's a comforting lesson for despairing children—and adults.

Father, give me strength to stand firm in the face of teachers or others who would burden my children with adult fears they cannot handle. Help me to tenderly discover whether my children have already been made fearful and if so, to tell them where they can lay their too-heavy burden: in the arms of the One who encouraged little children to come to him: your Son.

HOLY WHODUNITS

TO READ: JEREMIAH 17:9-10

The heart is deceitful above all things and beyond cure. Jeremiah 17:9

The great Christian apologist G. K. Chesterton once wrote that he learned more about the depths of human depravity from a simple priest in an isolated village in the English countryside than he'd ever known: "I did not imagine," Chesterton said, "that the world could hold such horrors."

That country priest became the inspiration for one of the most popular mystery series of all time: Chesterton's Father Brown mysteries.

Father Brown is a rotund, bumbling man of the cloth, yet he has the uncanny ability to solve even the most puzzling crimes. Why? Because his faith gives him insight into the human heart—and its capacity for evil.

In a story called "The Secret of Father Brown," the priest explains that he is able to identify sinners because *he* is a sinner: "I try to get inside the murderer . . . think his thoughts, wrestle with his passions," Father Brown explains. And he adds, "When I am quite sure that I feel exactly like the murderer myself, [then] I know who he is."

In "The Hammer of God," the murderer is a priest who has killed his brother by dropping a hammer onto him from the parapet of a church. Father Brown guesses the truth by observing what had been the daily habits of the two brothers and then putting himself in the place of the priest, who is angry over his brother's blasphemous attitude toward God.

The secular world sometimes dismisses Christians as naive—people who don't understand the real world. But Chesterton's Father

Brown shows us that Christians ought to understand evil better than anyone else: We never romanticize evil as just a product of a disordered environment because we know intimately the depths of our own sin.

On the other hand, Christians are also profoundly optimistic. We know that even the worst evil has a remedy—in the Cross. And so Father Brown never treats his criminals as mere beasts, as less than human. He always confronts them with the opportunity for repentance and treats them as people still capable of responding to divine grace.

The next time you're in a bookstore, why not pick up some Father Brown mysteries and lend them to unsaved friends who love mystery novels? Then discuss the stories together. The books will give your friends a greater understanding of a Christian worldview. And you'll all enjoy the stories about an absent-minded priest who prods the police and converts the criminals.

Father, make me willing to help friends and neighbors submerged in sin—people with whom I can empathize because I offend you in my daily life. And then help me move beyond empathy to a message of redemption, telling a fellow sinner about the One who can cure our sinful hearts.

AUGUST 27

CHALLENGING
SCIENTIFIC FRAUD

TO READ: GENESIS 1:14-23

*God created the great creatures of the sea and every living and moving thing
with which the water teems.* Genesis 1:21

In the early twentieth century—during the Scopes Trial, for instance—
evolution was the new theory challenging settled opinions about divine creation. But now, Darwinian evolution has become the established view, and those who want to consider alternatives have become
the innovative thinkers challenging the status quo.

Nowhere is this stunning role reversal more apparent than in the
story of Roger DeHart, a high school biology teacher in Washington
State who wanted to tell his students about evidence that casts doubt
on aspects of Darwinian evolution. The evidence that DeHart hoped
to discuss wasn't fringe stuff. It was material already published in scientific literature.

For example, biology textbooks have long featured drawings of
various animal embryos that purported to show similarity. This
was widely taken as proof that the species in question shared a
common evolutionary ancestor. But the drawings are seriously
inaccurate. They omit many details and falsely suggest similari-
ties among embryos. Harvard paleontologist Stephen Gould
called the drawings "scientific fraud," and he said that we should
"be ashamed and astonished by the century of [their] mindless re-
cycling" in textbooks.

It sounds like something students ought to know about, yet when
DeHart wanted to bring Gould's article about the fraudulent drawings into his classroom, the school administration forbade him to do

so. He wasn't even allowed to discuss Gould's article or question the drawings in the school district's officially mandated textbook.

The censorship didn't stop there. DeHart wanted to tell his students about the Cambrian Explosion, the sudden appearance of the major groups of animals about 550 million years ago. The Cambrian Explosion has long been a puzzle for Darwinian evolution. Again, DeHart was not permitted to bring in any supplementary materials offering an alternative explanation. It didn't matter that the issue is part of ongoing scientific debate. DeHart's students weren't allowed to see or hear anything that challenged textbook orthodoxy.

It's an amazing, even shocking, story—shocking because most people assume that science ought to be a search for the truth about the natural world, not indoctrination into wishful thinking. Christians need to find ways to bring the truth about evolution's flaws to our nation's children. If kids aren't allowed to learn about these flaws in their schools, we need to get creative—as Christians have always had to do when the censors come knocking: You might consider inviting local kids to an after-school youth meeting featuring a science teacher from a private school. Or think about starting a science club committed to teaching kids alternatives to established—and scientifically invalid—opinion. And then invite the kids to graciously challenge their science teachers with the facts.

Those who covered the Scopes Trial deliberately portrayed Christians as backwoods Neanderthals who were trying to force their biblical "fairy tales" on everyone else. How ironic that today it's the preachers of Darwinist evolution who are coming across as Neanderthals—so-called scientists who refuse to allow the latest scientific theories into the classroom.

Lord, give me courage and creativity to challenge those who would deny the truth to those they teach. May we overwhelm hostile teachers and administrators, both with scientific evidence for your design and with proof of your love— love they witness through our own loving behavior.

THE LIMITS OF KNOWLEDGE

TO READ: 2 CORINTHIANS 11:1-6

I am afraid that just as Eve was deceived by the serpent's cunning, your minds may somehow be led astray. 2 Corinthians 11:3

Today is the birthday of Johann Wolfgang von Goethe, Germany's greatest poet and writer.

Goethe's best-known work is *Faust*, which retells a legend that explores the moral limits of human power. Today, two hundred years after Goethe wrote it, *Faust* seems eerily prophetic.

The Faust legend tells the story of a man who yearns for infinite knowledge and godlike power. Eventually Faust turns to black magic and makes a pact with the devil, who grants him the knowledge he craves in exchange for his soul. That's where we get the concept of "making a Faustian bargain."

In earlier versions of the legend, Faust is condemned to hell for his Promethean overreaching, his yearning to "be like God, knowing good and evil," as the serpent put it in the Garden of Eden (Genesis 3:5). "Faust covets divine status," explains literary critic Roger Shattuck, and in the end he is suitably punished.

But in Goethe's version, Faust is not condemned. In other words, Goethe "calmly usurps the Lord's role and reverses the verdict," Shattuck writes. "Here is our modern Adam, raised up to heaven by a chorus of angels for conduct more proud and defiant than what earned the original Adam banishment from paradise."

The message is that there is no forbidden knowledge, nothing beyond human reach—even if it costs us our souls. Goethe has reversed the very essence of the story; he has abandoned the classical view that knowledge has a moral dimension and that it can sometimes cost us our humanity. This classical perspective looks back to Adam and Eve, whose grasping for the knowledge of good and evil meant disobedience and, ultimately, death.

By contrast, with Goethe we begin to see a distinctively modern view: The search for knowledge is sacrosanct and nothing—not even moral considerations—should limit it. Scientific progress is the new summum bonum, the supreme good that trumps all other values. Modern science unleashed first the atom and now the gene, yet how often do we hear anyone ask what price we will pay for these technologies? Ours is a Faustian generation if ever there was one.

Reading Goethe's play will help you better understand the intellectual challenges we face today and how easily our minds can be "led astray," as Paul warns. It serves, as well, as a reminder of the universal temptation to substitute our own will for God's, just as Eve did, and that we pay a high price when we fall prey to the cunning arguments of our own generation—one that is ready to sell its own soul for the sake of scientific knowledge.

Lord, how often I am tempted to exchange my will for yours. Help me to remember that you do not offer yourself on my terms and conditions but only on yours—and your terms demand submission to all your laws, including the command against attempting to become like gods ourselves.

PROTECTING THE MORAL ECOLOGY

TO READ: EZEKIEL 23:11-21, 48-49

She saw men portrayed on a wall, figures of Chaldeans. . . .
As soon as she saw them, she lusted after them. Ezekiel 23:14-16

Some forty years ago police arrested store owner Sam Ginsberg for selling pornography to a sixteen-year-old boy. Ginsberg claimed that antipornography laws violated his First Amendment rights. The Supreme Court disagreed. In a ruling that sounds quaint today, Justice William Brennan said that parents are entitled to the law's help in protecting the well-being of their children. Moreover, he added, the state had its own interest in safeguarding children from abuses that might prevent their growth into well-developed citizens.

Today, as Princeton philosopher Robert George observes, a great many people would disagree, embracing instead the dissenting view of Justice William Douglas, who ridiculed porn foes as people who are "propelled by their own neuroses."

Tragically, as George writes in *The Clash of Orthodoxies,* many modern judges agree with Douglas. Yes, pornography is shocking and offensive, they acknowledge, but "putting up with being shocked and offended is the price we must pay for the great blessing of freedom of expression."

But, George reminds us, pornography's harm is not in its capacity to shock and offend but in its tendency to corrupt and deprave. Laws regulating pornography are and always have been about preventing moral corruption. This view challenges a key tenet of the liberal secular worldview in that it presupposes that pornography is a source of moral corruption.

Christianity teaches that God intended sexual relations to serve both unitive and procreative functions within the bonds of marriage. Pornography corrupts because it undermines our capacity to understand sexual relations as anything other than self-gratification. In the name of freedom it teaches us to regard our own bodies and the bodies of others as merely instruments of sexual pleasure. Ultimately, pornography leads to sexuality that is impulsive, selfish, and out of control. It enslaves people to their own basest desires.

Intellectually honest defenders of an alleged right to pornography admit that porn damages the interests of nonusers and harms the community. Liberal philosopher Ronald Dworkin writes that access to pornography "sharply limits the ability of parents to bring about a cultural structure . . . in which sexual experience generally has dignity and beauty."

If we know someone who has been harmed by pornography harmed—a wife hurt by her husband's addiction or a child damaged by online filth—we know how much pornography degrades people. We especially know this if we have a secret porn habit ourselves. If we do, we must fight not only a cultural battle but a personal one as well, begging God's power to break that addiction.

We shouldn't let the multibillion-dollar porn industry—or judges—get away with claiming that we're simply prudes or neurotics. We must make the argument that pornography corrupts our children and degrades our entire culture.

Lord, your Word is clear that we degrade ourselves when we lust after depictions of the human body. Help me to resist the siren call of pornography and join efforts to rebuild a culture in which sexuality enjoys the dignity you intended.

A U G U S T   3 0

THE WAR AGAINST BOYS

TO READ: GENESIS 1:27-28

So God created man in his own image . . . ; male and female he created them.
Genesis 1:27

The Cleveland Avenue School in Atlanta has all the amenities you would expect a new school to have: computer equipment, an up-to-date library, and modern classrooms. It has everything except a playground.

No, that wasn't an oversight. The school was designed that way in order to make little boys behave more like little girls.

In 1998, Atlanta eliminated recess in its elementary schools. Other cities, such as Philadelphia, retained something called recess, but it bears little resemblance to the unstructured playtime most of us enjoyed as kids.

Why are schools doing this? In *The War against Boys: How Misguided Feminism Is Harming Our Young Men,* Christina Hoff Sommers says that educators today are intolerant of boys' acting like boys—moving, making noise, and engaging in raucous play. This intolerance goes beyond the need for order and discipline. The rule is "no running and no jumping," and boys who engage in normal, active play frequently face punishment or are sent home.

It is revealing that 95 percent of the kids on Ritalin today—a drug used to treat hyperactivity—are boys. As Michael Gurian, author of *The Good Son: Shaping the Moral Development of Our Boys and Young Men,* puts it, "If Huck [Finn] and Tom [Sawyer] were in today's schools, they would be labeled ADD, having attention deficit disorder, and drugged."

Behind this campaign against what Sommers calls youthful male exuberance is, in her words, "misguided feminism." Many feminists insist that it is maleness itself—defined by characteristics like aggressiveness, competitiveness, and assertiveness—that causes violence.

This view has found a receptive audience in the field of education, which is dominated by women. The result is a commitment to what Sommers calls feminizing boys: policing characteristically male behavior and getting boys to participate in "characteristically feminine activities."

As a result, our sons think there's something wrong with being a boy.

This war our culture is waging on boys is not only cruel, it's also culturally disastrous. When God made us male and female, it was in part an acknowledgment that the attributes of both sexes were intended to complement each other and achieve results that neither sex acting on its own could achieve.

Feminist author Camille Paglia understands this. She writes that masculinity is "the most creative cultural force in history." To be more precise, it is the masculine role as provider and protector, as restrained by clear standards of right and wrong, that has produced the civilization we know.

We ought to help our neighbors understand that a generation of boys who are taught that there's something intrinsically wrong with being male will not be able to act as the kind of responsible and creative force Paglia describes. And we must examine our own minds to discover whether we have unthinkingly accepted the false teachings of misguided feminists—feminists who either pretend there is no real difference between men and women or claim, in effect, that girls are good and boys are bad.

Lord, help me to identify unbiblical teachings I may have absorbed that may lead me into destructive attitudes toward the boys in my life. Give me your wisdom, I pray, to help the children I know—males or females—to delight in the way you created them.

BOGUS BELIEF

TO READ: LUKE 12:51-53

They will be divided, father against son and son against father, mother against daughter and daughter against mother. Luke 12:53

For ten years Darrell Lambert was active in the Boy Scouts in Port Orchard, Washington. In 2002, he attained Scouting's highest honor: the rank of Eagle Scout. After beginning college studies, Lambert continued to be active as a Scout volunteer, helping younger kids learn how to build campfires and read a compass.

But during a Scout leader training session, Lambert got into an argument with another Scout over religion. Lambert announced that he was an atheist—and walked out.

His announcement was no small matter. The Boy Scouts is a faith-based organization. Every Scout takes a vow of reverence; every Scout pledges his duty to God. As Mark Hunter of the Chief Seattle Boy Scout Council put it: "Advocating a belief in a Supreme Being has been a core value of the Boy Scouts" for nearly a hundred years. "The twelfth point of the Scout Law is 'reverent,' and that includes being faithful in your religious duties and respecting the beliefs of others."

Lambert says he knew all this when he joined the Scouts as a child. It was not until he studied evolution in the ninth grade that he concluded that God did not exist. But instead of resigning from the Scouts, Lambert says he began "mouthing" the words to the Scout oath. Sometimes he went ahead and just pledged his duty to God, knowing that he was telling a lie. But, he says, it really didn't seem to matter. That alone would be grounds for dismissal, a point the media have ignored.

The Chief Seattle Council told Lambert he had ten days to

reconsider his religious beliefs or leave Scouting. During the ensuing media frenzy, the usual suspects began attacking the Scouts on the same tiresome grounds, that they are intolerant bigots. But who are really the bigots here?

The Supreme Court has ruled that the Scouts is a private organization and thus has the right to set its own standards for membership. And, of course, those who disagree with the Scouts' policies are free to start their own scouting groups.

Lambert's story is an inversion of sorts of Christ's warning that if we follow him, we may drive wedges between ourselves and others whose companionship we value. Lambert pretended to believe in God so he would not be kicked out of an organization built on Christian principles; Christians, by contrast, are tempted to *deny* Christ in order to keep jobs, friends, club memberships, and family relationships. Lambert's lies are a reminder that we must never pretend to believe things we do not—or pretend *not* to believe things we know to be true—even if the price is high.

The Scout leaders' courageous stand has meant the usual abuse from the media, but it should earn them praise from those who believe that a Scout's oath, his duty to God, and his own character are nonnegotiable.

Father, give me the courage to boldly confess my belief in you. May I always remember that the earthly losses I may incur for doing so are small indeed compared with the eternal reward you have prepared for me: your everlasting companionship.

WORKING-CLASS HEROES

TO READ: PSALM 128:1-6

You will eat the fruit of your labor; blessings and prosperity will be yours. Psalm 128:2

One of the hottest-selling postage stamps in recent years features three New York City firefighters, in their hard hats and heavy gear, hoisting the American flag at ground zero. These are exactly the kinds of hardworking people Labor Day was designed to honor.

Christians have a special reason to celebrate this holiday, which honors the fundamental dignity of workers: We worship a God who labored to make the world—and who created human beings in his image to be workers. When God made Adam and Eve, he gave them work to do, cultivating and caring for the earth.

In the ancient world the Greeks and Romans looked on manual labor as a curse, something for lower classes and slaves. But Christianity changed all that. Christians viewed work as a high calling—a calling to be coworkers with God in unfolding the rich potential of his creation.

We can trace this high view of work throughout the history of the church. In the Middle Ages, the guild movement grew out of the church. It set standards for good workmanship and encouraged members to take satisfaction in the results of their labor. The guilds became the forerunners of the modern labor movement.

Later, during the Reformation, Martin Luther preached that all work should be done to the glory of God. Whether ministering the gospel or scrubbing floors, any honest work is pleasing to the Lord. Out of this conviction grew the Protestant work ethic.

Christians were also active on behalf of workers in the early days of the industrial revolution, when work in factories and coal mines was hard and dangerous. Children were virtually slaves—sometimes even chained to the machines.

Then John Wesley came preaching the gospel, not to the upper classes but to the laboring classes, to men whose faces were black with coal dust and women whose dresses were patched and faded.

Wesley preached to these people, and in the process he pricked the conscience of an entire nation. Wesley's teaching inspired two of his disciples, William Wilberforce and Lord Shaftesbury, to work for legislation that would clean up abuses in the workplace. At their urging, the British parliament passed child-labor laws, safety laws, and minimum-wage laws.

Here in America we've lost the Christian connection with the labor movement. But in many countries—from Canada to Poland—that tradition still remains.

So go ahead: Buy a few of those postage stamps that show gutsy firefighters hoisting the American flag. It's great to celebrate these faithful workers. But this Labor Day, remember as well that all labor derives its true dignity as a reflection of the Creator and that whatever we do, in word or deed, we should do all to the glory of God.

Lord, I pray for your blessings on those who toil—sometimes in danger—on my behalf. Bless and protect those who labor on behalf of the unborn, the handicapped, and the elderly. Help me to remember that my own work daily reflects on you—and that even the most profitable employment that does not glorify you is an eternal waste of time.

WORSHIPPING FALSE GODS

TO READ: DEUTERONOMY 13:1-11

It is the Lord your God you must follow, and him you must revere. Deuteronomy 13:4

The Raelians, a cult that worships UFOs, have threatened to sue the federal government for interfering with their plans to clone a human being; the Food and Drug Administration insists that experiments such as the Raelians' must meet with its approval—which it won't give.

The Raelians claim that the FDA's refusal violates their beliefs that human beings are the product of genetic experiments performed by extraterrestrials millions of years ago and that therefore, cloning people holds the key to eternal life.

Incredibly, the beliefs of the Raelians aren't as far from the American mainstream as you might think.

Nearly forty years ago, *Time* magazine asked on its cover, "Is God Dead?" The answer seemed to be that even if he wasn't, belief in the supernatural was on the way out. More than three decades later, Americans have embraced "belief" in a big way—so much so that social critics and historians are referring to our times as another "great awakening." But while belief is surging, what exactly are people believing?

Between 1976 and 1997, the number of Americans who believed in astrology grew from 17 percent to 37 percent. During the same period the percentage of Americans who professed belief in reincarnation nearly tripled, from 9 percent to 25 percent. Crystal-ball makers doubtless are glad to hear that the number of those who put stock in fortune-telling nearly quadrupled, from 4 to 14 percent.

In addition, up to half of all Americans believe in necromancy (conjuring up the dead), and millions believe in lucky numbers, alien visitations, and alien abductions. Clearly, this kind of spiritual awakening stands in marked contrast to the great awakenings of the eighteenth and nineteenth centuries. Those spiritual movements were grounded in historic Christianity. When men and women sought "spiritual growth," they turned to the God of the Bible.

But today, it's as simple as ABC—Anything But Christianity. In their attempt to find spiritual fulfillment without Christianity, Americans have become undiscerning about what they believe. If it enables a person to feel spiritual without having to bother with being religious, no belief is too off-the-wall for some people.

We should expect this. As G. K. Chesterton noted, when people cease believing in the biblical God, the problem isn't that they believe in nothing; it's that they believe in everything. Irrationality and even superstition become the order of the day.

This situation leaves the church with both an opportunity and a challenge. All of this misplaced belief is a tacit acknowledgment of the "God-shaped vacuum" within each human heart. Our challenge is to help our neighbors understand that superstition cannot fill up this vacuum. It can be filled only by relationship with the God of history—the one who created the vacuum within us.

Lord, let me never become intrigued by and drawn into that which you call evil. Give me the words to speak to those who engage in evil activities—séances, astrology, and fortune-telling—without realizing that they are evil because they violate your command to follow you alone.

THE IMITATION OF CHRIST

TO READ: MATTHEW 14:1-12

Prompted by her mother, she said, "Give me here on a platter the head of John the Baptist." Matthew 14:8

In the second century A.D. the Christian martyr Polycarp stood before the Roman proconsul. Recant Christ, the proconsul demanded—or face death by fire. Polycarp's response: "What are you waiting for? Bring on what you will."

Polycarp demonstrated that nothing, not even his own life, meant more to him than his steadfast devotion to Christ. His death was a heroic one; by standing firm in his faith, he demonstrated that the perfect expression of heroism is a courageous imitation of Christ.

Today, strength of conviction alone is often confused with heroism. Thus, even outlandish personalities such as basketball player Dennis Rodman receive praise for their courage, even begrudgingly from those who don't like them. Why? Because they insist on being true to themselves. That kind of personal courage may be laudable, but is it heroic?

Consider the man who prefers to die rather than give up his pocket money to a thief. He surrenders something that is truly precious for something ultimately insignificant. The soldier who fights for an unjust cause may have herolike convictions, but he exercises them in the service of what is ignoble or even wicked. That's courage, not heroism.

The steadfast courage of the great saints of the church gives us wonderful examples of what Dick Keyes identifies as genuine heroism. In *True Heroism in a World of Celebrity Counterfeits,* Keyes writes that while courage itself is not heroism, it is an indispensable ingredient of heroism.

This becomes especially clear when we consider Jesus as an example of heroism. He resisted the temptation to go his own way. He persevered in his ministry, knowing it would ultimately lead to a painful and humiliating death. He courageously bore the scorn and threats of his opponents. He endured a rigged trial and made no attempt to escape his fate. Jesus showed us that a true hero demonstrates not only courageous devotion but also devotion to what is true and praiseworthy.

Our Christian faith may call us to be heroic in the truest sense, so we need to provide the children in our churches examples of people who exhibit true heroism.

In America it's unlikely we'll be numbered among the Christians who, like John the Baptist and others throughout the centuries, have given their lives for Christ—and who are suffering martyrdom even today. But even in the United States, the Christian life is not without cost, and we, too, must learn to be courageous under fire. We are not to seek out persecution and suffering, but when they come, they provide an opportunity to experience God's grace in even greater fullness.

Lord, grant me the wisdom to respond to attacks on my faith in a manner consistent with your purposes: with a courageous refusal to compromise no matter what the cost, or with a gentle answer that turns away wrath—and which may ultimately bring my assailants to your throne.

SEPTEMBER 4

OVERCOMING BAD IMPRESSIONS

TO READ: MATTHEW 9:1-13

When the Pharisees saw this, they asked his disciples, "Why does your teacher eat with tax collectors and 'sinners'?" Matthew 9:11

We live in a time when Christians receive a lot of media attention. Unfortunately, it's not always favorable. In fact, favorable portrayals of Christians in film and on television are almost nonexistent today, and that can keep people from considering the gospel. Bad impressions don't matter for our sakes, but we should care about how they reflect on Christ and the gospel.

In *Fearless Faith: Living beyond the Walls of "Safe" Christianity,* John Fischer reexamines a believer's role in the world and concludes that some sort of public-relations campaign will never change bad impressions; only personal relationships can change them. That's a problem because so few Christians cultivate ongoing relationships with non-Christian friends.

Studies reveal that two years after conversion, most Christians have lost all normal contact with friends outside the church. Many Christians today can't name one non-Christian—someone they would call a friend—with whom they do anything on a regular basis. Some would say that living a holy life requires this kind of separation. Yet no one lived a holier life than Jesus, who was called a friend of sinners because of the company he kept.

It's easy to be around those who believe what we believe; it's a different thing being around those who challenge our faith and whose lifestyle and language may offend us. But as Howard Hendricks said years ago, "I can't think of a better place for a non-Christian to sit down and light up a cigarette than in the home of a Christian where he can hear about and experience the love of God."

Fischer describes the experiences of a pastor who served as a short-term missionary in France. Part of his job was to knock on four thousand doors and to leave a card that the home owner could fill out and mail in for a free Bible and study guide. Out of four thousand homes there was not a single response. Reflecting on his experience, the pastor said that if he had the opportunity to do it all over again, "I would move into that neighborhood and love my neighbors."

The fact of the matter is that we're already living in the neighborhoods; we don't need to go to France or anywhere else. All we must do is open our front doors and get to know our neighbors.

God's plan for reaching the world is simple: It involves followers' making friends with people who don't know him yet. We Christians must break out of our self-segregating patterns and engage the culture by engaging people—one at a time.

Lord, if I hesitate to befriend an unsaved neighbor, help me to remember that it is not the healthy who need a doctor but the sick.

LOSING GROUND

TO READ: JAMES 5:1-6

Look! The wages you failed to pay the workmen who mowed your fields are crying out against you. James 5:4

Everywhere you look—in factories, offices, the military—you see mothers of young children. Given how hard they and their husbands work, you might think dual-income families would enjoy a high standard of living. But recent reports suggest that the income of the average household has remained largely stagnant and that some families are even losing ground. What accounts for this phenomenon?

The author of a book about the family says we can blame the loss of a "family wage."

In *There's No Place Like Work*, Brian Robertson says that a family wage allows one parent to support a family on just one income. The concept is based on the belief that it's vitally important that we keep married mothers from having to work.

Ironically, it was the early feminists who fought hardest to keep mothers at home. From the start of the Industrial Revolution, factory owners had their eye on women as a cheap source of labor. In order to keep industry from forcing mothers into the workplace, women's groups and labor unions designed and fought for the family wage.

Thanks to their efforts, by the 1960s more than 80 percent of industrial employers paid a wage that was sufficient to support a family.

Then modern feminism was born. Housewives were told that they were wasting their brains by staying at home. Millions of women listened—and went to work. The results were dramatic. New laws barring wage and employment discrimination leveled wages, and the family wage all but disappeared. By 1987, only 25 percent of all jobs paid enough for one wage earner to support a family. Today, Robertson writes, the family wage is "effectively dead."

Worse, as the family wage ceased to be the norm, prices were adjusted to dual-income family standards. "The price of family necessities now reflects an economy in which most wives work," Robertson notes.

The result is that keeping mom at home is becoming a luxury few families can afford. Big businesses encourage moms to work by offering on-site day care, counseling for stress, and cafeterias that prepare take-home dinners. What they won't support, Robertson says, is "paying one parent enough to support a family on a single income."

But Robertson warns that this antifamily attitude may ultimately backfire. Corporate America may wake up one day to find it has undermined the primary source of productive labor. The traditional family motivates its members to excellence at work. But today companies are spending more and more money trying to solve their employees' emotional problems—because so many families are in chaos.

We need to help our neighbors understand why the concept of the family wage, rather than mere economic growth, is still the best measure of a society's economic well-being.

That's why we need to fight for policies that recognize what those early feminists taught: Families—not profits—must come first.

Lord, teach me to take my values from your wisdom and not allow myself to be manipulated by the culture around me, making decisions about work and family that I, and my loved ones, may eventually regret.

AN OLD ERROR IN A NEW PACKAGE

TO READ: ACTS 20:22-32

[Paul said,] "I know that after I leave, savage wolves will come in among you and will not spare the flock." Acts 20:29

One of the best places to catch a glimpse of celebrities in Los Angeles is inside an old church in Beverly Hills. There, A-list superstars such as Demi Moore, Britney Spears, and Madonna sing hymns at pep-rally tempo and shout hearty "Amens!"

Has revival finally broken out in Hollywood? Not quite. There is a revival of sorts, but it's a revival of an old error: Gnosticism.

The "pep rally" service is held every Friday night in L.A.'s Kabbalah Center, a former church. Kabbalah is a medieval form of Jewish mysticism. According to Israeli journalist Yossi Klein Halevi, the "preoccupation" of Kabbalah is "understanding and ending humanity's exile from God." Ending this exile entails not only meditation but also keeping the commandments of Judaism, which help to "sanctify" the material world.

If you have difficulty imagining film stars keeping the moral and ethical demands of the Old Testament, you're not alone. Halevi says that what's going on at the Kabbalah Center has more in common with other California-based religions like Scientology than with medieval Judaism. What's being taught to the celebrities "doesn't merely trivialize Kabbalah; it inverts its intention."

Traditionally, the goal of meditation is to "annihilate the ego, not reinforce it," but in L.A., "the spiritual quest isn't about God, but the seeker." Even when people are encouraged to give to others, it's for selfish reasons. As one "disciple" told Halevi, respecting the dignity of another person "has nothing to do with being a good person. It's about not hurting myself. Not because God told me to be nice to others, but because my life becomes better."

Most Jewish scholars consider the Kabbalah Center to be, at best, an oversimplification of an important mystical tradition; at worst, it's a fraud. Gnosticism, which has plagued Christianity since before the ink of the Scriptures was dry, teaches that secret and esoteric knowledge holds the key to salvation.

In *The American Religion: The Emergence of the Post-Christian Nation*, Yale professor Harold Bloom argues that many Americans, even some professing Christians, are Gnostics of sorts. Their religion is based on personal experience and has little room for tradition or authority. The goal of their religion is "to be alone with God or Jesus."

While Bloom was rightly criticized for overstating the case, it's undeniable that many Americans are in the market for what have been called "do-it-yourself God kits." These kits enable people to feel good about themselves without making objective moral demands. They promise valuable knowledge without forcing adherents to confront questions of truth.

In other words, it's a religious system perfectly suited for the spirit of our age. That's why it's standing room only at the Kabbalah Center.

The popularity of Gnosticism is a sobering reminder that the wolves are still out there, ready to devour our faith. We must put ourselves under the protection of church leaders who are rock solid in their devotion to scriptural truth—and expose the perverse teachings of those who invade our flocks.

Father, protect me from false teachings if they begin seeping into my church—or into my heart. May I never forget the price your Son paid in blood to bring us the truth—or my duty through the power of your Spirit to protect it.

SEPTEMBER 7

FUNDING FAITH EFFORTS

TO READ: LUKE 19:1-10

[Zacchaeus said,] "Look, Lord! Here and now I give half of my possessions to the poor, and if I have cheated anybody out of anything, I will pay back four times the amount." Luke 19:8

In El Salvador a few years ago two earthquakes left thousands of people homeless. To the rescue came Samaritan's Purse, a Christian relief organization. With the help of U.S. funds, it assisted victims in building temporary housing—combining elbow grease with evangelism.

The Salvadorians didn't have a problem with that—but American liberals did.

By all accounts Samaritan's Purse did a great job helping earthquake victims. It received hundreds of thousands of dollars from the U.S. Agency for International Aid, money that helped earthquake victims build new shelters.

But what stuck in liberal craws was the fact that Samaritan's Purse distributed religious tracts to those they helped. Even worse, it held prayer meetings before showing Salvadorians how to build their homes. That was only natural. As Dr. Paul Chiles of Samaritan's Purse explained, "When we build things, we say we build it with the love of Jesus, because that's why we are here."

Samaritan's Purse helps the needy whether they accept the gospel message or not. And as Chiles told the *New York Times,* its mission "was understood and accepted by the federal government." But the group's dual mission—saving souls and preserving lives—is not accepted by others. According to the *Times,* some American aid officials have "serious reservations" about the evangelism Samaritan's Purse engages in. Some bureaucrats and *New York Times* reporters even hinted that Samaritan's Purse was engaged in something not quite legal.

That's nonsense. There's nothing illegal or unethical about faith groups having voluntary Bible studies before they start projects. The Salvadorians themselves weren't complaining. One earthquake victim told the *Times* that hearing the Word of God from Samaritan's Purse "is a comfort and helps give us strength."

So if evangelism helped console Salvadorians, and if Samaritan's Purse followed the rules, what's the problem? It's that influential secularists don't like the witness these faith-based programs provide—the testimony to the power of Christ to transform lives.

For example, Teen Challenge drug-treatment programs have an 80 percent cure rate, far higher than that of secular programs. In Boston, Christian groups working together brought down the youth-homicide rate dramatically, something no secular group has been able to do. Criminals who complete Prison Fellowship's InnerChange Freedom Initiative program come back to prison in far fewer numbers than inmates who do not take part in the program.

Secular liberals hate these ministries even though those who benefit from them thank God that they exist.

The controversy over faith-based initiatives ought to remind us to take stock of our own lives: Do our actions reflect the difference we claim Christ makes—as it did with Zacchaeus?

As churches become more involved in solving America's social problems—many of which are caused by government programs designed by secular elites—we'll no doubt hear plenty of bogus attacks on government's support of faith-based solutions. Christians must understand what's behind all the yelling and learn how to answer the charges. It's not that faith-based ministries don't work; it's that they do—all too well.

Father, let my life demonstrate the difference faith in your Son makes—a difference that witnesses to your transforming power.

A DOSE OF PRAYER

TO READ: JAMES 5:13-18

Is any one of you sick? He should call the elders of the church to pray over him.
James 5:14

An elderly woman checked into Georgetown University Hospital with a serious diagnosis: congestive heart failure. Just one week later she had bounced back dramatically. Her doctor declared himself "astounded."

According to the *Washington Post,* the doctor credited the woman's amazing recovery to intercessory prayer. The patient's family had prayed with her; a deacon from her church had prayed for her, and the physician himself, Dr. Dale Matthews, had prayed for her regularly.

Was this just coincidence? Or can we really detect the results of prayer in people's lives?

Skeptics say that answers to prayer are nothing more than the power of suggestion. The Committee for the Scientific Investigation of Paranormal Claims lumps prayer with things like spoon bending; it argues that any evidence that prayer produces real benefits comes from believers who "fudge information, consciously and subconsciously," in their efforts to support their faith.

But recent studies prove that it's the skeptics who may be fudging the evidence—or at least ignoring it. These studies demonstrate that prayer has a measurable impact on a patient's recovery, even if a patient doesn't know he's being prayed for.

An article by cardiologist Randolph Byrd in the *Southern Medical Journal* reports a dramatic experiment in prayer. Byrd asked prayer groups to intercede for nearly four hundred patients in the coronary care unit at San Francisco General Hospital. To avoid any placebo effect (patients' feeling better for purely psychological reasons), neither the patients nor their doctors knew which patients were the objects of prayer. Byrd found that the patients who were prayed for had fewer complications and were five times less likely to require antibiotics than patients who were not prayed for.

The late Dr. David Larson, a psychiatrist, collected data on the health effects of religious beliefs and practices, including prayer. One documented study shows that religious commitment is associated with lower blood pressure and lower rates of hypertension.

This is not to say that believers automatically get miraculous recoveries whenever they pray. After all, prayer is not a magical incantation that puts God in our power. Prayer is communication with the living God, who responds to each of us individually.

Yet it's exciting that medical science can detect the impact of the spiritual world on the physical world. Many Americans think of religion as something confined to the internal realm of feelings and experience. They simply don't conceive of faith as connected with the so-called real world—the world confirmed by science.

That's why studies that track the power of prayer on physical healing are so exciting. They remind us of the need to bring every concern, every fear, before the loving God we serve. And when we talk to our non-Christian neighbors, we can demonstrate that faith has real and measurable results in the everyday world.

Lord, thank you for evidence that you hear and respond to the prayers of those who call out to you on behalf of desperately sick people. May I always remember that there is never a time when you are not available to hear me when I pray.

SICK, TWISTED PEOPLE

TO READ: LUKE 11:33-36

Your eye is the lamp of your body. When your eyes are good,
your whole body also is full of light. Luke 11:34

Are Christians sick, twisted people?

If you watch enough Hollywood films, you may begin to think so.

In the film *Hannibal,* a character named Mason Verger has just one goal in life: to catch up with the cannibal who chewed off his face and feed him to flesh-eating pigs. It's a sick and twisted goal, and it may not surprise you to learn that Verger is the film's only Christian character.

In the historical film *Quills,* about the Marquis de Sade, it's a Catholic priest who performs the vilest sexual acts; Sade is portrayed as the persecuted victim of a puritanical society.

Another film, *The Pledge,* portrays Christianity as a religion for killers. In *The Cell,* a Christian upbringing causes a character to become a serial killer. Celluloid missionaries are almost as bad. In films like *Black Robe* and *At Play in the Fields of the Lord,* Christians bring not salvation but disease and death, slavery and hypocrisy.

As Christian screenwriter Brian Godawa notes in *Hollywood Worldview: Watching Films with Wisdom and Discernment,* in films like these, "Christianity does not merely lead to mental breakdown in [individuals]; it also leads to the breakdown of society." Christians as sick, twisted people who got that way are portrayed as repressing their natural desires; their moral codes lead to intolerance, wife beating, and murder.

About the only good thing you can say about these films, spiritually speaking, is that they reveal the fact that humans—whether they admit it or not—are deeply religious. We can't help thinking about

God and trying to come to terms with him. As Godawa points out, elements of Christianity are often "deconstructed or reinterpreted through countervailing worldviews," but significantly, those elements are not ignored. In fact, Godowa writes, films that attack or redefine God may be more honest than those that simply ignore him. The filmmaker is "at least admitting [God] is an issue." Ignoring him "leaves the impression that He is . . . irrelevant to our reality."

The good news is that every now and then, Hollywood gets religion right. A recent remake of *Les Miserables* offers a poignant picture of Christian grace, forgiveness, and redemption. Parents ought to watch some of the better films with their kids. And all of us need to be discerning viewers, avoiding films that will only darken our minds.

When it comes to films that portray Christians as warped and wicked people—well, we ought to learn about these films as well. That way we can help the young people in our lives—and their unbelieving friends—understand why so many filmmakers treat Christianity as a violent, oppressive religion, fit only for sick and twisted people.

Lord, many form their opinions of you and your followers through deceitful films that distort the truth. May I be a lamp that illuminates your love in my words and actions so that those who see you only through depraved celluloid images will recognize that they have been lied to—and seek the light of your truth.

OUR CULTURAL MANDATE

TO READ: COLOSSIANS 1:15-23

God was pleased to have all his fullness dwell in him, and through him to reconcile to himself all things. Colossians 1:19-20

"Won't engaging the culture interfere with fulfilling the great commission? Isn't our job to win people to Christ?"

That pastor who asked those questions had just heard a talk about the need for Christians to plunge themselves into the great cultural battles of the day and was concerned that doing so would interfere with the "real" job of the church.

Yes, Jesus calls Christians to fulfill the great commission. But he also calls us to fulfill the *cultural* commission. Christians are agents of God's *saving grace,* bringing others to Christ. But we are also agents of his *common grace:* We're to sustain and renew his creation, defending the created institutions of family and society and critiquing false worldviews.

Scripture is clear on this matter. In Genesis we read that for five days God created the universe. On the sixth day he created human beings—and ordered them to pick up where he left off. They were to reflect his image and have dominion, but from then on, the development of the creation would be primarily social and cultural: It would be the work humans performed as they obeyed God's command to fill the earth and subdue it.

The same command binds Christians today. We bear children, plant crops, build cities, form governments, and create works of art. While sin corrupted God's created order, it did not obliterate it. And when we are redeemed, we are both freed from sin and restored to do what God designed us to do: create culture.

Remember, every part of creation came from God's hand. Every part was drawn into humanity's mutiny against God, and someday God will redeem every part. This means we must care about all of life. In Colossians 1, Paul notes that everything was made by and for Christ and that everything will be reconciled by Christ. It is clear that Christians are saved not only *from* something (sin) but also *to* something (Christ's lordship over all of life).

This is why Christians must never limit themselves to evangelism alone, standing by while our culture is hijacked by alien philosophies hostile to the created order. Look at the issues before us: gay "marriage," an oxymoron that will undermine the family; cloning, the creation of life in man's image; abortion; and terrorism driven by religious extremists, to name a few.

If Christians do not act on the cultural commission, there soon will be no culture left to save. But when we do our duty, we can change the world—as British abolitionist William Wilberforce did.

Yes, Christians must evangelize, but each of us must also work out our role in the common grace in our lives, bringing God's righteousness to bear against the crumbling structures of a fallen world.

Father, in a culture sagging under the weight of crushing sin, show me where I can best use my gifts in fulfilling the cultural mandate—not trying to repair every rotting beam myself but helping renovate one or two disintegrating planks, glorifying you by restoring your creation.

HEALING THE WOUNDS

TO READ: MATTHEW 27:45-56

*Among them were Mary Magdalene, Mary the mother of James and Joses,
and the mother of Zebedee's sons. Matthew 27:56*

Today is the anniversary of the most vicious terror attack in America's history—and of the beginning of a war on those who commit such heinous acts.

The wounds will never fully heal for the relatives of the three thousand people who perished in the World Trade Center towers, at the Pentagon, or on a lonely Pennsylvania field. Hundreds more Americans have died fighting Islamic terrorism in the years since in Afghanistan, Iraq, and elsewhere. The families of our fighters, often raw with grief, are asking the same question grieving families asked on September 11, 2001: "How could God let this happen? If he really loves me, why didn't he save *my* child, *my* husband, *my* sister?"

We must show great tenderness when our neighbors ask these questions. When it comes to understanding God's purposes, "we see but a poor reflection as in a mirror" (1 Corinthians 13:12). But we do know that God loved us so much that he made us free moral agents, able to choose either good or evil. The first humans, Adam and Eve, exercised that choice and chose to disobey God—what Christians call the Fall—and humanity has been bent toward sin ever since.

On September 11, we saw an example of the consequences of the Fall: raw, naked evil committed by men who made evil choices.

Could not a loving God have erased the consequences of sin? Yes, but then we would no longer be free moral agents. Without consequences, there are no real choices. God cannot simultaneously offer us a choice and then compel us to choose one option over another, which is what would happen if he stopped all evil.

"But," people say, "how do we cope with monstrous evil? How do we respond when it strikes our own homes and hearts?"

The answer may be found in the words of the Archbishop of Canterbury, who spoke at a memorial service for the British victims of September 11. "I am reminded," he said, "of a dear friend who lost his three children in separate accidents. One day I asked him: 'Have you and your wife never asked God why?'

"'Of course I have asked God why,' his friend gently replied. 'But I soon discovered that is not the right question. The proper question is how? How may I use my suffering to help others and to point the way to God's love?'"

We must continue praying for the victims of terrorism, for the safety of those who are bravely fighting against it, and for their anxious families. And we should keep in mind that in a fallen world, evil affects everyone of us—including the friends and family of Jesus, who saw him suffer an excruciating death on the cross.

In the midst of our grief we must remember—as did the bishop's friend—to ask the right question: Not *why?* but *how?*

Lord, in moments of deep despair, when my heart is raw with pain, bring to my mind the comforting words of Paul, himself no stranger to torment and trouble: "Neither death nor life, neither angels nor demons . . . nor anything else in all creation, will be able to separate us from the love of God that is in Christ Jesus our Lord."

THE RUBBLE DECLARES THE GLORY OF GOD

TO READ: 1 SAMUEL 31:1-13

They took their bones and buried them under a tamarisk tree at Jabesh.
1 Samuel 31:13

For years, skeptics have assailed the Bible as a book of pious pronouncements and claimed that science would ultimately prove the Scriptures unreliable.

The question of the historical reliability of the Bible was a major stumbling block for journalist Lee Strobel before his conversion. So, as Strobel writes in *The Case for Faith,* he turned to theologian Norman Geisler for help.

First, Geisler said, thousands of archeological finds back up the accuracy of the Bible. The stories of Abraham, Isaac, and Jacob, for example, were once considered legends—but archeological evidence has done much to corroborate them.

The same is true for the Genesis account of Sodom and Gomorrah. The tale of God's destruction of these cities for their sexual sin was once dismissed as a myth. But "evidence has been uncovered proving that all five of the cities mentioned in Genesis were, in fact, situated just as the Old Testament said," Geisler said. And archaeologist Clifford Wilson says there is "permanent evidence of the great conflagration that took place in the long distant past."

Archaeology has corroborated many other biblical details, as well. There's evidence confirming the Jewish captivity. Every Old Testament reference to an Assyrian king has been proven correct. During the 1960s, an excavation confirmed that the Israelites could indeed have entered Jerusalem by way of a tunnel during the reign of King David.

Biblical accounts of the burial of Saul—once thought by "experts" to be in error—have also held up under secular scrutiny. Critics used to say there was no evidence that the Hittites existed. But now, Geisler says, "archaeologists digging in modern Turkey have discovered the records of the Hittites."

As for the New Testament, Geisler notes that "archaeology has confirmed not dozens, but hundreds and hundreds of details from the biblical account of the early church. . . . Even small details have been corroborated, such as which way the wind blows, how deep the water is a certain distance from shore, what kind of disease a particular island had, [and] the names of local officials."

The evidence is now so overwhelming that historian Sir William Albright concludes that critics of New Testament accuracy hold "antiquated views" that are "pre-archaeological." Oxford University historian A. N. Sherwin-White says the evidence confirming details in the book of Acts alone is so staggering that "any attempt to reject its basic historicity must now appear absurd." This leaves Christians with an exciting apologetic argument: If archaeology proves the Bible's accuracy in thousands of historical details, why would it be any less accurate in its other claims?

Have you ever wondered why "the experts" are so eager to denounce the Bible on such flimsy intellectual grounds? When they trot out their latest sophisticated arguments, do you ever feel embarrassed to admit you believe the "unsophisticated" teachings of the Bible?

The Bible's historical accuracy is a reminder that while "the heavens declare the glory of God," there's also plenty of evidence among the rubble and ruins.

Father, thank you for archaeological evidence that confirms the truth of your Book. Even in the absence of such evidence, may I never be ashamed to admit that I firmly believe that your Word is truth.

STAR TREK AND THE CHURCH

TO READ: EZEKIEL 33:10-16

How then can we live? Ezekiel 33:10

A few summers ago a Christian writer named Carlos visited Star Trek: The Experience while vacationing in Las Vegas. While immersing himself in all things Star Trek, he struck up a conversation with another visitor, a truck driver from Reno.

Carlos later realized that the conversation, with its instant bond, common vocabulary, and vital interest in the subject was just like the experience Christians call fellowship.

This observation applies to more than just *Star Trek* fans. Popular culture, particularly electronic media, is increasingly the only thing that many Americans have in common—our one binding experience—and as such, it has emerged as the principal shaper of American culture.

The process has been under way for nearly a century. During the Battle of the Bulge, American sentries asked three questions designed to distinguish Americans from German infiltrators. Two of the questions were about popular culture, an indication of the influence sports, popular music, and films held on the American imagination.

This hold wasn't exclusive. A 1948 survey asked Americans which person they most wanted to emulate. Franklin Roosevelt and Clara Barton topped the list, with only 14 percent of the respondents naming an entertainer.

By 1986, every person in the top ten, save then–President Ronald Reagan, was a movie or television star. This survey illustrates the increasing hegemony of electronic media over American consciousness.

The emergence of this dominance coincided with the weakening of other institutions that traditionally shaped what Americans thought and believed: families, local communities, and especially churches. It's no coincidence that the institutions eclipsed by popular culture and electronic media were those that exercised moral authority and trafficked in norms and standards. Our culture had rejected both.

But rejecting these institutions isn't the same thing as rejecting what they traditionally provided—ideas about morality and meaning. It simply means that something else, something probably ill-suited to the task, will have to take their place. That something is popular culture, especially movies, television, and music.

If the only thing electronic media did was provide Americans with shared references and experiences, it would be cause for concern, but it does far more: It shapes our ideas about what's important and what a life worth living looks like.

It's hard to imagine something less qualified to fulfill this function than the entertainment industry. That's why it's imperative that Christians be concerned about more than media vulgarity, sex, and violence. We must also understand both the messages contained in our popular culture and how media shapes our beliefs. Then each of us must do our part to shore up traditional structures—family, church, and community—that offer rock-solid answers about how we should live.

Lord, help me to be a part of building strong and loving fellowship among those with whom I interact: family, neighbors, colleagues, and church friends. May I so cherish this fellowship that my family and friends will seek wisdom for living, not from actors, sports figures, and anonymous Internet buddies, but from your Word and your followers.

FOR WHOSE SAKE?

TO READ: 1 CORINTHIANS 11:3-16

In the Lord, however, woman is not independent of man,
nor is man independent of woman. 1 Corinthians 11:11

In an ABC interview with Diane Sawyer, talk-show host Rosie O'Donnell, who has three adopted children, announced that she is a lesbian. Nevertheless, O'Donnell insisted, "I know I'm a really good mother, and I have every right to parent [these children.]" Anyone who thinks otherwise is wrong.

ABC apparently agreed: No one challenged or contradicted O'Donnell. But the truth is, children do not fare as well in homes headed by homosexuals.

According to several independent studies by respected authorities, children raised by homosexuals are more likely to become promiscuous and engage in substance abuse. They are at higher risk of losing a parent to AIDS and are more likely to commit suicide.

In contrast, children raised in homes with married heterosexual parents enjoy greater health both physically and emotionally. They do better in school, commit fewer crimes, and are less likely to live in poverty. As Glenn Stanton writes in *CitizenLink*, children raised in such homes "do far better in every measure than children who grow up in any other family situation."

There's also the question of whether kids raised by gays are more likely to become gay themselves. One study showed that gay parents "may be four times more likely to produce homosexual children." One teenager who was interviewed said that when she had conflicts with her boyfriend, her lesbian mother "would tell me to try girls."

Rosie O'Donnell's assertion that she has "every right to parent [these children]" exposes what this debate is really about. It's not about what's good for kids. It's about the demands of homosexuals for their so-called rights.

O'Donnell is leading an effort to overturn state laws against gay adoption. State authorities need to listen to the real experts: people raised in gay homes. People like Jakii Edwards, who told *CitizenLink* that while gays' intentions may be good, "it does hurt the children to come up in gay homes. When a child [sees] mom kissing mom and dad kissing daddy, it leaves the child . . . with gender identity issues. We question whether we have to be gay like mommy [or daddy] is gay.

"It causes a lot of turmoil," Edwards says, and she adds that nearly everyone she knows who was raised by a gay parent "has major anger issues."

The Scriptures tell us that God intended men and women to complement each other, both within marriage and as parents. These teachings should serve as warnings to all of us: God gave us instructions about sex, marriage, and parenthood. He does not give us permission to ignore them—or rearrange them—into something more closely matching our own desires.

Jakii Edwards is a reminder that if we really care about the needs of children, we'll aggressively promote healthy, two-parent, heterosexual families. After all, what made June Cleaver and Donna Reed great moms was not the fact that they wore aprons and pearls. It was that they were married to their children's fathers.

Lord, when I am most tempted to defy your teachings, help me to remember that you gave us instructions about sexuality and parenthood for a reason and that if I ignore them, then I—and my children—may pay a tragic price.

SEPTEMBER 15

BALANCING ACT

TO READ: HEBREWS 2:5-9

You crowned him with glory and honor and put everything under his feet.
Hebrews 2:7-8

It was the first day of spring, and the sight that greeted one Maryland couple was enough to drive even a pacifist to a gun store. The Morses had carefully planted eighty tulip bulbs the previous fall. Two days after the last winter snow melted, they went out to see how their tulips were doing. What they found were row upon row of gnawed stumps. Hungry deer had chewed up every tulip in the yard.

It's a familiar complaint wherever woodland is turned into habitat for humanity. It's a recipe for disaster—and sometimes for venison.

Some people say we should let hunters deal with the problem. Others insist that the real problem is people: They view the great outdoors as a pure, harmonious place where nature, including all those adorable animals, would be much better off if humans would just get lost. But should we really put the welfare of Bambi and Thumper ahead of human interests?

How you answer that question depends on whether you think that nature is meant for man or man is meant for nature.

Theologian Michael Novak writes in *National Review* that humans "are made by their unique endowment of liberty to be provident over their destiny." One important way to exercise this providence is to take care of our habitat.

But those who attempt to do so often find themselves up against environmental militants who seek to elevate nature *above* humanity. They see nature—the pristine mountains, lakes, and forests—as a sublime, purer order that rebukes the order man has made, Novak writes.

The fact that throughout history nature has exercised cruel, killing dominion over man has been repressed. Nature is now viewed implausbily as simply beneficent. This, Novak says, "is the great psychic drama being played out in the modern environmental movement. Mythic elements of great power are involved in it."

This means that Christians must proceed cautiously when it comes to the claims of the professional environmentalists. Many of the "underlying arguments are not about policy only, but about quasi-religious visions of the pure, the good, and the nurturing." These visions are dangerous because they diminish the value of humanity. Some radical types even advocate killing humans to make more space for other species.

In contrast, the Scriptures give us a high view of nature without sacrificing a high view of human life. Genesis teaches that we are created in God's image and that we are charged with caring for the rest of God's creation. The sad truth is that many Christians tend to forget about the stewardship part. If we want to turn over a new leaf, we must seek out the most accurate, nonpoliticized information about environmental problems. Then we must get behind realistic strategies to solve them.

So the next time you catch deer chomping on your tulips, the answer is to look not for a gun but for solutions that recognize both a high view of humanity and the biblical injunction to care for God's creation.

Father, so many of us have forgotten your plan for the relationship between humans and animals. Teach us how to strike a holy balance between the animals you created and the humans your Son died for.

DISCRIMINATING CHRISTIANS

TO READ: ROMANS 6:1-23

We know that our old self was crucified with him so that the body of sin might be done away with, that we should no longer be slaves to sin. Romans 6:6

Eight-year-old Martin Thompson couldn't wait to join the Boy Scouts, but when Martin's parents discovered his interest, they told him absolutely not. Their reaction reveals how successfully the radical gay lobby has convinced Americans that homosexuality has no moral component.

The Boy Scouts of America doesn't accept members or leaders who engage in homosexual conduct—and that's why Martin's parents objected. "Our family does not agree with discrimination against . . . homosexuals," Martin's mother told him. The family then went to a meeting of the Anne Arundel County, Maryland, school district and tried to get the Scouts thrown off school property, a typical tactic of the "tolerance" crowd.

Martin's father read a statement Martin had written, which said, "I don't want the Boy Scouts to come to my school because my school allows everyone to come. . . . But . . . not everyone is allowed in the Boy Scouts."

Of course, Martin's school does *not* allow everyone to attend. It discriminates against people who are too old or too young and against anyone who lives outside the school district. It discriminates against children of the right age who *do* live inside the school district if they are not capable of performing the required work.

Evidently this type of discrimination doesn't bother Martin's parents. They may view it as appropriate because it violates no moral laws. However, they seem to be teaching their son that homosexual conduct violates no moral laws either—but that objecting to it does. They equate the upholding of biblical principles with gay bashing.

The argument that homosexual behavior breaks no moral law is predicated on the belief that homosexuality is a normal condition. Even some Christians believe that God created homosexuals, just as he created heterosexuals. The question is, did God create people with homosexual desires, or is homosexuality a consequence of what makes our world a broken place—the Fall?

Many secularists claim that homosexuality is genetically determined, but these claims ignore the empirical evidence to the contrary. Researchers looking for a gay gene periodically announce new evidence for it, but the evidence evaporates when other researchers study it.

David Persing, a molecular genetics researcher and a Christian, says the biblical teaching that all of nature is fallen includes our genetic heritage. As a result, we all have inborn tendencies toward various forms of sinful behaviors, from alcoholism to eating disorders to homosexuality. But this fact does not excuse us from having to make a choice to do right or to sin. Christianity calls all of us to struggle against our natural tendencies. Whatever those inclinations are, we still have room for making real moral choices.

Father, thank you that through the gift of your Son you have forever freed every single human being from the bonds of slavery to every imaginable form of sin— if only we are willing to accept that freedom.

SEPTEMBER 17

BALANCING THE SCALES

TO READ: EXODUS 21:12-32

You are to take life for life, eye for eye, tooth for tooth, hand for hand, foot for foot, burn for burn. Exodus 21:23-25

Few people have offered a more astute analysis of the crime problem than C. S. Lewis in his essay "The Humanitarian Theory of Punishment."

According to the so-called humanitarian theory, the criminal is not truly guilty of any crime; instead, he is sick. This theory gave birth to a criminal justice system that sought to rehabilitate offenders rather than punish them. To accommodate those who supposedly needed to be healed of criminal behavior, America built huge new prisons in the sixties and seventies and jammed them full. Then the therapists were brought in.

This is precisely the picture Lewis painted more than thirty years ago: He described modern psychotherapists roaming the halls of prisons in their white coats, remaking the inmates "after some pattern of 'normality' hatched in a Viennese laboratory."

The huge jump in crime exposes the fallacy of this approach. But the worst aspect of this theory is that it strips man of his dignity: It suggests that he is no longer a moral agent who may be held responsible for his actions. Instead, he is a patient—an object to be manipulated for social goals. It's a dehumanizing view of the person.

In contrast, Lewis recognized that crime has moral roots; it involves wrong moral choices. While this may seem obvious, few criminologists of our day are able—or should we say *willing*—to recognize this simple truth. Not only did Lewis recognize the moral dimension of crime itself, but he also saw the implications of stripping a sense of moral culpability from our *response* to crime.

519

To deny that man is a moral agent capable of right or wrong is to deny his rationality. Through sin a man is separated from God, but the humanitarian theory of punishment denies that he even bears the *image* of God. In Lewis's words, "To be punished, however severely, because we have deserved it, because we 'ought to have known better,' is to be treated as a human person made in God's image."

The Scriptures teach that people are responsible for their own actions; they must be held accountable and punished for morally wrong choices. Punishment is not primarily about pragmatic goals; it's about justice. Prisons are thus not primarily for therapy; they exist to confine and punish.

This is the view each of us must have of our own transgressions: We must not make excuses for our choices. We must instead acknowledge our moral guilt and be willing to accept appropriate consequences.

When it comes to lawbreakers, we must teach our neighbors why treating criminals as if they were sick is anything but humane. To demand that the punishment fit the crime is, as Lewis put it, to treat the criminal "as a human person made in God's image."

Lord, let me not succumb to the secular view that sinful behavior is the fault of everyone but the sinner. Give me the moral courage to own up to my own shortcomings, blaming neither sickness nor circumstance, and then to seek forgiveness and reconciliation.

THE ENEMY WITHIN

TO READ: PROVERBS 12:5-8, 13, 17-22

There is deceit in the hearts of those who plot evil. Proverbs 12:20

In the classic science fiction film *Invasion of the Body Snatchers,* aliens from outer space invade people's bodies as part of a plan to rule earth. One wonders if a certain abortion advocate was watching this film when she hatched a bizarre new abortion argument.

Political science professor Eileen McDonagh has written a book called *Breaking the Abortion Deadlock: From Choice to Consent.* McDonagh notes that many Americans have come to believe that human fetuses are actually human beings. That's a biologically accurate view, of course. But from a pro-choice perspective, it's dangerous.

To deal with this development, abortion supporters must find arguments that can justify the use of deadly force against these tiny humans. And that's what McDonagh has done. She's found her argument in—of all places—the law of self-defense.

McDonagh writes: "Even in a medically normal pregnancy, the fetus massively intrudes on a woman's body and expropriates her liberty." If the woman does not consent to this use of her body, McDonagh reasons, "the fetus's imposition constitutes injuries sufficient to justify the use of deadly force to stop it [just] as in rape, kidnapping or slavery." After all, McDonagh explains, if a woman has the right to defend herself against a rapist or kidnapper, she should also have the right to use deadly force to expel an unwanted fetus.

There you have it: Abortion is no longer murder—it's self-defense against an invading alien.

Of course, McDonagh's whole argument is patent nonsense. The law permits the use of deadly force only when a person has a reasonable fear for his life or physical safety. And the argument that the unborn child simply arrived without warning rests on the assumption that the mother did nothing to invite the fetus, that it simply showed up out of nowhere and attacked her—just like those aliens in science-fiction films.

But when men and women consent to sexual relations, they are, in effect, issuing an invitation. As the late Christian essayist Sheldon Vanauken puts it, "A pregnant woman is a *hostess*. When, through carelessness or design, the invitation has gone out and . . . the happy guest is inside the home, is that the time to . . . poison the guest in the name of controlling one's own house?"

McDonagh's "attack fetus" argument is so absurd that one wonders if anyone—even McDonagh—takes it seriously. The answer is yes, they do. Once people demand autonomy—the right to be their own gods—there is no limit to what they will do to justify their acts. That's what is really at stake here: freedom from any restraints.

Proverbs reminds us of the human tendency to lie in order to hide evil intent. That's certainly true for abortion proponents, who have lied for decades about the humanity of the fetus, leading to tragic consequences for millions of women and their unborn babies.

We have to be on our guard against this desire to deceive when we hear bizarre new arguments for abortion—arguments that treat babies as alien body snatchers.

Father, if I am every tempted to talk others into wrongdoing with a plausible-sounding lie, may I recall how much you detest lying lips—and keep mine shut.

READY TO FACE DEATH

TO READ: 1 PETER 1:3-9

In [God's] great mercy he has given us new birth into a living hope through the resurrection of Jesus Christ from the dead. 1 Peter 1:3

For decades Americans feared that the Soviets would annihilate us through a sudden nuclear strike. Today, those worries have been replaced by fears of terrorists' getting their hands on powerful weapons and using them to murder thousands—even millions.

How should Christians respond to threats of sudden, massive death? How do we keep our fear under control?

In a 1948 essay called "Living in the Atomic Age," C. S. Lewis asks how Christians ought to live in an age when atomic weapons—just invented at that time—might destroy the earth. His answer is that we ought to live just as we would have "in the sixteenth century, when the plague visited London almost every year" or as we would have a thousand years before that, when Viking raiders might have landed any night and cut our throats. In other words, the threat of disaster has always hung over humanity, and Christians in every age must be ready to face death.

Of course, what is different about atomic weapons is their ability to wipe out virtually *all* of humanity in one fell swoop. But even that leaves Lewis unruffled. What did you think was going to happen to the human race, he asks, had we *not* invented atomic weapons?

According to the second law of thermodynamics—which describes how the universe is winding down—the story of humanity will come to an end someday, with or without atomic bombs. This simple fact is a matter of real concern only if material existence is all there is.

"We see at once ... that the important question is not whether an atomic bomb is going to obliterate 'civilization,'" Lewis writes. "The important question is whether 'nature' . . . is the only thing in existence."

If nature is all there is—if there is no God—then nuclear war will simply speed up the inevitable. It makes little difference whether we are exterminated or not because, as Lewis puts it, life is nothing more than a "meaningless play of atoms in space and time."

But if there is a God who made us for a purpose—why, then, Lewis says, we need not worry about world destruction, because our true home is elsewhere. Global catastrophe will simply serve to send us to that home more quickly.

If the world is destroyed by atomic weapons, Lewis writes, let the bombs "find us doing sensible and human things—praying, working, teaching, reading, listening to music, bathing the children, playing tennis, chatting to our friends over a pint and a game of darts—not huddled together like frightened sheep and thinking about bombs."

Do you find yourself worrying about death—from nuclear war, terrorist attacks, car accidents, or cancer? We need not, and should not, fear death: We should instead rejoice in the knowledge that those who love God through Christ will live forever in his presence.

Lord, may I not spend one more moment fearing that I, or my loved ones, will die—knowing as I do that death is the doorway to joyous eternity in your presence for all who put their confidence in you.

A REALISTIC PORTRAIT

TO READ: HEBREWS 4:12-16

*We do not have a high priest who is unable to sympathize with our weaknesses,
but we have one who has been tempted in every way, just as we are—
yet was without sin.* Hebrews 4:15

Have you ever come across novels that appeared to be populated entirely by Precious Moments figurines? They're full of treacly, sentimental characters who seem to live in the one place on earth not affected by the Fall.

Then there's the alternative: novels full of graphic sex, violence, and nihilism that offer no redemption from the world's evil. Christian novelists need to avoid both of these extremes.

One author who has done this beautifully writes about a sleepy southern town called Mitford in the hills of North Carolina. The author is Jan Karon, and as Gina Dalfonzo notes in *BreakPoint Online,* Karon's books are flying off the shelves.

Mitford, Dalfonzo writes, is "a town where getting the Internet installed on one's computer is a big deal . . . where old friends regularly meet for lunch at the only diner for miles around, and where people . . . show up at each other's doors to borrow a cup of sugar."

The characters range from Uncle Billy Watson, an old man known for his corny jokes, to Sadie Baxter, the feisty, warm-hearted town benefactress. They interact with Father Tim Kavanaugh, a priest in his sixties who struggles with personal problems while opening his heart and home to an abandoned child.

Critics charge that Karon's readers are addicted to escapism and that the stories are cornpone. What these critics are missing, Dalfonzo writes, is Karon's ability "to blend innocence and realism."

For instance, there's nothing escapist about Uncle Billy's struggle to cope with his schizophrenic wife. Other characters endure life-threatening diseases, abusive spouses, loneliness, and poverty.

Yet throughout the stories, Dalfonzo writes, "the grace of God is present in Mitford as we see it through the eyes of its priest." Hope permeates the books.

This realistic literary balance between hopeless evil and sentimental mush is not always welcome. As Christian novelist Flannery O'Connor put it, "By separating nature and grace as much as possible," the average Christian reader "has reduced his conception of the supernatural to pious cliché and has become able to recognize nature in literature in only two forms, the sentimental and the obscene." O'Connor adds: "We lost our innocence in the Fall of our first parents, and our return to it is through the redemption . . . brought about by Christ's death and by our slow participation in it." Sentimentality skips this process, leading the reader to "an early arrival at a mock state of innocence."

Karon's ability to avoid this trap is one reason her books are literature, not just novels, and one reason they appeal to Christians and non-Christians alike.

Why not consider reading one of Karon's books—or giving one to a friend who is not a Christian? You'll be getting a story that is populated not by Precious Moments figurines but by the simple, sinful people of Mitford, where the God of all grace is marvelously at work.

Father, thank you for literary reminders that, as the author of Hebrews notes, while none of us is without sin, we have a sympathetic Savior to turn to for comfort as we journey back to innocence through him.

SEPTEMBER 21

RULES FOR A REASON

TO READ: 1 CORINTHIANS 7:1-9

If they cannot control themselves, they should marry, for it is better to marry than to burn with passion. I *Corinthians 7:9*

The June 2003 issue of the *Washington Monthly* ran an intriguing article by journalist Elizabeth Austin titled "In Contempt of Courtship." Happily married herself, Austin nevertheless found it depressing to study today's dating habits. Everywhere she looked, from popular culture to real life, dating was portrayed as hard, boring, thankless work, more like "applying for a new job" than having fun.

"When did we start to consider dating a synonym for hell?" she asked. "Wasn't the sexual revolution supposed to make courtship more fun? Yet everywhere we look, we see single people bemoaning the loneliness, the despair, the just plain drudgery of dating."

This led Austin to an astonishing conclusion: Maybe the sexual revolution, far from being the solution to a problem, was actually the cause of far bigger problems between men and women. It's not that Austin believes in saving sex for marriage, but, she admits, "the way it's been done lately, courtship isn't any fun. That's because there is currently only one broadly accepted rule of courtship: . . . If either party declines sex on the Third Date, it's a clear sign that the relationship is going nowhere."

Austin thinks that when you get right down to it, that's a sad way to live, and she's right. Imagine starting a sexual relationship that fizzles out after a few dates and having to go out and find someone else with whom to start another one—one that will probably also fizzle out. No wonder people dread dating these days!

Even Austin, with her mockery of "Rules girls," has to admit that she misses the days when single people took some time just to get to know each other rather than treat each other as something to be used and thrown away. After all, she writes, "in all forms of human behavior, there are rules." And they're not there just to keep us from having fun, as Austin's single friends are slowly and painfully learning. They're there to protect us. As Wendy Shalit explains in *A Return to Modesty: Discovering the Lost Virtue*, we all know that we need rules—so much that when we discard them, we end up longing to have them back and even trying to make up new ones.

Austin bases her argument "not on morality but on sheer utility." We Christians base ours on the fact that our loving Creator designed us for something much better than a string of broken relationships and unhappy memories. But it's interesting that both sides have reached the same conclusion. If Elizabeth Austin follows her train of thought to its logical conclusion, she may learn something from those women she dismisses as hopelessly prim and proper. Their lives are demonstrating an important truth: God's Word isn't just a set of arbitrary rules; it's a guide to the way the world really works.

Lord, thank you for courtship rules that protect us from degradation and despair. May I never succumb, in desperation for a date, to behavior you condemn. Whether single or married, I pray for your strength in resisting the siren call of sinful sexual liaisons.

DECONSTRUCTING RAND McNALLY

TO READ: JOB 38:1-11

The Lord answered Job . . . "Who is this that darkens my counsel with words without knowledge?" Job 38:1-2

When you're driving somewhere and get lost, you grab your handy road map. After all, it's an accurate representation of the local roads, which means you can count on it to show you how to get from point A to point B.

But today, postmodernism, which challenges all beliefs in objective truth, has even found its way into mapmaking. Some recent books argue seriously that maps don't reflect objective truth about the world but merely political interests. In short, postmodernism is invading what once seemed to be the most objective, two-dimensional means of representing the world: the field of cartography.

Of course, maps have always reflected the understanding of the times. Medieval maps showed a world that hardly extended beyond the Mediterranean and greatly exaggerated the size of the Holy Land. And in the late 1980s, the National Geographic Society chose a new projection of the world that portrayed the Soviet Union as much smaller—and less threatening—than it appeared in maps made during the Cold War.

But today these examples are being taken as the rule rather than the exception as postmodernists reject the very notion that we can represent the world objectively. In the words of geography professor David Woodward, we must "move beyond the idea of a map as a mirror of the world." Instead, maps should be "treated less as representational devices than as rhetorical devices," expressing the mapmakers' personal and political agendas.

Geographers are echoing the words of postmodernist philosopher Richard Rorty, who argues that we can no longer treat the human mind as a "mirror of nature." The idea that the mind is like a mirror or a camera, passively recording impressions of the world, stems from the Enlightenment, when many Western thinkers rejected divine revelation as the basis of human knowledge. Instead, they proposed that the human mind is capable of a "God's-eye" view of reality—an objective, neutral stance that transcends individual circumstances.

This was nothing less than the idolization of the human mind, and today that idol has crumbled. Postmodernism has exposed the flaw in the Enlightenment worldview by pointing out that each of us is limited and finite, conditioned by our social and historical context. It's now clear that apart from God's Word, humans have no transcendent "God's-eye" view of the world. As a result, postmodernism ends up in skepticism and despairs of finding any genuine truth.

Yet the spread of skepticism opens up an opportunity for Christians to make a powerful apologetic argument for what historian Paul Johnson calls "the necessity of Christianity." The only way to ground an objective view of truth is if God has given us his transcendent perspective—a genuine "God's-eye" view of reality.

If we press the case for biblical truth, we just might get cartographers away from doing postmodernist philosophy . . . and back into the business of making real maps.

Lord, when I am tempted to celebrate the wisdom of my own mind instead of falling down before yours, remind me that I cannot have a "God's-eye" view of reality apart from you.

THE MOVIEGOERS

TO READ: 1 CORINTHIANS 2:1-15

The man without the Spirit does not accept the things that come from the Spirit of God, for they are foolishness to him, and he cannot understand them, because they are spiritually discerned. The spiritual man makes judgments about all things, but he himself is not subject to any man's judgment. 1 Corinthians 2:14-15

Writer and film director Nora Ephron once declared that movies are to contemporary Americans what books were to previous generations. Movies shape the way we feel and the way we think.

This is why, warns screenwriter Brian Godawa in *Hollywood Worldviews: Watching Films with Wisdom and Discernment,* Christians should watch films with "wisdom and discernment." They must "understand what they are consuming and the nature of their amusement." This is especially true because films reflect worldviews, most of which are at odds with a Christian worldview.

For example, on the surface, the Oscar-winning film *Gosford Park* is a costume drama about the relationships between the British upper class and its servants. Once you get beneath the surface, however, you see that the moral universe the film depicts can best be described as nihilistic.

The world of *Gosford Park* is one in which all social and moral conventions are arbitrary, so much so that one character literally gets away with murder without any objection from the other characters or, for that matter, from the audience. The story unfolds in such a way that viewers can't help but accept the justification for the killer's actions and, even worse, the characters' indifference to the victim's death.

As Godawa notes, the best response to the insidious quality of many contemporary films is discernment. Discernment enables Christians to avoid two undesirable extremes—extremes that

Godawa labels *cultural anorexia* and *cultural gluttony*. Cultural anorexia means the avoidance of the culture altogether—but that leaves Christians incapable of "interacting redemptively" and causes them to miss good things in our popular culture. Cultural gluttons, on the other hand, ignore the way popular culture affects us for good and evil. They take it all in indiscriminately, consuming everything in front of them.

The best way to acquire discernment is through knowledge—and by asking probing questions. If you step into a movie theater now and then or rent DVDs, you may want to read Godawa's book, *Hollywood Worldviews*, which explains how to recognize the worldview messages in films. It's a reminder that when you go to the movies, you're often getting more than entertainment and popcorn. The lights may go down in the theater—but don't let them go down in your mind.

Lord, give me the gift of your discernment, that I may be neither a cultural anorexic—starving myself of culture—nor a cultural glutton, gorging myself on unhealthy cultural fare.

DELIVER US FROM EVIL

TO READ: JOHN 8:1-11

[Jesus said,] "If any one of you is without sin, let him be the first to throw a stone at her." John 8:7

A few years ago Virginians were horrified by the murder of Eric Van Nederynen, a fifteen-year-old Boy Scout who was shot and killed while walking to a neighborhood store. Why would anyone want to kill a popular boy who volunteered at soup kitchens and took part in church mission trips?

As his family mourned the loss of this promising teen, his friends—including some Christians—were no doubt asking themselves, *Why did God allow this evil thing to happen?*

The existence of suffering and evil in the world are among the most troublesome issues we face.

Albert Einstein believed that there had to be a God who created our incredibly complex universe, but he could not believe in the God of the Bible. Einstein argued that God could not be all good and all powerful at the same time.

Some people have tried to resolve this dilemma by arguing that God tolerates evil because he is not all good. Others, like Rabbi Harold Kushner, who wrote *When Bad Things Happen to Good People*, have concluded that God can't prevent evil—even though he would like to—because he is not all powerful.

But the Bible is very clear: God is all-powerful, and he created a good universe. He created human beings in his image, but he also gave us a free will. That means we all make our own moral choices.

The first man, Adam, responded to Satan's temptation and chose not to obey God. That is, he did the opposite of what a good God chose for us. At that moment, the opposite of good—or sin—entered into the world, and human nature was thereafter bent toward evil. We call this the doctrine of original sin.

Like a plague, evil has spread throughout history as the result of free moral choices. But God is not responsible for this evil. We are. Ultimately, evil exists because humans refuse to accept the good that God offers. It's important that people understand this concept because so many today are prone to deny the reality of the Fall. Some people believe that Adam and Eve are just symbols for all humanity and that the Fall is just a symbol of the sin that traps us. The truth is that the Fall is an actual historical event. Through an act of will, the first man and woman rejected God's way.

God could have made us incapable of sin, but then we would be less than human. We would be like robots or puppets, incapable of making free moral choices. We can choose to love God, or we can choose to defy him; this is the basis of our human dignity.

Lord, may my faith never falter when evil comes calling. Rather than draw me away from my trust in you, may the evil around me bring me closer to a holy and all-powerful God who, through the gift of moral choice, is preparing a people fit to spend eternity with him.

GOD IN THE CLOSET

TO READ: ACTS 6:8-12; 7:51-60

At this they covered their ears and, yelling at the top of their voices, they all rushed at him, dragged him out of the city and began to stone him. Acts 7:57

Imagine this scene: In a conference room at a major publishing company the author of a new civics textbook is having a tense meeting with his editor.

"There's a problem with your explanation of the Declaration of Independence," the editor says. "Where it says men are 'endowed by their Creator with certain unalienable rights,' you say it means that rights are given to people by God. We can't say 'God,' so that has to come out. Another thing: In the chapter on the civil rights movement, it's okay to mention that Martin Luther King Jr. was influenced by the Hindu sage Mohandas Gandhi, but you also say he was influenced by Jesus. That has to come out too."

University of Texas Professor Jay Budziszewski, author of *The Revenge of Conscience: Politics and the Fall of Man,* says that Christians face unofficial pressure to conceal the fact that the biblical faith has implications for every sphere of life. The shapers of opinion react with amazing hostility to the mere mention of God.

The story about the textbook author is true, and Budziszewski tells a similar story about himself. When he was a new scholar, a reviewer recommended against publishing one of his early books because he was rash enough to write that what we believe about God makes a difference in how we should live. Ironically, the reviewer liked the book, but he said, "God does not belong in political theory," and went on to blame the author for the massacre of the Huguenots in 1572, something that happened 380 years before Jay was even born.

What can explain such irrational hostility to the expression of biblical truth? Why do the custodians of culture react with such disapproval to the mere mention of God? Budziszewski's answer is that they are caught up in the Fall of man, the age-old rebellion of the human race against its Creator. The Fall means more than just doing wrong. We humans have a practical, an intellectual, and a strategic problem: We do wrong, we think wrong, and even our efforts to deal with wrong are corrupted by wrong.

The worst comes when we refuse to admit our sin sickness, because then we cannot bear even the mention of the God whom we have rejected. Because we deny our disease, we refuse its only cure.

Have you ever encountered someone whose hostility to your mention of your faith seemed wildly out of proportion to what you said? How did you respond? Although it's tempting to bark back at people who denigrate our beliefs, we ought to pause for a moment to consider where the antagonism is coming from—and respond accordingly.

If we Christians are ever going to counter the root cause of man's hostility to Christianity, we must understand the root cause: rebellion against God himself.

Lord, when I discuss my faith with those in rebellion against you, may I never forget that my ultimate goal should be not to offer witty ripostes but to model your love and truth so that they will forsake their sneering attacks and abandon themselves to you.

TAKING CARE OF BUSINESS

TO READ: 2 PETER 1:3-11

Through these he has given us his very great and precious promises, so that through them you may participate in the divine nature and escape the corruption in the world caused by evil desires. 2 Peter 1:4

Imagine you're on the board of directors of a large corporation. What do you do if the CEO of the company, a great leader who has made the company very profitable, is caught in adultery? Do you overlook the indiscretion? Do you fire him on the spot? Or do you come down somewhere in the middle?

Dr. Scott Rae, associate professor of biblical studies and Christian ethics at Talbot School of Theology, Biola University, has focused much of his career on medical and business ethics—exploring questions like the one posed above.

Rae argues that those in the business world must make ethical decisions with an eye on virtue, not education. After all, highly educated individuals who knew right from wrong caused the infamous ethical scandals of recent years. They simply chose to do wrong. There was no lapse of knowledge: There was, instead, a lapse of virtue. Rae argues that the success of capitalism depends on virtue, for without trust, honesty, and cooperation the entire free-market system falls apart.

As Rae puts it, "The founders of our nation believed that the democratic experiment would work only if the citizens are virtuous. Contrary to popular belief, total liberty was never their intent. Rather, their vision was one of 'ordered' or 'restrained' liberty, that is, freedom tempered by morals and character."

"Since business in a free-enterprise system is a cornerstone of democracy," Rae adds, "we should all be worried about the future of the free-market economy [and democracy itself] if virtue isn't once again taken seriously in the public dialogue about morality."

Rae believes that three theological norms exist for business ethics: holiness, justice, and love. *Holiness* in business ethics refers to being set apart from the surrounding culture or environment. That doesn't mean leaving the business world but rather standing against its corrupt values. *Justice* is the mark of a person who meets the standards set by God's character and who is innocent of intentional wrongdoing. The third norm, *love*, is necessary because without it, relationships with employees, company leaders, suppliers, customers, and shareholders become strained and break down.

If we want to avoid business scandals in the future, we need to learn to think biblically about all of life and to share these truths with the people around us—across the dinner table, over the backyard fence, and beside the water cooler at work—and we must grab hold of the promises and power of God ourselves in every decision we make, business or otherwise, in order to "escape the corruption in the world caused by our evil desires."

As for that imaginary CEO caught in adultery, Rae concludes that adultery on the job robs him of his moral authority—and therefore, he should go.

Lord, plant in me a desire to add to my faith the qualities that will make me productive in my knowledge of you and keep me from falling into sin and spiritual bankruptcy.

IT'S ABOUT TIME

TO READ: ECCLESIASTES 3:1-14

There is a time for everything, and a season for every activity under heaven.
Ecclesiastes 3:1

In Jonathan Swift's *Gulliver's Travels,* the Lilliputians see Gulliver's pocket watch and conclude that it must be his god because Gulliver told them that he never did anything without consulting it first.

Is the clock your god? There may be no other part of our lives so thoroughly co-opted by a secular worldview than our notion of time. We say time is a gift from God, but most of the time we treat time as a club rather than a gift.

To properly understand time, we need richer language than the language of business management. We need biblical language that reflects the God who grants us life, hour by hour, minute by minute.

In the global economy there are no more days; there is simply productivity—24/7. Time in the global economy never slows down, never rests, and has no rhythm but the relentless beat of commerce.

That is not the biblical idea of time. God has built a rhythm into the world and into humanity. Eugene Peterson, the author of *Working the Angles: The Shape of Pastoral Integrity,* points out that in the Bible a day doesn't begin with sunrise—it begins with sun*set*. The day begins when we go to sleep. We wake up and join God in the work of the day he began while we were sleeping. We don't begin the day; rather, we wake up and step into God's rhythm of grace, a day already in progress.

This idea that day begins when I go to sleep is a vital worldview concept. Life, success, and productivity don't, in the final analysis, depend on us. They depend on God. That understanding allows us to rest—to rest in our sleep knowing that God is at work, and to rest on the Sabbath. Because we believe in the providence of God, we can affirm that we have enough time, and we can then receive the day as a gift.

There are at least four applications for this biblical view of time: First, we should honor our bodies by keeping sensible schedules and getting the rest we need. We have enough time to work, rest, love our families and friends, worship, and exercise.

Second, we must build into our schedules prayer and meditation on God's Word. Keeping God and his Word at the forefront of our minds helps us develop the biblical notion of time.

Third, we can say no. Our overscheduled lives are testimony that our notion of time has not been formed by a biblical worldview.

Finally, we can enjoy the freedom of the Sabbath, that foretaste of our eternal rest with God.

A biblical perspective on time will revolutionize the way we live, play, rest, worship, and work. So the next time you look at your watch, take a moment to remember who your God is and how he has providentially given you all the time you need.

Lord, help me to trust you with the hours and minutes you have entrusted to me, remembering that you have given me all the time I need to carry out your plans and purposes for my life.

LOVING OUR ENEMIES

TO READ: JOHN 2:11-17

He made a whip out of cords, and drove all from the temple area, both sheep and cattle; he scattered the coins of the money changers and overturned their tables.
John 2:15

The attacks on September 11 were scarcely over before Christians began weighing in on how America should respond. For many, going to war was simply not an option: After all, didn't Jesus say, "Blessed are the peacemakers?" Remember, warned a letter writer to the *Atlanta Journal-Constitution*, "Christ was an absolute pacifist."

But as William Bennett reminds us in *Why We Fight: Moral Clarity and the War on Terrorism*, Jesus was nothing of the kind. It's true that Jesus told us as individuals not to resist evildoers and never to avenge ourselves. But there's a difference between commands to us as individuals and the role of the state in society. Bennett notes that in one of Jesus' few unmixed utterances of praise, he "lauded the faith of a Roman centurion, a soldier and a man of violence," who asked Jesus to heal a dying servant.

Jesus himself engaged in at least one act of violence. In John's Gospel we read that Jesus became enraged when he saw people turning the temple into a place of trade. He made a whip and drove the money changers out, overturning their tables and pouring their money onto the ground. In Luke's Gospel, Jesus tells his disciples to sell their cloaks if necessary in order to buy swords.

In Romans, Paul admonishes Christians to obey government authorities—authorities that God has authorized to use force to overthrow evildoers. Both Paul and the apostle Peter instruct the church that human institutions are sent by God "to punish those who do wrong."

"Nowhere in the New Testament do we find force itself held up for explicit praise," Bennett acknowledges, but "neither are the [biblical] writers so unworldly as to posit that the answer to every human conflict is to turn the other cheek." Indeed, he adds, it was to elaborate the why and how of force that the church developed the doctrine of just war.

Augustine, the first just-war thinker, explained that the belligerents in a just war must "intend the advancement of good, or the avoidance of evil." Bennett writes that Augustine recognized that "there are times when not resorting to force leads to evils far greater than the one we oppose."

Have you ever been confused by conflicting messages about the morality of violence? As our nation continues its fight in the war on terror, we need to thoughtfully consider the teachings of Scripture on this matter. And we must learn how to defend—sometimes to fellow Christians—the proper use of force, recognizing that in some cases the most honorable way to be a peacemaker is to take up arms against evil.

Father, I beg your protection of those who risk their lives to keep mine safe. Grant our leaders wisdom as they make decisions regarding the proper use of military force. Have mercy, I pray, on the souls of those who die fighting in just wars, advancing good by overthrowing evil.

SEPTEMBER 29

A CONSPIRACY OF SILENCE

TO READ: 1 THESSALONIANS 2:1-12

We were gentle among you, like a mother caring for her little children.
1 Thessalonians 2:7

Should children be raised by their parents—or by "experts" who know what they're doing?

Anna Freud, the daughter of Sigmund Freud, was a child analyst who thought that well-trained professionals could do a much better job of rearing children than their parents could. During World War II she got a chance to prove it.

In the 1940s, London was full of children left homeless by the German blitz. Anna Freud opened the Hampstead War Nurseries to care for these children. Only the best-qualified people were allowed to work there. The nurseries were run according to the latest theories in child psychology.

What was the result? As Brian Robertson writes in *There's No Place Like Work*, "In these controlled conditions—about as favorable as could be imagined—the children fared [far] worse . . . than those raised in average families." The children lagged behind on speech skills and were more aggressive and less cooperative than their counterparts who were raised in a family setting.

According to Robertson, Freud considered the nurseries "definitive proof that there was no adequate substitute for maternal care." Subsequent studies overwhelmingly confirm what Freud experienced. Robertson notes that children reared in day care "exhibit some of the same debilitating emotional . . . cognitive, and even physical problems" displayed by orphans.

Now, consider the fact that we've known for some sixty years that

543

children are much better off at home than within the walls of even the best-run day-care center. So why are people still trying to prove that day care is just as good or even better than maternal care?

The reason, Robertson writes, is that the evidence goes against "the reigning feminist orthodoxy regarding child care." This orthodoxy has led to a conspiracy of silence regarding the importance of maternal care. Radical feminists and academics make it nearly impossible to talk about how damaging nonmaternal care can be. As noted baby expert Penelope Leach candidly puts it, "There is a cover-up going on." Leach says the evidence that children are far better off in the care of their mothers is suppressed for "fear of upsetting the parents who don't provide it."

Some of the most evocative images in the Scriptures reveal how important child nurturing is. Deuteronomy 32:11 tells us that God's love is "like an eagle that stirs up its nest and hovers over its young, that spreads its wings to catch them and carries them on its pinions." This verse reveals just how strong the nurturing instinct is, even among animals.

If feminists really cared about children, they would make sure that every new mother understood how harmful day care can be. They would support policy changes to allow more families to make it on just one income or for moms to work from their homes.

Christians need to get the truth out about the superiority of mother care over day care. The church must do something else, as well: We must be as supportive as possible of mothers whose circumstances make it difficult or impossible to give up day care.

Lord, when I make important decisions about work and family, help me to overcome the temptation to lie to myself in order to justify doing what I want to do instead of opening my heart to what you want me to do.

DECEPTIVE RHETORIC

TO READ: GENESIS 24:50-67

Isaac brought her into the tent of his mother Sarah, and he married Rebekah. So she became his wife, and he loved her. Genesis 24:67

A few years ago abortion-rights groups ran an advertisement in several newspapers featuring pictures of an automatic and a manual transmission. The caption read, "Everybody likes choice." Comparing automobile purchases to the most important moral issue of our time may seem absurd, but enemies of the traditional family often appropriate the language of the marketplace to make their point.

As economist and author Jennifer Roback Morse explains, the assault on marriage "uses the rhetoric and language" of choice and the marketplace. It does so for the same reasons that pro-abortion forces use this rhetoric: It's "very seductive."

The goal of what Morse calls the "lifestyle left" is to create "perfectly autonomous persons who are not connected to each other in any permanent way." As a result of this "deconstruction of the family," the state would enjoy more power. Of course, putting it in these terms would not make the idea very marketable. So instead, the "lifestyle left" has "repackaged" its arguments in terms that Americans find more agreeable: the language of the marketplace. Thus, marriage ceased being a covenant or a solemn vow and became a "contract." This rhetorical shift led Americans to see marriage as a voluntary agreement between two adults. If marriage is a contract, then the parties are free to negotiate the terms of their agreement, enforce those terms, and terminate the agreement whenever they choose.

It's easy to see how this shift damaged the family. It not only opened the door to no-fault divorce, but it has done the same for cohabitation and same-sex unions. If marriage is simply a contract, then it's impossible to limit the terms of that contract to one man and one woman in a life-long committed relationship. Instead, anything goes.

There are other critical ways in which viewing marriage as a contract hurts families. This view "undermines the basis of generosity and self-giving" so essential to family life. On a construction site, a welder can tell the foreman, "It's not my job," if the foreman asks him to do some carpentry. The same response by a husband to a request from his wife is a sign of a dysfunctional marriage.

In other words, there are no job descriptions in marriage. Yet this is precisely where the "marriage as contract" rhetoric—and the worldview it produces—is leading us. Instead of seeing marriage and family as a joint effort lived out before God and the community, people see it as a "deal." And as with all deals, the name of the game is to make sure that you get the best of the bargain.

Christians must be aware of, and avoid, the temptation to abuse language in order to manipulate others and get what we want. And we must be ever vigilant against those who twist language and rhetoric to suit their purposes—purposes designed to deceive and seduce.

Lord, your Word says you hate liars, and when we see our neighbors deceived by the language of lies into committing sin, we understand why. Keep me from the temptation to embellish the truth—or hide it—or twist it—through the use and abuse of speech.

FLAT-EARTHERS

TO READ: PROVERBS 26:18-28

A malicious man disguises himself with his lips. Proverbs 26:24

"It's about time someone stood up to the Flat-Earthers who want to push their beliefs in the schools."

The comment came from *Kansas City Star* columnist Mike Hendricks, who was letting the world know what he thought about the decision by the Kansas State School Board to let local public schools decide how much Darwinian evolution to teach.

The phrase *Flat-Earthers* is intended to suggest that Christian beliefs are behind the times and out of touch with modern science and rationality. After all, didn't medieval Christians cling to the idea that the earth was flat? Didn't it take the voyage of Christopher Columbus to convince backward Christians that the earth is spherical?

Actually, no.

Augustine, who lived about a thousand years before Columbus, knew that the earth was round. In the thirteenth century, Thomas Aquinas, the most profound and prolific of the medieval theologians, observed that it was possible to empirically demonstrate the spherical shape of the earth. His proofs were both mathematical and physical. For example, he suggested that lunar eclipses allow us to infer the spherical shape of the earth.

Throughout the centuries many other church fathers taught that the earth is spherical. So where do people get the idea that Christians were Flat-Earthers?

It was a fable cooked up by Enlightenment propagandists. In *Inventing the Flat Earth: Columbus and the Modern Historians*, Jeffrey

Burton Russell explains that in the early nineteenth century, Enlightenment thinkers bent on discrediting the church invented the myth that medieval Christians taught the idea of a flat earth. It was essentially a calumny—indeed, a libel—designed to discredit the Christian heritage of the Middle Ages.

Of course, medieval Christians did not have the vast information that modern science has since revealed. But those men were not fools, and they were certainly not anti-intellectual. On the contrary, men such as Augustine and Aquinas helped put into place the tradition of careful, dispassionate inquiry in the quest for truth, a tradition that is one of the great glories of Western civilization. Modern scholarship—including modern science—would not have emerged without them.

Today the term *Flat-Earthers* is still in vogue. Hundreds of years after the Enlightenment, our opponents still seem to prefer to fight with insults instead of facts, whether the debate is about evolution, abstinence education, or stem-cell research.

As we observe Columbus Day this month, we need to take the opportunity to communicate the truth about the reason Columbus believed the earth was round: He was following in the tradition of Christians such as Augustine and Aquinas. And make sure your children understand that the term *Flat-Earthers* is the invention of the elites who lived hundreds of years ago—people who were just as afraid of Christian arguments then as the intellectual elites are today.

Father, let me not be found keeping quiet when I should be speaking out, simply because I'm afraid of secular insults. Help me to remember that your Son suffered the insults of the "learned teachers," and if I am to follow him, I must be willing to suffer the same.

BIG MACS AND BIG MONEY

TO READ: EXODUS 32:1-4, 19-24, 30-35

"Do not be angry, my lord," Aaron answered. "You know how prone
these people are to evil." Exodus 32:22

A woman I'll call Karen Smith measured five feet, six inches tall and
weighed 270 pounds. Why did she weigh twice her healthy weight?
Was it the result of genetics? poor nutrition? lack of exercise?

No, Smith claimed that she was obese because "her regular diet included an Egg McMuffin for breakfast and a Big Mac meal for dinner." She and other overweight people sued McDonald's.

Their complaint may sound ridiculous, but it points to a serious
problem: the increasing amorality of the law.

Chris Rangel, who runs a Web site devoted to medicine and public policy, doubts Smith's description of her eating habits. He
writes, "There is just no physical way for [her] to reach . . . 270
pounds . . . by eating an Egg McMuffin for breakfast and a Big Mac
for dinner." Basic nutritional guidelines lead Rangel to estimate
that Smith is probably consuming close to three times the calories
she alleges in her complaint.

But even if Rangel is right, it doesn't matter—at least not in today's
courts. Historically, even if you assumed that fast food caused obesity,
plaintiffs such as Smith could get nothing in court. That's because of
legal doctrines known as "assumption of risk" and "contributory negligence." If a plaintiff knew the risks of a behavior and acted anyway, or if
through her own negligence she contributed to her injuries, she was
not permitted to recover damages.

For many years these doctrines allowed tobacco companies to prevail in court. After 1964, when health warnings appeared on packs of

cigarettes, smokers knew the risks associated with smoking. This changed when lawyers borrowed a concept from our therapeutic culture: addiction.

John Banzhaf, who played a key role in tobacco litigation, told *USA Today* that the concept of addiction was "a breakthrough" that led to their success in court. Portraying plaintiffs as addicts allowed juries to disregard questions of individual self-control and assumption of risk. Instead, they held the corporations responsible. What's more, the concept of addiction is so elastic that it can cover almost any activity; it was only a matter of time before it applied to other "deep-pockets" industries.

Fast-food companies stand to become the Big Tobacco of the new millennium.

While this may please "Karen Smith," it should concern the rest of us. Our confidence in the law stems from the belief that law is about justice and is grounded in objective morality. Because of this, we know what society expects of us, and just as important, we know when we fall short of those expectations.

People have always been tempted to blame others for their own behavior. The biblical Adam did it; so did Aaron and Saul. But when slippery ideas such as addiction overrule common sense and prudence, our confidence in the rule of law is eroded.

Lord, if I am tempted to blame others when I indulge in sin, remind me that you will hold me accountable—even if society's laws do not.

WHO KNOWS BEZALEL?

TO READ: EXODUS 31:1-11

The Lord said to Moses, "See, I have chosen Bezalel . . . and I have filled him with the Spirit of God . . . to make artistic designs for work in gold, silver and bronze, to cut and set stones, to work in wood, and to engage in all kinds of craftsmanship."
Exodus 31:1-5

Ordinarily when we read about God's Holy Spirit filling someone, we know that God is equipping that person for some great spiritual task. But why did God fill Bezalel with the Spirit? To work on the Tabernacle, the early Hebrew tent of worship.

From the surrounding passages we can extract several biblical principles that apply to art. First, *God cares about beauty.* In Exodus 28 the Lord tells Moses to make garments for the priests to wear—garments "for glory and for beauty." This ought to be the slogan of every Christian artist, musician, and writer: that we work for the glory of God and for beauty.

Second, *being an artist can be a vocation from God.* Exodus 35 explicitly says God "called" Bezalel "by name" to his work. As Gene Edward Veith says in *State of the Arts: From Bezalel to Mapplethorpe,* we normally think of people being called to the ministry or the mission field. But the Bible teaches that every occupation—including that of an artist—can be a calling from God.

Third, *artistic ability is a gift of God.* Several times in Exodus the text speaks of various craftsmen as people to whom "the Lord had given ability." Those with artistic talent should not hide it under a bushel; it is a gift from God to be cultivated for the service of God and our neighbors.

Many Christians never think much about art—unless they're

outraged at the National Endowment for the Arts (NEA) for funding some blasphemous project like Andres Serrano's photograph of a crucifix in a jar of urine. But the call of God is not just to run around putting out fires after the secular world has started them. God calls his people to lead the way in renewing our culture by creating "artistic designs," things "for glory and for beauty."

Lord, thank you for the variety of artistic talents you have given. Help me to remember that creating art that glorifies you is a worthy calling. Show me ways to support Christian artists who are struggling to learn their craft, and teach me to appreciate works of art created by painters, sculptors, and stained-glass makers who worship you through the work of their hands.

OCTOBER 4

DUH!

TO READ: LEVITICUS 19:1-4

Each of you must respect his mother and father. Leviticus 19:3

A working mother asks her seventh-grade daughter, "So, what do you think of my presentation?"

"It's Stone Age," the daughter answers with a sneer.

The dialogue, from a radio ad for Canon copiers, raised the hackles of real-life parents. The girl goes on to tell her mom that she really should have used a Canon copier. Aren't all copiers pretty much alike? her mom asks. You can almost see the daughter rolling her eyes.

"Hel-*lo!*" she says sarcastically. Clearly, Mom is a little dense, and the girl rapidly identifies a few more of the Canon copier's features.

Mom is impressed. "How'd you get so smart?" she asks.

To which her daughter replies, "I'm a graduate of grade seven. *Duh!*"

It may have been that final insulting "Duh!" that sent listeners over the edge. Dozens called Canon to complain that the girl was a smart aleck.

Why would advertisers think it's a good idea to use sassy kids to push products?

Today, thanks to television, glibness, one-liners, and put-downs are what sell. Sociologist Todd Gitlin writes in the *Wilson Quarterly* that as the influence of church and family has waned, television has begun setting the tone and temper of our culture. "On TV both children and adults speak with an unprecedented glibness . . . the one-liner, developed for ads, is the premium style," Gitlin adds. In commercials, parents "are typically shown as . . . well-meaning bunglers who are set straight . . . by their sons and daughters."

Unfortunately, real-life children are watching—and mimicking—what they see. And what they're learning flies in the face of scriptural teaching and universal rules of civility.

The Bible admonishes children to speak respectfully to their parents and to other adults. Scriptural writers recognized that the family is by nature a social curb, a restraint on the sinful dispositions of children. It's the context in which children cultivate social virtue. The point of ads like the Canon commercial is that children do not need to recognize and defer to any social order, even that most fundamental social unit, the family. In fact, the ad suggests that children, rather than needing correction and direction, are on equal footing with their parents—or even superior to them.

Under the guise of cuteness, ad makers are attacking the parent-child relationship and, by extension, the social order itself. The biblical command to honor our parents represents the need to recognize the social order God has created.

When we see or hear commercials like the Canon ad, we need to take time to tell those companies to mind their commercial manners. Sometimes complaining works: When people called Canon to complain about that smart-alecky girl, the company altered the ad. Now when the mother asks the girl how she got so smart, her daughter answers, "Guess I inherited it."

That's a glib one-liner parents can live with.

Lord, in my dealings with all of the people in my life, help me to remember that you want me to treat others not with contempt but with civility, not only when it's easy but also when it's hard.

OCTOBER 5

GRACE FOR THE
STRAIGHT PATH

TO READ: GALATIANS 3:19-29

The law was put in charge to lead us to Christ that we might be justified by faith.
Galatians 3:24

In *Is the Father of Jesus the God of Muhammad?* theologian Timothy George describes the major differences between Christianity and Islam.

One of the critical differences is in the view of salvation. Islam and Christianity have radically different answers to the question of how we attain God's favor and paradise when we die. George writes, "The *Qur'an* says Adam forgot to walk the right way. Sin is forgetfulness, heedlessness, a failure to remember. This forgetting to obey is the result of inherent weakness, not active rebellion against God. . . . Once Adam repents, as he does, God quickly forgives. From that time on, Adam lived a perfect life."

If the sin is forgetfulness, the solution is remembering. So one of the pillars of Islam is the practice of *Salat,* the practice of ritual prayer five times a day. To help people remember, Islam teaches, God sent 124,000 prophets from Adam to Muhammad. And the Islamic law, or *Shariah,* enforces remembering and should be applied to "legal, political, and economic structures, as well as one's personal life."

In this view of salvation, George writes, humans "are fully capable of determining their own eternal destiny by their own exertion, discipline, and devotion. Redemption is not a category Islam recognizes. Every Muslim is his or her own redeemer."

But, George argues, if all we need is guidance to walk the straight path to God, then why, 124,000 prophets later, does everyone—including Muslims—stray from the path? If we all have the power to be good, why do we experience so many moral failings? Why do we know what's right and still do what's wrong?

The Muslim answer to the nature of human sin is as inadequate as its solution. The Islamic view is that we are sinners because we sin. If you stop sinning, you're no longer a sinner. But Christians know that we sin because we *are* sinners. Our hearts are twisted.

Christians believe that Adam didn't *forget* to obey. Instead, remembering perfectly well what God required, he still rebelled, and in so doing, he broke the relationship of love he had with God. George tells us that Allah forgives easily because human sin does not affect him deeply. But in the Bible, George writes, our sins clearly offend God and grieve him.

If there is to be a restored relationship, it can be only by the sheer generosity of God, who offers his Son as a sacrifice for the sins of his people.

An integral part of a Christian worldview is an understanding of the nature of sin. That understanding is also necessary if we're to intelligently answer our neighbors when they assert either a Muslim worldview or an easygoing ecumenism that denies the need for Christ.

Lord, you command us to have a ready answer for questions about the faith we embrace. Make me willing to learn enough about Islam—and to love Muslims enough—that I will be able to witness to them about the truth that can set them forever free from sin.

BROKEN RELATIONSHIPS

TO READ: ESTHER 2:1-20

Mordecai had a cousin named Hadassah, whom he had brought up because she had neither father nor mother. Esther 2:7

"Religion in all its forms [is designed to] continue the oppression of women" by "invoking the words and deeds of the exclusive male deity."

These angry words are from *Lesbian Nation,* written by feminist Jill Johnston, and her views are typical of how feminists view Christianity.

Why do so many feminists reject the masculine God of the Bible? A Christian psychologist says it may be because their earthly fathers rejected *them.*

In *Faith of the Fatherless,* Paul Vitz argues that rejection of God is linked directly to a defective relationship involving one's earthly father. By defective, Vitz means the father has died, abused his child, or abandoned his offspring.

But Vitz says that men and women behave very differently *after* they reject God. For men, Vitz writes, "God seems to function primarily as a principle of justice and order in the world." He functions "only secondarily as a person with whom one has a relationship." Vitz says this explains why atheistic men search for substitute gods through principles like reason, science, socialism, or existentialism.

But for women, it's their relationship with God that is primary. When women reject God, they attempt to replace him with other relationships.

Vitz writes: "It is not the idea of a god per se that they reject," but rather "the god of a particular relationship." As a result, they take up a new enthusiasm—like feminism—that offers "important new relationships to take the place of God the Father."

These women tend to put a strong emphasis on "sisterhood," and many embrace lesbianism. In addition, Vitz notes, "feminism is well known for its redefinition of God as female: the Goddess, or God the mother."

The backgrounds of modern feminists gives credence to Vitz's theory. For example, Jill Johnston was born out of wedlock; her father never tried to contact her. Her obsession with her father is woven throughout her writings.

Vitz offers insight into why intense atheists are so angry at God. It's because they've been deeply wounded by fathers who rejected, denied, hated, abused, or abandoned them.

Contrast these fathers with how Mordecai treated his adopted daughter, Esther. He made daily efforts to find out how she fared at court. He advised her wisely, and in return, Esther loved and obeyed him, even when she no longer had to. Mordecai's care for Esther ultimately prevented a Persian holocaust.

Modern Christian men must lovingly minister to fatherless children within their congregations, teaching them what it means to be loved by an earthly father figure.

That masculine love will go far in pointing them toward an eternal relationship with their heavenly Father.

Heavenly Father, help me to be a wise and loving father to the children you have placed in my care. May I be open to fathering, in some way, local children who lack fathers or to helping suffering adults I know whose own fathers let them down and who are afraid to trust you.

DOMESTIC PUBLICITY

TO READ: PHILIPPIANS 2:12-18

Do everything without complaining or arguing, so that you may become blameless and pure, children of God without fault in a crooked and depraved generation, in which you shine like stars in the universe as you hold out the word of life.
Philippians 2:14-16

William Wilberforce is remembered as the parliamentarian most responsible for ending the British slave trade. But to the people of his own generation, he was the man who changed the way the British viewed their role as parents. He's an example of the priorities every father—even busy political fathers—ought to have.

Wilberforce did not marry until he was nearly forty. But as Kevin Belmonte notes in *Hero for Humanity*, once Wilberforce became a husband and the father of six children, he took up his new responsibilities with relish.

"At any given moment," Belmonte writes, "one might visit his home and find the master of the house . . . refreshing himself by throwing a ball." It was not unusual for him to excuse himself "from important deliberations with fellow MPs to go out on the lawn and have a race with the children." It was not unusual for Wilberforce to scoop up his offspring and take them on a picnic, to see a juggler, or to visit a toy shop.

As Belmonte observes, Wilberforce's hospitality says much about his "ability to make goodness fashionable."

As Wilberforce's brother-in-law James Stephen eloquently noted, "Witnessing his domestic life is one of the best cures I know for prepossessions against religion [and] the best human incentives to the practice of it." And he added: "There is something peculiar in Wilberforce's character and situation that seem to point it out as the design of Providence that he should serve his Master in this high and special walk and should have, so to speak, a kind of domestic publicity—that he should be at home, a candle set on a candlestick, as well as abroad, a city built upon a hill."

Belmonte says it was through Wilberforce's example that British households "increasingly . . . became places where parents spent more time with their children, educating them, praying with them, reading with them, and playing with them." Eventually, Wilberforce resigned his powerful seat in the House of Commons in order "to take a more active role in educating and rearing his children."

Sadly, these days too many Christians in business or politics neglect their families. Wilberforce is a reminder of what every Christian father should be in spite of great demands on his time. For the sake of his children—and for the sake of his witness—he must be "at home, a candle set on a candlestick, as well as abroad a city built upon a hill."

Father, wherever you place me, let others be inspired to follow you by the way I carry out my responsibilities at home and abroad, helping make goodness—and the One who created it—fashionable in a depraved generation.

CLUELESS

TO READ: 1 KINGS 14:21-24

There were even male shrine prostitutes in the land; the people engaged in all the detestable practices of the nations the Lord had driven out before the Israelites.
1 Kings 14:24

When Pope John Paul II summoned American cardinals to Rome to discuss the sexual abuse of minors by priests—and how church officials handled it—many in the mainstream media proclaimed that neither the Vatican nor the bishops "get it." There is much to criticize in the way the church handled this sorry affair, but it's clear that the Catholic Church's critics are as "clueless" as they accuse the church of being.

For instance, the Reverend Paul Shanley was charged with molesting at least fifteen boys. Attorneys for Shanley's victims allege that church officials knew about the allegations against him yet continued to allow him to work in proximity to minors.

Some of the most damning evidence lay in eight hundred plus pages of documents that show the archdiocese was aware of the accusations against the priest. One of the victims' attorneys pointed out that the documents indicate that the officials knew about Shanley's "views on gay love." The documents tell us that Shanley was not only attracted to boys; he also publicly advocated sex between adult men and boys. Worse, Shanley attended meetings of what became the infamous North American Man-Boy Love Association, or NAMBLA.

The attorney's use of the expression "gay love" and the references to NAMBLA point to an aspect of this story that many in the media are intent on ignoring. Rod Dreher of *National Review* has written,

"What we're seeing is gay men who cannot or will not [control themselves physically] around teenage boys."

The fact is that at the root of these scandals is the homosexual subculture that has grown up among priests, but to say this openly is anathema to many commentators and reporters. As a result, they report on the documents as proof of misconduct by church officials, but somehow they scarcely mention Shanley's promiscuous and predatory homosexuality.

We also see this doublethink at work in reports about another Shanley-related document: a letter he wrote to former Cardinal Humberto Medeiros complaining about being forbidden to "[encourage] gay unions" and to give his opinion on the morality of homosexual acts. Reporters cited the letter as proof of malfeasance by the church, but again, they left out the issue of Shanley's homosexuality.

George Orwell, of *1984* fame, once wrote that he lived in an age when stating the obvious was the first duty of intelligent men. We live in such an age. We must be prepared to state the obvious: that homosexuality, not celibacy, is the problem in the Catholic Church. We must state it even when the media insists on ignoring it, for we must not allow their cluelessness to become ours.

Lord, your Word tells us that disobedience to your commands will always carry a tragic price. I pray for your healing for all who have been harmed through sexual abuse and that the truth about the origins of such abuse will be revealed.

OCTOBER 9

THE DENIAL GAME

TO READ: ISAIAH 40:21-26

Lift your eyes and look to the heavens: Who created all these? Isaiah 40:26

A few years ago, feminist Naomi Wolf admitted that although feminists pretend not to know that fetuses are babies, in reality they know it quite well. She confessed that abortion is real sin, and feminists have known it all along.

The problem is, Wolf wants women to keep having abortions. If they feel bad about them, women can hold candlelight vigils at abortion facilities afterward to show their sorrow.

How could anyone hold such a cynical, callused view? The problem is that Wolf is in denial too. She simply pretends not to know that God will not be mocked.

In *The Revenge of Conscience: Politics and the Fall of Man,* Jay Budziszewski reminds us that human beings have been playing the denial game ever since the Fall, feigning ignorance of the moral facts.

The Bible mentions five ways (apart from direct scriptural revelation) in which God has made his moral requirements known:

First, the witness of conscience. In Romans 2:15, Paul says that even pagans know God's moral law because it is "written on their hearts, their consciences also bearing witness." Sin comes not from ignorance but from stubbornness, for they "suppress the truth" (Romans 1:18).

Second, the witness of God-ward longing. In Acts 17 we read that the Athenians built an altar to "the unknown god." At some level, they knew their idols could never save them, but they had an intuition about a mysterious Holy One who could. This is a universal intuition, which tells us that we were made for God, not for ourselves.

Third, the witness of God's handiwork. All of nature and even our bodies proclaim his eternal glory.

Fourth, the witness of the harvest. The Bible warns that every sin is linked with consequences: Whatever we sow, we reap. We may pretend ignorance, as people pretend ignorance of the harvest of the sexual revolution. But the evidence is there.

Fifth, the witness of our design. God makes some of his intentions plain through the way he made us. Our physical design informs us that man was made for woman, not for man, and our emotional design reminds us that children are gifts, not curses.

Ultimately, no one is ignorant of the moral law, no matter how much he or she may deny it. Has anyone ever played the denial game with you? Have you ever played the game yourself? We need to understand and teach others that denial is really just self-deception. Because God's law is written in the skies . . . and on our hearts.

Father, how often I am tempted to pretend that what I want to do is acceptable in your eyes. Help me to listen to the witness of my own conscience and obey not my own evil desires but your holy commands.

OCTOBER 10

SORELY NEEDED WISDOM

TO READ: GENESIS 11:1-9

They said, "Come, let us build ourselves a city, with a tower that reaches to the heavens, so that we may make a name for ourselves." Genesis 11:4

What is the role of the Bible—Genesis, in particular—in twenty-first-century American life? Do words written more than three millennia ago have anything to tell us about how we ought to live our lives today? The answer, according to Leon Kass, author of *The Beginning of Wisdom: Reading Genesis,* is "absolutely."

Kass's book is the product of twenty-five years of studying Genesis and teaching it to his students at the University of Chicago. Those experiences led Kass to appreciate the "moral sensibilities and demands of the Torah," although he confesses that his practice is still "wanting." But he is no longer confident about the sufficiency of "unaided human reason" to answer life's most important questions.

The impact of Genesis isn't limited to the personal. Kass, who is Jewish, says that what he calls the "crisis in modern thought," especially in moral and ethical realms, stems from our culture's disregard for the lessons Genesis teaches. We have a "need for wisdom" in this area, one that requires a "serious examination" of the Bible, starting with Genesis.

Even a reader who doesn't believe in the inspiration of Scripture has to admit that the first eleven chapters of Genesis are without peer in their accurate depiction of the "human predicament"—our strengths and our weaknesses, our nobility and our folly.

As Kass puts it, the stories in these chapters tell "what always happens"—whether the subject is the relationship between spouses, between siblings, or between man and God.

For instance, Kass's chapter on the story of Cain and Abel, "Fratricide and Founding," is a powerful antidote to our culture's sentimental and even utopian view of human nature. Genesis's account of how pride, jealousy, and anger cause us to prey upon one another is much more true to life than what we hear from contemporary "experts."

Given the insight and accuracy we see in Genesis regarding the human condition, it's reasonable to think that the book's insights on what it means to be human are likewise worth examining. Its account of what makes man unique and the dignity that flows from that status, like its portrayal of our faults, rings far truer to human experience than secular alternatives.

The understanding of human nature and human dignity we get from Genesis has implications for nearly every aspect of our culture: bioethics, human rights, religious freedom, war, and peace.

The alternatives to the biblical worldview have all failed, leaving us with the crisis Kass mentions: We are unable to find answers because we no longer remember the real questions: Who are we? Where did we come from? How are we supposed to live?

To find the answers, we, like Kass, need to start at the beginning with the stories written three thousand years ago—in Genesis.

Lord, let me never become so educated, so sophisticated, so successful, that I think I no longer need to read the simple stories in your Word—stories that teach me how to live this life in preparation for the next.

FROM SKULL BASHER TO BRAIN HEALER

TO READ: PSALM 68:1-5

A father to the fatherless, a defender of widows, is God in his holy dwelling.
Psalm 68:5

Fourteen-year-old Ben was on the fast track to prison. The African-American youth had no father, was failing every class at school, and had a ferocious temper. He once tore open a classmate's forehead with a rock and even threatened his own mother with a hammer.

But instead of ending up in prison, Ben landed in a hospital—one of the most prestigious in the world. Today he is Dr. Ben Carson, chief pediatric neurosurgeon at Johns Hopkins University Hospital.

How did he turn his life around?

The first person to stop Ben's one-way trip to disaster was his mother. She took him to church and turned off the TV. Mrs. Carson, who had only a third-grade education, made her son read several books a week and write reports on them. Within eighteen months, Carson recalls, "I went from the bottom of the class to the top of the class."

One thing his mother couldn't control, though, was Ben's terrible temper. One day he became outraged at another boy. "I had a large camping knife," Carson recalls, "and I tried to stab him in the abdomen." But the blade struck the boy's belt buckle and broke. Suddenly Ben realized what he was doing. Horrified, he ran home, locked himself in the bathroom, and fell to his knees. "Lord," he prayed, "I cannot control this temper. It's up to you—I'm giving it over to you."

Ben spent three hours closeted in the bathroom, wrestling with God in prayer and Scripture meditation. When he finally emerged, his temper was gone—never to return.

In that cataclysmic experience, Carson realized how God could actually be the father he had lacked. He already knew God was his *heavenly* Father. But, Carson said, "I began to understand that I had [also] adopted God as my *earthly* father—somebody that I could go to, somebody who, if you allow him to . . . [would] control your life, would make it something special."

Carson *did* put his life under the Father's control. He graduated from college and medical school with top grades, and today he is a world-renowned neurosurgeon. When Siamese twins were born joined at the head some years ago, it was Dr. Carson who flew to Europe to perform the remarkable surgery that separated them.

How differently Carson's life might have turned out. Apart from God's grace, Carson says, "I could easily have ended up in prison."

Christian men need to get involved in the lives of fatherless kids in their congregation who desperately need father figures. And we can buy copies of Ben Carson's autobiography, *Gifted Hands,* and give them to school libraries or to fatherless youngsters we know. Stories like Carson's will teach children about the God who promises to be "a father to the fatherless."

Oh God, help me to remember that I can always come to you, not only as my heavenly Father but also as I would to an earthly father. Show me, I pray, how I might model your heavenly love to a child who has never known a father's love.

OCTOBER 12

HUNTING WITCHES

TO READ: MARK 14:53-65

The chief priests and the whole Sanhedrin were looking for evidence against Jesus so that they could put him to death, but they did not find any. Many testified falsely against him, but their statements did not agree. Mark 14:55-56

For many, the image of women burned to death for practicing witch-craft is a potent symbol of both Christian intolerance and Christian irrationality. But as a new book demonstrates, nearly everything we've been told about Christianity and witch hunts is wrong.

Feminists like Andrea Dworkin and Mary Daly claim that up to nine million European *women* were burned at the stake for witchcraft. And even nonfeminist historians write about how the witch hunts "consumed millions of innocents."

Historian Rodney Stark calls these claims nonsense. In *For the Glory of God: How Monotheism Led to Reformations, Science, Witch-Hunts, and the End of Slavery*, Stark estimates that the number was closer to sixty thousand. What's more, many of those killed—perhaps a third of them—were *men*.

Their accusers weren't fanatical clerics who were seeking to sup-press heresy. On the contrary, in Spain, home of the infamous Span-ish Inquisition, there were far fewer trials for witchcraft than there were by secular officials in the rest of Europe. And those brought to trial were far less likely to be executed. In fact, the Spanish Inquisition sometimes brought charges against the accusers instead.

This pattern was repeated throughout Europe. When church offi-cials intervened in witchcraft trials, it was usually to protect the ac-cused, not to persecute them. In an overwhelming number of cases, the witch hunts we've read so much about took place in isolated areas where church and government authority were weakest. This lack of authority enabled local officials and citizens to perpetrate injustice.

Moreover, what Stark calls the period of "frantic" witch-hunting took place during the late Renaissance and the Enlightenment, periods when Christian influence over European culture began to wane. While Christians tried to protect the accused, anti-Christian Enlightenment figures like Thomas Hobbes and Jean Bodin supported the prosecution and execution of so-called witches.

As Stark shows, it is untrue to lay the blame for the travesty of witchcraft trials solely at the feet of Christianity. In fact, the only reason to ignore the historical record is if you want to smear Christianity as the "relentless opponent of reason and science."

Christianity has been a proponent, not an opponent, of reason and tolerance in Western civilization. People who distort the historical record through their own intolerance and irrationality are the true heirs of the witch-hunters.

People have falsely accused Christ's followers for two thousand years. Christ himself was falsely accused by those who hated his message. Christians must understand this and be prepared to have lies told about us, as well, when we become active in culture-war battles. We need to pray both for boldness in battle and for God's guidance in responding to the inevitable lies.

Lord, what a joy it is to learn the truth about your followers down through the ages. Give me the strength to endure false testimony against myself, if it comes— and the wisdom to respond to it wisely.

MIAMI'S BUS TO NOWHERE

TO READ: MARK 10:1-10

Anyone who divorces his wife and marries another woman commits adultery.
Mark 10:11

When the courthouse in Miami's Liberty City neighborhood was closed for renovations, Miami-Dade County Circuit Court Judge Joel Brown had an idea. The county was already using a bus to bring government services into local neighborhoods. Why not use the bus as a rolling divorce court as well?

So once a month the bus pulls into a Liberty City parking lot, and those who want an uncontested divorce line up outside. On the bus, Judge Brown presides and grants the divorces. Time expended per divorce: two minutes.

"I didn't expect something to be so unbelievably convenient," said a young woman who had been married three months. A man in his sixties who had been married more than two decades agreed: "It was quicker to get divorced than to get married."

The bus is a sadly appropriate symbol of a way of thinking that's become all too common. A book called *The Starter Marriage and the Future of Matrimony* examines a growing trend of young adults to divorce after just a few years of marriage. Author Pamela Paul found several factors instrumental in these marital failures. For instance, many grew up in broken homes with little understanding of how marriage works. But more significantly, Paul writes: "A fundamental shift in public opinion took place [during the 1970s], producing a new truism: 'People should not stay married if they're not happy.'"

Viewed in this light, divorce buses, starter marriages, Internet divorces (another hot trend), and no-fault divorce in general are themselves just a small part of a larger social movement toward self-gratification and self-fulfillment at any cost. According to this philosophy, personal happiness takes precedence over honoring one's commitments to God and to other people, which is why Miami's divorce bus is so popular.

After speedily dissolving their marriages on the bus, some newly divorced people were already planning to look for someone new with whom to share their lives. But their addiction to personal freedom makes it doubtful that they will ever find real marital satisfaction. They're still looking for someone to make them happy.

In this area, as in so many others, Christians must understand—and consciously reject—our culture's teachings. In order to create healthy and permanent marriages, we need to make sure our churches offer programs, such as Marriage Savers, that have proven their worth, and encourage couples to seek them out.

In a culture that combines a love of convenience with a lack of commitment, we must make sure we don't imitate our secular neighbors—people who don't consider the hard work and sacrifice it will take to build the kind of marriage they say they want. For those people, their first trip to the divorce bus is unlikely to be their last.

Father, into the lives of young brides and grooms who enter marriage so hopefully, I pray you will bring someone who can articulate an understanding of what it takes to create lasting happiness in marriage and of the One who created men, women, and marriage.

OCTOBER 14

BLACK AND WHITE AND EXTINCT ALL OVER

TO READ: GENESIS 9:1-17

[God told Noah,] "The fear and dread of you will fall upon all the beasts of the earth and all the birds of the air . . . ; they are given into your hands." Genesis 9:2

What's the top attraction at major zoos around the world? The giant panda. These bears are what biologists call "charismatic megafauna;" that is, large animals that people care about. Biologists regard this endangered species as a symbol of man's relationship to nature. They're correct, but not in the sense they think.

Biologists estimate that there are at most fifteen hundred giant pandas living in the wild, all in southwestern China. The most common explanation for the panda's plight is human encroachment on their habitat.

But it's not quite that simple, as viewers of a Discovery Channel program, "Panda Nursery," learned.

Most bears will eat almost anything, but giant pandas eat only bamboo leaves and stems. Not only is bamboo not very nutritious, but the panda's digestive system—designed for meat—cannot digest more than 20 percent of what it eats. Thus, pandas must spend most of their waking hours eating huge amounts of bamboo.

Compared to other bears, panda pregnancies are rare. In the case of twins, a panda mother will abandon one sibling, leaving it to die. The species' ineptitude at reproduction has forced humans to intervene, breeding and raising the young of a species that can't do it on its own.

In other words, if pandas survive, it will be only because human beings have made their survival a priority. Humans refrain from activities that hurt the panda's chances of survival and take active measures, like breeding programs, to perpetuate the species.

This is the right thing to do, but it's hardly the Darwinian thing. It wouldn't be happening if human beings were, as Darwinists like Richard Dawkins claim, "just another animal." If we took Dawkins's worldview seriously, pandas would be merely another species that lost out and became extinct because it was beaten by a more adaptable contender. There would be no more reason to regret the panda's demise than there is to lament that there are no wooly mammoths in downtown Denver.

Among the millions of species on earth, only humans ponder their obligations to other species. As Leon Kass of the University of Chicago notes, this fact is the obvious reply to people who insist that we are just another animal. We intervene for animals like the panda because we instinctively know that man has a moral obligation to act as stewards of nature—an obligation that arises from a biblical—not a Darwinian—understanding of man and his place in the world.

Genesis says God gave the animals into our hands. We Christians have not always honored God's command to be stewards as we should have, but when it comes to pandas, our efforts give witness both to our own God-given humanity and to our concern for his creation.

Lord, thank you for the delightful diversity of your creation. Show me ways in which you would have me support efforts to nurture the birds and beasts and fish you created so that we will not forever lose them.

HARRY POTTER

TO READ: DANIEL 1:1-21

Daniel resolved not to defile himself, . . . [and] God had caused the official to show favor and sympathy to Daniel. Daniel 1:8-9

Only the battles over church music have generated the level of controversy we've witnessed over the Harry Potter craze. Some Christians worry that the books will lead children into involvement in the occult; others, just as sincere, say the books teach their children valuable moral lessons.

Should Christian kids read the books and see the films or not?

A Christian expert on Potter-mania says, "It depends."

Connie Neal, a veteran youth pastor and mother of three, has written *What's a Christian to Do with Harry Potter?* Neal says parents must use great discernment in deciding whether to allow their kids to read the Harry Potter books. Children with an unhealthy interest in the occult probably shouldn't. Other parents have prayerfully decided that their children would benefit from the moral lessons the Potter books teach.

Neal's belief that in some cases it's acceptable and even beneficial for Christians to read secular novels comes from her reading of the book of Daniel. Daniel was a teenager when he was taken from Jerusalem to live in Babylon. There he studied at a school that trained Babylon's magicians, astrologers, and sorcerers. The actual practice of sorcery and astrology was, of course, forbidden by God, but Daniel not only studied these subjects, he outperformed all his classmates.

When King Nebuchadnezzer asked him, "Are you able to tell me what I saw in my dream and interpret it?" Daniel responded: "No wise men, enchanter, magician, or divier can explain to the king the mystery he has asked about, but there is a God in heaven who reveals mysteries. He has shown King Nebuchadnezzer what will happen in days to come."

Daniel had immersed himself in his culture's pagan literature and teachings, but he didn't defile himself because of his deep devotion to God. As Connie Neal told *BreakPoint*, "God put Daniel in Babylon to be a light in the darkness—and he was. He was not afraid to read literature that resounded in the hearts of the people with whom he lived. He used his familiarity with this pagan culture to reveal the true and living God." Neal knows some kids who have done the same in our own post-Christian culture—with the Harry Potter books.

However we may feel about Harry Potter books and films, our kids will likely be exposed to them, so we need to teach them to be as discerning as Daniel. And we must be every bit as discerning when it comes to our own consumption of books, television, and film. We must ask ourselves, *Will my exposure to this lead me into sin, or will it help me to lead others to Christ?*

Lord, I pray for your protection in a culture that grows increasingly pagan. Teach me how to use the literature, trends, and teachings of my society to be a light in the darkness—without letting the darkness defile me.

WHERE'S THE REMOTE?

TO READ: 1 CORINTHIANS 7:32-38

*If anyone thinks he is acting improperly toward the virgin he is engaged to . . .
and he feels he ought to marry, he should do as he wants. 1 Corinthians 7:36*

LeRoy Sullivan is the pastor of the Bread of Life Church, a small African-American congregation in Kansas City, Kansas. When Sullivan learned about Mike McManus's Marriage Saver programs, he thought they made a lot of sense—especially the teachings about cohabitation.

Many couples think that living together is a good way to find out whether or not they're really compatible. But the truth is, living together is more likely to destroy a couple's chances of a good marriage. Almost half of all couples who cohabit break up before the wedding day. Couples who live together before marriage are 50 percent more likely to divorce. In addition, studies show that one of the best ways to eliminate childhood poverty is for parents to marry before having children.

Pastor Sullivan took a hard look at the evidence and then a hard look at his own congregation. He saw seven couples whom he knew were living together. From the pulpit Sullivan made a strong, biblical case for marriage. Living together, he told his flock, "is not part of God's plan. You need to marry or separate."

Most of the couples listened and tied the knot. But one cohabiting couple resisted his efforts—at least, the man did. His girlfriend told Sullivan, "Sam won't marry me, and he won't move out."

One night Sullivan showed up on the couple's doorstep. "Hi, Pastor, what are you doing here?" Sam greeted him.

"Lucinda tells me you won't marry her and won't move out either," Sullivan responded. "Now, that's not right." Glancing around the living room, Sullivan commented, "That looks like the most comfortable chair. I'm going to sit here until you move out. Now, where's the remote?"

Dumbfounded, Sam asked, "Pastor, you're not really going to sit there all night, are you?"

"Of course not," Sullivan cheerfully responded. "At midnight, Elder Jones is relieving me!"

Sam moved out that night.

It's sad that taking such a strong stand on marriage is controversial within urban communities, where marriage is an almost forgotten institution. According to McManus, to many nonwhites, promoting marriage sounds like a white man's message. But Pastor Sullivan knows that marriage is a big part of the answer to the social ills that plague America; he believes the church ought to be a force in building godly families. And that's why he's willing to go to such extremes to encourage it.

We Christians need to make sure that when it comes to our own living arrangements, our witness to the world is above reproach. And we should make sure our friends and children have the facts about cohabitation. A good place to find them is in Marriage Savers. You'll learn why living together, which is so common in our culture, sets up families for poverty, violence, and divorce.

Lord, thank you for pastors who love their flock—and your commands— enough to go the extra mile. I pray that my own lifestyle will be a quiet witness to my commitment to your teachings about sex—principles you gave us for our protection and for the good of our children.

ME, MYSELF, AND I

TO READ: 1 KINGS 9:1-9

[The Lord said to Solomon,] "If you walk before me in integrity of heart and uprightness, as David your father did, . . . I will establish your royal throne over Israel forever." 1 Kings 9:4-5

If you took your teenage daughter to the movies, what would you see? Laura Sessions Stepp, who writes on trends among adolescent girls, saw something that bothered her.

In the *Washington Post,* Stepp writes, "If you're a young Hollywood heroine today, you lip-sync your way to rock stardom overnight . . . win passage of a bill by giving [cosmetic] makeovers to members of Congress or solve murders by posing as a stripper cop. . . . You entertain, but you don't inspire, at least the way movies used to." For these young women, she says, "power lies largely in how you look and what you buy. . . . Perfection through consumption, that's the (young) American Way."

Stepp has put her finger on a problem just as important: the encouragement of selfishness among our youth.

Movies like the Charlie's Angels franchise, *Legally Blonde 2,* and *The Lizzie McGuire Movie* may pretend to teach about independence and maturity. But the truth is that real "character development" is out; consumerism and feel-good messages are in. Or as Stepp puts it, "Life revolves around these young women." Instead of stories about girls who grow up facing real challenges and learning how to help others, we get fictional girls whose main concern is "me, myself, and I."

There's more than one factor at work here. For one thing, at a time when many adults act more irresponsible than teenagers or want to stay juvenile, our definition of maturity has changed. For another, feminist leaders have long pressured both our educational system and our popular culture to try to make up for a supposed lack in girls' self-esteem.

But the biggest factor may be that teenagers today have more spending money. It's good marketing strategy to present the consumer with an image of herself the way she'd like to be: glamorous, independent of parental and moral restraints, easily able to overcome all obstacles. It's bad strategy to suggest she still has much to learn about the world, that there's life beyond adolescence, and that developing strong character is more important than instant gratification.

When frivolity and egotism become trendy among impressionable teens, we need to inoculate our kids against their attractions. We should help them understand that there is far more to life than self-interest—qualities such as humility, good character, and self-sacrifice.

First, though, we need to make sure that we're demonstrating these qualities ourselves—not aping the behavior of adolescents. The stories of the kings of ancient Israel reveal how important it is—both to a nation and in the eyes of God—to model integrity and righteousness to our own children and to the children of others. Are we doing that?

Father, may I never forget that every day I am modeling some kind of behavior to the children around me. Make me willing to walk before you "in integrity of heart," knowing that your eyes—and the eyes of children nearby—are observing my example.

REDEMPTIVE REALITY

TO READ: 1 CORINTHIANS 15:51-58

Where, O death, is your victory? Where, O death, is your sting? 1 Corinthians 15:55

Roberto Benigni, who wrote, directed, and starred in *Life Is Beautiful*, is a comic genius who has been called the Italian Charlie Chaplin. But the subject of his 1997 film, the Holocaust, is anything but funny.

Benigni's character, a sad-sack waiter named Guido, courts the affections of a local schoolteacher and through various hilarious adventures wins her heart. They marry and have a son.

Then things take a dark turn: Father and son, who are Jewish, are sent to a concentration camp. Guido, who's been irrepressibly joyful throughout, doesn't let even this monstrous turn of events get to him. To shield his son from the horrors they're going through, Guido concocts a wild story, telling the boy that the whole experience is really just an elaborate game. They'll have to play very, very hard to win, he says, but if they succeed, the boy will win a magnificent prize: a real tank!

It's a measure of the film's brilliance that the humor is never mawkish or inappropriate. Still, that didn't stop some critics from expressing horror at the idea of a comedy set in a concentration camp. They called it "profoundly unsettling" and said it "trivializ[ed] the Holocaust."

How did Benigni dare to use humor in a film about a great moral evil? He did it by expressing the Christian idea that there's more to life than what we see. In the scene in which the father is being led away to be killed, he spots his son and makes a funny face. The message is that there is something that triumphs over even death, some transcendent reality that, even in this ultimate moment of gravity, enables Guido to make his son laugh.

Most of our cultural leaders operate from a purely naturalistic perspective that says material existence is all there is. For them, since nothing transcends this world and its horrors, pretending that we can laugh even in the midst of the Holocaust is offensive and absurd. But Scripture teaches that there are eternal things. Do we understand the value of these things? If we do, we will not be cowed by even the most appalling earthly circumstances.

Benigni seems to understand this profound truth. Things like courage, self-sacrifice, and love are all part of being made in God's image and are more real than our sufferings. That's why, when faced with the horror of the Holocaust, Guido can still make you smile.

Life Is Beautiful is not the gospel story, but it does point to the gospel because it's about how God's redemptive reality trumps the very worst this world has to offer.

Lord, thank you for filmmakers who use their gifts to illustrate Christian truth: There are unseen purposes and realities that transcend our sufferings.

OCTOBER 19

LIFE IMITATES ART

TO READ: EXODUS 37:1-9

The cherubim had their wings spread upward, overshadowing the cover with them.
Exodus 37:9

Christians constantly bemoan the lack of wholesome fare on television, but Martha Williamson rolled up her sleeves and did something about it. She wrote and produced a successful prime-time television show that brought serious Christian themes to a wide television audience. The show was called *Touched by an Angel,* and it ran for nine years on CBS. With this hit show, Williamson gives us a wonderful model of how we are to obey the biblical mandate to redeem the surrounding culture.

To carry on the fine work that people like Williamson are doing, we need to start by analyzing what's wrong with popular culture today. Why is so much television and pop music woven through with themes of immorality and rebellion?

The answer is that popular culture, like all the arts, is shaped by worldviews. Up until the Enlightenment, people saw art as a way of expressing profound truths—not necessarily literal truths, yet even symbols and metaphors reflect something true about reality—like portraying angels with wings or saints with halos. Beauty itself was seen as a kind of truth.

But in the Enlightenment, a new theory of truth was born: the idea that the only real knowledge derives from what we can see, touch, and measure scientifically. Since angels and halos cannot be seen or measured, out they went. Beauty itself is an ideal that we cannot measure scientifically, so out it went, too—relegated to the realm of subjective fantasy.

But if art was no longer about truth, then what *was* it about? Many artists began to define art as the creation of an abstract, idealized world, and from that ideal world they hurled down thunderbolts upon the real world for all its shortcomings. Thus was born the idea that art is about criticism and revolt, a means of shocking conventional society. Filtered down to the popular level, this view of art inspired movies and rock music that today launch a relentless attack on traditional values.

If Christians want to help halt the degradation of popular culture, we must understand that the degradation is not merely a result of declining public tastes. It is a direct result of a change in worldview. Instead of merely decrying the decadence, we need to roll up our sleeves and offer positive alternatives, imitating the inspiring success of Martha Williamson and others.

C. S. Lewis once said that the only way to drive out bad culture is to create good culture. We need to recognize that artistic talent is a gift from the Lord—and that developing those talents is the only way to create good culture.

Lord, let me not be discouraged by the overwhelming ugliness of the culture I live in. Give me the determination to develop my creative gifts to the fullest so that I may nudge my neighbors closer to you, using beauty to point to your truth, just as the ancients did. May I never forget that our mandate to redeem the culture is not a request but a command.

OCTOBER 20

IN HIS STEPS

TO READ: HEBREWS 13:15-21

Do not forget to do good and to share with others. Hebrews 13:16

Have you seen kids wearing bracelets with the initials *WWJD*—"What Would Jesus Do?" The story behind those bracelets begins a century ago, when a minister named Charles Sheldon wrote a novel titled *In His Steps*. The setting is a city called Raymond. One Sunday morning at First Church, Pastor Henry Maxwell is preaching a sermon about how to follow Christ's example of sacrificial love.

The service is suddenly interrupted when a tramp stands up. He's been out of work for a year, he says, yet not one person in Raymond has helped him find another job. Twisting his shabby hat in his hands, the tramp says, "I was wondering if what you call following Jesus is the same thing as what he taught. What do you mean when you sing 'I'll go with him, with him, all the way?'"

"I get puzzled," the tramp adds, "when I see so many Christians living in luxury and remember how my wife died in a tenement. It seems that there's an awful lot of trouble in the world that somehow wouldn't exist if all the people who sing such songs went and lived them out. I suppose I don't understand. But what would Jesus do?"

At that point, to the congregation's horror, the tramp collapses and dies.

The following Sunday, the minister makes a stunning proposal: He's looking for volunteers willing to pledge themselves for an entire year to do nothing without first asking, "What would Jesus do?" Some fifty people make the pledge, and a remarkable series of events begins to occur.

The editor of the local newspaper has been accepting lucrative ads from saloons. Would Jesus do this? No, he decides—and cancels the ads. A young singer gives up a promising career to sing at tent meetings on Skid Row. An heiress takes in a homeless woman, to the horror of her fashionable family. A businessman decides Jesus wants him to make his tenements as warm and comfortable as his own home.

Some of these people pay a high price for their obedience. They lose jobs, fortunes, family, and friends—just as Jesus warned. But they also learn the joy of following faithfully in his footsteps.

A few years ago, a Holland, Michigan, youth leader was so inspired by this classic story that she had bracelets made bearing the letters *WWJD* and gave them to the kids in her church. The idea caught fire, and today millions of kids wear them.

If your kids don't know the story behind the bracelets, give them a copy of *In His Steps*. Long after they've given up wearing the bracelets, through all the trials and temptations of life, the story may inspire them to ask that one, quiet question: What would Jesus do?

Father, thank you for the inspiration of a century-old novel that puts a modern twist on Christ's teachings. May it inspire me, as well, to ask each day, What would Jesus do?

THE GRAND SEZ WHO

TO READ: AMOS 1:3-12

This is what the Lord says: "For three sins of Damascus . . .
I will not turn back my wrath." Amos 1:3

The United Nations International War Crimes Tribunal indicted former Yugoslav president Slobodan Milosevic for crimes against humanity, and according to the *Washington Post*, going after him was the right thing to do.

But Milosevic's case raised awkward questions for the modern world: By whose law should he be tried? Is law, especially international law, even possible in a world that rejects the idea of absolute truth?

The Nuremberg trials after World War II, which gave us the term *crimes against humanity*, set an important legal and moral precedent: that there exists a standard of decency legally binding on all nations irrespective of culture, creed, or history. By charging Nazi leaders with "crimes against humanity," the UN implicitly rejected notions of moral and cultural relativism. Instead, we declared that there is a universal moral standard.

But some sixty years later, do we still accept the idea of a universal standard that is binding on all nations? What gave the international community the moral authority to sit in judgment on Milosevic?

The answer is that there no longer is any moral authority because the leading nations of the world have rejected the basis for that authority—ultimately, the law of God. Without a basis in divine law, human law is only a matter of opinion, imposed by force.

The late legal scholar Arthur Leff put it this way: "Without the ultimate warrant of divine revelation, all claims to authority are vulnerable to 'the grand sez who?'" We say that ethnic cleansing is wrong. To which Milosevic and his ilk respond, "Sez who?" We say that raping and massacring civilians is wrong. "Sez who?" If it's merely my opinion versus yours, claims to international justice are really nothing more than a power play.

This is a vivid illustration of what law professor Phillip Johnson calls the "modernist impasse." The modern mind demands freedom from moral restraints for individuals but then demands a strong moral code for society in order to justify punishing barbarians. But that moral conjuring trick just won't work. You can't deny a transcendent moral order when it's inconvenient and then try to pull one out of a hat when you need one.

The book of Amos implies human awareness of God's moral order as God judges the ancient Israelites. Yet many deny its existence today—at least when it comes to themselves.

The modernist impasse provides Christians with a wonderful opportunity. When people tell us that they're horrified by a dictator's crimes, we can explain that they must face an uncomfortable fact: that condemning these horrors requires us to submit to an objective moral standard, one that judges our own lives as well. And that means acknowledging that there is an absolute moral standard—one that comes from God himself.

Father, let me not be found hypocritical when it comes to your laws, excusing my own "small" sins while condemning the crimes of another. Thank you for the blood of your Son, which covers the misdeeds of all if we are willing to confess them to you and seek your forgiveness.

THE PASSION IN MUSIC

TO READ: MARK 15:16-32

[The soldiers] put a purple robe on him, then twisted together a crown of thorns and set it on him. And they began to call out to him, "Hail, king of the Jews!" Again and again they struck him on the head with a staff and spit on him. Falling on their knees, they paid homage to him. And when they had mocked him, they took off the purple robe and put his own clothes on him. Then they led him out to crucify him.
Mark 15:17-20

For nearly two millennia the Gospels' passion narratives have inspired memorable works of art, a recent example being Mel Gibson's film *The Passion of the Christ*.

Gibson acknowledged this artistic tradition when he said that he wanted his film to be a "Caravaggio in motion." His reference was to the sixteenth-century painter whose use of contrasting light and dark gave his depiction of biblical scenes a sense of urgency and intensity.

It's almost impossible to imagine the history of Western painting without the art inspired by the Passion. Da Vinci, Tintoretto, Giotto, and El Greco are but a few of the great artists whose definitive works depict the events of Holy Thursday and Good Friday.

What's true of painting is certainly also true of music. Johann Sebastian Bach set the Passion narratives in Mark, Matthew, and John to music. Unfortunately only the latter two survive. Of these, it is his *St. Matthew Passion* that sits atop the Western musical canon.

First performed on Good Friday in 1729, the work is almost sacred opera. Soloists sing the words of Jesus, Judas, and Pilate while another soloist, called the Evangelist, narrates the story. These interactions are punctuated by choral settings of well-known hymns.

Two-and-a-half centuries later, another Christian composer, Arvo Pärt, also set St. John's account of Christ's Passion to music. The influential music magazine *Gramophone* called the result, *Passio,* a work "that transcends the doubt and nihilism of [our] age."

While Bach and Pärt are telling the same story and share the same faith, the results are very different. One reviewer has characterized *Passio* as music of "massive stillness." Where "Bach celebrated the human voice for its expressiveness, Pärt turns it into an instrument."

Bach's expressiveness and Pärt's stillness combine to help the listener more fully appreciate what happened on that first Good Friday. That's why Christians owe it to themselves to become better acquainted with the composers' works and the other art inspired by the Passion—art that can help us transcend "the doubt and nihilism of [our] age."

Father, thank you that we who live two thousand years after your Son's Passion are able to draw closer to you through the creativity of hundreds of composers, painters, sculptors, and writers—artists who, through two millennia, have revealed their devotion to you through the gifts you gave them.

FERTILITY FAIRY TALES

TO READ: GENESIS 16:1-12

The angel of the Lord also said to [Hagar]: "You are now with child and you will have a son. You shall name him Ishmael, for the Lord has heard of your misery."
Genesis 16:11

A few years ago, a series of controversial advertisements went up on buses in New York, Chicago, and Seattle. The subject of the ads was women's reproductive health. And for once that phrase was being used in the service of truth.

The ads were sponsored by the American Infertility Association and the American Society for Reproductive Medicine. Their message was straightforward: "Women in their twenties and early thirties are most likely to conceive." The longer a woman postpones having children, the less likely she is to ever have them.

This may seem obvious, but as *Newsweek* put it, infertility specialists were "alarmed" at what they saw as a "widespread lack of understanding" about the relationship between aging and infertility. They were concerned about their patients' "false sense of security about what science can do."

Pamela Madsen, executive director of the American Infertility Association, told *Newsweek* that American women have bought into a feminist myth that "they are in complete control of their reproductive lives and they can do it all." Along with the bus ads, her group distributed thousands of pamphlets to doctors' offices. The campaign, called Protect Your Fertility, hoped to replace myths with facts.

The problem is that many people aren't interested in inconvenient facts. Women who were raised to believe that they could "have it all" resented the reminder of their biological limitations; some characterized the ads as coercive and even sick.

But conception is not something humans have complete control over. And as the biblical story of Abram and Sarai reminds us, the inability to conceive a much-desired child can lead to heartbreak—and a willingness to go to extreme measures to become a parent.

The ad controversy exposes the dishonesty of radical feminists. They treat children not as ends in themselves but as lifestyle enhancements. Childbirth is an afterthought, something women get around to after they've done everything else they wanted to do. But a woman's biological makeup is under no obligation to accommodate the feminist agenda—an agenda that has serious consequences, as crowded fertility clinics reveal.

Feminists who become enraged at reminders that women do not have absolute control over their fertility are expressing a desire for radical autonomy over their sexuality. Their determination to overcome the God-given limits to their fertility or, as in the case of abortion, to reject fertility when it's inconvenient, reveals a desire to shake their fists in the face of the God who designed them—in effect, to become god themselves.

Christians must carefully consider the philosophy behind cultural teachings about sexuality. If we listen to those who have a fanatical commitment to "the right to choose," we may tragically lose our choice to one day have a much-desired child.

Lord, over the years we have been exposed to a steady drumbeat of secular sexual doctrines that reject your wisdom. Help us to sort out the lies from the truth and to accept the way you designed our bodies.

OCTOBER 24

ENGLAND IS TAHITI

TO READ: PSALM 19:1-6

The heavens declare the glory of God. Psalm 19:1

G. K. Chesterton once told a story about "an English yachtsman who slightly miscalculated his course and 'discovered' England while under the impression that it was an island in the South Seas."

The yachtsman "landed (armed to the teeth and speaking by signs) to plant the British flag on that barbaric temple which turned out to be the pavilion at Brighton."

Chesterton was discussing the way in which we cast off the truths we learned as children, only to rediscover them later, if we are fortunate, as adults. What we dismissed as simple often turns out to be far more profound than we ever imagined.

Stephen M. Barr, a theoretical particle physicist at the University of Delaware, says that what is true about people is also true about science. In *Modern Physics and Ancient Faith,* Barr tells us that after the "twists" and "turns" that science took in the twentieth century, it, like Chesterton's yachtsman, wound up in "very familiar surroundings": a universe that "seems to have had a beginning . . . [and is] governed by laws that have a grandeur and sublimity that bespeak design."

Instead of man's being merely the result of a "fortuitous concourse of atoms," we now know that the "universe and its laws seem in some respect to balance on a knife's edge"—exactly what is needed for the possibility of life. If there were even a slight deviation here or there, we wouldn't exist.

These and other "recent discoveries have begun to confound the materialist's expectations and confirm those of the believer in God," writes Barr.

Notice he said "materialist's," not "scientist's." As Barr makes clear, sciences like modern physics can and must be separated from materialism—the belief that nothing exists besides matter.

The assumption that you have to accept a materialist worldview in order to do science is simply wrong. Nevertheless, philosophical materialism has become so identified with science that scientists and the general public often have trouble telling them apart. This is why the discoveries Barr describes come as a surprise and why many within the scientific academy—scientists who are engaging in ingenious, almost fanciful attempts to interpret the evidence in a way consistent with the materialist worldview—resist their implications.

It's a reminder that science, far from being the enemy of faith, is at war only with those who, against the evidence, still insist that "England is Tahiti."

Lord, let me not be deceived or intimidated by those who, using the authority of science, deny that you are the creator of the heavens and the earth. Help me to use scientific discoveries to witness to the truth to my skeptical neighbors: that the universe declares your authorship and your glory.

OCTOBER 25

JESUS SHALL REIGN

TO READ: COLOSSIANS 2:6-12

See to it that no one takes you captive through hollow and deceptive philosophy, which depends on human tradition and the basic principles of this world rather than on Christ. Colossians 2:8

In *The Clash of Civilizations and the Remaking of World Order,* Samuel Huntington predicts that demographics will decide the outcome of the clash between Christianity and Islam. "In the long run," he writes, "Muhammad wins out."

In this instance, Huntington is wrong. For the foreseeable future there will be many more Christians than Muslims in the world. As Penn State professor Philip Jenkins writes in *The Next Christendom: The Coming of Global Christianity,* predictions like Huntington's betray an ignorance of the explosive growth of Christianity outside the West.

For instance, in 1900, there were approximately 10 million Christians in Africa. By 2000, there were 360 million. Conservative estimates see that number rising to 633 million by 2025. Those same estimates put the number of Christians in Latin America in 2025 at 640 million and in Asia at 460 million.

According to Jenkins, the percentage of the world's population that is, at least by name, Christian will be roughly the same in 2050 as it was in 1900. By the middle of this century there will be 3 billion Christians in the world—one and a half times the number of Muslims. In fact, by 2050 there will be nearly as many Pentecostal Christians in the world as there are Muslims today.

But at that point, only one-fifth of the world's Christians will be non-Hispanic whites. The typical Christian will be a woman living in a Nigerian village or in a Brazilian shantytown. These changes will be more than demographic. Jenkins points out that those he calls "Southern Christians"—who live in Africa, Latin America, and parts of Asia—are far more conservative theologically and morally than their counterparts in the West.

Thus, as Christianity becomes more "Southern," it becomes more biblically orthodox. While people like Bishop John Shelby Spong and Templeton Prize–winner Arthur Peacock insist that Christianity must abandon its historic beliefs to survive, it is precisely these historic beliefs that attract our "Southern" brethren.

That's why in Spong and Peacock's own Anglican communion, African bishops are ordaining missionaries to reconvert the West.

This story of Christianity's explosive growth is one of the great untold stories of our time, one that repudiates those who say that Christians must compromise their beliefs to remain relevant. The opposite is the case. Biblical orthodoxy is winning converts while churches that have lost their biblical moorings languish.

Assuredly, Muhammad will not win out. God is at work throughout the world. Everywhere the gospel is proclaimed, it is changing lives and societies.

Lord, bless the millions across the globe who are turning to you. Encourage the leaders of these flocks, who stand faithfully for you and for your Word despite poverty, persecution, and Western criticism. Show me ways I can help meet the needs of these believers—my brothers and sisters—faraway and unseen but whom I will one day meet face-to-face in your Kingdom.

THE *DRACULA* WITNESS

TO READ: 2 TIMOTHY 1:8-12

This grace was given us in Christ Jesus before the beginning of time, but it has now been revealed through the appearing of our Savior, Christ Jesus, who has destroyed death and has brought life and immortality to light through the gospel. 2 Timothy 1:9-10

A teacher at a Christian school told her students to choose a book for an October book report. An eleven-year-old named Trevor made an unusual choice: He asked to read Bram Stoker's *Dracula*.

Trevor's teacher was horrified. She was thinking, no doubt, of the many bloody film versions of this classic story.

She needn't have worried. This century-old gothic novel *is* frightening—but in a weird sort of way, it's actually an apologetic for the gospel.

In 1897 Bram Stoker wrote his gothic novel about a vampire he named Dracula. The book was loosely modeled on the life of a Transylvanian prince who literally drank the blood of his enemies. Stoker's novel condemns Dracula for seeking to prolong his life outside the power of Christ—and horrifically illustrates the evil that results when people try to do so. Stoker makes clear that even the most malignant evil is subject to the power of Christ: The vampires *must* retreat before the cross.

Most of the film interpretations of Stoker's classic accept this premise. For example, in the 1931 film version of *Dracula* starring Bela Lugosi, the vampire leaps back in fear whenever a cross is displayed. And the 1992 film treatment called *Bram Stoker's Dracula* stars a Scripture-quoting, cross-waving Anthony Hopkins as the doctor who tries to save a young woman from Dracula's supernatural clutches.

But at least one vampire story mocks the power of Christ. In the film version of Anne Rice's book, *Interview with the Vampire*, a vampire jokes that he's actually "quite fond of looking at crucifixes."

The message is clear: The power of Christ is inferior to the power of Satan.

This perversion of biblical truth expresses our culture's obsession with finding meaning in life outside of Christianity. That's why we're seeing writers and filmmakers promoting the view that Christ can be dismissed from the promise of immortality—that we can reject him without suffering terrible consequences.

If we watch these films, we ought to spend a few minutes asking ourselves if there are any areas in our own lives in which we try to find meaning and purpose without Christ.

If your own kids have a penchant for horror fiction, encourage them to read Bram Stoker's *Dracula* instead of Anne Rice. And then discuss the book's Christian themes with them—and perhaps with their friends, as well.

Unlike today's vampire fiction, Stoker's creepy classic is a reminder that true immortality comes through the shed blood of Jesus Christ alone.

Father, during a season in which my neighbors are focused on stories of the supernatural, show me ways I can use them to witness to you—and to the glorious immortality offered through your Son alone.

BATHROBE GAMBLING

TO READ: MATTHEW 22:34-40

Love your neighbor as yourself. Matthew 22:39

The Casino of the Kings has everything a gambler could want: poker, roulette, slot machines, and more—twenty-four hours a day. What's more, you can gamble the day away without even getting dressed. The Casino of Kings is one of more than three hundred Internet gambling sites—sites that demolish what few barriers remain between a casino and a gambler's money.

Government officials are concerned because operations such as The Casino of Kings, which is based in the Caribbean, operate outside the reach of state and federal regulators. A dollar bet online is a dollar that's *not* being bet at one of America's state-sponsored gambling venues, where states get a cut of the profits.

The government may be worried about money, but Christians ought to be more concerned about how Internet gambling removes another inconvenience that used to stand between citizens and vice. National Public Radio commentator Jim Sollisch drew an analogy between online gambling and online pornography. As Sollisch noted, it used to be that boys who wanted to buy a copy of *Playboy* had to deal with the disapproving glance of the store clerk. That inconvenience could be a powerful deterrent. These days, boys can privately peruse much worse pornography on-line—for free.

Likewise, anyone who wanted to gamble had to at least take the trouble of getting into his car and driving somewhere, often out of state. This inconvenience probably stopped a lot of people from gambling. Not anymore. Now you can gamble away your savings from the comfort of home.

The lesson here is that part of discouraging people from engaging in foolish behavior is making that behavior difficult. In fact, this is one of the essential functions of law. The Christian philosopher and theologian Thomas Aquinas taught that man has a natural aptitude to act morally, but his aptitude must be trained. That training occurs through social conventions, the threat of shame, and the threat of punishment for immoral conduct.

When it comes to discouraging Internet gambling, a good place to start is to get behind legislative proposals that would require Internet service providers to block access to these overseas gambling sites.

Critics argue that technology will make it almost impossible to enforce such laws—that if a site cannot be accessed through one provider, operators will find another way to make the site accessible.

That may be true. But the inconvenience involved may keep some people from gambling on a whim. And that's why Christians should support laws curbing Internet gambling.

Because even if our neighbor is bent on ruining his life through gambling, loving him means, at the very least, making sure he has to get out of his bathrobe to do it.

Lord, teach me to love your law enough that I will faithfully obey it even in the absence of outer restraints. Help me to love my neighbors, known and unknown, enough to make it difficult for them to destroy their lives—to love them so much that I am willing to tell them how to save their lives by turning to you.

RAYMOND'S ODYSSEY

TO READ: GENESIS 39:1-23

[Joseph said to Potiphar's wife,] "How then could I do such a wicked thing and sin against God?" Genesis 39:9

When Raymond McCarty appeared in court, the judge came up with an unusual sentence.

McCarty was found guilty of violating a court order to avoid a former girlfriend. The judge sentenced McCarty to four months in the Santa Rita, California, jail.

And then he *really* threw the book at him: He told McCarty he had to read the ancient Greek poem *The Odyssey* by Homer—and submit to the court a five-page book report.

It was the deputy district attorney, Chris Lamiero, who came up with the idea that McCarty read about the adventures and moral challenges faced by the Greek hero Odysseus during his journey home from the Trojan War. Upon his return, Odysseus slaughters the men whom he finds harassing his wife, Penelope.

Lamiero said he chose *The Odyssey* for its timeless lessons of honor and integrity—values he believes McCarty is a little short on.

Lamiero has stumbled onto the right idea. In *Books That Build Character,* William Kilpatrick and Gregory and Suzanne Wolfe describe how great stories help build great character. "Through the power of imagination, we become vicarious participants in the story, sharing the hero's choices and challenges," the authors write. We "identify ourselves with our favorite characters, and thus *their* actions become *our* actions."

In this way, the stories can become a dress rehearsal for our own life choices.

By giving us good characters to admire, stories also help educate the moral imagination. Virtue, you see, isn't just about knowing how to be good. To change behavior, we need to *love* the good. As we read in *Books That Build Character,* "stories can create an emotional attachment to goodness, a desire to do the right thing."

There's a reason that Jesus himself delivered his most profound teachings in the form of stories about farmers planting seeds, women finding coins, sons who go bad and then repent. His listeners could identify with these characters.

To quote again from *Books That Build Character,* in times of real-life pressure or temptation, "the half-forgotten memory of a story can rise to our aid."

That's why we ought to make sure that we, and the children in our lives, are reading good literature with moral themes—including the biblical story of Joseph and Potiphar's wife—literature that can move them toward right thinking and behavior, no matter what the cost.

As for Raymond McCarthy, who knows? The next time he thinks about harassing women, he just might recall the moral lessons that Homer taught. And if he doesn't—well, maybe he'll at least remember what Odysseus did to the men who bothered *his* wife.

Lord, no matter how busy I think I am, help me to make time to read to the children in my life—inspiring them to such an attachment to goodness that they will—when temptation steps in their path, respond as did Joseph: "How then could I do such a wicked thing?"

A BULWARK
NEVER FAILING

TO READ: PSALM 46:1-11

God is our refuge and strength, an ever-present help in trouble.
Therefore we will not fear. Psalm 46:1-2

In a few days millions of kids will be knocking on doors and calling, "Trick or treat!" Many Christian families will instead celebrate Reformation Sunday—the commemoration of Martin Luther's posting his ninety-five theses on the Wittenberg door.

Luther started the Protestant Reformation—something Catholics probably won't be celebrating. But he made at least one contribution all Christians can rejoice in: his great hymn drawn from Psalm 46, "A Mighty Fortress Is Our God."

Luther wrote this hymn nearly five hundred years ago in the midst of the religious and political upheaval of the Reformation. Then in 1723, Johann Sebastian Bach harmonized and lengthened Luther's hymn.

A man named Carlos, who happens to be Catholic, can testify to the mighty way God can use Luther's hymn to remind his people that, in the midst of life's greatest trials, God is always there.

Carlos has a young son, a wonderful little boy named Joshua. He's the apple of his father's eye, but tragically, Joshua is autistic.

Although Joshua has made great progress, he still has a long way to go. Joshua's father lives with the knowledge that there are many things he can never take for granted, like watching Joshua graduate from college, marry, or have children.

Most of the time Carlos copes fairly well with his son's autism. But there are days when he feels overwhelmed. One day, after bringing his son home from yet another appointment with a specialist, Carlos began to sob. In the depths of his despair, something—or Someone—told him to listen to Luther's great hymn. That Someone, Carlos is convinced, was the Holy Spirit.

As he listened to the great opening line, *Ein feste Burg ist unser Gott,* "a mighty fortress is our God," the world began to look less bleak.

Carlos's troubles were still there. But he no longer felt alone or overwhelmed. His fear was replaced by the assurance that he could take refuge in the same mighty fortress that had sheltered the psalmist—and Luther and Bach. He was reminded that while our strength may fail us, our Lord will not. Within a half hour, a five-hundred-year-old hymn had turned despair into hope and isolation into communion with our Lord.

This is the power that the great music inspired by our faith can have upon us.

This weekend, why not pick up a good recording of Luther's classic? Let those beautiful chords and words ring out and remind your own soul that our God is indeed "a bulwark never failing."

Lord, how marvelous that music written five hundred years ago can still move, inspire, and comfort. I ask that your hand direct today's composers and lyricists, that they, too, may create great melodies and lyrics that remind us that you are, in times of trouble, our refuge and our strength.

WORSHIPPING BEHIND BARS

TO READ: MATTHEW 25:31-40

I was in prison and you came to visit me. Matthew 25:36

We sometimes read about judges who go to prison for graft or corruption. But a Michigan judge goes every month—to preach and pray with prisoners.

Judge Gershwin Drain of the Wayne County, Michigan, Circuit Court began visiting inmates because the same offenders kept turning up in his courtroom again and again. It was obvious that simply sending men to prison was doing little to break the cycle of crime. In the judge's words, "Crime is a spiritual problem, and the real answer to crime requires changed hearts and lives."

So one Sunday each month Judge Drain joins his friend the Reverend James Owens in leading two Protestant services at Detroit's Mound Road Correctional Facility. The inmates—thieves, murderers, drug dealers—greet the judge with bear hugs. The inmate choir opens each service with gospel songs, and the prison classroom echoes with shouts of "Praise the Lord!" The men then open their Bibles to hear the lesson.

Since many inmates have had poor role models, the judge makes a point of discussing biblical men of great character such as Joshua. He then encourages the men to develop the character qualities they learn about. And the judge doesn't walk out of those prison gates without each week inviting the men to accept Christ.

Jesus says we will be judged by how much compassion we show to those who live on the fringes of society. He made a special point of including prisoners. Etched in Judge Drain's mind are the words of Jesus: "I was in prison and you visited me."

Judge Drain's own visits have become a labor of love. "When I'm worshipping with [these men]," he says, "there's no other place on Earth I'd rather be."

The feeling is shared by the men. Samuel Martin, an inmate who is serving a fifty-to-one-hundred-year sentence for rape, says, "We love the judge for coming to pray with us, when even some families don't visit."

Even the men Judge Drain put behind bars are glad to see him. Maurice Reynolds, whom Drain sentenced to life in prison for murder, explains that Drain is coming to prison not as a judge "but as a brother in Christ." And that, Reynolds says, "makes it very easy to accept him."

How many of us take seriously Jesus' command to visit those in prison? If we want to lower the crime rate, we've got to do more than simply lock criminals up. We must lead them to transformed hearts and lives through faith in Jesus Christ.

Father, forgive me for ignoring the less appealing commands of Christ. Help me to remember that many of those behind prison bars and razor-wire-topped fences are my brothers and sisters in Christ. Guide me into ways of serving them, their lonely spouses, and their needy children.

AVENGING MONSTERS

TO READ: PROVERBS 6:20-35

A man who commits adultery lacks judgment; whoever does so destroys himself.
Proverbs 6:32

What's behind our culture's fascination with the horror genre?

In *Horror: A Biography,* E. Michael Jones advances a fascinating thesis: Horror fiction, he argues, grew out of the sexual decadence of the Enlightenment.

Few people embraced debauchery more eagerly than English poet Percy Shelley. Shelley's first wife killed herself after he abandoned her to live with Mary Godwin. Shelley then victimized his new wife, Mary, even encouraging her to sleep with his friends.

As tragedy followed tragedy, a remorseful Mary became disillusioned with radical ideals. But she could not relieve her conscience, Jones writes, because she didn't understand repentance. "Literary catharsis seemed the only way" to purge her soul.

So Mary began writing *Frankenstein.* According to Jones, Mary's experience explains the genesis of horror films. We recognize, as she did, that the moral order is true, but if we suppress that, it comes back in our imagination as an avenging monster.

This was evident in *Frankenstein.* Dr. Frankenstein wants to play God, to create life on his own terms—just as Percy Shelley had created an Enlightenment sexual ethic. But instead of designing a superb new species, Frankenstein gives life to a murderous monster.

The avenging monster from the id, as Jones calls it, took new form during the second phase of the Enlightenment—a time when syphilis had contaminated European blood. Tragically, adulterous husbands often infected their innocent wives. *Dracula*—a novel about a vampire who infects the blood of innocent girls—symbolizes this deadly plague. *Dracula's* author, Bram Stoker, had syphilis himself.

As with *Frankenstein,* the true story of horror in the author's life—that is, sexuality divorced from the moral law—"is repressed and replaced by a monster who points to the [truth]."

A century later, another vengeful monster emerged in the wake of the modern sexual revolution: the creature in the 1979 film *Alien.* The monster's creator, H. R. Giger, denies he procured an abortion for his mistress. And yet, Jones notes, "his art is full of images of abortion and dead babies." Giger's conscience sought relief by creating a fetus-monster for *Alien.* At the film's end, a female astronaut kills the monster in a manner that strikingly resembles a suction abortion.

The warning of these stories echoes that of Scripture: that sex disconnected from the moral order is horrifying.

It's a sobering reminder in a culture that holds up fornication, adultery, homosexual encounters, and even pedophilia as normal and appropriate. If we are tempted to violate the laws set down for sex—if we think we can avoid unpleasant consequences—we will be in for a monstrous surprise.

Lord, how fascinating to have the inadvertent witness to the truth of your laws by those who deliberately violate them. I pray that these literary and cinematic witnesses will serve as a warning to those who have not yet broken the link between sex and your moral order—but who are thinking of doing so.

SUMMONING OUR COURAGE

TO READ: ROMANS 1:14-19

The righteous will live by faith. Romans 1:17

As a young German monk, Martin Luther was haunted by an acute sense of his unworthiness before God. But by studying the Scriptures, he learned that Christ himself had already suffered the penalty for Luther's sins. Christ had satisfied the demanding justice of a holy God. The passage that struck home for Luther was a line from Romans: "The righteous will live by faith."

At that moment, he wrote in his diary, "I grasped that the justice of God is that righteousness by which through grace and sheer mercy God justifies us through faith. . . . I felt myself to be reborn."

Luther's study of the Scriptures led him to press for reforms in the church. His urgent appeals to follow Scripture eventually led to his trial for heresy before the assembled religious and political powers of the day. Ordered to recant and knowing that his very life was at stake, Luther stood trembling before the assembly. "My conscience is held captive to the Word of God," he said in a shaking voice. "I cannot and I will not recant anything. God help me! Here I stand. I cannot do otherwise."

What compelled this solitary monk to take such a bold stand?

First, he realized that Christianity is no mere creed. It is a description of ultimate reality, rooted in Jesus Christ. The Scriptures are the very revelation of God and give us a truth that is absolute and universally valid. Believing this gave Luther the power to stand against the power structures of his day.

Second, Luther allowed the truth of God to inform his entire worldview. As he read the Scriptures, he realized that God demands justice and righteousness in all the created order. God's people are called to bring that justice into every area of life. We are to see the whole world through God's eyes, bringing righteousness both to individuals and to the structures of society.

This new perspective led to reforms not only in the church but also in politics, law, education, the arts, and sciences. It undergirded the principles that would eventually lead to Western democracy. It stimulated social reforms. It inspired art and music.

How desperately modern Christians need to grasp that same comprehensive worldview that lights up all aspects of life. If all of us were to perceive all of life through the lens of divine justice and righteousness—if we were to summon up the courage to take our stand, as Luther did—then we, too, might dare to dream of a reformation, one that could restore our flagging church and bring real justice to our failing culture.

Lord, help me to see the entire created order through the lens of your truth—and dare to dream of helping heal it.

WHY CHRISTIANS MUST VOTE

TO READ: DEUTERONOMY 16:18-20

Do not pervert justice. Deuteronomy 16:19

According to a recent report, only a third of evangelical Christians actually vote in the nation's elections.

This is appalling. Christians, of all people, ought to go to the polls, because voting is not just a right—it is a spiritual duty.

That was the message Rev. Curt Young gave his flock one Sunday a few years ago, just before an election. Young's church in Silver Spring, Maryland, is just a stone's throw from the White House, the Supreme Court, and the halls of Congress. Young wanted his congregation to know that the Scriptures have a lot to say about our responsibility to choose wise and ethical leaders.

For example, in Deuteronomy 16, Moses tells the Israelites: "You shall appoint judges and officials for each of your tribes . . . and they shall judge the people."

The term "judges and officials" covered all government leaders at that time. In addition to hearing cases and rendering decisions, they set public policy. They could even call up the military in times of crisis. Given these heavy responsibilities, it is not surprising that the criteria for selecting judges were strict. These were to be people who feared God, who were committed to the truth, and who hated dishonest gain.

When Moses commanded the Israelites to appoint God-fearing leaders, he wasn't just talking to a handful of citizens who felt like getting involved, Young says. The command was directed to all citizens. And modern Christians are under the same obligation to choose leaders who love justice. Our commitment to righteousness ought to come before our commitment to our pocketbooks or Social Security or Medicare.

Ironically, the Scriptures warn that if we value prosperity over justice, we will end up losing both. Moses told the Israelites to "follow justice and justice alone." He follows this command with a promise: Commit to justice, and the people will "live and possess the land the Lord your God is giving you." In other words, if you want prosperity, choose leaders committed to justice.

Today, unjust laws are passed all the time—laws that threaten the unborn, undermine the family, and endanger the elderly. Laws that protect pornographers and threaten our religious freedoms.

In the Old Testament, God often sent people to find particular individuals to become leaders. That was the case with the prophet Samuel, who chose David to lead Israel. Today in our modern democracy, free citizens act as God's agents for choosing leaders, and they do it by voting. The Bible says that God ordains these leaders to provide God's function for government, so we have a responsibility when we go to the polls.

Before the polls close on Election Day, we Christians must get out of our pews and into the polling booths—and do our sacred duty.

Lord, let me not be found making excuses for not troubling to vote for righteous leaders on Election Day. May I never forget that the election of God-fearing men and women—people who will not pervert justice—depends partly on me.

A SPECIAL INSTRUMENT OF GOD

TO READ: GENESIS 37:15-28

His brothers pulled Joseph up out of the cistern and sold him for twenty shekels of silver to the Ishmaelites, who took him to Egypt. Genesis 37:28

Most of us think we know the story of the first Thanksgiving. But did you know that God used an Indian named Squanto as a special instrument of his providence?

Historical accounts of Squanto's life vary, but historians believe that around 1608—more than a decade before the Pilgrims arrived—English traders sailed to what is today Plymouth, Massachusetts. When the Wampanoag Indians came out to trade, the traders took them prisoner, transported them to Spain, and sold them into slavery.

It was an unimaginable horror, but God had an amazing plan for one of the captured Indians, a boy named Squanto.

Squanto was brought by a well-meaning Spanish monk, who treated him well and taught him the Christian faith. Squanto eventually made his way to England and worked in the stables of a man named John Slaney. Slaney sympathized with Squanto's desire to return home and promised to put the Indian on the next vessel bound for America.

It wasn't until 1618, ten years after Squanto was kidnapped, that he returned to America. But when he arrived in Massachusetts, heartbreak awaited him. An epidemic had wiped out Squanto's entire village.

We can only imagine what must have gone through Squanto's mind. Why had God allowed him to return home, against all odds, only to find his loved ones dead? A year later, the answer came. A shipload of English families arrived and settled on the very land once occupied by Squanto's people. Squanto went to meet them, greeting the startled Pilgrims in English.

According to the diary of Pilgrim governor William Bradford, Squanto "became a special instrument sent of God for [our] good. . . . He showed [us] how to plant [our] corn, where to take fish and to procure other commodities." He "was also [our] pilot to bring [us] to unknown places for [our] profit, and never left [us] till he died."

When Squanto lay dying of a fever, Bradford wrote that their Indian friend "desir[ed] the Governor to pray for him, that he might go to the Englishmen's God in heaven." Squanto bequeathed his possessions to the Pilgrims "as remembrances of his love."

Who but God could so miraculously convert a lonely Indian and then use him to save a struggling band of Englishmen? It is reminiscent of the biblical story of Joseph, who was also sold into slavery—and whom God likewise used as a special instrument for good.

Have you ever suffered a great loss or tragedy and wondered why God allowed it to happen? We may not learn the answer for years. Sometimes we're not given the answer in this life. But we can take comfort in the knowledge that we worship a God who is both great and good—One who loves us and who can and does bring good out of evil.

Father, in every circumstance of my life, whether I understand your purposes or not, may my attitude be a witness to my trust in you.

IS ANYTHING REALLY EXTRA-CHRISTIAN?

TO READ: PSALM 24:1-10

The earth is the Lord's, and everything in it. Psalm 24:1

When you ask some people what they believe, they say they're agnostic. But what they usually mean is that they don't have enough evidence to decide whether or not God really exists.

Thomas Huxley, who was know as "Darwin's Bulldog," coined the word *agnostic* in the year 1870. Huxley was an atheist at a time when it was socially unacceptable to be one, so he found a more comfortable word to describe himself: agnostic. In Huxley's sense, agnosticism means there's no credible scientific evidence for the existence of God. So if God does exist, he's irrelevant.

Huxley championed Darwin's evolutionary theory tirelessly—not because he felt Darwin was infallible but because Darwin's theory helped Huxley ignore the Creator. Privately, he admitted that the fossil record seems to suggest that sharks have always been sharks and crocodiles always crocodiles, but Huxley believed it was "more profitable to go wrong than to stand still." Huxley hid his doubts from laymen, making bold statements like, "The whole evidence is in favour of evolution, and there is none against it."

To Christians alarmed by Darwin, Huxley was reassuring. During a lecture to the Young Men's Christian Association, Huxley declared that the sciences "are neither Christian, nor unchristian, but are extra-Christian." It's precisely this contention that holds many Christians hostage today.

To say that science is somehow outside the scope of Christianity is to suggest that Christianity is not a total worldview. Huxley's implication is clear: Christianity deals with the unseen and with faith; science deals with cold, hard facts and reality. Don't worry if Darwin's description of reality seems to contradict your faith: Just place each one in its own compartment and let it be.

When Christians accepted this point of view, they retreated. Suddenly they couldn't take faith into the laboratory or, by logical extension, into other "secular" places like the courtroom, the classroom, or the media.

Today's marginalization of Christianity is a direct result of our failure to understand our faith as a total worldview. We've lost our voice in the public square because we forgot, as Psalm 24:1 says, "the earth is the Lord's, and everything in it." God is sovereign over all of reality.

Once Christians understand this, they are prepared to enter the debate. And students who view their faith as a worldview can stand firm in their faith on college campuses, even in the face of atheism.

Darwin's Bulldog caused problems all right, but he also clarified the debate—because nothing is "extra-Christian." Remembering this helps us understand the sovereignty of God and the all-embracing scope of our Christian worldview.

Lord, help me to remember that those who want to shut religion out of the science classroom are often people who have shut you out of the rest of their lives as well. When I encounter them, guide me in making the case for the truth that the earth is yours—and that you created everything in it.

NOVEMBER 5

STANDING YOUR GROUND

TO READ: ECCLESIASTES 12:9-13

Of making many books there is no end, and much study wearies the body.
Ecclesiastes 12:12

A professor at a well-known liberal arts college was infamous for holding up a Bible on the first day of class and asking, "How many of you believe this book is the Word of God?" One or two students would sheepishly raise their hands. The professor would then say, "Here's what I think of this book!"—and he would throw it out an open window.

This childish display took place on a campus that, like so many in the United States, had solid Christian roots. Hostility to biblical faith is common today on both secular and even some religious campuses, says Jay Budziszewski in *How to Stay Christian in College*. Consider the story of a student named Frank. When Frank expressed a Christian point of view in a course on family law, a female student shouted, "Why don't you just shut up!"

The professor merely smirked and said to Frank, "I guess she told you!"

Or consider Kathy. In her ethics course, the textbook said there are two approaches to morality: supernaturalistic theories, which base morality on God, and naturalistic theories, which try to derive morality apart from God. The textbook then excluded supernaturalistic theories from the discussion. When Kathy asked the professor why, he replied, "We don't have time for superstitions."

Then there's Keesha. On the first day of her graduate seminar on public policy, the teacher announced that every point of view was welcome. Keesha looked forward to an open debate on abortion. But the second day the teacher opened class by saying, "All of you here are too intelligent to be pro-life, right?"

Sad to say, such tactics of intimidation are common in today's university classroom—and it's important for Christian students to learn to see through them. Telling a student to "just shut up" is the logical fallacy of *"argumentum ad baculum,"* or "argument to the stick"; that is, abusing someone instead of reasoning with them.

Dismissing Christian ideas as mere superstition is another fallacy—the fallacy of "begging the question," which really means assuming a point instead of proving it. And asking students if they're too intelligent to hold a Christian view is the fallacy of the "complex question," which means posing a question that one cannot answer without incriminating oneself: a question like, "Have you stopped beating your wife?"

College-bound Christians need to be intellectually prepared to see through such tactics these days and to demonstrate that Christianity is more rational as an explanation of reality than any of its competitors in the marketplace of ideas.

Christian students—and the rest of us—don't have to be intimidated if we can think rationally, because God's truth is far more reasonable than any of the logical fallacies thrown about today in college classrooms.

And it's the truth we all can live by.

Lord, give me the courage to stand up for your truth in every circumstance. May I never be confused or confounded by those who spend their lives coming up with self-serving alternatives to your truth and forcing them on others.

PRETTY STONES
AND DEAD BABIES

TO READ: ISAIAH 5:18-23

Woe to those who call evil good and good evil. Isaiah 5:20

At a Pittsburgh abortion clinic the walls are lined with pink paper hearts containing heartfelt messages from mothers to their aborted children. And at the end of every preabortion counseling session, the patient is given a pretty, colorful stone to take with her.

This novel approach to abortion is the trademark of a group of abortion clinics called the November Gang. A story in *Glamour* magazine explains that at these clinics, "intensive counseling is offered to patients. . . . Despite being staunchly pro-choice, counselors venture more willingly into areas like grief and regret than at most abortion clinics." They talk with the women about religious and psychological issues and let the women talk about their feelings toward their unborn babies.

According to *Glamour*, "One of the questions November Gang clinics sometimes ask patients is, Can you see abortion as a 'loving act' toward your children and yourself?" Faced with that query, "a lot of them are totally taken aback," says clinic director Debi Jackson. "Then they actually think about it, and they're like, 'Yeah, that's what I'm doing. I do love this child, but I can't [have] it right now.'" If a woman asks if God will forgive her, a counselor will turn the question back to her: "Do you think there are any things that God considers completely unforgivable?"

These abortion-clinic employees are coaching patients to twist their own words, emotions, and moral understanding so that they can feel justified doing something that they are clearly acknowledging is wrong. In language full of sentiment, these women are gently encouraged to put their own short-term needs first and not to think about what's best both for their babies and for themselves in the long run.

The pink hearts signed "Mommy," the "baptism ceremonies" held after the abortions, the stones that women are told to "imbue . . . with whatever meaning they choose"—all these things that are meant to heal and comfort are rendered duplicitous by the brutal act taking place.

Language can be deadly when it is not used in service of the truth. If we encounter women who have been deceived in this way, we need to lovingly tell them the truth: that abortion "counselors" manipulated them and called the evil of abortion good in order to make money. Then we must point these women to the One who offers not a pretty stone but salvation—and comfort to all who mourn.

Lord, teach me how to comfort a friend or family member who was deceived by abortion industry lies. Give me words of wisdom and sensitivity, that I might lead one who grieves a baby's death toward you, "the way and the truth and the life."

NOVEMBER 7

CHERISHING OUR CHILDREN

TO READ: GENESIS 48:8-16

Joseph brought his sons close to him, and his father kissed them and embraced them. Genesis 48:10

Like all Steven Spielberg films, *A.I.* was heralded by a blitz of media hype. The film was the product of Spielberg's collaboration with the late Stanley Kubrick, a legendary filmmaker who had worked on the concept for years but died before filming began.

Set in a somewhat distant future, *A.I.* (which stands for "artificial intelligence") is the story of David, a sort of cybernetic Pinocchio. Created in the image of a scientist's own lost son, David ushers in a new technological era. Like other androids, he can think, but unlike other mechanical beings, or "mechas," David can also feel. Most remarkably, he's programmed to love.

David is given to a couple whose own son is comatose and whose recovery is uncertain. The mother, distraught at the loss of her child, resists when her husband first brings David home. But after her initial hesitation, she decides to initiate the program to make David love her. They enjoy a brief and joyful time as mother and son.

But while David's love is hardwired, her own love comes with no such guarantees. When the couple's real son recovers from his coma and returns from the hospital, David finds himself without a home. And like Pinocchio, he sets out to become a real boy—in the hope that his mother will love him.

A.I. paints a disturbing picture of a world in which others are seen merely as instruments for satisfying our desires. Interestingly, response to this collaboration of two of Hollywood's greatest geniuses was cool to say the least. Critics discussed the problem of conflicting visions between Spielberg and Kubrick or the issues raised by creating artificial intelligence. But audiences may also have found that *A.I.* hits a little too close to home.

This film debunks the claim that when children are fewer in number, they will be treasured. When the only children society makes room for are "wanted children," then all children are, by definition, reduced to an extension of their parents' desires.

And *A.I.*'s critique extends beyond parenting. The impulse to create children for the parents' fulfillment also animates the drive for human cloning and stem-cell research. Conspicuously forgotten in today's lust for scientific breakthroughs is the humanity of the children being manufactured and destroyed.

Scripture teaches that parenting is a sacred trust and that the patriarchs greatly valued their offspring. Yes, children are delightful and bring us great joy, but they're also a weighty responsibility. They exist for their own sakes, with dignity in their own right, simply by virtue of being human.

A.I. is a film people will be talking about for a long time—and that's good. Let's pray that we learn its lessons before the fictional plot becomes a horrifying reality.

Lord, how often your Word tells us that children are a great blessing. May I never forget it. Help me to view the children around me as you do: not as possessions but as persons made in your image.

THE SOUL OF SCOUTING

TO READ: JUDE 1-25

These men speak abusively against whatever they do not understand. Jude 10

In a cover story called "Scouts Divided," *Newsweek* promised to tell readers "how a stand against gays is dividing an American institution." Instead, it demonstrated how the worldview of the media affects how journalists do their job.

According to *Newsweek,* a "growing number" of "moms, dads . . . and teenage boys" are challenging the Scouts' policy "because they love scouting." The article tells us about a Des Moines woman who took the uniform she wore as a chairwoman for a Cub Scout pack and put it the garage. Another man is considering removing his son—who has special needs and has "blossomed" as a result of his scouting experience—from the Scouts altogether on account of their policy.

The problem, as social scientists like to say, is that the plural of *anecdotes* isn't *data.* And *Newsweek*'s handful of stories does not constitute proof of a dissident movement within scouting. It's true that the number of kids in scouting dropped in 2000, but *Newsweek*'s own graphics indicate similar drops as recently as 1995.

To quote the social scientists again, correlation isn't the same as causation. The fact that two things happened at the same time does not prove that one caused the other. There are other factors responsible, like demographics, which *Newsweek* did not explore; such an exploration wouldn't be consistent with the slant the magazine's writers and editors wanted to give it.

The same is true when it comes to telling readers about the increased financial support for scouting or how attempts by United

Way chapters to strong-arm the Scouts into changing the policy has resulted in more people designating the Scouts directly as the recipient of their contributions.

Articles like this are the product of a worldview shaped by the sexual revolution, a worldview that can't imagine a legitimate reason for the Scouts' policy. Unable and perhaps unwilling to comprehend the Christian view—and unable to imagine intelligent people agreeing with a policy based on traditional Christian morality—they are attacking it in the manner described in Jude: speaking "abusively against whatever they do not understand."

Clearly, we need to be knowledgeable about issues of importance to Christians and not swallow everything we read. We must not only know the real story but also be able to lovingly correct misinformation and misrepresentation.

In the long term, we must strive to create a stronger Christian presence in the media. Stories like the supposed growing disdain for the policies of the Boy Scouts will proliferate as long as there are so few Christians in America's newsrooms. And the divide between journalists and the rest of us, who hold a traditional worldview, will only continue.

As the *Newsweek* story illustrates, America *is* a nation divided . . . by worldview.

Lord, you taught us not to throw pearls before swine, but you also tell us to "snatch others from the fire and save them" and to "show mercy" to doubters. When it comes to neighbors confused about why we believe as we do, give me the words and the wisdom to respond as I ought.

NOVEMBER 9

RESISTING
FORBIDDEN FRUIT

TO READ: LUKE 15:11-32

When he came to his senses, he said, "How many of my father's hired men have food to spare, and here I am starving to death!" Luke 15:17

The Lion, the Witch, and the Wardrobe is the first volume in C. S. Lewis's famous Chronicles of Narnia series, which features four British children during World War II who are magically transported into the world of Narnia. There they are given the heroic task of helping to undo a curse cast by an evil witch, which has kept the land frozen in perpetual winter. Through the younger boy, Edmund, Lewis portrays what happens when we give in to temptation—and how we can be forgiven and restored.

Soon after arriving in Narnia, Edmund is separated from the other children and encounters the White Witch. She offers him a magical candy that he finds addicting; eating it puts him under her power. As ethics professor Vigen Guroian writes in *Tending the Heart of Virtue,* "This encounter with the White Witch and the taste of her forbidden food marks the start of [Edmund's] long, lonely journey into the darkness." Soon his "temptation becomes an uncontrolled obsession, and he is no longer able to enjoy good and legitimate pleasures."

With deadly accuracy Lewis paints a picture of the way sin affects us. It doesn't announce itself as sin; it draws us in with something that seems pleasant and comforting but becomes addictive, blinding us to what is good and attracting us to what is evil.

The story form makes these concepts come alive. As Guroian writes, "Edmund's behavior is wholly believable and existentially compelling for young people. They can relate to the vortex-like inner

625

force that swallows him up into his dark night and descent into a personal hell."

The charms of the magical candy eventually wear off, and Edmund begins to realize how cold and miserable he is. The turning point comes when the boy is finally moved to compassion for someone besides himself. The selfish addiction is broken, and "just as the snow that covers Narnia begins to melt," Guroian writes, "Edmund's heart turns back to goodness."

Through the story, children "see that, while it is difficult, admitting one's mistakes and errors is the right thing to do and may lead to forgiveness and true happiness."

The story echoes the parable of the lost son, who succumbs to sin and then comes to his senses, repents, and returns home to his overjoyed father.

Read *The Lion, the Witch, and the Wardrobe* to the children in your life. And you might want to get a copy of *Tending the Heart of Virtue* for yourself. It will teach you how to use the power of literature to tend the hearts of children—to help them understand the gospel and then respond to the Savior.

Lord, I pray that you will bring me to my senses in every area where I have succumbed to sin—or am tempted to. Thank you for loving me so much that no matter how many times I falter, you always accept my repentance with joy—and forgiveness.

A BIBLICAL VIEW OF WORK

TO READ: 2 THESSALONIANS 3:6-15

If a man will not work, he shall not eat. 2 Thessalonians 3:10

Have you seen those bumper stickers that read, "I Owe, I Owe, So Off to Work I Go"? Is that all there is to the working life? Earn money to spend money, in an endless, pointless cycle?

The book of Genesis gives us a biblical view of work. From the beginning, there was God's work of creation. God looked at the work of his hands and called it good.

God created humans in his image, so it is part of our nature to work as well. As soon as God had created Adam, he gave him physical work—tending the plants and animals in the garden—and intellectual work, naming and classifying the creation.

Clearly, work was part of Paradise *before* sin corrupted the world. So Christians don't work just to earn money—we work because it is an expression of our created nature.

Most ancient civilizations did not see it that way. The ancient Greeks and Romans saw work, especially physical labor, as a curse. In fact, the Greek word for work is *ponos,* which means "sorrow." But Christianity saw work as something ennobling, an expression of the divine image.

When Paul said that men who refused to work should not be allowed to eat, he wasn't being harsh; he was teaching us that work is good for us and for our communities.

In the middle ages, Christians formed guilds to ensure high-quality work within their trades; monks and scholars saw no indignity in laboring for their keep.

When Martin Luther nailed his ninety-five theses to the door of the Wittenberg chapel in 1517, one of the things he declared was a high view of work. He denied that religious leaders have a superior calling and declared that all work—whether building houses or running a business or raising children—is equally important in God's eyes.

This view of work came to be known as the Protestant work ethic. It included virtues like thrift and industry and paved the way for democratic capitalism. The merchant's work, done to the glory of God, is good too.

The Puritans and other early settlers brought this ethic to the New World. They cleared land, dug ditches, and built houses, all for the glory of God. Eventually their descendants, steeped in that tradition, created the greatest economic power on earth.

If you catch yourself disdaining the work you are called on to perform—if you are tempted to perform it poorly because you dislike it—remind yourself that you should work diligently because you are working for God's glory. And if you find it impossible to honor God in your work, that may be a sign that you should labor at something else.

Father, may I never insult the Creator of all work by performing my own work badly. May I earn my wages honestly, and may my work at all times reflect not simply the need to pay my bills but the fact that I glorify you through work well done.

BONZO WAS RIGHT

TO READ: PROVERBS 13:13-24

He who spares the rod hates his son, but he who loves him is careful to discipline him. Proverbs 13:24

In the classic comedy film *Bedtime for Bonzo,* a young professor, played by Ronald Reagan, brings home a monkey to prove a point: that a stable, two-parent home, where children are taught right and wrong, can keep kids from a life of crime.

At first, the chimp drives Reagan's character to distraction, throwing cereal in his master's face and stealing jewelry. But in the end, Bonzo proves the professor's point: He returns a stolen necklace because his "parents" have taught him that stealing is wrong.

The film is lighthearted fun—with a profound message: Families do shape character and thus have a direct impact on crime.

The empirical evidence supporting this view is overwhelming. Researchers at the National Institute of Mental Heath who studied high risk, inner-city neighborhoods found that when kids grow up in safe, stable families, only about 6 percent of them will become delinquent. In contrast, 90 percent of children reared in unstable, one-parent families will become delinquent. Clearly, it's not poverty or race that is the chief cause of crime; it's the lack of moral training during morally formative years.

The problem is aggravated when a parent goes to prison. The leading indicator of a young person's future criminal behavior is having a parent locked up. One study found that 84 percent of boys who become serious juvenile offenders have a parent or a sibling in jail. If something doesn't change, generation after generation will continue to go into the family business: Crime, Inc.

At its root, crime is a moral problem. And conversion—bringing kids to a personal relationship with Jesus Christ—is the best way to turn wayward juveniles around.

Conversion is the key to keeping families together, as well. In areas of the world where churches most aggressively evangelize, family breakdown declines. The church's most immediate challenge is to reach out with the gospel to kids and families at risk.

Faith-based efforts—not government programs or bigger prisons—can deal directly with the problem of family breakdown. We must also work hard for measures that strengthen the family and fight the cultural forces that are corrupting it. When state legislators propose repealing easy-divorce laws, get behind them. If your local video store carries trashy movies, write to the owners or organize pickets. If a soap company advertises on raunchy TV programs, boycott it—and let the company know why you're washing your hands of its product. If gay groups donate *Heather Has Two Mommies* to your local school library, raise the roof until it's removed—or have your church group check the book out on a rotating basis so children won't be exposed to it.

Our children deserve better than to be surrendered to settings that prepare them for a life of crime. The only institution that can provide this crucial moral training is the fragile, but irreplaceable, family.

Just ask Bonzo.

Lord, if I am ever tempted to break up my family or spare myself the difficult job of disciplining my children, remind me of who will end up paying the cost: everyone.

FIGHTING HISTORICAL VANDALISM

TO READ: PSALM 133:1-3

How good and pleasant it is when brothers live together in unity! Psalm 133:1

In an article in Focus on the Family's *Citizen* magazine, Douglas Phillips described how he took his family to Plymouth, Massachusetts, a few years ago and was shocked at what he found. Atop Cole's Hill, the burial ground for Pilgrims who died that first hard winter, Phillips was startled to see a city truck pull up and men pile out carrying shovels.

"We're placing a new monument for the city," the men told him.

"What does it say?" Phillips asked.

"We aren't sure," they answered. "We were just told to dig the hole. Someone else will put the marker in tonight."

"Most revolutions are staged at night," Phillips wrote, so he wasn't surprised the next day to find stone markers all over Plymouth designating Thanksgiving as a day of mourning—a day to recall how the Pilgrims murdered and stole from their Indian neighbors. That afternoon, demonstrators—mostly white college kids—celebrated their victory by defacing the traditional monuments. Plymouth had transformed a tale of religious freedom into a story of genocide.

The historical reality is totally different. While it's true that later settlers abused the Native Americans, the Pilgrims and the Wampanoag Indians lived together in peace for fifty years. They signed covenants, bought and sold property, and fought against mutual enemies. In fact, Paul Jehle of the Plymouth Rock Foundation says the Pilgrims—as Christians—modeled the right way to interact with a native population—unlike later settlers, who did not share their commitment to Christian principles.

Activist groups don't distinguish between the Pilgrims and later Europeans because the postmodern obsession with group identity has led to the cult of victim politics, which in turn has led to deliberate distortions of history.

This is a field in which Christians have a unique contribution to make. Christians view history as a cornucopia of complexity because we understand the doctrine of original sin. We know that because the human race is fallen, people are capable of great evil. But because we are made in God's image, we are also capable of great good.

That's why society may remember a single person or group for both good and bad behavior. In fact, when we hear a version of history that portrays an entire group as all bad or all good, we should suspect that we're not getting the whole story.

The modern obsession with group identity and victimhood encourages us to see those assigned to other groups as our enemies—neighbors who are members of another religion, race, or culture. When we interact with them, we ought to recall the relationship between the Pilgrims and the Indians and model not hostility and hatred but brotherly love. As the psalmist notes, a willingness to get along with others makes for a pleasant and peaceful life.

Lord, help me to overcome my discomfort with neighbors and colleagues who are in some way different from me—and who may feel uncomfortable around me for the same reason. Make me willing to reach out to those who are unfamiliar, offering both my friendship and your love rather than retreating into the comfort of familiar friends.

THE ABUSE OF LANGUAGE

TO READ: NAHUM 3:1-7

Woe to the city of blood, full of lies. Nahum 3:1

During every national political campaign, the expression *anti-choice* is thrust repeatedly into commentaries, political ads, and talk shows. Its use illustrates the political mischief the misuse of language can cause, because the term is clearly used to obscure rather than illuminate the truth.

First, what does it mean to be anti-choice? Are we supposed to believe that a candidate is against allowing people to make choices? Of course not. People make hundreds of choices every day. Some are insignificant, such as whether we'll have eggs or cereal for breakfast. Others involve choosing between right and wrong, such as deciding whether or not to tell the truth. No one running for office opposes this kind of human freedom.

Second, calling someone anti-choice is hypocritical. Those who are clamoring for the protection of "choice" are working overtime to restrict other people's choices. They want to restrict smoking; they argue for laws against talking on cell phones while driving; and they lobby for more restrictions on gun ownership.

So if the expression *anti-choice* is nonsensical and hypocritical, why do abortion lobbyists and the press insist on using it? They do so because they hope to divert our attention from *what* is being chosen. Choice is a morally vacant concept. The morality of a choice lies in what we choose. No one wants to acknowledge that they're pro-abortion, so they claim they are actually pro-choice.

Likewise, labeling someone "antiabortion" would focus our

attention on the reality of abortion; this is why abortion supporters prefer to call their opponents "anti-choice."

This use of words like *choice* and *anti-choice* is a smokescreen, a warping of words to make a political point. A similar process was involved when the word *gay* became a code word for a particular sexual lifestyle. Co-opting a term with generally positive connotations makes it easier to attack as bigots those who hold a biblical view of homosexuality.

George Orwell, author of *1984,* understood the uses and abuses of language. In his essay "Politics and the English Language," Orwell said that "the great enemy of clear language is insincerity. When there is a gap between one's real and one's declared aims, one turns as it were instinctively to long words and exhausted idioms, like a cuttlefish spurting out ink."

Today, instead of using long words, the insincere turn to euphemisms and obscure phrases. But corrupt language leads to corrupt thought. It's an attempt to deceive, and today, as in Nahum's time, deceit is invariably linked to other sins—which is why God hates lies and why Jesus condemns Satan as "the father of lies."

Christians must help clear away the linguistic fog that obscures what's really at issue. More than anyone else, we understand the power of words and the need to treat them with respect.

Lord, open my eyes to deceptive language that exchanges truth for a lie. May I never use such language myself or fall prey to the phrases others employ in an effort to strip sinful actions of the evil you assigned them.

ENGLAND'S GREAT POET-PRIEST

TO READ: JUDGES 16:23-31

Samson said, "Let me die with the Philistines!" Then he pushed with all his might, and down came the temple. Judges 16:30

A few years ago a poll declared James Joyce's *Ulysses* the most important English-language novel of the twentieth century. Also in the top ten were D. H. Lawrence's *Sons and Lovers* and Nabokov's *Lolita*. All three books contain explicit sexual passages or themes; in fact, both *Ulysses* and *Lolita* were initially banned in the United States.

The choices of these books are a clear sign of the degradation of Western culture. Only a generation ago, the most influential works of English literature were not only morally uplifting but also often explicitly Christian. In *Invitation to the Classics*, Os Guinness and Louise Cowan challenge Christians to rediscover the classics and reclaim our glorious heritage of literature, including the works of one of the greatest writers of all time: the English poet John Milton.

Born in 1608 and raised in a pious Christian home, Milton considered entering the clergy but eventually decided to serve God as a kind of poet-priest. Today, among poets, he is generally ranked second only to Shakespeare. Milton's first mature poem, which he wrote when he was barely twenty-one, is titled *On the Morning of Christ's Nativity*:

> *This is the month, and this the happy morn,*
> *Wherein the Son of heav'n's eternal King,*

Of wedded Maid and Virgin Mother born,
Our great redemption from above did bring.

The joy of Milton's Christian faith could not be more evident.

Milton's most famous work is his epic poem *Paradise Lost,* which he wrote after he had gone blind. The poem deals with the story of Adam and Eve and Satan in Eden. It attempts, in Milton's famous words, "to justify the ways of God to man." Its sequel, *Paradise Regained,* tells the subsequent story of Jesus' redemption of Adam's sin. Milton also wrote a long poem about Samson, titled *Samson Agonistes.* Almost all his works are replete with Christian ideas and references.

Why don't more Christians know about Milton? For one thing, Milton, like many great writers of the past, can be difficult to read. And unfortunately, we Christians often aren't much more self-disciplined or rigorous about what we read than nonbelievers are.

Another reason is what Guinness calls "the centuries-old strain of cultural philistinism within the community of faith," one that "rejects the importance of literature and art." He reminds us that the apostle Paul "was thoroughly trained in classical languages, literature, and philosophy."

Guinness says that Christians have "a unique responsibility to guard, enjoy, and pass on [the Classics] . . . not least because [we] are privileged to share the faith that animated the majority of [them]."

He's right. If we find it difficult to do this on our own, we ought to encourage one another by forming book clubs. After all, many of us already gather in small groups to study books that are far less challenging—and in some cases perhaps, far less worthwhile.

We Christians owe it to ourselves to discover and celebrate our great literary heritage.

Lord, you have given us the great gift of literature, often the fruit of the labors of men and women who knew you. Give me a strong desire to learn and grow by reading these works. Make me willing to tackle the difficult over the undemanding, the uplifting over the degrading, and the excellent over the explicit.

BELIEVERS IN BUSINESS

TO READ: LUKE 22:7-23

He took bread, gave thanks and broke it, and gave it to them, saying, "This is my body given for you; do this in remembrance of me." Luke 22:19

Fr. Robert Sirico, president of Acton Institute, likes to quote theologian Paul Tillich, who said, "Christianity is the religion of which socialism is the practice." After all, the reasoning goes, isn't it all about sharing rather than working as a result of the "profit motive"?

But American Christians, of course, work in a free-market context. And maybe that misunderstanding about socialism is why so many of them find it hard to see their work as a calling. And yet, notes Fr. Sirico, Tillich is wrong. The notions of making money and private enterprise have a strong biblical foundation.

Fr. Sirico highlights the story of the Creation from Genesis. In that text, God formed man from dust, a *material* substance, and breathed life into him—the breath of God, a *divine* substance. God looked at his creation—a combination of corporeal and spiritual reality—and declared it good.

In the New Testament, Sirico says, Jesus commanded his followers to remember him through the Lord's Supper. In Communion, God supplies the grain and the grapes. Man supplies the kneading and crushing, that is, the human effort, to make bread and wine. This material and spiritual union of God's creation and our effort conveys dignity to human work. God allows us to mold his creation by our efforts.

Christians need to reaffirm the goodness of material things and at the same time emphasize our dependence on God and the moral reflection on all human action.

Only a free-market system takes the goodness of material creation and the value of work seriously. It also takes into account the social nature of humanity. In the market, those who produce goods and services offer what they have made to others in order to meet the needs of supplier and customer. This is a positive good.

There are flaws in a free market because the market reflects the sinfulness of its users. And capitalism can't survive without a conscience, without the reflection of Christian truth in the market. Sirico stops short of declaring a free-market system biblical, but he argues that it is the system most compatible with biblical values and principles when it is tied to religious faith.

Because material creation is good and human work and effort are good, Christians ought to see business as a holy calling and be willing to defend it against those who view the union of God's creation and man's effort as intrinsically evil.

Lord, let me not be misled by those who attack business and businesspeople as being inherently sinful. May I remember that every time I buy or sell, I must put integrity above all else, not only because I am either helping or harming society with every transaction, but also because I am bearing witness to what or whom I ultimately serve: the love of money or the love of God.

SEEKING GOD'S COMFORT

TO READ: PSALM 23:1-6

Even though I walk through the valley of the shadow of death, I will fear no evil, for you are with me. Psalm 23:4

In a certain section of the bookstore you'll find a batch of books that just might give your children nightmares.

Let's Talk About Staying in a Shelter, one title cheerfully suggests. Others invite tots to talk about what happens when their parents die, divorce, or get thrown in jail. In *Daisy,* a book about domestic violence, a little girl talks about how her father punches and kicks her.

These books are part of a trend among children's book authors to confront kids with the harsh realities of life. The idea is to use stories to help children deal with their own problems.

Children's author Maurice Sendak says parents should not try to protect children from the dark side of life. The worst crime we can commit against children, Sendak argues, "is not teaching them to survive" in a world of AIDS and drive-by shootings. Sendak himself wrote *We Are All in the Dumps with Jack and Guy,* a story about homeless kids who live out of a cardboard box.

Do these books really do any good? In *Books That Build Character,* William Kilpatrick and his coauthors, Gregory and Suzanne Wolfe, say that the problem with issues-oriented books is that they offer children "no self-forgetfulness, no room to stand back and get a larger view." Instead, these books cater to anxiety and self-absorption. As a result, Kilpatrick writes, it's questionable whether they work even on a therapeutic level.

A better approach to helping kids explore life's difficulties, Kilpatrick maintains, is to use fantasy, because fantasy provides the necessary distance. Kilpatrick relates the true story of a ten-year-old boy who struggled with cancer. As the child's mother recalls, "At first he was very upbeat, but after several painful treatments, his optimism faded. We were afraid that he was ready to give up. We were really afraid for his life."

Then, his mother says, the boy "came upon the story of the labors of Hercules in a book of myths, and he read it and reread it, and it seemed to give him back his spirit."

Kilpatrick explains that "the story of Hercules allowed the boy to transcend his fears and to cast his personal struggle on a mythic level. He was probably fortunate "that some well-meaning adult didn't hand him a book about a boy with cancer. That sort of thing often serves only to increase the depression."

Today more than ever, Christian parents must keep a close eye on what their children read and help them find books that will develop their moral imagination: books that serve as literary springboards to transformed lives.

Lord, give me discernment to choose books wisely for the children in my life, especially when they are struggling with difficulties. And when I myself am battling the demons of depression, sickness, or sorrow, remind me of the comfort that you are eager to provide, both through prayer and through the words of your Holy Book.

THE ROUTE TO
SELF-ESTEEM

TO READ: ZEPHANIAH 2:1-3, 8-11

Seek humility. Zephaniah 2:3

Lawyers for a man accused of taking part in a triple murder had his defense all ready. They planned to say that twenty-two-year-old Darwin Godoy had a defective personality: He suffers from low self-esteem.

This is just another example of how deeply the self-esteem movement has infiltrated our culture. According to a prominent psychologist, however, there's no real evidence that self-esteem, or the lack thereof, has any such impact on behavior.

Paul Vitz, author of *Psychology as Religion: The Cult of Self-Worship,* says that people blame low self-esteem for everything from drug abuse to teen pregnancy to murder. Self-esteem programs have infiltrated our schools, where educators believe that if they can just raise the self-esteem of their students high enough, the students' problems will go away.

So, teachers tell students over and over again how important and special they are. And the curriculum reinforces this message, telling students to say and write positive things about themselves. The problem is, it doesn't work.

Self-esteem, Vitz says, is "a complex notion, defined and measured in many different and ambiguous ways." But no matter how you define it, the evidence does not support the idea that high self-esteem by itself offers any benefit. In fact, psychologists often find that an inferiority complex is a much greater motivator for high achievement.

Gloria Steinem, for example, a high-achieving leader of the feminist movement, freely admits that she suffers from low self-esteem. But self-doubt didn't slow her down any more than it has slowed others who've achieved success.

Then there's the study that compared mathematical skills of children from different countries. As reported in the national media, the kids who ranked highest—the Koreans—scored lowest in self-esteem, while the kids who scored highest in self-esteem—the Americans—ranked lowest in math skills. Clearly, all those self-esteem lessons didn't help the American students add and subtract better.

The best way to raise self-esteem is through genuine accomplishment. That's because, according to Vitz, self-esteem is "primarily an emotional response to what we have done, and to what others have done to us." If you want to feel good about yourself, then "do good to others and accomplish something for yourself."

As Christians, we ought to have a high sense of self-worth because we know God made us in his image and sent his Son to die in order to save us.

Self-respect is one thing, but the self-esteem movement is something altogether different. It promotes self-worship. It teaches that unless we love ourselves, we will be unhappy. But Paul Vitz warns that this assumes that God will not love us as we need to be loved. It's a form of "practical atheism," and it can lead to sobering consequences: As Samuel Johnson said, "He that overvalues himself will undervalue others, and he who undervalues others will suppress them."

Father, help me to glorify you by making the most of the abilities you have given me. When I am tempted to esteem myself too highly, remind me of the words of your Son: "Blessed are the meek."

THEOLOGY AND
THE TRINITY

TO READ: JOHN 14:15-24

I will ask the Father, and he will give you another Counselor to be with you forever—the Spirit of truth. John 14:16-17

Within minutes of watching Muslim terrorists fly airplanes into the World Trade Center, the Pentagon, and a field in Pennsylvania, Americans were asking, "Who are these people? What do they believe?"

In response, theologian Timothy George wrote a book called *Is the Father of Jesus the God of Muhammad?* George answers his question with a yes and a no.

Islam and Christianity are both monotheistic; that is, both are founded on the belief that there is only one God. The Christian understanding of God, however, is vastly different from that of Islam because of the Christian doctrine of the Trinity.

George writes, "The Father of Jesus is the only God there is, and in that sense, He is the God of every person who has ever lived, including Muhammad." He adds, however, that "bare monotheism alone is not enough. It yields a god who is a unit, not a unity. It gives us a deity that is infinite, but not personal."

Thus, although the *Qur'an* affirms that Allah loves, his love is conditional, and it's something he does, not something he is. In contrast, Christians affirm that God *is* love. His love is unconditional and integral to the very being of the one God who is eternally three. The Father, Son, and Holy Spirit are eternally bound together in perfect love.

George writes, "What makes God God is the relationship of total and mutual self-giving by which the Father gives everything to the Son, and the Son offers back all that He has to glorify the Father, the love of each being established and sealed by the Holy Spirit, Who proceeds from both."

If God is just a unit, says George, then he "created the world in order to fill some deep deficiency within His own being"; that is, he needed to be known. The Trinity has no such need. Within the Trinity are love, knowledge, intimacy, and relationships. God freely chose to create and to love. "The doctrine of the Trinity," says George, "tells us that relationality—personality—is at the heart of the universe."

George also reminds us that in the church today the Trinity is perhaps our most neglected doctrine, and that needs to change. It needs to change because our own spirituality is dangerously deficient without an understanding of the Trinity: The doctrine of the Trinity "is the necessary theological framework for understanding the story of Jesus as the story of God."

Islam is growing in the United States and around the world. When we talk with Muslims about faith, conversations about the Trinity are unavoidable: On college campuses young Muslims are handing out tracts saying that Christians worship three Gods. We need a credible answer for our Muslim neighbors. Do you have one?

Lord, make me willing to love my Muslim neighbors enough to study what they believe so that I can lovingly and effectively share your truth—both for the sake of the souls they seek for Islam and for their own souls' sake.

PILGRIM FATHERS
AND KIDS

TO READ: PROVERBS 23:22-26

The father of a righteous man has great joy; he who has a wise son delights in him.
Proverbs 23:24

Why did the Pilgrims really come to America? Most people think they came seeking religious freedom. They did, in part, but they also came because their teenagers were giving them fits.

In 1608, the Church of England was the established church. Christians who objected to aspects of the official church were called Separatists, and they were often thrown into prison for worshipping in their own way.

Determined to worship as they saw fit, a group of these Separatists escaped to Holland in the spring of 1608. Among them was seventeen-year-old William Bradford, who was to pen a famous journal of their adventures. But after a dozen years of living among the Dutch, the Separatists were becoming desperate. It was difficult to make a living in Holland. Bradford recounts in his journal that many of them found it difficult to endure the "great and continual labors" and were getting old before their time. Fellow Separatists in England who observed their backbreaking trials actually preferred prison there to liberty in Holland.

Most lamentable of all, Bradford writes, many of the Separatists' children in Holland were losing their faith. They were influenced by the "great licentiousness of youth in that countrie" and were being drawn away by evil examples. Some of these young people were even leaving their families and living dissolute lives, Bradford records, "to the great greefe of their parents and dishonor of God."

It seemed clear to the Separatists that they needed to seek religious freedom in a land that not only offered an easier living but also would not corrupt their children. After much prayer they began to plan their historic journey to America.

The story of the Pilgrims illustrates the fact that parents have always had to contend with cultural influences that tempt their children away from faithful obedience to God. In the seventeenth century those temptations likely took the form of saloons and prostitutes. Today's kids are surrounded by a culture that celebrates recreational sex, drug use, and rebellion against God's laws.

We moderns don't have the luxury of packing up our children and moving to another country—assuming we could find one free of temptations. Still, we have to do everything we can to keep the corrosive forces of American culture from eating away at the character of our youth. We can do that by limiting their exposure to immoral films, music, video games, and television programs.

And when they're older, we need to help them understand the worldview implicit in these products: that the culture war is a cosmic struggle between the Christian worldview and the various secular and spiritual worldviews arrayed against it.

This Thanksgiving, when your kids are devouring their pumpkin pie, point out that the Pilgrims did not come to America just to find religious freedom. They already had that in Holland. The Pilgrims embarked on that dangerous journey to an unexplored continent for another important reason, as well: They came for the sake of their children.

Lord, let me be as committed to my children's spiritual well-being as the Pilgrim parents were to theirs. Make me to be willing to give up whatever I must to rear wise children "who delight in you."

DIGGING OUT THE TRUTH

TO READ: JEREMIAH 47:1-7

The Lord is about to destroy the Philistines, the remnant from the coasts of Caphtor.
Jeremiah 47:4

In modern English the word *Philistine* refers to an uncouth or uncultured person. The term is taken from the name of the people who were Israel's biggest rivals in the period between the Exodus and the reign of King David.

Until recently many scholars doubted the existence of the Philistines. But as is the case with so much of the biblical text, the more archaeologists dig, the more they confirm the historical character of the biblical narratives.

In *Is the Bible True? How Modern Debates and Discoveries Affirm the Essence of the Scriptures,* author Jeffrey Sheler writes that recent archaeological discoveries have both proved the existence of the Philistines and revealed much about how they lived. Ancient Egyptian inscriptions indicate that the "Sea Peoples"—the ancient Near Eastern name for the Philistines—most likely came from the island of Crete.

The Bible says the Philistines were originally from the land of Caphtor. Sheler points out that scholars believe Caphtor is another name for Crete.

The Bible characterizes the Philistines as the best metalworkers in the ancient Near East, and they exercised a virtual monopoly in the sword-making trade. The archaeological record has substantiated this characterization, confirming both the Philistines's skills in metallurgy and the advantage that their superior weaponry gave them in their battles with the Israelites as described in 1 Samuel.

Sheler documents that there is a remarkable consistency between what the Bible says about the Philistines and what archaeologists are finding. This consistency prompted William Dever of the University of Arizona to say that "all [the archaeological findings] 'fit' the many biblical allusions so well . . . and show that a post-exilic editor cannot simply have invented these passages, that they are genuinely archaic."

Archaeology is debunking the once dominant idea that books such as Judges and 1 Samuel were the product of some post-exilic writer's fertile imagination. The author of these books wasn't inventing some glorious past for Israel; he was working with real history—both oral and written.

So many finds in recent years have lent credence to the biblical text that critics are becoming suspect of the archaeologists' motives. According to an article in *Biblical Archaeology Review*, "archeologists have been . . . heavily criticized [for] being biased, for trying to prove the Bible." But, the magazine points out, they're simply following where the evidence leads.

Many people, Christians and non-Christians alike, believe that science is the enemy of biblical faith. But these discoveries in the desert show that scientific knowledge can buttress biblical faith. We need to familiarize ourselves with these exciting discoveries and introduce them to our neighbors who don't know Christ. As it turns out, the true Philistine today is someone who dismisses the Bible without first looking at the evidence.

Father, thank you for archaeological evidence that points to your truth and exposes the wrong thinking of those who deny your actions in history. May this evidence lead our children to wonder about the motives of those who try so hard— and so angrily—to prove that you don't exist.

THE CORROBORATION
OF CHRIST

TO READ: LUKE 24:28-49

It is true! The Lord has risen and has appeared to Simon. Luke 24:34

The Gospels contain many eyewitness accounts of the life of Christ. But in *The Case for Christ*, former journalist Lee Strobel asks, "Are there writings outside the Gospels that affirm or support any of the essentials about Jesus?"

For the answer, Strobel went to Edwin Yamauchi, former president of the Institute for Biblical Research. Let's be honest, Strobel told him. Is there really much corroboration of the events in Jesus' life outside the Bible?

Absolutely, Yamauchi replied. "We do have very, very important references to Jesus in Josephus and Tacitus. Josephus was a first-century Jewish historian who, because of his collaboration with the Romans, was hated by his fellow Jews. In the *Testimonium Flavianum*, Josephus writes of Jesus' life, miracles, death, and resurrection. Josephus wrote, 'On the third day [after his crucifixion] he appeared to them restored to life.'"

Yamauchi explained that "Josephus corroborates important information about Jesus: that he was the martyred leader of the church in Jerusalem . . . who had established a wide and lasting following, despite the fact that he had been crucified."

Tacitus, the most important Roman historian of the first century, was an unsympathetic witness to the spread of Christianity. So his testimony is especially credible. Tacitus wrote that an "immense multitude" held so strongly to their beliefs that they were willing to die rather than recant.

Yamauchi notes that the Jewish Talmud, finished in A.D. 500, also mentions Jesus. Although it calls him a "false messiah," the fact that it mentions him at all is a corroboration of his life in ancient Israel.

Finally, Yamauchi cites the writings of the apostolic fathers, "the earliest Christian writers after the New Testament." Among them was Ignatius, who went to his execution claiming that Jesus rose from the dead "and that those who believe in him would be raised too," Yamauchi said.

Put together the writings of Josephus, the Roman historians, Jewish writings, and the apostolic fathers, "and you've got persuasive evidence that corroborates all the essentials found in the biographies of Jesus." And, he added, "even if you were to throw away every last copy of the Gospels, you'd still have a picture of Jesus that's extremely compelling—in fact, it's a portrait of the unique Son of God."

In the information age it's sometimes hard to separate truth from falsehood. So it's not surprising that people are often skeptical. We need to help our neighbors understand that there's plenty of evidence that corroborates what the Gospels say. In addition to the historical evidence, we need to be sure that we offer skeptics plenty of contemporary evidence in the form of our obedience to the God we say we worship—evidence that points to the fact that Jesus is exactly who he said he is: the Savior.

Father, may my life exhibit the same joyful excitement demonstrated by your first followers when your Son opened their minds to who he was, why he had to suffer, and how those who loved him were now to follow him.

CHALLENGING MODERN
MYTHMAKERS

TO READ: MATTHEW 28:1-15

You are to say, "His disciples came during the night and stole him away."
Matthew 28:13

On November 22, 2003, Americans observed the fortieth anniversary of the tragic death of President John Kennedy. Television networks marked the occasion by trotting out the latest assassination-conspiracy theories—and reheating the old ones—even though there's no longer any doubt, as Peter Jennings noted, that Lee Harvey Oswald was acting alone when he killed the president.

Viewers were also treated to Oliver Stone's 1991 film *JFK*, which critics blasted as paranoid and error riddled. Stone's thesis is that Kennedy was secretly planning to pull U.S. troops out of Vietnam. To prevent this, a megaconspiracy involving the CIA, the FBI, the Mob, the Dallas police force, and the whole "military-industrial complex" plotted Kennedy's assassination.

Stone used a slick blend of cinematic techniques to make this implausible thesis seem plausible. He moved from real footage to black-and-white reenactments so smoothly that even alert viewers find it hard to tell the difference. To young people raised in the celluloid age, Stone's scenario looks like real history.

When critics challenged Stone about his reckless disregard for historical truth, he admitted that *JFK* is "not a true story per se." But he told *Newsweek* that what filmmakers care about is not historical truth but cultural myth. In other words, who cares if the portrayal of Kennedy is inaccurate in the mundane, factual sense? It can still be true in what Stone calls "a mythic sense"; it can still convey "a larger issue."

For Stone, the larger issues have to do with politics. Stone is an aging 1960s radical, and he still sees everything through the ideological grid of the sixties. To him, the world is divided between young idealists and the "Establishment." Any story that conveys this basic worldview seems to fit Stone's definition of mythic truth, even if it fudges on the historical facts.

This is a strange, divided notion of truth, but it's nothing new. It's the same idea that has led to academic decay at our colleges. There, it goes by the name of deconstructionism, the belief that there is no objective interpretation of history. History means whatever the individual takes it to mean.

Stone admits that he was interested not in historical accuracy but in what Kennedy's death symbolized for him. In short, Stone deconstructed Kennedy. He used the medium of film to convey what the events meant in his private, subjective world.

Critics are right to worry that young viewers will absorb a false picture of what happened, but what is worse is the film's deeper message: that there is no objective truth, historical or otherwise—no objective reality.

If you want to help the young people in your church understand the concept of deconstructionism, you might consider giving them a cinematic example: Pop some corn and rent *JFK*. Then show them exactly how Stone went about creating his "mythic truth"—a truth based on historical lies.

Lord, your Word warns that false versions of history lead to tragically real consequences. May this knowledge strengthen my commitment to complete truthfulness in my own life and compel me to speak out against cultural lies.

NOVEMBER 23

THE RIGHT TO ROAM

TO READ: ISAIAH 32:9-20

My people will live in peaceful dwelling places, in secure homes, in undisturbed places of rest. Isaiah 32:18

In England, as in America, we often hear that "a man's home is his castle." No matter how humble or grand, your property is your own and no one may invade it. But a few years ago the British government announced plans to compel landowners to allow access to their private property under a "right to roam" declaration. Eighty percent of Britons supported the idea.

This declaration would affect primarily aristocrats who own large estates, and it seems clear that not many people are concerned about the property rights of wealthy dukes and earls. Hikers already have access to private property in the United Kingdom as long as they stay on marked trails, but now they want more.

You may be asking, "Why should we worry about it? Isn't this just a British problem?"

We should worry because what happens in Britain is often a bellwether for what happens here. Those on the left in any nation, including the U.S., are always stirring the pot of class warfare. The debate over private property really has far more to do with power politics than with the rights of hikers.

But wealthy aristocrats won't be the only ones upset with new "right to roam" laws because they're no longer the only ones with big estates. Will rock stars want strangers roaming their property? What about oil sheiks, who already spend millions keeping spectators away? And where does this "right to roam" stop? The castles on those estates are historic. Should ramblers have the right to rummage through them, too?

For that matter, is it really fair that so few people have so much? Why should Madonna, for instance, be allowed to own multiple mansions—including one in England—while so many people languish in public housing? Many countries have solved the "fairness" problem by dividing land and redistributing wealth, but you wouldn't want to live in any of those countries.

The sanctity of one's home and the principle of private property in general are rooted in Scripture. In Isaiah 32:18, God says, "My people will live in peaceful dwelling places, in secure homes, in undisturbed places of rest." That peacefulness won't last long if strangers are allowed to wander all over others' property, playing soccer and leaving trash behind.

Sea changes always occur incrementally. It starts with a small incursion on the rights of people no one else sympathizes with. Today it's their backyard, but someday it may be yours or mine.

We need to be vigilant about defending our homes and land, or one day the "right" of others to roam where they choose may eventually become the right to trespass—right across our own property.

Lord, I pray that envy will not lead me into thinking that those who are wealthy deserve to have their privacy and property violated while mine should be protected. Give me wisdom when it comes to proposals that could result in a loss of domestic peace and security for all of us.

NOVEMBER 24

LIVING THE BIBLICAL WORLDVIEW

TO READ: MICAH 6:6-8

He has showed you, O man, what is good. And what does the Lord require of you? To act justly and to love mercy and to walk humbly with your God. Micah 6:8

In the spring of 2002, then House Majority Whip Tom DeLay of Texas, speaking before a large audience, remarked, "Christianity offers the only viable, reasonable, definitive answer to the questions 'Where did I come from?' 'Why am I here?' 'Where am I going?' 'Does life have any meaningful purpose?' Only Christianity offers a way to understand that physical and moral border. Only Christianity offers a comprehensive worldview that covers all areas of life and thought, every aspect of creation."

DeLay spoke these words to three hundred evangelical Christians at the First Baptist Church of Pearland, Texas. Nevertheless, Rev. Barry Lynn, executive director of Americans United for Separation of Church and State, assailed him for daring to proclaim his personal beliefs—in a church setting no less. Lynn told the *Washington Post* that DeLay's remarks show that the congressman "lacks appreciation for the religious pluralism" of the United States and that "this is particularly disturbing because he, as a top-ranking member of Congress, represents people from the whole spectrum of religious faiths and nonbelievers, not just Christianity."

In reality it's Barry Lynn's position that is disturbing. If tolerance of all religions is the standard, where is Barry Lynn's tolerance for Tom DeLay's beliefs? Evidently not all religions are entitled to the same broad-mindedness.

In his book *Earth Restored: Calling the Church to a New Christian*

Activism, author and evangelist John Barber addresses the need for living a biblical worldview at a time when people are promoting the privatization of religion. "A biblical worldview is seeing the world as God sees it," Barber writes. "It is thinking God's thoughts after him in all areas of life. While many people think that God's Word applies only to areas like prayer, personal evangelism, and inward holiness, a biblical worldview assumes that the Bible also speaks to education, art, business, politics, technology, and more."

DeLay's speech may have been a problem for some because he not only speaks about the benefits of a biblical worldview, he also lives it. He refuses to separate his Christian faith from his role as a congressman. He speaks his mind, and he lives his faith.

If the debate over DeLay's speech tells us anything, it tells us that private religion isn't what frightens some people. It's the public face of Christianity that scares them. The message is "Stay in your churches, fast and pray, and we'll tolerate you. But if you dare to express your faith in the public square, you will pay."

In an age in which private life is increasingly separated from public life, Christians need all the more to model a biblical worldview. We must, as Barber puts it, constantly "think God's thoughts after Him in all areas of life."

Lord, your Word says that those who meditate on your law day and night are blessed. May I never be afraid to think or speak or act on your truth simply because others threaten to make my life miserable if I do. Give me the grace "to act justly and to love mercy and to walk humbly" with you in every area of my life.

WHEN ART BECOMES GOD

TO READ: PSALM 33:1-22

Sing joyfully to the Lord, you righteous; it is fitting for the upright to praise him.
Psalm 33:1

Beethoven's magnificent setting of the *Ode to Joy* appeals to people everywhere. One could argue that people love the symphony simply because of the lyrics that celebrate universal brotherhood and because of the beauty and emotion of the music.

But music professor Esteban Buch thinks there's more to it than that. In *Beethoven's Ninth: A Political History,* Buch writes that the "career of the *Ode to Joy* . . . can be read as a fable on the moral value of Western art. All who have invoked the *Ninth Symphony* have begun by experiencing its beauty and ended with the need for its morality; because they revered the Beautiful and because they believed that they knew the Good, they have made that Beautiful the symbol of the Good."

But as Buch notes, people have different ideas about what "good" means. Thus, "the communists hear in *[the Ninth Symphony]* the gospel of a classless world [while] Catholics hear the gospel itself. Hitler celebrated his birthdays with the *Ode to Joy,* and yet the same music was used to oppose him, even in concentration camps. . . . Lenin even said that Beethoven's music was dangerous because it made him want to be kinder to his fellow human beings!"

Humans need art to inspire and delight us, to train our imaginations, and even to point us toward God. But even the most inspiring art cannot take the place of faith.

Many of the nineteenth-century Romantics made the mistake of replacing belief in God with belief in art. Art was to be the new god that raised humanity to a new level. Unfortunately, the century that followed dashed their hopes: The art that was intended to make us all moral human beings could easily be used by evil men for their purposes. Instead of changing their hearts, it was twisted to promote their own perverted concepts of goodness.

The Romantic view of great works like Beethoven's *Ninth Symphony*, elevating faith in mankind above faith in God, ultimately leads to pessimism and despair. Beethoven biographer Maynard Solomon writes, "If we lose the 'dream' of the *Ninth Symphony*, we will have nothing left to balance against the crushing terrors of modern civilization." But that's true only if there is no god higher than Beethoven. Only when we see art with a proper perspective—as a reflection of the glory of God, not as a god in itself—can that art truly inspire and uplift us.

What is the role of music in *your* life? Does it lead you toward God—or away from him?

Lord, the words of the psalmist—that it is "fitting for the upright to praise [you]," reveal both that we should praise you and why we should: because you are our help and our shield. Let me never be found worshipping your beautiful creation rather than the divine Creator, in word, deed, or song.

WORSHIPPING GOD WITH OUR MINDS

TO READ: JOB 22:12-14

Is not God in the heights of heaven? Job 22:12

To paraphrase a popular ESPN show, these four things everyone knows are true: Before Columbus's first voyage, people thought the world was flat. When Copernicus said the earth revolved around the sun, his conclusions came out of nowhere. The "scientific revolution" of the seventeenth century invented science as we know it. And the false beliefs and impediments to science are Christianity's fault.

There's just one problem: All four statements are false.

Rodney Stark writes in *For the Glory of God: How Monotheism Led to Reformations, Science, Witch-Hunts, and the End of Slavery* that "every educated person" of Columbus's time, especially Christian clergy, "knew the earth was round." More than eight hundred years before Columbus's voyage, church historian the Venerable Bede taught this, as did Thomas Aquinas. The most popular medieval text on astronomy was *The Sphere*—not a title you would choose for a book that claimed the earth was flat.

As for Copernicus's sudden flash of insight, Stark quotes historian I. Bernard Cohen, who called that idea "an invention of later historians." Copernicus "was taught the essential fundamentals leading to his model by his Scholastic professors"—that is, Christian scholars. That model was "developed gradually by a succession of . . . Scholastic scientists over the previous two centuries." Building upon their work on orbital mechanics, Copernicus added the "implicit next step."

Thus, the idea that science was invented in the seventeenth century, "when a weakened Christianity could no longer prevent it," is false. Long before Isaac Newton, clergy like John of Sacrobosco, author of *The Sphere*, were doing what can only be called science. The Christian scholastics, not Enlightenment thinkers, invented modern science.

Three hundred years before Newton, a cleric named Jean Buridan anticipated Newton's First Law of Motion, which states that a body in motion will stay in motion unless otherwise impeded. It was Buridan, not an Enlightenment luminary, who first proposed that the earth turns on its axis.

In Stark's words, "Christian theology was necessary for the rise of science." Science happened only in areas where Christianity shaped the worldview, that is, Europe. Many civilizations had alchemy and astrology; only Europe developed chemistry and astronomy. That's because Christianity depicted God as a "rational" being who created a universe with a "rational, lawful, stable" structure. These unique beliefs led to "faith in the possibility of science."

So where did all those myths come from? Stark explains that "the claim of an inevitable and bitter warfare between religion and science has, for more than three centuries, been the primary polemical device used in the atheist attack of faith." Christianity's opponents have used bogus accounts to discredit Christians and to position themselves as "liberators" of the human mind.

Stark's book is a reminder of how far the best-educated enemies of Christ will go in order to discredit his followers.

Lord, we sometimes forget your command to worship you with our minds. Help me to educate myself so that I am as convinced in my mind as I am in my heart of what is true. Then may my life and words, like those of your followers in centuries past, provide a convincing witness to the presence of the "God in the heights of heaven."

THE ANTIDOTE FOR "DISEASED PHILOSOPHIES"

TO READ: 1 PETER 3:13-22

Always be prepared to give an answer to everyone who asks you to give the reason for the hope that you have. 1 Peter 3:15

In *The Dumb Ox*, G. K. Chesterton's biography of St. Thomas Aquinas, Chesterton compared Aquinas to that other thirteenth-century spiritual giant St. Francis of Assisi. These saints enjoyed unexpected popularity during Chesterton's lifetime: Francis during the materialistic last decades of the nineteenth century and Aquinas two decades later.

These revivals prompted Chesterton to write that "each generation seeks its saint by instinct; and he is not what the people want, but rather what the people need."

Chesterton would never have called himself a saint. Yet like Francis and Thomas, he, too, has come to be regarded as what his and our generation needed: an antidote for the nonsense of the age.

Chesterton's opponents held him in such high esteem that after his death one of them, George Bernard Shaw, said that the world wasn't thankful enough for him. That kind of respect, Dale Ahlquist writes in *G. K. Chesterton: The Apostle of Common Sense*, comes from Chesterton's writing something about everything—and saying it in an intuitive, incisive, and often funny manner.

Few people have ever diagnosed the lies and foolishness that beset the modern world the way Chesterton did. Ahlquist writes that "Chesterton argued eloquently against materialism and scientific determinism, against relativism, agnosticism and atheism, and other diseased philosophies that have infected the halls of academia for more than a century."

These same "diseased philosophies" infect us today. The difference is, they've found their way out of the halls of academia and into everyday life. And that's why Chesterton is more relevant today than he was in his own lifetime.

There were those in his time who, as in ours, extolled technological, political, and economic progress. Chesterton replied that progress cannot be a goal or an ideal. The word *progress* is simply a comparative term that tells us nothing about what we should be considering superlative. For that, he said, we need a "definite creed and a cast-iron set of morals."

Regarding the contemporary fascination with paganism, Chesterton reminds us that paganism as it was actually practiced was very different from the way we romanticize it now and inferior to what replaced it: Christianity. The truth is that neither Chesterton's contemporaries nor ours would really want to live in a pagan world.

Every Christian interested in making the case for the Christian faith to his neighbors needs to get acquainted with the "Apostle of Common Sense." In Chesterton, you'll find the only sure antidote for the infection plaguing our culture: a reasoned defense of Christian truth.

Lord, let me be obedient to your Word—in always having an answer for everyone for the hope that I enjoy. May I explain my belief in such a way that my diverse and needy neighbors can understand it, defending your truth with gentleness, respect—and humor.

NOVEMBER 28

TWISTING REALITY

TO READ: PSALM 146:1-10

I will praise the Lord all my life; I will sing praise to my God as long as I live.
Psalm 146:2

The Heritage Foundation recently published a study showing a link between the sexual activity of teens and their mental health—and the news isn't good. In sexually active girls ages fourteen to seventeen, the rates of depression (which the study's authors define as "unhappiness," not clinical depression) are more than three times higher than for those who have not been sexually active. Sexually active boys "are more than twice as likely to be depressed as are those who are not sexually active." And both boys and girls who have been sexually active are more likely to commit suicide.

Robert Rector, coauthor of the study, is quick to point out that the study, which was based on the National Longitudinal Survey of Adolescent Health, does not show conclusive evidence of a "causal link" between sexual activity and depression. Such a cause-and-effect relationship, he says, would be "impossible to prove."

Some people are skeptical about the study as a whole. Tamara Kreinin of the Sexuality Information and Education Council of the United States (or SIECUS), which promotes "safer sex" education, thinks it's important to focus on other factors as well when studying teenage depression—factors like family problems and abuse.

Kreinin may be right. But the study's authors did control for certain "social background factors," like "gender, race, age, and family income." Moreover, nearly two-thirds of the sexually active teenagers surveyed expressed regrets about having sex too early. This suggests that "early sexual activity leads to emotional stress and reduces teen

663

happiness." Regardless of whether unhappiness causes early sexual activity or the other way around, they say, "teens should be told that sexual activity in teen years is clearly linked to reduced personal happiness."

Unfortunately, nothing will deter some people from selling the "safer sex" message to young people. Organizations like SIECUS and Planned Parenthood insist that there is no way to stop teens from having sex and that the best we can do is teach them to use condoms.

The fundamental problem with that perspective is one of worldview: Do we believe that a loving Creator designed us to glorify him and enjoy his gifts or that we are merely biological accidents with no transcendent moral law? If "human sexual relationships are predominantly emotional and moral rather than physical in character," as Rector and his team put it, we will teach young people to treat themselves and each other with respect. But if we ignore the emotional and moral aspects and tell them to treat sex simply as recreation, we create a generation with no self-worth, and we ought to expect the unhappiness, depression, and even suicide that follow.

Are you ever tempted to twist reality to suit your own desires? If so, be warned: for adults and teens alike, the consequences are serious—even deadly. But when we live as God intended, we find that our obedience doesn't subtract from our total happiness—it adds to it.

Father, thank you for evidence that confirms your truth: We should not put our trust in the "wisdom" of mortal men—especially the promoters of sexual wantonness.

DISCERNING CULTURAL TRENDS

TO READ: COLOSSIANS 1:6-14

We have not stopped praying for you and asking God to fill you with the knowledge of his will through all spiritual wisdom and understanding. Colossians 1:9

C. S. Lewis was born on this day in 1898, and forty plus years after his death it is startlingly clear that he was not only a keen apologist but also a true prophet for our postmodern age.

Lewis wrote his book *Miracles* in 1947, before most Christians were aware of the emerging philosophy of naturalism, which says that there is a naturalistic explanation for everything in the universe.

Naturalism undercuts any objective morality, opening a door to tyranny. In *The Abolition of Man*, Lewis warned that naturalism turns human beings into objects to be controlled and turns values into "mere natural phenomena" that can be selected and inculcated into a passive population by powerful Conditioners. He predicted a time when those who want to remold human nature "will be armed with the powers of an omnicompetent state and an irresistible scientific technique."

Why was Lewis so uncannily prophetic?

One reason is that Lewis was a professor with a specialty in medieval literature. This gave him a mental framework shaped by the whole scope of intellectual history and Christian thought. This framework liberated him from the narrow confines of the worldview of his own age, which meant that he was able to analyze and critique it.

Lewis once wrote than any new book "has to be tested against the great body of Christian thought down the ages." Because he was steeped in that body of Christian thought, he quickly discerned trends that ran counter to it.

How many of us are familiar with that same panorama of Christian ideas "down the ages"? How many of us know the work of more than a few contemporary writers? How will we stand against the destructive intellectual trends multiplying in our own day?

The problem is not that modern evangelicals are less intelligent than Lewis. According to Mark Noll, author of *The Scandal of the Evangelical Mind*, the problem is that our sharpest intellects have been channeled into biblical scholarship, exegesis, and hermeneutics. While this is a vital enterprise, we rarely give the same scholarly attention to history, literature, politics, philosophy, economics, or the arts. As a result, we are less aware of the culture than we should be, less equipped to critique it, less capable of being a redemptive force in our postmodern society.

We Christians need to liberate ourselves from the prison of our own narrow worldview and immerse ourselves in Christian ideas "down the ages." The best way to celebrate Lewis's birthday is to be at our posts, as he liked to say, with renewed spirits and with probing and informed minds.

Father, give me a desire for the knowledge of your will and your wisdom. May I fully use the mind you have given me, bearing intellectual fruit that will bring others out of the dominion of darkness and into the light of your truth.

FILMS OF FAITH

TO READ: LUKE 3:1-14

Produce fruit in keeping with repentance. Luke 3:8

When Italian filmmaker Franco Zeffirelli adapted Charlotte Brontë's classic gothic novel *Jane Eyre* in 1996, it opened to rave reviews across the United States. *Jane Eyre* is a remarkable film that might never have been made but for a near-tragic automobile accident that forever changed the celebrated director's life.

For more than fifty years Zeffirelli has enjoyed one of the most extraordinary artistic careers. He has made his mark both on the opera stage and behind the camera. And despite the scorn of his detractors, he has done so without compromising—or hiding—his Christian principles.

Much of Zeffirelli's early work anticipated Hollywood's "great books" craze. His first film was an adaptation of Shakespeare's *The Taming of the Shrew*. Next came *Romeo and Juliet,* which won two Academy Awards in 1968.

Zeffirelli's brilliant career almost came to a tragic end on an Italian highway in 1971. While driving to a soccer game with actress Gina Lollobrigida, Zeffirelli lost control of his Rolls Royce. He miraculously survived the accident, and believing that God had spared his life, he recommitted himself to his childhood faith.

Zeffirelli's work immediately began to reflect the effects of his conversion. His first postconversion film was *Brother Sun, Sister Moon,* the story of St. Francis of Assisi. Critics dismissed the film, but it was tremendously popular with audiences worldwide.

Five years later Zeffirelli made the television miniseries *Jesus of*

Nazareth. Unlike other contemporary portrayals, *Jesus of Nazareth* presents the same Jesus that every Christian knows from the pages of Scripture: He heals the sick, feeds the hungry, and in the ultimate miracle of all, is shown being raised from the dead.

Zeffirelli's Christianity has led him to take positions on artistic and social issues that alienate him from the artistic establishment. He is an outspoken opponent of abortion and sexual license, especially in art. He decries the nihilism that passes for sophistication. According to Zeffirelli, our culture has convinced itself that "art has to make you feel guilty. You must suffer or else it is not art." This "annihilates the real purpose of art, which is expanding freedom, imagination, creativity—not mental constipation."

Zeffirelli's contention that art is about being made in the image of God, not about fashionable nihilism, has earned him the scorn of the Italian cultural establishment. While *Jane Eyre* was receiving high praise in North America and Britain, Zeffirelli's fellow Italians awarded the film only grudging approval.

The distinct and dramatic difference between Zeffirelli's pre- and postconversion work is a reminder that no matter what field we labor in, our faith should make a difference in how we view and perform our work.

And when it comes to films, we ought to support those that reflect what is good and noble and inspiring to us all.

Lord, thank you for the witness of changed lives—lives that bear the fruit of repentance. I pray that those who observe my own life's drama will see a similar witness, one that excites a curiosity about the God I worship through my work.

TELL THE STORY
OF THE GLORY

TO READ: LUKE 2:1-7

She gave birth to her firstborn, a son. She wrapped him in cloths and placed him in a manger, because there was no room for them in the inn. Luke 2:7

The Christmas carols begin every year about mid-November, and by December 25 all you want for Christmas is a good pair of earplugs. You hear them at the shopping mall. You hear them in elevators. You hear them when you're put on hold while ordering duck decoys for Uncle Herb.

The result is that even our most beloved holiday hymns have lost their power to move us because of the sheer, endless repetition. They have become the musical equivalent of plastic reindeer. Besides, it's hard to capture the mystery of Christmas when everyone from Miss Piggy to Alvin and the Chipmunks is warbling these familiar tunes.

This Christmas, why not consider spending some time exploring unfamiliar holiday music—ancient carols that help us understand how Christians through the centuries have communicated the meaning of Christmas through song.

For example there's a three-hundred-year-old English carol called "Up! Good Christian Folk, and Listen." The song includes these lyrics:

> *Tell the story*
> *Of the Glory.*
> *God came down*
> *At Christmastide.*

In barely one minute this carol tells us almost everything we need to know about Christmas.

669

Then there's the fifteenth-century German carol "Lo! How a Rose E'er Blooming." This hymn covers most of the same theological and aesthetic ground as "Silent Night," and it emphasizes an essential part of God's nature—his faithfulness:

> *Isaiah 'twas foretold it,*
> *The Rose I have in mind;*
> *With Mary we behold it,*
> *The virgin mother kind.*

Through the prophets, God promised that a Savior would arise from the line of Jesse. In the fullness of time, as the apostle Paul put it, God kept his promise.

Reflecting on the meaning of the Incarnation should be the goal of every Christian in the days leading up to Christmas. The church has traditionally used this season to recall Jesus' first coming and to meditate on his second coming. Music is a rich part of this tradition, which is why exploring faith as expressed through song is a wonderful way to begin meditating on the real meaning of Christmas.

So when the commercialized, overworked sound of Miss Piggy attacking Christmas carols makes you want to say, "Bah! Humbug," try sampling some of the music that has brought Christians closer to God for hundreds of years—music that "tells the story of the Glory."

Father, help me to locate and listen to music that moves me to meditate deeply on your glorious gift to humanity—the gift of your Son, the Savior of the world.

VULGARIANS AT THE GATE

TO READ: EPHESIANS 5:1-12

You were once darkness, but now you are light in the Lord. Ephesians 5:8

Turn on your television set any night of the week, and you'll see entertainment that would have delighted the most bloodthirsty citizen of ancient Rome.

One reality-based program featured a 9-1-1 call made by hysterical children whose father had just shot their mother—five times. Another showed a screaming woman being mauled by a polar bear at a zoo.

Welcome to the world of "shockumentary" television, a new—and popular—breed of programming that turns real-life tragedy into entertainment.

But Christians ought to hit the mute button long enough to ask themselves what impact these shockumentaries are having on us.

The early church faced something very similar: They took a strong stand against the bloody gladiatorial games. In the second century, Bishop Tertullian criticized Christians who enjoyed these spectacles, and warned that their own degradation would result from nourishing a "passion for murderous pleasure."

A story from Augustine's *Confessions* helps us understand why. Augustine had a friend named Alypius, who was disgusted by the brutality of the gladiatorial games. He vowed to avoid them. But one day Alypius met some friends who persuaded him to join them at the arena.

Augustine writes that the arena "was seething with the lust for cruelty. Alypius shut his eyes tightly, determined to have nothing to do with these atrocities. If only he had shut his ears as well! For an incident in the fight drew a great roar from the crowd."

Alypius could not contain his curiosity. He opened his eyes, and, Augustine says, "his soul was stabbed with a wound more deadly than any which the gladiator had received in his body." Alypius reveled in the gore, drunk with bloodlust. He was hooked, and would return to the arena again and again.

The Roman playwright Seneca warned that when we make sport of maiming and killing human beings, we render ourselves less humane. We destroy the respectful kindness, the *humanitas,* characteristic of the virtuous person.

Modern research bears him out. Criminologist James Q. Wilson describes studies that link violent television with real-life copycat crimes. Clearly, programs that turn human suffering into entertainment coarsen us, making us less sensitive to the pain of others. They destroy our humanitas—our compassion toward those for whom Christ died.

Father, in this season when we remember that the Light of the world came among us, give us grace to walk in the light as he is in the light.

THE GOD OF
WOODEN PLOWS

TO READ: JOHN 13:1-15

He poured water into a basin and began to wash his disciples' feet. John 13:5

Back in Galilee in the second century, the Christian apologist Justin Martyr said that during his lifetime it was still common to see farmers using plows made by the carpenter Jesus of Nazareth.

Think about it: The second Person of the triune Godhead spent much of his earthly life working in a woodshop. By that act alone, God forever established the significance of *our* work in this world.

In *The Call*, theologian Os Guinness reminds us that even the humblest work is important if it is done for God. "How intriguing," Guinness writes, "to think of Jesus' plow rather than his Cross—to wonder what it was that made his plows and yokes last and stand out." Clearly, they must have been very well made if they were still in use in the second century.

Today, Christians typically exalt spiritual work above manual work. After all, what's making a plow compared with preaching to multitudes, feeding the five thousand, or raising someone from the dead? But the very fact that Jesus *did* make plows—and make them well—suggests that any work can be done to the glory of God. Any work can be a genuine calling.

A calling, Guinness writes, is anything we do "as a response to God's summons and service." When God calls us to some task—even if it's something the world sees as lowly—that task is invested with what Guinness calls "the splendor of the ordinary."

"Drudgery done for ourselves or for other human audiences will always be drudgery," he writes, but "drudgery done for God is lifted and changed."

Accepting drudgery is one of the ways we practice discipleship—learning to offer it up to God. "We look for the big things to do—[but] Jesus took a towel and washed the disciples' feet," Guinness writes. "We like to speak and act out of the rare moments of inspiration—[but] he requires our obedience in the routine, the unseen, and the thankless." We his followers must be willing to take on the humble and thankless tasks as well—and not become impatient with changing diapers, doing homework, or taking out the trash.

If you think that God is calling you to engage in menial work, just remember that for a season the One who turned water into wine and raised the dead to life . . . also made wooden plows.

Lord, today I offer my work up to you, to the praise of the glory of your grace.

THE NAKED BABY

TO READ: MATTHEW 2:1-12

On coming to the house, they saw the child with his mother Mary,
and they bowed down and worshiped him. Matthew 2:11

The 1996 Christmas stamp reproduces part of a 1712 painting by Italian artist Paolo de Matteis. The stamp features a blue-robed Madonna gazing down at the Christ child kicking his heels on her lap.

But while Luke tells us Mary dressed the baby in swaddling clothes, de Matteis didn't dress him at all—and that's what threw postal authorities into a tizzy.

As columnist Peter Rexford explained in the *Washington Times,* "Someone at the Postal Service thought the Christ child, [minus his] swaddling clothes, was too anatomically explicit." And so, Rexford writes, "with a few strokes of an airbrush," a postal service "artist transformed the child into an asexual being."

Fortunately, postal authorities reconsidered the matter and "came to their artistic senses," as Rexford put it. When the stamp was released, the baby's manhood, so to speak, had been restored.

The controversy is more than a modern tempest in a teapot. Since the time of the early church, artists have struggled to depict both the humanity and divinity of Jesus.

Medieval artists tended to focus on Christ's deity. In many a Byzantine church we see mosaics of a stern, majestic Christ coming in judgment. During the Victorian era, artists emphasized Christ's humanity through paintings of the "gentle Jesus."

But the greatest religious artists manage to portray both Christ's deity and his humanity—and that's what Paolo de Matteis does. The artist shows Jesus as a real, human child, squirming in his mother's arms. The artistic purpose of showing the baby naked was to empha-size his full humanity. The Madonna looks lovingly down on her in-fant, as mothers throughout the ages have always done. This is a moving, human scene.

And yet the scene also is charged with symbols of Christ's divinity. The baby's head is surrounded by a halo of light—a symbol of grace. The halo illuminates the face of his mother, symbolizing the fact that Mary herself is transformed through her Son's grace. The baby's ex-pression is exalted as he gazes not at his mother but heavenward. His tiny arms are outstretched in the position of the crucifixion. Mary is wrapping him in a cloth, an image that anticipates the pietà, when Mary would wrap the body of her crucified son for burial.

The message of the painting is clear: This baby is God in the flesh . . . a divine Child destined to one day die for our sins.

Lord, thank you that you were not ashamed to come among us as a man and to live and die for us, so that we might live for you.

PLEASE DON'T SEND ME

TO READ: ISAIAH 41:1-29

Do not fear, for I am with you. . . . I will strengthen you and help you. Isaiah 41:10

When she retired, Debbie Roeger prayed that God would show her how she could serve him. She had just one request: "Please God," she prayed, "don't send me into prisons." But that's exactly where God sent her. Debbie's story is an exciting one of how ordinary people can make an extraordinary difference in criminal justice.

Not long after praying her prayer, Debbie saw an ad for a Prison Fellowship conference on Restorative Justice. She didn't really want to go, but she felt God was calling her to attend. There, Debbie met Gary Sims, who was in charge of prison religious services in central Ohio, where Debbie lived. Gary told her about a pilot program at Ohio's Marion Correctional Institution in which forty-eight prisoners—Christian, Jew, and Muslim—were learning how to demonstrate respect and tolerance for one another.

Debbie had a sudden, clear sense God was calling her to Marion. Debbie has a master's degree in human resources and is a trained mediator. God wanted to use her background and experience in a new, unexpected way.

At Marion, the warden invited Debbie to develop a conflict-resolution program. And over the next eighteen months, Debbie trained twenty-four inmates to mediate disputes between their fellow inmates. She also worked with prison staff, teaching them how to mediate workplace disputes. Inmates now feel better equipped to handle conflicts and to use the skills informally in all sorts of situations.

Debbie was then asked to teach conflict resolution skills to the entire prison population. As Debbie notes, "It's tremendously powerful in what it can accomplish in terms of trust, self-esteem, and conflict resolution." One inmate commented, "I've never trusted anyone in my life, but this program taught me to trust."

And Debbie learned to trust too—to trust that God would give her the courage to accomplish his will wherever he sent her. "The first time I stepped into prison, there was no small amount of fear in my heart. God gave me Scripture from Isaiah 41: 'So do not fear, for I am with you; do not be dismayed, for I am your God. I will strengthen you and help you.'"

Today, Debbie says, "Some of the strongest prayer partners I have are men in prison. God has given me a family of brothers at Marion who love me as a Christian sister."

Lord, help me to remember that you love those in prison and have commanded us to remember them.

DECEMBER 6

THE POACHED-EGG PARADOX

TO READ: MATTHEW 16:13-20

"What about you?" [Jesus] asked. "Who do you say I am?"
Simon Peter answered, "You are the Christ." Matthew 16:15-16

C. S. Lewis famously said that anyone who believes Jesus was a great moral teacher but not the Son of God has a difficult choice: Jesus can't be a moral teacher if he lied about being the Son of God. So one either has to take him for who he said he is or dismiss him as a lunatic—on the level of a man who thinks he's a poached egg.

This witticism makes some people laugh. But not former journalist Lee Strobel. Is it possible, he wondered, that the man millions of Christians worship was actually out of his mind? For the answer, Strobel went to distinguished psychologist Gary Collins. Standing in Collins's office, Strobel pointed to a nearby mental hospital. Over there, he said, "I'm sure we'd find some people who claim that they're God. We'd say they were insane. Jesus said he was God—was he crazy too?"

"No," Collins laughingly replied.

But Strobel persisted. After all, he said, "people suffering from delusional psychosis may appear rational much of the time, yet can have grandiose beliefs" about who they are. Some attract followers who worship them. "Maybe," Strobel suggested, "that's what happened with Jesus."

Maybe, but it's unlikely, given the evidence.

When a psychologist attempts to determine a patient's mental health, Collins said, he doesn't just consider his words but also his emotions. Disturbed people frequently show inappropriate depression, anger, or anxiety. "But look at Jesus," Collins said. "He never

679

demonstrated inappropriate emotions. For instance, he cried at the death of his friend Lazarus—that's natural for an emotionally healthy" person.

But, Strobel countered, Jesus erupted in anger at times. Yes, Collins replied, "but it was a healthy kind of anger." It was directed against "people taking advantage of the downtrodden by lining their pockets at the temple. . . . This was a righteous reaction against injustice."

The Scriptures offer plenty of other evidence that Jesus was, psychologically speaking, perfectly normal. Disturbed people often cannot carry on logical conversations. But Jesus "spoke clearly, powerfully, and eloquently," Collins said.

Strobel then pulled out the trump card. Some of the people who actually knew Jesus concluded that he was raving mad, he said.

Sure they did, Collins replied, but these were not mental-health professionals making a diagnosis; they were religious leaders outraged by the claims Jesus made.

Collins is right. Two thousand years later, people are still outraged by Jesus' claims. But in the face of modern science, it's getting harder and harder for them to credibly claim that Jesus was mentally ill.

Oh Lord, you are the Christ—my Savior and my God! In this Christmas season, may I wholeheartedly worship you and rejoice in who you are.

FINDING FORGIVENESS
AT PEARL

TO READ: MATTHEW 5:38-48

Love your enemies and pray for those who persecute you. Matthew 5:44

Jacob DeShazer was on KP duty in California when he first heard of the attack on Pearl Harbor. Furious at what the Japanese had done, he resolved to retaliate personally. And in April 1942, he got his chance—as a B-25 bombardier when Doolittle's Raiders attacked Tokyo.

During that fateful run, DeShazer's plane ran out of fuel and the crew bailed out over enemy territory. DeShazer was captured and spent the next forty months as a POW. With plenty of time to think, Jake wondered: What makes people hate each other? Doesn't the Bible say something about loving our enemies?

He asked his jailers for a Bible and eventually got one. He read it with fascination. Ten days into his study, he asked Christ to forgive his sins. He remembers, "suddenly . . . when I looked at the enemy officers and guards, . . . I realized that . . . if Christ is not in a heart, it is natural to be cruel. . . . [My] bitter hatred . . . changed to loving pity." Remembering Christ's words from the cross in Luke 23:24, "Father, forgive them, for they do not know what they are doing," he asked God to forgive *his* torturers too.

Fourteen months later, in August 1945, paratroopers liberated DeShazer from his prison cell. After the war, a chaplain on General MacArthur's staff wanted something to help heal the animosity between the U.S. and Japan. He approached Don Falkenberg of Bible Literature International, who had read DeShazer's testimony shortly after his release. Soon the story was being circulated as a booklet called, "I Was a Prisoner of Japan."

And here's where the story outdramatizes Hollywood. Japanese Navy pilot Mitsuo Fuchida was chief commander of the historic December 7 raid on Pearl Harbor. He had advised against raiding the American base, but when given orders to proceed, Fuchida led the assault. Years later he was in Hiroshima the day before the atom bomb was dropped. His life was spared when headquarters summoned him to Tokyo.

When the war ended, Captain Fuchida returned to his farm near Osaka. Later, stepping off a train in Tokyo, he was given a copy of DeShazer's pamphlet that stimulated him to read the Bible. And despite his Shinto heritage, he accepted Christ as his Savior.

How marvelous are God's ways? An American airman is taken prisoner, is converted, and his testimony leads his captors' ace pilot to Christ.

The Japanese captain and the American sergeant later became friends and partners. Together and separately, over a thirty-year span, they saw tens of thousands of Japanese converted.

Father, thank you for your great love for me. Help me to grow in love, even for those who hate me.

MORE THAN PRETTY MUSIC

TO READ: ISAIAH 40:1-5

Every valley shall be raised up, every mountain and hill made low. Isaiah 40:4

What is the one piece of classical Christmas music known by even the most musically illiterate among us? Handel's *Messiah*. Performances of this sacred oratorio fill concert halls even today, 250 years after it was composed.

When *Messiah* premiered in Dublin in 1742, the demand for tickets was so great that the newspapers made an unusual request. Editors asked that ladies who planned to attend refrain from wearing hoop skirts and that gentlemen leave their swords at home. This would free up more space and allow more people to be seated.

Handel was inspired to write *Messiah* by Charles Jennings, an aristocrat who wrote the words for many of his oratorios. Jennings gave Handel what he described as "a Scripture collection," whose subject "excels every other subject. That subject is 'Messiah.'"

Jennings's lyrics, or libretto, as musicians call them, consist of fifty-three Scripture verses, most of them from the Old Testament. The passages tell the story of Christ: his birth, his life and passion, and his second coming.

As British music scholar Nicholas Kenyon notes, Jennings's libretto "sets out the central truths of Christian faith with a concision and balance never equaled before or since."

Of course, none of this would matter without Handel's music. For twenty-four days Handel locked himself in his room, refusing food and company, and feverishly worked on *Messiah* around the clock.

The result was some of the greatest and most beloved music of all time. But *Messiah*'s greatness lies not merely in the beauty of the music. Its greatness also lies in the way the music illuminates the text. An example is the tenor aria called "Every Valley." If you have a copy of Handel's *Messiah*, listen to the way Handel draws a musical picture of a verse from Isaiah. Notice the emphasis on the word *exalted* and the way *crooked* wanders, in contrast to the single note of *plain*.

For another example, listen to the awe and dread in the alto's voice as she sings Malachi's question: "But who shall abide the day of his coming?"

Chances are, there will be a performance of *Messiah* in your own community this Christmastide. Why not invite an unsaved friend to take in a performance? The combination of words and music creates a wonderful opening to share the gospel with your friends.

In modern-day America, as in Dublin 250 years ago, the performance of Handel's *Messiah* is likely to be crowded, so please . . . leave your hoop skirts and swords at home.

Father, thank you for the glorious music of this season and for coming to us in this valley of the shadow of death so that we may dwell on the heights with you.

RATIONAL ROMANCE

TO READ: PROVERBS 7:1-27

With persuasive words she led him astray; she seduced him with her smooth talk.
Proverbs 7:21

Fifteen-year-old Kevin was watching the classic film *The Godfather.* Halfway through the film Kevin asked a question that reminds us that the only rational view of romance is the Christian one.

In the film, the godfather's son, Michael, falls in love with a beautiful Sicilian girl. We see the courting couple walk off together. But they're not alone. A few steps behind are a dozen of the girl's female relatives.

Kevin asked, "Why are all those women following them?" His father laughed and replied, "They want to make sure nothing inappropriate happens." And he added teasingly, "That will be *you* in a few years, Kevin!"

If only it were so. In a society like ours, it's hard to guard our children because everywhere kids look, they see the celebration of out-of-wedlock sex. On television and in movies, premarital sex is depicted as normal and usually consequence-free, even though in real life there are often severe consequences.

In the midst of the cultural sewage, how can we teach our kids how to have pure relationships, build strong marriages, and avoid divorce? In his book, *Marriage Savers,* Mike McManus says the church needs to take an active role in helping teenagers understand the practical benefits of chastity.

The church's first message to dating couples ought to be strong and clear: If you want a good marriage, don't have premarital sex. The National Survey of Family Growth found that women who lost their virginity prior to marriage had higher divorce rates—in one study, 71 percent higher.

It's convincing evidence that those who follow biblical sexual ethics are building a happier, more secure future for themselves and their future spouses and families.

The reason is simple: Dating couples who abstain from sex are more likely to build spiritual, emotional, and intellectual companionship. Plus, they're building the self-restraint crucial to being successful spouses later on. After all, sexual temptation doesn't disappear once you're married.

To reinforce the abstinence message, we ought to let our kids in on a little secret: One survey indicates that faithful married couples have better sex lives than anyone else.

These days, most of us can't send a pack of relatives along to keep an eye on the kids when they date. But we *can* communicate the truth about abstinence and involve our churches in programs like Marriage Savers that teach young people the facts.

If we want to help our kids stay chaste and build stronger marriages, this is an offer we can't refuse.

Protect our children, Lord, and help us to find ways to teach them the dangers of sex outside of marriage and the delights that result when they reserve sex for marriage alone.

MORE THAN DUCT TAPE

TO READ: ROMANS 12:1-8

Do not conform any longer to the pattern of this world, but be transformed by the renewing of your mind. Romans 12:2

The woman stood in a Grand Rapids, Michigan, courtroom awaiting sentencing for murdering her husband. Her grief-stricken son struggled to find the words to express his feelings: "Delete. Delete. . . . Consider yourself deleted from our lives."

His use of computer language was not only sad and oddly humorous; it was also an example of how technology shapes the way we think and live.

Most Christians regard a technology's morality as a function of its use. For example, using the Internet to download pornography or spread Nazi propaganda is evil. But absent immoral uses, the thinking goes, the Internet has no moral or spiritual impact.

Quentin Schultze, a professor of communication at Calvin College, begs to differ. In *Habits of the High-Tech Heart: Living Virtuously in the Information Age,* he writes, "Information technologies are not just tools but also value-laden techniques." We not only use them to help us organize our lives, but we also increasingly "rely on them to understand nearly every aspect of our lives."

Stated another way, these technologies and the culture that springs from their use answer the question, "How now shall we live?" And, Schultze says, if we are not careful, technology's answers will become ours.

If this sounds alarmist, consider what one industry executive told Schultze: The goal is for technology not only to change *how* we do things, such as writing and editing, but actually to change the *kinds* of things we do.

Avoiding this worldview trap begins with understanding what Schultze calls "cyberculture," the "values, practices, and beliefs of people who spend a lot of time online."

For example, cyberculture places a premium on efficiency and control. That's okay for a data retrieval system. The problem comes when people apply that reasoning to their own lives and "assume that doing things quickly and effectively is more important than doing them carefully, thoughtfully, and ethically."

Another troubling aspect is what Schultze calls cyberculture's "libertinism." This refers to the online world's "strident individualism" and lack of respect for any moral order. On the Internet, Schultze says, "the individual alone [is] the only arbiter of truth and justice."

The most obvious example of this libertinism is Internet pornography. Attempts to restrict or regulate even the most explicit material are categorically rejected as infringing on the rights of the individual.

Schultze does not advocate giving up information technologies. He says, instead, that we must make a self-conscious effort to cultivate Christian ideas about virtue and community. Only then can we avoid the cyberculture trap.

Transform our thinking, Lord, that we may see the world as you do, and live in it by your grace and truth.

THE WORD AT CHRISTMAS

TO READ: JOHN 1:1-14

The Word became flesh and made his dwelling among us. John 1:14

Hundreds of sermons will be preached during Christmas on "the Word became flesh" at Bethlehem. The "Word" is Jesus Christ, the Son of God, who came to earth to bring salvation.

But why do the Scriptures use the term *the Word* to refer to Jesus? And what prompted the apostle John to use it to identify Jesus as Lord and Creator, and the only begotten Son of God?

The people of Jesus' day would have been familiar with this use of *the Word.* Prophets from Elijah to Malachi were recognized as bearers of the divine message of truth. They proclaimed the word of God to the people. That word was authoritative; it came from God himself, and thus it demanded a response.

By the time John wrote his Gospel, the term had taken on philosophical meaning as well. For the Greeks, *word,* or *logos,* referred to a spiritual reality that was all pervasive. This Greek word *logos* is the root of words like *logic, logarithm, prologue, eulogy,* and many more and is related to the first principles of the universe.

But while Greek philosophers thought of the logos as an impersonal force, they nevertheless believed it possessed dynamic power. The word made sense of everything in the cosmos.

When John referred to Christ as "the Word" in John 1:1, he combined these concepts. The *logos* is the authoritative utterance of God, and it's also an all-pervasive spiritual reality—and, therefore, the truth. John brings the Hebrew and Greek ideas together in one person: the child born in Bethlehem.

John says, "In the beginning was the Word, and the Word was with God." Nothing about that phrase would have seemed unusual to the people of that day. But the apostle goes further when he says, "The Word became flesh and made his dwelling among us." And, he says, "we have seen his glory, the glory of the One and Only, who came from the Father, full of grace and truth." Now, this was new!

Here was the personal God who walked in our midst. Then John records how Jesus proved he was the Word and power of God. He walked on water, healed the blind, stilled the storm, and rose from the dead.

This Christmas, help your family develop a new appreciation for who "the Word became flesh" really is: He's the Creator who existed before time. He's the Logos who made heaven and earth and who steers the stars in their courses. He is the Truth that is ultimate reality.

Help me to know you better this Christmas season, Lord, and to love you more completely.

WHAT'S IN A NAME?

TO READ: LUKE 1:26-38

You will be with child and give birth to a son, and you are to give him the name Jesus. Luke 1:31

For years, Richard John Neuhaus has tracked the trend in baby names. In *First Things,* he writes that if we go by names, it appears that parents take their sons more seriously than their daughters. Neuhaus found that parents tend to grace their boys with names with clear biblical or religious significance—names like Michael, Christopher, Jonathan, Daniel, and John. But parents give their daughters "cute, toy-like names—names of jewelry stores and soap stars." Among them are monikers like Tiffany, Brittany, Ashley, and Samantha. Few parents give their girls names that reflect character like Prudence or Constance, or biblical names like Ruth and Elizabeth, writes Neuhaus.

"As reflected by the names chosen, people obviously take boys more seriously than girls," Neuhaus writes, and he adds: "Maybe it's not among the top ten problems in American society, but I can't squelch the suspicion that it's not unimportant."

According to the experts, Neuhaus is right. Susan Seligson writes in *Redbook* that "an increasing amount of research suggests that our names and our destinies may be inexorably intertwined." Often, Seligson says, the prophecy in a name becomes uncannily self-fulfilling. For example, one study showed that girls with exceedingly feminine names like Lucy and Rose "did in fact have more girlish personalities." And although it's hard to prove, she says, "our personalities may also evolve to fulfill the subtle mandates our names carry."

Amy and Leon Kass, professors at the University of Chicago, write in *First Things* that the naming of children is an expression of the parents' best hopes and dreams. Parents may memorialize a worthy ancestor, historical figure, or biblical character, hoping certain qualities associated with that person will rub off on the child.

In Scripture a person's name was often intimately linked with what God planned to do with his or her life. For example, at the command of the archangel Gabriel, our Lord was named Jesus, which means "God will save us."

According to the Kasses, the act of naming imparts a blessing to the child whereby parents "dedicate themselves to the work of making good the promise conveyed in the good name thus bestowed."

This means that Christians should name their children with care. If we desire to raise a godly seed, as the Puritans put it, we need every resource available to us, including names that point to the kind of character we seek to instill in our children.

Of course, what we name our children is not nearly as important as how we rear them. We should teach them how to make good names for themselves, whatever their given names may be.

Most important of all, we must teach our Michaels and Jonathans, and our Tiffanys and Ashleys, how to identify their own names with the name above all names—Jesus Christ.

Father, help me to always live up to the Name I claim to worship: that of Your precious Son.

RECYCLED MUSIC

TO READ: PSALM 108:1-5

I will praise you, O Lord, among the nations; I will sing of you among the peoples.
Psalm 108:3

For much of his life, Johann Sebastian Bach was in charge of music at St. Thomas Church in Leipzig, Germany. But Bach had many other responsibilities as well—including raising twenty children—which may explain why he developed a few shortcuts when he wrote his *Christmas Oratorio:* He often recycled old material into new musical pieces—just as the writer of Psalm 108 did.

Of course, this did not render the great master any less creative. True creativity does not require us to work from scratch, to create complete novelty. Instead, creativity consists in taking what God has given us and cultivating and developing it to its highest form.

In composing the *Christmas Oratorio,* Bach recycled virtually every solo from sacred music he had composed earlier. Other parts, such as choruses and instrumentals, were mixtures of new and old.

But some sections were completely original, such as the opening chorus. If you own a copy of Bach's oratorio, listen as the choir, representing the angels, urges us to "Rejoice! Exult and Praise what the All Highest has done today!"

Later in the oratorio, Bach invites us to contemplate the paradox of the Incarnation: that the King of heaven saw fit to become a tiny baby born in a stable. We hear a powerful bass marveling that "the Great Lord and mighty King . . . who maintains the whole world, must sleep in a hard manger."

Today, Bach's notion of creativity has largely been lost. Contemporary artists are children of the Romantics of the nineteenth century, who focused on the self as the creator, the artist who spins out something completely novel and unique. As a result, most artists today equate creativity with novelty—even subversiveness.

But Bach's music stands as a powerful reproach to that notion. He used creativity to enhance traditional Christian belief, incorporating scriptural texts and basing his musical forms on Lutheran hymns or the church's classic liturgy.

Bach signed all his work "SDG," shorthand for *soli Deo gloria*—"to God alone the glory." Bach knew that God is the one who inspires true creativity and that he works through the efforts of the composer. This is a lesson that all of us need to take to heart in our own work.

So this Christmas let Bach remind you that all of our work should be done to the glory of God. Then our lives will likewise be illuminated with the beauty of true creativity.

Fill me with your Spirit, Lord, and lead me in songs of praise, joy, and thanksgiving for all you have done for me.

DANGEROUS GUESTS

TO READ: ESTHER 4:4-16

"I will go to the king, even though it is against the law. And if I perish, I perish."
Esther 4:16

The late Philip Hallie was a Jewish professor of ethics who spent years researching a depressing topic: human cruelty. He found himself exhausted and demoralized by the many stories of Nazi atrocities. Then one day he came across a story about the small French village of Le Chambon, whose inhabitants saved thousands of Jewish people from the gas chambers. It was a tale of quiet courage that moved Hallie to tears—and inspires us even today with a vision of true heroism.

The story begins when twenty members of the local police arrived at Le Chambon to hunt down Jews who had gone into hiding. The Huguenot pastor, Andre Trocme, stepped up to the police captain and announced that the village would not hand over a single Jew.

It was an incredibly courageous thing to do. The Nazis had slaughtered entire villages for lesser offenses.

Over the next four years, the people of Le Chambon rescued several thousand Jews, including many children. As Dick Keyes writes in *True Heroism in a World of Celebrity Counterfeits,* "Although several of the villagers were arrested, and some lost their lives, there was no record of them betraying a single one of their dangerous guests during the entire occupation."

Thinking of the story later that night, Hallie again began to weep. He later wrote that his tears this time were "an expression of moral praise." He found the story healing and inspiring. As Keyes puts it, "A moral consciousness deep within him was responding to a story of excellence and was demanding to be recognized."

The villagers of Le Chambon deserve to be called heroes. What is a real hero? It is someone who gives us a vision of moral excellence.

In a cynical age like ours, many of us no longer have heroes. But without heroes, we're left with no clear vision of moral excellence. Without heroes we have no one to inspire us to rise up beyond our own mediocrity and our cynicism. We have no one to teach us how we ourselves can act heroically.

How do we teach children about decency, courage, and honor—about right and wrong? Give them stories, role models that reflect genuine moral excellence. Stories that move them to behave like the villagers of Chambon, with quiet nobility.

Lord, I thank you for the many stories of moral excellence you have provided for us. When I am tempted to moral cowardice, I pray you will bring to my mind stories that will inspire in me the courage to do the right thing—no matter what the consequences.

SECULAR SHORTFALLS

TO READ: 1 PETER 1:3-9

These [trials] have come so that your faith—of greater worth than gold, which perishes even though refined by fire—may be proved genuine and may result in praise, glory and honor when Jesus Christ is revealed. 1 Peter 1:7

When tragedy strikes, does your belief system meet the challenge, or does it let you down? Christian psychologist Dr. Paul Vitz says that how Christians handle suffering can reveal the truth of Scripture—and expose the shortfalls of the secular worldview.

Vitz is the author of *Psychology as Religion: The Cult of Self-Worship.* In it he says that modern psychology is deeply committed to narcissism, egoism, and worship of the self—a phenomenon he calls "selfism." This commitment has turned psychology into religion—a form of secular humanism based on the rejection of God in favor of self-worship.

Selfist theories assume that self-gratification is the only ethical principle. The idea is to "actualize" ourselves through creativity and self-absorbed focus on our own needs and desires. But selfist philosophy falls apart when its followers begin to experience any kind of suffering.

Christianity acknowledges the reality of evil, with all of its attendant agony, heartbreak, and death. But Christians also believe that when we commit ourselves in obedience to Christ, suffering can actually bring us into a closer relationship with him. This view, Vitz says, is "at the very heart of Christianity, as represented by the passion of the cross followed by the joy of Easter."

By contrast, "selfist philosophy trivializes life by claiming that suffering" and death lack intrinsic meaning. Suffering is treated "as some sort of absurdity, usually a man-made mistake that could have been avoided by the use of knowledge to gain control of the environment," Vitz writes.

This view seems plausible enough when life is going well—but it becomes less convincing when people begin to suffer sickness, decline, or the loss of loved ones. After all, what do you say to the ambitious man who discovers, at age forty, that he's dying of cancer? What do you say to the couple whose only child was killed by a drunk driver?

Says Vitz, "Does one say, 'Go actualize yourself in creative activity'? For people in those circumstances, such advice is not just irrelevant, it is an insult."

For years, psychology as religion has wreaked havoc on our culture, with its fanatical focus on self-fulfillment. As our neighbors discover the shallowness of a life lived for personal glory, Christians must be ready to lovingly offer the true source of life filled with meaning.

And that begins by focusing, not on ourselves, but on the God who sent his only Son to suffer and die so that we might be forgiven and live in peace with him.

Thank you, Lord, that all our sufferings in this world are not in vain, but that by them we may draw closer to you.

HIDE AND SEEK

TO READ: JOHN 18:28-40

"What is truth?" Pilate asked. John 18:38

One day in a college classroom, students were discussing the medieval theologian Thomas Aquinas and his teachings about God. One student became noticeably agitated. Finally, he stood up and asked permission to leave.

Later he explained his strange behavior. "I'm not interested in finding truth," he confessed. "All I care about is what has immediate practical value for me."

The incident is a reminder that the truth can be scary; and truth about God is the scariest of all. Like the student who left class, some people actually prefer not to know the truth.

In his book *How to Stay Christian in College,* Jay Budziszewski says even on the college campus—a place historically committed to the search for truth—there's a lot of hiding from truth.

When Christians understand this, they can respond better when their faith is under attack. When Pilate asked, "What is truth?" do you think he really wanted an answer? No, not on your life! He didn't even wait for Jesus to respond. His question was a cynical dismissal intended to cut Jesus off.

Thinking Christians on campuses can influence students to seek truth. Budziszewski tells the story of a conversation between a Christian professor and a student named Tom, who was arguing that all morality is relative.

"How do we even know murder is wrong?" Tom asked defiantly. The professor saw the question as nothing but a smokescreen. The

Bible teaches that the moral law is written on every human heart. That means everyone really knows murder is wrong—whether we admit it or not. So the professor pushed Tom by asking, "Are you in real doubt about whether murder is wrong?"

Tom was evasive: "Many people might say it's all right."

"But I'm not asking other people," the professor pressed on. "Are you at this moment in any real doubt about murder being wrong?"

There was a long silence. "No," Tom finally admitted. "No, I'm not."

"Good," the professor said. "Then we don't have to waste time asking whether morality is relative. Let's talk about something you really are in doubt about."

Tom at that moment realized his smokescreen had been blown away, and he agreed to discuss his real questions about morality and religion. It was a turning point in the conversation—and perhaps in Tom's life as well.

Many of the ideologies Christian students encounter in college are smokescreens, set up not to find truth but to hide from anything that threatens people's comfort zones—and Christians must learn to tell the difference.

Lord, so many young people have closed their hearts to you. Prepare me now— through reading and thinking, conversation and prayer—to witness to them through the avenue of their minds, that they may eventually understand and accept your truth.

DECEMBER 17

MAKIN' A LIST,
CHECKIN' IT TWICE

TO READ: PROVERBS 22:3-6

Train a child in the way he should go, and when he is old he will not turn from it.
Proverbs 22:6

Is the child on your Christmas list asking for a video game this year? If so, be careful: The game he wants just might be a "murder trainer."

This is no exaggeration, says Lt. Col. Dave Grossman, a former West Point psychology professor and Army Ranger who now teaches at Arkansas State University.

In his research in "killology," the study of killing in combat, Grossman has found that the vast majority of soldiers, even in "kill or be killed" situations, are very reluctant to shoot. But kids today, he warns, are learning just the opposite: that killing is okay and that a well-aimed bullet solves problems.

During warfare, Grossman says, only about 15 percent of soldiers actually do any killing. And most of these feel revulsion when they do it. The other 85 percent either refuse to fire or deliberately miss the target.

In recent years, the military has devised techniques to raise the firing rate to 90 percent, using techniques based on the behavioral psychology of Pavlov and B. F. Skinner.

Pavlov, you may recall, taught dogs to salivate when they heard a bell ring. Combat training uses the same kind of conditioned response to make soldiers stop thinking with the forebrain and react with the midbrain: the reflexive, animal-like portion of the brain. In other words, they're conditioned to respond to a moving target with a "don't think, just shoot" reaction.

How does that work? Grossman explains: "The soldier stands in a foxhole with full combat equipment, and man-shaped targets pop up briefly in front of him. These ... eliciting stimuli ... prompt the target behavior of shooting. If the target is hit, it immediately drops, thus providing immediate feedback."

Disturbingly, many video games use the same techniques, but without the controlling restraints of the military environment. Soldiers only shoot and kill on orders, and firing without orders brings serious punishment.

But what happens when kids play violent video games? They learn the same hair-trigger behaviors and an us-versus-them attitude, but without the context of obedience to a command.

One expert calls violent video games "murder trainers." Grossman agrees, saying that violent media are not just conditioning people to be violent but are also developing hand-eye coordination of the trigger finger—teaching the very mechanics of killing.

So when you shop for that special child this Christmas, check his list twice. Know which games are actually dangerous devices no child should have. And make sure the children in your life know why they can't have these games: It's because they teach kids to kill.

Lord, give parents and grandparents wisdom and sound judgment as they shop for children this Christmas season.

SAVING CHILDHOOD

TO READ: MATTHEW 18:1-6

If anyone causes one of these little ones who believe in me to sin, it would be better for him to have a large millstone hung around his neck and to be drowned in the depths of the sea. Matthew 18:6

A class of first-graders is having a discussion, and what are they talking about? The letters of the alphabet? The sounds animals make? No, nothing so innocent. These six-year-olds are discussing sex-change operations.

It seems the mother of one of the little tykes doesn't want to be a mommy anymore; she wants to be a daddy. And the teacher has decided that the upcoming operation is just the topic for circle time.

The incident is one of many examples cited in a book by talk-show host Michael Medved and his wife, Diane, a clinical psychologist. It's called *Saving Childhood,* and it traces the ways our culture seems bent on destroying childhood innocence.

What is it about contemporary theories of education that would allow adults to seriously think sex-change operations would be an appropriate topic for six-year-olds?

The answer is that "the very idea of parental protectiveness" has been shot down, say the Medveds. It's been "overwhelmed by relentless pressure from a society that seems determined to expose its young to every perversion and peril." The supposedly enlightened view is that the kids are going to face these issues eventually, so why not prepare them?

But that logic is flawed. Imagine telling a four-year-old about schizophrenia or torture or serial killings. Sure, they're going to face a world where such horrors occur, but exposing them before they're capable of processing what these things mean is not helpful— in fact, it's actually harmful to their emotional development. It overwhelms them with a sense that the world is a dangerous, uncontrollable place.

What kids really need, the Medveds write, is just the opposite: a strong sense of security. In those early years, their own bodies and minds are developing so rapidly that they crave "anything that anchors them, that offers them comfort and stability to undergird their development."

In other words, the best way to prepare children to face the adult world is to let them be children—to give them a safe and secure environment to grow up at their own pace.

Today parents need to be especially diligent in giving their kids a sense of security. The danger is coming from all sides—not only from movies and TV shows that expose them to sex and violence but even from well-meaning teachers.

It's time to find ways to keep our children innocent and protected, just as God intended.

Lord, your Word tells us that children are a gift from you. Help me to protect children from those who would expose them to unfit ideas and images.

JIHAD FOR JESUS

TO READ: 1 PETER 2:9-15

Live such good lives among the pagans that, though they accuse you of doing wrong, they may see your good deeds and glorify God on the day he visits us.
1 Peter 2:12

The faithful had had enough. They were tired of seeing their beliefs ridiculed. And they were tired of seeing the infidels appropriate *their* holiday and strip it of its religious significance.

So they did what any dedicated follower of the Prince of Peace would do: They beat up Santa Claus and his elves.

It's one of the funniest scenes in a book by Chris Fabry, *Away with the Manger*. And it's a reminder that Christians cannot win people's minds at the cost of losing their hearts.

The setting for *Away with the Manger* is the mythical town of Hartville. Under pressure from the village atheist, the town council has voted to dilute the nativity scene near city hall. Beside the Holy Family and the shepherds, the city fathers have added nativity characters the Gospel writers forgot to mention: namely, Frosty the Snowman and Rudolph the Red-Nosed Reindeer.

A huge controversy erupts. One group, led by the town atheist, accuses Christians of wanting to cram their beliefs down people's throats. The Christians accuse their opponents of stealing their holiday.

Civility completely breaks down; the tension in the air lends an ominous new meaning to the words *You better watch out.*

In the end, a Christmas Eve crisis over a lost child forces both sides to come together. In the process, they begin to see how silly they've been. And that's the author's point. While the annual crèche-and-carol wars involve serious issues, they don't exempt Christians from behaving like Christians. As Chris Fabry told the *Washington Times,* "We could win all the battles [over Christmas displays] in the courts," but in the process we'll lose the battle for people's hearts.

At stake in the culture war is the existence of truth itself. The most effective witness to Christian truth is a life that, as Peter writes, causes men "to glorify God." The late Mother Teresa, for instance, made the case for "the truth which is in Jesus" far more effectively than the most learned theologian.

Behind all the humor, that's the message of *Away with the Manger:* Ultimately, the battle for our neighbors' minds will be won through their hearts.

Heavenly Father, help me to never bring shame on your name through my speech or behavior, remembering always that far more important than winning points is winning hearts.

GOING TO THE DOGS

TO READ: ISAIAH 9:2-7

The people walking in darkness have seen a great light. Isaiah 9:2

Susan Hellauer, a singer with the vocal ensemble Anonymous 4, was walking in New York's Riverside Park a few years ago when a fan stopped her. The woman told Hellauer that Anonymous 4's recordings had helped calm a dog who was struggling to give birth to a litter of puppies. Hellauer was taken aback, but she managed to say, "How wonderful."

The story is amusing, but it's ironic that a pregnant pooch would appreciate what many evangelicals have lost sight of: our Christian musical heritage.

Anonymous 4—Susan Hellauer, Ruth Cunningham, Marsha Genensky, and Johanna Maria Rose—specializes in the music of the high Middle Ages—what historians call the Age of Faith.

Anonymous 4's recording *On Yoolis Night* is a medieval music celebration of Christmas. The carol "Alleluya: A Nywe Werke," sung in Middle English, tells us that "a new work has come on hand, through the might and grace of God's messenger, to save the lost of every land."

Another release, *A Star in the East,* surveys Hungarian medieval Christmas music. As Hellauer explains, Christianity replaced Hungary's pagan gods and hymns to the earth but kept sacred song at the heart of Hungarian spiritual life.

Close your eyes and imagine yourself in a cathedral in thirteenth-century Hungary during Christmastime. You would hear, in song, the words of the prophet Isaiah foretelling the coming of God's Messiah and affirming the promise that "the people that walked in darkness have seen a great light."

Unhappily, music that once communicated the gospel is now frequently marketed as "mood music," used to calm everyone from pregnant dogs to people undergoing root canals. While happy for any sales, members of Anonymous 4 hasten to add: "You're supposed to really listen to this stuff."

Good advice—especially for Christians. Sadly, much of today's Christian music is simply watered-down versions of popular music. Musically speaking, we've inherited a collection of gourmet recipes but insist on eating fast food every night. As you prepare for the holidays, why not take a medieval musical tour—one that will help you understand how the worship of our God led to the creation of a culture envied by the world?

If we lose that understanding, we shouldn't be surprised when more than our musical heritage eventually goes to the dogs.

Lord, help me to be willing to seek you not in the mediocre but in the magnificent.

THE FIRST AND ONLY ABOLITIONISTS

TO READ: PHILEMON 1:8-18

Perhaps the reason he was separated from you for a little while was that you might have him back for good—no longer as a slave, but better than a slave, as a dear brother. Philemon 1:15-16

Christianity was born into a world where chattel slavery, one person owning another, was the cornerstone of the economy.

Ironically, many famous historians, including those most critical of Christianity, were indifferent about the role that slavery played in antiquity. Edward Gibbon called the "cruel treatment" of slaves "almost justified by the great law of self-preservation."

Western Christianity saw matters differently. Its spread through western Europe was accompanied by calls for an end to chattel slavery. Saint Bathilde, the wife of the seventh-century Frankish king Clovis, was canonized, in part, for her efforts to free slaves and end the slave trade.

The result of hers and similar efforts was that, by the eleventh century, slavery had been effectively abolished in western Europe. The lone exceptions were areas under pagan or Muslim control.

So why did slavery make a comeback in the Americas? As historian Rodney Stark writes in *For the Glory of God: How Monotheism Led to Reformations, Science, Witch-Hunts, and the End of Slavery,* the problem was that people stopped listening. The distance between the Americas and western Europe, coupled with the rise of nation-states and commercial interests, meant that Christian teaching about the evils of chattel slavery was less likely to be heeded.

The failure to obey this teaching doesn't change the fact that, according to Stark, the "moral predisposition" to oppose slavery was unique to Western Christianity. It certainly didn't exist in the Islamic world, where legal slavery existed until 1981 and where informal slavery still exists.

This "moral predisposition" was why the second successful abolitionist wave in the beginning of the nineteenth century was led by William Wilberforce and other Christian politicians. And in this country the abolitionist campaign which brought about an end to slavery was led by Christians as well.

What Stark calls the "moral potential for an antislavery conclusion" lay uniquely within Christian thought. Despite the Bible's apparent acknowledgment of slavery, what the Bible taught us about God and man led Christians to conclude that the holding of another human in bondage was a sin. This religious appeal is why the British taxed themselves to abolish slavery in the West Indies.

Unfortunately, the truth that Christianity, almost alone, led to the abolition of slavery is not being told in our schools—and never will be unless Christians speak out. If we don't set the record straight, who will?

Lord, give me opportunities to glorify you by telling others why Christians have always led efforts to abolish slavery: because in Christ, "there is neither Jew nor Greek, slave nor free, male nor female."

A CANDLE IN
THE DARKNESS

TO READ: DANIEL 3:8-29

*If we are thrown into the blazing furnace, the God we serve is able to save us
from it, and he will rescue us from your hand, O king.* Daniel 3:17

In 1989, Laszlo Tokes was the pastor of a fast-growing reformed
church in the city of Timisoara, Romania. His powerful preaching
had caught the attention of communist officials, and they began a
strategy of suppression. They stationed police officers around his
church and hired thugs to attack him. Finally, just before Christmas,
they decided to send him into exile.

But when the police arrived to hustle Pastor Tokes away, they were
stopped cold. Around the church stood a wall of humanity. Christians from around the city—Baptist, Pentecostal, Orthodox, Catholic—had joined together to protest.

All through the day they held their post. As it grew dark, a Baptist
student named Daniel Gavra pulled out a packet of candles, lit one,
and passed it to his neighbor.

Then he lit another. One by one the burning candles were passed
out among the crowd. Soon the darkness of the December night
was pierced by the light of hundreds of candles. When Pastor
Tokes looked out his window, he saw a sea of faces lit up by a warm
glow.

That night, he said later, was the "turning point in my life." He
would never forget the sight of believers from all denominations joining hands in his defense.

Two days later, police finally broke through the crowd and dragged
Pastor Tokes away. But that was not the end. The people now

streamed to the city square and began a full-scale demonstration against the communist government.

Finally, panicked communist officials ordered troops to open fire on the crowd. Hundreds were shot. Young Daniel felt a searing pain as his leg was blown off.

Yet the brave example set in Timisoara inspired the rest of the nation. Within days the entire population of Romania had risen up and the bloody dictator Ceausescu was gone.

For the first time in half a century, the people of Romania celebrated Christmas in freedom.

In the hospital, Daniel Gavra celebrated while learning to walk with crutches. His pastor came by, offering sympathy, but Daniel wasn't looking for sympathy.

"Oh, Pastor," he said softly. "I don't mind so much the loss of a leg. After all, it was I who lit the first candle."

What mighty things the church can do when we stand shoulder to shoulder with our brothers and sisters, ready to fight evil—including evil leaders who command us to worship them instead of God—prepared to give our limbs and even our lives to light a candle in the darkness.

Light your church, O Lord, with the brightness of your Spirit, and let us shine boldly in a dark and needy world.

A REVISIONIST GRINCH

TO READ: MATTHEW 2:1-18

A voice is heard in Ramah, weeping and great mourning,
Rachel weeping for her children. Matthew 2:18

"Every Who Down in Who-ville Liked Christmas a lot,
But the Grinch, Who lived just north of Who-ville, Did NOT!"

It's one of Dr. Seuss's most amusing books about a grumpy creature who tries to steal Christmas. But now a film succeeds in doing what the Grinch fails to do: It really does steal Christmas.

How the Grinch Stole Christmas, starring Jim Carey, opens with the residents of Who-ville frantically buying gifts and trying to out-decorate one another. On Christmas Eve, the Grinch dresses up as Santa Claus, climbs down Who chimneys, and steals the gifts, the trees, and even the Roast Beast.

But here is where the film deviates from the book. Dr. Seuss relates that on Christmas morning, every Who, tall and small, joins hands and begins to sing joyously. Clearly, the gifts and trimmings are superfluous to their celebration.

Hearing them sing, the Grinch thinks, "Maybe Christmas doesn't come from a store. Maybe Christmas . . . perhaps . . . means a little bit more!"

Just what that "little bit more" consists of is left to the reader's imagination. But in the film, the Whos react exactly as the Grinch anticipated: They're outraged that their gifts have been stolen—and there's nothing left to celebrate. It takes little Cindy Lou to teach them that Christmas is indeed about a little bit more: Christmas, it turns out, is all about . . . families!

But saying Christmas is all about families is as hollow as those cards and commercials claiming Christmas is about "love," or "peace," or maybe a six-pack of beer.

Our consumer culture says the meaning of Christmas is found in parties, presents, and extravagant self-indulgence. What would happen if a real-life Grinch really did steal the trappings of Christmas? Would we have anything left to celebrate?

Well, if the cultural grinches have stolen the meaning of Christmas, then—like the Whos of Who-ville—we'll just have to get it back. But we mustn't make the mistake of latching onto the wrong thing. Shopping is not the answer, nor is a frenzy of good works.

Christmas is about Christ himself. Our celebration ought to include quiet moments in his presence—thanking him for his sacrifice for us and basking in the gift of his love. If we leave Christ out of the celebration, we are, as G. K. Chesterton observed, celebrating December 25, not Christmas.

We must remember that "unto us a child is born" and "he is Christ the Lord." That's something no Grinch can steal.

O God, Herod could not steal Christmas, and neither can a materialistic culture. Fill our hearts with the joy of the living Christ.

O COME, ALL YE SHOPPERS

TO READ: LUKE 2:8-20

*The angel said to them, "Do not be afraid. I bring you good news of
great joy that will be for all the people." Luke 2:10*

It was Christmas Eve, and the first of fourteen thousand townspeople
began streaming through the building's huge double doors. A beam of
light shone down from above, highlighting an elaborate Nativity
scene. Marble angels gazed down upon the largest pipe organ in the
world. As people settled into their seats, the organist struck a chord
and led the crowd in singing the first hymn: "O Come, All Ye Faithful."

Surprisingly, this spectacular Christmas celebration took place,
not in a modern mega-church, but in a department store. It was an
annual attraction that drew shoppers to the leading Philadelphia department store, Wanamaker's, from the 1910s to the 1950s. It illustrates how America's Christmas consumerism has some of its roots,
ironically, in our own Protestant tradition.

As strange as it may seem today, Christmas was not always treated
as a holiday in America. In the seventeenth and eighteenth centuries,
few Americans really celebrated Christmas. Influenced by their Puri-
tan heritage, Congregationalists, Presbyterians, Baptists, and Meth-
odists viewed Christmas Day with suspicion, regarding it as a Roman
Catholic invention with dubious origins. The emphasis on the Nativity, they believed, grew out of devotion to Mary.

Protestant reluctance to celebrate Christmas had one major side effect. In his book *Consumer Rites,* Princeton professor Leigh Eric
Schmidt writes that keeping Christmas off the church calendar
helped pave the way for its inclusion in the secular calendar. While
clergy downplayed Christmas, businessmen and department-store

magnates like John Wanamaker stepped in where angels feared to tread, fostering the celebration of Christmas in the marketplace instead of the church.

This is shocking news. Could the roots of Christmas consumerism be in our own tradition? History suggests that Christmas became such a commercialized holiday, in part, because Protestants did not make it a holy day.

This year—instead of just griping about the commercialization of Christmas—let's make up for our past errors by filling our churches. If we present to the world a joyful, worshipping community, they'll be drawn to the real thing—not a manufactured substitute. If our candle-lit churches and cathedrals are full of Christians demonstrating real harmony and love, then nothing in those glittering shopping malls can possibly compare.

Father, help me to put aside Christmas shopping long enough to consider which of my unsaved neighbors I should invite to a Christmas service at my church this year. Teach me to celebrate Christ's birth as the angels did—rejoicing together and sharing the Good News with those who need him.

A BABY VERSUS THE WORLD

TO READ: ROMANS 12:14-21

Do not be overcome by evil, but overcome evil with good. Romans 12:21

Father Jerzy Popieluszko was a young pastor who once delivered the dynamic messages that stirred the Polish people to overthrow their Communist oppressors.

Father Jerzy's sermons were neither fiery nor eloquent. Yet his monthly masses, dedicated to the victims of Communist persecution, attracted tens of thousands of Polish people. He never preached revenge or revolution. He preached the power of good to overcome evil.

It was a passion that dominated his own life as well. In 1980, martial law was declared in Poland. Tanks and troops clogged the streets, until the entire country was one vast prison. Jerzy hated the occupation as much as his countrymen, but he fought it using God's weapons—overcoming evil with good. On Christmas Eve, Jerzy slogged through the snow and handed out Christmas cookies to soldiers in the streets.

Even in his death, Jerzy was victorious. In 1984 he was kidnapped by the secret police. In churches across Poland, people gathered to pray. Steelworkers demanded his release, threatening a national strike. Fifty thousand people gathered to hear a tape of his final sermon.

Then the blow fell: Jerzy's body had been found in the river. He had been brutally tortured, his eyes and tongue cut out, his bones smashed. Yet the gentle pastor had taught his people well: After his funeral, hundreds of thousands of Poles marched through Warsaw—right past secret police headquarters—carrying banners that read, "We forgive."

They were assaulting evil with good. And under the impact, the Communist regime soon crumbled.

The message Jerzy preached has always been God's strategy for overcoming evil. The supreme example is the Incarnation itself—which we celebrate today—when God himself entered human history to overcome the evil of sin.

America is not in the grip of a Communist regime as Poland was, yet Christians are battling a hostile secular culture. And we often wonder how we can fight more effectively. The answer is that God's people are to fight evil using God's strategy and weapons.

When God wanted to defeat sin, his ultimate weapon was the sacrifice of his own Son. On Christmas Day two thousand years ago, the birth of a baby in an obscure village in the Middle East was God's supreme triumph of good over evil.

Lord, when I am tempted to respond to hatred and insults with anger and abuse, help me to remember the weapon of the Cross: overcoming evil with good.

SYNCRETISTIC SERVICES?

TO READ: 1 KINGS 12:25-33

After seeking advice, the king made two golden calves. He said to the people,
"It is too much for you to go up to Jerusalem. Here are your gods." 1 Kings 12:28

Just after Christmas a few years ago, a newspaper story appeared titled, "Many churches wrap Kwanzaa into their Christmas services."
The article quoted several pastors who favored including Kwanzaa
celebrations in their holiday worship.

Kwanzaa is a seven-day holiday that runs from December 26 to January 1. It has no roots in antiquity, but is the invention of Dr.
Maulana Karenga, who heads the Department of Black Studies at
California State University, Long Beach. Karenga created Kwanzaa in
1966, mixing elements of African harvest festivals with sixties radical-
ism and the civil rights movement. The seven principles of Kwanzaa
set forth by Karenga include unity, self-determination, cooperative
economics, and faith. Faith is defined as, "To believe with all our
heart in our people, our parents, our teachers, our leaders, and the
righteousness and victory of our struggle."

Karenga's official Kwanzaa Web site states that, while celebrating
Kwanzaa includes "special reverence for the creator," and is "spiritual," "it
is important to note Kwanzaa is a cultural holiday, not a religious one."

The site adds: "You should not mix Kwanzaa holiday or its symbols, values, and practices with any other culture." That's in part because Kwanzaa was established as an alternative to Christmas, which
was viewed as a Western holiday. Christian worship would seem to violate the intent of Kwanzaa's promoters. But if public schools and
civic ceremonies are any indication, Kwanzaa is gaining equal standing as a third holiday, alongside Christmas and Hanukkah.

The good news is that many African-American pastors say they're rejecting Kwanzaa. One inner-city pastor said that Kwanzaa had all the trappings of a manufactured holiday and that most people he knew—Christian and non-Christian—had no interest. Another said that it was an issue in a few churches in his area, but that pastors dealt with it by making a clear distinction between a celebration of ethnic and cultural heritage and the celebration of the birth of Christ.

But Christians need to be on guard. The church is always vulnerable to syncretism. Santa kneeling at the manger, church Easter-egg hunts, inviting an imam to speak from the pulpit, and dozens of other examples show how easily we mix cultural rituals with our Christian faith. We must remember that worship is not for a cultural celebration, but for the celebration of the one eternal God who created and rules all cultures.

Father, keep us from being drawn into "new things" merely because they are interesting, entertaining, or convenient. Help us to guard the truth that is in Jesus.

SHOULD WE HAVE PERFECT BODIES?

TO READ: ROMANS 8:20-25

The creation was subjected to frustration . . . in hope that the creation itself will be liberated from its bondage to decay. Romans 8:20-21

It's a humbling experience we've all had on the way to the morning shower—looking at our bodies in the mirror. Even the physically fit can spot areas for improvement.

But do our imperfections prove that we evolved by natural selection? An article in *Scientific American* makes that very claim.

Entitled "If Humans Were Built to Last," the article by S. Jay Olshansky, Bruce Carnes, and Robert Butler argues that the human body reflects the mindless process of natural selection, not purposeful design. The authors argue that many of our physical shortcomings exist because natural selection causes us to survive "just long enough to reproduce." Once we've passed on our genes, they say, our bodies start to fall apart.

If we had been intelligently designed, they add, we should last much longer. And we wouldn't choke on food, suffer detached retinas, or endure a host of other ailments.

This argument for naturalistic evolution echoes the teachings of eighteenth-century philosopher David Hume, who argued that the miseries of human existence are best explained by "blind nature," not design. But this misrepresents what intelligent design really says.

First, intelligent design does not say that any currently existing organism should be perfect. Every designed system in our present universe is subject to physical laws and involves trade-offs with a wide range of functional requirements.

Consider, for example, your throat. The esophagus (the passage to the stomach) and the trachea (the passage to the lungs) come together at the top of the throat. When you swallow, a structure called the epiglottis closes to cover your trachea.

Sometimes, when people take large bites of food, or if they're inebriated, the epiglottis may not close properly, and they choke.

Olshansky and company argue that if our throats had been intelligently designed, this wouldn't happen. A better design would have placed the trachea higher, near the nasal passage. Or would it?

You see, it would be impossible to speak if air only passed through your nostrils, not your mouth. Catching a cold could be a life-threatening illness, because congestion would block the only pathway for oxygen.

Yes, humans occasionally choke. But there is no evidence that another system would work better.

The Christian worldview tells us not to expect perfection. While God created the world, it's also fallen—a world with illness and pain and decay, waiting to be redeemed by God's new creation.

We should remember that the next time we look in the bathroom mirror. If your current model is due to expire, don't worry: There's an incomparably better one coming!

Thank you, Lord, for your great wisdom in making our bodies and for your steadfast love in saving our souls.

CHRISTIANITY IS LIFE, ISLAM IS DEATH

TO READ: PSALM 83:1-5, 13-16

Cover their faces with shame so that men will seek your name, O Lord. Psalm 83:16

Since the early 1990s, an estimated 100,000 Algerians have died in a civil war that pits the Algerian government against Islamic extremists, who target anyone expressing what they call "non-Islamic" views.

At the top of their list of targets is Algeria's Christian community. In 1996, seven Trappist monks were kidnapped and then beheaded by Islamic militants, an act that Pope John Paul II called "despicable." Less than three months later, as if to emphasize their disregard for world and Christian opinion, they assassinated the Catholic Bishop of Oran. All of this is part of their promise to "eliminate" all Jews, Christians, and other non-Muslims from Algeria.

You would think that such a campaign would deter conversion to Christianity, but reports out of Algeria suggest the opposite. Since the beginning of recorded history, a people called the Berbers have lived in North Africa. The Berbers, who are referred to in ancient Egyptian records, were originally pagans, but many of them eventually embraced Christianity in the first centuries after Christ as the gospel spread across Roman North Africa.

Then, in the seventh century, the Muslim army conquered North Africa. Within a century, the Christian presence there disappeared. The Berbers, like nearly everyone else in North Africa, became Muslims. Now that's beginning to change. A recent issue of *Middle East Quarterly* tells us "people of all ages are converting to Christianity" in Kabylie, the heart of Berber culture. Despite obstacles that forced pastors to work in "absolute secrecy," "the number of [Berbers] who have embraced Christianity has grown rapidly."

What lies behind this spate of conversions? The *Quarterly* cites the deterioration of the "image of Islam" as a factor in "the rise of conversions to Christianity." Berbers have seen the atrocities committed in the name of Islam and they asked the question that many Westerners don't dare ask: Does the problem lie with extremists, or is the problem inherent in Islam itself?

The Berbers have seen the impact of Islam on the lives of ordinary people, and they have summed up the difference between the two faiths in startling fashion: "Christianity is life; Islam is death." These Berber conversions should remind us to pray for Muslims. Islamist extremists are causing Muslims to rethink what they believe. As a result, conversions to Christianity are occurring in North Africa, Iran, and elsewhere.

Thrillingly, Christianity's message of God's love and grace through the Cross stands in such marked contrast to Islam that people are choosing life over death.

Lord, as we look ahead to a new year, we pray that many Muslims come to know, in the words of the psalmist, that you alone are "the Most High over all the earth."

FAMOUS FOR NOTHING

TO READ: COLOSSIANS 3:1-4, 15-17, 23-24

Whatever you do, work at it with all your heart, as working for the Lord, not for men. Colossians 3:23

As you walk down the red carpet, a frenzied mob swarms around you, demanding your autograph. The paparazzi are snapping your picture, nearly blinding you. Every ten feet, a television crew stops you for an interview.

Have you just become the hottest newest star? No, you're at Tinseltown Studios, a new theme park in Anaheim, California. For forty-five dollars the studio will treat you as though you really *were* a star. It's the latest manifestation of our celebrity culture, where "image is everything."

The next stop at Tinseltown is an auditorium filled with gorgeous models who are dying to have their picture taken with you. For an additional fee, you can go into an editing room and have yourself edited into a scene from a famous movie. The audience then votes on the best performance, and the winners go on stage to accept their awards.

Is it worth forty-five dollars to pretend you're a star for a few hours? Susan Scanaliato, a seventeen-year-old acting student, put it this way: "Walking up on the carpet, all these people coming up to you and treating you like you're in the real movies—that's our dream." Pathetic words, but they certainly capture our culture's obsession with celebrity.

But this falls far short of the classic, or Christian, understanding of happiness. Deal Hudson, editor of *Crisis* magazine, describes the classical idea of happiness as the product of good character and virtue. For example, taking years to learn the craft of acting—and becoming a fine actor in the process—could indeed make someone happy. In fact, the ancient Greek word for happiness, *eudaimonia*, means the formation of character and the development of our potential over a lifetime.

But Hudson reminds us that "the word *happiness* was stripped of its moral meaning in the 20th century." Today our concept of happiness has more to do with feeling good and getting what we want. But there is no substitute for the sense of accomplishment that comes from doing a job well. A good actor gets joy from acting well, not just from getting awards. And that's true in every sphere of life.

This is a lesson we need to be teaching our kids. Being famous isn't important. In fact, many famous and powerful people are very unhappy. Working hard at our craft, whether it's acting, accounting, or homemaking, is what really matters. And this is what the apostle Paul meant when he said we should do everything as unto the Lord.

Lord, help me to desire your pleasure—to please and serve you and to make you known—and not the fleeting pleasures of adulation, fame, or fortune.

RESPECTING CAESAR

TO READ: 1 PETER 2:13-25

Show proper respect to everyone: Love the brotherhood of believers,
fear God, honor the king. 1 Peter 2:17

How do Christians live under a government whose policies we sharply disagree with—even one whose positions we find morally offensive? The answer is surprisingly simple. Except in the most extraordinary circumstances, we're to live the same way we would under a government we do agree with.

In 1 Timothy 2, Christians are commanded to pray for those in authority. Why? Because, as Paul explains in Romans 13, government officials are God's servants to preserve order and administer justice in the public arena. Notice that Paul doesn't limit his description to good rulers. In fact, he wrote these words during the reign of Nero, one of the cruelest, most vicious Roman emperors.

Whether our rulers are good or bad, whether we agree or disagree with their policies, our duty is the same: to respect and pray for them. That doesn't preclude criticizing their policies, of course, but even criticism should flow from an attitude of prayer.

Now, respecting our leaders does not preclude disobeying the powers that be, but we may disobey only when to obey would mean disobedience to God. For example, in the Old Testament, Daniel refused to obey the king's command to worship idols. Christians were thrown to the lions in the first century, you'll recall, because they refused to say that Caesar—not Jesus—is Lord.

Clearly, civil disobedience must be chosen whenever civil magistrates frustrate our ability to obey God. However, when we take this course, we must do so without resorting to violence. And we must be prepared to bear the consequences that a wicked magistrate will mete out against us, as Peter and John told the Sanhedrin when they refused to stop preaching the gospel.

Some sixty years ago, German theologian Dietrich Bonhoeffer did just that. He resisted the Nazi government and was ultimately martyred.

So, yes, there are times when Christians must stand against an unjust regime. God ordains leaders, but they must act within the scope of the authority he has given them. If they repress religious freedom, or slaughter the innocent, or trample human rights, they're violating God's trust. They're failing to carry out their biblically ordained duty to preserve order and to promote justice. And then, they're no longer entitled to our allegiance.

Lord, remind us to pray for our leaders. Bless and use them, Lord, for your good and glorious purposes.

DOING THE RIGHT THING

TO READ: GALATIANS 6:2-10

As we have opportunity, let us do good to all people, especially to those who belong to the family of believers. Galatians 6:10

The year was 1968, and Kenneth Swan was a young army surgeon, just arrived in Vietnam. One of his first cases was a nineteen-year-old soldier who had been blown up by a grenade, losing his eyesight and both legs. It took seven long, grueling hours at the operating table to put him back together.

Dr. Swan was surprised the next day to find his fellow surgeons sharply critical of him. For not doing a good job? No—for doing the job at all.

"That kid was so badly mangled," they told him, "you shouldn't even have bothered to treat him. He would have been better off dead."

For the next twenty years, Swan was haunted by those words. Had he had done the right thing in trying to save that soldier's life?

Swan determined to find the soldier he had patched up so many years before. It took more than two years to locate him.

And what he found was nothing short of astonishing.

Yes, the man is blind and in a wheelchair. But he is not languishing in any hospital. He is married and has two daughters. He attended college, learned to scuba dive, and trained to help others with debilitating injuries.

The former soldier has a zest for life—and a faith in God. When a reporter asked him about his success in life, he responded simply, "I give the credit to God."

What a testimony.

And it's a great example of the life-changing power of compassion.

But without a sense of duty to a higher standard—a commandment, for example, to treat life as sacred—moral decision making is often driven by purely utilitarian considerations.

Each of us has a right to expect that no effort be spared to preserve our own lives and those of our loved ones. And the Christian worldview provides us with the *basis* for that expectation. We believe all are created in the "image of God." And *all* life—not just that which is judged "worthy"—should be treated as a gift from God.

Whether through medical missions, humanitarian relief, or fighting the killing of the unborn, Christians have historically borne witness to the dignity of human life. We can learn from Dr. Swan's example and never hesitate to act with compassion—to do the right thing.

Give us more love, O Lord, and make us alert to the opportunities to do good to everyone we meet.

ABOUT THE AUTHORS

Charles Colson, chairman of Prison Fellowship Ministries, is a highly respected author, speaker, and columnist. He has written more than twenty-five books, including *The Good Life, Born Again, Burden of Truth, The Body, Loving God, Kingdoms in Conflict, How Now Shall We Live?* and *Gideon's Torch* (a novel, with Ellen Vaughn). Colson was also the 1993 recipient of the prestigious Templeton Prize for Progress in Religion, given for extraordinary leadership and originality in advancing humanity's understanding of God.

Anne Morse is a senior writer at the Wilberforce Forum in Reston, Virginia. She frequently writes for *National Review Online, Crisis, Touchstone,* the *Women's Quarterly,* Beliefnet, *World,* and *Boundless.* She and her husband have two sons and live in Unity, Maryland.

Look for these insightful worldview books by CHARLES COLSON wherever fine books are sold

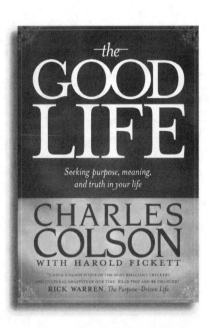
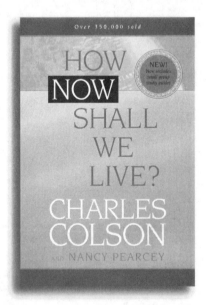

Expose the lies of our culture:

Lies That Go Unchallenged: Popular Culture

Lies That Go Unchallenged: Media and Government

Apply the Christian worldview to your life:

Tough Questions about God, Faith, and Life

Hearts and Minds

How Now Shall We Live? Devotional

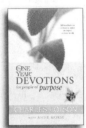

The One Year Devotions for People of Purpose

Developing a Christian Worldview series

Discover *How Now Shall We Live?* worldview issues in a format for individual and group study:

Science and Evolution

The Problem of Evil

The Christian in Today's Culture

A complete *How Now Shall We Live?* adult and youth video curriculum
is available from LifeWay Church Resources:
Customer Services, MSN 113
One LifeWay Plaza
Nashville, TN 37234-0113
Fax: 1-615-251-5933
Catalog orders: 1-800-458-2772
Order from online catalog at www.lifeway.com/shopping